Funny Valentine

Matthew Ruddick

Published by

MELROSE BOOKS

An Imprint of Melrose Press Limited
St Thomas Place, Ely
Cambridgeshire
CB7 4GG, UK
www.melrosebooks.co.uk

SECOND EDITION 2013
First edition Melrose Books, 2012

Cover designed by Catherine McIntyre
from a photograph by Graziano Arici, used with permission

ISBN 978-1-909757-22-6

Printed and bound in Great Britain by:
Martins the Printers, Spittal, Berwick upon Tweed

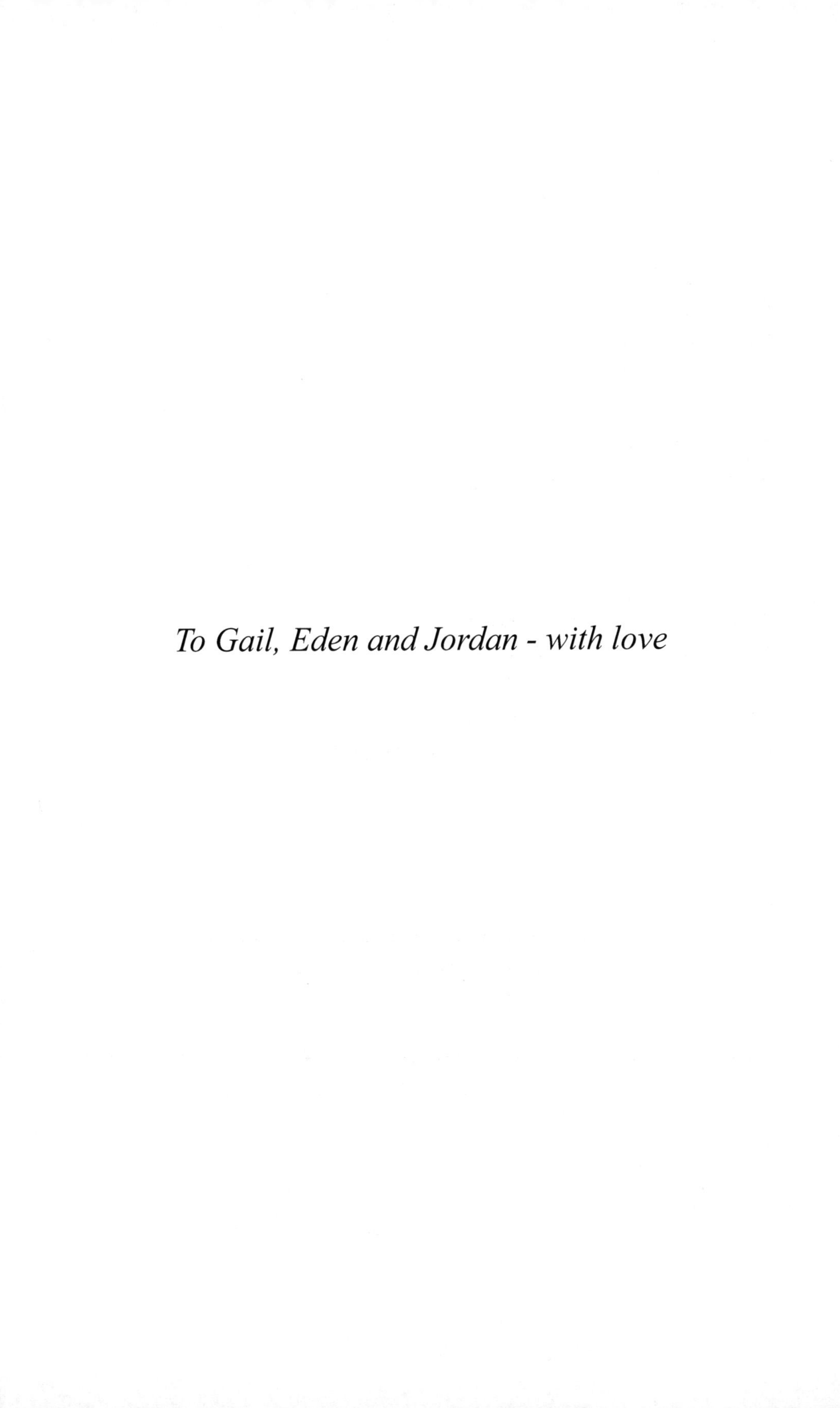

To Gail, Eden and Jordan - with love

Contents

Prologue

"The only thing I could tell you is that I've always felt it's very important to try and swing and find the pretty notes." Chet Baker

In 1981, Lisa Galt Bond signed a contract with Chet Baker to co-author his memoirs under the working title of *Hold The Middle Valve Down*, which was taken from 'The Music Goes Round and Round', a hit for Tommy Dorsey in 1936. Despite the best efforts of her literary agent, Charles Neighbors, the book, which was admittedly somewhat flimsy, met with a negative response. One editor at Macmillan wrote back, and claimed he found Chet's life "too much of a downer to make a commercially successful book".[1]

I felt much the same way reading James Gavin's 2002 biography, *Deep In A Dream*. The book was very well researched, drawing on a large number of original sources, but ultimately it was a depressing story, a tale of squandered talent and a harrowing descent into drug addiction.

In many respects, Chet Baker's life story was a tragedy. He was blessed with movie-star looks and a wealth of natural talent, but struggled to cope with his early taste of success. When a young pianist in his band died of an overdose on his first European tour in 1955, he felt as though he was being held responsible. Jazz critics were also starting to turn against him at this time, and he tried to bury his pain through increased use of narcotics. "It's so sad, he had such a great musical mind," said bass player Jon Burr, a former addict himself. "He played so in tune that notes became transparent, a transcendental quality that he was capable of, but only under certain conditions. He could have had the world. This was a guy who didn't send money home to feed his children, because it was going up his veins. This is a tragic story."

Whilst there is no denying the tragedy in Chet Baker's life, I felt that *Deep In A Dream* focused more on Chet's lifestyle, rather than the music he left behind. I wanted to paint a more balanced portrait, and as I talked to people who knew him in the 1940s and early 1950s, before his addiction took hold, old wives and girlfriends, and musicians that had played with him over the years, I discovered many of them felt the same way.

In short, I felt that three key elements were missing from the story.

The first we might classify as the 'human' element. Ruth Young, who was Chet's girlfriend for ten years from 1973, felt that "the more human you can make him, the more you're going to have a warm reception for what you do".[2]

Talking to friends from his teenage years, I uncovered a young man that was laid-back yet fun-loving, possessing a natural charm, a good sense of humour, and an infectious laugh. He was occasionally inclined towards reckless, rebellious behaviour, whether it was climbing the cliffs at Redondo Beach or his race-car approach to driving. And whilst his delinquent behaviour was only one small facet of his personality, it still filtered into his playing. "Don't we use terms like bold, audacious, daring, defiant, to describe his music?" asked bass player Bob Whitlock, an original member of the Gerry Mulligan Quartet. "Of course we also use terms like sensitive, lyrical, moving, soaring, warm and soulful."[3]

In later years, it was hard for most people to get past his addiction. Orrin Keepnews, owner of Riverside Records, encountered Chet in the late 1950s, when his addiction was hopelessly out of control, and wanted nothing to do with him. He regarded Gavin's biography as "honest, interesting and therefore disturbing".[4]

But others were upset by the account they read, and felt there was another side of Chet that had not been portrayed. "Chet was a beautiful man," said drummer Colin Bailey, who played with Chet in the mid-1960s. "The stuff they wrote about him in that last book was horrible, complete horse crap. He was so pleasant all the time when I played with him. He always showed up for the gigs, I never saw him do anything wrong. And I loved playing with him."[5]

Chet's addiction meant that he was frequently anti-social; he periodically resorted to crime, he was prone to wild mood swings, and his behaviour was occasionally abhorrent, particularly in the way he treated women. But beneath this he was still a soft-spoken, gentle soul, loyal to his friends and still capable of turning on the charm. In addition, there was a vulnerability to his character that still attracted certain types of women, generally those who felt they could mother him or change him; indeed, this was another facet of his character that also came across in both his playing and singing.

The last word on this subject, for now at least, goes to Micheline Graillier, the daughter of Belgian jazz saxophonist Jacques Pelzer, and one of Chet's closest friends. "If Chet was as bad as they say in that book, nobody would have invited Chet to stay," she laughed. "He was a sweetheart, really."[6]

The second element that seemed to be missing from *Deep In A Dream* was an appreciation of the music. Reading the book, one felt that Chet had been on a steady decline since the mid-1950s, and produced little music of any consequence after his comeback in the early 1970s.

To be fair, a number of musicians feel this is a fair reflection of Chet's output. "I found it marvellous to listen to him and to play with him," said alto saxophonist Bud Shank, who had known Chet since his teenage years. "The tragedy is he stopped developing when he became addicted. We lost a star. We will never know what he could have achieved otherwise. Since the '50s it's all gone downhill for him ... That's all there is to it, as everyone knows."[7]

In the same vein, the jazz trumpet player Wynton Marsalis was equally dismissive of Chet's playing in the 1980s. "On a good night—and there weren't enough of them—towards the end of his life, in his 50s, Chet was playing jazz as well as anybody has ever played it," said Mike Zwerin, a musician who played with Miles Davis on the legendary *Birth Of The Cool* album, and who worked as a music critic for the *International Herald Tribune* for many years. "It's not a popular thing to say to Wynton Marsalis. I told him once, and he looked at me as if I was crazy."[8]

Chet was convinced that he continued to develop as a musician in his later years, and I would be inclined to agree. If one listens some of his recordings from the late 1970s and early 1980s, there were significant changes to both the style of music he was playing, and to his soloing, which continued to evolve. "He never forgot to develop his own style," noted bass player, Riccardo Del Fra. "The way he played the trumpet in his last six or seven years is special and original, and completely different to the way he played when he was young."[9]

He started to experiment with a 'drummerless' trio, which is heard to good effect on the recordings he made for SteepleChase in 1979, and again in his classic trios with Riccardo Del Fra and Michel Graillier, and Philip Catherine and Jean-Louis Rassinfosse in the early–mid 1980s. This approach required a bass player with good timing, but allowed Chet to develop long, uncluttered lines in his solos. On a good night, as a consequence, he could astonish with an endless stream of ideas.

Chet's tone also changed in his later years. This had less to do with the dentures that were fitted in the late 1960s, after his beating in San Francisco, and more to do with kidney stone problems he was suffering in 1977, which caused him to play in a more defensive posture, producing an aerated tone. Chet enjoyed the softer, melancholic sound that this produced, and used it to good effect on some of his later recordings, such as 'Mr B' in 1983.

The Dutch author, Jeroen de Valk, did a fine job of highlighting some of the gems that can be found amongst Chet's later recordings in his book *Chet Baker: His Life and Music*. I would also note that the authors of the splendid *Penguin Guide to Jazz*, Brian Morton and the late Richard Cook, found themselves constantly re-evaluating Chet's later recordings as the years went by, surprised at the high quality of some of his recorded output. In the discography at the back of this book, I have highlighted ten Chet Baker records that I would consider essential; of those ten, six stem from his 'comeback', post-1973. As Mike Zwerin suggested, there may not have been enough good nights, but when Chet was on form, those nights were very good indeed.

Thirdly and finally, I felt there was something slightly heroic about the way Chet stayed true to his principles from a musical perspective, no matter what misfortunes he suffered in his personal life. Some might suggest he was quite the opposite, given the way he neglected his family. But he was honest about the importance of music in his life, even from the early days. The photographer William Claxton once asked Chet, in front of an old girlfriend, what the most important things in the world were to him. "Oh, I don't know for sure, Clax. I guess my horn—and my new Caddy—and well, of course, my music. I guess that's about it." His girlfriend overheard this conversation and stormed off, saying, "Well thanks a lot, *Mister* Baker!" With that, she slammed her hand on to the bonnet of his brand new car. Chet looked at Claxton, shook his head and smiled. Then he shouted out, "I forgot to mention my dog! I love my good ol' dog, Bix."[10]

In later years, of course, drugs competed head-on with the music, but on the good nights, the music prevailed. Ruth Young laughed when she heard Claxton's anecdote. "I always felt I was secondary to the music and the drugs, but I felt I inched up just ahead of the car!"[11]

But even amid the chaos of his personal life—battling his demons, struggling to cope with his addiction, living out of a suitcase, never looking more than a few weeks ahead—he maintained a belief in his unique vision of jazz music. He once summed up his approach to a master class of young German musicians. "The only thing I could tell you," he said, "is that I've always felt it's very important to try and swing and find the pretty notes." Chet may have been understating the simplicity of his approach, but the reality is that he used understatement to good effect in his music, exploring the sense of space as he played.

So rather than dwell on the tragedy in Chet Baker's life, or think about what he might have achieved if he had stayed clean, I have tried to place a considerable emphasis on the elements that created this deeply flawed musician, and the significance of his musical legacy—which is still being felt, almost twenty-five years later.

Chapter One

PRINCE OF COOL
1929-1946

"All too often celebrities are reduced to one-dimensional caricatures. Public perception ends up defining the very boundaries of character, the circumference of the soul. This is too easy. There is always much more to a person than what the public gets to see, and never was this truer than in the case of Chet Baker."—Carol Baker[1]

More than Louis Armstrong, Charlie Parker and Miles Davis—in fact, more than any other artist in the history of jazz—photographers were drawn to Chet Baker. Of course it helped that, in his younger days, Chet was blessed with an extraordinary face. But there was more to his appeal than this. "Baker cooperated by striking a variety of poses that always seemed easy and natural," noted photographer Lee Tanner.[2]

Over the years, Chet's good looks diminished. He inherited his father's lined face, which was sculpted by the Depression, periods of prolonged unemployment and years of heavy drinking. Chet added his own life experiences—which included drug abuse, prison sentences and a vicious beating, which eventually resulted in the loss of his front teeth. In his final years "he looked like twenty miles of bad road," recalled bass player Ron McClure, "like an old sea captain that had been left out in the sun." Yet photographers were drawn to him more than ever, as demonstrated by movies made by the fashion photographer Bruce Weber and the French director Bertrand Fèvre in the final years of Chet's life.[3]

The camera's love affair with Chet Baker began through the work of William Claxton, a young photographer whose images were to grace the cover of Pacific Jazz records, and contributed to the image of 'West Coast Jazz'.

Claxton recalled one evening in June 1952 at The Haig, a tiny jazz club in downtown Los Angeles, where he was shooting pictures of the

Gerry Mulligan Quartet, a group that was beginning to gain a reputation as one of the hottest acts in town. "After that first night at The Haig, I rushed home to develop my film," he wrote. "Later on, in the early hours of the morning, I began making prints of Gerry Mulligan and his quartet. All of the musicians were young and nice-looking. [Drummer] Chico Hamilton was downright handsome. Yet the face that stood out was the young trumpeter, Chet Baker. As the latent images began to appear in the developing tray through the pale red darkroom illumination, it was Chet's face that came through like magic—a photographer's dream—a photogenic face. Now I finally knew what that mysterious term, photogenic, truly meant".[4]

Over the course of the next five years, Claxton would capture Chet's image in a wide variety of settings—recording in the studio, relaxing with his fellow musicians between takes, live on stage, at ease in the company of his wife, or girlfriend, posing for the camera or lost in a reverie, the music reducing him to a dream-like state.

Lost in music: A Pacific Jazz recording session with Jack Montrose and Herb Geller. Photograph by William Claxton / Courtesy Demont Photo Management, LLC

Carol Baker was once asked if Chet felt the need to live up his "charismatic, photogenic" image. "No, he used to chuckle about it," she explained. "Chet was Chet. You know, people compared him—when we were in Italy, Jack Palance was there and if so, he looked like a Jack Palance, and things like that. No, Chet was very quiet, actually, quite a shy person. It was very difficult. Unless Chet had a big interest in you and pursued you, he was very quiet."[5]

If Chet had no interest in his own image, what is the significance of analysing his photogenic appeal? Is there not a danger that we make the same mistake, reducing him to a one-dimensional caricature?

In fact, these early images of Chet are important for a variety of reasons. Firstly, it is worth remembering that his later drug dependency made it difficult for many people to get close to him. Many of his oldest friends did not recognise the portrait of the washed-up heroin addict that was painted in James Gavin's biography *Deep in a Dream*. "Chet was lots of things—passionate, self destructive, a magnet that attracted women—and men of all kinds," noted the poet and singer Rod McKuen, who befriended Chet in the mid-late 1950s. "He was faithful as a friend and one of the 20th century's great and most influential musicians. Best of all, he had an offbeat sense of humor that the press and other observers never seemed to acknowledge. Of course, his unique talent and sometimes bad behaviour—nearly always directed against himself—surely got in the way of any assessment of the true man."[6]

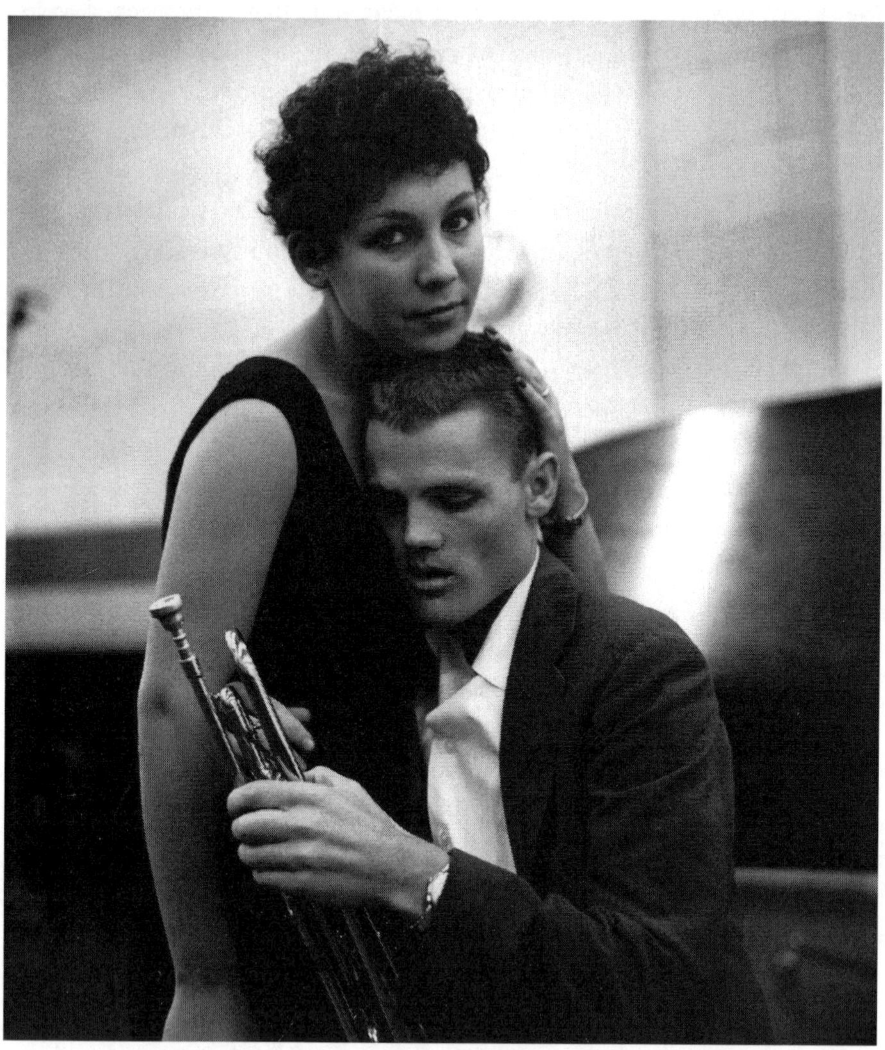

Vulnerable: Chet Baker and Liliane Cukier, 1954.
Photograph by William Claxton / Courtesy Demont Photo Management, LLC

William Claxton's images of Chet offer a tantalising glimpse of Chet's underlying character in his early years, before his dependency took hold.

Chet's high cheekbones, square jawline and carefully sculpted hair made him look superficially handsome, but there was more to his appeal than this. In a number of the images his eyes are closed; he looks almost angelic, a little-boy-lost. One famous photograph shows his then girlfriend,

Liliane Cukier, holding him close to her chest, as though he needed to be protected, mothered even. In this respect, Claxton had unknowingly captured an important element of Chet's character—he had been spoiled as a child, and needed a woman by his side to look after his needs. It is interesting to note that when his final girlfriend, Diane Vavra, finally plucked up the courage to leave him, Chet struggled to live without her and died just a few months later.

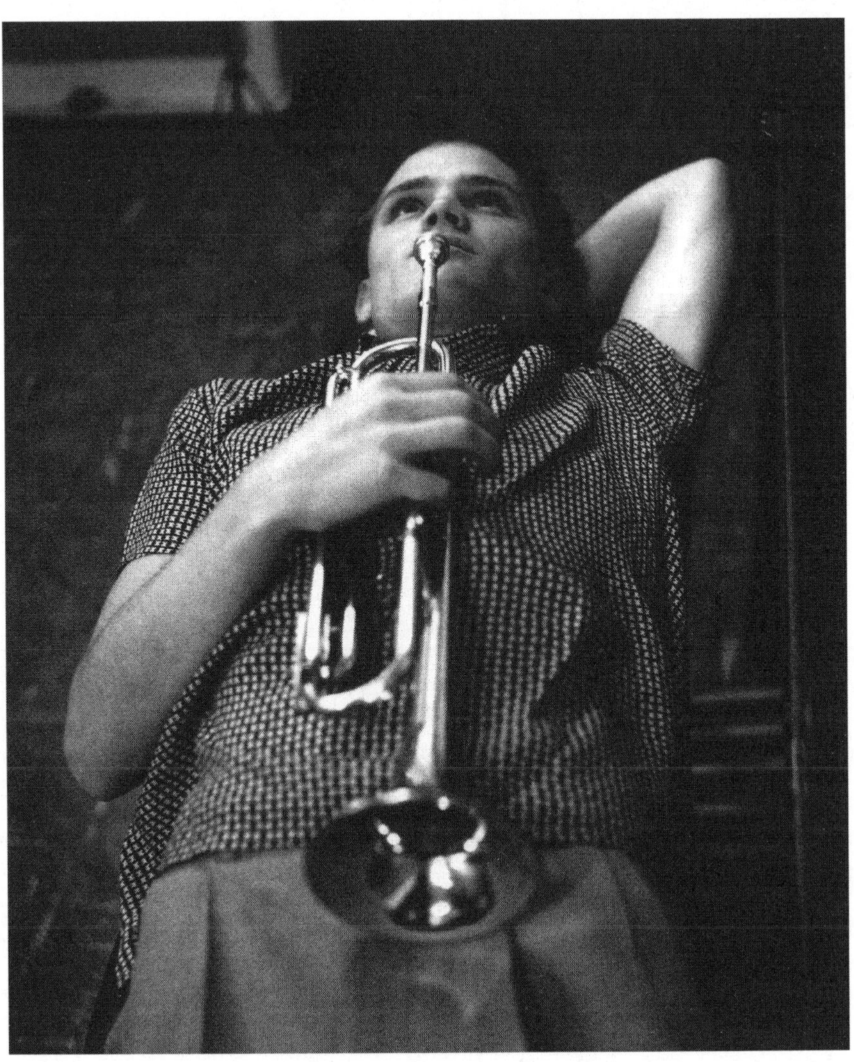

Playful: Chet Baker in 1954
Photograph by William Claxton / Courtesy Demont Photo Management, LLC

With his eyes open, there were suggestions that Chet was not as angelic as he might appear. There was a mischievous twinkle in his eyes, a glint that never completely disappeared, even as the lines on his face multiplied in later years, and his cheeks shrivelled into his face. The playfulness might manifest itself in a number of ways—the boyish enthusiasm he applied to pursuits such as driving, climbing and sailing, the childish behaviour he would occasionally exhibit in the studio, letting out a shriek on his trumpet or clowning around during a photo shoot, or when he simply used his eyes to flirt with a young admirer.

His sense of humour was also apparent in his enigmatic smile—little more than a half-smile, really. In fact, it was carefully designed to avoid revealing his missing front tooth. Chet rarely let his guard down in front of William Claxton, a professional photographer, but when he did it revealed a less photogenic, less 'cool' side to Chet's image. "One funny thing … as long as I knew Chet, he had one missing tooth in the front that made him appear charming and dopey at the same time," the photographer recalled. "And the missing tooth never showed up in any of his pictures."[7]

Half-smile: An early publicity shot, 1954.
Photograph by William Claxton / Courtesy Demont Photo Management, LLC

Claxton's iconic images of Chet, coupled with the vulnerable, delicate sound of his trumpet playing, and the hushed, melancholic tone of his singing voice, cemented his reputation as the 'Prince of Cool', a title later used for a compilation of his Pacific Jazz recordings.

Secondly, it is worth noting that Chet's 'cool' persona was one with which both women and men could identify. As Claxton himself later noted, "Chet was loved by women and admired by men; but he was also loved by men and admired by women. It was understandable why women liked him and his art. He was handsome, seemingly innocent, boyish and sexy. But I think men liked him because he was masculine and yet sensitive, and wasn't afraid to express his sensitivity—a kind of freedom that many men wish they had."[8]

This in turn helps to explain his meteoric rise to fame—from an under-employed musician, struggling to find regular work in the early 1950s, to a sideman with the Gerry Mulligan Quartet in late 1952, to poll-winner in his own right by the end of 1953. By early 1955 he was even offered a role in a minor Hollywood movie, a career path he chose not to pursue.

But there was a tragic flipside to this turn of events. Whilst his good looks helped to him to become a star in his early twenties, it was a status he never felt comfortable with for a variety of reasons. His growing reputation was at odds with his quietly spoken, reserved demeanour. "Amidst extravagant acclaim Chet has retained the shy, charming personality that so reveals itself when he plays ballad tunes like 'My Funny Valentine'," noted *DownBeat* magazine in the summer of 1953. When the inevitable critical backlash began in the years that followed, his fragile personality found the pressure hard to bear.[9]

There are interesting parallels with today's obsession with pop 'idols', whether we examine the meltdown of Britney Spears, who was ill-equipped to cope with the tabloid focus on every aspect of her life, to the English R&B singer Amy Winehouse, who seemed irresistibly drawn towards self-destructive behaviour. *Newsweek* magazine went as far as to describe Winehouse as "a perfect storm of sex kitten, raw talent and poor impulse control"—words which, with a slight change of emphasis, might equally have been applied to the young Chet Baker, fifty years earlier.[10]

A third reason that Chet's image was so important was that it led to accusations from his peers that his success was primarily due to his appearance, rather than his abilities. Miles Davis, in particular, was incensed by Chet's early success, convinced that he had copied his own style. When Chet won the prestigious *DownBeat* magazine year-end poll in 1953, Miles complained that Chet was being treated as "the second coming of Jesus Christ". And Miles was not alone. His pianist in 1954, Horace Silver, famously dismissed

West Coast jazz as "faggot-type jazz"—a less than subtle dig at Chet Baker and his band. Likewise Dinah Washington was scathing about his abilities as a singer. "Is that a singer or someone just kidding?" she asked in a 'blindfold test' in *DownBeat* magazine in 1959. "I don't know who it is, but the diction is terrible." Of course, she knew exactly whom she was listening to—she wanted to make the point that she considered his abilities to be over-rated.

To some extent this view of Chet Baker has persisted. "He was the living embodiment of a certain stereotype of the jazz musician as drug addict/cool guy," claimed the vibraphonist Gary Burton, who played with Chet briefly in the mid-1960s. "He was a kind of genial version of James Dean, good-looking and boyish, always getting into trouble, getting through life by using his charisma, more than talent or hard work. But that's just my opinion.[11]

If Miles Davis felt that Chet did not deserve his early success, Gary Burton felt that he took his success for granted. He lacked the discipline of young trumpet players that he admired, such as Freddie Hubbard, Lee Morgan and Blue Mitchell. He rarely rehearsed, and was content to practice on the bandstand. In addition, he was periodically guilty of allowing his 'chops' to get out of shape, not playing for weeks at a time. Whilst these are valid observations, it is harsh to deny his considerable natural talent, or imply that his skills deteriorated—or even stagnated—after his initial brush with fame. "The evolution was in Chet's soloing, the way he brought emotion out in the music," noted the Belgian bass player, Jean-Louis Rassinfosse. "He showed that you can use the same material, but tell different stories every time."

The final way in which Chet Baker's look was significant is that, like that of James Dean, it had an enduring appeal that has kept his legacy in the spotlight. It was his image, for example, that captured the imagination of the fashion photographer, Bruce Weber, who came to fame as a result of his homoerotic images used in advertising campaigns for the likes of Calvin Klein. Weber came across Claxton's photographs of Chet on the cover of his 1955 album *Chet Baker Sings and Plays*.

Bruce Weber used Chet's version of 'Blame It on My Youth' on the soundtrack of his first movie, *Broken Noses*, a documentary about a boxer by the name of Andy Minsker, who failed to make the big time, and made a living teaching the sport to teenage boys. Weber seemed captivated by images of faded beauty, and took his obsession with Chet Baker one stage further when he spent one million dollars of his own money to make a documentary about the ageing trumpeter in 1987, just one year before his mysterious death. *Let's Get Lost* presents a highly stylised vision of Chet Baker's life, but met with considerable critical acclaim.

A newly restored print of the movie was screened at the 2008 Cannes Film Festival, twenty years after Chet Baker fell to his death in Amsterdam. "The enduring fascination of *Let's Get Lost*, the reason it remains powerful even now, when every value it represents is gone, is that it's among the few movies that deal with the mysterious, complicated emotional transactions involved in the creation of pop culture—and with the ambiguous process by which performers generate desire," wrote Terrence Rafferty in the *New York Times*.[12]

This analysis of Chet's public perception might help to explain his early rise to fame, or even his continued popularity, but as Carol Baker suggests, it only scratches the surface of what he was like as a person. To gain a deeper understanding of this complex, damaged individual, we need to go back to his childhood days in the Midwest.

* * * *

Whilst Chet Baker is often regarded as the epitome of West Coast 'cool', his roots lie in Oklahoma, a state that had been ravaged by the Great Depression. His father, Chesney Henry Baker, had endured a miserable upbringing. He was born on January 24th 1906, in Snyder, Oklahoma—a small town that had been devastated by a tornado just one year earlier. His father, George Baker, abandoned his wife and their five children when he left home for another woman. His mother, Alice Baker, went on to marry a local farmer who was known as 'Grandpa Beardsley'. Grandpa Beardsley had a bad leg, and walked with a stick. He soon developed a dislike for Chesney, and beat him with his cane on a regular basis. As a result, Chesney left home when he was eighteen, and continued to harbour a hatred of both his father and stepfather.

For the next few years, Chesney scraped a living as a musician. He was a big fan of jazz music, and had taught himself to play the banjo, an instrument that was frequently used in ragtime and early jazz recordings. His hero was the Texas-born trombone player, Jack Teagarden, and Chet later recalled that his father could whistle some of Teagarden's best-known solos whilst improvising on the guitar. Chesney also enjoyed listening to Bix

Beiderbecke, a cornet player whose cool, romantic tone was quite distinct from the more vibrant sound of his contemporary, Louis Armstrong.

With few jazz bands in rural Oklahoma, Chesney found work as a singer and guitarist with a western swing band, a swinging country-and-western group that played throughout Oklahoma and the Midwest. In 1928, the band was booked to play a dance in Yale, Oklahoma, a small oil town about forty miles west of Tulsa. It was there that he met Vera Moser, the eighteen-year-old daughter of a local farmer.

Vera's father, Salomon Wesley Moser, was born in Iowa, but in 1899 he took part in the Oklahoma land rush. The government had been under increasing pressure to open up lands controlled by Native American tribes, and this pressure intensified after the completion of the first railroad across the land in 1872. The government eventually purchased about two million acres of 'unassigned lands', claiming that local tribes had not settled in those areas. The land run started at noon on April 22nd 1899, with an estimated 50,000 people lining up to claim a parcel of the fertile farming land. Moser evidently claimed around eighty acres, and started a farm. His wife, Randi, was a blind, Norwegian immigrant. Vera Pauline Moser, born in 1910, was the second youngest of their seven children, all of whom helped them to tend the farm.

Vera later recalled how handsome Chesney Baker had looked when they met, and photos reveal a tall, wiry man with slicked back, sandy-coloured hair and a hard mouth. Vera, by contrast, was a plain looking woman with dark brown hair, a round face with a high forehead, and small, deep-set eyes. The young couple married after a brief courtship, and settled down in a small house in South B Street in Yale.

In mid-1929, they found out that they were expecting a child. With Chesney touring with the band for several weeks at a time, Vera went home to live with her parents until his return, shortly after 'Black Tuesday'—the stockmarket crash of October 29th 1929. Chesney Henry Baker Jr, named after his father, was born on 23rd December 1929—an early Christmas present, she used to say. With his chubby cheeks and hazel eyes he initially looked like a small version of his mother, but in later years he increasingly resembled his father, inheriting his slim build and lined forehead.

As the new decade began, it became clear that the stockmarket crash had heralded the end of the 'Roaring Twenties'. The Great Depression started to take hold across the country. Farming communities were hit harder than most, with commodity prices plummeting, and few alternative sources of employment. Chesney Sr had struggled to make ends meet during the good times, and soon found himself out of a job. "No one could afford to go dancing anymore," Chet later wrote in his memoirs, "since just trying to survive was hard enough."[13]

Chesney was willing to accept any work to support his young family, and eventually took a job in an oilfield, smashing old boilers with a sledgehammer for just twenty-five cents an hour. When the refinery closed, another victim of the recession, Chesney had little choice but to move his family to Oklahoma City, the state capital.

On the face of it, Oklahoma City had avoided the worst of the devastation seen in the state's rural communities. Oil had been discovered just outside the city, and by 1930 there were 800 oil derricks south-east of the city, making it the world's second largest oilfield. Another major discovery was made in late March, throwing 3,000 barrels of oil into the air on an hourly basis until it was finally contained. In the city itself, the Rock Island and Frisco railroads had resulted in a thriving business community, whilst two new skyscrapers—the 33-storey First National Centre and the 32-storey Ramsey Tower were racing to completion—the tallest buildings west of the Mississippi. The local newspaper published upbeat articles about how the city had avoided the worst of the recession—"Sixteen Million Dollars in Downtown Buildings in One Year!" it claimed in one front page article as late as 1931.[14]

Chesney and Vera felt a sense of renewed optimism, and initially rented a small house in downtown Oklahoma City. Chesney found part-time work at the local radio station, WKY, where he joined the house country music band. They used to open the day with one hour of music, starting at 6 a.m. Chet later claimed that one of his earliest memories was sitting in a chair, listening to his father sing on the radio. He was clearly absorbing the music, even at a young age, and later told a prospective biographer that he learned his first tune, 'Sleepytime Gal', when he was just two years old.[15]

Another time Chet revealed to Maarten Derksen, a colleague of the Dutch promoter Wim Wigt, that he himself once sung on the radio with his father. Whilst no recording has ever surfaced, it is entirely possible that this story is true; after all, tapes have recently surfaced of Charlie Haden singing on air with his family, aged two, from 1939.

These were relatively happy times for the Baker family. Chesney Sr was making enough money for them to get by, and he would occasional invite his musician friends back to the house to jam in the evenings, enjoying a few drinks and smoking a little marijuana on the porch.

Sadly the good times were not to last for long. The economic downturn caused the closure of numerous local businesses, and even the oil industry started to suffer, with Governor Murray shutting the Oklahoma City field in 1931 due to 'wasteful overproduction'. Liberty Bank was bailed out by a number of local businessmen in 1930; other banks were not so lucky, and were forced to close in 1932 and 1933. The local Building and Loan Association survived, but its assets declined by 60% between 1929 and 1935.[16]

Chesney lost his job at the radio station over this period, and never again found work in the music industry, the love of his life. He struggled to find regular work in the months that followed. "My old man did get other jobs, but he was a failure at each one," Chet told a tabloid journalist in the 1960s. "He didn't mind admitting it—I mean the jobs, but not the music. He would never admit he was a failure as a musician and always blamed the 1929 depression."[17]

By 1935, the family was struggling to make ends meet, and were invited to stay with Chesney's sister Agnes, and her husband Jim, the whole family crammed into a spare room at the back of the house. Jim had been stationed in Belgium during the First World War, and had suffered from serious lung damage after a mustard gas attack. Jim had found work through the Works Progress Administration (WPA), a body established to provide jobs during the Great Depression. He was offered a job in the city parks department, a job he enjoyed, as the clean air was good for his weak chest. The couple had no children, and Aunt Agnes was delighted to look after young Chet while Vera looked for work. "She and Jim were the two most gentle people I think I have ever met," Chet later recalled. "In all the time I spent with them, I don't remember either of them getting angry or raising their voice. 'Darn' and 'shucks' were about their limit when it came to cursing."[18]

Around this time, Chet started to attend the Culbertson Grammar School in the north-east side of the city. He appears to have enjoyed his studies at an early age, claiming to have got good grades in every subject, and never to have missed a day at school. With Chet in school, Vera found work in a local ice-cream factory. In his memoirs, Chet later recalled that his mother used to bring home a different flavour every night—a rare treat during these tough times.

Every summer vacation, Chet would spend an idyllic few weeks on his maternal grandparent's farm, where they grew corn, potatoes, and a variety of fruit, including watermelon and persimmon. "There were cows, pigs, horses, chickens, ducks, cats and dogs—and usually at least two or three nephews or nieces to play with as well," he said. "There was a hayloft to play hide-and-seek in, and I vividly remember all the childhood smells the barn had. When I got a little older, I would accompany my dad and an uncle or two through the blackjack trees in search or rabbits or a squirrel, and possibly a quail or two."[19]

It's interesting to note that Chet has little to say about his parents in his memoirs; even in later years, he would typically limit himself to one or two lines—"My father was a good musician. He had a good ear and good timing," he told one French interviewer. But as with Chet's eloquent trumpet solos, the notes that he left out are just as important as the notes he played. Whilst he rarely had a bad word to say about his upbringing, it is notable that most of his happy memories from his early childhood concern his aunt and uncle, and the time he spent on his grandparents' farm over the summer months.[20]

There is considerable evidence, however, that his parents' relationship started to deteriorate around this time. The pressure of struggling to find work was taking its toll on Chet's father, Chesney Sr. The lines around his eyes started to deepen, and he started drinking heavily, a problem that would continue to plague him until his death in 1967.

He also used to smoke weed on a more regular basis, particularly when Vera was out of the house. In one interview, Chet revealed that he had first seen his father smoke marijuana when he was just seven years old. "Well, my old man was a pot-head," he claimed. "One day, I was up late in bed, mother was out somewhere, and the old man was in the parlour with some of his cronies. I could hear their voices as they talked, but after a while, there was silence. I crept downstairs and took a peak through the keyhole. My old man and his pals were lying back in their chairs with their eyes closed … the room was filled with white smoke and its pungent smell reached me through the door and made me feel sick."[21]

Chesney's heavy drinking and love of marijuana suggest he may well have suffered from an addictive personality. Studies have shown that stress is the factor that is most often associated with drug and alcohol dependency.[22]

Nor was this the full extent of Chesney's behavioural problems at this time. Diane Vavra, Chet's girlfriend in the early 1970s, and again after 1982, remembered a revealing conversation she had with Chet's mother in 1986. He had taken her on a visit to Oklahoma to see his mother and children. In a quiet moment, Diane confided to Vera that Chet used to beat her. Vera went on to explain that on one occasion she was out driving with Chesney, when he accused her of flirting with another man. As they argued, he flew into a terrifying rage that culminated in his losing control of the vehicle, and turning the car on its side. "I never felt the same way about him after that," she confessed.[23]

Chesney's vile temper was made worse by his drinking, and on numerous occasions he beat both his wife and his young son. "He made no secret about the fact that his father beat him," said Ruth Young. "Chet always wanted to be close to his father, but he was afraid of him."[24]

The behaviour of Chet's father in his formative years goes a long way towards explaining the problems that plagued Chet himself in later life. In 1983, the *New York Times* published a series of articles on the causes of addiction. In one of these pieces, focused on the addictive personality, Dr Leon Wurmser, a psychiatry professor, notes that the potentially addictive child may well have been physically abused by parents who are often themselves dependent on drugs or alcohol. "The legacy of brutality leaves the child in a helpless rage," Dr Wurmser says. "He does not view authority, which has been represented by the parents, as something which should be respected, but as capriciously cruel. The child can feel completely out of control and is racked by feelings of violence toward those around him. For him, the use of narcotics can be a way of trying to suppress the highly aggressive feelings that have resulted from his early trauma."[25]

The fact that Chet suffered from severe problems with drug addiction have been well documented, and will be discussed at length later in this book. He smoked prodigious amounts of marijuana in his youth, long before he turned to heroin, and was using heroin on a regular basis—albeit in limited doses—long before his ill-fated European tour in 1955.

Dr Wurmser also touches on an interesting point when he highlights the issue of rage. For the most part, Chet was a mild-mannered individual, albeit an individual with a number of antisocial character traits, but he was prone to losing his temper, often at the slightest provocation. His life is littered with examples—from road rage to fist fights to onstage tantrums.

Unfortunately, Chet also inherited his father's abusive streak. Carol Baker, Diane Vavra and Ruth Young all suffered as a result of his violent behaviour at some time. He was also abusive to his own children, particularly to Paul—his second child by Carol Baker. Vavra even went as far as to claim that Chet admitted to once beating his own mother. This story adds a disturbing twist to Vera's comment in the movie *Let's Get Lost*, in which she claimed that her son was "exactly like his father".[26]

Vera's response to her husband's behaviour was to lavish all her attention on her young son. She started a new job as a saleslady at F.W. Woolworth in downtown Oklahoma City, and used her employee discount to treat him to new clothes. Photographs of Chet as a young child show him with unnaturally well-oiled hair, suggesting his mother had spent considerable time working on his appearance. Carol Baker confirmed that Vera used to pamper her son, and revealed that her behaviour did not change, even as Chet grew older. "Chet was an only child, and a spoiled child," she said. "His mother spoiled him completely! She did everything for him. Until the end of his life, she treated him like a ten-year-old. Whenever Chet came to visit, she said, 'Chet, you need a haircut. Chet, you look terrible. Chet, why don't you wear something decent for once?'"[27]

Ruth Young viewed Vera's relationship with her son as bordering on the obsessive. "I sensed that she was totally preoccupied with her son, and I don't think it was completely natural," she revealed. "Whether it was because of her own dashed hopes for a better future Chet might have provided, it's hard to say, but she was certainly not having an easy time of things. She wasn't able to deal with the failed relationship with her husband; he was beating her, and that was a time you didn't complain."[28]

Despite his parents' significant shortcomings, Chet never sought to blame them in any way, even in private. Ruth Young asked him at length about his upbringing in the years that they were together, but Chet was reluctant to hold them responsible in any way. "He was not so much forgiving, as tolerant," Ruth revealed. "In *Let's Get Lost*, you hear Vera describe their relationship, but you never hear him talk about his mother. Chet's version of his parenting was that it was minimalist. He made no secret about the fact that his father beat him. He didn't seem to take exception to either one of them, which made me revere Chettie even more—he could put it aside, and get on with things. He was level enough to say, 'This is the hand I was dealt.'"[29]

In 1939, Chesney Baker landed a new job through the WPA, working as a timekeeper on a construction site, keeping track of the hours worked by the labourers. Whilst the wages were low, it meant that Chesney and Vera were earning enough between them to move out of his sister's house and into a place of their own. They rented a two-bedroom apartment over a restaurant near the centre of the city. It was here that Chet got his first glimpse of sex. He evidently heard moaning sounds coming from the restaurant below, and scrambled on to the balcony to see if he could see what was going on. He leaned over the railings, and caught a glimpse of the restaurant owner lying on top of one of the waitresses. At that moment, the railing gave way, and Chet fell several feet to the ground below. He dusted himself down, and ran away as fast as he could, but the experience evidently traumatised him.[30]

Chesney's work with the construction company only lasted a few months, it seems, another victim of the sluggish economy. At this point, he made the decision to join the thousands of 'Okies' making their way to California in the hope of securing a better future, as described in John Steinbeck's acclaimed 1939 novel *The Grapes of Wrath*. In the meantime, Vera and Chet stayed behind in Oklahoma City, moving back in with Aunt Agnes and her husband Jim.

A few months later, Chesney sent word that he had secured a job at Lockheed, the aircraft manufacturer based in Burbank, California. Aircraft production had soared as a result of the Second World War, and Chesney was hired as a parts inspector. He rented a modest home at 218, Everett Street in nearby Glendale, and arranged bus tickets for Vera and Chet to join him. The Greyhound bus took them along 1,400 miles of the fabled Route 66, passing through Texas, New Mexico and Arizona before ending in California. It's easy to imagine that Vera felt a sense of optimism, despite the arduous journey, as the family looked to make a fresh start on the West Coast.

Those hopes looked to be well grounded. The house in Glendale was more spacious than anything they'd been accustomed to in Oklahoma City, and was located in a quiet, residential neighbourhood. Chesney seemed to finally accept that he was not destined for a career in music, and was enjoying his new job. He had bought a 1936 Buick, and used to drive to work every morning. Vera found work at the downtown branch of W.T. Grant, a now defunct discount store where she worked on the sales floor. Chet, meanwhile, attended the nearby Glendale Junior High School. He was even allowed to skip a half-grade, supporting his assertion that his grades had been good in Oklahoma.

Whilst Chet makes no mention of it in his memoirs, he was bullied at school after he moved to California; in fact the bullying continued into high school, even after he had spent time in the Army. He was small for his age, and his classmates teased him over his well-groomed, 'mother's boy' appearance and his accent, which betrayed his Oklahoma roots. Chet's response mechanism was to develop a violent temper of his own, a behavioural pattern that continued in adult life, when it was frequently exacerbated by chemical imbalances. He also became intensely competitive, determined to prove himself on the sports track or in the swimming pool.

Outside of school, Vera thought that Chet showed considerable aptitude towards music. He continued to listen to jazz on the radio, often accompanied by his father. Chesney no longer picked up his guitar, but used to sing along, and was joined by his twelve-year-old son, who soon memorised the words. His voice had not yet broken, and sounded angelic to his mother's ears. She encouraged him to join the school choir, and later brought him along to local talent contests at Clifton's, a restaurant near the store in which she worked. In later years, Chet baulked at the memory. "When I was about twelve or thirteen years old, she used to drag me around to these things," he explained to the editor of one jazz magazine. "At that time we had talent contests and things like that, you know. Not just music—tap dancers, harmonica players, accordion—and I got up there and I was very small for my age and sang these ballads with a high little voice. I never did win. I came in second once to a girl tap dancer."[31]

Vera encouraged Chet to sing popular songs such as 'I Had The Craziest Dream', originally sung by Helen Forrest in 1942, and 'That Old Black Magic', a hit for Margaret Whiting in 1943. The fact that these songs were hits for female vocalists did not seem to have occurred to Vera, who simply loved the songs. In later years, however, Diane Vavra raised questions about his mother's motives. "Maybe some kind of Oedipus thing was going on," she said."[32]

Vavra overstates the case; Vera may have been misguided, obsessive even, but only wanted to show off her son's good looks and burgeoning talent to her friends. Chesney was evidently concerned by this turn of events, however, and worried that this would make the bullying worse. He took matters into his own hands by stopping by a pawnshop on the way home from work and buying a trombone, hoping that Chet would be able to emulate his hero, Jack Teagarden. Whilst his aims were admirable, the trombone was clearly too large for a child of Chet's size. "I'd been playing it for a couple of weeks without much success," Chet wrote in his memoirs. "Being small for my age,

I just couldn't reach the bottom positions very well, and the mouthpiece was too big for my lips."[33]

Chesney was disappointed, but on his thirteenth birthday replaced the trombone with a trumpet. Chet later revealed that his father had coldly placed the trumpet on the table, without saying a word. The mouthpiece was better suited to Chet's size, and he was able to produce some basic sounds immediately. In the weeks that followed, Chet intuitively figured out how to play a number of tunes, even if his fingering was technically incorrect. Vera later boasted that it only took two weeks for Chet to replicate Harry James's fast solo on 'Two O'Clock Jump'. Vera was always inclined to romanticise these memories over the years—she once claimed he started playing at the age of two—but it was clear that Chet had a phenomenal ear, and demonstrated an amazing natural ability, even at this age.

Chet enrolled on an elementary instrumental course at Glendale Junior High, but he found himself getting bored after a few weeks. He mastered the basic exercises within minutes, and demonstrated little interest in studying musical theory. Part of the blame probably lies with Chet's father, who had taught himself how to play the banjo and guitar. Vera confirms this view in the movie *Let's Get Lost*. "His father just wanted him to be a natural musician," she told director Bruce Weber, "but his father really held the reins on him."

Chet's early promise on trumpet nearly came to nothing after a bizarre accident broke his front left tooth. One of his school friends evidently threw a small stone that ricocheted off a nearby lamppost, hitting Chet in the mouth. The tooth had to be removed, and Chet found he could no longer control the windflow into the mouthpiece in the same way. In the weeks that followed, Chet was able to alter his embouchure and continue playing. He noticed that the missing front tooth made it more difficult for him to reach the high notes, but over time he adapted his playing style to suit his more limited range. Vera was concerned by her son's appearance and took him to the dentist, who fitted him with a false tooth. Chet found it cumbersome, however, and opted to keep his lips closed, concealing the missing tooth. This resulted in the shy, inscrutable smile that so beguiled his admirers in the years that followed.

Whilst Chet's father was still a big fan of Bix Beiderbecke, Chet's earliest influence was Harry James whose flashy playing style made him easily identifiable. James joined the popular Ben Pollack band in 1935, but started to make a big name for himself when he joined Benny Goodman's orchestra in 1937. He started his own band in 1939, hiring a young Frank

Sinatra as vocalist, before scoring a top ten hit with 'You Made Me Love You' in late 1941.

Over the next few years Chet started to lean to more jazz-oriented players, including Roy Eldridge, Harry 'Sweets' Edison and Louis Armstrong. It has been suggested that Bobby Hackett, a disciple of Bix Beiderbecke, may also have been an influence on Chet's playing, but he vehemently denied this was the case. "For me, Bobby Hackett didn't reach far enough," he explained. "He played the melody very nicely, but there wasn't too much real improvisation, I don't think. He could play very pretty. That's what endeared him to many people, he played very simply. If I had to do that every night I'd be bored to death in a month's time."[34]

In 1944, at the age of fifteen, Chet lost his virginity. He was close friends with two brothers at Glendale High School, Leo and Bennett Little, who lived in a residential hotel in downtown Glendale. On one occasion he visited them after school, and they were joined by a fifteen-year-old girl by the name of Barbara. She apparently asked the three boys whether they had ever had sex, and when she learned of their innocence, offered to sleep with all three of them. Mrs. Bennett was due home from work, so the four of them made their way to a tree house situated at the rear of the hotel, conveniently shielded from the road by two advertising hoardings. The brothers encouraged Chet to go first, then laughed at him when the experience was over in a matter of seconds. Chet later told a prospective biographer, Lisa Galt Bond, that the experience left him humiliated, and afraid to sleep with another woman for a considerable period of time.

Chesney Baker lost his job at Lockheed the following year, after a violent dispute with his boss at the factory. In the months that followed, he struggled to find another job, in part because of his chequered employment history, but also because he was much older than many of the returning servicemen, who offered a cheap source of labour. The family found it hard to get by on Vera's modest income, and eventually took up the offer of help from two old friends from Oklahoma, Bob and Tillie Coulter.

The Coulter family lived in Hermosa Beach, a small seaside town just north of Redondo Beach. Chesney and Vera moved into their spare room, whilst Chet shared a bedroom with their son Brad, who was around the same age. Vera was able to transfer her job to a local branch of W.T. Grant's in nearby Inglewood, close to Los Angeles International Airport, whilst Chesney continued to look for work.

Chet found the move unsettling—it was his third school in three years, and came at a time that is generally considered critical from an educational standpoint. Hermosa Beach offered more in the way of distractions than suburban Glendale, and he started to skip classes, spending his time laying on the beach, climbing the cliffs at nearby Palos Verdes, and diving for abalone. Music was another distraction; in addition to playing in the marching band at his new school, he started to play in a dance band a couple of evenings a week.

An obsessive mother, an abusive father: Chet aged twenty-one, Hermosa Beach.
Courtesy of Ruth Young

In the meantime, Chet found the atmosphere at home stifling. His father eventually found work as a cab driver, but the hours were antisocial and the pay was poor. He took out his frustrations on both Vera and Chet, beating them on a regular basis, and could regularly be found drowning his sorrows in a local bar. Vera sensed that her son was unsettled in this environment, and tried to compensate for Chesney's behaviour. Her smothering approach only served to drive Chet away from her, however. He started to look for part-time work, just to get out of the house, and soon found a job at the local bowling alley. In the absence of automatic pin-setting machines, Chet used to pick up the pins by hand and reset them, earning regular tips because he worked so quickly.

Chet turned sixteen in late 1945, and started to develop a keen interest in cars—a passion that would continue throughout his life. Chet spent his weekends working on old cars with Brad Coulter, who had become a good friend. "He built a little model of a Spider with a shortened drive shaft that went like hell—when it ran," Chet wrote in his memoirs. Chet also borrowed his father's Buick to go drag racing at night, despite the fact that he did not yet have a licence. His school friends were impressed. "He drove like a race car driver—very fast, and he'd go into places I would never drive," recalled Jack Sheldon, who was two years below Chet in high school. Chet's parents were increasingly concerned by his delinquent behaviour, however. They had learned that he was skipping classes, and noted that his grades were also starting to suffer.

The arguments intensified when they found out that Chet had been stealing gas; he had become adept at inserting a piece of rubber tubing into the gas tank of another car, sucking on the tube to create a vacuum, and siphoning the gas into his father's Buick. His father told him in no uncertain terms that he needed to finish high school, and would do as he was told to while he lived under the same roof. Chet responded that he was bored at school, and didn't even want to live at home.

Chet made no attempt to modify his behaviour in the weeks that followed. As a result, Chesney suggested to Vera that it might be best for him to sign up for the Army, which would at least impose a sense of discipline. Vera burst into tears, scared of losing her precious son, but gradually came round to the idea. When they told Chet about their idea, he responded positively. The Army gave him a sense of independence, an escape route from the repressive conditions of home life. He signed up for an eighteen-month period on

November 5th 1946, just a few weeks short of his seventeenth birthday.

The night before he was scheduled to leave for basic training, Chet went out on a date with a girl called Gloria. By now he was a qualified driver, and his father gave him permission to borrow his car. At the end of the evening, Chet drove her to a quiet spot near her house, and they made love frantically in the back seat of the car. Gloria knew that Chet was leaving next day, and handed him a small photograph of herself so that he remembered her, kissed him, and then ran back into the house. It seemed like a perfect way to begin his new life of freedom.

Chapter Two

EVERYTHING HAPPENS TO ME
1946–50

"... When I heard Dizzy and Miles, everything changed for me, and I found myself getting further and further away from the 'sweet' Harry James style of playing, and trying to phrase things in, I guess—for lack of a better word—a 'hipper' way."— Chet Baker[1]

A few days after signing up, Chet made his way to Fort Lewis in Pierce County, Washington. It was one of the largest Army facilities in the country, set in over 80,000 acres of dense woodland. Since the end of the Second World War, the base had been used first as a separation centre, discharging war veterans, and from May 1946 as a training centre for young men scheduled to be sent overseas for occupational duty.

Chet joined thousands of other fresh-faced recruits in undergoing two months of ground-force training. They learned how to march, complete with heavy backpacks, how to use rifles and hand-grenades, as well as more mundane functions such as guard duty and kitchen patrol. The intense training and cold, wet weather came as something of a shock to Chet after his laid-back lifestyle at home. "I guess I had gotten used to the Southern California climate," he admitted, "where just a short time ago I'd spent so much time lying on the beach or skin-diving along the cliffs of Palos Verdes."[2]

Despite the tough regime, he had no regrets about joining the Army. Like many of the other recruits, it gave him his first taste of independence, and he had no desire to return to the stifling conditions of life at home with his parents. In early December, just one month after his arrival, he was summoned to see the company commander. The officer explained that they had discovered that he was only sixteen years old, and that he had the right to request a discharge, even though his seventeenth birthday was just weeks away. Chet declined the opportunity, and returned to the barracks.

Chet befriended a recruit by the name of Dick Douglas, who came from Pasadena, California. At nineteen, he was more than two years older than Chet, who was impressed by both his physical strength, particularly in the gymnasium, and his intelligence. As luck would have it, they were amongst a handful of soldiers from Chet's regiment selected to ship out to Western theatre of operations, where they would be based in Berlin; most of them were sent to Japan and Korea, which sounded even more alien, more 'foreign', to someone of Chet's background.

After completing two months of basic training, the new recruits were given a thirty-day leave, after which Chet and Dick took a bus to Camp Kilmer in New Jersey, twenty miles south of New York City. It was here that the troops were vaccinated, and picked up their supplies for their overseas posting. The ten-day boat trip to Germany that followed left an indelible print on Chet's mind. "The trip included the usual forty-eight hour crap game, which I did not participate in, since the majority of the money always seemed to end up in the pockets of two or three guys. There was vomit everywhere, and you could not escape the smell of it, no matter where you were on the ship. Since there wasn't anything alcoholic to drink, some of the guys mixed Aqua Velva (aftershave) with fruit juice. Everyone was getting loaded and fighting. Some went blind from the noxious aftershave mixture. Altogether, it was a trip I could not easily forget."[3]

The ship eventually docked at Bremerhaven, the port city of nearby Bremen. The troops disembarked and were transported to a nearby aircraft hanger, glad to get their feet back on dry land and enjoying the icy, fresh German winter air. Next morning, after breakfast, there was a mad rush to get to the bulletin board to find details of where they would be stationed. Chet expected to be separated from his friend, Dick Douglas, but was pleased to discover they would both be based at the same compound in Berlin; Chet was given a clerical job as a typist, whilst his friend was given a comfortable role as theatre manager, responsible for the troop movie theatre.

Next morning, a train took them across the snow-covered countryside to a Russian checkpoint on the outskirts of the city. Chet had not appreciated the depth of devastation that had taken place in Berlin, noting that whole blocks of the city had been completely flattened. "Russian tanks had roamed the streets of the city, taking revenge for what the Germans had done in

Russia," he noted in his memoirs. "They had left some blocks intact though, and used these to house their own troops."

The city had been divided into four sectors after the war, occupied by the Russians, Americans, British and French. Chet was based in the district of Zehlendorf in the American sector, which was one of the greener suburbs of the city, where the housing had been less badly damaged. As he later discovered, the local inhabitants, many of them elderly and younger children, had been forcibly evacuated from their homes to make way for the occupying troops.

After being shown around the Office of Military Government, where he had been assigned, he wandered round the nearby Onkel-Tom district. He was encouraged to hear the sound of band music coming from one of the blocks, and saw a sign outside reading '298th AGF Band' [Army Ground Forces]. He went inside and introduced himself to the unit's staff sergeant, who suggested he come back next morning, when he would be introduced to the band's first trumpet player, Paul Martin. After hearing Chet play for a few minutes, Martin said, "That's enough, Chet. I'll have the sarge [sergeant] make out a transfer request." Chet was evidently surprised the audition was so straightforward. "They must have been desperate for trumpet players," he later remarked.[4]

"The 298th Army Band consisted of ninety-eight musicians, and we had special uniforms and they looked really sharp," recalled fellow trumpeter Sebastian 'Sebby' Papa, who played alongside Chet. The band enjoyed a fairly comfortable lifestyle. A typical day would start with reveille in the morning, which took place in the campground across the street, rehearsal during the day, before playing retreat every night. "We ate with the officers," said Papa. "We were treated like kings."[5]

Chet was not familiar with all of the tunes in the band's repertoire, but his ear was good enough that he could pick things up after just one run-through. "That didn't matter, because he had a great sound," recalled Papa. "He was seventeen years old and played like no other trumpet player in the band, even then."[6]

The 298th Army Band on parade in Berlin, 1947
Photograph courtesy of 'Sebby' Papa

Jim Coleman, an old family friend of Chet's, who is an amateur trumpet player himself, is convinced that this was a crucial period in the development of Chet's playing. "You know what they do in the Army—they practice eight hours a day," he explained. "During the Vietnam era, I looked into joining the Air Force; they promised that I would never leave New York, and they told me exactly what I would do in my four years in the Air Force. I would report every morning at eight o'clock, and from nine until five I would practice the trumpet, singly and with other musicians. Most normal people are never going to practice for eight hours a day. Charlie Parker went into a period of wood-shedding in the late 1930s, where he would lock himself up for up to twelve, fifteen hours a day and do nothing but practice. I don't even know what kind of discipline that takes. Courtesy of the US government, this is what happened to Chet. And he became a brilliant musician at this point."[7]

Outside of the daily routine, the band would travel out to Tempelhof Airport every week or so to play for dignitaries and high-ranking officials, as well as visiting movie stars such as Wallace Beery and Victor McLaglen.

On 3rd April 1947 the band played for General Lucius D. Clay on his arrival in Berlin to become the High Commissioner. The band also sneaked on to the grounds of his mansion three weeks later, on April 23rd, to surprise him with a rendition of 'Happy Birthday'. The General was surprised and flattered by the gesture, and invited the whole band to breakfast.

Chet's only complaint was when the band had to wait around in the biting cold. "It wasn't so bad in the spring … ," he wrote, "but the long German winter was a bitch, and it was rough standing out on the runway for up to three hours, often in four or five inches of snow, just to honor the arrival of these guys, most of whom could really not have cared less about the music that awaited them."[8]

The 298th 'Big Dance Band', Chet Baker back row, second from left. Photograph courtesy of 'Sebby' Papa.

The 298th Army Band also had an informal 'Big Dance Band', headed by Sergeant Robert Badgley, a fine trombone player. When it became apparent that Chet was having problems reading music, Chet asked Bob Badgley if he could help. "He came for one lesson, and never returned," Badgley recalled. "He never learned to read, and never developed the desire to learn. Consequently, as far as I knew, he always faked his way through his performances."[9]

According to 'Sebby' Papa, the dance band used to play once a week at Club 48, a bar that had been established for the American soldiers. It had forty-eight marble-topped tables, each of which was engraved with the outline of one of the American states. The dance band rarely played outside Berlin, but did once enter a big band contest in Frankfurt. "I believe they came in second," he vaguely recalled.

Club 48 also served as one of the main social venues for the soldiers. "The first night there, Badgeley took me out to the Club 48, and not being a drinker got loaded on the dark German beer," said Papa. "I don't remember getting back home." The Army seems to have had a calming effect on Chet's rebellious behaviour, as most of his colleagues remember him as a quiet-spoken man, who didn't socialise with many of the other soldiers. "He was on the shy side, and didn't have many friends," Papa confirmed. "Mostly other trumpet players."

Chet continued to see his old friend, Dick Douglas, who was enjoying an enviable lifestyle running the movie theatre. "Dick had a staff of Germans working for him, his own office, a private room in the basement fixed up with a parachute that draped from the ceiling, colored lights, a bar, and his own 16mm projector. Need I say more?" Douglas was also active in the black market business, trading cigarettes, coffee, chocolate, soap, even cameras, all goods that were otherwise hard to come by. Coffee and cigarettes doubled as currency around Berlin. "Any soldier could flag down a VW with a German driver, as long as the driver was alone, and he'd take you anywhere for five to six cigarettes," Chet later recalled.[10]

Between rehearsals, Chet enjoyed playing cards, chess, table tennis and bowling. As the weather started to get warmer, he started to spend more time by Lake Wannsee on the edge of Zehlendorf where he would rent a boat with friends such as Dick Douglas and one of the band's saxophonists, Howard Glitt. Out on the water they would listen to broadcasts on the Armed Forces Radio Service on a portable radio, listening to the latest tunes by Stan Kenton and his orchestra. "It was the first modern music I'd heard, and I couldn't believe it," Chet wrote in his memoirs. "This was the year that Stan came out with 'Intermission Riff', 'Artistry in Percussion,' etc. And since we had a dance band made up of musicians from the Army band that played at the (NOO) club, we were all interested in what was happening on the music scene."

Stan Kenton had formed a fourteen-piece big band, the Artistry in Rhythm Orchestra, in 1941, recording tunes such as 'Artistry in Rhythm' (1943) and 'And Her Tears Flowed Like Wine' (1944). The band's sound became more 'progressive' after the war, when Kenton recruited the Italian composer, Pete Rugolo, who contributed many key arrangements, and helped the band to move up the popularity polls. June Christy also joined the band at this time, replacing Anita O'Day on vocals. The band continued to make the odd novelty record, presumably to keep Capitol Records happy, but also recorded a number of classics, including the titles that Chet refers to, along with 'Artistry in Boogie', 'Artistry in Bolero' and 'Concerto to End All Concertos' (all 1946).

Chet Baker (far left) with friends from the 298th Army Band: Photograph courtesy of 'Sebby' Papa.

Chet was also drawn to modern jazz in the form of bebop, as pioneered by the likes of Dizzy Gillespie and Charlie Parker. The new sound was in stark contrast to 'swing'; it was more stripped back, typically relying on two or three horns as the front line, with piano, bass and drums providing rhythmic support. Arrangements were sparse, with the front line typically playing the melody in unison, but the soloist no longer felt the need to keep to the stated chord changes. As a consequence, improvised lines grew faster and more complex. "To gauge the full extent of this change, one need merely study the melody line to 'Donna Lee', Charlie Parker's reworking of the standard, 'Indiana'," suggests Ted Gioia in his hugely informative book *The History of Jazz*. "The melody of 'Indiana' is conventional, staying close to chord tones at all times, but Parker's piece immediately moves into deeper waters: almost every bar features one or more altered tones—an augmented fifth, a major seventh played against a minor chord, a flatted ninth leading to a sharpened ninth, and the like. The composition as a whole is nothing less than a textbook example of how bop harmonic thinking revolutionised the flow of the melodic line in jazz."[11]

Chet would have listened to Charlie Parker's early recordings with Dizzy Gillespie, which included 'Salt Peanuts', 'Billie's Bounce' and 'Now's The Time', as well as Parker's legendary early recordings for Dial, which featured the nineteen-year-old Miles Davis on trumpet, which produced classics such as 'Ornithology' and 'Night in Tunisia'. These recordings had a profound effect on Chet, and the way in which he played. "When I first started playing, Harry James, of course, was a very big star with the trumpet. Roy Eldridge, Charlie Shavers, Sweets Edison also impressed me—and Louis Armstrong, of course," he later explained. "But when I heard Dizzy and Miles, everything changed for me, and I found myself getting further and further away from the 'sweet' Harry James style of playing, and trying to phrase things in, I guess—for lack of a better word—a 'hipper' way."[12]

During the warmer summer months, Chet pursued his passion for sailing, often going out on the lake alone while his friends from the band went out in the city, looking for girls. "For four months I hadn't thought much about chicks," he later wrote. "I'd say to myself, 'Why should I go out of my way to look for women when I'm sure that if I wait, it will be so much better?'" He had traded in some packets of cigarettes for a gold ring, complete with a large aquamarine stone and two sapphires, and later swapped the ring for a small motorboat. Most weekends he drove out to the lake, parked up by the shore, and took the motorboat out about fifty metres to a buoy, where a forty-foot sailboat was moored.[13]

One weekend, Chet decided to go out on the boat, in spite of the overcast weather. As he set sail, he noticed an attractive German girl wading in the water, holding her dress above her knees to keep it from getting wet. Chet told numerous versions of the story in the years that followed, but in short, he asked her if she wanted to join him. Moments later, the heavens opened, and the two of them ended up making love on the boat out in the middle of the lake.

Chet saw their relationship as the beginning of a summer romance, but the German girl, Gisella, and her sister, were apparently on the lookout for a wealthy officer to marry them, and take them to live back in the United States, away from the poverty of post-war Berlin. When it became apparent that Chet was neither wealthy, nor officer material, she quickly lost interest. Next time Chet paid a visit he was met by her mother, who informed him that Gisella had married a Russian officer. In his memoirs, he seemed to remember the episode fondly. "I'll never forget her," he concluded, "and how she made my fantasy come true." On other occasions, he sounded bitter, once confiding to a prospective biographer that the mother had lied to him, and that she had eventually married another trumpet player in the 298th Army Band.

The story is significant to the extent that it helps us to understand Chet's attitude towards women. Chet had an old-fashioned, chauvinistic view of how women should behave, shaped by his upbringing in Oklahoma, and the example set by his parents. For the most part, his mother had behaved dutifully towards Chesney Sr, putting up with his heavy drinking, and long periods where they were short of money, and she was the main breadwinner. When she did complain about his drinking, or smoking pot with his friends, they would argue violently, Chesney Sr beating her on a regular basis.

Chet's previous relationships with girls, back in California, had tended to be short-lived, adolescent affairs; in his limited experience, however, the girls had been looking for the same thing as him—sex, rather than romance. Chet regarded his affair with Gisella in quite different terms; a relationship he had been prepared to "wait" for, a "fantasy". And when she didn't see the fantasy in the same way, he was not sure how to react. It left with him with a deep distrust of women that he was never able to shake off, an emotional immaturity he never grew out of. When he became addicted to heroin, which frequently left him impotent, it added a sense of inadequacy to the equation, fuelling intense jealousy over the most insignificant of issues.

In late October, Chet was treated for appendicitis; the doctors discovered that his appendix had perforated, and as a result he spent sixty days in the hospital, after which he was sent back to Camp Kilmer to be discharged. "I was ready," he later recalled. "It was time to go home."[14]

While he had been in Europe, Chet's parents had moved to Hermosa Beach. Vera had been promoted to floor supervisor at W.T. Grant's, and had put aside enough money to put down a deposit on a small, two-bedroom house—the first house they had ever owned. 1011 16th Street was situated close to the top of the hill, with a clear view down to Highway 101, and the golden beach beyond.

Vera was delighted to have Chet back home, and when he enrolled at the local high school, Redondo Union, she was convinced that the Army had instilled a new discipline in her son, and that his days of delinquency were behind him. The school boasted one of the largest campuses in California, and was known for the strength of its high school football team. Within a few days, Chet auditioned for the high school concert band. One time, the band's conductor George Cather requested they play 'Ruslan and Ludmila', a classical piece by Glinka, a Russian composer. The band's first trumpet player, Gene Daughs, watched with astonishment as Chet barely played the piece first time around, and simply listened to the music. Second time, however, he didn't miss a note.

Chet's good looks soon endeared him to the high school girls, but he was less popular with the jocks, who used to pick on him. "He got into fights all the time," recalled his friend Bernie Fleischer, who played clarinet in the band. Chet soon learned to defend himself, and despite his small frame, he could pack a fair punch.[15]

When he graduated from high school in the summer of 1948, his parents encouraged him to sign up for El Camino Junior College in nearby Lawndale. Chet's status as an ex-GI entitled him to free tuition, and he elected to major in music, taking English as a minor.

His music professor was another ex-GI, a twenty-three-year-old by the name of Hamilton Maddaford. Chet was expected to study sight-reading and harmony, but as happened in Germany, Chet quickly lost interest.

Chet played in the El Camino College Warrior Band, where he was occasionally allowed to solo, but he soon grew bored of playing marches. As far as he was concerned, the real education came after school, when he and Bernie Fleischer would sit at home listening to bebop 78s, playing the solos over and over until they could repeat them, note for note.

In early 1949, Chet started to sit in at a small jazz club in Hermosa Beach. One of Chet's friends, Andy Lambert, played double bass, and occasionally played at a small club by the name of High Seas as part of a trio. "He was in his thirties, and had been in the Navy, where he had lost a leg," Chet recalled in his memoirs. "He now got around nicely on a wooden peg. We became friends, and he invited me to come into the club and sit in with his band."[16]

Lambert also introduced Chet to grass. Chet had witnessed his father smoke pot as a child, and remembered being sickened by the smell. Several years later, when he was fourteen or fifteen, his father confessed to being a 'pot-head', but even then, Chet had no desire to try it. His attitude changed when he saw Andy and the other members of the band outside the club, smoking a joint. He asked if Chet wanted to join them. "I readily agreed—did I want to be taken as a square?"[17]

He later tried to explain the appeal of marijuana in an interview with an Italian magazine. "Everything becomes beautiful and pure, serene and pleasant … the nerves are relaxed, worries fade away. Time takes on new meaning. There's no need to worry because the hours, the days, the years are all for you, at your service … everything is easy, everything is possible."[18]

Andy Lambert and the band's guitarist, Gene Sergeant, introduced Chet to a pianist by the name of Jimmy Rowles. Rowles was an experienced musician, who had worked with Lester Young, Benny Goodman and Woody Herman. He was best known for his work with singers, however, and at this time he was accompanying Peggy Lee at Ciro's on Sunset Boulevard. Rowles was well-known amongst the jazz community for his extraordinary repertoire, and once Chet had been introduced, he was a regular visitor at his house in Culver City, dropping by on his way home from college, even waking him up in the morning if his classes didn't start until later. He asked the pianist to play certain tunes, listened intently, and then tried to reproduce the tune by ear. Rowles was astounded by his ability, and within a few weeks, offered to take Chet to another jazz club after he had finished work.

Chet's style was still raw and fiery at this time, and when Rowles took him along to a jam session, he made an immediate impression. "People kept saying, 'Where the hell did you get this guy?'" he said. "Nobody had ever heard of him, and he was up there blowing these guys out."

The LA jazz scene that Rowles introduced to Chet was quite segregated at that time, with musicians still divided into a 'white union' and a 'coloured union'. The black jazz musicians tended to congregate around the clubs on Central Avenue, which at that time was LA.s equivalent of Harlem; a thriving community of businesses, shops, restaurants, bars and nightclubs. Jazz was just one part of the bustling nightlife, which also featured theatre, dance, vaudeville and R&B. The Central Avenue scene was probably at its peak in the 1930s and 1940s; African-American celebrities from across the nation—names like Joe Louis, Duke Ellington, Louis Armstrong, Jackie Robinson and Jack Johnson—would congregate there if they were in town.

"Central Avenue was like Harlem a long time ago," confirmed Art Pepper. "As soon as evening came, people would be out on the streets, and most of the people were black … it was a beautiful time ... the women dressed up in frills and feathers and long earrings and hats with things hanging off them, fancy dresses with slits in the skirts. Most of the men wore big, wide-brimmed hats and zoot suits with wide collars, small cuffs and large knees, and their coats were real long, with padded shoulders. They wore flashy ties with diamond stickpins; they wore lots of jewellery; and you could smell powder and perfume everywhere. And as you walked down the street you heard music coming out of every place."[19]

Art Pepper ended up with a job at the Ritz Club; a small bar hidden behind an empty storefront. "The music started at two in the morning and went on all night," he recalled. "People would come and sit in: Jimmy Blanton, probably the greatest bass player that ever lived … Art Tatum came in; Louis Armstrong, Ben Webster, Coleman Hawkins, Roy Eldridge, Johnny Hodges, Lester Young. You can imagine what a thrill it was to be in the same room as these people."

Whilst Chet would occasionally venture to Central Avenue, he preferred a club called the Showtime, located on Sepulveda Boulevard, Encino, in the San Fernando Valley. He would drive out there with a revolving circle of friends—bass player Hersh Hamel, fellow trumpet player Jack Sheldon, clarinet player Bernie Fleischer, pianist Gordy Swain, drummer Bob Neel—to name but a few. "We'd always go out to the Showtime," confirmed Jack Sheldon, then just sixteen years old. "They had a jam session there run by Herbie Harper, the trombone player, every Monday night. Everybody would come to that; all of Stan Kenton's band, Maynard Ferguson, Art Pepper, we'd always play there. All the cats!"[20]

Whilst Sheldon suggests that all the 'cats' were present, those that he mentions by name were all white. "The Showtime was mostly white musicians, from what I can remember," confirmed saxophonist Bill Holman. "By that time, Central Avenue was starting to wind down, but there were probably still sessions going on that the black musicians went to." There were exceptions—saxophonists Wardell Gray and Teddy Edwards attended on an occasional basis—but for the most part, the Showtime was every bit as segregated as the Musicians' Union.[21]

The segregation was maintained by Herbie Harper, a twenty-nine-year-old trombonist, who carefully selected who would be allowed to play from the crowd of eager young musicians. He would then allocate each group a forty-five-minute set in which they could demonstrate their ability. As a result, the Monday night jam was regarded, at least by the white musicians, as one of the most elite sessions in town. "It got to be so popular that you'd have to call up the guy who ran it in the afternoon to make an appointment to play!" laughed Bill Holman. "For young people starting out it was the place to meet people and be heard, so it was very popular, and they had a big crowd every week. Everybody would stand around, listen to the new guy, see what they thought, and see if he had anything or not."[22]

A number of Chet's friends were never invited to play at the Showtime. Jack Sheldon, who later established a very successful career of his own, made it to the stage, but was soon asked to leave. "It was real hard for me," Sheldon admitted in the movie *Let's Get Lost*. "I never knew where I was, and I would always forget what bar we were in."[23]

One consequence of the selection policy was that the Showtime became a showcase for some of the emerging West Coast talent—saxophonists like Art Pepper and Herb Geller, trumpet players such as Shorty Rogers, Maynard Ferguson and the Candoli brothers, pianists such as Russ Freeman and Lou Levy, bass players including Red Mitchell and Joe Mondragon, and drummers such as Shelly Manne and Bob Neel—all paid their dues at the Monday night jam session.

In his memoirs, Chet recalled that it took several weeks before he was invited to play. "The first few times I went out there, I was not allowed to play, but then finally I was allowed to sit in one time, on just one set—you see, it was rather cliquey … After a while, I finally got to play a whole set; then two sets, and eventually it became my gig and everyone had to ask me if they could get in."[24]

According to his friends, Chet's playing was impressive, even in those early years. "Chettie was just a genius right away; he was so talented," Jack Sheldon remembered. "He had completely his own sound. Very inventive, he played so well. I didn't hear too many other people play that way. When I was with him he never practiced, but I heard from several people that he practiced all the time when he was in the Army."[25]

Bill Holman, who first met Chet at the Showtime, confirmed this view. "He was playing French horn at the time, and everybody was astounded that he could play jazz on the French horn," he recalled. "Chet's playing stood out even then; he played all the good notes."[26]

On other nights, Chet would get together with a small group of friends, and drive from club to club, looking for somewhere to play. "We played all over LA," recalled Jack Sheldon. "We had a little band with Hersh, Bob Neel, I played piano sometimes, sometimes Gordy Swain played piano. We'd just go round the nightclubs saying, 'Can we play tonight?' Sometimes they wouldn't want us to play loud, so we developed a way of playing real soft, which was kind of the way we played there for a while. It gave us a lot of control over the playing."[27]

According to bass player Hersh Hamel, the personnel in the band would vary from night to night, depending on who was available, and who had transport. "We used to go out playing all the time," he said. "Sometimes out of seven nights in the week, we'd be playing five nights, and we had a different place for each night. Even if we weren't working we'd be, like, together as a group of guys: myself, Jack Montrose, Art, Sammy Curtis, sometimes Chet Baker, sometimes Jack Sheldon, Bill Perkins, Gene Rowland, Bob Braucus, Bob Neel. Sometimes Shorty Rogers even came along. Some nights we'd play at the Samoan in East LA, right in the Barrio, off Whittier and Atlantic. We knew the owner there, he was very mellow, and he liked us to come in. Al Leon had a place for us to play in El Cerrito."[28]

By this stage, Chet was spending so much time playing in clubs at night that his college work was starting to suffer. In music, his major, his playing was considered to be good, but he was only given an F for his sight-reading. In his other subjects, which included English (his minor), political science and psychology, he scraped by, managing low passing grades.

Over the summer vacation, Chet divided his day between visits to Jimmy Rowles, where he continued to absorb many of the tunes that later became part of his repertoire, getting high with his friends, and spending time down by the beach, where he loved to sail and climb the cliffs by Redondo Beach. By night, he'd borrow his father's car at every opportunity and look for a club in which he could play, not returning until the early hours. One evening, after a gig at Hermosa Beach, he and Bernie Fleischer were walking along the Esplanade when they passed a catamaran moored just off the beach. Chet suggested they steal the boat, and sail to Catalina, an island twenty-six miles off the coast of California. Fleischer thought he was crazy.

That summer he also started to frequent a bar called Esther's down at Manhattan Beach. The pianist Matt Dennis, who had worked as a composer and arranger with the Tommy Dorsey band, had a regular job at the club. "He was a hell of a nice guy," Chet recalled, "and I'd always ask him to do his tune, 'Everything Happens To Me'." He fell in love with the song, and in later years, he may have come to empathise with the sentiments expressed in the lyrics.

> *"I make a date for golf, and you can bet your life it rains,*
> *I try to give a party, and the guy upstairs complains.*
> *I guess I'll go through life, just catching colds and missing trains,*
> *Everything happens to me."*[29]

It was at Esther's that Chet met Sherry, a small, pretty Mexican girl. Chet fell deeply in love with her, and they were virtually inseparable over the vacation period. Towards the end of summer she broke the news that she was pregnant. At first, Chet's parents were understanding, and even offered to have Sherry move in to their small house in Hermosa Beach while they figured out what to do. Given that Chet was still at college, and had no regular income, they decided it would be best for both of them to terminate the pregnancy.

Soon after, however, they put pressure on their son to break things off with her altogether. In his memoirs, Chet speculated they might have been worried she would get pregnant again, but in all likelihood his narrow-minded parents didn't want to see him marry a Mexican girl. Chet's mother had a similar reaction when he started dating a Jewish-French girl, Liliane Cukier, several years later. Either way, Chet was genuinely upset to split with her, and still looked back on their romance fondly some twenty years later. "I sure missed having her around and remember her from time to time with warmth and affection. I hope that she found happiness and love with someone worthy of her."[30]

When Chet enrolled for the fall semester, he dropped English, and only signed up for music appreciation and orchestra. He soon started skipping classes, and his teacher warned him that he'd never make it as a professional musician without the proper grounding. Within a few weeks he made the decision to drop out of college altogether. "At the end of a year-and-a-half

I failed that [course] and I still play by ear," Chet explained in an interview with Les Tomkins. "Although I can read, I don't know the chords. I just hear them, you know, but if you ask me what the name of it is, I wouldn't be able to tell you".[31]

Chet's mother was disappointed when he dropped out of college, and told him that he needed to find a real job, and start paying his way. He found a job with a Latin dance band in a hotel in downtown Los Angeles, where he became friends with the band's bass player, Bob Whitlock. "I had heard him one time out at the Showtime," Whitlock recalled. "I was just totally amazed; he sounded like a mix of Fats Navarro and Miles Davis, with a little bit of Dizzy. His playing was more aggressive than he became known for; when he started with Gerry, he was thought of as being 'cool', part of the 'cool school'. But at that time, his playing was fiery. I was just knocked out; I couldn't believe this young guy was playing like that."[32]

Whitlock hailed from Roosevelt, Utah, and at eighteen years old, he was one year younger than Chet. Despite his tender years, he had already been married and divorced from his high-school sweetheart. "I had just gotten over an early marriage—I was eighteen, I guess, and was having a hard time getting over this girl. I really loved her, but her parents were very wealthy, and didn't approve of me at all. They succeeded in busting up our marriage."[33]

With their mutual love of music, Chet and Bob hit it off right away. "Chet had just been through a similar scene where his parents had disapproved of a girl, a little Mexican girl that he had got pregnant. He really liked that girl. Anyway, we had a lot in common. We got talking after the show, and then we went out to a jam session in East LA, and we were out until the sun came up!"

Over the next few weeks, they started hanging out together, both on and off the bandstand. Bob remembers him as a cool, laid-back, fun-loving individual at this time. "There was just a kind of openness and wildness about him then," he recalled. "He had a fantastic sense of humour, and maybe the most infectious laugh I've ever heard. He was a very funny guy when he was young, believe me."[34]

Chet's wild streak exhibited itself in a number of ways. He was still inclined towards mild misdemeanours, whether it was 'borrowing' someone's boat for the evening, or siphoning gas from a fuel tank. He also exhibited a sense of daring that would frequently astonish his friends. "We used to walk the cliffs down at Redondo Beach, just for something to do. Most of us would creep along, making sure our footing was right, whereas Chet would go shooting down there like a mountain goat. You'd think, 'What the hell is he doing, he's going to kill himself.' I mean, it's a long drop there. He acted like he was indestructible. He used to drive the same way. If there were a parking place with just a foot and a half to spare, he'd get in there somehow. I knew a lot of people who'd never get in the car with him. He was an amazing guy. Dare him to do anything, and it would be done."[35]

Bob Whitlock is convinced that Chet's playing was an extension of his personality. "As far his being 'different as a musician and a person', nothing could be further from the truth," he explained to the writer Gordon Jack. "His playing was the mirror image of his personality. It's true that he often exhibited rebellious, juvenile delinquent, hot-rod kid behaviour; but that was just one small facet of his personality. It would take a much larger palette than that to do a portrait of Chet.

He went on to explain how Chet's daring, his willingness to take chances, impacted his playing. "Most of us play by ear assisted by some knowledge of harmony and counterpoint. Since Chet didn't have the benefit of these tools, he was forced to do it all by ear. And therein lies the key to his genius. Naturally there's a price to pay with this approach. It requires the bravado to run through minefields and the courage of Hannibal because the perils are endless. The reward comes in the form of refreshing vitality, breathtaking melodic invention, freedom from exasperating clichés, extraordinary sensitivity to shading and colour, and a lyricism second to none. Not a bad trade-off if you're willing to take the risks, and Chet greeted the challenge like a gladiator."[36]

Chet once explained his thought process to Bob. "'Every now and then I just put my finger down and blast, play a dissonant note, and then use my ear to fight my way out of it'," he revealed. "And when he did that, he could amaze you," said Whitlock. "It was part of the way he played, and it's one of the most exciting things about his playing. He improvised at all times, and would try stuff that the average trumpet player wouldn't even attempt. And some things that perhaps he shouldn't have even attempted! It's like he put himself on the spot so he had to come out with something original. Most of us are just too self-conscious to do that."[37]

After a few weeks, Chet learned that Bob needed to find a new place to live, and suggested he move in to his parent's house at Hermosa Beach.

Chet's mother, in particular, wasn't happy about the arrangement, as the house was barely big enough for the three of them. "Chet's mother was naïve, almost silly, I thought," said Whitlock. "Straight off the Oklahoma farm. She expected him to be a nice little boy—I mean, how naïve can you get. He had his eye on the big time, he was a flamboyant, a racy kind of guy. She talked him to him like he was at Sunday school, and he was going to be a minister someday. It was really bizarre."[38]

Bob found Chet's father, Chesney Sr, somewhat easier to get on with because he was a musician himself, and a big fan of the trombone player, Jack Teagarden. "I could never figure out how the hell they got together," he recalled. "He was more of a lady's man." On one occasion, however, he witnessed another side to Chet's father's behaviour—a violent, unpredictable temper that had resulted in his beating his son in earlier years. "I remember Chet wrecking his father's car; not very bad, but his father really got hot, I tell you. He was scary to me. He told Chet, 'I don't care what the hell you think you're doing. You can take that trumpet, go stick it in the drawer. I want you to go out and earn the money to pay for this car'. And Chet did. He went to work in a little machine shop there in Hermosa, separating bolts, putting one in this bin, one in that bin! He was as loyal as could be, until he'd saved the money to pay for the car.[39]

This incident hastened Chet's desire to move into a place of his own, and in late 1949 he and Bob Whitlock rented the guest cottage of a mansion in Redondo Beach. The young musicians were playing regularly, but paid work was still hard to come by, so they invited two other friends to move in with them and help share the rent. "We got Bob Neel to come in with us, and Larry Bangham, a really good piano player. He played a little too complicated for his own good; he was a Joe Albany type of player. We had a built-in band; a rhythm section and Chet. We played night and day, and would play little gigs if we could get them. That's how I really developed my playing—I got a lot of playing under my belt."

From the musician's perspective, the cottage was ideally located. It was an old building, with thick concrete walls, and this, coupled with the sound of the surf crashing against the cliffs below, drowned out the sound of the music. Even when other musicians would stop by the house in the early hours of the morning, and they played until the sun rose, they never experienced any problems with the police.

In *As Though I Had Wings*, Chet suggests that the drummer Jimmy McKean lived in the cottage, but this is incorrect—he was one of many musicians that used to drop by on an occasional basis. "He was a good little drummer—very cool, very reserved. He was a very considerate drummer, using a lot of brushes, rather than drowning people out, which a lot of drummers did at that time." His drumming made a considerable impression on Chet, who tended to favour less obtrusive drummers. There was a degree of envy, too; McKean drove an MG sports car, which Chet admired. He was also reportedly blessed with "one of the biggest wangs this side of the Sierra Madres."[40]

Musicians weren't the only visitors to the cottage. Another regular guest was Manuel Vardas, who was a big pot dealer. Chet recalled Manuel as a "completely spaced-out guy, a non-musician whose main object in life seemed to be to find out how much grass he could smoke up before the second coming of Christ." He was frequently accompanied by his friend, Don Sparky, who Whitlock remembered as a complete 'weed-head'. "But Chet was one of the biggest 'weed-heads' of all time," he laughed. "He loved his weed, I tell you! He didn't even smoke. He hated cigarettes, thought they were disgusting! But he used to smoke weed until it was coming out of his ears."[41]

Manuel and Don encouraged the musicians to help their own enterprise in return for a steady supply of weed. "We never had less than a kilo or two around," Chet remembered. "Sometimes we'd all sit around a low coffee table with piles of clean grass in front of us and loose papers at the ready, seeing who could roll the most joints in an hour."[42]

But there was a dark side to the drug scene, with some individuals always looking for additional ways to get high. According to Jack Sheldon, Jimmy McKean started shooting formaldehyde.

Don Sparky also started to experiment, which eventually led to his demise. "He will be remembered by a few Inglewoodians for his antics in the drug scene, which eventually killed him," noted Chet in his memoirs.

Bob Whitlock had also started to dabble with heroin, which would eventually result in a full-blown habit that he struggled to shake off for more than twenty years. "The first time Chet ever got loaded on heroin, I was responsible," he admitted. "I was no big junkie, or anything, but I'd used it a few times. Chet happened to be along one time, and I asked him if he wanted to try it."

Chet had already demonstrated that there was little that could scare him, and he watched intently as Whitlock showed him how to spike himself.

“He got as sick as a dog,” the young bass player recalled. “He vomited and vomited. It was nothing like he’d imagined—I guess he was looking for the sort of high he got smoking pot. I thought to myself that he’d never do that again.”[43]

Chapter Three

CHET BAKER AND CHARLIE PARKER 1950–52

"(Bird) treated me sorta like a son. I can see now how helpful and understanding he was. He stayed with the tunes I knew well, and he avoided the real fast tempos he used to like so much."—Chet Baker[1]

By 1950, the West Coast jazz scene—which was always more disparate than the term suggests—was starting to change. Bars on Central Avenue were starting to close down, one by one. Part of the decline was a result of ongoing economic development as the city became wealthier, and socio-economic patterns began to change. But as Ted Gioia points out in *West Coast Jazz*, there were also more sinister developments taking place. "The Los Angeles Musicians' Union helped to speed up the process by threatening to fine members playing for free at local jam sessions."[2]

Jazz on Central Avenue, Los Angeles, c.1950: Courtesy of Clayton Museum, California.

In the 1986 documentary *Blues for Central Avenue*, saxophonist and flautist Buddy Collette also blamed the closure of the clubs on racism within the L.A. police force, suggesting that officers "didn't like the idea of some people, especially the young white ladies, coming down and mingling in the clubs."

Other African-American musicians went further, suggesting that the white jazz musicians had copied their music, their language, even their clothes. "The white people, they learned from us and took what we knew and went on," claimed trumpet player Harry 'Sweets' Edison.[3]

In the years that followed, their resentment would intensify, as they watched lesser musicians win valuable recording contracts and studio jobs. Chet Baker, who won popularity polls ahead of more accomplished black musicians such as Louis Armstrong and Dizzy Gillespie, was singled out for criticism by certain narrow-minded musicians, jealous of his success. For the time being, however, the Central Avenue regulars adapted as best they could, looking for work in any club that would let them play.

One such club, which later became synonymous with the West Coast jazz scene, was The Lighthouse Café in Hermosa Beach. The bar, situated on Pier Avenue, a few sandy feet away from the beach, had been a popular haunt with local sailors before the war, but by the late 1940s, all that remained of its former glory was its tacky Polynesian interior, with grass mats on the wall, bamboo supports around the bar and a small bandstand. One Sunday, the bar owner, John Levine, was approached by an out-of-work bass player, Howard Rumsey, about offering live music on Sunday afternoons. "Don't you know that Sunday is the worst day in the week for the liquor business?" Levine replied. Looking around the half-empty bar, Rumsey said, "Well, I don't see how it can be much worse than it is right now." Levine admired his attitude and his vision, and agreed to hold a series of Sunday afternoon jam sessions, which began on 29th March 1949.[4]

Rumsey was a native Californian, born in the desert town of Brawley in 1917, making him significantly older than many of the musicians on the scene. His first professional job was with Vido Musso's band, where he met a young pianist by the name of Stan Kenton. He went on to become one of the original members of Kenton's band, which he eventually left in 1943. Drawing on his experience, Rumsey recruited a small band for the initial session. It was a less than illustrious line-up at first; Dick Swink on tenor saxophone, Don Dennis on trumpet, Arnold Kopitch on piano, Bobby White on drums, and Rumsey on bass.

"I hired the loudest musicians I could find," Rumsey reminisced. "We propped the front doors open and started to blast off." The sounds drifted down to the beach, attracting both jazz fans and young people in their swimwear, unaccustomed to hearing live music in the sleepy seaside town. "The people began to filter in," said Rumsey. "Pretty soon the place was full. There were more people than Levine had had in the entire preceding two weeks."[5]

After a few weeks, the Sunday jam sessions took off. Rumsey started to play his old jazz records for patrons, Tuesday through Thursday, and over time, live music was played six nights a week. Rumsey gradually upgraded the calibre of the musicians, too; Teddy Edwards took over on tenor saxophone in late 1949. Other black musicians, displaced by the fading Central Avenue scene, also took part. Sonny Criss and Hampton Hawes became regulars, and Wardell Grey was a frequent visitor.

Ken Koenig, who made a documentary about The Lighthouse, suggested that the club played a significant role in reducing the prejudices that existed in the early 1950s. "Many little beach towns were in fact primarily made up of white, working-class people who had very little contact with black people," he explained. "There was a dividing line in Los Angeles. So when black musicians would come down to Hermosa Beach, they found that they were outsiders. In addition, musicians, particularly jazz musicians at that time, had the reputation of being drug addicts, alcoholics, so there was also that prejudice that had to be dealt with. So Howard and John really did a lot of public relations events that would bring the public into the club to make it not so mysterious and the musicians not so strange, and that broke down some of the barriers at the time."[6]

Chet did not hold the jam sessions at The Lighthouse in the same regard as those at the Showtime. He was also less than impressed by the abilities of Howard Rumsey as a musician. "The only time it would swing was when another bass player sat in," he complained. "[He] was the only bass player I knew of [professional] who played right in the middle of the beat. If you tried to do it on purpose, it would be very difficult, but for Howard it was apparently no problem."[7]

Chet still played there most Sunday afternoons, however, because of the quality of the other musicians who would stop by the club to play. "[There were] people like Shelly Manne, Shorty Rogers, Hampton Hawes, Dexter Gordon, Sonny Clark, Frank Morgan, Stan Levey, Larance Marable, Bill

Holman, Art Pepper, Bob Whitlock, Monty Budwig, and many others."[8]

Bob Whitlock felt much the same way about The Lighthouse. "It wasn't that important as a venue," he said, "but it gave me the chance to work with the tenor player Steve White. He was a fabulous musician, one of the best on the West Coast, but he was a little crazy, a bit out to lunch! He could sound like you'd think Zoot and Stan Getz would like to sound—just utterly gorgeous. Then a second or two later, he'd be honking like a rock'n'roll player. As a result, he never became known for much of anything, but the musicians around town respected the hell out of him. I gained so much experience playing with him; he knew all these tunes, all the changes, all these charts, and he knew how to teach them to us. I was really lucky. They were seasoned musicians, and they taught me everything I know about harmony, how to back up soloists—it was a great education."[9]

By this stage, Chet was playing most nights; he would play at The Lighthouse every Sunday, the Showtime on Monday, checking out the scene at clubs such as Esther's at Manhattan Beach on the other nights. Still, he struggled to find much paid work at this time. "I had way more work than him, even though I was nowhere near the musician he was," recalled Bob Whitlock. "At that time there was more demand for bass players than bebop trumpet players. Only a few people in the jazz community knew what he was capable of. There just wasn't much work. Jazz was just starting to come alive—it hadn't yet become part of the mainstream."

According to his friend, Jack Sheldon, it was around this time that Chet first exhibited any interest in singing. "We used to know these girls out at Long Beach—they were sisters—and we'd go out there. They were kind of goofy girls, but they were real rich, so we used to love them! They used to have a piano and a recording machine. We used to sing together, with me playing the piano. Chet sang like he played, even then. He always could sing."[10]

Chet was so absorbed in his music, he had little time for anything else in his life. "Chettie wasn't very much interested in girls then," recalled the drummer Bob Neel. "They'd gravitate to him, but he was mostly fighting them off. He didn't seem to care about anything except playing his horn."

After the episode with Sherry, his Mexican girlfriend, Chet was more interested in casual sex than developing a serious relationship. Jack Sheldon still jokes that he used to help Chet find girls in those days. In the movie *Let's Get Lost* he laughed at the memory of Chet sleeping with the girlfriend of Gene Rowland, who worked as an arranger for Stan Kenton. "We were doing a job in the Miramar Hotel in Santa Barbara with this little band," he recalled. "And Bill Perkins was up there, and his mother was rich, and she had a house in the hills in Santa Barbara, so after the job we went up to his house. How slick Chettie was! And finally I had Ann Jasmine in the bedroom, and I was in bed with her. And I turned round for some reason, and when I turned back, Chettie was fucking her, and they were going! And she was saying 'Oh, Jack!' And so she thought I was fucking her, and it was Chettie who was fucking her. And ever since then, Ann has really liked me a lot!"[11]

Chet was certainly not looking for romance when he caught the eye of a young blonde girl who walked into The Lighthouse a few weeks later. "I'd seen her a couple of times before and had told myself that I would hit on her if she came in again," he wrote in his memoirs. "When the set broke, I worked my way through the packed club until I was beside her. I can't remember what I said exactly, but within half an hour we were parked in her father's new Buick along the cliffs of Palos Verdes."[12]

Charlaine Souder was twenty years old, and worked in a local dress shop. Chet later described her as a "sharp-looking blonde, well-built and very self-assured". Chet's friend, Bob Whitlock, remembered her in a similar light, describing her as a "stylish, fun-loving" girl. "She wasn't beautiful," he recalled, "but she was very attractive."[13]

Chet was taken aback by her forward nature, and her considerable sexual appetite. "We made it a lot during the next two to three months," he boasted. "She loved to be screwed, and I loved screwing her. Once, in front her house in Lynwood, we made it nine times in three hours." He kept his friend Bob Whitlock entertained with details of their exploits. "We used to joke about it," he laughed.

As the weeks went by, Chet and Charlaine became virtually inseparable. Their relationship was always volatile, however. She was flirtatious by nature, and when Chet saw her talking with other guys, he would assume the worst, and fly into a rage. "She was very sexy, and she flaunted it, there were no two ways about it," said Bob Whitlock. "She used to make Chet jealous, drive him crazy. I think that's one of the reasons why he behaved like he did later."[14]

In the meantime, Chet's reputation as a musician continued to spread like a Californian forest fire. "I first got to know him in the early 1950s," the alto saxophonist Herb Geller remembered. "There was some jam session in North Hollywood, at The Stagecoach as I recall. I was amazed, because he obviously didn't know formal harmony; he couldn't tell you what chords he was playing. But his ear, and more important his reactions, allowed him to hit a wrong note and bounce off it, and turn it into a great phrase."[15]

Off the bandstand, however, he was also developing a reputation as something of a delinquent. "Chettie was already into a little larceny then," confirmed Jack Sheldon to author James Gavin. "I gave him a flugelhorn that I had checked out of City College, and he never gave it back. It was like stealing gas—he thought it was alright to do that."[16]

On one occasion, Sheldon recalled, he and Chet were driving home after scoring pot when they were pulled over by the police, who were investigating a nearby robbery. Sheldon was able to stuff the drugs underneath the passenger seat, but was unable to hide a rifle he had inadvertently left on the back seat. "We were just wild kids, driving in a car, but we weren't doing anything," he said. "I had a .22 rifle with me. They took us to jail, handcuffed us together. When we got to the station, the cops told Chettie, 'We know your father'. They let us drive home eventually."[17]

Some of Chet's old friends were scared by his reckless behaviour, and in particular, his love of marijuana.

Fleischer recalled Chet being busted for possession at this time, and thought that was probably behind Chet's decision to re-enlist in the Army in late 1950. "The judge gave him a choice of re-enlisting or going to jail," he claimed. "This was during the Korean War, and the judge probably thought he was giving Chet a death sentence. Chet's police records indicate no such case ever coming to court, however; it's possible that he was caught smoking at this time, and let off with a warning, but this does not appear to be the cause of his relocation to San Francisco.

In the book *As Though I Had Wings* Chet implies that he decided to rejoin the army after an argument with his girlfriend. "I had it bad for Charlaine," he wrote, "but I wasn't alone. There was another dude who liked her action. Charlaine and I eventually argued over this and some other stuff, and because of this I reenlisted directly into the Sixth Army Band up in San Francisco, a three-year commitment."[18]

Bob Whitlock thought that this account sounded entirely plausible. "I was only eighteen years old, and not the best critic, but I was smart enough to know he was the best trumpet player around. Nobody could touch him. But he was playing around beach towns—there wasn't much work for white jazz musicians at that time. I think he went back into the Army to go up to

San Francisco. Chet was a crazy guy when he was young, and made crazy decisions sometimes."[19]

The Sixth Army Band was based at the Presidio, a park on the northern tip of the San Francisco peninsula. It was an idyllic location, backed by wooded hills, and with views overlooking the Golden Gate Bridge and the bay. Chet was lucky not to have been posted overseas, since the Korean War had broken out in June of that year, and eventually claimed the lives of more than 30,000 U.S. servicemen.

The officer in charge of the band was CWO Nathan Cammack, and the band's conductor between 1950 and 1952 was none other than André Previn. During this period, the band performed at General MacArthur's triumphant homecoming parade on 17th April 1951, an event that was televised. It is not known whether Chet played on that day, but it seems likely—if so, it may well have been his first televised appearance. The band also appeared when a defence treaty was finalised between the United States, Australia and New Zealand on 1st September 1951. The treaty was signed at the Presidio itself, and band played the national anthems. Three days later, President Truman addressed the nation from the War Memorial Opera House in San Francisco at the Japanese Peace Treaty Conference; again, the Sixth Army Band was present, and is thought to have played the national anthem.

In addition to major ceremonies, the Sixth Army Band was quite active in the surrounding area—playing at recruiting drives, county fairs and opening ceremonies. They also played at local high schools and colleges, and performed occasional concerts for wounded veterans at the Letterman Hospital in San Francisco. They also played a weekly radio broadcast; this is likely to have been performed by a smaller version of the band, and it is not known whether Chet played on these broadcasts.

Chet had to endure an early start, waking up at dawn to blow reveille before rehearsing with the Army band in the morning. After lunch, however, he was pretty much left to his own devices. Most afternoons were spent playing the trumpet with some of his fellow band-members, playing cards, or looking for a quiet corner where he could smoke pot.

Most evenings, Chet was free to leave the base and head into the city. In the months that followed, he developed a routine, leaving the base at midnight in search of a jazz club where he could play. "It didn't take me long to find out where everything was happening," he later recalled.[20]

He soon met the Latin jazz musician Cal Tjader, who was a regular at a club called Facks. Tjader was a fan of Chet's playing, and used to let him sit in on a regular basis. Later in the evening, Chet would make his way to jam sessions at after-hours clubs like Bop City and Jimbo's, which didn't get going until the early hours of the morning. There he would run into saxophonist Frank Foster, one his colleagues from the Sixth Army band, fellow trumpet player Kenny Dorham and saxophonist Norwood 'Pony' Poindexter, who went on to play with Lionel Hampton, Stan Kenton and Count Basie. Chet would finally finish playing around five-thirty in the morning, get back into his car, and rush back to base in time to blow reveille.

Stories of Chet's exploits in San Francisco made their way back down the coast to his friends in Los Angeles. "He was playing all the time up there, at clubs like Facks and Bop City," recalled his close friend Bob Whitlock. "It was good to hear the stories, because he was starting to get appreciated up there, playing with some real people. He left little doubt in your mind that he was going places."[21]

Whilst Chet was enjoying the change of scenery from a musical perspective, he found himself missing Charlaine, and the two of them wrote to each other on a regular basis. When Charlaine made it clear that she was no longer seeing her old boyfriend, they reunited, and Chet proposed to her. It was a hasty decision, much like his plan to move to San Francisco in the first place, and one they both lived to regret. They married in front of a justice of the peace in Las Vegas, and returned to San Francisco as man and wife.

The early months of their marriage were happy. As a married man, Chet was allowed to move off base, and the young couple found a small, one-bedroom apartment on Lombard Street. Chet would be free most afternoons, and used to return home to see his wife. He tried to grab a few hours of precious sleep early evening, but at midnight he would wake up, and make his way to the clubs, with Charlaine usually by his side.

One regular haunt in early 1951 was the Blackhawk, where pianist Dave Brubeck headlined with his newly-formed quartet. Chet was a fan of the band's alto saxophonist, Paul Desmond, who possessed a warm, lyrical tone that was in sharp contrast to most of the bebop players on the scene. "He had such a delicate way of playing, so melodic," Chet later noted, and his style may well have exerted some influence on Chet's own sound. Chet used to sit in with the band from time to time, apparently against the wishes of Brubeck himself. The saxophonist used to push the pianist to allow him to play, suggesting that the admiration was mutual.[22]

After a few months of this punishing routine, both Chet and Charlaine longed to lead a more normal life. Whilst Chet had signed up for three years, he had heard stories about fellow musicians who had bluffed their way out of the Army, demonstrating that they were unfit for service. "One guy put himself into a trance, and while I didn't see this myself, I was told of his being carried out of the band barracks by two medical corpsmen … The other guy told the bandleader that there was a little man inside of his flute who was playing all of the wrong notes. They both got out."[23]

Chet's own plan was less elaborate, but he hoped that it would be successful. In the autumn of 1951, he informed the Army psychiatrist that he was afraid to go to the bathroom in front of the other men, and had started to use an area behind the barracks, concealed by a dense row of bushes. "Of course they checked all that out and found out it was true," he explained in the movie *Let's Get Lost*. "And that helped a great deal. That, and the multiple-answer questionnaires that they give you. They ask you if you want to be a mechanic, or a florist, or work for the forestry department. And I would always pick the most feminine one. And I told them I smoked marijuana, and played bebop."[24]

The psychiatrist explained that it would take as long as two weeks to evaluate the results, after which he would be informed of the Army's decision. Unfortunately for Chet, the plan backfired; one week later he was informed that he would be transferred to Fort Huachuca in Arizona. "There I was, plucked out of my comfortable San Francisco routine, and separated from my wife, plopped down out in the middle of nowhere," he complained in *As Though I Had Wings*.

In his memoirs Chet speculated that he might have been transferred because of his poor sight-reading, or because the Army was trying to root out troublemakers. It's doubtful that the transfer had anything to do with his sight-reading; the 77th Army Band had just been reconstituted in Fort Huachuca on 1st November 1951, having previously been active in the Philippines after the Second World War. The Army was searching for recruits for the newly formed band, and Chet, who was looking to leave the Sixth Army Band, was an obvious candidate.

Chet is thought to have arrived in Fort Huachuca in November 1951, shortly after the Army band had reconvened. The installation was situated in Cochise County in South-East Arizona, some fifteen miles north of the border with Mexico. The base had been used to train infantry divisions during World War II, but was essentially closed in the late 1940s. The base gained a new lease of life after the start of the Korean War, with the arrival of the Signal Corp. The 77th Army Band followed just a few months later.

The band consisted of a disparate group of musicians, many of whom had been relocated from other units. One of the clarinet players, Bob Freedman, who later became a highly successful arranger, remembers Chet's arrival. "A lot of the guys in the band knew of his reputation as an outstanding jazz player," he recalled. "Mostly we were of, at best, average talent with skills to match. There was one outstanding flute and piccolo player who went on to some degree of success. In contrast, there was a guy who I don't think could read music. He was reputed to have had Mafia connections (and could easily have been cast in a movie in that kind of role) and played bass drum only."[25]

The Warrant Officer in charge of the band was a strait-laced individual by the name of Jones, who Freedman remembers as a good conductor, and fairly tolerant of the men's behaviour. "The fussbudget Master Sergeant who was his second in command was a fairly incompetent percussionist who was the subject of a lot of ridicule from those of us who were very young and who thought of ourselves as musical geniuses," he said. "Warrant Officer Jones openly came to the sergeant's defense and pretty much put an end to that nonsense."[26]

The band's day-to-day routine was incredibly relaxed, just as it had been in San Francisco. "I don't recall our ever doing calisthenics or being required to fire weapons," said Freedman. "In fact, we didn't have weapons." After reveille, there were rehearsals, marching practice, and time allocated for individual practice and maintenance of the instruments. Most of Chet's time was spent playing his horn. "Like nearly every other aspiring young jazz musician, he would play along with recordings of guys he admired—including Miles Davis," he added.

Freedman is also dismissive of Chet's reputation as a poor sight-reader who knew nothing about chord changes. "I was aware of no evidence supporting either of those claims," he said. "In fact, in direct opposition to those theories, he wrote a wonderful one-chorus arrangement of 'The Continental' for six brass (three trumpets and three trombones) and rehearsed the group very knowledgeably in the barracks. He wrote with the same type of musicality that was in his playing. I believe that his supposed lack of knowledge of chords rose from the fact that he would rather just hear things and respond to them instead of intellectualizing them."[27]

The band's only other recurring duty was at the end of the day, when the musicians played just outside the barracks. "Another sign of Mr Jones' tolerance was that we often got out of that," said the clarinetist. "The barracks was on a stretch of flat desert and often we would be able to see seasonal rain clouds coming our way from miles off. If the storm hit at the time we were supposed to play, the event would be canceled. We got very good at weather prediction and often were out of our uniforms and into civilian clothes long before our duties would have been required."[28]

The 77th Army Band rarely played off base, suggesting there was little need for the unit in such a remote location. Freedman remembers one parade in Tucson, and the occasional concert at the officer's club, but most of the time was spent playing informally on the base. "A couple of times we left the Army base in pursuit of jam sessions in towns within drivable distances," he recalled. "There really weren't any piano players around, so even though I was playing clarinet in the band, Chettie found out that I could comp passably well so I went with him to play piano. It seemed that people everywhere knew who he was. The thing I remember most clearly about his playing in sessions was the extended length of time he'd let go by if the right lick or note wasn't occurring to him. Very few players have that kind of confident patience."[29]

Chet was obviously missing his wife Charlaine, but Bob Freedman remembers Chet as a friendly, easy-going guy. "The outstanding thing about Chettie was how nice he was," he told author James Gavin. "He was just a sweet guy. He had this wide open face, and he trusted everybody."[30]

In his memoirs, Chet reminisces about the cheap marijuana that was available off base, with the Mexican border just a short drive away. "There was a moderate amount of marijuana use in the band, but I never saw or heard of anything stronger," confirmed Bob Freedman. "Even smoking pot was more in the nature of kids smoking cigars behind the barn because they knew they weren't supposed to do it."

Chet's innocent appearance and love of marijuana made him easy prey for the less scrupulous members of the unit. Henry Freda, the company clerk, tried pushing to Chet on numerous occasions, as did 'Big John', the tall Italian rumoured to have mob connections. There is no evidence to suggest that Chet sampled heroin during his short spell in Arizona, although Freda did seek him out in later years, after he had come to fame with the Gerry Mulligan Quartet.

Chet's spell in the 77th Army Band lasted just two months. He remembered one Army psychiatrist in San Francisco advising him that if all else failed he could consider going AWOL for a period of one month, before turning himself into the Army, where he would probably be given a discharge. "Every trumpet player in the Army band pulled bugling duties," recalled Bob Freedman. "On the evening that Chettie made his unauthorised departure from Fort Huachuca he was on his way to the base's flagpole to play the bugle call known as 'retreat'. As he was leaving the barracks he came over to where I was and said goodbye in an unusually expressive way. That was it. A while later we got the news that he had turned himself in to one of the Army's psychiatric wards in California after having remained AWOL for the requisite amount of time necessary to be considered for such evaluation."

Chet hitchhiked his way from Arizona to Los Angeles where he reunited with his wife. "I enjoyed a wonderful month with my young and beautiful wife," he later recalled. "Charlaine was living in a small bungalow behind her father's Lynwood home. We spent a loving, leisurely month together. Each night I'd pick Charlaine up from the dress shop where she'd found work and we'd go somewhere."[31]

Around this time—in January 1952—Chet reunited with his close friend, the bass player Bob Whitlock. They decided to form a quarter with the drummer Bobby White, and a pianist by the name of Russ Freeman. Born in 1926, Freeman was three years older than Chet. He had cut his teeth playing with the trumpet player Howard McGhee, and had even played with Charlie Parker for a few months in 1947, after the saxophonist had been released from the Camarillo State Hospital. He recalled running into Chet on several occasions at jam sessions in the late 1940s. "Our friendship and musical association started around 1952," Freeman later recalled. "Chet lived in Lynwood with his wife, and they had this little house-behind-a-house where Chet and I played together, days and nights."[32]

"We practiced day after day," confirmed Whitlock, "and had this Quartet ready for work long before I got a call to work with Gerry Mulligan. We played over at Chet's house in the backyard; he had a piano in the back room which we could wheel out into the open air if it was nice weather." Russ Freeman even offered Whitlock the chance to rent a room from him and his wife Marion. "Which I did, for the best part of a year, all the time I was in the Mulligan Quartet."[33]

Plans for the quartet of their own were effectively put on hold when Chet had to return to San Francisco to turn himself back in to the Army, most likely in mid-February 1952. "I had explained everything to (Charlaine) about what I'd done in Presidio with respect to my attempt to get out of the Army," he later revealed. "She knew that what I had to do was not going to be pleasant, but that it was the only way."[34]

Chet returned to the Sixth Army Band base, where he was referred to the same young psychiatrist who had advised him to go AWOL just a few months earlier. He explained that if Chet had not been transferred to Arizona, his test results would have warranted an automatic discharge. The test results were not valid in Arizona, however, and as a consequence he was liable to be disciplined for insubordination.

This was not what Chet had been hoping for, and the psychiatrist escorted him to the office of the MPs, who suggested he be placed in the stockade. His punishment consisted of collecting garbage and gruelling exercise routines. In his memoirs, Chet claimed that some of the soldiers were so desperate to escape their ordeal that they tried to get high by sniffing gasoline-soaked rags. "I saw that, and said I've got to get out of here," recalled Chet in *Let's Get Lost*. "You know, there's got to be a better way. So I kind of put myself in a trance, and nobody could get through to me for hours on end, you know, I'd just sit there, staring into the distance. And they gave me a cephanol, and put me in a private cell that night. And the next day I was transferred to the nearest psychiatric ward."[35]

He later recalled hearing the screams of men receiving shock treatment, before watching the guards carry the unconscious soldiers back to his cell. Another man, suffering from shell shock, used to keep the other patients awake at night, shouting, and trying to attack an imaginary enemy.

Chet was questioned by the ward doctor on a daily basis, and after about three weeks was granted an honourable discharge from the Army, which claimed he was "unadaptable to Army life". He was transferred to the Army hospital's regular ward for outpatients, and a few days later, was glad to return home to Los Angeles, where he was again reunited with his wife.

By the spring of 1952, when Chet returned to Los Angeles, the jazz scene had continued to evolve. The changes that were taking place at The Lighthouse in Hermosa Beach were in many respects a microcosm of a new movement that was beginning to emerge. Earlier that year tenor saxophonist Teddy Edwards, who had been the star attraction at the club for two years, was given two weeks' wages when a new line-up became available. He was replaced by Milton 'Shorty' Rogers, a trumpet player who had been playing with Stan Kenton, and Jimmy Giuffre, a saxophone and clarinet player who had written arrangements for Woody Herman's big band. The new look line-up of the Lighthouse All-Stars was completed by founder member Howard Rumsey on bass, and Shelly Manne on drums.

"This largely unnoticed shift in personnel marked a symbolic turning point distinguishing the new 'movement' of the 1950s from the Central Avenue-dominated scene of the 1940s," wrote Ted Gioia in *West Coast Jazz*. "The black bebop-drenched sound, inspired by Parker during his lengthy California sojourn, now took a back seat to the white, heavily-arranged music that would become known simply as West Coast jazz."[36]

The change was exacerbated by the emergence of new record labels such as Pacific Jazz and Nocturne Records, which were established to capture the new sound. "The jazz out of New York was heavy and black," Teddy Edwards later complained, "and the jazz out of the west was light and white. But of course, that only really applies to the records. Suddenly there were no more recording dates for black West Coast musicians like Hampton Hawes, Sonny Criss, Wardell Gray, Dexter Gordon and me. We had no more work. Just because we played powerfully. The West Coast kids were afraid that we would blow them out of the studio. The Lighthouse? That's me. I was in the original line-up of the Lighthouse All Stars. I was the one that made The Lighthouse successful. Bud Shank was still sitting at home practicing. He didn't once dare unpack his horn when there was a jam session."[37]

In the years that followed, the 'West Coast' label was used by certain musicians, including Miles Davis and Roy Eldridge, to dismiss Chet's playing style. But to the credit of Teddy Edwards, who had witnessed Chet's development first-hand, he dismissed such crude generalization. "The only personality among them was Chet Baker," he told Bob Rusch. "He was unique although he was still a kid. I heard him playing when he still wore short pants … he was a teenager, and already he played everywhere. I also saw him appearing that time with Stan Getz. Stan was seventeen. Chet already played exactly the way he played later. The same pretty sound. He always had a splendid sound. I liked his playing much better than that of the other so-called West Coast players."[38]

When Chet returned to Los Angeles, the plans to form a quartet with Bob Whitlock, Russ Freeman and Bobby White appear to have gone on the back-burner—at least for the time being. While Chet was in San Francisco, Bob Whitlock received a phone call from a girl by the name of Gail Madden, asking him if he would like to come to an audition with Gerry Mulligan. Whitlock was familiar with Mulligan's arrangements on the *Birth of the Cool* sessions, and was flattered that he had been considered. At the time, Gerry was playing with a tenor saxophonist and trumpet player he had met in Albuquerque, so when Chet returned from San Francisco he started to look elsewhere for work.

Despite his burgeoning reputation as a musician, Chet was still scuffling for work at this time. He continued to look for jam sessions he could join at every available opportunity. One such session took place on March 25th at the Trade Winds at Inglewood, an undistinguished club with a tacky Polynesian-style décor. Somebody made an amateur recording of Chet jamming with the saxophonists Sonny Criss and Wardell Gray on 'Out of Nowhere'. The recording was later released, together with other tunes recorded that evening, on an album called *Live at the Trade Winds* (Fresh Sound Records).

Around this time, probably in April, Chet landed a job with the saxophonist Stan Getz; it may be this gig that Teddy Edwards witnessed when he referred to Getz being just seventeen years of age—in fact, Stan was twenty-five years old, almost three years older than Chet. Stan Getz was already a star at this time, having topped both the *Metronome* and *DownBeat* polls in 1950. He had just recorded *Moonlight in Vermont*, which became a big hit later that summer. But Stan's early success had taken its toll, and he was already nursing a serious heroin addiction. In later years, a number of musicians held Getz responsible for getting Chet hooked on heroin—indeed, he seems to have offered him the drug as early as April 1952. "At this point, I had still never been strung out on the stuff, but I had tried it a few times, and usually, since it was pretty good quality back then, ended up really loaded and puking my guts up," Chet wrote in his memoirs. "I promised myself over and over that I would never take it again."[39]

In the meantime, Bob Whitlock and Bobby White had landed a gig with the tenor saxophonist Vido Musso. The Sicilian musician was known for his solo on the Stan Kenton hit 'Come Back To Sorrento', and was looking to assemble a band of his own. The band played for three weeks at the Tiffany Club, starting on 23rd April. In mid-May, the band is thought to have played another gig at the 5/4 Ballroom, a huge club on the corner of 54th and Central. Chet was recruited to join the band for that gig. In his memoirs Chet recalls that he was recruited by his old roommate Jimmy McKean, who was playing drums, and that Gil Barrios was on piano. This is almost certainly incorrect, as Whitlock was fairly certain that Bobby White played drums. "We played for several nights at the 5/4 Ballroom," the bass player recalled. "It was one of the most fun things you can imagine. There must have been over one hundred people—a sea of happy, black faces, all dancing. It may not have been the greatest music in the world, but it was a hell of a lot of fun!"[40]

It didn't take long for Chet's wife, Charlaine, to discover that she was starting to take second place to music in Chet's life. Rather than taking her along to jam sessions, as he had in San Francisco, he would frequently leave her behind. She tried to make her feelings known by provoking Chet, flirting with his close friends, knowing that it would make him insanely jealous.

On at least one occasion, Charlaine went one step further, and slept with Chet's friends. "One time I went over there, I think I was in the Air Force," said Jack Sheldon. "I went over there to visit. I used to drink a lot then, so I brought a bottle of port wine. Charlaine and me went in the bedroom and locked the door so Chettie couldn't get in. We drank the port wine, and we were fucking in the bedroom. He didn't seem to get too mad. We stayed in there for quite a while. Charlaine was a real good sport!"[41]

Thereafter, the marriage gradually started to unravel, Charlaine seeking to attract his attention by making him jealous, knowing that he would fly into a rage, and Chet later seeking revenge, openly parading his conquests in front of his wife.

In May 1952, the whole jazz community was buzzing with excitement at the forthcoming arrival of Charlie Parker, who was booked to do a short tour of the West Coast. It marked his first return to California since his troubled visit in the late 1945, which culminated in his being committed to the Camarillo State Hospital, charged with acute alcoholism and narcotic addiction.

The intervening years were Parker's most fertile period; he recorded extensively in a wide variety of settings—with his own small ensemble, with strings, with Latin musicians. He also toured Europe on two occasions, in 1949 and 1950. With regular work, and a recording contract with Norman Granz's Verve Record label, he should have enjoyed a degree of financial security. But drug addiction took its toll on the saxophonist. Asked about why he was constantly looking to borrow money, Parker once rolled up his sleeve and said, "This is my home, this is my portfolio, this is my Cadillac."

Years of drug addiction and alcoholism had left him bloated—topping the scales at over two hundred pounds, and he looked far older than his thirty-one years. Just three years later, he would be dead.[42]

Shortly before Bird's arrival, the studio pianist and arranger Donn Trenner was asked to assemble a band for the forthcoming tour, which was due to commence at the Tiffany Club on 29th May. He recruited the drummer Larance Marable, and a bass player, Harry Babasin. When Parker arrived in Los Angeles, he requested a trumpeter be added to the line-up, and the pianist recalls calling Chet Baker.

Chet's memory of the occasion is quite different, embellishing the anecdote with additional flourishes on each retelling of the story. "One day during the summer of '52 I returned home to find a telegram under the door," he wrote. "It was from (record producer) Dick Bock, I believe, saying that Charlie Parker was auditioning for trumpet players for some club dates in California. The audition was to take place that same day at three o'clock at the Tiffany Club. I rushed over, arriving a little late, and I could hear Bird from outside as he ran through a tune with some trumpet player. Pushing into the darkened club, I could make out Bird up on the stand, flying through the blues. I sat for a minute or two, looking around the room. I recognised many trumpet players and lots of other people I knew who somehow had found out about Bird being there. I saw someone move up to the bandstand and say something to Bird. I felt uncomfortable and very nervous as he asked the crowd if I was in the club, and would I come up and play something with him. He had by-passed all these other guys, some of whom had much more experience than I had and could read anything you put in front of them."[43]

Chet was reportedly asked to play two tunes, both of which he knew; the first was 'The Song is You', the second a blues tune written by Bird himself, called 'Cheryl'. "After Cheryl, he announced that the audition was over, thanked everyone for coming, and said that he was hiring me for the gig," Chet claimed.

A number of musicians have cast doubt upon Chet's version of the story. Neither Donn Trenner nor Larance Marable recalled an audition, and Chet's friend Jack Sheldon—one of the musicians Chet has claimed was at the club—denies being present at the Tiffany Club that day.

There can be little doubt that Chet exaggerated the story over time, but another witness—the photographer William Claxton—clearly remembers other trumpet players stopping by the club, hoping for a chance to play with Bird. "We shot the last two sets that night and then stayed on until the early hours as various musicians dropped by, hoping for a chance to sit in with the soaring Bird, whose playing was fantastic … he and various musicians jammed until about three in the morning, much to the enjoyment of his adoring young fans. At the end of the last impromptu set we found ourselves out on the dark sidewalk in front of the club. Chet said goodbye, and disappeared into the night with a pretty, blonde, young lady."[44]

Charlie Parker was hungry, and disappointed to see that most of the restaurants were already shuttered for the night. Claxton's parents had a big house in the hills outside Pasadena, and were away for the weekend, so the young photographer took the liberty of inviting Bird back to their house for breakfast. "My house guest stayed on all the remaining hours of dawn, all day Sunday, until late Sunday night. We fed him, waited on him, and treated him like a king. Between swims in the pool and feeding sessions (he had an enormous appetite), he sat on a big lounge chair like Buddha with all of us, his young fans, at his feet."[45]

It was during this time that Claxton asked him why he chose Chet Baker to accompany him—again implying that there must have been other trumpet players auditioning that day. "Bird answered my question quickly and concisely: 'Pure and simple … I mean, that young cat just played pure and simple, know what I mean? Somethin' about him and his playing was like that, and I felt it in just a few seconds of his playing. I knew he was right'." Parker went on to elaborate about the qualities he had heard in Chet's playing at the club. "'Yeah, that little white cat is kinda Bixelated—you know, a kind of Bix Beiderbecke quality. Reminds me of some of those old Bix records my Mama used to get for me. Like Bix, Chet's blowing is kinda sweet, gentle, yet direct and honest'. After hearing Bird say that, we all paid considerably more attention to this new, young guy with that bright, all-American face."[46]

Most of the other musicians felt the same way. "Being chosen by Charlie Parker was like a pronouncement by God," recalled Chet's friend Bob Whitlock. Only Art Farmer, a respected and experienced trumpet player himself, sounded bitter about what had taken place. Years later he complained to the saxophonist Bob Mover that he and his brother had even put Bird up in their apartment, and were dismayed to see him not give the job to one of "his own".[47]

Chet played with Charlie Parker for two and a half weeks at the Tiffany Club. The drummer Larance Marable later recalled that Bird went out of his way to help the young trumpet player. Parker "sort of nurtured him along. He told Chet what notes to hit on the ends of tunes, how to play a cadenza—everything." Bob Whitlock witnessed a similar side to Bird's character. He subbed for Harry Babasin for two whole nights at the Tiffany. "One evening we were playing 'Cheryl'," he recalled, "which has some chromatic changes unique to that particular song. After Bird and Donn Trenner had taken their solos, I played my own solo. I played a walking bit, but I knew the changes, and started to incorporate them into my solo. After a bit, Donn Trenner came back in, but Bird shut him up, and let me keep playing. I thought 'I'm free to go here!' Bird's attitude about the whole thing was great for me."[48]

Bird also acted as a father figure to Chet off the bandstand. Every night, at the Tiffany Club, and later at Billy Berg's and the 5/4 Ballroom, the saxophonist attracted swarms of drug dealers, all aware of his reputation. When they turned their attention to the young trumpet player, Bird brushed them away, warning Chet to steer clear of drugs.

In return, Chet showed his mentor the sights of Los Angeles, driving him to the beach of the cliffs at Palos Verdes, areas where he had spent much of his youth. "Bird would get out along the cliffs and stare out to sea, or watch the waves breaking on the rocks below for half an hour." The summer sun seemed to take the saxophonist away from his own troubles, if only for a few minutes, but by night that was forgotten once more. "He was snorting up spoons of stuff and drinking fifths of Hennessey," Chet recalled. "It all seemed to have little or no effect on him. I wondered at the stamina of the man." Chet also invited Charlie Parker to jam at the back of his house in Lynwood, where they were accompanied by Russ Freeman on piano, Bob Whitlock on bass and Bobby White on drums.[49]

Bob Whitlock remembers that Parker was impressed by his young protégé. "He was amazed that Chet could do what he did without the harmonic training that a lot of players had," he said. Still, there were times when Chet would struggle to keep pace with the sheer flow of ideas coming from Bird. A bootleg of a jam session that took place at the Trade Winds club in Inglewood, where they were joined by fellow alto saxophonist Sonny Criss, finds Chet sounding somewhat hesitant, but determined not to be overwhelmed by the occasion.

From mid-June, the band embarked on a short tour of the West Coast, accompanied by both the Dave Brubeck Quartet and Ella Fitzgerald, taking in San Diego, North Bakersfield, Seattle and Vancouver. The tour was scheduled to finish in San Francisco, where they were booked to play a two-week stint at the Say When club on Bust Street. On the third night of their engagement, the group made a TV appearance as part of a telethon, raising money for muscular dystrophy. Returning to the club after the show, Bird stepped up to the microphone at the end of the first set, and announced that he would be passing the hat around the club to collect money for the charity, and that the club's owner had agreed to match whatever money was collected. "He did this, of course, completely on his own, without having spoken to the manager of the club, who was a tough guy name Dutch," Chet later recalled. "Anyway, after the money was collected, Bird walked over to the bar, with all the eyes and ears in the joint focused on his counting out the money. The total came to $125. Naturally Dutch refused to kick in his $125. People began yelling, banging on the tables, etc—there was almost a riot."[50]

The band was fired as a result of this incident, and the tour came to a premature end. Later that night, Bird apparently fell asleep in his hotel, cigarette in hand, and set fire to his mattress. Chet remembered being woken by the sound of sirens, watching the fire department tossing the charred mattress on to the street.

In the meantime, Bird returned to New York. Legend has it that on his return he called both Dizzy Gillespie and Miles Davis to tell them about his 'discovery', saying, "There's a little white cat out in California who's going to eat you up." The story may well be apocryphal, but we do know that Bird was genuinely impressed by Chet's abilities, and that Miles exhibited an irrational hatred of Chet, even before they finally met in the fall of 1953.

For his own part, Chet returned to Los Angeles in late June, but it was far from a triumphant homecoming. He landed a job with the veteran clarinet player Freddie Fisher and his New Orleans-style band, the Schnicklefritzers. "After playing with Bird, it was like one extreme to the other," he noted. His old friend Jimmy McKean was playing drums, and recommended Chet for the job. "They played at a place called the Glider Inn at Seal Beach, just a few miles south of Long Beach," recalled Bob Whitlock. Freddie Fisher's act was more vaudeville than jazz, combining 'fun' versions of standards, comedy songs and jokes. "I never saw the band, but I remember people comparing him to Spike Jones," he continued. "I do remember Chet telling me how much fun it was, not from a musical perspective, but that Freddie was a funny guy."[51]

His fortunes started to change in early July, however, when he received an unexpected phone call from Gerry Mulligan, asking him if he wanted to join him onstage at a small club called The Haig, just off Wilshire Boulevard. He had mixed feelings about the invitation; bad memories still lingered from their initial encounter, which had been a disaster, but with few offers of regular work, he figured he had nothing to lose by giving it another shot. It was a decision that would change his life forever.

Chapter Four

THE GERRY MULLIGAN QUARTET 1952–1953

"It was a very unique group in as much as there was no piano and it left a lot more open space. The piano covers up a lot. The piano is an orchestra itself and when you're playing behind an orchestra, sometimes you get lost in it. But without it, everything was very clear, and the space was there and the feeling was there."—Chet Baker[1]

Chet walked into the rehearsal with Gerry Mulligan, relaxed and nonchalant as ever. He put his trumpet to his lips, and let out a series of piercing shrieks, his regular warm-up procedure. "Don't you ever blast like that again, not under my roof!" shouted Mulligan. Chet was embarrassed and upset, unaccustomed to the saxophonist's disciplined ways. "Go fuck yourself!" he yelled, then stuck his trumpet in his bag, and walked out.

It wasn't the most auspicious of starts to what was to become one of the most celebrated pairings in modern jazz. But then Gerry Mulligan and Chet Baker were always the odd couple. Mulligan was a formally trained musician, who favoured tight musical arrangements that had been well-rehearsed. He had a strict, paternal manner, in part inherited from his father, a trait that also made him very business-minded. Chet, by contrast, played almost exclusively by ear. His laid-back demeanour, a product of his West Coast upbringing, belied a stubborn, sometimes childish streak. The music industry meant nothing to him; he just wanted to play. But for a short time—just one year—they generated a chemistry that both musicians struggled to replicate in the years that followed.

Although forever associated with the 'West Coast jazz' tag, Gerald Joseph Mulligan was born in Queens, New York, on 6th April 1927, the fourth and youngest son of an industrial engineer. His father changed job on a regular basis, relocating the family to Marion, Ohio, where he worked for the

Marion Power Shovel Company, then to Chicago, on to Kalamazoo, before finally settling in Philadelphia. The moving took its toll on the family. "No sooner did I get to know children in one town than we'd move someplace else," he later recalled. "I became very insecure in my relations with other people as a result."[2]

Unlike Chet Baker, he had an extensive formal musical training, encouraged by his authoritarian Irish father. His first instrument, a ukulele, quickly gave way to piano. He spent a great deal of time at the house of his African-American nanny, Lily Rowan, who gave him an early exposure to jazz. "She had a player piano and I used to love that. She used to have all kinds of things, like Fats Waller rolls, so I used to lean against the piano bench with my nose at keyboard height pumping away, playing the stuff."[3]

Attending the local Catholic school in Kalamazoo, Mulligan's music teacher, a trumpet player, taught a variety of different instruments, and he switched his emphasis from piano to clarinet. The school orchestra also provided him with his first opportunity to try his hand at arranging. "It was a fairly ungodly instrumentation: one clarinet, one violin, one drum, one piano player—seven or eight of us," he later remembered. "I had the desire to write something for us, so that was my first arrangement. I was fascinated with the tune 'Lover', with its chromatic progression that I felt was beautiful. So I tried to write out an arrangement of 'Lover', very simple with a lot of whole notes and quarter notes, and I tried to get the moving parts and all that stuff for our little instrumentation. Well, I ultimately never heard it because the school was taught by nuns, and like a fool I put on top of each sheet the title 'Lover'. A nun took one look at the title and that was the end of that. We never even played the thing. So that was the abrupt end of my burgeoning writing career."[4]

Mulligan later added the tenor saxophone and finally, the baritone saxophone to his repertoire, before reaching the decision to focus his attention on the baritone, in part duc to thc influence of Harry Carney, who played in Duke Ellington's band. In 1944, aged just seventeen, he left home to join the Johnny Warrington radio band, then the Tommy Tucker big band, writing arrangements for both. Mulligan returned to New York in 1946, joining the Gene Krupa big band as staff arranger, where he attracted attention by composing and arranging 'Disc Jockey Jump', a 1947 hit. Around this time, Mulligan also met Claude Thornhill, another New York-based bandleader. Thornhill's main arranger was Gil Evans, who was beginning to make his mark with an original big-band sound, depending partly on instruments more often associated with classical music, such as the French horn and the tuba.

Gil Evans introduced Mulligan to a number of like-minded young musicians, including Lee Konitz, who played alto sax with Thornhill's band, pianist John Lewis, who was working as an arranger for Dizzy Gillespie's band, and Miles Davis, at that time best known for his work with Charlie Parker. Between engagements the musicians used to crowd into Evan's basement apartment, situated behind a laundry on West 55th Street.

"I was over at Gil's place most of the time. It finally got to the point where Gil and I were taking turns using the piano and taking turns sleeping, and there were people in and out of the place all the time," said Mulligan. "Day and night we'd have people over there, and so there was no schedule like with normal people. When guys would come, we would be up and have breakfast or eat something if we felt like it, and one of us would be using the piano. This went on winter and summer. It got really cold down there, so we were bundled up in overcoats and blankets sitting at the piano taking turns writing. More than anything, it was just an outgrowth of these endless or open-ended conversations that were always going on."[5]

Regular visitors included George Russell, John Lewis, Lee Konitz, John Carisi, Max Roach, Blossom Dearie, and members of the Thornhill band, whenever they were in town. Charlie Parker and Dizzy Gillespie were even known to drop by, and occasionally the arranger Johnny Mandel. "We would always be sitting round, talking about music, or arguing about something," Miles recalled in his autobiography. "I remember Gerry Mulligan being very angry at this time, about a lot of shit. But so was I, and we would get into arguments sometimes. But Gil was like a mother hen to all of us … he was a beautiful person who just loved to be around musicians. And we loved being around him because he taught us so much, about caring for people and about music, especially arranging music."[6]

At this time, Evans was experiencing some friction within Thornhill's band, in part because of the attention he was receiving, whilst Davis was disillusioned by the tensions that existed within the Parker band, and the constant disputes over money. Miles was also "looking for a vehicle where I could solo more in the style that I was hearing. My music was a little slower, and not so intense as Bird's."[7]

Before long, Gil Evans, Gerry Mulligan and Miles Davis started to discuss forming a new band. Evans and Mulligan, as arrangers, were keen to experiment with a scaled-down version of the Thornhill group, convinced that they could match the tone and harmonies of the eighteen-piece big band with just nine instruments. Between them, Gerry Mulligan and Gil Evans spent most of the winter of 1947–48 working on the instrumentation for a nine-piece band.

The horn section was centred on the trumpet sound of Miles Davis. As Mulligan explained, "We wound up holding it down to one trumpet because if Miles were to be the trumpet his sound was so personal that we didn't really want to have to blend it with another trumpet sound. Let the trumpet sound be his; and it really fit. It became an easy thing for me to write for because I could hear Miles melodically much more easily than I could hear a trumpet player who was really playing an open trumpet sound."[8]

The original plan was to recruit Danny Polo on clarinet, but Mulligan and Evans came to the conclusion that, much as they loved his sound, it was probably impractical. "Danny was always on the road with the Thornhill Band and there wasn't anybody else that we wanted on clarinet," explained Mulligan. To add depth to the lower range, Mulligan and Evans decided on the French horn and tuba that Evans had pioneered in Thornhill's band, trombone and Mulligan's baritone saxophone, using an alto saxophone to balance the higher end of the range.

Having decided the instrumentation, the three of them had to recruit the other band members. John Lewis, a regular guest at Evans's apartment, and with a shared interest in arrangement, was an obvious choice as pianist. Lewis had been a member of Dizzy Gillespie's bop-style big band since 1946, where he had developed his skills as both a composer and arranger. Al McKibbon had replaced Ray Brown in Gillespie's band in 1947, and joined the new band on bass. Max Roach was a drummer with Charlie Parker's quintet, where he worked with Davis, and had been one of the regular guests at Evans's apartment.

The tuba was a potential problem, as Carisi noted, as they needed "to get a tuba player that could play delicately enough, that wasn't a German-band-sounding tuba."[9] They eventually settled on Bill Barber, a member of Thorhill's group, who came recommended by Evans. Sandy Siegelstein, a French horn player, was also poached from the Thornhill band, although by the time of the group's concert at the Royal Roost, Junior Collins had replaced him. First choice trombonist J.J. Johnson was on tour when the band formed, and Davis initially recruited Michael Zwerin, an eighteen-year-old college student. Zwerin was present at the group's New York concerts in September 1948, but was replaced by Kai Winding for the group's first recording session, and eventually by J.J. Johnson for the two later sessions.

The biggest debate appears to have been over the alto saxophonist, with Miles Davis favouring the more bop-oriented Charlie Parker disciple, Sonny Stitt, and Mulligan preferring the more delicate sound of Lee Konitz. Mulligan was keen to develop a sound that was quite distinct from the hard bebop sound of Parker and Gillespie, and was concerned that there were already too many bop-based musicians in the band, including Davis himself, Roach, Lewis and McKibbon. He eventually persuaded Davis that Konitz's 'cool' tone was more in keeping with the compositions he was working on.

Davis later likened the instrumentation to a choir. "I was the soprano voice, Lee Konitz was the alto. We also used the French horn for alto voicing and the baritone sax for the baritone voicing, and the bass tuba for bass voicing … I wanted the instruments to sound like human voices, and they did."[10]

The role of Miles Davis in the formation of the *Birth of the Cool* band has always been a matter of debate. Whilst Evans and Mulligan decided on the instrumentation, Davis was the one who was motivated enough to get the band out of the apartment, and into the rehearsal hall, a view that Mulligan confirmed. "Miles was really the practical one. It's a little hard for some people to realise that, but Miles always wanted something of his own and he really had the desire to have his own band and make a place for himself in the music scene. He loved the sound of the Thornhill Band and when he heard this idea we were talking about with the instrumentation, he thought that could be it. So he was the one who started making the phone calls, getting the guys together, picking out the players, reserving the rehearsal studios, and generally assuming the role of a leader. And that's how we started actually playing together, because I think if it had been left to the rest of us we probably would have kept on theorizing and writing and never have gotten around to doing anything."[11] Davis confirmed this view of events in his autobiography, describing how he "hired the rehearsal halls, called the rehearsals, and got things done … I got us some jobs, and made the contact at Capitol records to do the recording."[12]

The new band only played one engagement, supporting the Count Basie band at the Royal Roost on Broadway and 47th, playing a two-week stint in late August and early September 1948. In the words of Konitz, the concerts were not a resounding success. "It didn't sound that great. Changes in personnel, and not much opportunity to rehearse, and it was very delicate music."

The more bebop-oriented members of the band, most notably Miles Davis himself, also had problems adapting to the chamber-type arrangements in a live setting. "If you start stretching out too many solos on those arrangements—to me this always happens in arrangements anyway—if the solos are too long then the composed parts lose their continuity; they lose their connection with each other," noted Mulligan. "And that's what Miles started to do in the club, play more and more choruses on the things, so that the band never really solved those problems, and Miles wasn't considering them. John Lewis used to get really mad at him because he wouldn't assume the responsibility and wouldn't consider the band—because the band was a unique thing. It's not like going into the club with a sextet. It functioned well as a rehearsal band, because as a rehearsal band you're in an altogether different world than when you're out functioning as a working group in front of an audience. It's an altogether different kettle of fish and it takes focus and concentration, and it takes consideration."[13]

The reaction of the audience and critics was also mixed. No doubt this is partly explained by the fact that the music played was quite distinct from that of Basie's swing band. In addition, many of the leading jazz critics were still enamoured of the bop style, and did not seem to know what to make of the textured arrangements.

Still, Basie himself seems to have liked what he heard, describing how "the slow things sounded strange and good", and more importantly Pete Rugolo of Capitol records was impressed, and signed up the band to record twelve sides once the recording ban had ended.

Ralph Watkins, the owner of the Royal Roost, had only taken on the band as a favour to Davis, having been impressed with his work with the Parker quintet. For most club owners, it was uneconomical to take on a nine-piece band, particularly when the music they played was regarded as experimental. As a consequence the nonet effectively disbanded after the Royal Roost concerts, with the members returning to their other bands, and Zwerin returning to college.

The band effectively regrouped in late January 1949, with Kai Winding replacing Zwerin, and Al Haig and Joe Shulman replacing Lewis and McKibbon, respectively, both of whom had returned to Gillespie's band,

and were away touring. The band recorded four songs at the first session, returning to the studios in April 1949, and again in March 1950, to fulfill their contract, each time with slightly modified personnel.

To begin with, Pete Rugulo had difficulty capturing the band's unique sound. "He told me at one point when we took a break, 'Gerry, we are having a hell of a time in the control room and I don't know what to tell the engineer. We just really are not getting it'. I said, 'Well, I don't know what to tell you about how to record it because I don't know that much about the microphone and the techniques. All we're trying to do is get a natural balance between the six horns'. We were trying to blend with each other and we were set up so that we were all facing in on the microphones, so ideally we should have been able to hear each other to a certain extent. I think probably what they needed to do—I don't know if they had the facilities then before any kind of stereo—was to have more microphones than we used. I don't know what the limitations were on the equipment, but that's really what it seemed like it needed."[14]

Once the technical difficulties had been resolved, the recording sessions proceeded smoothly, according to Mulligan. "Miles was brilliant on those things, Miles and Lee both. Absolutely brilliant, the way they played in and out of the arrangements—wonderful. That made everything worthwhile. Another thing that made it worthwhile was Max Roach on the first date. The first set of dates was really wonderful. He was far and away the best drummer for the thing because he could approach the things as a composer and he took the kind of care with playing with the ensemble that showed his compositional awareness."[15]

The music was originally released on four 78-rpm singles in 1949 and 1950, and was not available in long-play format until May 1954, under the title *Birth of the Cool*. The critical reaction was mixed, at least initially. *The New York Times* published an unfavourable review, whilst Winthrop Sargeant, a classical musical writer for *The New Yorker*, questioned whether the music should even be labelled 'jazz'. "The music sounds more like that of the new Maurice Ravel than it does like jazz. I, who do not listen to jazz recordings day in and day out, find this music charming and exciting … If Miles Davis were an established 'classical' composer, his work would rank high among that of his contemporary colleagues. But it is not really jazz."[16]

Even if the critics were unconvinced, musicians were increasingly won over by what they heard. Tadd Dameron, a prominent band lead and arranger, who had invited Davis to join his band around this time, described 'Boplicity', released in October 1949, as "one of the best small group sounds I've heard."

The music also started to impact musicians on the West Coast. As drummer Shelly Manne recalled, "the main influence on West Coast jazz, if one record could be an influence, was the album that Miles Davis made called *Birth of the Cool.* That kind of writing and playing was closer to what we were trying to do, closer to the way a lot of us felt, out on the West Coast. What we wanted to do was to be represented by that album. It had a lot to do with not only with just improvisation and swing. It was the main character of the music we liked—the chance for the composer to be challenged too. To write some new kind of material for jazz musicians where the solos and the improvisation became part of the whole and you couldn't tell where the writing ended and the improvisation began. The spaces were right, it was lighter, maybe a little more laid-back kind of music. Maybe a little cooler, but still swinging. I felt that it was a good period, a creative period at that time."

The *Birth of the Cool* records also had a profound impact on Chet Baker, and his close friend, bass player Bob Whitlock. "Chet and I used to sit and listen to those records together and marvel at the arrangements of Gil Evans and Gerry; they were like something out of the blue, you know. It wasn't like the brassy big band sound at all; it was very different, very subtle. There was a clarity and buoyancy to the arrangements. And the voicing between the horns was very unusual. There was some lightweight dissonance that most of us weren't used to. It was fresh and delightful. We weren't so much taken by the soloists as the ensemble playing. The closest thing we had to that out here on the West Coast was Shorty Rogers, people like that, but it didn't even come close. It was very influential."[17]

Whilst the nonet effectively disbanded after these recordings, the musicians learnt from their experience, and had greater success developing these ideas on their own. Miles continued to refine his unique sound, and by the mid-1950s, had evolved into the most important bandleader of his generation. Lee Konitz had been working for some time with Lennie Tristano, a blind, Chicago-born experimental pianist, and together with saxophonist Warne Marsh, they devised their own unique take on 'cool' jazz. John Lewis, the pianist, teamed up with vibraphonist Milt Jackson, eventually forming the Modern Jazz Quartet in 1952, developing a style that is frequently described as 'chamber jazz'. Finally, Kai Winding the trombonist, started to work with saxophonist Stan Getz, and experimented with a number of small group formats.

As a consequence, the influence of the *Birth of the Cool* sessions gradually seeped out into the mainstream, arguably finding greatest traction on the West Coast, influencing the 'cool' sounds that took hold in the early–mid 1950s. The music press also warmed to the band over time, with the *New York Times* reversing its initially lukewarm response to the music, and *DownBeat* magazine going as far as to analyse the solos of both Davis and Konitz.

After the nonet disbanded, Mulligan found work harder to come by, and struggled to finance a burgeoning heroin habit. In 1950, he started to play at the Red Door, a midtown Manhattan rehearsal space. It was here that his girlfriend Gail Madden, a pianist and percussionist, apparently encouraged him to experiment with a sound that he would later make famous – a pianoless quartet. The band featured Mulligan on baritone, Tony Fruscella on trumpet, Phil Leshin on bass, and drummer Walter Bolden. Unfortunately, the band never made it out of the Manhattan walk-up, and Mulligan was left to further develop these ideas when he reached California.

In the meantime, he found occasional work as an arranger, continuing his apprenticeship with Claude Thornhill, and contributing scores to the big band of Elliot Lawrence. He also recorded a solo LP, *Mulligan Plays Mulligan*, for Prestige Records in August 1951. The recording was originally attributed to The Gerry Mulligan All Stars, a tentet including Latin-style percussion, and much lighter in tone that his work with the Miles Davis nonet.

Shortly afterwards, Mulligan decided to leave New York. His drug addiction was starting to get out of control, and he was struggling to find regular work. He decided to sell his horns, and hitchhike to California with his girlfriend. "I did some playing along the way using borrowed horns, mostly tenors, and I remember playing in a cowboy band in a roadhouse outside Albuquerque for a while," he said. "I was lucky because I knew a guy who was teaching at the university there, and he helped me keep body and soul together."[18]

Upon arrival in Los Angeles, Gail Madden introduced Mulligan to her former boyfriend, the arranger Bob Graettinger. Graettinger was in the process of recording 'City of Glass', his most famous composition, with Stan Kenton's orchestra. Mulligan evidently impressed Kenton, and was invited to write for the band. "Even though it wasn't my ideal band or style or anything, I was very glad to get the job and did my best to try to satisfy Stan. I wrote a lot of charts for him at that period. I remember that the first thing I wrote for him was very contrapuntal, I was trying to do a thing that built an ensemble sound out of all the unison contrapuntal lines, and it built up to a nice solid ensemble chorus. Stan didn't really like it very well, so he said if I rewrote it he would take it, so I did. I put the tune 'Walking Shoes' on the first part and used the out chorus from the piece that was there. That was alright. He made sure that I understood that the other guys were to do the concert stuff, and what I was writing would be the dog work, writing the dance arrangements, which was alright with me because I liked the tunes. I did the best I could with them. I'm not sure how much he liked them. I threw in a few originals along the way."[19]

Mulligan struck up a friendship with the orchestra's trumpeter, Milton 'Shorty' Rogers, whose own work was heavily influenced by the *Birth of the Cool* sound. "I did some playing with Shorty Rogers at Balboa," Mulligan later claimed, "with people like Art Pepper, Wardell Grey, Coop and June Christy. Shorty was very nice and always used me whenever he could."

Another early acquaintance on the West Coast—from around March 1952—was the twenty-one-year-old bass player Bob Whitlock. "Gail Madden called me, and asked me if I'd come to an audition with Gerry. I was tickled pink—I would have done anything." Whitlock was surprised to find that Mulligan was struggling to find regular work. "It was kind of rough; you would have expected him to find all kinds of work, but he had some pretty rigid principles. He figured he could blaze a new trail." The rehearsal with Mulligan was just as a duo, and whilst the young bass player found the experience somewhat daunting, it was a musical success. "The first thing he said to me scared the life out of me. He said, 'Play a four bar introduction'. I had this thing I'd memorised that Al Haig used to play with Stan Getz, and I played that as an introduction. Gerry came in, cooking, and we hit it off real well."[20]

Gerry introduced Bob to two musicians he had met in Albuquerque, Bill and Ty, who played tenor saxophone and trumpet, respectively. Then Bob Whitlock suggested they recruit Gil Barrios on piano. "Gerry didn't really know too many guys out here," he said. "He knew Jimmy Rowles real well, but he was busy doing studio work most days."

Mulligan arranged for the band to rehearse at the Cottage Italia, a small bar and restaurant in the San Fernando Valley whose owner encouraged musicians to stop by and play. "It was a different era then; guys would be happy to play for free, just to get the experience of playing," explained Whitlock. "He wound up getting three of four sets a night; guys would line up to play, and couldn't even get on the bandstand. So it was a good place to go, just to keep your chops together between gigs. That was what it was all about in those days; we were young, full of enthusiasm, and didn't give a damn about money, we really didn't. It was all about playing what we could play, and hoping we could go somewhere with it."

Shortly after the band started playing at the Cottage Italia, Gerry was approached by the disc jockey Gene Norman, who asked him if he wanted to record an album. He booked a small studio on Vine, in the centre of Hollywood. "We did a few tunes, mostly Gerry's arrangements, but none of it came out very well," Whitlock remembered. "The album was real sorry, and convinced Gerry that he had to replace the two guys from Albuquerque." The record was shelved, and to date has never been released.[21]

A couple of weeks later, some time in April, Bob Whitlock suggested that Gerry audition Chet Baker as a replacement. "He said, 'Bring him in, I'll listen to him'," recalled Whitlock. "I thought, 'Chet's going to love this'. But the rehearsal was a disaster. Chet had this terrible habit of blowing so hard to warm up that he'd practically blow your ear-drums out. I don't know why he did it; a lot of people didn't like it, but Chet wasn't one to care what other people thought. Gerry went off, and said, 'Don't you ever blast like that again, not under my roof!' He got very uptight about it, and left Chet feeling very embarrassed. Chet told Gerry, 'Go fuck yourself!' then stuck his horn in his bag, and walked out. I sat there with my mouth open."[22]

Around this time, Gerry secured occasional work at The Haig nightclub on South Kenmore Avenue, just off Wilshire Boulevard. The Haig was a tiny, converted bungalow, complete with its original white picket fence, hidden behind the elegant Ambassador Hotel, which hosted established stars like Frank Sinatra at its prestigious Coconut Grove nightclub. "It only held seventy or seventy-five people," recalled tenor saxophonist and arranger Jack Montrose. "It was so tiny that when they had a customer ordering a drink, they had to send someone out to the liquor store to get some inventory. It was not really prepared for business."[23]

The Erroll Garner Trio was headlining at The Haig at this time, with Paul Smith taking over on the off nights. Gerry Mulligan initially started playing with Paul Smith, but when the pianist left for another gig, Mulligan took over the off nights as leader.

Over the next two months, Mulligan experimented with a number of different musicians. One of the earliest line-ups consisted of Gerry Mulligan on baritone saxophone, Art Pepper on alto, Gil Barrios on piano and Alvin Stoller on drums. This only lasted a couple of weeks, however, before Marty Paich took over on piano, and Bobby White on drums. At various times, the rotating group of musicians also included Jimmy Rowles and Fred Otis on piano, Red Mitchell and Joe Mondragon on bass, and Chico Hamilton and Lloyd Morales on drums. "Gerry was trying people out, but had nothing to offer anybody, except Monday night," said Whitlock.

The first draft of the Gerry Mulligan Quartet emerged from these Monday night jam sessions. Listening closely to Mulligan's musical experiments was an earnest, bespectacled young man, Dick Bock, an executive of Discovery Records who dreamed of starting his own label. On the afternoon of June 10th, he made arrangements for Gerry to record at the Laurel Canyon bungalow of recording engineer Philip Turetsky. "Gerry asked Jimmy Rowles, Red Mitchell and Chico Hamilton to meet up at Turetsky's house where I had access to his Ampex tape recorder and one RCA 44-B microphone," he later recalled. Rowles failed to turn up for the recording session, but the trio went ahead, recording three songs, with Mulligan filling in on piano as well as baritone saxophone.[24]

Shortly after this first recording session, Mulligan had a change of heart about his failure to hire Chet Baker. Bob Whitlock cannot be certain, but suspects that pianist Jimmy Rowles had something to do with this. "I know Jimmy Rowles had a record deal. I think Jimmy contacted Gerry to see if he wanted to do a record date he had cooked up. I know that Jimmy loved Chet's playing, and he may even have called Chet before he called Gerry. I remember Gerry hadn't heard how good Chet sounded with Charlie Parker, and he took it upon himself to go down there and listen. And when he got there, he was just amazed, and was sorry that he'd blown up on Chet like that."

In early July, once Chet had returned to Los Angeles after touring with Bird, Mulligan invited Chet to join him onstage at The Haig, an event witnessed by Dick Bock. "He came in, and just sat in. It was so pure, and so natural, you know, that natural talent, that it started to change the whole picture there."

A week later, Mulligan approached Bock about another recording session, this time with Chet on trumpet. "Soon after that meeting Gerry decided to attempt to record with Jimmy Rowles again. So, together with Chet and Joe Mondragon, we met at the Universal Recording Studio in Hollywood on the evening of July 9th 1952. Out of this session came Kern and Harbach's 'She Didn't Say Yes'. This is the only recording session without drums and with piano." Bock's memory may have let him down on this point as the session was almost certainly recorded at Phil Turetsky's bungalow. The sound of Jimmy Rowles's piano dominated the session, and Mulligan was again dissatisfied with the results.

Bass player Bob Whitlock was deeply disappointed not to have been invited to the initial recording sessions. "I knew nothing about it until after the fact," he later revealed. "Chet didn't mention anything about it, and that really hurt me. They were Jimmy's arrangements, and Joe was Jimmy's bass player, but that was little consolation. For a few months I had invested a lot of time and energy with Gerry and it was a hard thing for me to swallow. It was then that I seriously began to entertain other offers."[25]

Mulligan continued to experiment with the sound, his girlfriend Gail Maddon occasionally contributing ideas about percussion. "One of the things that gave me a lot of confidence to do that was that when we were still in New York and Gail and I were organizing some things, we organized a record date with Prestige, but the rhythm section that she had (with maracas that kind of made a swishing sound, that she made go with the cymbal sound) had no piano in it. So, because of the things she had tried, it gave me kind of an idea of what I might try and what not to do and so on."[26]

Whilst Gerry found her contributions helpful, Chet was less favourably disposed to her input. "A couple of weeks later I was called in for a rehearsal with Mulligan, which turned into a big hustle between Gerry and some chick who had come with him from New York," Chet recalled in his memoirs. "She played the maracas—somewhat—but mostly she was just a pain in the ass for Gerry and kept anything from happening with her bullshit."

Gerry Mulligan eventually settled on the experienced Forestorn 'Chico' Hamilton on percussion. The thirty-year-old drummer was a veteran of the Lionel Hampton, Duke Ellington and Count Basie big bands. His style was not to everyone's taste, but as Bob Whitlock explained, he had the characteristics that Mulligan was looking for. "Chico's drumming wasn't always liked back then, and he got a lot of criticism. I will say one thing for

Gerry; he stood up and made clear that was what he wanted. Chico rarely played anything but brushes; he was also very facile with his fingers, doing stuff on the drums, even the cymbals, with his hands. He had done that with Lena Horne, and it was considered very good showbusiness with her; Gerry saw it as good showbusiness as well, and it also gave him a little variety."[27]

Gerry arranged another rehearsal, this time without his girlfriend. "He got in touch with me a week later and we set up another meeting, this time at my house," Chet wrote. "Chico Hamilton, Bob Whitlock, Gerry and myself were present. The group clicked immediately under Gerry's direction."[28]

But Chet oversimplifies matters—the initial rehearsal did not go as smoothly as he suggests, and further sessions were arranged at the apartment of saxophonist Buddy Collette. "Chico Hamilton, their drummer, wanted to know if they could rehearse at our apartment," he said. "The first rehearsal didn't sound too great, because they didn't know how to play without the piano. It was a shifting of the gears."[29]

Whilst Gerry Mulligan was already experimenting with a pianoless quartet, the owner of The Haig, John Bennett, effectively forced the final decision on him. For some months Errol Garner had been the principle attraction at the club, and Bennett had managed to squeeze a nine-foot concert grand Baldwin on the club's tiny stage. " I remember when they had that grand piano, two of the legs were on the grandstand and the far leg was on a box!" laughed Whitlock.[30]

The Red Norvo Trio had been booked to replace Errol Garner from mid-July, and was scheduled for a lengthy engagement. At this time the band consisted of Red Norvo on vibraphone, Red Mitchell on bass and Tal Farlow on guitar. "They were now in a quandary over what to do about the off night because they didn't have a piano and they certainly weren't going to rent a grand piano to play on the one night," Mulligan explained. "John Bennett, who was one of the owners of the place, said, 'What they should do is get one of those little sixty-six-key studio uprights for the off night'. In the meantime Dick had said that he would like me to put a group together to play the off nights. I said, 'Great', but when John said this about the piano I said, 'No, I don't think I want a studio upright. Thank you. Let me think of something else'. I started to try different things with a bass guitar, drums, and horn—various ways of approaching a rhythm section without a piano."[31]

Whilst Mulligan makes it sound like a rational decision to proceed with the pianoless quartet, it was a decision made out of desperation. The band was only working Monday nights at that time, and was struggling to make any kind of living. If he had insisted Bennett bring in an upright piano just for the Monday night, he might easily have lost the slot. Dick Bock remembers asking Mulligan about what he was going to do without a piano, and being told that the band could play without one. "He didn't want to lose the gig—at that point he was really scuffling. And so it turned out to be a pianoless quartet."

As another Monday night gig approached, Mulligan remembered watching Chico Hamilton loading his drum kit into the back of his car. "All the time we rehearsed we only had a small set, maybe a snare drum and high hat, a standing tom-tom, and one top cymbal on a stand—no bass drum, no set of tom-toms—and so it was a minimal set. And I remember the first time we had been rehearsing down at a house that Chet rented in Watts, and we were getting ready after rehearsing to pack up to go up into the city to play the job, and I looked in the back of Chico's car. He had a whole set of drums back there. I asked, 'What have you got your drums here for?' He said, 'Well, we're going to work tonight'. I said, 'Yeah, but you're not going to use all that stuff are you?' He said, 'Certainly'. I said, 'No man, you must play with same stuff you've been rehearsing with, because this is the sound of the group. It's going to be different if you come in with a whole set of drums'. He finally gave in, so that's what he played on: the snare, the sock cymbal, the one standing tom, and the one standing cymbal, and he played a good deal of the time on brushes. But he used to do things in solos that put me away."[32]

Onstage at The Haig, the group's early teething problems were plain for all to see. "Their first night was just horrible," Dick Bock remembered. "There were these long stretches where there were just bass and drums, where Gerry and Chet were just trying to figure out what they were doing."

The musicians initially found it difficult to play without the harmonic underpinning of the piano. "The first few nights weren't that great," recalled bass player Bob Whitlock. "Gerry would play, then Chet would play, then all of a sudden Chico and I would be alone, and there were only a couple of alternatives; either I would go into solo mode, and Chico would brush away, so the only rhythm going was the brushes. And if I'm playing a solo, there's no harmonic background, nothing to give any definition to what I'm playing. I'm telling you, I would get up on the bandstand on some of them warm summer nights, and the horns would get out of tune with the bass. I'd be spending half my time cranking the tuning peg. It could really sound bad, a group without any harmonic foundation when you're not perfectly attuned. There was a very low comfort level there for a while."[33]

The group persevered, with Chet quickly grasping that if he were to fall in behind Gerry's baritone, in the same way that Gerry accompanied his own solos, it gave the rhythm section a great deal more freedom. "Gerry could play counterpoint with anyone, because he was fabulous at that," explained Bob Whitlock. "He had been a good arranger for many years, and he could fall in behind anyone and accompany them. But other musicians couldn't do it with him. Chet was the first guy who took that on actively. Chet was so impressed with Gerry's ability in that respect that he decided he was going to get good at it. And he did; Chet ended up playing some fabulous counterpoint. And finally Gerry noticed that it worked if he played a little counter-line to my solo. And then it got more comfortable, so I would start playing more walking solos. Eventually we got to the stage where all three of us would be playing counterpoint to one another, and it just got more interesting. All of a sudden, people liked what they were hearing, and the more they liked it, the more we liked it, and we got comfortable with each other. And that's kind of the way it happened. It didn't happen overnight."[34]

Dick Bock could hear the difference, and felt the group was ready to record its first single. With two thousand dollars in savings, and a further two thousand from his friend Roy Harte, who owned a drum shop in Hollywood, he now had enough funds to launch his own record label, Pacific Jazz. "On the afternoon of August 16th 1952, at the Turetsky bungalow again, we recorded the memorable 'Bernie's Tune' and 'Lullaby Of The Leaves'. That record, released as a single in the fall of 1952, put Pacific Jazz in business," said Bock.[35]

The record was well received, and the group was rewarded with a prestigious gig at San Francisco's Blackhawk club, opposite Dave Brubeck, starting in early September.

By that stage, Bob Whitlock had decided to leave the band, opting to join Vido Musso, the Italian saxophonist, who was offering more regular work. "I left the band after a while, because all I had was the Monday night. I needed some income—I mean, Christ, I was making no money. Vido Musso called and asked me if I wanted to go up to San Francisco. I went up to the Say When, and while I was gone, Gerry hired Carson to replace me."[36]

The twenty-one-year-old Carson Smith only had one week to rehearse with the band, but the hard work had already been done, and he quickly grasped what was required of him. "Carson Smith on bass had a particular feeling for the function that he was doing," Mulligan later claimed. "He realised that he was doing two things at once; it was like being part of the ensemble plus part of the rhythm section. Because everything was supported by the bass, since you didn't have a piano stating the chords, it had to come from the combination of the bass, bass line, and whatever we were doing with harmonies."[37]

In many respects, the Blackhawk gig proved to be the band's major breakthrough. The influential jazz writer Ralph Gleason, who wrote for the *San Francisco Chronicle*, and was the West Coast editor of *DownBeat* magazine, witnessed their performance. Impressed by what he had heard, he described the band as "certainly the freshest and most interesting sound to come out of jazz in a long time." His favourable review ensured a capacity crowd for the remainder of the engagement.

Dave Brubeck was also blown away by the unique sound of the quartet, and recommended them to the West Coast label Fantasy Records, much to the disappointment of Bob Whitlock. "If I had known Gerry was going to get a job up there, I never would have gone! As it turned out, we were up there at the same time. Eventually Fantasy Records offered them a deal, and Carson took my place. In the meantime I was working with Vido Musso, and I was madder than hell!"

The resulting session for Fantasy produced four outstanding tracks; two of the tunes were named after local DJs, thereby ensuring heavy rotation on the local San Francisco radio stations. 'Line For Lyons' was named after KNBC's Jimmy Lyons, an early champion of Dave Brubeck. 'Bark For Barksdale', meanwhile, was named after 'Big' Don Barksdale. A third track, 'Carioca', was a Latin-tinged dance tune taken from the movie *Flying Down to Rio*, which featured Fred Astaire and Ginger Rogers, Baker's airy trumpet gliding over the tune as effortlessly as Astaire moved across the dance floor.

Searching for a final song to complete the session, bass player Carson Smith suggested a Rogers and Hart ballad that he had recently come across, entitled 'My Funny Valentine'. The song was originally performed in the now obscure musical *Babes in Arms*, sung by Mitzi Green in the role of Susie Ward, and was later sung by Judy Garland in a 1939 film version of the musical. Smith later recalled that his colleagues were not familiar with the tune, so he sang them the melody. His recollection does not ring entirely true on this issue, as Chet and others had been playing the tune around L.A. for a number of years before this.

Smith and Mulligan then developed a relatively simple arrangement that highlighted the aching tone of Chet's trumpet. Mulligan later attributed the success of the arrangement to Carson Smith, saying, "a lot of the good ideas in the early quartet were his. For instance, the idea of doing 'My Funny Valentine' with that moving bass line, which makes the arrangement, was Carson's."[38]

In retrospect, it is clear that Gerry Mulligan was setting out to provoke Bob Whitlock with these comments. He would have been well aware that the distinctive descending chromatic line was written by Richard Rogers himself, rather than Carson Smith. In the same interview he even goes on to describe Carson Smith as the band's "original bass player", undermining the enormous contribution of Whitlock to the formation of the quartet's distinctive sound. "It's no secret that Gerry resented me for leaving the group," Whitlock later explained. "Even though I returned within a few weeks he never really got over my having the audacity to leave in the first place. I left because I didn't see anything on the horizon with Gerry, and I was getting desperate for some income. If that was disloyal, then so be it. But for God's sake, to flat out deny someone's existence for the better part of a year with such casual disdain some forty years later seems a bit extreme! Pardon me, but I have to wonder what kind of person does a thing like that."[39]

Whilst Mulligan attributes the success of the arrangement to the bass line, the record's success predominantly reflected the lyricism of Chet playing. His soft, mournful tone gives the tune a haunting quality that has not dimmed with the passing years. Carson Smith agreed that Chet's tone was the key to the record's success. "After Fantasy released those records, everybody knew that this new voice of Chet Baker was the thing," he said. "All of a sudden everybody was talking about Chet."

'My Funny Valentine' went on to become a big hit, both on the airwaves and with the jazz critics, helping to establish the reputation of the quartet. In *DownBeat* magazine, Ralph Gleason raved over the band's "fantastic, fugue-ish, funky, swinging and contrapuntal sound." He singled out Chet Baker for special praise, suggesting that once he worked out how "to project his personality to the audience and not rely on the music completely, he should be sensational."[40]

Returning to Los Angeles in late September, John Bennett was quick to cash in on the quartet's newfound success, signing them up for four weeks to headline at The Haig; it was a period that would eventually stretch into several months as the group continued to grow in popularity.

Whilst Carson Smith played adequately on the Fantasy session, Chet preferred the playing of Bob Whitlock, and suggested Gerry called him to see if he wanted to return to the band. He had no hesitation. "After a few weeks of 'Come Back To Sorrento', I was ready to return as Gerry's gardener," he laughed.[41]

The quartet now had the opportunity to work together on a more regular basis, no longer limited to Monday nights, and the group's dynamic continued to evolve. Gerry's musical relationship with Chet, in particular, moved to another level, as they started to play off one another, each trying to anticipate what the other would play. As Mulligan later recalled: "Chet and I would sometimes play tunes that we never even discussed, and one or the other of us would just start playing it. We would wind up doing something with it that would sound like an organised arrangement, so people couldn't really tell whether we had worked it out or not. We were also able to do something that, to this day, I don't think that many people are successful at—make convincing endings. We could go into some kind of a chord extension, a sequence at the end of a piece, that sounded like we worked it out. Each one could hear where the other was going and wind up making sense out of it, so that it sounded like it was written. Sometimes a whole night would go by, and we wouldn't discuss what we were playing, and we would hardly play anything that we would normally play on other nights. We would just play a whole bunch of different things. And that was one of the joys of playing with Chet because we were able to work together so easily in that way. I had never experienced anything like that before and not really since."

Local musicians flocked to the club to hear the new group that all the critics were talking about. The pianist Russ Freeman, who was working at The Lighthouse club, remembers witnessing the quartet at this time. "A lot of things that were being done on the West Coast were, in retrospect, really not very good. But Gerry and Chet were astonishing. They had a rapport between them that was unique—like an intuitive conversation. You'd think 'Well, they've got this stuff worked out—he's going to come in here, and *he's* coming in *here*'—but it wasn't that way at all. Whatever they played, it was different every time."

Bill Holman, an arranger himself, was also impressed by the way the quartet coped without a piano. "Not having a chordal instrument seemed to take a lot of the urgency away from the music. They could really relax, and listen to each other. Of course, Gerry had the musical knowledge, which, together with the bass, enabled him to make some sort of harmonic implication. And Chet, amazingly, went along with what Gerry was trying to do. Some guys would probably have rebelled a little bit, because Gerry could be kind of a taskmaster. But Chet really fitted in well—two strong personalities managed to co-exist. The group was just great."[42]

Despite their chemistry on the bandstand, the musicians did not get on particularly well offstage. Chet used to socialise with his old friend Bob Whitlock. "He was my closest friend," the bass player explained. "We would spend whole days together, and we always knew we could count on each other." Chet and Gerry were never tight, with Gerry despairing of Chet's youthful antics, and their relationship gradually deteriorated as the band ran its course.

Chico Hamilton found Gerry Mulligan's manner to be somewhat intimidating. He also chose to keep his distance, to some extent, because of the saxophonist's involvement with drugs. "He and Chet were both a little bit into the drug thing," he told Gordon Jack, author of *Fifties Jazz Talk*. "If you are not a 'druggie', and you are hanging out with people who are, they can manifest an 'outsider' thing to you, no matter how nicely it's done."

Despite Bob Whitlock's own battle with drug addiction, the drummer treated him as a younger brother. "Every so often after work he would take me to one of those after-hours speakeasies on the South side where everyone knew him," he said. "I liked Chico, and was always happy to see him coming down the pike."[43]

Dick Bock was only too aware of the quartet's rapid development, and having missed out on the group's breakthrough recording, which came out on Fantasy, was keen to return to the recording studio. The band cut six new tunes over two days in mid-October; together with the original 78-rpm single, recorded two months earlier, there was enough material for a ten-inch LP. Mulligan wrote half of the new tunes, which comprised 'Nights at the Turntable,' 'Walkin' Shoes' and 'Soft Shoe', all of which were taken at a mid-tempo, designed to highlight the interplay between the two horns. Chet contributed a tune of his own, an uptempo number called 'Freeway', with two standards completing the line up.

"Gerry wrote practically all of the originals himself, but on standards, show tunes and ballads he not only encouraged but expected everyone to improvise on arrangements," Whitlock explained. "That was the beauty of it. The arrangements were not static. Just no anarchy, please! When everyone was on the same page, it could be very exciting. Having said all that, it was Gerry's inimitable presence that drove and defined the character and flavour of the group."[44]

Chet plays with greater confidence and creativity at this second session for Pacific Jazz, a result of the growing chemistry within the band, and the fact that he was beginning to feel more at ease in the confines of the recording studio. The producer, Dick Bock, once suggested that the group's initial success was partly down to him, claiming "when we made the first quartet records, [Chet] was still pretty immature, and I had to do a lot of editing and splicing to make complete solos without any fluffs."

Chet reacted angrily to this suggestion, turning on his early mentor. "He's full of shit. I never had any solos spliced. The only credit that man deserves is that he was able to borrow three hundred dollars [sic] from Roy Harte, who had a drum store there in Hollywood, to rent the studios and pay the union wages for the record date. He knows nothing about music whatsoever in any way."[45]

Chet's reaction seems unduly harsh, particularly given the support Bock offered him in later years, when he had a family and a drug habit to support. When the jazz record producer Michael Cuscuna unearthed the original master tapes in the early 1980s, he did indeed find numerous splices. Pianist Russ Freeman confirmed that this was considered common practice at Pacific Records. "My rationale was, recording is very difficult," he reasoned. "Go into a studio, and somebody points a finger at you and says, 'Ok, make magic'."

The ten-inch LP was well received in the jazz press, winning a four-star review from the influential *DownBeat* magazine. "Mulligan's baritone, Chet Baker's trumpet, Chico Hamilton's drums, and Bob Whitlock's bass share the credit about evenly. Mulligan, who presumably did most of the arrangements, deserves an extra salvo for his economical and efficaciously simple use of the limited instrumentation. A couple of his originals [sic], notably Freeway, have quite a melodic charm too."[46]

The magazine's only note of reservation concerned the absence of piano on the recording, noting, "we can't hear anything in the music that wouldn't have sounded even better with a piano rounding out the rhythmic underline…"

Mulligan was incensed by these comments. He had gone to the trouble of explaining his rationale for recording without a piano in the liner notes to the record. "I consider the string bass to be the basis of the sound of the group; the foundation on which the soloist builds his line, the main thread around which the two horns weave their contrapuntal interplay. It is possible with two voices to imply the sound or impart the feeling of any chord or series of chords, as Bach shows us so thoroughly and enjoyably in his inventions." The band's unique sound owed more to King Oliver and the Dixieland sound than Bach, of course, as Mulligan himself acknowledged, but by bringing Bach into the equation, he presumably hoped to undermine his critics.

More than fifty years on, it's perhaps worth pausing to analyse why the Gerry Mulligan Quartet was so well regarded at the time. Firstly, from a simplistic perspective, the music provided a stark contrast to bop. The ordered, sometimes chamber-like arrangements were an extension of the 'cool' sound pioneered by Mulligan, Evans and Davis in the late 1940s, but stripped back to the bare essentials. It sounded fresh and original then, a cool, fresh breeze after the storm of bop, and has stood the test of time remarkably well. Secondly, the absence of a piano allowed the musicians to improvise without the safety net of predictable chord progressions; as Chico Hamilton noted, it forced the musicians to listen to one another, providing support where necessary, but also the freedom to explore new directions. Such an arrangement was well suited to Chet, who played by ear, and could respond with ease to anything suggested by the other musicians. Thirdly, it's worth remembering that, in addition to being a superb arranger, Mulligan was a composer of some note; tunes like 'Nights at the Turntable' and 'Walkin' Shoes' were minor gems, with a relaxed, easy swing and a clean, uncluttered sound. Last, but not least, the band's success can be partly attributed to Chet Baker himself; he may have lacked the technical prowess of a Dizzy Gillespie, but he was still a phenomenal musician with a quite unique sound—a star in the making, even at the tender age of twenty-three.

Soon after the recording session, the Quartet travelled to San Francisco for a return engagement at the Blackhawk, which started on 21st October, and lasted for two-and-a-half weeks. Bobby White took the place of Chico Hamilton for that particular gig. Bob Whitlock cannot remember the reason for Chico's absence, but wondered if he might have been offered an engagement with his former employer Lena Horne, which would have been far better paid.

Back in Los Angeles, the press controversy over the 'pianoless' quartet continued to attract a range of musicians to The Haig. "The greatest guy that I saw come there was Leonard Rosenman, who wrote the music for 'East of Eden'," said Bob Whitlock. "He wrote some really beautiful passages. I figured that if a guy like that is coming in, we must be on the right track."[47]

Some of the biggest names in jazz continued to drop by, too, many of them asking to sit in as the night wore on. "Buddy Rich was just unforgettable," Walter Norris recalled. "The first title he sounded like Buddy Rich, the second title he sounded like he'd been working with the group for a year. He just adapted that quickly, he was an exceptional talent in that way. Stan Getz came in. There was a whole evening of Oscar Pettiford playing cello; Gerry was just shaking his head in disbelief. The recordings of Oscar playing cello could never equal that night. It was a club that when you played, you felt very uninhibited."[48]

The club also started to attract a smattering of celebrities around this time. "William Holden dropped by with Deborah Kerr one evening," recalled Bob Whitlock. "They were magnificent, just beautifully behaved. They sat right up close to the bandstand, and they hardly made a sound—they were so courteous. I remember thinking, 'I've been so many times to the movies to see these people, and now they're coming to see us!' I got a real kick out of it."[49]

Gerry Mulligan took full advantage of celebrity guests in the club, acknowledging them from the stage, and thanking them for coming, which in turn encouraged them to bring their friends. "Gerry was very adept," said Whitlock. "He was a much better politician than people gave him credit for."

After a while, Mulligan started to play on his reputation as a perfectionist. "He would just wait for anyone to make a noise, or clink a glass, or laugh, or do something out of line," said Bob Whitlock. "He thought it was Carnegie Hall, or something. Anyone caught talking at the table, bam, he'd read them off. And you know what? People loved it. It was like when Miles Davis turned his back on people at concerts. They just seemed to get a kick out of it. Gerry used that as a gimmick; he couldn't wait to stop the band and chastise a member of the audience. That's how we became known as the 'Chamber Music Society of Lower Wilshire Boulevard!'"[50]

The press liked to pick on Mulligan over his treatment of paying customers.

Bill Brown, who wrote the 'Jazz Beat' column in the *L.A. Daily News*, wrote, "We heard Mulligan at The Haig recently and were appalled by the speech he made to the 'parvenue' customers … his records are better than his live performances because the speech is omitted … a new sound is alright, but so is the H-bomb."[51] Mulligan was savvy enough to know good publicity from bad publicity, and had the last laugh as the lines continued to form outside the tiny club.

Of course, Mulligan was not the only band member to attract attention. Chet's playing continued to develop over this period, a fact noted by the many visiting musicians. "He was like a comet blazing, he was unstoppable'" recalled tenor saxophonist Jack Montrose. "There was nothing he couldn't play or do. He was a phenomenon." A young Herb Alpert, just seventeen years old, was also blown away by Chet's natural ability. "Chet could play with lightning speed, those even eighth notes," he noted. "It was mystifying to most trumpet players, because we all got the feeling he didn't really practice."[52]

Gerry could not help but notice the attention Chet was receiving, and tried to give people the impression that it was he who had discovered the young trumpet star. "That didn't sit well with Chet at all," remembered Whitlock. "Any time Gerry tried to promote that idea, Chet would step in and shoot it down. I'm sure they respected each other musically, but they weren't the best of friends."

It wasn't only the local jazz community that was drawn to the rising star; pretty soon Chet was attracting the attention of jazz fans, eager to talk to the hip musicians, and young ladies, desperate to attract the attention of the handsome trumpet player. But in many respects, he was ill-equipped to deal with the attention he was now receiving. "When you have such early success, maybe you don't question yourself and your music in a way in which you would if you don't have that early success. I don't think he questioned anything," said jazz pianist Walter Norris. "He just went straight ahead with his life. He was very decadent in that respect. He was not an intellectual, he was not thinking heavily about anything. He was just very carefree."[53]

Whilst Gerry revelled in the spotlight, and played up to the audience, Chet tended to be shy, almost cold, with strangers, and struggled to engage them in any kind of meaningful conversation.

One form of escape was with the women who sought his attention. After two years of tantrums and jealous rages over Charlaine's flirtatious behaviour, Chet took a childlike pleasure in gaining revenge, openly parading his conquests in front of his tearful wife, who sat alone at the bar. "Chet got famous when we started playing at The Haig," recalled Bob Whitlock. "Movie stars started to come in, and things started to change radically for him. All these women used to come on to him. I don't want to be crude, but he was banging everything in sight."

Chet's behaviour didn't endear him to the band's drummer, Chico Hamilton. "He was a brilliantly talented juvenile delinquent and not someone I could get next to, because I couldn't abide his attitude," he told Gordon Jack. "He was married to a lovely lady named Charlaine at the time, and he was just a chauvinistic pig to her. At intermissions, she would be waiting at the bar for him while he was in the back seat of someone's car with a groupie, and if she dared to ask where he had been, he would kick her ass. That didn't appeal to me, and whatever else he was interested in also didn't appeal to me. Sometimes he would come into work with his mouth all cut from having been in a fistfight during the day, but that was Chet. The paradox was he could be incredibly sensitive in his playing."[54]

Chet's other release was marijuana, and despite Gerry's concerns, he regularly smoked a joint between sets, oblivious to the risks of the police patrols in the area. Chet's reputation as a pothead finally caught up with him just before Christmas, the night of his twenty-third birthday, when a policeman caught Chet and Bob Whitlock smoking weed in Chet's car between sets. As Chet later described the incident, "It happened one night during a break. I was sitting in my car in the parking lot getting high with two other musicians when a police car came through, and seeing us, stopped."[55] One of the cops was from Oklahoma. "He got talking to Chet," recalled Whitlock, "found out he was from Oklahoma, and said to him, 'Well, I'm going to search the car, and if you're telling me the truth, and this is all you've got, I'll let you off with a warning'. He proceeded to search the car, and he found a whole lid in the side panel of the door, and took us off to jail."[56]

Chet and Bob spent the Christmas holiday in jail. Chet ended up taking the rap, and had Bob cut loose. In the end, he was lucky to only receive three months' probation given his previous brushes with the law. But when the two musicians returned to the club a few nights later, Bob Whitlock was astonished to find that Gerry held him responsible. "All the time we were at The Haig, all through 1952, I was using [heroin] pretty good," remembered

Whitlock. "Gerry was also using, but he was using on the sly. If you can imagine, we did not even know what he was doing! I remember being amazed. We had a ferocious bust-up in The Haig one night, and I thought we were going to come to blows.

"'I quit!'

"'No, you're fired!'

"'No, I quit.'

"We were like a couple of children," he said. "Unfortunately it went so far there was no redeeming it. All this time he was using, so that's what he was so mad about—that they might turn up the heat on him! I knew he had used in the past, but I thought he was keeping pretty clean. I don't know how he hid it as well as he did."

Mulligan's secret was safe for now, but just four months later, his own world would come crashing down, and with it, the future of the quartet itself. In the meantime, Whitlock returned to his hometown of Utah, vowing not to return to the West Coast until he was clean. "It was a good thing for me, in a way. I was getting really out of line with the drug thing. Three of my cousins were out visiting from Utah for the Christmas holidays. So three or four days after New Year's I got in a car with them and went back to Utah. They almost kidnapped me; I guess they saw me potentially getting in a lot of trouble. I didn't come back until midway through 1953."[57]

Bob Whitlock was replaced by Carson Smith, and in early January the quartet returned to the studio to cut four more songs for Fantasy Records, sufficient to both fulfil their contract and to fill a ten-inch LP. The band recorded two Mulligan originals, 'Limelight' and 'Turnstile', as well as covers of 'The Lady is a Tramp' and 'Moonlight in Vermont'. The album, which included four tunes cut the previous September in San Francisco, received a four-star review in *DownBeat* magazine. "'Tramp' shows to what humourously effective use these guys can put their two horns and two rhythm [sic]. 'Vermont' has Chet backed by what sounds like two horns—actually Mulligan blowing and drummer Chico Hamilton humming. Bassist Carson Smith lends plenty of tonal colour to this one. 'Limelight', another rapid GM original, is mostly unison in the first chorus. Baker casts his beatful bread upon the waters again to strong effect, and Chico has a couple of discreetly underplayed spots. Both sides conclude with a snatch of Mulligan's theme, which, peculiarly enough, sounds like Dixieland."[58]

Around this time, Chet started to have an extramarital affair with an old friend by the name of Joyce Tucker—the daughter of Jack Tucker, who owned the nearby Tiffany Club. Joyce had worked as a child actress in the movies, and later worked as a model in New York. "I ruined my father's life when I fell in love with Bird at twelve, and played 'Embraceable You' one hundred and forty-seven times in a row. He heard this, and understood. He had been a dancer on Broadway, my mother had been a dancer on Broadway, and he ended up by opening the club."[59]

Her early love of jazz saw her meet a number of musicians in New York, including Gerry Mulligan and her childhood hero, Charlie Parker. "I saw terrible things when I was very young. When I was about fourteen I knew Donna Lee; you know Donna Lee, the Bird tune? I knew her; she was a gorgeous young thing, did heroin, and before you knew it, she was gone. She died very young."[60]

Back on the West Coast, she met and married a young clarinet and saxophone player, Marvin 'Marv' Koral, who went on to become a member of Tommy Dorsey's band. She first encountered Chet playing at the Showtime Club, and she and her husband went on to become close friends with Chet and Charlaine.

By 1952, Joyce had got a job working as a camera girl at the Ambassador Hotel, just across the road from The Haig. "My father's club was on one side of the Ambassador Hotel, and The Haig was on the other side. I was working in the main showroom, where they had all of the biggest people, and I was working as a camera girl, not as a musician. I was the only camera girl there, which was a great job because it was like 9–12 p.m., and I was in the middle of all the music after that. It was probably late 1952 or early 1953 when we started having an affair."[61]

What started out as a surreptitious affair, some stolen moments in the back of Chet's parked car, soon became more serious, the couple making excuses to their partners to go out on romantic day trips along the California coast. "He started singing when we used to go for long drives in the car," Joyce recalled, still relishing the memory. "His singing was much like his playing." Chet's reckless nature made it difficult to keep a lid on their secret for very long. Russ Freeman remembered attending a party one evening, and seeing Chet lying on the floor, Joyce by his side, shouting, "I wanna fuck!"

Taking chances like this, it was only a question of time before one or other partner found out about the affair. After a few months, Chet received a tearful phone call from Joyce, informing him that her husband had found out, and gone crazy. "A half dozen of us drove out to the Korals' house," remembered bass player Carson Smith. "She opened the door, and Marv had trashed the entire place. He had dumped the refrigerator over, torn up the stove, ripped open the sofa, cut open the mattresses on the bed, broken all the windows. It was unbelievable. He'd gone absolutely nuts."

Joyce remembered that Chet felt guilty over what happened, and is convinced that this is the reason why Chet never wrote about their affair in his memoirs. "We had a love affair that was nasty, because the four of us were good friends. It was one of the only things that no matter what stuff he did, he was embarrassed about; that's why he never wrote about it. It ended up quite badly." The affair devastated Marvin, and the following year he left Los Angeles to move to Las Vegas, Nevada, where he later led several orchestras.

In the meantime, Gerry Mulligan had started work on a more ambitious project, arranging music for a larger band once more. "I started the tentet as a rehearsal band to have something to write for," Mulligan recalled, and persuaded John Bennett to let him use the club during the daytime. Chet does not seem to have been that enthused by the new project at first, preferring to avoid rehearsals and spend his time with Joyce Tucker, or hanging out with friends. Chet's attitude didn't sit well with Gerry, who felt that he was putting in the hard work while Chet went skiing and hiking, and he initially brought in Pete Candoli on trumpet. When it was time to record, Chet was available, and Candoli was relegated to second trumpet. "In the event, Chet wound up playing most of the lead parts anyway," said Mulligan, "And I had Pete who was a high note man on second trumpet!"

The tentet album was recorded for Capitol records, rather than Pacific Jazz, suggesting that Bock was less enthusiastic about Mulligan's experiment. The circumstances under which the band ended up recording for Capitol were confused, as Mulligan later revealed, and go some way to explaining why the band only recorded on the one occasion. "After a time, Gene Norman, a Los Angeles promoter and disc jockey, came to me and said he'd like to record the band. Since no one else had suggested recording us, I said yes. The irony, as I found out later, was that Gene had no American Federation of Musicians' recording license of his own and planned to offer the date to Capitol if he could record on their license. Bill Miller of Capitol told me later that he had heard about the band from musicians and was planning to come to The Haig to discuss recording when Gene came to him with his proposal.

Since Bill felt it would be unethical to pursue the project directly for Capitol we ultimately did the album for Gene … I have the feeling that if we had been recording for Bill Miller we might have [had] some more albums to show for our work."[62]

"The tentet is essentially my original quartet with Chet Baker combined with the ensemble instrumentation of the Miles Davis Nonet," Mulligan explained. "Musically I think the ensemble worked perfectly with the quartet concept and the band was very easy to write for. I would like to have pursued it further at that time, but c'est la vie." In terms of both instrumentation and sound, the tentet was indeed similar to the *Birth Of The Cool* band, consisting of two trumpets, two baritone saxophones, alto saxophone, valve trombone, French horn, tuba, bass and drums. The other notable feature of the tentet was the continued absence of piano on most tunes, although Mulligan himself contributed piano to the odd track. On the original liner notes, Mulligan notes that "the piano seems to get in the way. The group swings better without it."

Chico Hamilton was astonished to see how Mulligan's mind worked when arranging for the larger group. "I remember he did something really wild when we recorded those tentet things," he later recalled. "We rehearsed one of the pieces, and after we made a take on it, we listened to the playback. Gerry flopped down to the floor in the middle of the studio, concentrating in a really dramatic, Christ-like pose, with his arms outstretched and his eyes closed. When the recording was finished, he got up off the floor and said, 'OK, guys—pencils'. He then proceeded to dictate a new road map for the chart, which completely rearranged it, and when he counted us in, it was like a brand new piece of music. His writing had a magical quality, and he probably influenced both Bill Holman and Bob Brookmeyer, because he was a fantastic arranger."[63]

The resulting album was far closer in style to the *Birth of the Cool* band than Gerry's own tentet recordings from 1951. Both the tentet and the 'Cool' groups recorded 'Rocker', and the arrangement is strikingly similar, although Mulligan does remove the thematic variation he had written for the close of the earlier recording. There are also strong similarities between the Gil Evans arrangement of 'Moon Dreams', recorded in 1950, and Gerry Mulligan's 'A Ballad'. 'Walkin' Shoes' was the only tune recorded by both the quartet and the tentet, although the influence of the quartet also comes across on the Mulligan original, 'Westwood Walk'.

The record was eventually released in October 1953, by which time the quartet had effectively disbanded, and it is partly for this reason that the recording is not better known. *DownBeat* magazine awarded the record a five-star review. "The rich diversity of orchestrated tonal hues is what gives this set its fifth star. The solos, though secondary, are almost completely, and justifiably, monopolised by Mulligan and Chet Baker." The parallels with the *Birth of the Cool* sessions were also noted. "Gerry switches to piano on three tunes, including the attractive 'Ontet'," noted the reviewer. "(The) latter is based on the last chorus of 'Godchild', which he scored for the Davis date."[64]

At around the same time as the tentet recording took place in late January 1953, probably in an attempt to appease Bock, Mulligan suggested that Pacific Jazz record the quartet live at The Haig, with a view to an eventual album release. One evening the alto saxophonist Lee Konitz, an acquaintance of Mulligan's from Claude Thornhill and *Birth Of The Cool* days, stopped by the club, and sat in with the band. They recorded six songs, and encouraged by the instant bonding of the musicians, Konitz joined them for two further studio sessions.

The precise date of these historic recording sessions remains unclear. As Michael Cuscuna explains in the CD release of these sessions, released as *Konitz Meets Mulligan*, "because of the liner note information given by producer Dick Bock, it was assumed that these three sessions took place in the June of '53. But actually, several of the titles were released months before then. And in June, Konitz was thousands of miles away from Los Angeles earning his living with the Stan Kenton orchestra."

The live recording almost certainly took place on January 25th, the date provided on the original liner notes to the twelve-inch album *Lee Konitz Plays with the Gerry Mulligan Quartet.*

Lee Konitz sounds far less introspective than on his studio recordings from this era, and appears to have enjoyed his freedom from the confines of the Kenton band. Gerry Mulligan seems content to allow the alto saxophonist the majority of the solos, and Konitz takes full advantage, delivering lengthy and seemingly effortless improvisation on up-tempo numbers such as 'Too Marvelous for Words' and 'Bernie's Tune'. On the two ballads, 'Lover Man' and 'These Foolish Things', Konitz returns to the more relaxed style with which he is usually associated. Chet sounds less assured than usual on these recordings, perhaps unhappy at having to share the spotlight with Gerry's old friend.

The Gerry Mulligan Quartet with Lee Konitz at The Haig: Photograph by William Claxton / Courtesy Demont Photo Management, LLC

There is greater uncertainty over the timing of the subsequent studio recordings. Three tracks were probably recorded at around the same time, most likely in the Turetsky bungalow on January 30th, the date listed in Jorgen Jepsen's *Jazz Records*. That said, he confuses the studio and live recordings in this discography, so the uncertainty remains. Either way, 'Lady Be Good', 'Sextet' and 'I Can't Believe That You're In Love With Me' were released in May as part of a ten-inch LP, so the timing looks about right. Three other studio cuts were made with Konitz, and whilst the date is not known, the session may have taken place as early as February 1st, again in the Turetsky studio.

The studio recordings were well received by *DownBeat* magazine, which described the record as "as inspired a session as we've heard in months. Though we briefly resented the addition of another horn to the compact quartet, Lee's tremendous contribution soon dispelled the feeling. 'Sextet' is a bubbling Mulligan original on which all three men, in near perfect rapport, play the line in unison before soloing. 'Lover Man' is all Konitz with Gerry and Chet supplying only some murmuring background. Lee's faultless technique and lovely sound were never in better evidence … ".

Despite *DownBeat*'s four-star review, the studio recordings sound a little anaemic after the fiery live recordings, the solos kept short to fit in with the three-minute format of the 78-rpm single era.

As January came to a close, drummer Chico Hamilton told Gerry of his intention to quit the band to go back to work with singer Lena Horne. "Chico was offered quite a bit more money to travel with Lena," recalled Bock. "It was a difficult decision to make, but being the father of two children, he was obliged to go where he could earn more. Because The Haig was small, the quartet could not earn much more than union scale out of the operation." Hamilton was replaced by Larry Bunker, a versatile musician who was also adept at playing both the piano and vibes.

On the tiny stage at The Haig, the quartet continued to evolve, taking Mulligan's basic arrangements to new levels every night. "The early Fantasy records with Gerry's band are nothing compared with The Haig, when they had been playing those pieces every night for almost a year," recalled pianist Walter Norris. "I don't think they got along that well, but when they were on the bandstand playing, they intuitively sparked the other one to do something. They could make it work; in other words, it was a gamble, inspiring the other one to do something, and it turns into something which is a big surprise to them both. After the songs they'd be shaking their heads, as though they couldn't quite believe it had come off. Playing every night for that length of time they were so conditioned and in-shape, physically and mentally, that they could make it happen like magic. It was unbelievable."[65]

Still relatively clean-living, and in good shape physically, Chet's own playing continued to develop in this environment. "His solos were just sparkling with inventiveness and fire; I don't think Chet ever played like that since. I think that was his best period," said Norris.

As if the favourable reviews in the jazz press were not enough, *Time* magazine published a glowing review of the group's Haig concerts in early February, providing nationwide publicity for the group, and helping to broaden the appeal of the band beyond its traditional jazz audience, to lovers of classical music, too. The article included a photograph of Mulligan performing in a conservative suit and tie, and citing his influences as Stravinsky, Ravel, Prokofiev and Bach. In retrospect, the article sets the tone for the growth in popularity of jazz amongst white, college-educated Americans that took place in the mid-1950s. Mulligan also used the article to announce his future plans, which included an enlarged band and a nationwide tour. "I've got to keep moving," he said. "I've got to grow."[66]

The article was good for business, of course. "On weekends more people could be found inside waiting in line to get in than were actually inside," recalled Dick Bock. Walter Norris thought that the club's convenient location also contributed to the band's successful stint at The Haig. "The Haig was located about fifty yards off of Wilshire Boulevard; it was a dead end, and if the road had gone straight, it would have gone directly into the Ambassador Hotel, the Coconut Grove. The Brown Derby was one block away on Wilshire Boulevard itself; it was a very nice restaurant and club, everyone used to go there, it was very popular. Olly Hammond's restaurant, all night long, was very popular, and was next door. So there were a lot of people walking along the street, or pulling up there in cars, and The Haig was just around the corner. There were lines at the weekend to get in, people who'd eaten nearby and would drop in at The Haig".[67]

Chet's playing continued to evolve at The Haig: Photograph by William Claxton / Courtesy Demont Photo Management, LLC.

Soon after the *Time* magazine article was published, rumours began to circulate that Getz wanted to combine his own band with that of Mulligan. The story had its roots in Stan's Boston engagement at the Hi-Hat in December 1952, where he was playing with Bob Brookmeyer. One night, between sets, Getz was discussing the current jazz scene with Nat Hentoff, and the talk got round to Mulligan's quartet, which had impressed Getz. "I sat in with them when I was last on the coast and felt so good about the things Gerry was doing," Getz recalled. "I told Nat I'd like to do something combining the good features of both of our groups."[68]

Hentoff wrote a story around his conversation with Getz, which eventually appeared in *DownBeat* magazine on February 25th 1953. It was the first Mulligan had heard of any such plan, and he reacted angrily, sparking a minor war of words between the two bandleaders.

"I don't know just what Stan has in mind here when he talks of adding me and Chet to his combo, joining me, or whatever it is, but it's not for me. I have my quartet. Stan has his combo, and I'm sure it's good. But if we got together, we'd have a band with two leaders, unless Stan was willing to be just a figurehead—and I don't think that's what he had in mind," Mulligan wrote in a letter to *DownBeat* in mid-March. "For years I stayed in the background and wrote arrangements for many bands. Now, in the quartet, I have something that is all mine. I see no reason for sharing it with anyone."

The letter is an excellent illustration of Mulligan's sizeable ego, which would spill over from time to time and cause friction within the band. Stan Getz was not always the easiest of personalities to deal with, but on this occasion he chose to be tactful, and carefully revealed the roots of the misunderstanding to *DownBeat*. "It was half pleasant speculation on an ideal musical group, and half a serious thought toward a unit that could offer the musicians involved a happy working situation, a steady inter-flow of musical ideas and bookings and record dates, enough to keep the thing together," he explained. "The point I feel should be cleared up is this: Gerry seemed to feel that I was looking to absorb him or his group into an organization of mine and relegate him to the position of arranger and behind-the-scenes brain of the group. This wasn't anything like what I pictured."[69]

Getz went on to explain that if such a band were to form, Gerry would have a free hand with the music, equal billing and equal financial reward. The explanation seemed to appease Mulligan, and when Getz opened at the Tiffany Club on June 8th, Getz and his band were regular guests at The Haig, watching the Mulligan Quartet in action. "Stanley and I spent so much time over at The Haig that the owner of the Tiffany Lounge said we obviously liked it so much more there than at his club we were fired," Brookmeyer later recalled. "I had no alternative but to go back to Kansas."[70]

Dick Bock encouraged the quartet to return to the studio in late February, where they cut four tracks, 'Makin' Whoopee', 'Motel', 'Cherry', and 'Carson City Stage'. The first two cuts were released as singles that spring, and the entire session was later combined with the first of the Lee Konitz studio collaborations, and released as a full-length LP (PJLP-2) in May to favourable reviews.

Whilst the group was enjoying increasing critical acclaim, there were growing frictions within the band, most notably between Mulligan and Baker. The difficulties stemmed from a variety of sources, and cannot be attributed to any one factor. First off, the two musicians might have been known for their interaction onstage, but offstage they were two quite distinct personalities. Gerry was two years older, relatively well educated and had enjoyed an extensive musical training. By contrast Chet was far less academic, and for the most part, still played music by ear. He was also less communicative than Gerry, and prone to childish, immature behaviour, which did not dovetail with Mulligan's more regimented approach.

An example of the problems this caused occurred when it was time to plan new material for a forthcoming recording session. As the quartet's main composer and arranger, Mulligan was keen to rehearse new ideas and songs in the afternoons, before the band took the stage in the evening. He later complained that Chet would " … always have this pack around—Californians, surfer types—and there'd always be five or six of them. We'd get done and these guys would drive up to the mountains to ski. By the time they got there, the sun was up. They'd ski through the morning then go down to the beach and sail. By then, the day's gone by and Chet comes to the gig. He'd do that two, three days in a row, without sleeping, and his chops would dry out; he'd have trouble with chapped lips, and he'd start missing notes. I'd say to him, 'Chet, have you ever heard of sleep? It's a wonderful thing for your chops'."[71]

No one else can remember Chet having problems with his chops at this time; by contrast, he was playing every night, and was probably in the best shape of any time during his long career. The issue arose from Mulligan's desire for perfection, according to Joyce Tucker. "Gerry was so well polished musically, and was happy to rehearse one hundred times, even if he didn't play it the same," she recalled. "There was a resentment there somewhere."

Bass player Bill Crow, who worked with Mulligan from 1956, remembered experiencing similar problems. "Oh, he was an egomaniac. But very likeable. I think that was part of what gave him that star quality, that made it possible for the rest of us to work … But he set a different standard for himself. I mean, he was good, he could really play well and he really knew what he was talking about when he talked about music, but sometimes he tried to hold his musicians to a higher standard of dedication to his music than he held himself. He used to drive me crazy sometimes, but in retrospect I must say that without Gerry I probably wouldn't have learned as much about music as I did."[72]

Chet's behaviour used to antagonise Gerry, whether it was his tendency to hang out with his 'surfer' friends, firing water pistols at one another in the house, or his driving at breakneck speed around the city. "I don't think Gerry and Chet got along particularly well," Walter Norris later remembered. "Chet wasn't that easy to get along with, and Gerry was very sure of himself, and capable of one-upmanship. I remember once between titles, Chet turned to Gerry and said, 'I want a raise'. There was polite laughter in the audience, and Gerry said, 'We can talk about that later'. And Chet said, 'No, I want a raise before we play the next title!' He was making $100 a week, which was very good, but he said, 'I want $125'. Gerry turned to him and said, 'I'm not going to discuss this, and I'm not going to give you $125. We'll talk and argue later'. He announced the next song, and after it was over, Chet said, 'I want $125!' He was very primitive and stubborn when it came to bargaining. He sometimes acted a little bit like a spoiled child."[73]

The rhythm section also suffered their fair share of run-ins with Mulligan. He kept firing bass player Carson Smith, claiming he was not playing what he was looking for, only to rehire him once he had calmed down. Drummer Larry Bunker was upset and being forced to play the same way as his predecessor Chico Hamilton. "You did as you were told," he once recalled. "I think I reached the point where I didn't even have a pair of drumsticks. It was all brushes—that's all he wanted."

Mulligan's dominant behavioural characteristics were almost certainly exacerbated by his growing dependence on heroin at this time, which had got to the stage that it was no longer so easy to hide from other members of the band. Chet later claimed, "Gerry was not an easy person to get along with, especially since he was using. He was nervous and highly-strung, and sometimes I'd notice his long fingers would tremble as he played his horn."[74]

Gerry Mulligan had broken up with girlfriend Gail Madden some months earlier, and with Chet still continuing his affair with Joyce Tucker, Gerry started to date her best friend, Jeffie Lee Boyd, a vivacious brunette who worked as a waitress at The Haig. "She had worked at the Tiffany for my father before I knew her, really," recalled Joyce Tucker. "She went out for coffee with Gerry and they got married. She had no idea he was that into dope. She'd heard the stories, of course, but hadn't seen anything."

Gerry confessed his addiction on their honeymoon in Palm Springs, and announced his intention to go cold turkey. "I was supposed to help him," Jeffie explained. "I was such a moron, what did I know? So I locked him in the room and went to lay by the pool. He started screaming for the doctor, and I kept saying, 'No, you can't have the doctor'. I left him there for three of four days. When we went home, he returned to being a junkie."

While Gerry's marriage was getting off to a difficult start, alto saxophonist Herb Geller filled in for him at The Haig. "One time I got a telephone call from Chet saying that Gerry was going to be off for a couple of weeks," he remembered. "Gerry had eloped with one of the waitresses, so Chet asked me to take his place. The elopement, of whatever it was, didn't last long. I played with Chet for about two weeks; the same group, but with me on alto. We just jammed, as Chet didn't want to play any of the Mulligan tunes—I think we played 'Bernie's Tune'. He said, 'Let's play some standards, because I know lots of standards'. He called a tune like 'Have You Met Miss Jones' or 'I Could Write A Book'—a lot of Richard Rogers and Gershwin tunes. I'd say, 'Sure, I know that tune. What key?' He never knew what key it was in. Larry Bunker would always say, 'I remember, it's in E-flat, you're in E-natural, Chet, first and second valve position,' and calling out the bass notes for Carson Smith. Larry Bunker was really a fantastic musician."[75]

Mulligan returned to Los Angeles in late March, and a few days later the quartet returned to the studio with Pacific Jazz to record three more songs: 'Festive Minor', 'All The Things You Are' and 'My Old Flame'. Only the last of these songs was released at the time, the other two tracks remaining in the vaults until Mosaic Records released a box set of the complete Pacific Jazz and Capitol recordings of the quartet some thirty years later.

Early April brought some unwelcome visitors to The Haig—the tall, bulky Sergeant John O'Grady, head of the Hollywood Narcotics Detail, and his sidekick Ruby Diaz, a tough Hispanic detective who scared even the hardiest of drug dealers. The two thickset police officers stood out amongst the hip, jazz-loving crowd, and made for an uncomfortable atmosphere in the small club. Gerry secretly blamed Chet for their presence; he had been busted in December the previous year, and had subsequently encountered O'Grady on numerous occasions, hoping to catch Chet smoking in his car between sets one more time. The two of them had exchanged words, and Gerry was convinced that O'Grady was out to nail him.

But unbeknown to Mulligan, O'Grady had a far broader agenda, a McCarthy-like campaign to "protect society against the creeping menace of drugs". His childhood dream of entering the movie industry never came close to becoming a reality, and he took a perverse pleasure in targeting Hollywood entertainers, most notably the 'jazz' community. "I set out to destroy that crowd and damn near did," he later boasted in his memoirs. "I ran Charlie 'Yardbird' Parker, the great saxophonist, out of town. I could have nailed him. His arms were covered with track marks form heroin needles. But he was too old and too drunk and I decided it wasn't worth wasting the time …" Gerry Mulligan, who was beginning to show the telltale signs of using once more, and Chet Baker, who had only just completed his probation, were a far more enticing target, more likely to help him make his name.[76]

After a few days scouting the club, the detectives knew that Mulligan and Baker would be on their guard, and on April 13th they turned their attention to their home addresses. Chet's house was dark, but as luck would have it, Gerry's recent bride Jeffie was entertaining Chet's wife Charlaine that evening. The unscrupulous O'Grady drove his unmarked police car into the back of Jeffie's sports car, and rapped on the front door. When Jeffie answered the door, O'Grady explained that an accident had occurred, and offered to pay for the damage. As the young lady peered outside, O'Grady elbowed his way into the house.

Hearing the commotion, Chet's wife grabbed a small container of cannabis and locked herself in the bathroom. O'Grady pounded on the door, but seconds later the cool Charlaine emerged, acting as though nothing untoward had occurred. "There was just enough grass still floating around in the toilet so that if they wanted to get it out, they could legally file on someone," Chet later recalled. The furious detectives searched the premises, but found no other evidence of drugs or drug paraphernalia, so O'Grady charged the two women with possession of marijuana, a case that was unlikely to stand up in court, given the illegal entry.[77]

But O'Grady had more ambitious plans, and drove the two women back to The Haig, where he confronted the quartet backstage at the club. He made the band members take off their jackets and roll up their shirtsleeves. When Mulligan revealed fresh track marks on his arm, O'Grady knew he had his man. Gerry Mulligan's cool exterior gave way to tears, and he agreed to accompany the police officers back to the house. "I went inside and Gerry went with the cops down the driveway to the back corner of the house," recalled Chet. "And confusedly he gave them the evidence that they needed." The evidence included a small amount of heroin and a variety of drug paraphernalia, including hypodermic needles and burned teaspoons. Mulligan was too shattered to be discovered in this way to realise that if he hadn't led the police to his stash, they could only have charged him with using, a far less serious offence than possession.

The two couples were driven downtown, booked, locked up for an hour, and then released on bail, straight into the glare of the awaiting media. The following morning, the headline in the Los Angeles Mirror read, 'HOT LIPS BOPSTER, AIDE AND 2 WIVES JAILED; NAB DOPE'. The accompanying photo shows a broken Mulligan, a bewildered Chet and their scared wives, Charlaine trying to cover her face in her coat.[78]

At the resulting hearing, Gerry took the rap for the small amount of marijuana that had been recovered from the scene, and was also charged with the more serious offence of heroin possession. A trial date was set for June. "We all pleaded not guilty, went to court, and beat it—except Gerry," explained Chet. "It was like he was there one minute, and gone the next."

Mulligan split with Jeffie shortly after the arrest, both of them aware that they had rushed into marriage, and that she was not equipped to deal with his addiction. He returned to The Haig, telling the other members of the quartet that he was hopeful of beating the charges.

The owner of Pacific Jazz, Dick Bock, was less convinced, and booked a recording studio for what turned out to be the final studio recording sessions of the original quartet. At the first session, which took place on 27th April, the group recorded 'Love Me Or Leave Me' and two Mulligan originals, 'Swing House' and 'Jeru'. The former is based on the changes to 'Sweet Georgia Brown', whilst 'Jeru' is quite different in structure to the version recorded with the *Birth of the Cool* band, this time based on a conventional 32-bar, AABA arrangement, rather than an unorthodox structure. The second session produced a further five tunes, including 'Darn That Dream' and 'Tea for Two'. The two sessions were combined to produce a single LP, which was to be the second and final LP devoted solely to the quartet.

A few days later, just weeks after his split with Jeffie, Mulligan married one of his old girlfriends, Arlyne Brown. Arlyne was the daughter of Lew Brown, who was part of the old songwriting team of DeSylva, Brown and Henderson, composers of such hits as 'Sonny Boy', written especially for Al Jolson, and 'You're the Cream in my Coffee'. Chet was unimpressed with Gerry's choice of partner, describing her in vivid terms in his memoirs. "It seems Gerry was divorcing Jeffie and planned to marry Arlyne, which to my way of thinking had to be something like being in heaven one second and in hell the next. Arlyne was a short Jewish woman—not attractive. And looking as though she would gain weight easily; of course, I didn't know about her mind. She must have given Gerry something he needed but on a purely physical basis, Jeffie was sweet and beautiful while Arlene was just a drag."[79]

Despite their differences, Gerry thought enough of Chet to ask him to be best man at their wedding, but in the event Chet failed to show up. "Chet was supposed to be the best man at their wedding, and I was going to stand up for Arlyne, and be the lady-in-waiting, but Chet didn't show," recalled Joyce Tucker. "So I became the best man! 'Doe' (real name Dunya) Mitchell, who was married to Red Mitchell, became the lady-in-waiting. We were all very tight. The jazz scene was all very incestuous, with people having break-ups in music, just like they do with lovers."[80]

We get to hear the quartet on one final occasion in late May, when Dick Bock decided to record the band onstage at The Haig. It's not clear whether he intended to release a live EP or a full-length LP, but in the end, only three of the nine songs taped on May 20th were released at the time—'Five Brothers', 'I Can't Get Started' and a poignant version of 'My Funny Valentine'. The remaining tunes remained in the vault for thirty years, eventually released as part of a Mosaic Records box set. It's hard to see why these recordings remained unreleased for so many years, since Bock was pleased with the results. "The intimacy of the club, with its unpretentious atmosphere, created a bond between the quartet and its audience that can be felt in these 'in-person' performances." Listening to these recordings now, they clearly support the conventional wisdom that the quartet was more dynamic onstage than in the recording studio, where they were bound by strict time limits, and solos were kept to a minimum.

In June, his trial date fast approaching, Mulligan made the decision to go cold turkey, and try to quit heroin for good. He turned to his old friend Joyce Tucker—Chet's old girlfriend—to help him get through the painful process, and moved into her small house out in the valley. "He came to me and said, 'I have to get clean, I have to do it'," she said. "'But I have to be some place where I know that if I really go out my mind, I can reach what I need. I need to have a backyard where I can bury my stuff, leave it there for a few days. Will you do that for me?' I said, 'Of course, sure I will'. Not thinking that I could get busted for that!"[81]

While Mulligan took time off to sort out his drug problems, Stan Getz, whose Tiffany club engagement had just finished, filled in for Mulligan at The Haig. The club's owner, John Bennett, who had a vested interest in hiring a big name, suggested trying tenor saxophonist Stan Getz. Getz's successful partnership with guitarist Jimmy Raney had recently come to an end, and he was agreeable to the idea. On the face of it, it was a perfect match; two of the rising stars of the West Coast jazz scene, both known for their exquisite tone, both favouring a measured, lyrical approach to their playing, quite distinct from the frenetic, competitive style associated with bebop.

In practice, the recordings that exist of the Baker–Getz quartet suggest that there was little chemistry between the two musicians. This might be partly explained by the fact that the band was simply under-rehearsed; after all, Getz had stepped in at fairly short notice, and was playing with a fairly settled line-up that had played together most nights for the last several months. In addition to that, Getz would have been keen to impose his own playing style on the sound of the quartet, rather than simply ape Mulligan. On occasion Getz lends gentle support to Chet's solo, whilst at other times he seems to get in the way, as if to suggest impatience with the way the trumpeter was developing his solo.

One can sense the intense competition within the band on these dates. Chet Baker had effectively inherited the leadership of the band from Gerry Mulligan, and would have been keen to stamp his own authority on the band, no longer content to remain the sideman. In addition, he would have remembered Getz's egotistical nature, which had flared up some months before, when Getz proposed the idea of combining the Mulligan and Getz bands. In this sense it is notable, perhaps, that the set opens with 'My Funny Valentine', the tune most clearly associated with Baker as a soloist. Listening to the tune unfold, we hear the opening drum roll, the familiar, foreboding bass line of Carson Smith, then the fragile, haunting refrain from Chet Baker. Later we hear the background 'singing' of Smith and Bunker, a feature developed by the original quartet. Missing, however, is the haunting saxophone played beneath the solo. Whether this is by design, with Chet imposing his 'leader' status on the group, or reflects the petulance of Getz, who saw himself as the natural leader, it is difficult to say.

The songs selected for the set certainly appear to support the view that Baker saw himself as the group leader. Roughly one third of the songs recorded are associated with the Mulligan quartet, including 'My Funny Valentine', 'Half Nelson', 'All The Things You Are', 'Bernie's Tune', and the Mulligan-penned 'Soft Shoe'. At least two songs would have been familiar to Baker through his stint with Charlie Parker, including the Bird original 'Yardbird Suite' and the Miles Davis tune 'Little Willie Leaps'. Others hint at Baker's growing interest in the playing of Miles Davis himself, such as the inclusion of 'Move', which appeared on the *Birth of The Cool* album as well as 'Little Willie Leaps'. Most of the other songs were standards, such as the Gershwin tune 'Strike Up The Band', and the nostalgic Jerome Kern ballad 'Yesterdays'.

Given the understanding that had developed between Mulligan and Baker, the original quartet was always going to be a tough act to follow. Given time, Baker may have developed a similar relationship with Getz, but the saxophonist's surly nature suggested the partnership was never going to last for long. In fact it is notable that throughout his life, Getz was most closely associated with guitarists such as Jimmy Raney, João Gilberto and Charlie Byrd, and pianists such as Al Haig, Chick Corea and Kenny Barron, rather than fellow horn players.

The other notable feature of these recordings is that we get to hear Chet Baker stretch out as a soloist, clearly enjoying the freedom of playing outside the restrictive confines of Mulligan's tightly arranged songs. 'Soft Shoe' is an obvious example, the song clocking in at over six minutes, compared with the two-and-a-half minute studio recording. In addition, Chet sounds more comfortable than previously on up-tempo recordings, taking tunes like 'Strike Up The Band' and 'Winter Wonderland' at a vigorous pace, maintaining a fairly even tone throughout. It seems as though Chet was trying to deliberately distance himself from his reputation as a romantic ballad player, a view confirmed by the first recordings of the Chet Baker Quartet just six weeks later.

Dick Bock saw the potential of the Baker–Getz quartet, and recorded the Haig show, although the tapes were not published until the 1980s, since Stan Getz was still under contract with Norman Grantz's Clef and Norgran labels at the time. The recordings were eventually released as *West Coast Live* on the Pacific Jazz label.

At around this time, there were growing rumours circulating in the jazz community that Chet himself was starting to experiment with heroin on a more regular basis. He may well have been encouraged in this respect by Getz himself, a view held by Chet's friend, percussionist Bill Loughborough. "Stan was always trying to get him to shoot up," he recalled. "I always thought it was Stan that helped turn Chet into a junkie."[82]

Pianist Walter Norris confirms that it was well known amongst musicians that Chet was starting to use heroin more regularly at this time, and was dangerous to hang around with. "In June I got a call to go and play at one of his jam sessions on one of his off nights, a Monday night," he said. "I was the only one that came; there was no bass player and no drummer. They were probably afraid that either the police would be threatening, or they wouldn't get paid, or something. So Chet and I played for a little bit, and talked, had a long conversation. I think he was flattered that I would show up, since no one else did, so he was in a talkative mood. At that stage he was taking drugs, but not heavily; he was trying to protect himself somewhat, and take as little as possible. He was taking heroin, even in those days."[83]

It seems that Chet was able to keep his drug use under control at this time. "I don't remember Chet using when he was at The Haig; I would take a chance, and swear that he didn't—at least up until the time I left, which was January 1953," recalled bass player Bob Whitlock. "What he did after that, I couldn't vouch for. I got back in the summer, but I didn't notice any change in his behaviour."[84]

Mulligan, meanwhile, received word that his trial had been postponed until September, and returned to play at The Haig for a few more weeks, convinced that now he was clean, he was likely to escape with probation.

With Gerry's return, Stan Getz decided to reform his quintet. Aside from Bob Brookmeyer and John Williams, he had recruited bassist Teddy Kotick, one of bebop's finest, with an impeccable sense of timing and a vibrant tone. Kotick was working with both the Stan Getz Quintet and the Charlie Parker Quintet during this period. Drummer Frank Isola had played with Johnny Bothwell and Elliot Lawrence before joining Getz. The re-formed

Stan Getz Quintet opened at Zardi's club in Hollywood on July 21st 1953 for a successful run that lasted through the first week of September.

During their engagement at Zardi's, Getz and Brookmeyer used to head over to The Haig, as they had done during their engagement at the Tiffany Club. This time they sat in with the Mulligan Quartet, both onstage at The Haig, and playing together in their spare time. "I remember a jam session at somebody's house, probably Chet's, and Stan, Bob, Chet and I were in the front line. We worked really well together, improvising on ensemble things that were great," he said. "Stan decided we should all go out together as a group, only he wanted it to be his group! All of us just looked at him and said 'Why?' Musically it was too bad we couldn't do it, but personality-wise I don't think it would have worked. Stan was peculiar. If things were going along smoothly, he had to do something to louse it up, usually at someone else's expense."

Whilst Gerry blamed Stan for the differences, a more neutral Bob Brookmeyer saw it as a clash of egos between the two bandleaders. "It sounded simply wonderful with the four horns," he remembered. "And for a while it looked as though this might be a band, but neither Gerry nor Stan could agree who would be leader." Unable to resolve their differences, Gerry went behind Stan's back, and asked the trombone player to join his quartet. Assuming he would be given a suspended sentence, he was planning his first nationwide tour with the band that fall. "Gerry asked me to join him as arranger and soloist, to go on the road as a quintet with him and Chet," Brookmeyer recalled.[85]

In early August, the quartet's original bass player, Bob Whitlock, returned to Los Angeles from Utah, where he had tried to get clean, away from the temptations of the jazz scene. "It was the first time I'd seen Chet in months, and he said, 'Why don't you come to work tonight? You can have your old job back if you want'," he recalled. "Frankly, I wasn't even sure I wanted my job back, as Gerry and I were still at odds. But I thought I'd go along, see how things worked out, and if they offered me the job, I might think about it. When I got there, they went up on to the stage, and started playing the first tune or two."

At that point, Chet's wife, Charlaine, walked into the club and joined Bob at the all bar. "Chet and Charlaine were still together, but Chet was fucking everything that walked, two at a time," he said. "He was treating her like a dog, which was really sad. She was lonely. She and I had always had a subtle kind of attraction to one another; we'd always joked about it, but had never actually done anything."

She suggested they leave The Haig and head over to Zardi's, where Stan Getz's new quintet was playing. "I thought, 'Well, that's great. I don't have to stay all night, I can come back later and find out what's going on'. So we went over to Zardi's, and one thing led to another, and we ended up in a motel room. We didn't get back until 4.30, 5 o'clock in the morning. When we went inside the house, Chet was sitting at the kitchen table, glaring at me like he wanted to kill me. It was horrible. He was the first guy I went to see when I got back from Utah, and because of my own weakness, and the fact that I thought I could rationalise my behaviour—because of the way he treated her—I did a really stupid thing. I walked her in the house, saw the glare on his face, went out to my car, and drove back home to Long Beach. I figured he'd hate me for the rest of his life. And I think there was an element of truth to that."

In the end, Chet and Bob were able to bury their differences, and he toured with the Chet Baker Quartet in early 1955; but Bob felt there was always lingering resentment on Chet's part, an anger that eventually boiled over when their paths crossed in the late 1960s. "The very last time I saw him, we got into a savage fight that must have been related to that issue; a huge build-up of tension after years of being civil, like nothing had happened."[86]

Gerry Mulligan eventually appeared in court in September, and found himself facing the distinguished judge Charles W. Fricke. Fricke was best known for his controversial handling of a murder case involving twenty-two Mexican–American defendants in 1942, a case which became known as the 'Sleepy Lagoon' trial. More important to Mulligan was his reputation as a 'hanging' judge, a reputation which stemmed from the 1935 murder trial of Nellie May Madison, who stood accused of murdering her husband.

In the event, he treated Mulligan quite leniently. When Mulligan confirmed that the marijuana found in the house belonged to him, he reportedly leaned over to the saxophonist and whispered, "Son, you don't want to say that." In the event, he ignored the marijuana charge, but convicted Mulligan for possession of heroin, sentencing him to six months in the Sheriff's Honor Farm, an L.A. prison. A bitter Mulligan was led away, cursing his lawyers; he felt he'd done the decent thing, by taking the rap for the marijuana, but having led the police to his stash of heroin, he only had himself to blame.

As the band fell apart, some of the leading jazz critics started to question the success of the Mulligan Quartet, reassessing their hitherto positive assessments of the group's achievement. Amongst the first to do so was Nat Hentoff, in his 'Counterpoint' column in *DownBeat* magazine:

"The musically adventurous deserve support, but they're all served by indiscriminate adulation. I think specifically of the former Gerry Mulligan quartet. It was good, and the individual musicians were first rate, though even here Chet Baker has much evolving to do, new star though he be. But was the quartet really that brilliantly original? Weren't the chords more barbershop harmony than anyone except a few musicians publicly noted? Was the counterpoint that contrapuntal or was that revived praiseword used quite loosely at times? And don't the records—some of them—sound kind of dull on re-hearing?

As one who lauded the group loudly at initial hearings, I'm just wondering. Anyone for reflection?"[87]

Ralph Gleason, another early champion of the group's cause, took the issues raised by Hentoff to the next level, describing the quartet as "the most overrated small band in jazz". The group's over-stylised sound was "boring me silly", he wrote in *DownBeat*, two weeks later. "Mulligan with or without piano and with or without his pretentious explanations of what he's doing, is still a child when racked up against men like Duke."

The backlash was probably inevitable, given the critical praise heaped on the quartet over the preceding months. After all, critics then, as now, are always on the lookout for the 'next big thing'.

Unfortunately for Mulligan, Chet Baker was widely regarded as the next big thing. His first solo LP, recorded for Pacific Jazz with his own quartet, had received a five-star review in *DownBeat* magazine on its release in July. Two weeks later, before Mulligan's trial had even taken place, the same publication interviewed him for a stand-alone article, introducing him as "an international jazz sensation". By the end of the year, he had made his first vocal recording, and topped the *DownBeat* poll as best trumpet player, beating Dizzy Gillespie, Louis Armstrong, Maynard Ferguson and Miles Davis in the process.

Gerry Mulligan was released from the Honor Farm prison just after Christmas, that year. He ran into Chet on Hollywood Boulevard a few days later, and discussed a possible reunion. "We spoke right there on the street for a few minutes," revealed Chet in his memoirs. "I said that I'd work for Gerry again, and that I didn't care what we did—club dates, concerts, whatever—

but I wanted three hundred dollars a week. 'Not a lot of money under the circumstances,' I said."[88]

Mulligan told a slightly different version of events. "Instead of two musicians throwing their arms around each other and saying, 'Oh, man, I'm glad to see you, pal', forget it, man! Before he says hello or 'Merry Christmas' or anything, he says, 'Listen, I've been thinking about it, and I gotta have more money'. He asked me for three or four hundred dollars. Well, considering that we were getting twelve hundred a week, out of which I had to pay commissions, a couple of other musicians, expenses, hotels, transportation, taxes, I don't know where the hell he thought the money was coming from. I just laughed. It was like a scene out of a bad movie."

The manner of the break-up was somewhat ironic; years later, when they got together for their short-lived 1974 reunion, Chet would complain that Mulligan had taken advantage of him financially, receiving the bulk of the royalties from the subsequent recording. "I guess that's called taking care of business," he complained. Chet's manner may have been clumsy, his social skills lacking, but he was simply trying to take care of business. He was now a successful bandleader in his own right; he was offering to give up his solo career to put the original quartet back together, but in return he no longer expected to be paid as a sideman. Chet was probably close to the mark when he later dismissed Mulligan's attitude as resentful. "Gerry's so pissed off because I've been able to make it on my own, without him," he complained. "He can't hack that. I was supposed to be his trumpet player for life, I guess. He wouldn't give me a raise, and I'd just been voted the best trumpet player in the world."[89]

In the years that followed, Gerry Mulligan struggled to replicate the rapport he had developed with Chet Baker, hiring musicians such as valve trombonist Bob Brookmeyer and trumpet player Jon Eardley to effectively take on Chet's role. "All the years with Brookmeyer we were able to anticipate each other, but still not in the same way and not with the same ease that happened with Chet," he later admitted.

There were periodic attempts to reform the quartet, most notably when they recorded a new album in 1957, and when they played together at Carnegie Hall in 1974. Whilst there were occasional glimpses of the old magic, they found it hard to reproduce the chemistry that made the original quartet so special.

Years later, Bob Whitlock was asked to reflect upon what had made the group so popular in the early 1950s. "Showbiz, plain and simple," he concluded. "Gerry knew the importance of variety in material and treatment, and he had an uncanny sense for pacing. We played not only standards and originals, but everything from Latin sambas to themes from Disney movies. There was something for everyone, and the caliber of musicianship was always convincing. Also, it would be naïve to ignore some of the obvious gimmicks Gerry used—the slightest disturbance in the audience was his cue to stop the band in its tracks and make an example of the perpetrator. God, how the rest of the crowd ate it up!"[90]

Chapter Five

THE CHET BAKER QUARTET 1953–1955

"Herb, you know I just won the poll." I said, "Poll, what, the DownBeat *poll?" He said, "Also the* Metronome*; I won them all!" I was amazed, I had no idea he was attaining that pinnacle." (Chet Baker, talking to Herb Geller)*[1]

"Until now the great modern horn stars could be counted on the digits of one hand. To the names of Dizzy, Miles, Joe Newman, Shorty Rogers and Clark Terry must now be added an extra finger on the hand: Chet Baker has arrived" (*DownBeat* magazine, July 29th 1953).

For many years, jazz historians had assumed that the Chet Baker Quartet's first recording session took place on July 24th 1953. This was the date listed in the Mosaic box set of *The Complete Pacific Jazz Studio Recordings of The Chet Baker Quartet With Russ Freeman*, and Thorbjørn Sjøgren's book *Chet: A Discography*. This date is clearly incorrect; the bass player on the four tunes taped at the initial recording session was Bob Whitlock, who was in Utah in July 1953.

The roots of the Chet Baker Quartet go back to January 1952, when Chet went AWOL from the 77th Army Band. At that time, he formed a quartet with Russ Freeman on piano, Bob Whitlock on bass and Bobby White on drums. The band never really developed into a working unit at that time, primarily because Chet had to return to San Francisco to turn himself back in to the Army. By the time he had returned to Los Angeles, Bob Whitlock had been invited to work with Gerry Mulligan, and plans to form his own band were put on hold.

Dick Bock made the decision to record Chet as a solo artist in December 1952, when the Gerry Mulligan Quartet was at the peak of its popularity. It was a decision that didn't sit too well with Gerry Mulligan, and was a contributing factor to the increased tensions between Chet and Gerry in the months that followed. "Chet had suddenly, overnight, blossomed into a major star—or at least a very big fish in the small pond of jazz," Russ Freeman later recalled. "And I think Dick Bock wanted to take advantage of the fact that he had two stars—not just Gerry, but Chet too."

Chet opted to reconvene the Quartet that had rehearsed earlier that year. Dick Bock evidently had some reservations about using Russ Freeman, and was unsure that their styles would be compatible. "With Gerry, Chet was so free—it was as if there wasn't any space between the idea and the execution," he said. "Russ played differently to anyone else, so that it was difficult for me to accept at first. He didn't sound like Al Haig or any of the bop pianists that I liked at that time. But it wasn't long before I began to admire Russ because of his compositions. He wrote some great things, I think equally as memorable as Gerry's. And he was the perfect pianist for Chet at that time. He gave him an enormous amount of room."

Some discographies have suggested that Red Mitchell played bass on the first recording date, but Bob Whitlock has confirmed this is also incorrect, and that he plays on both dates. The first session, which took place on December 24th, produced just one usable track, 'Isn't It Romantic', suggesting that the group had not had enough time to rehearse. The quartet returned to the studio three days later, and laid down three more tracks. The empathy between Baker and Freeman is immediately evident, with Freeman comping for Chet, and Chet responding, as demonstrated by the round of four-bar exchanges on 'This Time The Dream's On Me'. Another highlight of the first session is Russ Freeman's Latin-tinged 'Maid In Mexico', which features a vibrant solo by Chet.

Given the obvious chemistry that existed between Baker and Freeman, it seems strange that no follow-up sessions were arranged for several months. After all, four tunes would only fill one side of a long-player. The most likely explanation for the delay was the departure of Bob Whitlock, who left the Gerry Mulligan Quartet in late December, and returned home to Utah in early January in a bid to clear up his heroin addiction.

Dick Bock revisited the idea of recording Chet as a solo artist in July 1953, most likely to hedge his bets ahead of Mulligan's forthcoming trial. He needed the band to record a few more tunes—enough to fill a ten-inch record. Bob Whitlock was still in Utah, so Carson Smith took his place; Larry Bunker, the drummer with the Gerry Mulligan Quartet, replaced Bobby White on the drums.

The second sessions, recorded in July 1953, further demonstrated Freeman's skill as a composer, with charming originals like 'Batter Up' and 'No Ties'. The highlights of the session, however, were a delightful take on Gershwin's 'Long Ago and Far Away', featuring Larry Bunker on brushes, and a gorgeous version of Burke and Van Heusen's 'Imagination', which *DownBeat* described as "beautifully simple and simply beautiful".

Pianist Walter Norris has suggested that studio recordings of the Mulligan quartet failed to capture the 'sparkle and fire' that was heard onstage at The Haig. Listening to these early recordings of the Chet Baker Quartet, however, one is immediately struck by the vibrancy of the playing. As Dick Bock suggested, Freeman's compositions shone in their own right, and his arrangements allowed Chet more space in which to improvise. Freeman was delighted with the results, and later remarked, "Chet Baker is the only one who could play my songs the way I hear them. He had such an innate feeling for them."

The record was pressed quickly, and Bock arranged for advance copies to be shipped to *DownBeat* magazine in time for its July 29th edition. The gamble paid off, and the record—still lacking a title when *DownBeat* went to print, but eventually released as *The Chet Baker Quartet* (Pacific Jazz 3)—was awarded five stars. Chet Baker was a star in his own right, which must have rankled Mulligan, whose trial was looming:

"Now it's for sure. Our suspicions that the twenty-three-year-old trumpet man from Yale, Okla., was a major new star are confirmed by the LP, which is a gasser from start to finish. The lad has the style, the sound, the command of the horn; almost as important, he has the perfect setting. Russ Freeman's piano, fleet and modern in both accompanying and solo roles throughout, is of immeasurable value to the overall results ..."

Whilst Chet continued to play with the Mulligan Quartet at The Haig, Bock arranged for Chet Baker to make his debut as a solo artist at LA's Carlton Theatre on August 12th. A well-orchestrated press campaign helped to further Chet's appeal as a solo star. On the same day *DownBeat* published a prominent article on the 'Story of Chet Baker—Horn Star who'd Rather Sing':

"Amidst extravagant acclaim Chet has retained the shy, charming personality that so reveals itself when he plays ballad tunes like 'My Funny Valentine', the song that has become associated with Chet much like Bunny Berigan's 'I Can't Get Started', and identification that will undoubtedly last throughout Chet's playing career."

Both Bock and Freeman were taken aback by Chet's ambition to become a singer, a subject that he had never previously raised.

"He is convinced that he is a better singer than he is a trumpet player. Being so convinced he will probably move others to succumb to his charms as a singer. His current plans include more recordings with the Gerry Mulligan Quartet and with his own Quartet featuring Russ Freeman, also some vocal recordings that will perhaps startle his jazz following."[2]

Chet's plans to record again with the Gerry Mulligan Quartet were put on hold indefinitely on September 11th, when Mulligan was sentenced to six months in prison. The saxophonist had not anticipated his prison sentence, but he was not the only one. Plans for Bob Brookmeyer to join the group were put on hold, a scheduled engagement at the Down Beat club in San Francisco was cancelled, and tentative plans for a nationwide tour were scrapped.

Bock considered various options, but there was no obvious replacement for Mulligan. The relationship between Stan Getz and Chet Baker had been strained, and besides, the saxophonist was busy with his own band. Chet had also already demonstrated that he was not a natural bandleader when Gerry eloped to Mexico with Jeffie. As a consequence, the remaining members of the Gerry Mulligan Quartet were left in limbo for a few weeks.

In mid-September, Chet accepted an invitation to play with the Lighthouse All-Stars down at Hermosa Beach. The band's original line-up had come to an end earlier that month when trumpet player Shorty Rogers left the band to form his own band, recruiting fellow All-Stars reed-player Jimmy Giuffre and drummer Shelly Manne to join him. Ironically Shorty Rogers and His Giants replaced the Mulligan Quartet at The Haig.

Howard Rumsey was quick to bring in replacements; he hired Bud Shank and Bob Cooper, both versatile saxophonists, and Swedish trumpet player Rolf Ericson to complete the front line. His real coup, however, was to recruit the East Coast bebop legend Max Roach to replace Shelly Manne on drums. Roach was an experienced musician, playing with Coleman Hawkins at the age of nineteen, and having recorded extensively with Charlie Parker in the late 1940s and early 1950s. He had also played on the *Birth of the Cool* sessions with Miles Davis and Gerry Mulligan.

"When Max Roach came in from New York to take over Shelly Manne's drum chair," said Rumsey, "he drove up with Charles Mingus and Miles

Davis in the car with him." Roach made a huge impact on the West Coast scene, right from the very beginning, and in the months that followed numerous East Coast stars sat in at The Lighthouse, most notably Charlie Parker.

Mingus's contributions were limited, given that Rumsey played bass, although he did sit in on the piano from time to time. Miles Davis made a bigger impact, however, agreeing to sit in with the new-look Lighthouse All-Stars on Roach's first weekend; when Chet Baker also agreed to join, The Lighthouse was set for one of the most exciting nights in the club's history.

The fireworks started before the show. Miles Davis had been out of action on the club scene for some time, battling his addiction, and by the time he made his way over to the West Coast, he had learned that his position as the rising star of jazz trumpet was in danger of being usurped by the young upstart that Bird had warned him about. Indeed, the *DownBeat* critics' poll, which had been published in late August, voted Chet the overwhelming winner in the category of 'new star', with a total of 115 votes; names like Shorty Rogers, Cat Anderson and Clark Terry trailed with just ten votes apiece. Miles was too established to feature in that particular category, but was disappointed to see that he ranked sixth in the main trumpet poll, equal with Chet Baker, and far behind poll winner Louis Armstrong, and names like Dizzy Gillespie, Bobby Hackett and Roy Eldridge.

Miles' mood darkened further as he stepped on to the bandstand to warm up for the evening's performance. A Chet Baker tune started playing on the club's jukebox, a song that Miles himself had just recorded, and planned to release. "The look on his face was unbelievable and he leapt off the bandstand and was slowly reeling about looking at everyone, saying Chet had stolen his charts, that there had to be a spy, and demanding to know who it was," recalled Sandi Hummer, a regular visitor to the club. "Stan Levey [Lighthouse owner] had to come from his home in Manhattan Beach to remove it from the juke box, as they couldn't find the other key, all of this before Miles even showed a hint of calming down."[3]

Chet Baker, Miles Davis and Swedish trumpeter Rolf Ericson at The Lighthouse Café, Hermosa Beach, CA 1953. (c) Cecil Charles/CTSIMAGES

Perhaps as a result of this incident, Miles and Chet do not appear to have shared the stage together. That does not seem to have spoiled what must have been an exciting evening, Max Roach making his debut with the All-Stars, Miles and Chet, guest pianists Russ Freeman and Lorraine Geller, and the return of old band members, Shelly Manne and Jimmy Giuffre. Miles was on fine form, playing with a hard-bop flair that characterised his early work. He blazes through 'A Night in Tunisia', at times sounding more like Dizzy than himself, only slowing the tempo for a delicate read of ''Round Midnight', a tune that would later help to revitalise his career.

Chet had been a fan of Miles from the *Birth of the Cool* days, and Cecil Charles Spiller, who recorded the night's events, also took a photograph of Miles and Chet backstage, the young Chet looking in awe at his hero. Determined not be overwhelmed by the occasion, Chet played with uncharacteristic fire, a reflection of both the 'jam session' nature of the club, and his determination to impress Miles. The highlight of Chet's set was a lively reading of 'Winter Wonderland', a tune that would become a regular part of Chet's repertoire with his own quartet.

Even after Miles Davis and Charles Mingus had returned home, Chet continued to stop by The Lighthouse, often accompanied by his friend,

Russ Freeman. One night he got into a heated argument with the eighteen-year-old trumpet player, Herb Alpert. Alpert was studying at the University of Southern California at this time, and used to play regularly at Cyrano's, a club near Torrance Beach in Hollywood Riviera. Sandi Hummer remembers being warned to stay clear of the club one evening, as the dispute between the two musicians got out of hand. "The biggest thing when we were going to The Lighthouse was walking in the door and Eddy the bartender, Stan Levey and Frank Rosolino telling us that we should leave and leave right away and get some buildings between us and The Lighthouse as there might be gun play," she said. "Chet and Herb Alpert were in a feud and gun play was threatened. Herb Alpert's fans were another concern, as he had a large Mexican following, wealthy high on the totem pole Mexicans, and they weren't about to let Chet shoot their man. Stan and Frank were the ones who were going to try to handle it all. So we left and didn't go back until we called and talked to Eddy and found out if things had settled down. Stan and Frank were furious about it. They were unhappy about it for quite a while. I don't remember if I saw him play The Lighthouse after that incident, but he could have, I'm just not sure."[4]

Given the success of his debut LP, producer Dick Bock suggested Chet form a permanent band with Russ Freeman. He was convinced that they would find it easy to get bookings, and saw Freeman as a responsible musician who could take care of business, in addition to acting as the group's musical director. "There was something in Chet's personality that was, I think, basically irresponsible—toward himself and toward anything else," he said. "That's probably the thing that upset Gerry the most, because Gerry was able to function as a leader, and his career is ample proof of his ability to do that. He always looked upon Chet as a sideman."[5]

Russ Freeman felt torn over the proposal. "I had ambivalent feelings," he remembered. "I thought the breakup was really unfortunate, but I liked the idea that Chet and I were going to get to play together. Gerry's things sound terrific still: they're lyrical—jazz *compositions*, and what these two were playing between them was just gorgeous."[6]

Chet got to know pianist Russ Freeman in January 1952. "Chet lived in Lynwood with his wife, and they had this little house-behind-a-house where Chet and I played together a lot, days and nights. There had been a time earlier when I had been pretty strung out. By 1952 I had straightened myself out and I was seeing a lot of Chet, and we were playing together every chance we could get."[7]

Russ Freeman was twenty-five at the time, and three and a half years older than Chet. He was born in Chicago in May 1926, and moved to Los Angeles in 1931. He had studied classically with an aunt between the ages of eight and twelve, before giving up. His high school dance band rekindled Freeman's enthusiasm for music a few years later. "I thought 'that looks terrific to me—I want to do that!' The band was pretty bad—just perfect for me—I fit right in! I couldn't read music and didn't know anything about chords or harmony. From then on, it was all self-taught."

Freeman learnt fast, and persuaded his mother to let him leave high school just one year later, aged sixteen, to join a big band. When things didn't work out, he returned to high school, and graduated in 1945. At this time, Freeman remembers Charlie Parker and Dizzy Gillespie coming to play at Billy Berg's in Hollywood. "Nobody had ever heard anybody play like that in the history of the world! We were just dumbfounded by the whole thing. We had sort of been fooling round with jazz up to then, but that really set things off."

Suitably inspired, Freeman went on to form a short-lived bebop band with saxophonist Dean Benedetti, best known for his amateur recordings of Charlie Parker solos. The band found it hard to get work, and Freeman spent most of his time trying to sit in on jam sessions that were taking place throughout the city. At one such session he met trumpeter Howard McGhee, who had worked with Charlie Parker in 1946, before Bird was committed to Camarillo State Hospital for acute alcoholism and narcotic addiction. The two eventually formed a band with Sonny Criss and Teddy Edwards on alto and tenor saxophone, and Roy Porter on drums.

When Parker was released in early 1947, he joined McGhee's band. "We worked a number of one-nighters and a lot of after-hours clubs, places like 'Jack's Basket' on Central Avenue," said Freeman. "Playing with Bird was an indescribable experience." Parker returned to the recording studios in February 1947, and although Dodo Marmarosa was probably the first-choice pianist in Los Angeles at this time, Russ Freeman replaced him for one session, recording 'Home Cooking'.

Freeman went on to work with Dexter Gordon in the late 1940s, and Art Pepper, Wardell Gray and Shorty Rogers in the early 1950s, and it was at this time that he started to run into Chet Baker. Freeman's first influence was Nat 'King' Cole, although bop pianist Bud Powell probably exerted a greater influence on his playing. "Nobody ever articulated on the piano the way Bud did, not even Nat Cole. Not many pianists realised that they could do what a horn player does as far as the various weights that are given to notes, and the phrasing, and the whole way of playing. Bud is the first one to have done that. Where he came from, I don't know, because he didn't play like anyone else."

As a songwriter, Freeman drew his inspiration from a variety of sources. "Mulligan once said to me, 'You're a songwriter,'" he recalled. "I wondered for a while what he meant and I realised that the things I wrote back then, with Chet, were very melodic, very lyrical. Part of that was the influence of Lester Young and Charlie Parker. Bud Powell too. Those were the major influences on me, the people who influenced me the most. Monk, too, in a way."[8]

Dick Bock lined up an engagement with Stan Getz at The Blackhawk, but before that began, he invited the Quartet, again featuring the rhythm section of Carson Smith and Larry Bunker, to return to the Radio Recorders studio in early October. The band was really starting to gel at this stage, and the session was highly productive, resulting in seven tracks.

Any suggestion that Chet was simply a disciple of the 'cool' school, incapable of playing with fire, is blown away by his playing on this session. He sounds liberated after the constraints of the studio sessions with the Mulligan Quartet, reveling in the newfound freedom of Russ Freeman's arrangements. Listen to his tumbling, freewheeling style on 'All The Things You Are', or better still, his explosive playing on Russ Freeman's 'Bea's Flat'. As Doug Ramsey later noted, transcriptions of Baker's solos were published not long after these records were released, urging readers, "to play with the records, in order to duplicate the nuances of Chet's artistry."

"Like hundreds of other aspiring young trumpeters, I had a crack at them," he said. "I was able to make my way, laboriously, through most of the music, but 'Bea's Flat' destroyed me. Nuances; hell, I couldn't get the melody line right, let alone the solo. Not at that tempo. Chet, of course, sails through it."[9]

A few days later, the Quartet made their way to San Francisco, where they started a month-long engagement at the Blackhawk, opening for Stan Getz. This booking represented something of a gamble from Dick Bock's perspective. His attempt to pair Baker and Getz earlier that summer had not proved to be particularly successful, a clash of egos rather than styles. "They were never tight," percussionist Bill Loughborough remembered. "Stan was an excellent player but not a particularly warm or friendly human being."[10]

The problems were compounded by the decision to have Baker and Getz share a motel room in order to save money. Again, Getz led Baker to temptation, encouraging him to shoot up. "Chet chippied with him at that time," recalled Loughborough, referring to the practice of using heroin on an occasional basis, without being physically dependent.

There were frictions onstage, too. Whilst Getz was nominally headlining at the Blackhawk, Chet's growing popularity meant that he quickly became the star of the show. As bass player Carson Smith later noted, "Stan couldn't bear having the spotlight taken away from him." A week or so into the engagement, Getz returned to Los Angeles, claiming he was suffering from a virus. Chet stayed on, but his temperament again suggested that he was ill-suited to leading a band. He showed up late one evening, and found the other band members onstage, playing without him. He stormed off, refusing to play, childish behaviour that upset the club's owner, Guido Caccianti. He later filed a complaint against Stan Getz for breach of contract, and told *DownBeat* magazine he was "a little annoyed at modern music's problem children," implying he was less than impressed by Baker's own attitude.

Back in Los Angeles, Dick Bock had booked the recording studio for October 27th. The resulting session included Chet's first vocal recordings, 'I Fall In Love Too Easily' and 'The Thrill Is Gone', and two instrumental takes of the Christmas song, 'Winter Wonderland'. Good as his playing was on that session, it is Chet's singing that inevitably grabs the attention. His singing is in many ways hard to separate from his playing style, a feeling intensified by the use of overdubbing, which allowed Chet to play gently beneath his own vocal. "My phrasing as a singer has been influenced a lot by my playing," he later claimed. "If I hadn't been a trumpet player, I don't know if I would have arrived at singing that way. I probably wouldn't have. I don't know whether I'm a trumpet player who sings or a singer who plays the trumpet. I love to do both."

In later years, Dick Bock tried to take credit for this idea, claiming to have heard Chet singing in a club in order to add variety to the performance. "I encouraged him to sing, and it turned out that he had an exceptional talent for it." Russ Freeman denied this version of events. "The first time I heard Chet sing? That was on his first vocal session for Pacific. He didn't sing on the stage so much, you know."

In fact, Chet had been singing for a number of years. His first known public performance—as an adult, at least—probably took place at a jam session, and was witnessed by the photographer William Claxton. "It was during a late-night, or rather an early morning, 'jam session' at Falcon's Lair," he recalled. "The Lair was a beautiful Spanish-style mansion high in the hills in the Benedict Canyon section of Beverley Hills. It was built by silent screen star Rudolph Valentino in the 1920s, but in the early 1950s it was remodeled by heiress Doris Duke. She added a state-of-the-art music room for her live-in boyfriend, pianist Joe Castro. Joe would stage 'jazz musicales'—sort of elegant jam sessions—and hosted many wonderful nights for the visiting jazz personalities. It was during one of these evenings that I heard Chet sing. He was seated at the piano alongside June Christy. Together they were singing softly a medley of standards while 'Coop' (Bob Cooper, June's husband) played beautifully in the background on his tenor sax. They sounded like two angels singing. The room became still while everyone listened. When they finished Cole Porter's 'Every Time We Say Goodbye', trumpeter Art Farmer called out, 'Yeah, yeah, that was beautiful! You know, Chet, you should sing on your next album'. June Christy agreed."[11]

Thereafter, Chet pestered Dick Bock to record him, and when he sensed the producer's reluctance, casually dropped a reference to his ambitions as a singer into a *DownBeat* magazine interview, knowing full well the ripples that this would cause. His former girlfriend, Joyce Tucker, confirmed that Chet had to push for what he wanted. "They didn't want to record him as a singer," she said. "Imagine that face being able to play … and then being able to sing! A lot happened too fast. He had always been broke, and Gerry paid very little. He didn't do it for any reason other than that he loved to sing. He had to talk them into recording him. And he insisted on it."

Russ Freeman was disappointed with the turn of events, and felt he had been relegated to a mere accompanist. He did admit, however, that his dislike of Chet's singing partly stemmed from his own bias towards singers. "I always found that male as well as female singers got too much attention. Maybe that was prejudice. I didn't like the idea of Chet singing at all."

Dot Woodward, Dick Bock's secretary, remembered a troubled recording session, with Chet's unsteady pitch resulting in numerous takes of each vocal, which probably helps to explain why only three songs were completed that day.

It's easy to pick holes in his vocal performance from a technical perspective. There's an adenoidal tone to his voice, which was never going to appeal to everybody, and his vowel pronunciation occasionally betrays his Oklahoma roots. His pitch is uncertain, to say the least—listen to the way he struggles with the high notes, two minutes into 'The Thrill Is Gone'. As with his trumpet playing, he is most comfortable in the mid-range, and occasionally struggles with the higher notes. His breathing patterns also reflect his lack of formal training, resulting in irregular pauses, mid-phrase.

But many listeners, myself included, are able to overlook his technical shortcomings as a singer, drawn in by the lovelorn, melancholic edge to his breathy voice. As with his trumpet playing on ballads such as 'My Funny Valentine' or 'Imagination', there's an underlying sadness and fragility to his tone that can mesmerise, a suggestion that he is drawing on deep emotions, baring the very depth of his soul.

An additional quality that many have identified, at least in his early vocal recordings, is one of innocence. Some years later, Rex Reed memorably wrote that Baker "sang with an innocent sweetness that made girls fall right out of their saddle oxfords." This is a view shared by Astrud Gilberto, whose own singing style was clearly influenced by that of Baker. "Chet had this little lost boy look and it came through in his singing." As we will later discover, age lent a certain gravitas and world-weariness to Chet's singing voice, and whilst dental problems and life itself took its toll on his tone, it still had the power to move listeners, even in his final years.

Whether Chet's singing really provided any insight into his soul is another question altogether. Ruth Young, Chet's partner for almost ten years, and a singer herself, feels sure that the lyrics held little meaning to Chet, despite his preference for romantic ballads. "None of the songs held any meaning to him," she said. "I don't think Chet approached his music from a romantic sense; I just think his sensitivity was such that it came out that way. I think he understood romanticism from the music, not the other way round. His troubled upbringing made it difficult for him to relate to people; if not for his natural musical affinity, I don't think he would have been able to relate at all, especially in any romantic manner."[12]

Jazz critics, then and now, are divided on the merits of Chet's singing voice. *DownBeat* magazine was one of the few magazines that was initially quite favourably disposed, described his singing on *Chet Baker Sings* as "very appealing", going on to add that "his intonation is good, and he has an admirable feel for the lyrical play of these excellent songs."

Others were less kind. Nat Hentoff later wrote that "his vocal prowess, though it had a short vogue, was such as to make Rex Harrison sound like a bel canto virtuoso." Jack Tracy, writing in *DownBeat* a couple of years later, was also highly critical. "I am still amazed, however, by the number of persons, chiefly feminine, who are gassed by him. His voice—much like Mel Torme's—husky, whispery, almost ephemeral. Saving grace is his sense of phrasing, almost always present in an instrumentalist who sings, but lyrics have meanings, and Chet doesn't seem to grasp them often enough."[13]

More recently, West Coast jazz historian Robert Gordon was utterly dismissive of Chet's vocal recordings. "Richard Bock seemed to get sidetracked by a bid for mass popularity. This resulted in an album entitled *Chet Baker Sings*, which is, from a jazz standpoint, an unmitigated disaster. The worst faults of Baker's trumpet style—a tendency towards introspection, a limited emotional and dynamic range—are multiplied tenfold by his soft, quavering voice. No doubt the singer's small-boyish vocals brought out the mothering instinct in some of the females of his audience, but hard core jazz enthusiasts were and remain turned off."[14]

Regardless of critical opinion, Chet's vocal recordings—particularly his early work on Pacific Jazz—have an enduring appeal. The records have remained in print for many years, and despite the views of Robert Gordon, are popular with hardcore jazz enthusiasts as well as more casual fans of jazz singing. It's interesting to note that his singing, not just his playing, has influenced a wide variety of jazz and pop musicians, from Kurt Elling to Curtis Stigers, from Georgie Fame to Elvis Costello.

We will analyse his influence as a singer in more depth later in the book. Dick Bock selected the best take of 'The Thrill Is Gone', and released it as a single (PJ615). Despite his reservations, the response was overwhelming, and before long he invited Chet back into the studio to rerecord 'I Fall In Love Too Easily', and to record enough additional material for a full album.

Sadly, the thrill had also gone from Chet's relationship with Charlaine, which had disintegrated into a series of bitter affairs, each seeking to gain revenge over the other. Chet never forgave her for sleeping with Bob Whitlock, and in a piece of footage that was edited out of the final version of the movie *Let's Get Lost*, referred to her as "a whore".

Chet's growing popularity won him a place on a prestigious ten-day tour in November, arranged by Gene Norman, joining forces with his old mentor

Charlie Parker, and pianist Dave Brubeck and his Quartet. "It was a tour with a rhythm section of Jimmy Rowles, Carson Smith and Shelly Manne," confirmed Ron Crotty, bass player with the Dave Brubeck Quartet. "They played a set with Chet, and a set with Charlie Parker. We went up and down the coast of California, had one gig in Canada, and played the final gig in San Diego."[15]

The tour took them up and down the West Coast, taking in Vancouver (unconfirmed, but probably 2nd November), Seattle (3rd), the University of Oregon (4th), Oakland (5th), Palomar Gardens in San Jose (6th) and the Embassy Auditorium in Los Angeles (7th), the Philharmonic Auditorium in Los Angeles, plus dates in Riverside and San Diego.

The tour allowed the young jazz audience the chance to see their first glimpse of the rising stars of West Coast jazz, and one of their final glimpses of Charlie Parker, whose health was on the decline. Dave Brubeck later recalled that Parker had pawned his saxophone by the time they reached Seattle, and had to borrow Paul Desmond's instrument. Piano player Jimmy Rowles also remembered Parker go off in search of drugs at every town they came to, wondering whether he'd make it back for the show. The bloated saxophonist, still only thirty-three, invariably made it, and called his protégé onstage to join him every night, proud of what the young trumpet player had been able to achieve.

Back in Los Angeles, Dick Bock booked the Quartet to play opposite Stan Getz at Zardi's, on the corner of Hollywood and Vine. In recognition of Chet's growing popularity, it was billed as a double-header. Chet asked saxophonist Herb Geller, a close friend of Russ Freeman's, to join them onstage at the club. "Around the second night we played, he didn't show up. He finally came in for the last set. He didn't offer any excuses, but all he said was 'Herb, you know I just won the poll'. I said, 'Poll, what, the *DownBeat* poll?' He said, 'Also the *Metronome*; I won them all!' I was amazed, I had no idea he was attaining that pinnacle."[16]

Chet did not top the *Metronome* poll until the following year, but he had indeed topped the *DownBeat* readers' poll with an impressive tally of 807 votes, far ahead of Dizzy Gillespie (664), Harry James (624) and Maynard Ferguson (501). Given the emergence of bebop, and the rise in popularity of West Coast jazz, it is perhaps not so surprising to see Louis Armstrong down in seventh place. But it must have rankled sixth-place Miles Davis to see Chet Baker, a relative newcomer, riding so high in the polls. Miles obviously felt that colour played a part, and whilst Chet's looks may have helped, it should be noted that Charlie Parker still topped Lee Konitz and Paul Desmond in the alto sax category, Ella Fitzgerald managed to hold off Peggy Lee, Doris Day and June Christy, and Nat Cole beat Frank Sinatra in the male singer category. Miles felt hard done by, and held a bitter grudge against Chet for years to come, making his feelings clear when they met again in New York the following year.

Another musician who held a grudge against Chet was Stan Getz, who continued to resent Chet's growing popularity. He eventually walked out from the engagement, just as he had in San Francisco, leaving the Chet Baker Quartet to play on alone. A *Time* magazine review from this period shows that the band was playing a mixture of songs from the Mulligan Quartet era such as 'Soft Shoe', standards that had long been a part of Baker's repertoire such as 'My Funny Valentine' and 'All The Things You Are', and new songs such as Russ Freeman's 'Maid In Mexico'.

Once it became clear that Chet Baker and Gerry Mulligan were not going to reform the quartet, Dick Bock started to make plans for the group's first nationwide tour. He was confident that this would broaden the group's appeal. He also knew that in pianist Russ Freeman he had someone who could keep Chet under control, both financially and musically. "He was really the musical director," he noted, "and he was largely responsible for the success that the quartet had as far as being able to be a unit to work. Not only did he pick the tunes, he wrote the tunes, he taught Chet what he needed to play them, he took care of business on the road."[17]

Herb Geller confirmed Bock's version of events. "Russ took charge of Chet," he said. "Chet couldn't do anything, couldn't organise the music, or make a program, or make out the payroll."[18]

The decision to embark on a national tour involved bringing forward a number of recording sessions that Dick Bock had proposed to Baker and Freeman. The tour was due to last several months, departing the West Coast in early March, after a final engagement at The Haig. As a consequence, Bock was aware that Baker would not be available for studio recordings until mid–late 1954. By that time, the dynamics within the group changed quite dramatically; Baker had started to take Freeman's role for granted, and his relationship with a young French girl had started to cause friction within the band.

"The first proposed session, a seven piece ensemble date, came about through my interest in the compositions of Jack Montrose," Bock later wrote. "Jack, a graduate of Los Angeles State College, had been writing for a rehearsal group which had been playing off nights at The Haig. It was there that Chet and I first became aware of Jack's unique ability as a composer and arranger."

Born on December 30th 1928, in Detroit, Michigan, Montrose attended high school in Chattanooga, Tennessee before moving to Los Angeles. After graduating college he started work with Jerry Gray's band, working on his compositions in his spare time, and rehearsing them with his part-time band at The Haig. The *Ensemble* session with Chet Baker was his first major writing assignment.

The rhythm section for the session consisted of Shelly Manne on drums, Joe Mondragon on bass, and Russ Freeman, with a front line that consisted of Chet on trumpet, Jack Montrose on tenor saxophone, Herb Geller on alto and tenor, and Bob Gordon on baritone. They agreed to record a selection of Montrose's original compositions and a number of standards that he had arranged for the occasion. "Dick Bock was basically looking for a showcase for Chet," recalled Jack Montrose. "The musicians were basically the band I was playing with at that time, with the addition of Russ Freeman, who was playing with Chet."[19]

The notes to the original album *Ensemble*, probably by Bock himself, describe Montrose's style. "Jack's approach to jazz composition closely parallels chamber music forms. He utilises the transparencies of linear writing combined with chamber music conciseness to create a well-developed, mature framework for jazz expression. Jack insists his music is neither programmatic nor descriptive, that his intention is to write so as to build compositions that are entities within themselves."

His approach to composition may help to explain why the music is not particularly emotionally involving. Many of the arrangements come across as too fussy, arguably too clever for their own good. The standout track is probably 'Goodbye', one of the three tunes not composed by Montrose himself. On this mournful ballad, a delicate solo by Baker is underpinned by subtle shading from the three saxophonists. 'Pro Defunctus' is perhaps the most successful of the up-tempo tracks, benefiting from a less intricate arrangement, which paves the way for Baker's strongest solo of the set.

In retrospect, Baker was accustomed to working with arrangers who played to his strengths, such as Gerry Mulligan and Russ Freeman, so it is perhaps not surprising that his soloing sounds less confident on some of the faster tracks, such as 'A Dandy Line'. Jack Montrose, who went on to work with Art Pepper, and play opposite Clifford Brown and Max Roach, later made the comparison of the two young trumpeters. "Chet would play a lot of wrong notes when he improvised, but in Brownie's improvisations, all of the notes were correct—like they were written down by Beethoven."[20]

Whilst Clifford Brown was undoubtedly a superior player from a technical standpoint, Montrose had considerable respect for Chet's intuitive abilities. He did note that Chet was something of an outsider within the West Coast jazz scene, even at this stage, and voiced concerns about his ability to withstand the pressure Bock was subjecting him to. "Chet was unique, and was quite separate from the rest of the people in the business," he revealed. "He was not concerned with the business, and could not have been more concerned about what he left behind, even at that time. He had no concept of how he fitted into the bigger picture. He wasn't concerned about anything. I don't think he could handle the success—he couldn't handle any of it."[21]

The ensemble set was swiftly followed by a recording session with a string section, an idea Bock had been discussing with Baker and Freeman for some time. As Bock later explained, the recording session came about quite by chance. "While Chet was rehearsing for the *Ensemble* date, Columbia Records, through Paul Weston, made Pacific Jazz an offer that was too interesting to dismiss. Because Chet is under exclusive contract to Pacific Jazz, Columbia wondered if we would agree to record a twelve-inch Long Playing album featuring Chet. We were to be allowed complete freedom to select the material, arrangers, instrumentation and even the cover artist."

The first recording sessions took place on December 30th and 31st, just eight days after the completion of the ensemble recording sessions. The rhythm section used was identical to the *Ensemble* date, and tenor saxophonist Zoot Sims was brought in as an additional soloist. Perhaps reflecting time constraints, Bock chose to work with a number of different arrangers for the recording sessions; Jack Montrose, Marty Paich, who was working as a pianist and conductor for Peggy Lee at the time, trumpeter Shorty Rogers, and Johnny Mandel, who had recently settled on the West Coast. A total of eight tunes were recorded over the two days—not enough for a twelve-inch LP—necessitating a return to the studio in February, when an additional four songs were recorded, this time with Bud Shank joining Baker as a soloist.

In the event, the use of a variety of different arrangers probably helped to make the resulting album *Chet Baker And Strings* more interesting than it might otherwise have been. Whilst some of the arrangements are somewhat cloying, the soloing is uniformly excellent, and interest is maintained through the inclusion of three more up-tempo numbers, 'Love', and two tunes penned especially for the session, 'A Little Duet For Zoot and Chet' by Jack Montrose, and 'Trickleydidlier' by Shorty Rogers. One gets the impression that Montrose had learnt from the previous session, and contributed arrangements that were more suited to Chet's playing than on the *Ensemble* album. The highlight of the album is probably 'The Wind', a Russ Freeman composition which was arranged for the session by Johnny Mandel, and went on to become something of a jazz standard.

Dick Bock has been accused of over-exposing Chet Baker at this time, recording him too frequently and in settings that were not always appropriate. The accusation that he made too many recordings seems a little harsh. First of all, he was running a fledgling record label, Pacific Jazz, which just one year earlier had struggled to raise the funds for a single recording session. Now he had a rising star on his roster, and could use Chet's success to sign and promote other new artists. Secondly, Chet was not a typical musician; as Jack Montrose himself commented, "he was not concerned with the business." When the UK music journal *Melody Maker* interviewed Chet around this time, he suggested that he would consider quitting the trumpet altogether within two years, citing his bad teeth and gums, and buy a boat. He wanted to "see things I've never seen … I want a fifty-foot sailboat to travel on and write music, heavier things … I've had coastal sailing experience around LA, and I intend to start studying navigation." Under the circumstances, it's easy to see why Bock was keen to record the young trumpet protégé while he still could.[22]

The suggestion that the settings Bock had chosen were not always appropriate is more reasonable. It was Dick Bock, rather than Chet himself, who took a shine to the arrangements of Jack Montrose; it's worth noting that Chet only revisited a handful of the tunes recorded on the *Ensemble* album, and rarely returned to the ensemble format either. Likewise, Chet was probably still too immature as a musician to record an album with strings. Dick Bock was aware that Charlie Parker had recorded with a string section, and thought it would send a signal that Chet Baker was now a major recording artist.

Chet Baker and Strings was released in July 1954, and was largely dismissed by the critics, with *DownBeat* magazine describing the results as 'soporific', and awarding it just two stars.

"Though some of the horn writing has its points, the scoring for strings throughout could double as background for *Young Widder Brown.* The arrangers involved are all obviously men of talent, so my speculation is that they were kept firmly and unwisely under wraps. Mr Baker, as Dorothy Parker once said of the young Katherine Hepburn, runs the gamut of emotions from A to B. The two stars in the rating are for the stubborn signs of life and vitality exhibited by Sims, Shank, and the rhythm section (when allowed). Also salvageable are Montrose's *Duet* and the theme (though not the arrangement or all of the execution) of Freeman's *The Wind.*"[23]

Despite the reservations of the jazz critics, *Chet Baker and Strings* went on to become one of Chet's most successful albums. The moody black and white cover shot, courtesy of William Claxton, certainly helped, capturing his chiselled features side-on, a few strands of his well-oiled quiff hanging down as he stared into space in the recording studio. The trumpet player Herb Alpert was also a fan, and Chet's melodic playing on this and other early Pacific Jazz recordings, undoubtedly helped to influence a number of Brazilian musicians, including João Donato and Antonio Carlos Jobim.

There was still time for one final recording session before the quartet hit the road, and the band returned to the Capitol Studio in LA in mid-February. Chet's debut recording as a singer, 'The Thrill Is Gone', had produced an enthusiastic response from the public, and Dick Bock agreed to record a ten-inch LP, *Chet Baker Sings*.

Russ Freeman was less keen on the idea, in part concerned that the idea was too commercial. "To be honest, I was never much of a fan of his singing," he later admitted. "It only distracted from what was going on instrumentally. But of course I did my job. I functioned as Chet's musical director. I picked out the pieces for him, I wrote the arrangements, and I also composed one or two numbers." If Freeman was indeed responsible for selecting the songs for Chet, he did an impeccable job, the follow-up session incorporating the exquisite 'Time After Time', 'I Get Along Without You Very Well' and 'I Fall In Love Too Easily', the bitter-sweet songs ideally suited to Chet's wistful style. In all, the session produced six brand new songs, including those discussed above, together with a rerecorded version of 'I Fall In Love Too Easily'.

The album was released in June of that year, and as discussed above, received mixed reviews. *DownBeat* magazine gave the record four stars, praising both his intonation and his feel for the lyrics. "My only objection to the collection," wrote Nat Hentoff, "is the same that I have for his playing in general both on records and in person. It's almost all small-scaled, and while often very moving within its limited compass, there's a lack of expressive range and never, so far as I've heard, is there any exultancy."

Dick Bock had no experience of organising a nationwide tour, and nor did Russ Freeman. The producer arranged for Chet to sign with Joe Glaser, the president of Associated Booking Corporation, now known as ABC Booking. Glaser was allegedly once connected to the Al Capone mob, and as manager of the Sunset Café in Chicago in the 1920s, he met a number of jazz musicians, including Louis Armstrong. He started to manage Armstrong in 1935, and maintained a close relationship with him until his death in 1969. Over the years he built up an impressive client list including Duke Ellington, Billie Holiday and Anita O'Day.

Glaser arranged for advanced publicity about Chet to be sent to a number of venues around the country. The two-page sheet included a section entitled 'What They Say About Chet Baker', which quoted from a number of publications, including a *Time* magazine article that had appeared in February. "Today, the liveliest center of developing jazz is California where a cluster of youngsters, still mostly in their 20's, are refining the frenzies of bop into something cooler, calmer and more coherent. At the top of this list stands twenty-five-year-old Chet Baker."

The departure date fast approaching, Russ Freeman suddenly realised he would be responsible for handling the group's finances for the next three months. With most of the band members bringing their partners, there was a great deal of responsibility on his shoulders, and he sought the advice of the experienced sound engineer, Phil Turetsky, who taught him how to keep accounts and withhold taxes from the band's weekly paychecks. "Otherwise none of it would have happened," he said. "Chet wanted to play, but he wouldn't put himself out to do anything else."

Drummer Larry Bunker decided not to go on tour with the band, opting to stay in LA, where he was being offered regular studio work. He later claimed he was sick of playing quietly behind Mulligan and Baker. "I kept thinking, 'I wanna play like the guys in New York are playing. I wanna bash! Not play all those carefully crafted arrangements'. But that was the work, so that's what I did." Replacement Bob Neel, who came on board before the *Chet Baker and Strings* album, was asked to perform a similar role. "Chettie wanted somebody that would just keep time and stay out of his way," he later recalled, "and that's what I did."

Bob Neel's description is important, as it effectively defined Chet's relationship with drummers for the vast majority of his life. In the 1980s, in particular, he regularly experimented with a drummer-less trio, which often proved to be an effective vehicle for Chet's soft tone, provided the bass player could keep good time. The one period he opted to use a more dynamic drummer, Peter Littman, was influenced by his performing opposite Miles Davis at Birdland in New York—an event that took place on that first tour in the summer of 1954.

Having completed a final engagement at The Haig, the band members made their preparations to go on tour, knowing that they would not return to the West coast for three months. The tour was scheduled to start in freezing Detroit on March 2nd, so it was with some trepidation that Russ Freeman, Carson Smith and his wife Joan, and Bob Neel and his girlfriend Marion Raffaele, squeezed into Marion's Pontiac to start the long journey, their clothes and instruments packed into a small trailer hooked to the back of the car.

The tour got off to an eventful start. A few hours into the journey, and the tyres on Marion's old Pontiac gave out, and had to be replaced. Racing across California, trying to make up for lost time, driver Russ Freeman was given a speeding ticket. When they eventually reached Oklahoma, they ran into a violent sandstorm, the flying red dust making driving conditions near impossible. Just when they felt that nothing else could go wrong, they hit a violent blizzard on the outskirts of Detroit, and were forced to stay in a small roadside motel in the less than salubrious suburbs of the city.

Chet and Charlaine had left a day or so earlier, and met the other members of the band next day at the Rouge Lounge, a small music club and bowling alley in River Rouge, just outside Detroit. Freeman was not impressed with the venue, or its badly tuned spinet piano. "Just because Chet was a poll winner, it didn't mean we didn't play some real toilets," he laughed.

Fortunately the gig was less eventful than the journey, and the band received a rapturous welcome from the enthusiastic crowd, enjoying a dose of warm West Coast jazz in the icy winter months. The band played a number of tunes associated with the Mulligan Quartet, including 'Line for Lyons',

'Lullaby of the Leaves' and the inevitable 'My Funny Valentine', as well as Russ Freeman's own compositions, such as 'Russ Job' and 'Maid in Mexico'. Chet still enjoyed playing a number of Charlie Parker tunes, and 'Lover Man', 'My Little Suede Shoes' and 'My Old Flame' were frequently included in the set list. Finally, it's worth noting that the band tended to play a couple of tunes from the *Ensemble* album, composed by Jack Montrose, such as 'A Dandy Line' and 'Headline'. Russ Freeman, who was responsible for choosing the set list, may have selected these songs; Chet would appear to have been less keen on the Montrose compositions, and rarely played them after the band's debut tour.

After a fortnight, the band moved on to Boston, where they played a two-week stint at the Storyville club, before going on to the Blue Note in Philadelphia, where they played from the end of March through April 10th.

The atmosphere within the band at this time was "real good", according to Freeman. "There were difficulties sometimes of course, but that is inevitable. Here we were, eight of us on the road, four young men and four [sic] pretty girls. That easily leads to conflict. It also happens when young people go on vacation together. But we were always able to talk about it. Chet was somebody you got along with easily. He was an easy-going person. He was open to every suggestion. He made few demands. If there were problems, it was usually because of money or a girl. We didn't earn an awful lot if you take into account that we had trip and hotel expenses. There would be some grumbling if we stayed in bad hotels or had to play in funky clubs. Now the working conditions for jazz musicians in California have improved somewhat."[24]

One of the 'conflicts' that Freeman refers to was the tense relationship between Chet and Charlaine, whose marriage was effectively over by the time the tour started, according to the pianist. Night after night, Chet would find himself surrounded by young women at the club, eager to meet the handsome young musician, and tell him how much they admired his playing and singing. Chet and Charlaine had long used sex as a weapon against one another, and Chet continued to parade his numerous conquests in front of Charlaine, even as their marriage unravelled.

Onstage, however, Chet could forget about his personal problems and get lost in the music. Considering his lack of formal training, and the fact that he relied so heavily on playing by ear, his natural ability frequently amazed Russ Freeman. "Of course, we all play by ear when we play jazz," he explained, "but he had nothing to fall back on. If he had a bad night, which he did occasionally, he didn't have any way to say 'Well, okay, I'll just go back and cool it and sort of walk through this path'. He didn't know how to do that—he had to rely on what his ear told him to do. And if he was not on that night, then it didn't happen. But there would be certain nights, maybe once a week, when it was absolutely staggering. To the extent that I would sit there coming for him, listening to him play, and think 'Where did that come from? What is it that's coming out of this guy? You mean, I have to play a solo after that?'"

The tour continued, taking in such venues as the University of Michigan in Ann Arbor and the Colonial Tavern in Toronto. Reviews were extremely favourable, and the Quartet continued to play to capacity crowds. Several promoters submitted tapes of the various concerts to Richard Bock at Pacific Jazz records. Only the recording of the Ann Arbor concert was considered good enough for release, although airshots of the Boston concerts, some of which were broadcast on the radio, have also subsequently surfaced.

In mid-May, the band made its New York debut at Birdland, the so-called 'Jazz Corner of the World', which took its name from Charlie Parker's nickname, 'Bird'. Situated at 1678 Broadway, just north of 52nd Street, the club was owned by Morris Levy, and had a reputation as being one of the foremost centers of bop. It was somewhat ironic, then, that Chet found himself headlining at the club with the legendary Dizzy Gillespie, who had made his name with Charlie Parker, playing support. If Dizzy was upset by this arrangement, he was too much of a gentleman to show it; he recognised the commercial appeal of Chet Baker's band, and knew that Charlie Parker greatly admired the young trumpet player. Indeed, when Chet fell on hard times in the late 1960s and early 1970s, Dizzy Gillespie tried his best to help him, securing him his first booking in New York in several years at the Half Note club.

For now Dizzy stood at the bar and watched, admiring the fact that Chet had attracted more girls to the club than usual. One girl in particular caught his eye; an attractive, short-haired girl in a slinky black dress, her thick black eyeliner drawing attention to her dark eyes, and distinguishing her from the more traditionally attired bobby-soxers gathered around the stage. He introduced himself, and was taken aback to find out she knew exactly who he was.

Her name was Liliane Cukier, and she was a twenty-one-year-old French girl who had arrived by boat from Paris just two weeks earlier. She had fallen in love with jazz at a young age, rushing to the St-Germain clubs as soon as she had finished school, dancing to the music and hanging round with the local musicians. Before long, she was introduced to a number of the American jazz musicians living in Paris at that time, such as drummer Kenny Clarke. "Shortly after that I left home, and went to live in a famous hotel in St-Germain," she said. "It was unbelievable—only musicians lived in this hotel. The people that owned the hotel looked after the musicians; they were patient over money, cooked for them. There were musicians in every room, and everyone knew each other. I used to spend my nights with musicians; all we would do is lie down, listen to music, and smoke pot. They introduced me to a lot of music, Duke Ellington, Count Basie, Lester Young, Charlie Parker, Thelonious Monk and so on. And also to classical music, including Bela Bartok, Stravinsky and Ravel. The nights went like that. I liked the music, and the people that made it; I also liked this way of life. I was like a fish in water."[25]

Her parents despaired of her wild behaviour, hoping that she would soon settle down and get married. When she showed no signs of changing her ways, her father called his brother in New York, and arranged for her to stay with them for a few months at their apartment in Washington Heights. Liliane had no idea how she was going to earn a living in New York, but accepted the proposal, aware that New York was considered the center of the jazz world. "I took a trip on the very famous ship *The Normandie*. I arrived on a beautiful April morning, and the same evening, I stepped into Birdland on my own," she recalled. "I didn't know anybody, and I wasn't going to sit at a table, because it was expensive, so I stood at the bar. There was the Count Basie Band there with the Miles Davis Quintet; that was the program for two weeks. I knew some of the musicians from the Count Basie Band because they had come to Paris; I knew a couple of people, including Joe Newman."

Two weeks later, Chet Baker and Dizzy Gillespie took over at Birdland, and now here she was, talking to Dizzy Gillespie himself. The two became friends, with Dizzy inviting her backstage to play chess with him during the intervals, ignoring the sign that read 'No Ladies Allowed'. It was there she encountered a bloated Charlie Parker, sick from a heart condition and bleeding ulcers. He had just lost his daughter, Pree, to pneumonia, and was killing his pain the only way he knew, with heroin and alcohol.

Parker had fallen out with many other musicians, including his former protégé Miles Davis, who was tired of paying off Bird's drug dealers on his behalf. Parker knew he'd be welcomed by Dizzy Gillespie and Chet Baker, however, and made his way to the rear of the club, knocking on the dressing room door. "Bird saw us playing chess, and would advise me all the time, telling me how to play, which got on my nerves, because I knew more about chess than him," said Liliane. "The manager of the club, Oscar Goodstein, eventually told Bird to go, saying he had no right to be there. They had had problems before, which I wasn't aware of. I was very shocked. Carson Smith, who was standing behind me, went white. Bird said, 'Man, you named this place after me'. Nobody said anything."[26]

Chet was besotted with Liliane, attracted to her dark good looks, and her air of sophistication. "Liliane was like a breath of fresh air," he later wrote. "She was quick, beautiful, and played chess well." For the young French girl, it was not love at first sight, but the enjoyment of living for the moment. "I was not looking for a husband, or money—I was just trying to have fun! Chet fell in love with me there; later he would tell people how he fell in love with me at first sight. He started to look for me at intermissions in the Village. At the club he always had an escort—other musicians around him."

The atmosphere at the club changed quite dramatically following the arrival of a resurgent Miles Davis, who took over from Dizzy Gillespie as the support act. Newly clean, having recently kicked heroin in his hometown of St. Louis, he had returned to New York City earlier that year. There he recorded a third session for Blue Note, which was eventually released as *Volume 2* and *Walkin'*, with a razor-sharp band that included Horace Silver on piano, Percy Heath on bass and Kenny Clarke on drums. The band had really started to gel after spending two weeks playing opposite Count Basie, and by the time they hit Birdland, Miles Davis and his band felt as though they had a point to prove.

Miles had encountered Chet at The Lighthouse the previous summer. Whilst Charlie Parker had warned him of Chet's virtuosity, Miles was less than impressed. He was convinced that Chet had copied his trumpet sound, even ripping off songs that he had recorded. When Chet's debut solo recording received a five-star review in *DownBeat* magazine, and he won the prestigious year-end readers' poll, Miles complained bitterly that Chet was being treated as "the second coming of Jesus Christ."

The issues went deeper than that for Miles; West Coast jazz symbolised 'white' jazz. He sensed that white jazz musicians were getting paid more than their black counterparts for delivering what he regarded as a 'watered-down' sound; worse still, jazz critics and the general public seemed to buy into the conspiracy. "I guess it was supposed to be some kind of alternative to bebop, or black music, or 'hot jazz'," he argued, " … but it was the same old story, black shit was being ripped off all over again." The fact that Chet Baker could headline Birdland over more established musicians like Dizzy Gillespie and himself simply served to prove his point.[27]

Other members of Miles' band appeared to share his perspective. Pianist Horace Silver later told Nat Hentoff of *DownBeat* magazine, "I can't stand the faggot-type jazz—the jazz with no … no guts. And the discouraging part is that the faggot-type jazz is getting more popular than the jazz with real soul. The groups that play with a lot of guts are not making as much loot."[28]

The tension mounted as the Miles Davis Quintet took the stage. Miles played with a fiery passion on the more bop-oriented tracks, his solos sharp and concise, driven by one of the finest rhythm sections in the business. But he also demonstrated his versatility, not afraid to slow the tempo, and take on Chet on the ballads for which he was best known. The band left the stage to polite applause, the audience eager to hear the evening's main event.

Chet still had the utmost respect for Miles, and was taken aback when Miles walked straight past him, ignoring his outstretched hand. This marked the beginning of a pattern of behaviour between the two trumpet players that would continue throughout Chet's career; Chet admiring Miles, and craving his respect, and Miles ignoring him, criticising his abilities. Horace Silver behaved the same way, shunning both Carson Smith and Russ Freeman, barely exchanging a word with them.

By the time the Chet Baker Quartet took the stage, they all felt intimidated. Russ Freeman, the most experienced of the musicians, knew that he was no match for Horace Silver, whilst Bob Neel was being asked to play a more supporting roll, rather than drive the rhythm section; even if he had wanted to play in a more aggressive style, he knew he was outclassed by Kenny Clarke. "I started to feel inadequate back there," he later admitted. "I began to think that maybe we weren't the greatest jazz band in the world."

Even Chet was affected by the change in atmosphere. He tried to play with more aggression on the up-tempo numbers, but with his limited range, and lacking the support of a more dynamic rhythm section, it came across as half-hearted by comparison. His singing also sounded less assured, and whilst the audience was still behind him, he knew that his band was a pale shadow of the Miles Davis Quintet.

A young drummer called Ben Riley, who went on to play with Thelonious Monk in the mid-1960s, was in the audience that night, and witnessed the impact it had on Chet's playing. "Miles' band went on first; boy, that was a rough band to follow! But I noticed that in the second show, Chet was a little more forceful, a little more assertive, after listening to Miles. I thought, 'OK, he's got the message'."[29]

Miles Davis had also succeeded in winning over the critics with his performance. "Miles, largely through his own fault, has not yet fulfilled his early potential. He may now be on the way ahead again," wrote Nat Hentoff. "As the week ended and his embouchure strengthened, he was often the Miles of old in quality of conception with a new, drivingly emotional way of playing. On a ballad like 'It Never Entered My Mind', he cut Chet at his own specialty. For one thing, Miles' harmonic awareness, let alone his phrasing, is considerably keener. And on middle and up-tempo numbers, Miles, even when he occasionally fluffed, was a wholly alive, stimulating voice."[30]

Hentoff also highlighted the importance of the difference in rhythm sections. "In Chet's unit, drummer Bob Neel was just adequate," he wrote. "Bassist Carson Smith has a good tone, and is steady, and Russ Freeman, whilst no major jazz pianist yet, has individually intriguing conception at times. But as a section, Baker's rhythm entourage was static compared with the swinging, often elated, rapport amongst Percy Heath, Kenny Clarke and Horace Silver in Miles' outfit. And man for man, Miles' men were also superior. Even Freeman was pallid compared with Silver in terms of both ideas and beat, and Smith and Neel could take lessons from Heath and Clarke."

Chet himself came in for less criticism than his band, but was still considered inferior to Miles in terms of both execution and showmanship. "He is at least consistent on up-tempos and is best on ballads on which he usually creates an effective mood. But even on these he is not always able to sustain long tones, and in general, his execution is spotty." Hentoff also remarked on his apparent nerves, a factor that had not been apparent when he played opposite Dizzy Gillespie.

In many respects, the gig at Birdland marked a change in the relative fortunes of Miles Davis and Chet Baker. It heralded the triumphant return of Miles Davis, who hit his stride over the next two years, recording classic albums such as *Bags' Groove* and *Miles Davis and the Modern Jazz Giants*, before forming his classic quintet in 1955 with John Coltrane, Red Garland, Paul Chambers and 'Philly' Joe Jones. For the time being, Chet was still the public's favourite, but he started to lose favour with the jazz critics, who turned their attention to another rising star, the twenty-four-year-old Clifford Brown. In addition, Chet started to question his place at the top of the polls; he knew he was less gifted than Dizzy Gillespie and Clifford Brown, and craved the recognition of African–American musicians, some of whom—Miles Davis included—were dismissive of his talents.

If Chet was shaken by the encounter, and by Nat Hentoff's review, he didn't mention it to the band, or to Liliane. "Chet didn't talk; he didn't confide; he didn't reflect; he didn't discuss," she said. "I was the opposite."[31]

But Russ Freeman noticed the change in Chet's playing style after the gig. "For a while he got more into Miles' bag than his own," he noted. This can be heard on a number of Chet's subsequent recordings, including his blistering version of 'Night in Tunisia' on *The Tonight Show* in May 1955, and the early concert recordings from his subsequent European tour, where he openly admits to audiences that he was a big fan of Miles Davis, including a number of his songs in his repertoire.

It wasn't long before Charlaine discovered that Chet was seeing Liliane, catching them together in Chet's car outside the club between sets. She confronted Chet about his latest affair, and was shocked to discover that Chet was thinking of leaving her for Liliane. On hearing the news, she went back to the Bryant Hotel, picked up a handgun from her wardrobe, and returned to the club to confront the young French girl. "She wanted to kill me, because he was thinking of leaving her," said Liliane. "She threatened me with a gun on the steps of Birdland in front of Kenny Clarke. She asked me if I knew what a German Mauser was. I didn't take it very seriously." Liliane's cool response, and some calming words from Kenny Clarke, persuaded the tearful Charlaine to return to the Bryant Hotel. Next day, Chet bought her a one-way ticket back to LA, their stormy marriage finally at an end.

Chet went round to visit Liliane's uncle and aunt to introduce himself, and explain that he would like her to join him on tour. "My uncle couldn't believe it—this guy coming into his house saying that he was taking me!" she said. After completing the gig in New York, the Quartet headed for Atlantic City. Chet's legion of female admirers were glad to get the chance to see their hero in person, but disappointed to learn that he had a glamorous new French girlfriend. "I had this tight black dress that my mother had made me, and you could see my shoulders. I had come from St-Germain-des-Prés. My eyes were made up all around with black, I had no lipstick, and I wore no brassiere. The girls in the club were very interested, and used to follow me to the ladies room and ask me questions. Was I married to Chet? Why didn't I wear a brassiere? I was very surprised. I was very naïve, and surprised at the attitude of the American girls and the questions they were asking."

The other band members, and more importantly their partners, were also suspicious of Chet's new girlfriend. Her looks and make-up seemed foreign to them, and they found her difficult to talk to after the down-to-earth Charlaine, with few interests in common. "I liked Marian, Bob Neel's girlfriend," Liliane recalled. "She was warm, she was nice. But I don't think they really knew me at all. I found out later they called me 'Frou-frou', because I was a very inhibited young girl. I used to go to the ladies room all the time to see if I was looking alright. I was not very sure of myself. I was interested in music, I read books, I used to play chess."[32]

The next stop was St Louis, Missouri, where Joe Glaser had booked the Quartet to play for one week at a small club in East St Louis called the Glass Boy. "I remember we stayed in a big place, the Melbourne Hotel," said Liliane. "It was so hot, it was June; when you stepped out of the hotel air conditioning, it was like you got punched in the face." The week before Chet opened at the club, Max Roach had been playing there with Clifford Brown, and Chet got the opportunity to see what the fuss was about first-hand. "We went there to see their last night at the club," recalled Liliane. "And the air conditioning was broken, so I had water all over my body. We were the only white people in the club."

Liliane was naïve about racial segregation, which was still rife in St. Louis in the mid-1950s, and aroused considerable controversy when she invited African-American friends she had met in the jazz club back to the room she shared with Chet at the plush Melbourne Hotel.

The band moved on to Chicago next, where they played for three weeks at The Streamliner, starting on June 22nd. In mid-July, the road-weary band returned to California, where the tour came to an end, taking in such cities as San Jose (July 22nd), Santa Clara (July 23rd), Fresno (July 24th), Modesto (July 25th), eventually winding up in San Diego on July 28th. Thereafter they returned to Los Angeles, where Dick Bock had arranged a 'homecoming' gig, which consisted of a six-week stint at the Tiffany Club. Bock was on hand to record the quartet on August 10th; no live album was released at the time, but these recordings are now available as *Out Of Nowhere—Live Volume 2* and *My Old Flame—Live Volume 3*, which are a useful addition to the original *Jazz At Ann Arbor* release.

One week later—just one day after being released from prison for drug-related offences—Stan Getz joined the band for an informal blowing session at the club in the afternoon, with Shelly Manne replacing Bob Neel on drums. Neither Freeman nor Smith could remember the reason for Getz's presence, but it may well have been a rehearsal for a show at the LA Shrine three days later—a show which effectively marked Getz's 'comeback'. The fact that Dick Bock was present to record the session suggests that he still harboured hopes of bringing the two musicians together once Getz's contract with Norman Granz had elapsed. In the event, their only studio recording was an ill-fated session for Verve itself, recorded under Getz's leadership in 1958, and hampered by both musicians' growing addictions.

On 20th August, the Chet Baker Quartet appeared at the LA Shrine as part of a big jazz show, which also featured the Max Roach–Clifford Brown Quintet, Stan Getz and Cab Calloway. Stan Getz had yet to reassemble his band at this stage, and seems to have been backed by members of Chet's own quartet.

While the band was playing at the Tiffany Club, Chet stayed with his parents in their small house near Hermosa Beach. Chet's mother, Vera, was delighted to see her son, but was less than overjoyed to meet his new girlfriend. "When these people saw Chet coming in with me, rather than Charlene, who was a blonde Californian, they couldn't understand it," recalled Liliane. "This girl, coming from Paris, and the fact that I was Jewish. They never said anything, but they couldn't understand that I wasn't with Chet for his name or his money. I don't think they thought for a minute that I was genuine and sincere."[33]

Liliane found it difficult to relate to Chet's mother. She clearly doted on her son, but the young French girl had little in common with Vera, an unsophisticated woman from the heart of Oklahoma. She found it easier to talk with Chet's father, who was unemployed at this time. "He was more interested in music than she was, because she wasn't interested in music at all," she remembered. "I liked him a little more, because he was more into jazz." For the most part, she found it dull in California compared with life on the road. "I used to spend my time watching TV, and eating cookies, because

I didn't have much to do there. I lived there for two months until we went on the road again. Chet took me wherever he went, holding my hand, and I met all his friends, many of the Californian musicians."

In mid-September, Dick Bock suggested Chet return to the recording studio to make an album with a sextet. The front line consisted of Chet, Bud Shank on baritone saxophone and Bob Brookmeyer on trombone, supported by Russ Freeman on piano, Carson Smith on bass and Shelly Manne on drums. Bock invited a number of arrangers to contribute to the album, including Jack Montrose, Bill Holman and Johnny Mandel. As with the earlier *Ensemble* album, the playing is excellent, but the album as a whole is disjointed, and not really in keeping with the music Chet had been playing.

Bill Holman remembered the session, and expressed reservations about the manner in which such studio recordings were made. "Chet never saw the music before he showed up for the record date, so the music wasn't really a reflection of him," he said. "It was more of a reflection of the guys who wrote the music, with solos by Chet Baker. Everyone was responsible for the music, the writer, the arranger, as well as the soloist. A record producer would just call up an arranger and say we've got a record date with so many men. They were so fond of the word counterpoint after the Mulligan Quartet; that's when everyone learned the term. They'd say, 'Write some counter-pointal charts', because that's what 'West Coast' was starting to mean. You'd write the chart, bring it in, and that would be the first time anyone had seen it. Hopefully the artist would be able to read the changes, or hear them immediately, because the soloist never had the chance to get used to the music. That wasn't right."[34]

DownBeat magazine seemed to share these concerns, and described the album as "tightly constructed and thematically shallow."[35]

Their recording commitments completed, the band hit the road again in late September for a second nationwide tour, taking in Kansas City (late September), the Storyville club in Boston (mid–late October), Birdland in New York (late October to mid-November), the Comedy Club in Baltimore (late November), and the Blue Note in Philadelphia (early December), before returning to Birdland at the end of the year. It soon became clear that it would be hard to recreate the carefree atmosphere of the first tour. The stresses and strains of living out of a suitcase began to take its toll on the various band members.

Some of the problems stemmed from Chet's irresponsible attitude towards money. The story that perhaps best epitomises Chet's behaviour occurred in late 1954. Russ Freeman had been organising the weekly paychecks for the band, and had carefully put aside money that Chet owed the tax authorities into a separate account. When the tax payments were due, he transferred the funds, which amounted to approximately $3,500, into Chet's bank account. Although this money was needed to pay taxes on behalf of the band, Chet did not give this a moment's thought. Instead he flew to Detroit, and bought a brand-new racing-green Jaguar. He was a "naughty boy", Freeman later recalled, suggesting a mixture of fondness and frustration over the memories.

But Chet's immaturity also manifested itself in other, less amusing ways. When he left Hermosa Beach to go on the second tour, he took his dog, which had been looked after by his parents. He insisted to Russ Freeman that he would be able to take care of the dog on the road, despite the band's hectic schedule. When the dog proved to be too much of a burden, he simply left the dog in one particular town, his cruelty disgusting the pianist.

Chet's girlfriend, Liliane, was also the cause of friction amongst the young musicians and their partners. She clashed badly with Russ Freeman's new girlfriend. Freeman also found her behaviour divisive. "Chet at that time had a relationship with this French girl who tried to insulate him from the other band members," he said. "She pulled us to pieces."[36]

If the other band members had a problem with Liliane's behaviour, they don't appear to have raised it with Chet. "I was not really aware of what the other members of the band thought about me," she said. "Chet didn't speak much; he was a man that didn't explain. He never tried to understand, or to discuss. Who knows what he thought?"

Carson Smith's wife, Joan, also found out she was pregnant at this time, and returned to Los Angeles. After a few weeks, Carson felt lonely and was longing to join her.

Drugs were also a factor in the disintegration of the band. Russ Freeman, a former addict himself, discovered that Chet was chippying and tried to warn him of the dangers of addiction. "It started at the end of 1954, at the time we had the quartet together," he recalled. "Chet was incredibly popular already, and played well—I don't understand why he was so irrational. It had nothing to do with stage fright or anything like that. In that respect, he never had to worry. He started to use right around the time everybody else was stopping. Drugs were going out of fashion ... Chet was also the only guy who continued so long, while other junkies either quit or died. In the 40s and 50s, an awful lot of musicians died because of drugs. Art Pepper was the only other exception; he was addicted a very long time. He finally did manage to quit—but then he died as a result."[37]

Today, Liliane denies being aware that Chet was experimenting with heroin at this time. "When I lived with Chet, I never saw him touch anything at all," she insisted. "Chet drank milk, didn't smoke cigarettes, didn't drink alcohol. He did smoke pot from morning until evening, in large quantities. He always smoked good pot. He had this guy in Los Angeles that would supply him with Mexican pot. I was smoking pot before I met Chet. It's not like Chet took me into this kind of life; that was my kind of life."

If anything, she claims, she was the one who was taking heroin on an occasional basis. "The one who messed around a little bit was me; I was the one who touched it once in a while, but Chet never did. My use of drugs was periodic. It was not sufficiently present in our lives for us to ever argue about it."

Bass player Carson Smith would appear to support her on this point, telling James Gavin, "I was fooling around with heroin a little bit, and I could never get Chet to come near me then. He told me he was deathly afraid of needles and didn't see any reason to get on that shit."

Despite Liliane's vehement denial, there's plenty of evidence to suggest that Chet's use of heroin was increasing at this time. Firstly, we know that Chet had experimented with heroin in the past, despite his apparent fear of needles. His predilection for pot also suggests an addictive personality. Secondly, Russ Freeman, as a former addict, would have known the telltale signs. Thirdly, as the quartet began to disintegrate, the original band members were replaced by musicians with drug problems; saxophonist Phil Urso joined the band, Al Haig replaced Russ Freeman on piano, Peter Littman replaced Bob Neel on drums, and Chet's old friend, Bob Whitlock, rejoined the band to play bass—all four of them heroin addicts. Certainly by the time Paul Bley came on board for a gig in Los Angeles in February, he distinctly remembered the whole band being addicted.

Whether or not Chet was truly addicted at this time is open to debate. A number of musicians who played with him in 1955 were not aware of his heroin use, so it would appear that his drug use was, at the very least, under control. The real problems started in 1956, after his return from Europe, when his drug use started to escalate.

So why would Liliane deny that Chet was experimenting with heroin? It could be that Chet only took drugs with other musicians, and tried to keep her from knowing the truth. This seems unlikely, however, given that she was quite open about her own use of drugs, and given that she lived with him at this time. A more likely explanation, perhaps, is that she has become fed up with being blamed for Chet's addiction, particularly in the light of the events that would take place on his subsequent tour of Europe.

The return visit to Birdland at the end of 1954 should have been the highlight of the tour. The quartet was at the height of its popularity; the *DownBeat* readers' poll, published in late December, showed Chet Baker was still the nation's favourite trumpet player with 882 votes, ahead of Dizzy Gillespie (661), Harry James (449) and Roy Eldridge (417). If Miles Davis was starting to win over the critics, he hadn't yet won over the public at this stage; he ranked ninth, just below another West Coast favourite, Conte Candoli. Chet even ranked seventh in the male singer category, far below poll winner Frank Sinatra, but only fractionally below Louis Armstrong. Despite these positive signs, the band was being torn apart by the constant bickering, and New York marked the beginning of the end of the quartet.

Charlie Parker heard that Chet was in town, and used to stop by the club, at least until the manager got wise. Thereafter he began to show up at the Bryant Hotel on a regular basis, asking Chet if he could sleep on the couch. His condition had deteriorated significantly since the band's visit in May, several months earlier. In late September, he had voluntarily committed himself to the psychiatric ward at Bellevue Hospital, telling the admitting physician that he was severely depressed, and feared for his own safety. He was diagnosed as suffering from 'acute alcoholism and undifferentiated schizophrenia'. He had never fully recovered from the death of his daughter earlier that year, and was also disturbed by memories of his father's funeral. His heavy drinking also culminated in regular threats being made to his wife and children.

After his release, he struggled to get bookings in New York, and resorted to hocking his saxophone on a regular basis to fund his drug habit. Around Christmas time he was seen playing in a small cellar cabaret, Le Club Downbeat. "Charlie was shabbily dressed in a suit I remembered from earlier years. The suit had not been to a cleaner in weeks. Dirt creases showed on the cuffs and collar of a rumpled white shirt. Charlie was wearing carpet slippers. His face was bloated, and his eyelids so heavy that only half the pupils showed … when Charlie got round to playing it was evident that he was having trouble getting air through the horn. The saxophone tone, normally so clear and brilliant, had flabby spots."[38]

Chet and Liliane tried their best to help the ailing saxophonist. "He was sick, and had few places to go," Liliane said. She cooked meals for him, and listened in fascination as he told stories from his prime, and talked about the great musicians he had played with. One morning they were shocked to wake up and find he had already left the hotel, taking the cash from Chet's trouser pocket. Chet refused to confront him over this, and wasn't going to begrudge him a few dollars after all the help he'd given him in the early days.

Less than three months later, on 12th March 1955, the legendary saxophonist passed away. The official cause of death was given as 'lobar pneumonia', the coroner working on the assumption that he was in his mid-late fifties. He was just thirty-four years old.

The Birdland show also marked the beginning of Chet's relationship with saxophonist Phil Urso, a musical partnership that lasted on-and-off for the remainder of Chet's life. Urso had worked with a number of small group leaders in the early 1950s, including Jimmy Dorsey, Miles Davis, and Oscar Pettiford, and had just formed his own quartet, which played at Birdland on Monday evenings. One night, Urso stopped by the club and found an old friend, Gerry Mulligan, deep in conversation with Chet Baker. "I said, 'Gerry, please introduce me to Chet'. He said, 'Chet, this is a very good friend of mine, Phil Urso'. I said, 'I've been trying to meet you for a long time and play with you'. He said, 'Well, you got your horn?' I said, 'Yeah, it's over there in the booth'. He said, 'Well, come on up in the next set'. I got my horn, played 'Stella by Starlight', 'Have You Met Miss Jones?'—you know, standards. Chet liked the way I played."[39]

The twenty-nine-year-old Italian-American saxophonist had been on the scene for some time; born in Jersey City, he had grown up in Denver, Colorado, studying both clarinet and tenor saxophone. He came to New York in 1947, getting his first break with Elliot Lawrence the following year. It was there he met both Gerry Mulligan and Al Cohn. "Al Cohn's clarinet was not worth a dime," he laughed, "so when it came time for him to play a clarinet part, I just handed him my clarinet, and I played his clarinet part on my tenor. We became fast friends, and shared a room."

Al Cohn later introduced Phil to Woody Herman. "'Phil', he said, 'I want to stay in town, I'm going to leave Woody. Would you like to join the Woody Herman band and take my place?' 'I'd like that very much', I said. 'I've been dreaming of playing with Woody for years'. He arranged an audition. The band boy comes over to the Paramount and says, 'I need Phil Urso, I have to talk to him. Phil—you're wanted for an audition with Woody Herman over at the Capitol Theatre'. 'What time?' 'Three o'clock'. So I looked at my schedule and it was OK because I could get through the show at two. So I went down to the Capitol Theatre downstairs and sat in Al Cohn's chair. I read his part. He'd just got through writing a brand new chart for 'Music to Dance To'. I had to read that all the way through, and I passed the test. Woody's manager said, 'How much are you making with Elliot Lawrence?' I says, 'I'm on $120'. He said, 'Well this band pays $135. You're earning $135—Woody told me to hire you'. I spent around fifteen months with him. I left at the Palladium, and I flew back to New York."[40]

After that set, Chet invited Phil Urso back to the Bryant Hotel. They met Liliane in the lobby of the hotel, and went up to the room together. Chet selected a recording of 'Daphnis et Chloe', conducted by Toscanini, and put it on the record player in the hotel room—a sign of the effect Liliane was having on his musical taste. "I told Chet it was the most beautiful music that Ravel ever wrote, and he agreed," recalled Urso. "Then I pulled out my latest release I did for Savoy with Horace Silver and Brookmeyer. He said to let him keep it to listen to it and give it back next night because we had to get back to Birdland for our next set together."[41]

A couple of nights later, Phil Urso remembers Chet Baker and Russ Freeman had a big argument in the lobby of the Bryant Hotel. "Russ Freeman's lady friend didn't like Chet's lady friend, so Chet had to defend his lady friend, and Russ defend his. So eventually Chet says, 'You're fired'."

The band played out the rest of the evening as a pianoless quartet, with Phil Urso on tenor. Next day, Chet again invited him back to the Bryant. According to the saxophonist, he offered him a job on the spot:

"Well, how'd you like to come on the band?"

"Well, I'm doing OK, but I'd like to go on the road. How much does it pay?"

"I'll give you $175, and then we can go from there. Can you write some arrangements?"

"Sure I can."

"Every time you write a new arrangement, I'll give you some extra money."

"So when do we leave town?"

"As soon as we get through Birdland, which is next week."[42]

Back at Birdland, Miles Davis dropped in one night to catch his rival. As ever, Chet was keen to impress. "He was trying to be nice to Miles," recalled Phil Urso. "He copied a couple of things that Miles did, little improvisations, little clichés that Miles did. I'm not sure that Miles liked that." Later that evening Miles made sure that Chet knew exactly how he felt. "Chet was sitting at the table with some friends," said the saxophonist, "and Miles walked up and said, 'You suck!' And then he walked away. I wonder why he did that? Chet played awful good. He was one of the best trumpet players I ever heard, and I heard them all."[43]

Miles was probably just venting steam over the recent *DownBeat* poll, in all likelihood. Nevertheless, the fact that he heard Chet 'stealing' some of his phrases simply confirmed the impression he had already formed—Chet was copying his style, and was getting more recognition than he deserved.

Before they finished at Birdland, Joe Glaser booked the band to play on the prestigious *Tonight Show*, hosted by Steve Allen. Phil Urso asked Chet if he knew of any pianists who could fill in for Russ Freeman at such short notice. "He said, 'Al Haig's in town, let's try and find him'. I went down, and in the lobby I ran into Art Moneghan, and I said, 'Is Al Haig in town, Art?' He said, 'Yeah, I got his number, do you want it?' I called, and his lady friend answered the phone. She got him, and I said, 'Al, we need a piano player for tonight'. He says, 'Well, I don't have a white shirt. I don't have a tie'. I said, 'I've got a white shirt, what are you, 17, 18" neck, whatever'. I fixed him up with a tie, and he had a blue coat. We were all wearing blue coats."[44]

Al Haig was a wonderful pianist, but he was never going to provide the steadying hand that Russ Freeman had offered, and Chet required. Fellow pianist Paul Bley remembers coming across Al Haig at this time. "It was five in the morning in New York, and the window opens of a parked car. Al was inside, and said, 'Paul, how are you doing?' I said, 'Al, what are you doing up here?' On the back seat was his son, who was no more than four of five years old. I looked in the window and said, 'Shouldn't your son be in bed?' The son had rings under his eyes, if you can believe that—they were just living in the car."[45]

Interviewed by Steve Allen on the show, Chet revealed that he had lost ten pounds in weight during the preceding four months, logging over twenty thousand miles as the band toured the country. When asked about other trumpet players on the scene, Chet revealed that even if the East–West Coast divide concerned Miles, it meant little to him.

"You have a very pleasant sound," said Steve Allen. "I think you get a lot of educated people interested in jazz because you make a very pleasant noise. Let's take Dizzy Gillespie. He plays fantastic. But I have noticed that even people who know nothing about jazz can appreciate your sound, you know, they understand what the sounds mean. Dizzy has a … sharp, shrill sound. Does this disturb you, artistically, or is it alright for him?"

"Not in the least," replied Chet. "Dizzy is a big favourite of mine. Miles also."

In early January, the new Quintet set off for a gig at Baker's Keyboard Lounge in Detroit, with Phil Urso, Al Haig and his girlfriend all cramming into the car with Chet and Liliane. "The piano was in mint condition," remembered Urso, "and Haig, Smith and Neel played trio numbers, then Chet and I came on and we had a quintet of very good players, to say the least. Al Haig played super."[46]

Chet was also on fine form, according to Urso, his speed quite dazzling at times. "Chet played very melodic and very soft, he didn't try to hit too many high notes. He could get a high B out, a high C, but he wouldn't go over that. One night he did Cherokee, and it was so fast, it was unbelievable. I thought, 'There's no way I can follow that', so I handed over to Al Haig!"[47]

Midway through the Detroit gig, bass player Carson Smith handed in his notice, keen to rejoin his pregnant wife in Los Angeles. Chet placed a call to his old friend Bob Whitlock; they had fallen out when Bob slept with Chet's wife, Charlaine, but now that Chet had left his wife, he was prepared to forgive and forget. "I remember Chet called me from Detroit and said, 'Can you hop a plane and get out here? I want you to do this tour back East'," recalled Whitlock. "When he called me, I've never been so happy in my life. Not only did I want to play with him, I thought I'd lost him as a friend. I got on the first plane. Nothing was ever said, and Chet and I got very close again. We were friends for years and years."[48]

But as Bob Whitlock discovered, the atmosphere within the band was quite different to the carefree early days of the Mulligan Quartet, tainted by the same issues that caused Russ Freeman to leave the band just one month earlier. "The atmosphere in the band was kind of weird," he said. "The musicians would have been fine, left to their own devices; everyone was happy with everyone else. But the women in the band were causing more dissension than you could imagine. Now that might sound crazy, but that's a fact. There was this girl Alice that Al Haig went with, and neither Al nor Alice could tolerate Chet's girlfriend, Liliane."[49]

Pretty soon, Bob Whitlock also fell out with Liliane. Chet had invited him up to their hotel room, but when he opened the door, the young French girl was stark naked. "As we walked in, she grabbed her clothes, pulled them on, and then went off at me for walking in on her," he said. "I didn't even know she was in there. I wasn't ready for that, so I went off on her with all the venom I could scrape up. After that, I was strictly in Al Haig's camp! So there was all that going on."

Drugs were also a growing problem within the band, with Bob Whitlock, Phil Urso and Al Haig all addicted to heroin. "Every town we'd go to there was this big scene trying to score," recalled Bob Whitlock. "Every day we'd be giving someone our money, even to other musicians. I remember giving some money to 'Tootie' Heath, Percy Heath's brother, and he never came back." Whitlock also remembers Chet using occasionally, but not yet strung out. "I'm not saying he didn't touch anything—he used to snort a bit of coke or a bit of heroin from time to time, but he was not a junkie, believe me."[50]

Despite these problems, the musicians were usually able to get their act together on the stage, even without the steadying influence of Russ Freeman. "Some nights on the bandstand were just glorious—some of the best nights I can remember," said the bass player. "Al Haig was one of my favourite pianists, along with Bill Evans and Bud Powell. He played some outrageously beautiful things."

Unfortunately, this line-up of the Quintet didn't stay stable for long. Bob Neel was the first to quit; both he and his new wife, Marion, were former users, and found it difficult to be around so many addicts. The drummer handed in his notice, and returned to California. Chet invited Peter Littman, a young drummer he had met at a venue called The Stables in Boston, to replace him. "Chet was very enthusiastic about his playing," recalled Bob Whitlock. His hard-hitting, hard-bop style suggested that Chet was looking for a different sound, the influence of the Miles Davis Quintet becoming more apparent.

Others were more concerned about the turn of events. Dick Bock noticed that his protégé was struggling to hold a band together in the absence of Russ Freeman. Freeman himself noted that the band had now filled up with heroin addicts. He voiced particular concern over Peter Littman. "This guy was an asshole, addict or not."[51]

Next to go was Al Haig, who was fired en route from Cleveland, where the band had played at the Loop Lounge, to Detroit, where the band was scheduled to play at the Rouge Lounge. "Imagine how stunned and appalled I was to hear that Chet had just fired Al," recalled Bob Whitlock. "How could this be? Aside from being a highly admired and valued friend, Al was one of my all-time favorite pianists. We had known each other for only a couple of years, but I had been in awe of him ever since first hearing recordings of him in the mid-forties when he graced the groups of such giants as Bird, Dizzy, Stan Getz, among many others. And since joining Chet's group, we had spent long hours together most every day, around the clock. And here Chet was suddenly leaving Al high and dry, a stone's throw from the Canadian border, in a brutally cold winter, hooked to the gills—all over some petty nonsense with Liliane Cukier. It had nothing whatsoever to do with music! I remember musing to myself that anyone who ever heard Chet and Al play together would never forget the experience!" Bob Whitlock and Phil Urso, both addicts themselves, gathered together their few remaining dollars to give to Al Haig, whilst Bob also handed him his brand new wool overcoat, knowing that he would soon be returning to the West Coast.[52]

Chet and Bob took turns driving Chet's new Jaguar back to Los Angeles, where the Quintet was booked to play for three weeks at Jazz City. "We were spelling each other off at the wheel every few hundred miles, when I fell asleep at the wheel near the New Mexico/Arizona border," said the bass player. "I awoke with the car wildly careening all over the narrow highway as I struggled, frantically over-steering, for nearly a mile before I was able to bring it under control. When we finally came to a complete stop, Chet and I just sat there petrified, and stared at each other for what seemed an eternity, just glad to be alive, but too shaken to utter a sound. Needless to say, we had no problem reaching silent accord that a brief nap might be in order."

Chet had struggled to find a replacement pianist for the gig, and was eventually called by Canadian-born pianist Paul Bley, who offered his services. Bley was grounded in the East Coast jazz scene, having relocated to New York in 1950 to study at the Juilliard School of Music. While studying at Juilliard, he formed a band with saxophonist Jackie McLean and trumpeter Donald Byrd; he also had the opportunity to play with Charlie Parker at this time. He recorded his debut album in November 1953, backed by the prestigious support of Charlie Mingus on bass and Art Blakey on drums.

As a result, Bley had his doubts about taking a gig on the West Coast, but soon found that his reservations were unfounded. "I know the West Coast has a bad rap, at least it did at the time, because some of the players went to the studio and sort of betrayed their jazz beginnings by succumbing to the lure of very dull studio work—which any musician could have done," he said. "But in fact, having come from New York, playing with Bird and everybody, they were really good players. Peter Littman was a fantastic drummer, and I was collecting drummers at the time—Art Blakey, and so forth. They were burning; there was no such thing as super-relaxed stuff—the 'relaxed' tag came as a result of Chet's singing. In any case, Chet was really playing well, and the band played very hard bop."[53]

The pianist soon realised that most of the band were using, but having experienced similar issues on the East Coast, he was not particularly fazed. "The whole band was addicted; I'm surprised I wasn't," he remarked. "It wasn't new for me to be in a band full of people who were on. Having been sent down to New York to bring back Charlie Parker for a television show and a recording—*Bird on the Road*—I knew what I was dealing with."

Between sets, Chet gave Paul Bley a guided tour of the city, showing him the sights and testing his nerve. "We went for a ride in his convertible in a break at Jazz City. The thing that amazed me is that he never drove on the streets. He drove on the sidewalks, in the alleys, but he never went through the streets—so he never had a traffic problem," he laughed. "He could check out how much of a man you were by how fast he could go and seeing if you were still cool. If you put your hands up to your forehead and started screaming, you were chicken!"[54]

The quintet effectively disbanded after the gig at Jazz City. Bob Whitlock found it hard to cope with his addiction, and the stresses and strains of being on the road. "We'd be sick, and have to go onstage," he recalled. "It got to the stage where I couldn't wait to go home." He was also disappointed by Al Haig's departure, having enjoyed a close musical relationship with the troubled pianist. "That was the straw that broke the camel's back."[55]

Bob Whitlock decided to start his band with a view to saving enough money to go back to college, and formed a quintet featuring Zoot Sims, Jack Sheldon, Larry Bunker and Triggs Morgan. They were offered a gig at a small club called the Red Mill down at Long Beach. Whitlock found his former employer extremely supportive of the new band. "Chet took me completely by surprise by dropping in throughout the first two weekends as guest soloist, gratis, providing vital impetus for our early success. That is the kind of friend Chet was—totally unpredictable! For this gesture alone, I will be continually in his debt."[56]

The band stayed on at the Red Mill for several months. "When Zoot was out of town, as he frequently was, I would occasionally invite other guests, but more often, we found it more comfortable and rewarding to play as a quartet," said Whitlock. "I deeply regret that the band was never recorded." The band allowed him to save a little money, after which he left the jazz scene for a number of years, pursuing a career in academia. He studied for two years at the Brigham Young University in Provo, Utah, before being accepted into the Graduate School at UCLA. He spent three years at UCLA, working as a teaching assistant, while completing a Master's thesis on Webern's early instrumental music. His thesis won him a grant to study in Paris for one year, but his studies were interrupted by jazz, and a renewed addiction to heroin. By the time he renewed his acquaintance with Chet in the late 1960s, the two of them were full-blown addicts. "By then the music was just another means to earn money," he said. "I never thought we'd see that day when we were youngsters."

Saxophonist Phil Urso returned to New York, and Paul Bley also split. He had travelled to Los Angeles with the drummer Al Levitt, who had appeared on his second album *Paul Bley*, which had been recorded for EmArcy. "Charlie Mariano invited the two of us to go on tour with him," recalled Bley, "and so we drove to Palm Springs together."[57]

With Chet back in Los Angeles, Dick Bock was keen to record a follow-up to *Chet Baker Sings*, which had been a big hit for Pacific Jazz. Bock's market research had revealed that Chet had a large number of female fans who wanted to hear him sing, rather than play more jazz-oriented material. He suggested that the trumpet player should reunite with Russ Freeman for the next recording. Chet was able to patch up his differences with the pianist, and Carson Smith and Bob Neel returned to the fold, presumably hoping that Freeman would exert a degree of stability.

The new album, *Chet Baker Sings and Plays*, was recorded at two different sessions; the first, in late February, included Bud Shank on flute and Red Mitchell standing in for Carson Smith, and featured a string section, whilst the second session featured the regular quartet. One year after his first full vocal album, Chet's singing sounds more confident, his enunciation is still a little nasal, but far clearer. Highlights include a gorgeous reading of

Gershwin's 'Someone to Watch Over Me', with Chet sounding every inch the 'little lamb that's lost in the woods', and a dreamy vocal on 'This is Always'. The album also features Chet's only known recording of 'Let's Get Lost', the title track of the Bruce Weber movie.

Dick Bock asked photographer William Claxton to design the cover, which resembled a teenage girl's scrapbook, featuring photographs of Chet, one with Liliane, a single rose, a scrawled heart with the initials 'C.B.', a cartoon cupid and a photograph of young couple walking side-by-side along the beach.

Given the target audience, it is perhaps not surprising to find that the album received a mixed review from the jazz critics on its release. *DownBeat* magazine awarded the album "barely" three stars. "Chet doesn't have the equipment to essay [sic] a project of this size," noted Jack Tracy. "Saving grace is his sense of phrasing, almost always present in an instrumentalist who sings … "[58] The review in *Metronome* was no better, Bill Coss criticising Chet's "anemic singing", "weird phrasing" and "uneasy intonation".[59]

The jazz critics may have moved on to the next big thing, just as they did with the Mulligan Quartet some two years earlier, but Chet was still at the height of his popularity with the general public. The album sold well, and given Chet's film star looks, and growing audience of female admirers, it seemed inevitable that Hollywood would approach him to star in a movie.

"Chet Baker Signed For Important Role In Movie", read the headline in *DownBeat* magazine. "Tom Gries, director of *Hell's Horizon*, said the decision to use Baker was made after hearing his Columbia LP with strings and his more recent vocal work on Pacific Jazz. 'Of course, we gave him a screen test,' said Gries, 'And now we think we might have a very promising young actor'."[60]

Chet signed a contract with Gravis Productions, a subsidiary of Columbia Pictures, and filming took place over two weeks, starting March 7th. *Hell's Horizon* was set in the Korean War, and starred John Ireland as the commanding officer of a small team of men assigned to bomb a Communist-controlled bridge over the Yalu River. Chet played 'Jockey', an introverted, trumpet-playing gunner, a role which obviously required limited acting ability. "Without that horn he's stuck for an answer when you say hello," complained one of his roommates in the movie.

Poster for the 1955 movie Hell's Horizon*, which introduced 'Chet Baker and His Trumpet'.*

The plane sets off from Okinawa, but the mission is marred by poor weather and a fuel shortage, and although they bomb the bridge, they are attacked on their return journey, and forced to crash land. Jockey's corpse is eventually dragged from the burning plane by John Ireland, his trumpet laid to rest on his chest.

Whilst the role of Jockey was undemanding, the studio was sufficiently impressed by Chet's performance and presence that he was offered a seven-year contract by Columbia. Without hesitation, Chet turned down the offer. "I didn't like standing around for hours all day to shoot a few minutes of film," he reasoned. "All I want to do is play—that's all." The movie sank without trace at the box office, overshadowed by two big name war movies—*Strategic Air Command*, which starred James Stewart and June Allyson, and *The Bridges At Toko-Ri*, which boasted William Holden and Grace Kelly.

In retrospect it seems a shame that Chet was not given acting lessons by Columbia, or allowed to cut his teeth in a meatier role; after all, James Dean emerged at this time as a brooding teenage rebel, shooting *East of Eden* just as Chet was filming *Hell's Horizon*. James Dean resembled Chet in many respects—his photogenic good looks, his brooding presence, his iconic West Coast cool. But Chet had no interest in a movie career, just as he had no career path planned in the music industry, the perennial outsider.

In the end, it was their shared love of racing cars that brought a premature end to the career of James Dean, who crashed his Porsche Spyder in California on the afternoon of September 30th 1955. His death, aged just twenty-four, ensured that Chet would occasionally be referred to as the 'James Dean of jazz', not vice versa.

In mid-March, Chet Baker was invited to join a tour featuring the Dave Brubeck Quartet, singer Carmen McRae and Gerry Mulligan. Gerry Mulligan had disbanded his quartet with trumpeter Jon Eardley at this point, and was taking a 'sabbatical' to work on new compositions. As a consequence, he was short of work, and found himself in the embarrassing position of having to play with the band of his former sideman. Bob Neel and Carson Smith refused to go on tour, and to Russ Freeman's disgust, Peter Littman was invited to rejoin the band on drums, with Jack Lawler filling in on bass.

The tour opened at Carnegie Hall on March 12th, with Phil Urso reuniting with Chet for the occasion. Despite Chet's attempts to produce a more convincing East Coast sound, *Metronome* magazine was not impressed, referring to the "watered-down Miles and Zoot sounds from Chet and tenor Phil Urso." *Jazz Journal*, an English periodical, gave the band a more favourable review, however, with Douglas Hague suggesting that "Chet is above Miles in execution and taste," and that he had "never heard the beautiful work shown by Chet on slow numbers exhibited by Davis."[61]

After the Carnegie Hall show, Chet flew back to Los Angeles to complete the filming of *Hell's Horizon*, leaving Liliane and the band in New York. Shooting may have finished earlier than expected, so Chet had a few days to kill before he rejoined the tour. He evidently decided to join percussionist Bill Loughborough and his friends in Sausalito, just outside San Francisco. Loughborough lived on a barge that he shared with jazz guitarist David Wheat and a poet by the name of Gerd Stern. Another regular visitor to the commune was Marguerite Angelou, later known as Maya, who was then working as a singer and dancer in the local clubs. Their own thing included a steady supply of marijuana, some of which Loughborough baked into 'hash' brownies. Angelou later credited Chet with helping her to quit marijuana after a scary high speed drive home one night.

The hippy lifestyle came to an abrupt end when Chet had to return to New York. Loughborough remembers loading his 'boobams' (hand-made drums) into the back of Chet's Jaguar and racing to New York, where they picked up Liliane. From there they drove to Boston, with Liliane stretched out on the narrow ledge behind them, where they met with other members of the band.

The band reunited at the Celebrity Club in Providence, Rhode Island, where Bill Loughborough joined the quartet on percussion. Bill stayed for the next few weeks as the band's tour criss-crossed the country, including gigs in Toronto (18th–23rd April), Cincinnati, Houston and a benefit concert at the County Centre in White Plains on 28th April, a concert that also featured Lionel Hampton—who even played Loughborough's 'boobams'—and Errol Garner.

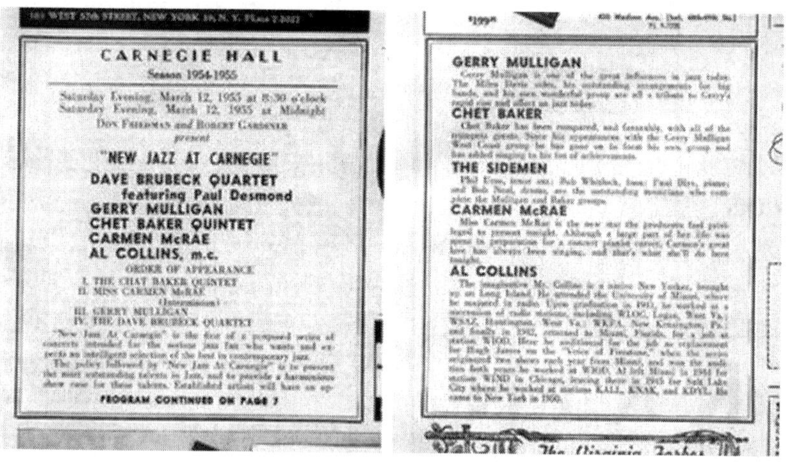

CARNEGIE HALL
Season 1954-1955

Saturday Evening, March 12, 1955 at 8:30 o'clock
Saturday Evening, March 12, 1955 at Midnight

present

"NEW JAZZ AT CARNEGIE"

DAVE BRUBECK QUARTET
featuring Paul Desmond
GERRY MULLIGAN
CHET BAKER QUINTET
CARMEN McRAE
AL COLLINS, m.c.

ORDER OF APPEARANCE
I. THE CHET BAKER QUINTET
II. MISS CARMEN McRAE
(Intermission)
III. GERRY MULLIGAN
IV. THE DAVE BRUBECK QUARTET

PROGRAM CONTINUED ON PAGE 7

GERRY MULLIGAN

CHET BAKER

THE SIDEMEN

CARMEN McRAE

AL COLLINS

Advertisement for the show at Carnegie Hall, March 1955. The line-up of the quartet had changed completely by the time the band reached New York.

In early May, the band—effectively a quintet with Bill Loughborough on board—embarked on a short tour of US colleges, supported by Gerry Mulligan. The band returned to New York in mid-May, where they were scheduled to play *The Tonight Show* on May 12th. That night, Chet tore through Dizzy Gillespie's 'Night In Tunisia', clearly out to prove a point to the critics who had dared to suggest he was a 'watered down' version of

Miles. "Chet was out to kick some ass," confirmed his former bass player Carson Smith. "He knew how many of those New York guys hated him. He was burning." His performance certainly made an impression on drummer Art Blakey, who visited Chet a few days later at the Bryant Hotel. "I didn't know this motherfucker could play like that," he admitted.

Chet may have won over some of the New York musicians, but a number of jazz critics were still looking to knock him off his perch. In late May, Chet played a two-week stint at Basin Street, again supported by Gerry Mulligan. On this occasion, Mulligan brought his own band—a short-lived line-up featuring his old friend Gil Evans on piano. Bill Coss of *Metronome*, who had earlier savaged the *Chet Baker Plays and Sings* album, was not impressed, and described Chet's appearance at Basin Street as disastrous. "His trumpet was weak, his singing almost insipid," he wrote.[62]

Chet must have wondered what he needed to appease the critics. Two years earlier, he had been labelled one of the "great modern horn stars". His band had lacked stability since Russ Freeman's initial departure, but the addition of Peter Littman had added a certain amount of steel to the rhythm section that had been lacking when he'd played opposite Miles Davis at Birdland. Chet's own playing was also stronger, as the performance on *The Tonight Show* clearly demonstrated.

Around this time, Liliane had a problem renewing her United States visa. She had arrived in New York in May 1954, and had initially been given a six-month visa. "After six months, I went to the immigration department to get an extension," she recalled. "Chet used to introduce me as Mrs. Baker, making out that we were married. Six months later, I approached a different guy at the immigration office, not the man I usually dealt with. When my application was denied, the original immigration officer came up to me and said, "Why didn't you come to me? You're a little Jewish girl, and I would have given it to you."[63]

They could have overcome this problem if they had chosen to get married. "But Charlaine wouldn't grant him a divorce without large alimony, California-style," Liliane explained. Chet tried to help her get a visa extension, and even wrote a contract for his girlfriend, employing her as a 'singer' for $52 a week. When this ploy failed, he asked his manager, Joe Glaser, if he had any suggestions. Glaser suggested that Chet consider a tour of Europe. He had recently arranged a successful tour for Billie Holiday, and had good contacts in Europe, including Jeffrey Kruger, owner of the prestigious Flamingo Jazz Club in London. Chet reluctantly agreed, although he had little interest in European culture.

The following month, the Chet Baker Quartet played at the second annual Newport Jazz Festival on Rhode Island, with Bob Carter replacing Jack Lawler, and Gerry Mulligan again appearing as a guest artist on 'Five Brothers'. "It was a pain in the ass—bad sound, screaming mobs, too many musicians milling around," recalled pianist Russ Freeman. "It wasn't a place for creating good music, most festivals aren't." In addition to his own set, Chet joined Clifford Brown and Gerry Mulligan onstage with the Dave Brubeck Quartet. On paper, it sounded like a dream line-up, but onstage it sounded like a mess, the musicians struggling to make themselves heard.[64]

Reviews of the band's performance by the jazz critics were mixed, but the quartet was a hit with the audience. "Chet Baker and his quartet were the surprising hit of the second annual Newport Jazz Festival," claimed the *Providence Sunday Journal*, "where traditionalists outnumbered modernists until Mr Baker came on the scene."

Whilst the line-up probably varied, the quartet is thought to have played a number of gigs over the summer, including a gig at the Blue Note in Chicago in early August. It was here that Russ Freeman informed Chet of his decision to quit the band, rather than join the tour of Europe, which was scheduled to start in September. "There were several reasons for it," he told Dutch author Jeroen de Valk. "Chet was addicted, his drummer was addicted, and there is always a division between musicians who are clean and those who are using. Addicts hang with other addicts. Our old friendship no longer existed. I finally had enough of bearing all the responsibility. Chet was the leader officially, but in practical terms I had to take care of everything. I (also) had constant headaches, a kind of migraine."

It is debatable as to whether Chet was a full-blown junkie at this stage, but he was certainly using on a more regular basis. Bob Freedman, who had known Chet since his Army days, remembers meeting him in Boston when he was on the tour with Gerry Mulligan in the spring of 1955. "Gerry wants me to get him some drugs," Chet whispered. "Do you know anybody?" Freedman knew that Gerry was clean, and was shocked by the change that had taken place in his old friend. "This was no longer Chettie—this was now Chet Baker," he said. "He was tougher-looking, with that paranoia that goes along with trying to do a drug deal, and knowing that if you got busted, you'd go to jail, so you don't trust anybody."[65]

Russ Freeman suggested that Chet hire a young pianist by the name of Dick Twardzik as his replacement. He was a close friend of the drummer Peter Littman, and had created a strong impression when they met in Boston the previous year. Freeman was impressed by the young pianist's unique style, which was influenced by classical music, as well as by bebop pianists such as Bud Powell. He also admired his skills as a composer, having worked with him on a solo recording in October 1954. Freeman was convinced that he would be an ideal foil for Chet, approaching harmony from a less intuitive, more intellectual perspective, and pushing the young trumpet star outside of his comfort zone.

But Twardzik was also fighting his own demons, having struggled to overcome an addiction to heroin. Had Freeman have been aware of this, it is doubtful that he would have recommended him to go on tour with Chet, who appeared to be on the brink of addiction himself. It was a potentially lethal combination that could either make or break Chet's career.

Chapter Six

CHET BAKER IN EUROPE 1955–1956

"The first time I heard (Dick Twardzik) play, I couldn't believe it. He was—he had somehow bridged the thing between classical and jazz."—Chet Baker[1]

Chet Baker and Russ Freeman first encountered Dick Twardzik at the Storyville Club in Boston in mid-October 1954. The Chet Baker Quartet was headlining at the club, returning for its second engagement of the year, and the baritone saxophonist Serge Chaloff was playing support. Chaloff's band featured the twenty-three-year-old Twardzik on piano. The slender young man with his high forehead and slicked back hair had an intellectual air about him, his dark, hooded sad eyes offering the only clue to his troubles.

The pianist sat in with Chet Baker for the final set of the evening, and both Baker and Freeman were impressed by the originality of his playing. "He told me that Bud Powell and Art Tatum were his favourite pianists, and I think that their influence can be heard in his playing, but certainly he had evolved an original style," recalled Freeman. "His playing struck me as being very fresh and uninhibited, especially harmonically."[2]

By that stage, Twardzik was known as something of a prodigy amongst local musicians, having been active on the Boston jazz scene since the age of just seventeen. Serge Chaloff admired his inventive playing, and hired the young man when he was still in his teens. He had also worked with Lionel Hampton, Charlie Mariano and Charlie Parker.

Russ Freeman wasted no time and placed a call to Dick Bock in Los Angeles, suggesting he arrange a recording of Twardzik for Pacific Jazz. Bock's budget was limited, and he proposed a recording be made at the studio of a young engineer, Rudy Van Gelder, in Hackensack, New Jersey. Van Gelder went on to become a legendary jazz sound engineer, recording for Blue Note and others at his studio in Englewood Cliffs. In 1954, however, he still worked as a full-time optician. He could only record on his days off—Wednesdays and Sundays—and used his parents' living room as a makeshift recording studio.

Dick Twardzik was delighted to have the opportunity to record with his own group, and recruited an old friend, Peter Littman, to play drums. With no bass player in mind, he asked if it would be possible to use Carson Smith for the album. A recording session was booked for 27th October. It seems likely that Twardzik and Littman drove down from Boston for the recording session, and that Freeman and Smith—probably joined by Chet Baker himself—drove down from New York, where the Quartet was now headlining at Birdland.

Dick Twardzik, with Peter Littman on drums. Photograph probably by Nick Dean. (From the Twardzik / Thompson Archive.)

The recording offers a tantalising glimpse of Twardzik's considerable talents, both as a pianist and a composer. The original Pacific Jazz LP opened with 'A Crutch for the Crab', a Twardzik original, the unusual syncopations suggesting the sudden movements of a crab, surprising and difficult to grasp. Twardzik offers an alternative explanation in the liner notes, suggesting the inspiration came from "watching the hands of the Polish pianist, Jan Smeterlin, as they scurried crab-like into the keys."

'Albuquerque Social Swim', another original, alternates his flowing melodies with sudden, unexpected stops, the pianist trying to capture the stilted conversation of Albuquerque socialites at a cocktail party he had attended. The standards were no less intriguing. He chose to play Gershwin's 'Bess, You Is My Woman', an unusual selection at this time, given that the recording by Ella Fitzgerald and Louis Armstrong did not appear until 1957, the movie and Miles Davis recording in 1959. Likewise, Thelonious Monk's ''Round Midnight' is given a subdued reading, bringing a hushed, delicate beauty to the tune.

Richard Twardzik was born in Boston on 30th April 1931, the son of a Polish immigrant, Henryk, who had moved to Buffalo at an early age, and worked as a stained-glass window artist. His mother, Clare, worked at drafting in the acoustics laboratory at Harvard, and later in the Massachusetts Institute of Technology (MIT) during the war.

Henryk and Clare shared a love of the arts; Clare painted watercolours in her younger days, and was engaged in technical drawing whilst working at the MIT. In addition to his day job, Henryk was a keen amateur artist. Whilst he is not known to have exhibited his work, he left behind an array of pencil sketches and oil paintings that offer some insight into Dick's formative years. In addition, they were both fans of 'traditional' jazz music.

Their young son exhibited an interest in music at an early age; with a phonograph in the background, the first words he uttered were "nice music". He started taking piano lessons around the age of nine, encouraged by his mother, and it wasn't long before he started to incorporate boogie-woogie into his fast-growing repertoire.[3]

In 1947, the family relocated to Danvers, Massachusetts, seventeen miles north-east of Boston. They moved into a large, sprawling building of historic significance, the Samuel Fowler House, which was open to the public in the summer months. According to his biographer Jack Chambers, the sixteen-year-old Dick Twardzik seems to have taken this opportunity to reinvent himself as an aesthete; he immersed himself in the arts, practising the piano for hours on end, and spending his spare time in art museums or attending classical concerts. "One of the forms his teenage rebellion took was an aggressively modern stance in music and art," noted Chambers. "He espoused Bartok over Beethoven, and Schoenberg over Schumann." Twardzik also changed his appearance, dressing in a more flamboyant style, a small pile of books under his arm.[4]

Around this time, Twardzik started to study piano technique with Margaret Chaloff—the mother of the legendary baritone saxophonist Serge Chaloff—who worked at the New England Conservatory of Music. Whilst she focused on classical music, she worked with many of the most important jazz pianists over the years, including George Shearing, Toshiko Akiyoshi, Herbie Hancock, Chick Corea and Keith Jarrett. She is likely to have instilled a greater discipline in his playing, and also aided his compositional skills.

Twardzik is thought to have started joining local jam sessions from 1948, aged seventeen—usually accompanied by his father. In late 1950 he had the chance to sit in with Serge Chaloff, who had recently returned to Boston after a spell with Woody Herman's Second Herd, one of the best known jazz orchestras. "It didn't seem possible that a fellow his age could be playing some of the music that was being played," he later recalled. "He sat in with us for a set and amazed everyone at the session with his fluent and original ideas."[5]

He ended up working with Chaloff on a fairly regular basis for almost eighteen months, through the spring of 1952, when Chaloff was busted for heroin possession. Whilst Chaloff skipped bail, his problems effectively kept him away from the jazz scene for more than a year. Twardzik landed a job working at the Hi-Hat jazz club, where he was the intermission pianist. It was there he encountered Charlie Parker, who played at the club in early March. The young pianist must have made a considerable impression, because when Parker returned to Boston in December 1952, he hired Twardzik for the engagement. This gave him the opportunity to work with not only Charlie Parker, but a rhythm section that consisted of Charles Mingus on bass and Roy Haynes on drums.

The engagement with Charlie Parker further enhanced Twardzik's reputation in the city, and he was asked to lead the house trio at the Hi-Hat. In the weeks that followed, this gave him the chance to work with a number of visiting horn players, including Lee Konitz, Zoot Sims and J.J. Johnson.

From the spring of 1953, however, Twardzik's progress seems to have been impeded by a series of personal problems, presumably related to narcotics. He had been using heroin on a regular basis since his stint with Serge Chaloff, and it is thought that local narcotics officers started to track him from this period. As a consequence he left Boston for three months in April 1953, presumably to escape the attention of the police. He travelled with friends to Mexico and New Mexico, a trip that included an ill-fated attempt to kick his addiction in a Mexican hospital. Whilst he returned to Boston over the summer, his personal problems were causing conflicts with his parents, and he again embarked on a road trip, this time to Miami.

By early 1954, Twardzik felt strong enough to return to Boston, where he accepted a job as the pianist with Lionel Hampton. He did not find the job particularly rewarding from a musical perspective, but it helped to raise his profile once more after a period of inactivity. In April 1954 he quit the band to rejoin Serge Chaloff, who had emerged from his period of hiding, and was starting to re-immerse himself in the Boston music scene. It was during this second stint with Chaloff that he met Chet Baker at the Storyville club in October 1954.

Later that year, Chaloff took the decision to go into rehab, first as an outpatient at a Brookline clinic, then as a private patient at the Bridgewater State Hospital, thirty miles south of Boston. During this period, Twardzik found work as the intermission pianist at The Stable, another Boston club. These were troubled times for the pianist, however. His girlfriend, a nightclub singer and pianist by the name of Crystal Joy, had taken the decision to accept a job in New York. He seems to have taken this badly, and his drug use spiralled out of control. By the time Chaloff returned to Boston in mid-February, it had become so bad that he insisted that Twardzik could not rejoin his band unless he cleaned up.

He initially tried to undergo cold turkey at the house of a friend, the photographer Nick Dean, and when this failed, he reluctantly agreed to check in to the Bridgewater State Hospital. Upon leaving hospital in June 1954 he told his old friend Herb Pomeroy that he would commit suicide if he ever got hooked on dope again. He returned in time to rejoin Chaloff for the Boston Arts Festival on 13th June, before going on tour in July and August. The tour finished at the Patio Lounge in Washington on Sunday,

21st August. Chet Baker was scheduled to start at the same club the following week, and to Twardzik's apparent surprise, he was offered the job as pianist on his forthcoming European tour.

Twardzik evidently had no qualms about accepting the job, and applied for a passport that same week. Chet Baker was one of the best known West Coast jazz musicians, and was starting to make a name for himself on the East Coast, too. He was also aware of the development that had taken place in Russ Freeman's playing over the preceding two years, and probably saw the opportunity of including some of his own compositions in Chet's repertoire. The idea of visiting Europe for the first time was an added bonus, given his interest in classical music and the arts in general.

His girlfriend, Crystal Joy, did not share his enthusiasm. Having finally undergone treatment for his drug addiction, she worried that the tour would leave Dick open to temptation. Her fears were compounded when she learned that he would be reunited with the drummer Peter Littman—an old friend from Boston, and a notorious junkie.[6]

On Monday, September 5th 1955, Chet boarded a TWA flight to Paris from New York's Idlewild—now known as JFK—with a view to spending a week or so with Liliane before meeting up with the rest of the band. Two days later his sidemen boarded the *Ile de France* in New York, all three still in their early twenties, travelling outside North America for the first time. They were seen off by Crystal Joy, who made her way to the cabin Twardzik was supposed to be sharing with Littman, only to find a small party in progress. "The room was supposed to be theirs but it was full of these groupie girls," she recalled. She left in tears, convinced that Twardzik was taking one of the girls to Paris with him. Later she recalled an eerie premonition. "They were all so out-of-it that I had a feeling it was over for him."[7]

"I think now that Dick started getting high from that first night," Chet later recalled, "but I was not to find out about this fact for some months." Bass player Jimmy Bond, who saxophonist Phil Urso described as "clean as a houndstooth", knew of Peter Littman by reputation, and kept to himself for the whole voyage, only running into Twardzik and Littman on deck on one occasion.[8]

When Chet arrived in Paris, Liliane was disappointed by his reaction to the elegant city. "He didn't seem very excited to be here," she recalled. Chet's formative years had been spent in Oklahoma, and his education had been limited, so he had no real preconception of European culture and history. Dick Twardzik, by contrast, was clearly impressed by the architecture, and sent postcards to his parents to show them what he had seen.

Chet was surprised to learn that jazz had quite a following in Paris. The pioneering New Orleans clarinet and soprano saxophone player, Sidney Bechet, had moved to Paris in 1951, and was regarded as a major star. There was also a burgeoning bop scene, pioneered by local musicians such as French pianists René Utreger and Martial Solal, and Belgian saxophonist Bobby Jaspar. When Liliane brought Chet to Caméléon, a small jazz club in the Latin Quarter, he was treated as a hero.

On 15th September, Chet drove out to Le Havre to meet the band off the boat, and brought them to Paris, which was to be their base for the next few weeks. The tour began in confusion, with Baker seemingly unaware of some of the bookings that had been made, and missing one or two concerts. Matters were not helped by the fact that media publicity for the tour had been poor. The French jazz press was primarily focused on the forthcoming concerts by Art Tatum, a tour that was later cancelled as a result of the pianist's illness. Chet did feature on the cover of the July/August cover of *Jazz Magazine*, but it made no reference to a European tour. The following edition only made brief mention of the tour in the form of a dispatch, but no dates were provided. "New York: Chet Baker and his Quartet will give a series of concerts in Europe in October, most notably in France". The September issue of *Jazz Hot* added to the confusion by implying the shows had been cancelled. "We'd been promised Mulligan and Baker for this autumn. It seems like we're about to be disillusioned, and we'll have to wait for better days."

The tour had been organised by two local promoters, Jeff Kruger and Joe Napoli, who were working in conjunction with Chet's US manager, Joe Glaser. Kruger was also the founder of the Flamingo Jazz Club, one of the leading modern jazz clubs in Europe. "I think I had just finished the Billie Holiday tour, and was working with Associated Booking," said Kruger. "As I recall, they had just signed Gerry Mulligan and Chet Baker, and asked me to help Joe Napoli, who lived in Italy, to put some dates together. They were more concerned with getting their commission than anything else."[9]

The confusion cleared up, the band made their way up to Holland, playing their first date at the Concertgebouw in Amsterdam, on September 17th. Baker began the concert by announcing the names of the band, correcting the programme notes that incorrectly listed Russ Freeman on piano and Bob Carter on bass. The programme also contained a list of sixteen tunes the band would apparently choose from; the list was presumably submitted by

Russ Freeman before he decided against joining the European tour, since it includes several of his own compositions. In the event, only two tunes on the list were played over the course of the next two evenings, the revised repertoire presumably decided in conjunction with Dick Twardzik.

The band opened with a brisk version of 'Tommyhawk', a Johnny Mandel tune that he had recorded for the Sextet album one year earlier. It is soon apparent that Chet is playing with more fire than previously; no doubt this was partly a result of his experience in New York, where critics had been dismissive of his playing style. It also reflects the more driving, forceful drumming of Peter Littman, whose hard bop-oriented style was quite different to that of Larry Bunker and Bob Neel, both of who had been used in a more supportive role.

Next up was 'Indian Summer', a new song in Chet's repertoire, and the first indication that Dick Twardzik was already beginning to exert some influence over Chet. The pace slows for 'I'm Glad There Is You', before Chet sang two vocal numbers 'But Not For Me', a tune he would regularly use to showcase his scat singing in later years, and 'My Funny Valentine', a song which many in the audience would have been expecting.

The band received a thundering ovation from the capacity crowd. The reviews of Chet's European debut were equally rapturous. The British music journal, *Melody Maker*, thought that Chet's playing was far stronger than on record.

"There was no yelling from a sensation-seeking audience, but deep silence during the numbers and long, warm applause after each one of them. Also, there was not the slightest bit of showing off from people on the stage. Chet and his men behaved as if they were doing a record session. They delivered their music, their true art, in all seriousness and sincerity. Chet's trumpet playing is at least twice as good as one would realise before hearing him in the flesh. On records he gives a fair impression of his feeling, his technical abilities and his beautiful tone. But onstage, the shy boy with the heavenly trumpet entices. The way he runs through the chords is almost incredible, and he never tries to impress by any other things than his musical qualities … Chet admitted he is a great fan of Miles, but I do not think anyone could say he copies him in any way. Chet announces his shows himself, and did so in the same way he sang—quietly, almost timidly. His voice is hard to compare with any other vocalist's. Like his playing, his vocals are serious, well considered and calm."[10]

Other newspapers also remarked on the contribution of Dick Twardzik. A reviewer in the Dutch daily *de Volkskrant* noted that Twardzik's "unabashedly romantic" approach "fits Baker's intimate playing wonderfully". *Jazz Journal* credited Twardzik with "a pleasant abundance of musicality", and *Rhythme*, another jazz magazine, praised Twardzik as "a highly original soloist who journeys into melody à la Dave Brubeck and possesses a lively swing."[11]

Next day the quartet made their way to The Hague for a concert at the Kurhaus, playing a similar set, again opening with 'Tommyhawk' and 'Indian Summer', before going into a lengthy reading of the ballad 'Someone to Watch Over Me.'

It's interesting to hear Chet's spoken introduction to CTA: "Now for our final number this evening we'd like to play another of the tunes from Miles Davis' *Blue Note* album. By now you must have gathered I'm quite a Miles Davis fan—my favourite trumpet player." Chet had clearly fallen under the influence of Miles Davis since the infamous Birdland concert in mid-1954; it was apparent from his playing, the selection of tunes that he played on the tour, and from the more dynamic rhythm section he had brought to Europe. Indeed, Miles would remain an important influence until the late 1950s, by which time Chet arguably felt he had nothing left to prove. Even then, he continued to seek the approval of Miles Davis at every opportunity, still stung by the early criticism of his playing.

Again, the reviews of the concert were mostly favourable, with writer Peter Swiens noting of Chet's singing, "Perhaps it's his mournful loneliness that makes such an impression, the sense that Baker really is 'lost in the wood', quoting from the Gershwin ballad, 'Someone To Watch Over Me'."

Later that evening, however, came the first sign of the problems that were to come. Twardzik was struggling to come to terms with the purity of the heroin he had scored in Amsterdam the previous day, and overdosed after the show. The incident took place at the Flying Dutchman, a nearby jazz club. Paul Acket, later the founder of the North Sea Jazz Festival, was in the audience and noted that Twardzik had nodded out on the stage. He was sitting on a chair behind the piano, drool running from his mouth. Luckily bass player Jimmy Bond was able to bring him round backstage, scrubbing his bare back with a brush to revive the pianist. After this incident, Chet asked the bass player to keep an eye on Twardzik and Littman, a role that he reluctantly agreed to. Deep down, however, he thought that Chet was a weak character, and should have exerted more influence over the young band.

A couple of days later, the band travelled to Germany, where they played a one-night stand in Mainz. A bootleg-style recording exists of the concert, now available on CD, and whilst the sound quality is poor, it does give us some insights into the ways in which the band was developing. The tape runs too fast, but on the opener, 'Walkin', one can still hear the power of Baker's playing at this time, the influence of Miles Davis, and the swing that Littman brought to the band. Chet's enthusiasm is audible, shouting "Yeah!" as the pianist completes a rousing, bluesy solo. Twardzik's classically-influenced introduction to 'All The Things You Are' is astonishing, just one example of the inventive touches that he brought to this wonderful, if short-lived, band.[12]

On 24th September, Chet attended an awards ceremony at the Amateur Jazz Festival in Zurich, organised by the local radio station. Chet played two tunes, 'Happy Little Sunbeam' and 'Moonlight in Vermont', accompanied by Elsie Bianchi (piano), Siro Bianchi (bass) and René Nyfeller (drums). The tunes appeared on a limited edition CD that incorrectly attributes them to Chet's regular quartet.

With no gigs planned for a few days, the band returned to Paris. Chet and Liliane spent time hanging around with some of the European jazz musicians, including the Belgian guitarist René Thomas and bass player, Benoît Quersin, both of whom were heroin addicts, and very familiar with the darker side of Paris nightlife. "They were hip and funny musicians," Liliane later recalled, "but I must say they helped turn Chet on to drugs."

Peter Littman and Dick Twardzik used the opportunity to go out and score; again, they were taken aback by the purity of the heroin available in Europe, with Littman later overdosing in his hotel. "One day in Paris I saved him, and brought him back to life," said Liliane. "At the time, Chet was still clean, and baby-looking."[13]

Next day, Liliane introduced Chet to Nicole Barclay, who together with her husband Eddie Barclay, had founded a record label, Barclay Disques. They recorded a number of American jazz stars visiting Paris including Thelonious Monk, Lester Young, Blossom Dearie and Charlie Parker. "She was the one who was into the music more than Eddie was," remembered Liliane. "Eddie was too, but she was the one who brought Charlie Parker to the label."[14]

The British promoter, Jeffrey Kruger, remembers meeting the Barclays at around this time, since they were heavily involved in the promotion of Chet's Salle Pleyel concert, booked for early October. "Eddie Barclay was like the Sinatra of France; elegant, a top showman," he said. "A quiet dinner as far as he was concerned was for fifteen to twenty people; otherwise it would be a formal dinner with sixty to eighty people. When they started the Barclay record label they used to deliver their records on bicycles, the two of them. But they were very shrewd. Eddie was more of a showman, the figurehead, whilst Nicole was the one that did the work. I have fond memories of Eddie—he was a gentleman."[15]

Baker signed a contract to record up to seven LPs with the French record label, and the first recording date was set for October 11th, when the band was scheduled to be back in Paris. Given that Chet was already signed to Pacific Jazz in the US, Nicole Barclay came to an arrangement with Dick Bock whereby he would control US distribution of the music recorded in Europe, a deal that worked well for both labels.

Over the next few days, the band spent their evenings playing all night, jamming at any club that would let them sit in. "Those jam sessions turned into a rally from club to club, depending on when they closed," recalled Louis Scali. "They'd start at the Caméléon, which closed at two, go on to the club Saint-Germain, which closed at three, and then finish up at the Tabou, which shuts its doors at five. It sometimes happened that, even later than that, they'd go on to blow at someone else's place, providing he was lucky enough not to have any irascible neighbours."[16]

On October 4th, the band was scheduled to headline at the prestigious Salle Pleyel concert hall in Paris, an event that was to be broadcast nationwide on French radio. Whilst the main newspapers *Le Monde* and *Le Figaro* made no reference to the show, *Combat* published an article on Chet Baker on the morning of the concert. "In less than a year, Chet Baker has gone from the relative obscurity of a military big-band musician to the status of an international jazz star," it claimed.

At this point, the British promoter, Jeffrey Kruger, decided to travel from London to join the tour, accompanied by the Tony Kinsey quartet, one of the bands scheduled to open for the Chet Baker Quartet. Beyond travelling with the English band, Kruger had other ulterior motives for joining Chet in Paris. "I decided to go with the band to keep my eye on things and to keep a watching brief on Chet's then manager, a street wise character called Joe Napoli," he wrote. "This way I could ensure my share of the monies due me for making certain arrangements and bookings were honoured. I also wanted to see a little of these great cities for myself and to meet as many new contacts in the European business market that I felt would be a very lucrative market for us to be involved in."[17]

The concert at Salle Pleyel was designed to be a showcase for modern jazz, and it was interesting to see Sidney Bechet, the veteran New Orleans jazz musician, in the audience to witness the changing face of jazz. The promoters had arranged a stellar line up; in addition to the Tony Kinsey Quartet from England, the show featured the best of the modern European jazz musicians, including the Martial Solal Trio and the Bobby Jaspar All Stars, which featured saxophonist Bobby Jaspar and guitarist René Thomas.

Some of the organisers had expressed concerns that Chet's ballads and quiet singing style might not carry in such a grand setting. As Alain Tercinet later recalled, "People expected a musician murmuring in the mist, and here stood an incisive, powerful trumpeter with a clear tone. Which detracted not at all from the poetic side of his playing." Kruger also remembers Chet as being well received, and was pleasantly surprised that the British group was also a hit with the French audience. It was also the first time Kruger had witnessed Dick Twardzik. "I thought Twardzik was one of the most talented pianists I had ever met," he later recalled. "He was laid back, very introverted, and played with his head down."[18]

Jazz Magazine published an article about the concert, abandoning its occasionally condescending tone to deliver a favourable review. "As soon as the curtain was raised, Chet Baker had won the game, agreeably surprising the audience with a punch and dynamism in his playing we'd hardly been used to from his records. Gifted with genuine technique, this musician still expresses himself with sincerity; there's nothing artificial at all."

The only real note of reservation came from the UK music press. *Melody Maker*'s Henry Kahn was less impressed. "Chet Baker was given the bird when he played at the Salle Pleyel on Tuesday night, but it was only a moderate 'bird'. The fans on the whole were kind to what was really a gruelling and rather lamentable performance."

The tour continued through October, taking in a number of punishing one-nighters in towns such as Rouen (October 5th), Louvain (October 6th), Strasbourg (October 7th) and Grenoble (October 8th), even playing Brussels and Antwerp on the same day.

Twardzik's biographer, Jack Chambers, notes that the young pianist wrote to his parents on a number of occasions over this period, as if to reassure them that he was healthy, and in good spirits. He sent his father, a stained-glass artist, a postcard with a picture of Strasbourg Cathedral.

> *Hi Dad!*
> *Today was a real thrill for me. This is the most beautiful church I have ever seen! The windows absolutely take your breath away! The greatest symphony in color. I can't begin to describe it. Truly one of the world's masterpieces. When I came in, many priests were singing so you see it was perfect.*
> *Love Dick*[19]

The sudden flurry of letters to his parents suggest that the young pianist had been shaken by his overdose in Holland, aware that he was slipping back into his old ways, and was making a concerted effort to change his lifestyle. "His boyish tone, evocative as it is of his tone a few years earlier, suggests that he might have been making some headway," suggests Chambers. "The postcards leave little doubt that he was feeling good about himself."[20]

The Quartet returned to Paris on October 11th, for what was to be the first and most significant of Chet's studio recordings on his first European tour. When Twardzik joined the band that summer, he told Baker that he would not be content playing standards, and introduced him to the compositions of his Boston mentor, Robert Zieff. Baker was evidently impressed with what he heard; he later remarked, "I found Bob Zieff's music a delight. Every line and harmony was different to the next, never going the way you thought it would, but somehow complete, logical and unique."[21]

Robert L. Zieff was born in Lynn, Massachusetts, in 1927, the son of Lithuanian refugees. After finishing high school, he was drafted into the Army at the end of World War II. Upon his return, Zieff studied trumpet and composition at Boston University, emerging with a Bachelor of Music. After graduating, Zieff found work in Boston, although he was always something of a peripheral figure on the booming local scene. Local favourites Serge Chaloff and Boots Mussulli, stars of the Woody Herman and Stan Kenton orchestras respectively, had recently returned to their hometown. Clubs like the Hi-Hat and Storyville were attracting the big names in jazz, and new clubs began to sprout up.

Zieff felt that bebop was showing signs of becoming formulaic, and was drawn to the more experimental elements of jazz, including the 'cool' sound of the Miles Davis nonet, and the Tristano 'school' from New York. His compositions attracted like-minded young disciples of his own, among them trumpeter and violinist Dick Wetmore and pianist Dick Twardzik. The musicians occasionally rehearsed at 905, Boylston Street—a musician's boarding house, close to the Berklee College of Music.

On the back of these rehearsals, Dick Wetmore assembled an experimental quartet that featured Dick Twardzik on piano, Jimmy Woode on bass and Jimmy Zitano on drums. The band primarily worked on charts contributed by Bob Zieff, and rehearsed under his supervision. After a few weeks, however, bass player Jimmy Woode missed three rehearsals before announcing he had received an offer to work with Duke Ellington. "I suggested another bassist, Bill Nordstrom, who didn't impress the violinist until a couple of rehearsals later, and was then very impressed," Zieff later recalled. "Woode went with Ellington for many years; however, the other bassist was much better!"[22]

Dick Twardzik was also suffering from personal problems at this time, as discussed earlier, and left Boston for a few months in the autumn of 1953. His place in the quartet was taken by Ray Santisi. The new look line-up, with Santisi on piano and Nordstrom on bass, recorded a ten-inch LP for Bethlehem in September or October 1953. The album was not released for two years, and was simply titled *Dick Wetmore* (BCP 1035). Whilst it received little publicity at the time, and was soon deleted, it is noteworthy because it featured many of the compositions that would be recorded by Chet Baker and Dick Twardzik two years later.

Years later the album was later rereleased under the title *Wetmore Plays Zieff*; Wetmore had apparently asked the record company for money for the composer, and as a result the producer, Creed Taylor, had left Zieff's name off the original sleeve.

Before he left for Europe, Dick Twardzik telephoned Bob Zieff, who had relocated from Boston to New York. He asked his mentor if he had any music that might be suitable for the Chet Baker Quartet. "I adapted what I wrote for Wetmore for Chet," Zieff later recalled. "Seven of the eight pieces. One didn't seem especially adaptable at the time ('Shiftful'). I sent one different piece ('Midforte'). Dick asked me for as much music as I had, and said they would record it. I gave him eight and said telegraph me if you need more."[23]

In early September, Twardzik arrived in New York, ready to set sail for Europe. On his way to the port, he stopped by Zieff's room in the Alvin Hotel, which was something of a musicians' hangout. "We went over the music together," said Zieff. "I would assume that he ran the (subsequent) record date."

As the band entered the Studio Pathé-Magellan in Paris, Dick Twardzik reached into his bag, and pulled out the arrangements that Zieff had given to him in New York. It's interesting to note that the band had not yet played any of the Zieff tunes onstage. They must have rehearsed extensively, however, since there are no alternate takes from the band's two days in the recording studio. Rehearsals would have been helped by the fact that Twardzik was familiar with all but one of the tunes, 'Mid-Forte'. In addition, Chet was a fast learner, absorbing the complex chord changes by ear, drawn in by the intricacies of Zieff's compositions.

'Rondette' sees Baker gliding through the changes effortlessly, his tone bright and clear, before Twardzik takes over, delivering an angular solo, in stark contrast to Chet's more melodic lines. As so often with these wonderful recordings, it's the contrast between the two styles that makes the whole so absorbing. Chet's solo on 'Mid-Forte' is astonishing, and when he hands over to Twardzik, the influence he has had on Keith Jarrett becomes quite apparent. The mood changes for 'Sad Walk' and 'Just Duo'; on both tracks the bowed bass of Jimmy Bond accompanies Chet's mournful refrain to good effect.

The band returned to the studio three days later to complete the album. They recorded three more Zieff compositions, including the wonderful 'Piece Caprice', which sounds almost Monk-like in structure. Dick Twardzik contributed one of his own compositions to the session, 'The Girl From Greenland'; it is similar in style to the rest of the album, in many respects, reflecting the hours of time he had spent playing and rehearsing with Zieff in Boston.

Chet was delighted with the results. "The originality and freshness of Zieff's line and chordal structure is going to please a lot of people, I think—at least musicians and serious listeners." Back in Los Angeles, however, Dick Bock was reportedly disappointed with the Barclay album. He only released six of the tunes recorded at the first recording sessions, pairing them with tunes recorded at later sessions on the European tour. The album was eventually released as *Chet Baker in Europe: A Jazz Tour of the NATO Countries*. He evidently believed that Bob Zieff's compositions were not commercial, and would not appeal to Chet's growing number of female fans, who were drawn to his singing voice.

He may have been correct on this last point, but he arguably misread the commercial appeal of the music. After all, the Paris sessions have remained in print for much of the last fifty years, reissued in numerous formats. They may not have sold as well as *Chet Baker Sings* or *Chet Baker with Strings*, but they almost certainly outsold records such as *Ensemble* and *Sextet* that Bock himself had supervised.

I would go as far as to suggest that the album recorded with Dick Twardzik in Paris, released as *Rondette* on Barclay records, ranks amongst his finest achievements in a recording career that spanned thirty-five years, and included almost two hundred recordings. In Bob Zieff he had found a composer of intricate, eloquent, original music that challenged the listener, and inspired him as a musician. And in Dick Twardzik, he had found the perfect partner from a musical perspective; a fine soloist and composer, but just as importantly, someone who was prepared to push him beyond his comfort zone: a pianist that approached harmonies from a less intuitive, more intellectual perspective, and constantly surprised Baker with his invention. In the words of Twardzik biographer, Jack Chambers, "he played staccato to Baker's legato, brains to his heart, thought to his feeling, and the sum was greater than the disparate parts."[24]

Composer Bob Zieff was delighted—and surprised—by the success of the recording session in Paris. "He and Chet were more than extraordinary in both the interpretation of the parts and in the improvisations. Chet had some technical trouble with the part on 'Piece Caprice'," he noted, "but outside of that it was a landmark. If you listen to his work with Gerry and with his own quartet afterward where he certainly plays well; he seems to have turned a corner with Dick Twardzik and my music. There were not many who could meet that challenge—and with such great artistic results—that goes for Dick Twardzik as well."[25]

Whilst Twardzik never had the chance to hear the Dick Wetmore recording *Wetmore Plays Zieff*, Bob Zieff thought that the versions recorded by Chet Baker and Dick Twardzik were far superior. "I felt the soloing was worlds apart between the Wetmore and Baker dates," he argued. "Amazing how fine the interpretation is on the Chet date."[26]

In between the first two recording sessions, Chet and Liliane travelled to London to promote Chet's forthcoming show at the Stoll Theatre on The Strand. Promoter Jeffrey Kruger had already brought Billie Holiday to the UK, and wanted to showcase other jazz stars, including Chet Baker. The main obstacle was an antiquated law designed to protect the livelihood of British musicians, which essentially prevented American musicians from playing their own instruments on British soil.

Kruger explained the root of the problem: "Cooked up years before by the President of the American Federation of Musicians, James Petrillo, with our own Musicians' Union, essentially it worked like this: no US musician could come and work in Britain unless a British musician was booked to play in the States under the same terms and conditions. This sounds fine until you stop and think about it. Imagine that Stan Kenton and Woody Herman wanted to bring their bands to England. Who could go to the States in exchange? Nobody at all, because even Dankworth, by far the most renowned of British jazz musicians, was totally unknown over there. So this apparently fair rule was tantamount to a total ban and deprived British fans of the chance of seeing their US idols—unless, that is, those fans were rich enough to travel to Eire or France where no such stupid rule existed."[27]

Kruger knew that there was significant demand to see American musicians perform in the UK. In addition to organising the Billie Holiday tour, he was lucky enough to witness a one-off appearance by Norman Granz's Jazz at the Philharmonic at the Kilburn State Theatre in London in 1953; the musicians were given special dispensation to perform a benefit concert to provide disaster relief for a major flood. In addition, he had seen the special transport arrangements that had been put in place for British musicians and fans to travel to Ireland to see Woody Herman and his band play in Dublin. Sensing a commercial opportunity, Kruger decided to take on the Musicians' Union, and press ahead with plans to bring Chet Baker and Swedish saxophonist Lars Gullin to London.

"I didn't take no for an answer," he later explained. "I booked Chet and Lars. I announced that I would be presenting them in concert in London. My telephone line must nearly have caught fire after that: stuffed shirts from the Musicians' Union shouting to me that I couldn't do that because it broke their rules. Me telling them in very direct terms that I was taking out an injunction restraining them from interfering. It was from that moment that I earned my reputation as a hard man to cross. I was also one of the biggest users of MU members and I threatened to not use MU members at the Flamingo Club or on my concerts and they knew I would do just this if I had to. The national press got hold of the story and I was able to maximise their coverage by bringing Chet Baker and his wife [sic] Liliane to London for a pre-concert promotional visit."[28]

Jeffrey Kruger found Chet introverted but polite on his first visit to the UK. "Chet was very laid back," he recalled. "He wasn't very forthcoming, and you couldn't get friendly with him—he wasn't that sort of person. But he did what he had to do, was very courteous, very cordial, and bemused by the farce of what was going on. He was a nice young guy."[29]

After the first recording sessions, and the promotional activity in England, the tour resumed. On October 15th, the band travelled to Stuttgart in Germany, accompanied by the Italian pop singer Caterina Valente, and the Swedish baritone saxophonist Lars Gullin. A twenty-minute bootleg recording was made of the concert, which has now been made available on CD (*Lars Gullin, 1955–56, Volume 1*). The concert sounds more informal than the earlier Mainz concert, and provides us with the last known recording of pianist Dick Twardzik. Gullin joins the band for a brisk romp through Charlie Parker's 'Cool Blues'. Next up is the Bob Zieff composition 'Brash', recorded just four days earlier. It is played by the Quartet alone, and offers a tantalising glimpse at how the band might have evolved had Twardzik lived. If Chet's solo sounds slightly hesitant, the pianist sounds at ease with the arrangement, producing a brief but imaginative solo; it's also interesting to note the audience reaction, which is extremely favourable. Gullin returns for a slightly plodding version of 'Lover Man', before Valente scats her way through a forgettable 'I'll Remember April'.

After the concert, Caterina Valente's record company proposed she make a recording with the Chet Baker Quartet. "After the concert, the record company proposed to record in the studio 'I Remember April' and 'Every Time We Say Goodbye', but the musicians refused to be part of it," recalled Eric van Aro, Valente's manager. Twardzik was particularly dismissive of the idea, it seems, but Chet was more amenable, and agreed to record the two songs as a duet, with Valente on guitar and vocal, and him playing trumpet.[30]

Most discographies list this recording as having taken place in Baden-Baden in Germany in March 1956, but van Aro believes it took place after the Stuttgart concert. The two songs were released as a single in Europe, and were later made available on a compilation, *Chet Baker: Compact Jazz* (Emarcy 840632-2).[31]

Chet Baker and Caterina Valente, Stuttgart, October 1955.
Photographer unknown.

Lars Resberg published a review of the Stuttgart concert in *Estrad*, and made thinly veiled references to the obvious drug use by certain members of the band. Interestingly, he chose to make more detailed observations in the December issue of the same magazine, written in the light of Twardzik's subsequent death.

"This feeling spread like an evil mist around Chet Baker's quartet, though not from the effects of liquor but of narcotics. The coloured bassist, whose name is Jimmy Bond, was doing no wrong. He was the only one in the band who neither injected, smoked nor drank. Chet himself wasn't in too bad a state either.

But the other two. The pianist Dick Twardzik, smiling and courteous when we first met, told some amusing anecdotes … Later, at a restaurant. "Just a sip of wine and some light food for me, thank you". Our conversation didn't proceed very well. He moved uneasily in his chair. Then a visit to the toilet, a long visit. When he eventually returned he was overwhelmingly cordial until I noticed that some of his spirited transmissions were dysfunctional. A few days later: a dead pianist in a narrow hotel room in Paris, from a heroin overdose …

And the drummer trying out sticks during a rehearsal … the expression on his face was macabre. It was the same celestial affliction you see on pictures of Jesus Christ in crucifixion. Then he dropped a stick. He noticed this after a while, and bent down slowly to pick it up. He remained in this position for so long that you expected him to fall down on his drums at any moment. But with immense effort he managed to rise to an upright position again, and started to play—a bit hard, but with a rhythmic spark, swinging and driving. And in a completely different world to us 'common' people …"[32]

Next day, the musicians left for Switzerland, where they were originally scheduled to play concerts in Zurich on October 16th and Basel on October 17th. A third concert, scheduled for Geneva's Victoria Hall, had apparently been cancelled. Twardzik was still in bad shape, and suffered another overdose backstage at Zurich. "In the middle of the party, he went into the bathroom and gave himself a fix," Chet later recalled. "He had already taken a shot earlier and had complained that he wasn't high. Now he gave himself an overdose. He just managed to come into the room and then went flat out on the floor. 'Give him a salt shot', someone cried, but somebody else had the better idea of getting an ambulance while most of the cats present cleared out."[33]

The precise details of this event remain unclear. Dick Twardzik's biographer, Jack Chambers, believes the incident took place some three weeks earlier in Geneva on 27th September. He admits that a number of the dates are not precise, however, and that he had to piece together parts of the tour schedule from postcards sent by the pianist to his family. The extensive liner notes to the box set, *The Complete 1955–1956 Barclay Sessions*, cast doubts on this date, and suggest that the band did not play any full concerts in Switzerland until mid-October.

Chet had a tendency to downplay the overdose in later interviews, suggesting that this was the first time he became aware of Twardzik's addiction. In the movie *Let's Get Lost* he claimed, "I didn't even know that he was using anything until a concert in Switzerland somewhere, in Zurich I think." This seems highly unlikely, given his previous overdose in The Hague. Jimmy Bond also recalled having to revive the unconscious pianist in his hotel room on more than one occasion. "He wasn't friendly when I woke him up, either," he told Baker biographer, James Gavin. "He'd still have the needle in his arm." Presumably Chet was trying to distance himself from the pianist's subsequent death less than one week later.

The suggestion that the overdose took place in Zurich is further supported by the young Swiss drummer, Daniel Humair, who had travelled by train from his hometown of Geneva to see the show in Basel. He remembers thinking that the drugs were beginning to take their toll on the young American musicians. "The quartet arrived wearing dark suits, and white shirts, and they were whiter-looking than their shirts—they were in a shape you wouldn't believe," he said. "I was so shocked by the physical state of those guys. In Europe, it was too easy to get dope; that's why they always played here. Coming out of Switzerland, still drinking milk, and being greeted by this vision, I think it saved my life. I understood early on what you shouldn't do as a musician."[34]

The band's poor physical condition, exacerbated by the long train journeys between each show, had also taken its toll on the music, the exuberance of the early shows in Amsterdam, The Hague and Mainz replaced by a drug-fuelled haze. "The music was absolutely fantastic, but it was a very weird kind of music, with almost no joy whatsoever," recalled Humair. "The bass player, Jimmy Bond, was good, and the drummer, Peter Littman, was a fantastic drummer. He was slightly crippled (he had one lung), but he was the first one playing those Tony Williams-like licks; he had a very modern way of playing the drums. He could have been a master. Both Dick Twardzik and that drummer were great. The concert was much more modern than the West Coast guys, who were basically studio guys."[35]

Back in Boston, Dick's girlfriend Crystal Joy was becoming increasingly alarmed by his behaviour. He had not sent for her to come over to Europe, as he had promised. On the two or three occasions he did phone her, she knew he was back on drugs. "I knew he was high," she said. "He sounded like he was underwater."[36]

Over the course of these dates, Chet Baker began to build up a rapport with the Swedish saxophonist Lars Gullin, and invited him to join the quartet for a second recording date in Paris a few days later. Chet later described how Gullin's playing style differed from that of Gerry Mulligan. "I was very impressed by him. He had a very melodic, liquid—yes a liquid way of moving through the changes, you know. The only baritone player that I was aware of was Gerry Mulligan. When I heard Lars, I thought, Jesus, there is another way of playing the baritone! Lars played with a lot more fire and a lot more authority in some ways than Gerry did. Gerry was more of an arranger on his horn than a soloist, although he did play some nice solos from time to time, but I thought Lars was really strong, a talented man."[37]

The band had evidently rehearsed some new material in Paris in mid-October, with Dick Twardzik taking care of the arrangements. "There was one night, after we'd played, when Bobby Jaspar and I went on to meet Chet and his rhythm section to try and decipher the tunes and Dick's arrangements before doing a session scheduled for the following week," recalled trumpet player Roger Guérin. "Chet wanted to hear the whole group, and see if it suited him. And it did."[38]

The band returned to Paris on 20th October, and that evening, they made their way to Club Tabou, a small basement jazz club on Rue Dauphine in the Latin Quarter. Jimmy Bond, weary from the endless train journeys, and mindful of the recording session next day, opted to stay behind at the hotel. Benoît Quersin filled in on bass, and the new-look quintet jammed into the early hours. Olle Lind later told Twardzik biographer Jack Chambers that Chet had told him it was one of the best gigs of his life. "Gullin was fantastic. Chet said he had only played with Gerry Mulligan before, and that he didn't know that anyone could play a baritone like Lars did."[39]

As the night wore on, other musicians joined the jam session. René Urtreger, the Belgian pianist, joined for a few numbers. The bass player, Eddie de Haas, who had recently returned to Paris from a gig on the Cote d'Azur, also made his way to the club. "I had a job in the Caméléon, and usually worked until 2 a.m. or so, and then all the jazz players would converge on the Tabou club and have jam sessions down there," he recalled.[40]

As so often, Dick Twardzik appeared lost in the music, an Arabian fez pulled down low over his brow as he leaned over the keyboard. "Twardzik was a very cerebral-type piano player, different from anybody else I had ever heard—very individualistic," recalled de Haas. "If you listen to his music now, you might not realise that he was different to everybody else, because there are so many different players nowadays that go even further out. At the time, Twardzik was definitely an enigma. He was good for Chet in the sense that he didn't always have to play his Broadway repertoire. Twardzik was an original."[41]

At some point before dawn, Eddie de Haas recalls Chet leaving the club with his girlfriend Liliane. "I don't recall Chet being there at the end of the evening," he said. "Chet would normally go his own way; he had a girlfriend, which the others didn't." Liliane confirmed this view of events, and remembers Chet spending the night with her.

An hour or so later, the remaining musicians went their separate ways, the dawn still two or three hours away. "We had finished playing at the Tabou at around five or six in the morning," recalled de Haas, "and Peter Littman and Dick Twardzik, who were staying at a different hotel to me, went to their hotel. They probably decided to get high one more time."

René Urtreger remembered a slightly different version of events, with Twardzik and Littman going their separate ways. He recalled walking with Twardzik to the Grand Balcon Hotel, rather than the Madeleine where he was staying, and assumed he was meeting a connection.

The following afternoon, the musicians waited in the Studio Pathé-Magellan for Twardzik to arrive, setting up their equipment, smoking cigarettes and discussing which tunes they would record. After an hour had passed, the musicians began to worry, and Bond decided to telephone the Madeleine Hotel, but there was no reply. At this point, Littman seemed alarmed, and volunteered to go to the hotel. He was joined by Jeffrey Kruger, the tour promoter, who assumed that Twardzik must have overslept. "I dashed up to his room to wake him," said Kruger. "The sight that confronted me as I flung open the door is one that I can't forget: Dick was lying on the floor with a needle sticking out of his arm. He had overdosed, not overslept, and he was quite dead."[42]

Littman panicked, rushing back to the recording studio and screaming hysterically that Dick was dead. Kruger told him to calm down, and quietly made plans for the musicians to leave Paris at the earliest opportunity. "I discreetly ushered the rest of the party out of the hotel, and told Joe Napoli to ensure everyone kept quiet," he wrote. "Only when the group were about to board our plane at Orly airport did I inform the authorities about Dick. This incident more than any other ensured that I would never get involved with the drug scene that is such a temptation in the world of jazz."[43]

Jeffrey Kruger was surprised to note that Chet appeared to show little emotion to the news of Dick's tragic death. "Chet listened, and just got on with things," he said. "I don't think it affected him like a cousin, or a brother, or how it should have, given their relationship. But he was laid-back, and I never saw him show feelings for anyone, including Liliane."[44]

Bass player Jimmy Bond agreed. "He was certainly distressed, but I don't think he was really in touch with what had happened," he later recalled.[45]

But Liliane knew that even if Chet kept his feelings bottled up inside, he was devastated by his friend's overdose. "Chet was very, very upset, because he loved Dick Twardzik," she said. "I think the fact that Dick died, and that Dick was into drugs, influenced Chet more than anything else about drugs. Dick's death didn't scare him away from drugs; there was a magnetism, he was attracted." That came later in the tour, according to Liliane, as Chet spent more time with the Belgian jazz musicians, most of whom were addicts themselves.[46]

Two days later, Chet's emotions were laid bare for all to see. He was scheduled to play a concert at the Stoll Theatre on London's Strand, supported by Tony Crombie and his orchestra. Jeffrey Kruger had reached a compromise with the Musicians' Union: Chet would be allowed to sing, but not play the trumpet, and could be accompanied by his own pianist. Lars Gullin was also given special permission to join as a special guest on baritone saxophone.

At the end of the evening Chet took to the stage in a grey suit, bowed, and with his hand shaking, took the microphone to address the audience. He announced that his pianist, Dick Twardzik, had recently died, adding that Raymond Fol was to replace him for the evening's performance. The show lasted just four songs before a tearful Baker left the stage, too upset to continue. *Melody Maker*'s Mike Nevard later reported that "He sang as though to himself, eyes closed, face screwed tight in concentration … At one point he stood watching Raymond Fol's hands caressing the keys. His mouth tightened and he swallowed. He bit his lip, flexed his shoulders, and went on singing."[47]

The audience reaction to Chet's performance was muted, which is probably not surprising under the circumstances. For Kruger, the event had been a success, despite the difficult circumstances; he had taken on the Musicians' Union, and won an important victory, drawing attention to the UK's arcane laws and making it easier to stage future performances by visiting jazz stars. "Of course, one or two of the newspapers picked up how farcical it was, and one of them even came up to the office and took a shot of Chet playing the trumpet," he recalled. "I think that got front page or, if not, page three of a national newspaper."[48]

The band flew back to Paris next day, where they were summoned to the police station, and subjected to a thorough interrogation. Whilst they had reported that Twardzik had died of a heart attack, they had removed his 'works' and a small amount of heroin from his room, and were well aware of what had happened. Jimmy Bond later recalled that he was "petrified" by the experience, whilst Chet reportedly sat there in a daze, still struggling to come to terms with his friend's death.

Whilst it has never been confirmed, it seems likely that Chet argued with Peter Littman over the cause of Twardzik's death; we do know that Littman was not present in the recording sessions held in subsequent days. Chet would have known that the two musicians regularly scored together, and may well have heard rumours that the two friends left the club together that night. Eddie de Haas, for example, strongly believes that Littman was present when Twardzik overdosed. "They both passed out, but Peter seemed to have a stronger constitution, and woke up, and found Twardzik still," he told me. "I don't know how long had passed, probably one or two hours. He tried to revive him, to walk him round the room, but to no avail."[49]

Back in Boston, Serge Chaloff also held Peter Littman responsible. When the drummer returned home later that year, the saxophonist confronted him over the incident, and punched him in the face in the middle of the crowded Jazz Workshop club.

Even if Twardzik and Littman did score together, it seems unlikely that Littman would have fled the scene that quickly. He had experienced overdoses before, and would have known how to attempt to revive him. But Twardzik's body was found with the syringe still hanging from his arm; he died alone. This interpretation is shared by Liliane, who is convinced that Littman had no role in Twardzik's death. "Dick was a junkie before he met Chet, he was a junkie after he met Chet," she said. "He gave himself an overdose."

Others, including Herb Pomeroy, have suggested that Dick Twardzik committed suicide. He dreaded returning to rehab, and may have taken his own life rather than face the difficult process of cold turkey. Again, this explanation seems unlikely. Aside from one passing comment to Pomeroy himself, there are no signs that he had suicidal tendencies. By all accounts he enjoyed playing with the band, and his written communication with his parents suggest a man who was enjoying seeing the sights of Europe. Moreover, there was no suicide note. "Twardzik would never have passed up the opportunity of dramatising his plight," concluded Jack Chambers, his biographer.

There have also been lingering suspicions that Chet was somehow involved in Twardzik's death. These stories seem to have stemmed from four primary sources. Firstly, from Dick's parents Henryk and Clare, who presumably felt they needed to blame somebody for his untimely death. We know that they wrote several letters to Chet, holding him responsible. "There was a lot of talk that I was responsible for Dick's death," Chet later admitted.[50]

Dick's girlfriend, Crystal Joy, also blamed Chet. She was convinced that Peter Littman would have known how to revive his close friend. Chet, by contrast, might have fled the scene, worried about the impact on his career. There's no real evidence to support this theory, however. Chet's girlfriend, Liliane, did admit that he was a weak character, and might conceivably have left the scene. "This is the way Chet would have reacted," she said. "I wouldn't have trusted Chet to come forward and call for help. I am sorry to say that." Yet she strongly dismisses any suggestion that Chet was present at the time of Dick's overdose. "I don't agree with these stories linking Chet to his death; unless I was blind and deaf, it didn't happen. Next morning he didn't look nervous or worried. I don't remember Chet getting up in the middle of the night. Chet was not a junkie at that time; that I can confirm. I slept with him, I went to bed with him, I lived with him; I think I would know."

The finger of blame was also pointed by Peter Littman himself, who told a number of Boston-based musicians that Chet had failed to revive Dick. This was certainly not an accusation he ever made to Chet's face; he healed his differences with Chet after they returned to the US in 1956. In all likelihood, Littman's accusation was simply the coward's way out; after all, he was a notorious junkie himself, and a known drug buddy of Dick Twardzik. Having been accused of failing to help his friend by Serge Chaloff, he may have found attack the easiest form of defence.

The final argument that Chet was somehow involved stems from Chet's own version of events, which tended to change over time. In his memoirs, he claims that he didn't find out that Dick had been using regularly until "some months" after his death. In the movie *Let's Get Lost*, however, he claimed he had no idea of Twardzik's habit until he overdosed in Switzerland. In a 1963 interview with *Today* magazine in the UK, we hear a third version of events. Here he claimed that Twardzik had asked his permission to shoot up in Holland on 17th September—some ten days earlier. "I told him he was a grown man, and had to decide for himself. I warned him not to let it become a daily habit."[51]

Should we be at all suspicious about Chet's varying explanations? I think not. Chet was well aware that Dick was a junkie long before the band set sail to Europe; given that he was being blamed for his death, and that the incident hit him hard, it is only natural that he tried to distance himself from events as much as possible. Dick's death had cost him dear; he had lost a friend, a great musician, and now he was being held responsible. In the end it was probably the biggest single factor that drove him towards a life of heroin addiction. The fact that the story changed over time is simply the reflection of a junkie's mind. The same thing happened when he was beaten in San Francisco in 1966; the exact circumstances varied each time he told the tale. Laurie Pepper, Art Pepper's widow, reported the same problem when compiling Art's autobiography *Straight Life*. "Art tended to tell an anecdote a little differently every time he told it, with different flourishes, sometimes with a different emphasis," she noted.[52]

The fact is that there is no evidence whatsoever linking Chet Baker to the death of Dick Twardzik. The young pianist died alone, the needle still in his arm, with no one there to revive him. It's sad to admit, but in the light of what we now know, it was probably the inevitable end to the young man's life, an original talent, not yet fully developed, cut off in his prime.

After talking to the police, Chet Baker and Jimmy Bond appear to have gone directly to the studio to start work on the second album for Barclay. Chet later defended his flurry of activity: "I was just trying to keep busy," he wrote in his memoirs. Nils-Bertil Dahlander, a Swedish drummer, replaced Peter Littman, who appears to have fallen out with Chet in the aftermath of Dick's tragic overdose. Chet had hoped that René Urtreger could fill in for Dick, but he was unable to join at such short notice, and was replaced by Gérard Gustin, a young pianist recently signed by Eddie Barclay. "I was proud someone had thought of me," he later recalled. "I felt excited about the idea of playing with the stars, but I dreaded it at the same time."[53]

With no time to rehearse, the band stuck to standards. Whilst they played an uptempo version of 'Summertime', there was an unmistakable air of melancholy hanging over the session. There's an aching sadness to Baker's playing on 'You Go To My Head' and 'Tenderly'; he may have struggled to express his feelings in words, but one can hear the emotion he was going through in his playing.

Next day the band returned to the studio once more. Nicole Barclay had asked if Chet was interested in recording with a sextet, playing arrangements by Pierre Michelot and Christian Chevalier. Chet agreed to do the session, and the band was joined by Benny Vaseur on trombone and Jean Aldegon on alto saxophone. René Urtreger was also available for the date, and replaced Gerard Gustin on piano. The band recorded just four songs that day, reflecting the amount of time needed to rehearse each tune. According to Alain Tercinet, who was present at the session, Chet's esteem for the arrangements was "boundless", and he rerecorded three of the tunes one year later for his *Big Band* album. The final track recorded that day was entitled 'In Memory of Dick', and had been composed by Bobby Jaspar. Chet plays well, but one can't help but feel that Twardzik himself would have made far more of the arrangement than René Urtreger, who was left with the unenviable task of filling his shoes.

On October 29th, Chet travelled to Lyon for the second edition of the Salon du Jazz festival, which took place at the Palais d'Hiver. The promoters advertised 'Bill Coleman, Chet Baker and Sidney Bechet leading the sixteen orchestras you'll be applauding'. The 'orchestras' included Raoul Bruckert and his band, the André Persiany orchestra, Albert Ravouna and his group and the Spree City Stompers, to name but a few. The bands alternated every thirty minutes on Saturday, starting at 9 p.m. and finishing at 5 a.m., and again next day, from 2 p.m. until 5 p.m. The show drew huge crowds, with many of the musicians jamming next door at the Whiskey à Go Go club between sets.

Chet was accompanied by Jimmy Bond, Maurice Vander on piano and Nils-Bertil Dahlander on drums, and excerpts of the concerts were later broadcast by Paris Inter radio on December 8th. *Le Progrès* advertised Chet as the star of the show, and his performance was well received.

Returning to Paris, Chet seems to have patched up his differences with Peter Littman—at least temporarily. With no concerts for a few days, the remaining members of the quartet used to jam regularly in the Club Tabou. Bass player Eddie de Haas remembers that Littman was instrumental in teaching another young drummer, Charles Saudrais, some of the tricks of bebop drumming. "Saudrais was left-handed, as was Littman, so there was a bond there," he remembered. "Charles made a fantastic amount of progress in those couple of months." He also noted that Jimmy Bond seemed to be drifting away from Chet Baker and Peter Littman at this stage. "Jimmy was hardly ever seen. He was the clean member of the band, and a businessman, and was probably working on his eventual return to Los Angeles."[54]

Shortly after this, Chet seems to have fallen out with Peter Littman once again, firing him after a gig at an Army base outside of Paris. “He was acting too strange,” Chet recalled in his memoirs. Littman was forced to sell his drum kit to Jean-Louis Viale to pay for his return flight, and Viale in turn sold his own drum kit to Charles Saudrais.

Work for the Quartet was starting to dry up. A number of planned concerts were cancelled, with promoters concerned about narcotics use within the band. As Jimmy Bond later noted, “Before we left the States, the page was black with concert dates. And they faded along the way. Maybe we were playing one or two a week.”

Kruger and Napoli were struggling to find replacement bookings, and in early November, they booked the band to play several gigs at US Army bases in the UK. Nils-Bertil Dahlander replaced Peter Littman on drums, whilst Maurice Camille Vanderschuern (Maurice Vander) filled in on piano. The tour was inevitably something of a let down after the early concerts. The audience consisted of US servicemen, many of whom were not jazz fans, and most of the halls were less than half full. “Some of them got up and left during the first number,” noted the *Melody Maker*. “Others stood about and talked during the 80-minute concert. By the finale, some thirty or forty had left the hall.” The new members of the band were certainly not of the same standard, either. “The pianist, a Frenchman, did not impress me … he lacked style and personality in his playing, and was an insignificant member of the Quartet.”[55]

Matters were not helped by a dispute between Joe Napoli and Jeff Kruger. According to Oli Stephenson, who was trying to book Chet Baker to play in Iceland at this time, Joe Napoli wanted to break away from Kruger, and work on his own. “Kruger worried that he was going to steal Baker as a client, so there were a lot of telegrams and letters going back and forth, and out to Iceland, because we had made previous bookings,” he said. “I decided to stick with Kruger, because I had heard some stories about Joe Napoli that were not very nice. I knew Kruger, and thought I would get further with him at that time, because I knew the people that worked for him, many of whom later worked at Ronnie Scott’s club.”[56]

Chet’s US manager, Joe Glaser, sided with the UK promoter and club owner in the dispute. “I know that I split with Napoli, and that Joe Glaser wrote him off, warning him never to come back to the States,” recalled Jeffrey Kruger, “and that was not an idle warning.”[57]

A musician’s strike in France appears to have disrupted Chet’s recording plans around this time; two quartet sessions for Barclay, one featuring René Urtreger on piano, the other with Maurice Vander, appear to have been scheduled then cancelled.

Jimmy Bond quit the band shortly after the UK tour, and returned to the West Coast. He reunited with Chet the following year, eventually quitting jazz to become a successful realtor. Years later, he still had fond memories of the time he spent playing with Chet. "Chet had probably one of the most generous talents of any musician that lived," he said. "He could play any tune he had ever heard. He had an uncanny sense of rhythm and melodic line. If he heard a chord, he could improvise whether he knew the name of the chord or not. He was a brilliant player. Chet at his best was as good as anyone."[58]

Without a band, Chet sat in with Bobby Jaspar's Quintet at the Club Saint-Germain on a couple of occasions. Jeffrey Kruger had been able to secure a number of bookings for the month of December, taking in Denmark, Sweden and Iceland. At relatively short notice, Chet had to put together a new group.

Jimmy Bond was replaced by Eddie de Haas, who had jammed with the band on numerous occasions at the Club Tabou in Paris. De Haas was born in the Dutch East Indies, now known as Indonesia, in 1930. He had studied guitar as a child, and played Hawaiian music in Java during the Japanese occupation. He moved to the Netherlands in 1947, where he took up the double bass. When Chet arrived in Paris in 1955, he had just come back from the French Riviera where he had spent the summer working with baritone saxophonist Jay Cameron and drummer Charles Saudrais.

Chet also recruited a number of French musicians to join the band. Jean-Louis Chautemps was a twenty-four-year-old tenor saxophonist, with considerable experience and a lyrical style. "I was kind of a poor man's Bobby Jaspar, fashionable and overrated," he later laughed. "When Bobby couldn't do the thing, or asked too much, they went to someone cheaper, and that was me. It wasn't really an audition, it all went on at the Tabou; I played with Chet, he said 'OK', and two days later we found ourselves in Reykjavik in Iceland where we stayed a few days."

Seventeen-year-old Charles Saudrais joined on drums; Chet knew that he had worked with Peter Littman, and had played with him from time to time in jam sessions. Finally, Raphel 'Ralph' Schecroun was hired to replace Maurice Vander; heavily influenced by Errol Garner, the pianist later changed his name to Errol Parker, and moved to the US.

Once again, Chet demonstrated his inexperience as a bandleader. Ralph Schecroun had little experience of playing in a band, having worked primarily as a solo artist, and his technical abilities were extremely limited. Charles Saudrais was also a poor replacement for Littman; at that stage in his career he lacked the experience and the subtlety of Littman, and his raucous style tended to dominate the proceedings.

The band rehearsed just a handful of times together, mostly at Club Tabou, before hopping on a train to Denmark on December 9th. Two nights later, the Quintet played at the Odd Fellow Palais in Copenhagen. Eddie de Haas remembers the gig was poor. "The piano player could only play in one or two keys, so that was a disaster," he recalled. "He was an Errol Garner-type player. He was a nice guy, but he was never one of the 'in-club', because he'd never played with the rhythm section. He had that pumping left hand, à la Errol Garner, and he'd played mostly solo jobs in Paris." A recording of the concert was later released on CD; it makes for fairly grim listening after the wonderful recordings with Dick Twardzik. Chet sounds uncomfortable from the beginning, playing with a rare anger for much of the concert.

After playing one show in Sweden, Chet flew back to Paris for another recording session with Barclay. The session took place on December 26th, and featured Bobby Jaspar on tenor saxophone, René Urtreger on piano, Benoît Quersin on bass and Jean-Louis Viale on drums. Unfortunately this fine band only had time to record four tunes, including 'Exitus' and 'Dear Old Stockholm' before Chet had to make his way to the airport and fly to Iceland to reunite with his band.

The remainder of the Quintet had spent a cold and lonely Christmas in Iceland. "Boy, Reykjavik was a trip!" laughed Eddie de Haas. "We had dinner in Reykjavik on Christmas Day evening. That was the highlight of the Icelandic trip."

Chet and Liliane arrived two days later from Paris, and the band played a concert at a small club in the centre of Reykjavik. Unfortunately, the club was only half full. "For the first concert there was much anticipation, at least in the group of jazz enthusiasts I used to belong to," recalled local promoter Oli Stephensen. "He came onstage and the first tune was 'Look for the Silver Lining'. He played the first chorus on trumpet, and then he started singing, and when he opened his mouth, you could hear the people who were not familiar with him and his music gasp for air, because one of his front teeth was missing. It didn't look very pretty, although of course, he was a good-looking man. His diction was affected by the missing tooth, so 'Look for the Silver Lining' was not so silvery as expected! The concert was fairly good, but with an Errol Garner-style pianist that Chet was uneasy with, it wasn't a classic concert."[59]

Having lost money on the first concert, Oli Stephensen arranged a second gig at the officer's club at the US Airforce Base in Keflavik, about an hour outside the capital. "We had to travel for a couple of hours to get to an airbase in an unheated military bus," recalled the bass player. "Boy, did we freeze our butts!"

Oli Stephenson remembers the gig as being more successful than the official concert in Reykjavik. "There was more of a club atmosphere, and Chet obviously felt much more at home," he said. "Although Chet did not feel at ease with the officers, it was a good crowd; it was not a typical all-male thing, and they had families and girlfriends there."

The atmosphere may have been better, but Eddie de Haas remembers the audience was more attuned to pop music, rather than jazz. "Maybe there was a small contingent of 5–10% of the military personnel who'd ever heard of Chet Baker," he said. "That was the sad part of it. I don't know what sort of entertainment they were used to, unless it was Bob Hope. But we were all Europeans, and we figured this is American music, everyone must have heard of Chet Baker by now. Jazz music must be *the* popular music. It didn't enter our minds that Elvis Presley had already taken over the market."[60]

The band was due to travel back to the city in the promoter's car, but were stopped and searched at the exit to the base. "It looked like the military police had been tipped off about him, and the affair in Paris," recalled Oli Stephensen. "We were ordered out of the car and they literally pulled it apart, looking for something they did not find. This took quite a while. Chet made no attempt to protest, and held back, knowing they would find nothing in the car. Chet was bored stiff waiting and sat down on the sidewalk next to Liliane, and started singing 'You are My Sunshine', complete with Southern twang; like a cowboy song. Meanwhile his drummer used the sidewalk as a snare drum, and drummed appropriate fills. It was very funny. I wish I had it recorded."[61]

As 1955 drew to a close, Chet Baker had plenty of reasons to be concerned. His first European tour had not exactly gone according to plan. He had lost Dick Twardzik, a good friend and a fine musician, and in the aftermath, his band had disintegrated. Since then he had been floundering; gigs had been cancelled, and he had found himself playing at US Army bases, rather than jazz clubs. He had also struggled to rebuild his band. Eddie de Haas and Jean-Louis Chautemps were fine musicians, but he knew that Saudrais and Schecroun were not up to the task.

Still, he looked to the New Year and sensed a chance to start afresh; Joe Napoli had arranged a tour of Italy, which was scheduled to last for up to two months. The band was booked to play hotels and clubs, rather than Army bases, which had tended to be a depressing experience for the musicians. Just as important, the experienced French pianist, Francy Boland, had agreed to join the band, which would make a big difference to the morale of the group.

The tour of Italy didn't get off to a good start, however. The band made their way from Paris to Milan at the end of December, where they were scheduled to play a two-week run at the elegant Hotel Duomo, starting on New Year's Eve. The hotel was filled with well-heeled guests, dressed in their finest clothes, who had come to drink and dance, rather than to listen to jazz. "A mass of festive drunks arrived to aggravate quite a common nightclub situation—a particular type of customer who never tires of asking for 'Maruzella' and 'La Pansé' while booing every French and American hit," wrote Giancarlo Testoni in *Musica Jazz*.[62] After a few tunes, the audience started to boo, and the manager asked the jazz musicians to stop playing. "Man, these Italians are hard to please—they want *dance* music!" Chet wrote to *DownBeat* magazine. "However, before we finished blowing, they sure swung."[63]

The band stayed on at the hotel for two weeks, before making their way down to Rome for a concert on January 19th. The show was supposed to be opened by the New Traditional Dixielanders, but the band's trumpet player and trombonist failed to show. At short notice, the promoter arranged tenor saxophonist Sandro Serra to open with his quartet, followed by a quintet led by vibraphonist Franco Chiari. Chet played two thirty-minute sets, before going off to jam with the local Italian trumpeter, Nunzio Rotondo.

The show in Rome was witnessed by music critic, Roberto Capresso, who later wrote in *Musica Jazz* that the playing was excellent, and that Baker himself was "extremely friendly and approachable". He was left puzzled by one incident, however, where Chet appeared to throw Charles Saudrais offstage during 'Chik-Eta', and took over on drums himself. Jean-Louis Chautemps dismisses this incident as a simple misunderstanding by the jazz critic. "You see, that's typical, because there, at that moment, it was all pure showbiz. Every night, Chet used to sit down at the same time, practically to the minute, in Saudrais' seat. It was planned like that. We played for two weeks at the Duomo in Milan, and fifteen times, at the same time, Chet sat down at the drums."[64]

Also in the audience was the young Italian trumpet player Cicci Santucci, who remembers being surprised by the strength of Chet's playing. "When Chet Baker came to Italy in 1956, it was a surprise," he said. "When we heard him on record, he played soft, always soft. When we heard Chet Baker live, he was very strong."[65]

The following evening, the band was invited to play as the guest of Dado Ruspoli, one of the leading figures of Italy's 'Dolce Vita'—the circle of beautiful people immortalised by Federico Fellini in his film about high society in 1950s' Rome. The band was a huge success with Rome's in-crowd, and played until 6.30 a.m. next day.

While in Rome, the band was introduced to Romano Mussolini, the son of the late Italian dictator. This was not the occasion of the famous incident between Chet and Romano Mussolini—that would come later, on Chet's second visit to Italy. Romano Mussolini was a jazz pianist, and the bass player from his band was kind to the band. "He showed us around the city, and did his best to make us feel at home," recalled Eddie de Haas.

Chet and Liliane liked to go shopping in Italy, although for quite different reasons. "Liliane loved to go shopping, Chet too," confirmed Jean-Louis Chautemps. "Oh yes, and he liked shoplifting … how shall I put it? He did it to put himself in danger. In the sense used by bad actors, the ones with no talent, who pretend that they have put themselves in danger. Chet had great fun doing that."[66]

The atmosphere within the band remained good, with Chet clowning around with the other band members. "Saudrais and Chet loved having a fight in their hotel, just to play around when they were stoned. It was a game. It would be stupid to use that to jump to any conclusions about their relationship," recalled the saxophonist.

Chautemps went on to draw an interesting parallel between Chet's driving and his playing. "We had some great experiences in the van. Chet used to drive. That's when you understand a lot of things. Seeing someone drive is extraordinary. You can see his thinking, his quickness and fluidity. Chet even drove a van like a sports car; he knew how to change down and all about double-declutching, and especially, he knew how to anticipate. He could see way in front of him on the road; he saw things before they happened. He drove by ear, which allowed him to change gears just at the right moment, with all that refined double-declutching. It was ingenious the way he changed down. He was immediately over there, on the horizon, and at the same time he was still here. What made you sit up when he was at the wheel was how fast he was thinking. Every note he played came out at just the right time."[67]

On 24th January, the band played two concerts at the Conservatorio Cherubini in Florence, a prestigious musical institution. The band was not immediately taken with the venue, which Eddie de Haas described as "an ice-cold church". By the time the afternoon concert was scheduled to begin, the atmosphere had warmed considerably. A busload of jazz fans had travelled from Lucca, and the show had completely sold out, with people even standing in the aisles.

The Italian photographer Cecco Maino introduced himself to Chet after the first show; he would later photograph Chet on his second visit to Italy, and got to know him well over the course of the next few years. "In the interval between the afternoon and the evening concerts we drove Chet to dinner up the hill to have a view of Firenze," he later recalled. "It was dark and crystal clear; the second bridge was still in ruins after the destruction caused by the retreating Nazis. Chet didn't utter a word but was evidently moved."

The concerts in Florence were recorded, and were originally released as *Exitus*, a two-volume set on an Italian record label, Replica Records. The recording is now available on CD, billed as the 'complete concert'; unfortunately it isn't, and still excludes instrumental versions of both 'My Funny Valentine' and 'I Cover the Waterfront', both of which were missing from the original LPs because of space limitations. Still, it's a chance to hear Chet play with Francy Boland, and it's immediately noticeable that Chet sounds more relaxed than he did with Ralph Schecroun, delivering lengthy solos and singing with confidence. Eddie de Haas was impressed by the reaction of the packed crowd. "Chet was received wonderfully everywhere we went," he said.

Chet stayed relatively clean in the aftermath of Dick Twardzik's death. "He smoked some pot, some hashish, but we all did that then. But that was about it," recalled Eddie de Haas. Around this time, the bass player remembers Chet arguing with his girlfriend Liliane over her own use of drugs. "It was at one of these concerts that Chet discovered his girlfriend wanting to get high with cocaine again," he said. "He blew a gasket, and threw all her paraphernalia into the toilet. At that time he was inclined to stay on the straight and narrow path. On the whole trip, including going to Germany afterwards—I never saw Chet so stoned I could tell he'd taken a shot of something. He was clean."[68]

Liliane does not recall this particular event, but does confirm that Chet's drug use during this period was occasional, not regular. "I remember one time in Italy he was looking for drugs; he wasn't hooked at that time. The people sold him some sugar," she said. "He eventually bought a big lump of opium which he smoked in the hotel next day, and it stank. It was very obvious!"

Jean-Louis Chautemps did smoke opium with Chet that day (Sunday 29th January), but confirmed that for the most part, Chet confined his drug use to hashish. "We didn't drink a drop. Well, we did, but he never did. No more than he took heroin, except once in Florence, not that he found it that interesting. Hash, on the other hand, yes he did. I'd already done hashish, it was the least a jazz musician could do then..."[69]

By this stage, Chet and Liliane's relationship was beginning to show signs of strain, in part the result of spending several months on the road. "Our relationship wasn't going so well; we were arguing a lot," she said. "Chet was a musician, and I was just a follower; I had nothing to do. I was not an actress at that time. I traveled, I met all the musicians, and I heard all the music. I had my records and my record player, which followed me everywhere. But I had nothing to do myself."[70]

Shortly after the shows in Florence, the band returned to Rome where they taped a television appearance at the RAI (Radio Italia) studios in Rome. Part of the footage can be seen in the movie *Let's Get Lost*, where it is mistakenly labelled as being filmed at the San Remo Jazz festival. Chet, looking elegant in a dark suit and tie, crooned 'You Don't Know What Love Is', a performance that helped to cement his growing popularity in Italy.

The remainder of the Italian tour had a somewhat ramshackle, improvised feel to it. "On 29th January 1956, the Hot-Club in Perugia organised a concert for Chet at the Sala dei Notari, a historic room on the Piazza del Duomo," recalled Adriano Mazzoletti. "Everyone was staying at the Hotel La Rosetta. On the 30th, I had a phone call from Bruno Berri from the Berri ed Ivaldi firm, an impresario in Milan who'd organised the group's Italian tour. He had problems with the other bookings, and so he asked me to keep Chet and his band in Perugia for another three days. They stayed in town but didn't play, except once at the house of Luisa Gelmetti, who was engaged to

Cleveland Moffett, an American amateur who played drums. On the morning of February 2nd they left Perugia on the train to Padua and they played the same night at the Teatro Verdi."[71]

After a performance in Turin, Chet appears to have been approached by the FBI, who may have been looking into Chet's behaviour in the light of Dick Twardzik's death. "Two guys came backstage before the concert," said Liliane. "They said they came from Manuel, Chet's pot connection in Los Angeles. There was one dark Italian-looking guy, one redhead. They said they had some pot, and rolled a joint, which we smoked. After half a joint I was so high that when Francy Boland played his introduction, I thought I heard the angels sing!"

The two men met up with Chet after the show, but he thought they were acting strangely. "Chet said, 'I don't know why, but I don't trust you guys'. One of them said, 'You're right not to trust us, because this is a bust!' There was a long silence, and then everyone laughed. We spent the whole evening with them, and they even took us to the station next morning. Looking back, I think these guys must have been with the FBI, and came to see whether Chet was addicted to drugs. He wasn't, and they left without taking any steps; he was not hooked, he was not dealing, but he was fiddling."

After completing the Italian leg of the tour, the band toured Germany, culminating in a three-night stay at the Storyville club in Frankfurt. Judging by Chet's letters to *DownBeat* magazine, which were not particularly revealing, the gigs appear to have been a success. "We closed last night here in Storyville after three packed nights. I have never seen such a packed club," he wrote. "You know there's a club in Koln we played, that sure brought me back to The Haig. It really swings."

Between dates, the band returned to Paris, in part to fulfill his contract with Barclay. On February 10th, for example, he entered the Studio Pathé-Magellan with his working band. They only recorded four tunes that day, in part reflecting Chet's growing frustration with the drumming of Charles Saudrais, who was eventually excluded from one of the tracks, 'Tasty Pudding'. He also recorded another session with Pierre Michelot and Christian Chevalier in mid-March.

Chet also ran into Gerry Mulligan in Paris, where Mulligan was playing at the Olympia, the same night as singer Jacqueline François. After the show, eyewitnesses remember seeing Chet jamming with his old partner, frustrated that they were playing behind the stage curtain, rather than in front of the audience.

In late March, Chet drove to Germany, where he made a studio recording in Baden-Baden with the Kurt Edelhagen Orchestra. Thereafter he reunited with Gerry Mulligan, joining him at the airforce base in Kaiserslauten, then at the Air Force Club in Landstuhl. The tour ended on a triumphant note, however, with Chet reuniting with Gerry Mulligan and Stan Getz, playing in front of 12,000 people in Berlin's Deutschlandhalle.

Chet's relationship with Liliane had also run its course. He told her of his intention to return to the US in early April. "Chet said he had to go back to America to play," she said, "and would arrange for me to come." A few months later, however, she received a letter from Chet saying that he had married a woman named Halema. "We looked very much alike; she was very beautiful."

Liliane later learned that Chet descended into drug dependency on his return to the US. "It was good that I never married Chet," she admits. "You can imagine what would have happened if I had stayed with him, because he got deeply into drugs, and eventually got Halema into drugs. I got out of trouble just in time. My relationship with Chet was a good one."

Liliane's love affair with Chet may have ended, but her love affair with jazz continued. She later married Gilbert 'Bibi' Rovère, a French bass player, and enjoyed romantic affairs with a number of jazz musicians in later years, including Dexter Gordon. She went on to become a highly successful actress in France, appearing in a number of movies, including *'Round Midnight*. She stayed in touch with Chet until the very end. "In later years, when Chet came to Paris, I went to listen to him play, because I loved his music," she said. "Every time he met me was in admiration because I never gave him any trouble, and we only had good memories. He used to tell everyone how pretty I was, and how he fell in love with me. So we stayed on very good terms, but no more."[72]

Chapter Seven

CHET BAKER & CREW
1956–1957

"Dick's overdose totally destroyed me. Destroyed me. Dick's parents felt it was my fault, even though I was completely unaware of the situation."—Chet Baker

In its heyday, a year was a long time in jazz, much as a year can be a long time in the world of popular music now. New stars emerge, new styles start to take shape, and the critics, as fickle then as they are now, are always on the lookout for the next big thing.

Chet Baker flew back to New York from Berlin on 4th April 1956. He had been gone for just seven months, but in that time his profile in the United States had started to diminish.

On the face of it, little had changed. West Coast jazz continued to thrive. Dave Brubeck had built on his early success, leaving the Fantasy label in 1954 to sign with a major label, Columbia, his face even appearing on the cover of *Time* magazine that same year. He continued to develop his appeal with his young, student audience, recording live albums such as *Jazz Goes To College* (1954) and *Jazz Goes To Junior College* (1957). At times the group struggled to find a balance between Brubeck's rhythmically complex, classically influenced, occasionally heavy-handed piano style and the more lyrical approach favoured by alto saxophonist Paul Desmond. In many respects the band's sound was cemented by the hiring of Joe Morello, an East Coast drummer, in early 1956, which set the stage for the band's crossover success following the release of *Time Out* in 1959.

Stan Getz had also started to emerge as a star in his own right. In July 1955, Getz had opened at Zardi's with a fine quintet that included Conte Candoli on trumpet, Lou Levy on piano, Leroy Vinnegar on bass and Shelly Manne on drums. The same band went into the studio with Norman Granz the following month and recorded *West Coast Jazz*; no matter that much of the material was 'East Coast' in style, including Miles Davis' 'Four' and Dizzy Gillespie's 'A Night in Tunisia'—the album helped to cement Getz's growing reputation, and paved the way for other successful albums, such as *The Steamer* (1956) and *Award Winner* (1957).

The East–West divide remained just as pronounced as when Chet Baker played opposite Miles Davis in New York in 1954. Miles himself remained vocal on the subject. In a *DownBeat* interview in late 1955, he dismissed the West Coast jazz scene, claiming that he found the music dull. "My general feeling about what's happening on the coast is like what Max Roach was saying the other night. He said he rather hear a guy miss a couple of notes than hear the same old clichés all the time. Often when a man misses, it at least shows he's trying to think of something new to play. But the music on the coast gets pretty monotonous even if it's skillfully done. The musicians out there don't give me a thrill the way Sonny Rollins, Dizzy and Philly Jo Jones do. I like musicians like Dizzy because I can always learn something new from him." He was particularly dismissive of pianist Dave Brubeck. "Do I think he swings? He doesn't know how. Frankly I'd rather hear Lennie [Tristano]. Or for that matter I'd rather hear Dizzy play the piano than Brubeck, because Dizzy knows how to touch the piano and he doesn't play too much."[1]

The jazz critics also played their part in talking up the East–West divide. Nat Hentoff described tenor saxophonist Sonny Rollins as the most influential player since the emergence of Stan Getz in the late 1940s and early 1950s. "Unlike the mesmeric Getz of that period, Sonny's approach is far from cool, and he is seldom lyrical. Sonny's style is hot, driving, deeply pulsating, and is rooted in Charlie Parker and before Bird, Coleman Hawkins."[2]

On the surface, then, little seemed to have changed while Chet Baker was in Europe. But there were a number of strong currents beneath the surface, pulling jazz in different directions, and in some cases, threatening its growing mainstream popularity.

One such change was the gradual fragmentation of jazz into a variety of different styles. The terms 'West Coast' and 'East Coast' jazz were convenient labels for jazz critics and certain musicians, but masked the constant exchange of ideas and personnel. Just as the 'Birth of the Cool' had influenced a number of the West Coast musicians, including Chet Baker, so Chet Baker had been influenced by his encounter with Miles Davis in New York. Likewise Sonny Rollins may have been "hot, driving, deeply pulsating", but in early 1957 he recorded an album entitled *Way Out West*, recorded in Los Angeles and featuring Shelly Manne on drums.

East Coast jazz was also starting to fragment, with bop under threat from the growing emergence of 'cool' jazz; this was somewhat ironic considering the origins of the *Birth of the Cool* in the New York apartment of Gil Evans. The pianist on those sessions, John Lewis, had found success with the Modern Jazz Quartet, which also featured vibraphonist Milt Jackson, bass player Percy Heath and drummer Connie Kay. The quartet made its debut in the early 1950s, developing a chamber-style music that moved jazz away from the clichés of bop, towards a more delicate, ensemble sound that owed as much to the string quartet as the bebop of Charlie Parker.

Miles Davis was also showing signs of moving away from 'bebop' towards a more 'cool' sound of his own, a fact that did not go unnoticed by bass player Charlie Mingus, who went as far as to write an open letter to Miles Davis in *DownBeat* magazine in late 1955. "How is Miles Davis going to act when he gets back and gets going again? Will it be like a gig in Brooklyn not too long ago with Max, Monk and me when he kept telling Monk to 'lay out' because his chords were all wrong? Or even at a more recent record date when he cursed, laid out, argued and threatened Monk and asked Bob Weinstock why he hired such a nonmusician and would Monk lay out on his trumpet solos? What's happening to us disciples of Bird?"[3]

Whilst the 'disciples' of Bird moved in their different directions, the jazz critics continued to keep their eyes open for changing trends and emerging stars. Chet's short-lived position as the critics' favourite trumpet player was under threat before he left for Europe, but the emergence of Clifford Brown and the 'comeback' of Miles Davis, left him in a vulnerable position, something he struggled to comprehend on his return from Europe.

Clifford Brown had joined Max Roach in the summer of 1954, and soon made a name for himself with his 'fat' tone, influenced by 'Fats' Navarro, and his astonishing control. His work with the Brown–Roach Quintet can be heard on such albums such as *Study in Brown* and *At Basin Street*, where his solos on tunes such as 'Cherokee' are taken at an astonishing pace. He was also a sensitive accompanist, as witnessed by his delicate yet vital contributions to the early solo recordings of Sarah Vaughan and Helen Merrill. Sadly, the Brown–Roach Quintet lasted for just two years, the trumpet player's life cut short by a car accident on the Pennsylvania turnpike which also claimed the life of pianist Richie Powell, brother of Bud Powell, together with Powell's wife. Clifford Brown was just twenty-five years old.

Miles Davis's comeback was cemented by his performance at the Newport Jazz Festival of 1955. He had only been added to the bill at the last minute, but his performance of Monk's ''Round Midnight' on mute trumpet won over the audience, even if Monk insisted that he had played it wrong. "When I got off the bandstand," Miles later said, "everybody was looking at me like I was king."[4]

As Chet was making preparations to head off to Europe, Miles opened at the Café Bohemia with an impressive new band featuring Red Garland on piano, Paul Chambers on bass and the young drummer 'Philly' Joe Jones. Miles was initially joined by Sonny Rollins on tenor saxophone, but his stay was to prove short-lived, as he left New York to focus on ending his drug addiction. Miles eventually settled on John Coltrane as his replacement, who was yet to make a name for himself as a major stylist.

The sharp contrast in style between the spare, mournful ache of Miles's muted trumpet and the probing, restless sound of Coltrane's tenor can be heard to good effect on ballads such as ''Round Midnight'. The quintet disbanded after a short time, in part because of Coltrane's heroin addiction, but not before they had recorded enough tunes to fulfill Davis's contractual obligation to Prestige Records, material that resulted in the albums *Steamin'*, *Cookin'*, *Workin'* and *Relaxin'*.

Signing with a major label, Columbia, Miles Davis made clear to producer George Avakian the full extent of his ambitious plans. "We found in each other a mutual interest in furthering the ideals of the nine-piece band. What direction this desire would take was uncertain, beyond the conviction that Gil Evans was the arranger we wanted. A series of discussions with Gil followed, out which grew the basic conception (largely Miles') of this album; within the framework he wanted. Gil developed the details which produce the remarkable texture of a large jazz orchestra, a texture unique in tonal quality and breaking away from the roots which are to be found in the Davis group of the late Forties."[5]

The resulting album, *Miles Ahead*, recorded in May 1957, was one of the high points of Miles' long recording history. Playing flugelhorn for the first time on album, Miles floats effortlessly over Gil Evans' melancholy arrangements with his soft tone and subtle, considered playing. Charlie Mingus was right all along: Miles Davis no longer sounded like a disciple of Bird—he had a concept that was all his own, a style that would be further developed on subsequent projects with Gil Evans, including *Porgy and Bess* and *Sketches of Spain*, and taken to new levels with *Kind of Blue*, recorded two years later in the spring of 1959.

Outside the sphere of jazz, there were significant developments in the world of popular music; developments that would have little impact for now, but as jazz continued to splinter, with elements moving towards the avant-garde, meant that jazz started to lose its position with the mainstream audience. Over in Europe, Chet's bass player Eddie de Haas had noted that Elvis Presley was starting to take over the market; weeks later, just three months before Chet Baker returned to North America, Elvis entered the RCA studios for the first time. Two weeks later, on January 27th, 'Heartbreak Hotel' was released as a single, with Elvis making his first national TV appearance the very next day. Rock and roll had arrived.

Whilst Miles Davis had a clear vision as to what he wanted to achieve, and the sort of musicians he wanted to work with, Chet wasn't looking beyond the next concert. On his return from Europe, Chet made his way to Boston, where he quickly patched up his differences with drummer Peter Littman. They hooked up with another old friend of Dick Twardzik, bass player Jack Lawler. They formed a quartet with pianist Johnny Williams and played a three-week gig at the Rouge Lounge in Detroit, starting on April 24th.

Around this time, Chet called his old friend, tenor saxophonist Phil Urso, who was happy to rejoin the band. Urso effectively took over as the de facto bandleader, recruiting a full-time band, working on arrangements and booking tour dates. As a consequence, Harvey Leonard took over from Johnny Williams on piano, and percussionist Bill Loughborough rejoined the band in mid-May, giving the band a fuller sound.

As a result of Phil Urso's efforts, the new-look sextet found themselves booked up for several weeks. The tour appears to have included one week in Toronto, one week at Peacock Alley, St. Louis (18th–26th May), The Showboat in Philadelphia (late May), Washington (4th–10th June), Cleveland and Chicago (20th June–4th July). Thereafter, they were scheduled to return to the West Coast where Dick Bock was planning a couple of recording sessions.

The tour was eventful in a number of respects. It was while Chet was playing in Detroit that he caught the eye of an elegant, short-haired, dark-skinned young lady named Halema Alli. Born in the US, but of East Indian origin, Halema possessed the same sultry, exotic good looks that originally drew him to Liliane. A shy, unassuming twenty-year-old, she lived at home with her parents, and was taken aback when this famous jazz musician started calling her from Toronto, the next stop on the tour.

Chet had been used to traveling with Liliane whilst away on tour, and was no doubt missing her now that he had returned home. One night he impetuously proposed to Halema, suggesting they get married immediately, so that she could travel the country with him. Flattered by the attention, and excited by the prospect of escaping Detroit, and seeing the rest of the country, she agreed. Years later, she struggled to explain her rash decision. "I ran away from home," she admitted. "I just left one day, don't ask me why. Nobody knew I was leaving. A girlfriend who helped me leave called my parents to tell them, so they wouldn't worry about me, and after I got married, then I told them."[6]

Chet drove from Toronto to Detroit with Peter Littman, picked up Halema, and then drove to St. Louis where they were wed by a Justice of the Peace. The marriage started well enough, with Chet showering his young bride with gifts, including a brand new Thunderbird for her twenty-first birthday. Chet tried to keep her away from the drug users within the band, who included Peter Littman and Phil Urso, but she was naïve about such things. Even when Chet started using more regularly in the weeks that followed, he took great care not to do so in front of Halema. "Chet never, ever used drugs in front of me," she said. "Ever."[7]

While the band was playing in Philadelphia, the twenty-year-old pianist Bobby Timmons, a Philadelphia native, sat in with the band. Chet Baker and Phil Urso evidently regarded him as a superior pianist to Harvey Leonard, who was fired. Whilst the liner notes to a recent reissue of the Chet Baker CD *Playboys* suggest that Harvey Leonard left the band in Los Angeles, this seems to be incorrect. Bill Loughborough recalled that Leonard reported Chet Baker to the Musicians' Union for compensation for the lack of notice, a story that is supported by an old friend of Timmons.

The following week, Chet finally got to meet the jazz composer, Bob Zieff. He had recorded an album of his compositions in Paris, *Rondette*, with the pianist Dick Twardzik, and they had left him with a lasting impression. On his return to the United States he contacted Zieff in New York and asked if he had any more music that he might record. For his own part, Zieff had been impressed with Chet's playing, and had no hesitation in giving him two more tunes, 'Slightly Above Moderate' and 'Medium Rock'. "He asked me to go down to Washington with the group where we rehearsed a number of my pieces to record when they got to LA," recalled Zieff. "I think Phil Urso or someone on the scene said Art Pepper didn't want to play my music—quite understandable since he had been living in musical cliché settings forever—although he was a very good and capable player. Chet was most unhappy with the way Bobby Timmons misplayed my music. Chet said that he knew Bobby was playing wrong chords, but that he could do nothing about it."[8]

Chet was still not a natural bandleader at this stage, even after his experience in Europe; the contrast with Miles Davis in that respect was quite remarkable. "Onstage, Chet was very relaxed," recalled Phil Urso, "but he used to let me run the band. If he couldn't think of anything, I'd come in with a refrain, and he'd know what that was. On other tunes that we played, he knew them, and he counted off. He tried to be a leader, and sometimes he was—but most of the time he wasn't! A lot of the times the piano player started, Chet would pick up on it, then I would come in with the harmony, and everything would come together."[9]

On their way back from Chicago to the West Coast, Phil Urso remembers Chet getting stopped for speeding. Tearing through a small town at ninety miles an hour, the police spotted him and gave chase. Chet put his foot down, accelerating to over 130 mph, the car sounding like a small jet about to take off. The police couldn't keep up, but phoned ahead to arrange a roadblock in the next town, where less than an hour later, Chet was hauled in front of the local judge. "I didn't think I was over 85," Chet told the judge in his quiet tone. "But the limit was 35," the judge explained. "What's the fine?" "$50 or two nights in jail." Chet always had a wad of bills, but that night the smallest he had was a one hundred dollar bill. He waved the bill before the judge and asked if he could make change.

The band arrived in Los Angeles, where Dick Bock had arranged a high-profile gig playing opposite rising star Art Blakey and his band, the Jazz Messengers. Bass player Jack Lawler hadn't made the journey out west, but was replaced by Chet's old friend, Jimmy Bond. "We were opposite Art Blakey and Jackie McLean," recalled Phil Urso. "I was good friends with Art Blakey. We used to listen to each other's bands, see what was nice, what was real nice. The improvisation was great."

Back on the West Coast, it was like Chet had never been gone. "When Chet sang 'They're singing songs of love, but not for me. The lucky stars above, but not for me …', boy, they ate it up, they loved it," said Phil Urso.

"You could see the girls' faces in the light; they already had him in bed! The way he sang, it was good for the ladies. The men kind of shook it off, they listened to it, but they couldn't wait 'til he put the horn to his mouth. That's what they came in for."[10]

After two weeks at Jazz City, the band moved across the street to the Peacock Club, where they played opposite Shorty Rogers. "Shorty Rogers had Bill Holman on tenor saxophone, who was doing some of the writing. And Shorty was also writing, so they had plenty of arrangements," recalled Urso. "So I approached Shorty and I says, 'We're a little short of charts, could you write a few for us?' He said, 'Sure, I've got the time'. So he wrote four of five for us, then Bill Holman wrote about three or four, so we finally got enough music to rehearse."

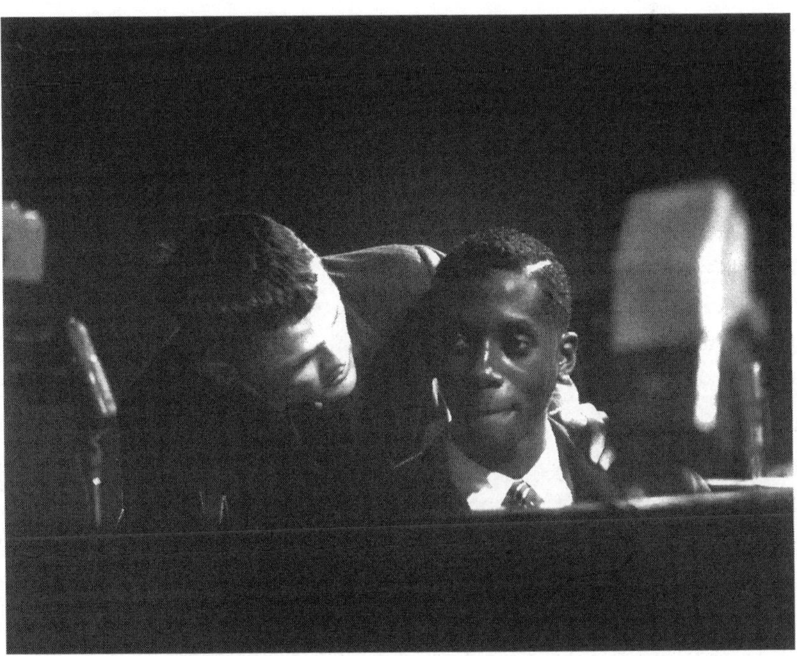

Chet Baker and Bobby Timmons, October 1956.
Stars of Jazz 1956 (c)Ray Avery / CTSIMAGE

By late July, Dick Bock thought the band was ready to record, and booked a week at the Forum Theatre in Los Angeles. He had not recorded with Chet for almost eighteen months, and was keen to make up for lost time. The main album that came out of these recording sessions, entitled *Chet Baker and Crew*, featured Chet's working band, which featured Phil Urso on tenor saxophone and Bobby Timmons on piano.

In addition to the Bob Zieff compositions mentioned earlier, the band also recorded a number of Phil Urso's tunes. 'Chippyin' gives us a fair indication of the drug use within the band, referring to the junkie slang—also referred to as 'chipping'—for the recreational or occasional use of heroin. Chet was also starting to use more frequently at this time, and since he refused to take drugs in front of Halema, he started to spend more time in the company of the other junkies within the band—Phil Urso, Peter Littman and Bobby Timmons. Chet's young wife was unhappy that he was spending so much time with the band, and Phil Urso wrote a tune, 'Halema', in an attempt to make her happy. "Phil has told me that she was a nice lady, but kind of jealous of Chet going out a lot, hence why the song was written by Phil," explained Graham Carter of Jazzed Media. "He wrote it to placate her but I don't think it did much good."[11]

Chet only recorded one vocal for the album, a version of 'Line for Lyons' with lyrics written by Bill Loughborough. "I was surprised when Chet recorded my lyrics," he revealed, "since it was clear Gerry would never allow it to be issued—although after his death it's been included in later CDs."[12]

The resulting album was quite different to Chet's previous outings with Pacific Jazz. Chet plays with the same full tone, the same drive, as he had demonstrated across Europe. It was a sound that had evolved since his encounter with Miles Davis at Birdland, but it was new to his American audience. "A new Chet Baker is unveiled," wrote Woody Woodward in the original liner notes. "This is not the Chet Baker heard with the Mulligan Quartet or at Ann Arbor. He has not changed radically. That sound is still there. Only the passage of time could bring about what has happened. He speaks with authority now, and with an electric spark that was not as evident in the past."

A photo shoot for the album cover was arranged on a boat off the coast of Los Angeles. Photographer William Claxton captures the spirit of the band looking relaxed and carefree as Chet leaned over the edge of the boat, his trumpet to his mouth, glistening in the summer sun. Only percussionist Bill Loughborough was missing from the photograph. "My wife had come to LA, and had to do something," he later recalled, "and that was more important to me than being on the cover of an album. I was more of a family person than a musician!"[13]

Chet Baker with (left to right) Jimmy Bond, Peter Littman, Bobby Timmons and Phil Urso, summer 1956. Photograph by William Claxton / Courtesy Demont Photo Management, LLC

The album was released to strong reviews. In *DownBeat* magazine, Nat Hentoff, who had occasionally been critical of Chet's soft tone and limited range, was impressed by the change that had taken place in his style since he left for Europe. "This may well be Baker's best LP so far. He plays throughout with more virility than often heretofore; his tone is fuller with a cheering diminution of wispiness, and withal, he has been able to retain the lyricism that is his primary identification." He awarded the album four stars.

Hentoff also recognised the contribution of the other band members, singling out Phil Urso for particular praise. "Urso's presence helps since Phil has an earthy, strongly swinging quality to his playing, and perhaps his own playing is the lifting agent in the proceedings. His own work is almost wholly derivative of Zoot-and-other-brothers but is pleasant and emotionally alive. In the rhythm section, Timmons impresses considerably—a modernist who articulates cleanly, and is thoroughly funky in a springy way, and thinks besides. Bond is also good—he cares for tone quality. Littman is a crisp, spearing, stimulating drummer. The boo-bams are only heard briefly; Loughborough ought to be invited back so we can hear more what these drums might contribute to a jazz combo."[14]

Dick Bock also arranged two other projects that same week. The first was to record some additional vocal tracks for a twelve-inch LP version of *Chet Baker Sings*, a project that reunited him with pianist Russ Freeman. It was not a particularly remarkable session; the highlight is probably Chet's reading of 'Like Someone in Love', which is beautifully phrased. We also get a rare opportunity to hear Chet play muted trumpet on 'My Buddy', although the vocal sounds somewhat under-rehearsed.

The second project saw Dick Bock attempt to pair Chet with alto saxophonist Art Pepper. Pepper had just completed a twenty-month jail sentence, and Bock was presumably hoping that the session would help Art to get his chops back in shape. He may also have felt that the pairing was a more commercial proposition than Chet's recording with Phil Urso.

Dick Bock's attempts at matchmaking were doomed to failure, just as they had been when he tried to pair Chet Baker and Stan Getz in the summer of 1953. There was no love lost between the two of them, with the saxophonist mistakenly blaming Chet for one of his early arrests. Time had done little to heal these wounds, it seems. There was some disagreement over the material, even before the two of them got together, with Pepper reluctant to play the Zieff compositions that Baker proposed. Pepper may also have refused to record with Chet's band, since an entirely different line-up was hired for the occasion—including Pete Jolly on piano, Leroy Vinnegar on bass and Stan Levey on drums.

The resulting recording session was something of a compromise; Chet and Art record five tunes as a sextet, a band that also featured tenor saxophonist Richie Kamuca. Thereafter, the group split, with Pepper supported by the rhythm section on his own composition 'Ol' Croix', before playing stripped-back versions of 'I Can't Give You Anything But Love' and 'The Great Lie' with just bass and drums. Baker, Kamuca and Jolly each play a 'solo' piece to round off the record, with Chet recording 'Sweet Lorraine'. The fragmented nature of the session meant that the album was not released at the time, with

Bock releasing several tracks on compilations over the years. With the aid of producer Michael Cuscuna, the whole session was eventually unearthed and released as *The Route*.

On the face of it, Chet's return to the United States had been a success. He was playing well, and for the most part his 'new' style had been well received by the influential jazz magazines. He had assembled an excellent band; Phil Urso's presence gave the band a harder, more bop-oriented feel. Bobby Timmons was technically less gifted than Dick Twardzik, but played with a sense of swing that was sometimes lacking in the original quartet. Peter Littman, for all of his faults, helped to cement the band, providing them with a more driving sound, an element that had been missing when they played opposite Miles Davis two years earlier. "We had an 'us against the world' spirit, and played successfully in quite a few places," recalled Bill Loughborough.

The growing use of narcotics within the band was beginning to take its toll, however. Loughborough remembers that Phil Urso, in particular, was beginning to take too many chances. He remembered one occasion when the saxophonist insisted on getting a fix while the band stopped at a gas station to refuel, walking back to the car from the bathroom, sucking the blood off the crook of his arm. Eventually Bill Loughborough had enough, and told Chet of his intention to quit the band. "I didn't want to be around when Chet, like so many of the era, had the overdose from which there was no recovery. We liked each other a lot and he understood my view on the matter," he said. "That was only part of it, however—I just didn't want to be a traveling musician. I was more interested in promoting the drums, and shortly after that, I went back into technology and didn't play for forty years."[15]

In later years, Chet gave various reasons for his increased use of heroin at this time. His autobiography *As Though I Had Wings* is not particularly revealing. "I began to get high more and more often," he says, "until finally I was hooked."

In a frank interview with a UK tabloid, from an article entitled "The Trumpet And The Spike—A Confession By Chet", he later described how he made the transition from marijuana to heroin. "What happens with pot is this; you smoke away regularly and sooner or later you find out its effect is going tamer and tamer. One day a friend was with me—I remember how it started well enough—and he said I should kick pot, which was kid's stuff. He took a spike and showed me how to use it and suddenly I was hooked.

I became a junkie. Spiking myself became a gesture as automatic as lighting a cigarette is with you. I did it thousands of times, squeezing the vein out and plunging the syringe. My veins became hardened and my arms became covered with sores—but I didn't care. A junkie never does. From then on I was on heroin and this is where things started to get hot for me, because in New York you can get as much pot as you like—it's as simple as stopping in the street and whistling—but with junk it's not the same. You have to have a connection, dig?"[16]

The article, suitably dressed up by the tabloid press, focuses more on the process of injecting heroin than the reasons behind his addiction. In an interview with *Jazz Hot* magazine in 1983, however, he offers some explanations for his behaviour. "I got married for a second time, and that was a big mistake. The fact that I was no longer as popular in the States as I had been before was maybe also a factor."

Chet's explanation doesn't sound particularly plausible, however. There's no doubt that he rushed into his second marriage, but photographs taken by William Claxton that summer suggest a couple that were very much in love at that time; the problems only started later, when Halema found out she was expecting a child, and Chet's drug use started to get out of hand.

The suggestion that he was no longer as popular also doesn't ring true. A number of jazz critics had started to turn against him before his departure for Europe, and if anything, he had started to make a more favourable impression on his return. The audience reaction to his gigs was also extremely positive, judging by comments from Phil Urso and Bill Loughborough. The critical backlash really started in earnest after Chet's drug-taking got out of hand; he was thrown off the 'Birdland Stars of '57' tour in the spring of that year, received a scathing review for his short-lived gig at Peacock Lane, and was given bad reviews for a number of lacklustre albums in 1958, such as *Stan Meets Chet* and *It Could Happen To You*. There can be no doubt that Chet's addiction and subsequent unreliable behaviour contributed to his decline in popularity, not the other way around.

It has been suggested that the escalation in Chet's drug use coincided with his growing concern that he was not being accepted by African–American jazz musicians such as Miles Davis, whose respect and approval he craved. Phil Urso admitted that one of the reasons behind his own use of drugs was to keep up appearances with musicians that he admired. "A little tiny snort to be company and be around them to learn the music."[17]

There may be an element of truth to this explanation, but for the most part Chet was content to take drugs in the company of the fellow addicts within the band, rather than with musicians such as Art Blakey and Jackie McLean.

There seems little doubt that the biggest single factor contributing to Chet's increased use of heroin was his lingering feeling of guilt over the death of Dick Twardzik. Twardzik's parents, Henryk and Clare, had sent him numerous letters accusing Chet of killing their son. Chet also claimed that Dick's girlfriend—Crystal Joy—had slapped him in the face when they ran into each other in New York, a claim she vehemently denied. The accusations eventually started to take their toll. "There was a lot of talk that I was responsible for Dick's death," he admitted in *Today*, a British tabloid.[18]

The timing of Chet's addiction suggests it was the accusation that he was somehow responsible for Dick's overdose, rather than the death itself, that drove Chet to seek refuge from the pain he was feeling. The closest we get to understanding the extent of his suffering comes from an interview with Jerome Reece in *Jazz Hot* magazine in 1983. "Dick's overdose totally destroyed me. Destroyed me. Dick's parents felt it was my fault, even though I was completely unaware of the situation," he admitted.[19]

According to Halema, Chet consulted a psychiatrist over his behavioural problems when he moved to New York in 1958. She later found out that the doctor believed Chet was using drugs to punish himself over the guilt he was feeling over Dick Twardzik's death. Unfortunately no amount of therapy appeared to soothe his troubles, and Chet sank even further into his addiction.

For the time being, at least, Chet's addiction was sufficiently under control that many of his friends—Halema included—did not notice that anything was wrong. Around this time, photographer William Claxton drove over to Chet's house at Redondo Beach with the aim of taking some pictures for a possible record cover. "When I arrived, a young woman named Halema greeted me at the door and looked so fresh and pretty in her summer dress that I *had* to include her in the pictures," he later wrote. "I took them next door to an unoccupied house that was in the process of being remodeled. I had them sit in a bare window seat, with the soft back light streaming through the window, and the mood was set."[20]

The resulting photo shoot included one of the Claxton's most celebrated images of Chet—his shirt off, looking fit and muscled, trumpet in hand, he looks longingly into the eyes of his wife. Halema, meanwhile, sitting on the white window seat, wearing an elegant linen dress, leans into Chet's right arm, gazing at the camera. The two of them look lost in the moment, and other photographs from the shoot reveal a young couple still very much in love. Sadly, it was not to last.

The band, minus Bill Loughborough, taped a KABC-TV show in Los Angeles on September 5th, where they played two songs—'Imagination' and 'Jumpin' off a Clef'. The quintet then drove up to San Francisco, where they played for two weeks at the Blackhawk, before finishing the month back at Peacock Lane in Los Angeles.

The following month Dick Bock had Chet return to the recording studio on two separate occasions. The first was to record a 'big band' album, which was inspired by the eight-piece band recordings Chet had made for Barclay in Paris. Dick Bock had never got round to releasing those recordings on Pacific Jazz. He was keen to capture Chet's 'new', lustier tone accompanied by a big band, and was no doubt happy to rerecord the same tunes, and avoid paying any licensing fee to Nicole Barclay. Seven tracks were recorded with a nonet, including 'Mythe', 'Not Too Slow' and 'V-line' which were composed and arranged for the March 1956 Paris session; a further three tunes were recorded by an eleven-piece band which included Art Pepper, Bud Shank and Phil Urso on saxophone. The arrangements are better suited to Chet's style than the earlier *Ensemble* and *Sextet* records, and swing easily.

Dick Bock hadn't given up on the idea of pairing Chet with Art Pepper, and brought the two West Coast jazz stars back into the studio once again in late October. To avoid any clash over the material for the session, Bock arranged for them to record an album of compositions by the saxophonist, Jimmy Heath. The result was what Heath later described as "an authentic junkie record".

"Art Pepper was just out of jail, Chet was arrested a week after the session, and piano player Carl Perkins would die two years later," he told Jeroen de Valk. "When the record was recorded, I was behind bars myself. In 1955, I was caught with narcotics and had to serve almost five years. Luckily I was allowed to keep my saxophone in the cell, and I composed a lot during the time. They had to come to fetch the music for Playboys from jail."[21]

Despite the band's condition, the session went smoothly. "The record date went very, very well," Phil Urso remembered. "Carl Perkins played piano with his left elbow up in the air! The date came off good." Although Chet Baker and Art Pepper were never close, there was far greater chemistry in their playing than in Chet's earlier recordings with Stan Getz. Phil Urso also plays well on the record, and contributes some bright, inventive solos. The album was eventually released on Pacific Jazz under the name 'Playboys', the original cover featuring a blonde model covering her bare breasts with a pair of glove puppets.

Dick Bock had recorded four albums of material with Chet in as many months. Was he trying to make up for time 'lost' while Chet was touring Europe, or aware that he was his biggest star was developing a heroin habit that was showing signs of spiralling out of control? One suspects the latter. Chet had argued with Peter Littman, a well-known junkie, during the making of *Big Band*, and Phil Urso was not always subtle over his addiction, as Bill Loughborough described.

The Pacific Jazz photographer William Claxton also noticed the changes in Chet's appearance and behaviour around this time. "It was during a recording session in 1956 that I realised the Chet Baker I had known was changing and moving into another world—a world of dependency," he wrote. "The drugs were taking over. Yet his playing seemed remarkably good in spite of this intrusion."[22]

On November 8th 1956, one week after the 'Playboys' record date, Chet was arrested for the possession of heroin—the first time he had been caught with 'hard' drugs. Beyond this, the details are a little murky. The Dutch author, Jeroen de Valk, noted that Chet was sentenced to two months at the Federal Hospital in Lexington, Kentucky.[23] Helen LaFaro-Fernández, the sister of bass player Scott LaFaro, and author of his biography, also suggests that a planned tour may have been delayed while "Chet cleared up his problems in Los Angeles". If Chet did spend time in Lexington at this time, the sentence would appear to have been cut short, as he was back in the studio in late November, and on the road again by November 27th.[24]

Before he hit the road, Dick Bock managed to find the time for one last recording session, a quartet date with the pianist Russ Freeman, which turned out to be their final collaboration. The precise date of the recording is not known. Most discographies list the date as November 6th, but the recording data kept by Pacific Jazz was notoriously inaccurate, and there have been suggestions that the date took place in late November.

The album, which also featured Leroy Vinnegar on bass and Shelly Manne on drums, was later released as *Quartet*, and was jointly credited to Russ Freeman and Chet Baker. The record opens with the stunning 'Love Nest', which was the theme to the popular *Burns and Allen* TV Show. After a number of aborted takes, Chet delivers a wonderful solo on muted trumpet. Another highlight is Russ Freeman's 'Summer Sketch', a ballad on a par with 'The Wind', and one of the pianist's favourite compositions. 'Say When', another Freeman original, features bright, vibrant solos from both Baker and Freeman, whilst Billy Strayhorn's 'Lush Life' is given a fairly straight reading.

Shelly Manne later remembered the session fondly. "Sometimes you go into a studio, and for some strange reason—the set-up is right, everything feels right, you can hear clearly, all your creative juices are flowing, and everything is perfect—it's kinda like magic almost. And those are the times you really make some great records … Russ and I had found almost a new way of playing in the rhythm section together—a kind of looser, freer way, where we were an integral part of melody lines and what was happening rhythmically, without just being stuck in the background … Leroy was such a strong walker; he gave us a foundation to lean on. And Chet was such a loose, free player that it worked perfectly with him."[25]

Quartet is probably the strongest of the numerous dates recorded with Freeman, in part reflecting the growing maturity of the musicians, but also because of the driving drumming of Shelly Manne on the more uptempo numbers.

After this recording session, Chet Baker appears to have hit the road with a new-look quintet. Chet had argued with Peter Littman during the recording of the *Big Band* album, and was replaced by Larance Marable. Jimmy Bond, the only clean member of the band, also decided to quit, and was replaced by the twenty-year-old Scott LaFaro, the influential bass player who made his name with Bill Evans.

Scott LaFaro had been playing with the Buddy Morrow orchestra, but was frustrated that the musicians were encouraged to stick to the charts, which allowed little room for improvisation. He sat in with the Chet Baker after hours one night at the urging of his tenor saxophonist, Phil Urso. At the end of the evening, Chet asked him to join the band, and embark on a short tour of colleges and small jazz clubs. "Scotty was finally realising what he had been working and hoping for," recalled Helen LaFaro-Fernández, "a gig with real jazz guys. He was thrilled out of his mind with this development and called home to tell Dad and his family his great news."[26]

The first confirmed date of the tour was at Frazier Hall at Idaho State

College on November 27th. A reviewer of the concert noted the tunes they played included 'Slightly above Moderate', 'Ray's Idea' and 'Tommyhawk'.

According to Suzanne Stewart, Scott LaFaro's former fiancée , Scott was concerned by Chet's heroin addiction. "Scotty phoned often during his time with Chet," she recalled, "complaining of Baker's irresponsibility and waste of his wonderful talent."[27]

Bass player Paul Warburton saw the Quintet play at Denver University in late 1956, and also witnessed Chet's condition at this time. "I remember being floored by that whole band, but particularly Scottie, because I was a bass player," he recalled. "They had chairs set up for Chet and Phil because they were so fucked up, they kept nodding out. But at that time I was naïve about the whole thing. I thought, 'My God, those poor guys are just so exhausted from being on the road'."[28]

There must have been other dates on the tour, but this period is not particularly well documented. Helen LaFaro-Fernández remembers her brother coming home for the Christmas, before rejoining the band in Florida in late December.

According to *DownBeat* magazine, the band started a two-week engagement at the Ball and Chain club in Miami on December 26th 1956. Thereafter, the Quintet joined a 'Modern Jazz For '57' package tour that also featured Art Blakey and the Jazz Messengers and vocalist Chris Connor, taking in cities such as Dakota, Kansas and Missouri. According to Helen LaFaro-Fernández, Chet's father acted as a chauffeur for part of this tour, driving some members of the band in his Cadillac. Chesney Sr must have been concerned about his son's condition following his November arrest, and wanted to protect his son from the influence of drug dealers. But with Phil Urso and Bobby Timmons facing addiction problems of their own, he would have found it difficult to keep his son away from drugs at this time.

Whilst driving through one of the Southern states, Scott LaFaro was shocked to witness some people throwing rocks at the car, protesting at the fact that people of a different colour were travelling in the same vehicle. "He could not tolerate intolerance," his sister recalled. "We grew up in an area that had a long history of concern about human rights issues. There were underground railroad and safe houses during the days of slavery. The women's rights movement had its start here. An African-American girl was queen of his high school prom. And while he certainly was aware that many were not so enlightened, this was his first brush with the realities of the situation."[29]

Whilst Chet was struggling with his addictions, fellow musicians also remember him for his sense of humour. Pianist Pat Moran remembers watching the band play at Peacock Alley in St. Louis in late January. "Chet was pretty funny," she recalled. "He had just made an album where he sang and after the gig that night, he sat on the bandstand and sang 'Look for the Silver Lining' to some girl. We were all cracking up. He didn't have a tooth in front, but was very handsome."

Chet's young wife, Halema, was less amused by Chet's antics. It was around this time she told Chet that she was pregnant, and was expecting their child in August of that year. By that stage, she was aware of Chet's addiction, and was worried how he would cope with fatherhood. "I don't think Chet was father material to begin with," she later revealed.

The public was still not aware of Chet's growing addiction, and in mid-February he looked clean and healthy when he appeared on *The Tonight Show* in New York. The band, with Belgian pianist Francy Boland sitting in for Bobby Timmons, played two songs—'Extra Mild' and 'C.T.A.'. Chet was also awarded Playboy's All Star Jazz Award, having placed second to Louis Armstrong. Chet also took the opportunity to tell the nationwide audience that he would be joining the 'Birdland Stars of '57' tour, which featured some of the biggest names in jazz, including the Count Basie Band, Sarah Vaughan, Billy Eckstine, Bud Powell, Lester Young and Zoot Sims.[30]

The sixteen-city tour had been arranged by Joe Glaser, who managed most of the artists. For the purposes of this tour, the regular Quintet was augmented by two additional musicians—trombonist Bob Brookmeyer, an old friend from the West Coast days, and German clarinet player Rolf Kühn, who had been working with Caterina Valente in New York.

The tour opened with two nights at the Carnegie Hall in New York City on Friday, 15th February. Whilst Chet opted to drive himself from New York to Boston for the third show, the rest of the band travelled by bus. "I was on the bus with Sarah Vaughan and Lester Young," recalled Phil Urso. "I sat in the back of the bus with Lester Young and he had a flask of scotch. So he said, 'How would you like a little taste of this, young fella?' He didn't know my name! It was chrome, and he had it already open. I took a big swig, and handed it back to him. So we start talking a little bit, and he tells me he enjoys being the soloist with Basie. Then he said he would lay down for a bit, where all the clothes were. I said, 'I'll see you later, Pres!' They were gambling in the aisle, Sarah and Joe Newman and the rest. The highest bill they were playing was $5, but they were mostly paying single dollar bills. Count Basie was up front with the bus driver, keeping an eye on him, making sure he wouldn't close his eyes, or anything."[31]

The third stop on the tour was supposed to be Memorial Auditorium in Rochester, New York, but Chet Baker and his band did not appear, due to a prior engagement in Philadelphia on February 18th. Helen LaFaro-Fernández remembers being disappointed that her brother did not appear in Rochester, which was less than fifty miles from the family home in Geneva, New York. Nevertheless, she travelled by train to watch the band play in Philadelphia. She talked to him between sets that night. "He was a bit down, expressing his dismay at Chet's drug use," she recalled. "Scotty, as he often did, shook his head in disbelief at how guys chose to 'screw up' so badly. Many did this mistakenly, he said. 'A lot of guys think that Charlie Parker was great because of his drug use—that it somehow added to his genius—and maybe it'll do the same for them. Yardbird was great in spite of his drug use'."[32]

Chet Baker and the band were scheduled to catch up with the Birdland Tour in Philadelphia next day. A rehearsal had been scheduled early afternoon, but as Scot LaFaro and his sister walked to the venue, two police cars pulled up outside the Auditorium. Given Chet's arrest in late 1956, narcotics agents had been tracking his movements. Six plain-clothes officers came backstage, and asked where they could find Chet Baker's group. When they eventually found them, saxophonist Phil Urso was caught trying to flush his stash down the toilet. "Everyone had to get undressed completely," recalled Rolf Kühn. "I had only been in the States for seven or eight months, and I was very straight. The police looked at me and started laughing, because I looked so healthy."[33]

Chet claimed he was clean, but the police found track marks down his arms. Upon further investigation, they found a bag of heroin in Phil Urso's saxophone case, and marijuana in the glove compartment of Chet's car. The two men were arrested, and spent the night behind bars. Manager Joe Glaser bailed them out next morning, but when the story hit the newspapers next day, he had little choice but to throw them off the tour.

Chet Baker pleaded guilty to possession of marijuana, and according to one Philadelphia newspaper was fined $500 and given one year's probation.

The first leg of the Birdland Tour finished in Canada in mid-March, after which a number of the stars—Count Basie included—embarked on a tour of Europe. Phil Urso later recalled that Chet Baker might have joined this tour without the band, playing with a different rhythm section. This seems unlikely, however. Chet's previous European tour had been well documented, but no photographs or recordings have emerged of a tour in 1956.

Whilst details remain sketchy, drummer Larance Marable appears to have quit the band at this time. Scott LaFaro told his sister that he intended to leave the group, and intended to return to Los Angeles. He did not return until April, however, suggesting he may have stayed on for a few more weeks. Phil Urso hired Philadelphia native Albert 'Tootie' Heath as Marable's replacement. Heath was the younger brother of bass player Percy Heath and saxophonist Jimmy Heath. Heath was shocked when Chet spent hours searching for drugs before a gig, often causing the band to arrive late. He even witnessed Chet nodding out onstage. "But the audiences loved him, so he could do no wrong," he said. "He could sit there and sleep, and people thought that was cute." Heath was also horrified by the way Baker treated his pregnant wife. "She was a beautiful woman, and she followed this guy around like a dog," he recalled. "He was in serious control of her."[34]

This new line-up appears to have been short-lived, however. Heath quit the band, and at this point, Scott LaFaro is thought to have returned to Los Angeles.

Remarkably, Chet appears to have been reinstated in the line-up for the second leg of the Birdland Tour, which kicked off at the Berkeley Community Theatre on 27th April. It may be that Joe Glaser held Phil Urso to blame for Chet's problems; after all, it was Urso that had been caught with heroin, not Chet. Certainly Chet seems to have appeared as a solo artist, with a supporting rhythm section—rather than with his own band. Joe Glaser was a hard-nosed businessman, and most likely he still saw Chet as a commercial proposition, despite his well-documented personal problems. Either way, Chet is mentioned in a review of the show at the LA Shrine on 29th April, and at the State Fair Auditorium on 9th May. He is also advertised as appearing in numerous newspaper articles and advertisements from this period.[35]

The 'Birdland Stars of '57' tour seems to have ended in late May, after which Chet is thought to have returned to Los Angeles.

Back in Los Angeles, Phil Urso helped Chet to assemble yet another new line-up. Pianist Bobby Timmons seems to have quit the band in April—certainly he appeared on a number of studio sessions back in New York in April and May. He was replaced by Elmo Hope, who had worked with Sonny

Rollins and Jackie McLean, but was forced to leave New York having lost his cabaret card. Doug Watkins is thought to have replaced Scott LaFaro on bass, whilst Heath was replaced by 'Philly' Joe Jones, a fiery drummer who had made his name playing with Miles Davis Quintet, a band that also featured tenor saxophonist John Coltrane. Miles Davis, a former heroin addict himself, knew that both Jones and Coltrane were using, and suspected the drummer of encouraging Coltrane's habit. In March 1957, he fired them both. "We went to play at Shelly's Manne-Hole, and Joe visited us one night and wanted to sit in," Phil Urso remembered. "Chet let him sit in, and when we got in the back room at the break he asked Chet if he could join. He said, 'Whatever you need, I think we can do it'."

Those words proved to be ominous, as Chet and 'Philly' Joe took to getting high together, their drug intake even scaring Phil Urso. "Chet was going off half-cocked by this stage, he just kept on doing it, and kept on doing it," he said. "I don't know if he was trying to imitate Bird, or what."[36]

'Philly' Joe even took to stealing from the band, using a credit card meant for band expenses to buy new tyres for his car, before selling them at another gas station a few miles down the road. Phil Urso, who was effectively acting as the band's road manager, finally had enough and decided to quit the band. He was replaced by the baritone saxophonist Pepper Adams.

The new Quintet—featuring Pepper Adams and 'Philly' Joe Jones—opened at Peacock Lane, a jazz club on the corner of Hollywood Boulevard and Western, in July 1957. By this stage, Chet's heroin addiction was out of control—the fact that his wife was eight months pregnant had no impact on his behaviour. His attitude was no better on the bandstand, either, lashing out at his fellow musicians. Doug Watkins usually took a solo in 'This is Always', but one night, before he was through with his solo, Chet grabbed the mike stand from him and dragged it across the stage to sing his final chorus.

John Tynan, a journalist from *DownBeat* was on hand to witness his disappointing display. "Judging by his behaviour onstage, the only performer who mattered at all was Baker," he wrote. "The leader's governing attitude is surly, unfriendly, strictly don't-give-a-damn ... Chet Baker, Established Star, is much less refreshing than Baker, Boy Trumpet Player. In the latter context he still has something of value to say—when he bothers to care."[37]

Elmo Hope seems to have been fired after the first Peacock Lane engagement, and was replaced by the twenty-two-year-old pianist Don

Friedman, a native of San Francisco, who had cut his teeth with Dexter Gordon and Shorty Rogers. Friedman was delighted to be playing with the likes of Pepper Adams and Chet Baker, but was shocked when he saw how Chet had changed from his younger days. "He was a scary guy—never around, always running off to score, very nervous," he later recalled.[38]

Friedman's first gig was the Blackhawk in San Francisco, starting on July 22nd. There he witnessed Chet and 'Philly' Joe getting high together. "They were hitting themselves in the foot, because the veins in their arms were so messed up," he explained. The young pianist was desperate to fit in with his musical idols, and pretty soon, he started 'chippying' with heroin too. Before long, he was also nodding out onstage.

'Philly' Joe Jones was fired after the Blackhawk gig—not for the first time, by all accounts, but certainly the last. Pepper Adams and Doug Watkins had also seen enough of Chet's behaviour, and quit the band.

Around this time, Chet returned to the studio to record a movie soundtrack for a documentary about James Dean, who had died two years earlier at the age of just twenty-four. Most discographies suggest this recording took place on November 8th 1956—the official date given by the record label, World Pacific (Pacific Jazz). This date cannot be correct, however. James Dean's last film, *Giant*, wasn't released until the very end of 1956, and the documentary includes footage from the premiere. As a result, the documentary can't have been scripted until early 1957. It's worth noting in passing that the documentary itself was co-directed by a young Robert Altman.

The soundtrack was composed by Leith Stevens, a former child prodigy and prolific soundtrack composer, and was arranged by Johnny Mandel and Bill Holman. Chet Baker and Bud Shank were the featured soloists on the album, but in all likelihood they had not heard the music before recording the session. "It was the same scene as the earlier sextet album," said Holman. "Chet probably came in, having not seen the music before. But with a film score, you're not expected to be that soulful, as opposed to a jazz score, where you're supposed to show your essence." The recording is thought to have taken place in two sessions—on 12th May and in July/August—with Chet appearing on the second of these sessions.

The album features some pleasant solos from Baker and Shank, and the CD reissue includes a rare vocal performance of 'Let Me Be Loved'. Nevertheless, this remains an inconsequential item within Chet's crowded discography.

Chet was due to play a return engagement at Peacock Lane in early August. He needed to recruit a new band at short notice, and asked Scott LaFaro and Larance Marable if they could help out. Tenor saxophonist Richie Kamuca was invited to join, and this became the latest version of Chet's ever-evolving Quintet. Once again, the line-up proved to be short-lived. Chet stopped to score on the way to the club, and turned up late for the first two nights. "I'd been ten to fifteen minutes late a couple of times," he admitted in his memoirs, "and the manager of the club told me the next time I was late, I was fired."[39]

But all Chet cared about was his next high. The next night he scored again on his way to the club, and turned up ten minutes late. As he parked his car, he noticed two policemen examining the arms of Don Friedman and Larance Marable, looking for track marks under the streetlight. Chet knew they were after him. He left Halema sitting in the car, and managed to sneak in the club without their noticing. The manager was waiting for him, pointing out that he was late again. "I guess this means I'm fired?" he asked. "Yes," he replied, so Chet walked to the stage, grabbed his trumpet from the top of the piano, and left through the club's back entrance.

He crept back to his car, and as he got in, he became aware of an unmarked black Ford making a turn on to Western. He told the heavily pregnant Halema to hold on tight, and accelerated to the end of the road, screeching left at the corner, then left again on to the freeway, losing the cops along the way. When the coast was clear, he dropped Halema off, leaving her enough cash to catch a taxi home. He told her he would meet her in San Francisco when things had calmed down, and drove to Balboa Bay. There he ran into an old friend, Bobby Gill, who was about to set sail for San Miguel Island, where he planned to dive for abalone. Chet figured he'd be safe on the boat, and that a few days in the sun would help to heal the numerous track marks on his arm. The days were fine, working on the boat and helping his friend, but the nights were tough, undergoing cold turkey and shivering in the cool evening breeze.

Chet left for San Francisco a few days later, where he reunited with Halema. She had given birth to a son on August 7th 1957, christening him Chesney Aftab Baker, his middle name the Pakistani word for 'sun'. In later years, Chet spoke fondly of his first child, but at the time he was too self-absorbed to pay much attention to his family. Even in his memoirs, he glosses over the event, which seems to have left little impression on him. "My son Chettie was born a couple of months later in San Francisco," he wrote. "No-one bothered me during this time. The next couple of years were difficult, however, with a continuous change of personnel in the band."[40]

Chet is thought to have returned to Los Angeles in mid-August. He had promised to help out his childhood friend Jack Sheldon, who was scheduled to make a big band recording. Unfortunately, Chet did not stay clean for long, and turned up at the recording studio in a dreadful state. "He came along to the session, and he'd just shot up a whole spoonful of heroin," Sheldon later recalled. "I was a little disappointed, he was so high, but he did good on it." The album was eventually released as *Jack's Groove*, and is periodically available on CD.[41]

While he was in town, Chet made some enquiries to find out what had happened to his band members outside the Peacock Lane jazz club. The police had evidently threatened Don Friedman, the youngest member of the band, that they would put him in jail if he didn't sign a statement admitting that Chet had supplied him with the dope. The frightened pianist panicked, and did as he was told.

Chet knew the cops would be after him, and came to the decision that they should leave California and make a fresh start in New York. Chet left his wife and son in San Francisco and drove to Las Vegas, where his car blew a valve. He stayed there for a few days with his old friend, Jimmy McKean, before calling his manager, Joe Glaser, and explaining what had happened. Glaser sent him a plane ticket, confident that he would soon find work on the East Coast.

But Chet wasn't thinking about the music; he figured it would be easier to score in New York, and that he'd get less trouble from the cops. He figured wrong.

Chapter Eight

CHET BAKER IN NEW YORK
1957–1959

"I didn't even bother to blow my horn much. I just pumped dope into me and dreamed my life away."—Chet Baker[1]

Jazz was thriving in New York in the summer of 1957. As discussed in the previous chapter, Miles Davis had renewed his acquaintance with arranger Gil Evans, and had just finished recording *Miles Ahead.* The importance of this recording cannot be overstated. "Although Ellington had written individual pieces based on and for certain soloists, *Miles Ahead* was the first concept album built around the sound of the soloist. It demonstrated Gil's belief that Miles extended the tradition of Louis Armstrong," wrote Bob Belden. "*Miles Ahead* contained not only stunning and virtuosic music, but carried the seeds of future breakthroughs as well. The trumpet solo sections of 'New Rhumba' and the song 'Blues for Pablo' predate 'Milestones' as the first examples of Miles soloing with only scales to improvise on. Tying all these songs together with musical transitions so that the entire album could be experienced as one performance (or suite) was also a programming innovation."[2]

John Coltrane, having been fired by Miles Davis, teamed up with pianist Thelonious Monk, whose New York cabaret licence had only just been renewed. The band, with Wilbur Ware on bass and Shadow Wilson on drums, began an extended run at the Five Spot in July, a partnership that helped to change the face of modern jazz, and revolutionised the career of the saxophonist. Monk's original compositions challenged Coltrane with their unexpected rhythmic leaps, but also enabled him to extend his solos within the structures the pianist had laid down. "Those of us who heard it will never forget the experience," Ira Gitler later recalled. "There were some weeks when I was at the Five Spot two or three times, staying most of the night even when I intended to catch just a set or two."[3]

Sonny Rollins, meanwhile, was in the midst of a creative surge that would result in some his finest recordings. After his fine West Coast recording *Way Out West*, he had returned to New York where he renewed his relationship with Blue Note records, delivering Volume Two in April 1957, and the more stripped back *Newk's Time*, recorded with Wynton Kelly on piano, Doug Watkins on bass and 'Philly' Joe Jones on drums in September of the same year.

Unfortunately there was a dark side to this surge in creativity. Whilst John Coltrane had emerged from the heroin addiction that plagued his first stint with Miles Davis, others were getting dragged into the abyss. The police were aware of the growing problem, and in late May, embarked on a citywide crackdown that resulted in 131 arrests, including alto saxophonist Jackie McLean, who was playing with Art Blakey's Jazz Messengers.

When Chet arrived in New York with his family he had nowhere to stay, and called upon pianist Francy Boland and bass player Eddie de Haas, two old friends from his European tour. The two musicians were sharing a large apartment on the Upper West Side, and thinking that Chet would share the rent, gladly invited him to stay. "I went to America to learn more about the music," recalled de Haas. "By the time I came to America in February 1957, Francy Boland was already in America, and had two small children, a boy and a girl. Francy had rented this large apartment, and he asked me to move in with him, because work was kind of slow, and I guess his funds were running low. On top of that, he got screwed out of some money that was owed him by Count Basie's manager. It was sad that a guy with a young family had to wait for his money, wait for his pay."[4]

Eddie de Haas renewed his acquaintance with Chet just four days after his arrival, travelling down to Philadelphia to watch Chet play on February 17th, prior to his arrest next day. "I only had a short time to catch up with him, and let him know I was here. Scott La Faro was playing with Chet at that time."

When Chet showed up in New York, the bass player generously gave up his room for Chet and his family. "He had married a different girl; he'd also had his first kid," he recalled. "I gave up my room, which had a private bathroom with a shower and took a small servant's room in the back of the apartment."

It wasn't long before Boland and de Haas realised that their former employer had a serious drug habit. Rather than look for work, Chet would spend much of his time either catching a cab to Harlem to score, or using Boland's telephone to beg friends for money. "Chet was stoned by then, and claimed that Phil Urso had turned him on; but listen, you either do or you don't," the bass player said.[5]

With both Francy Boland and Chet Baker out of work, Eddie de Haas was single-handedly providing for a household of eight people, including three small children. "I was the only person in that household that had a job. I was working, I believe with Billy Taylor, on 56th Street and 6th Avenue. "My salary was just $90 per week at that time," he recalled. "Of course, you couldn't see the kids go hungry, so I used to buy certain things for the kids; but there was a limit to what I could do. I filled the refrigerator with eggs and milk, and bought cereal. It got so bad that before I could get to refrigerator, the stuff was gone. I took it for a while, but eventually decided to move back down to the Village."[6]

By October, Halema had had as much as she could take. Chet was spending all of his money on dope, rather than providing for his young family. She called her parents in Detroit, who made arrangements for her to come home with her young child.

Chet stayed on in the apartment for a few more weeks with Francy Boland. The experience of losing his young wife finally brought him to his senses, and he started actively looking for work. He seems to have formed a short-lived band with Francy Boland on piano, Jimmy Gannon on bass and Dannie Richmond on drums. They were able to secure the occasional booking, including a gig at the Crown Propeller Lounge in Pittsburgh in late 1957.

"I know that Chet started working again, and that he showed some loyalty to Francy Boland, by hiring him for the job," Eddie de Haas later remembered. "They worked sporadically, but eventually Francy had to move his family into a hotel, because he could no longer afford the rent."

Chet could not afford to stay in the apartment on his own, and a few weeks later the landlord evicted him. He slept in his car for a few nights, and later moved in with one of his drug dealers. Halema telephoned a number of musicians, and eventually learned of her husband's whereabouts. She then called the composer Bob Zieff, who had an apartment in the West Sixties, and asked him to take Chet in for a few weeks to help him find his feet. "If he stays with you, I know there'll be some chance of him being straight," she said. Zieff reluctantly agreed to her request, but could do little to change Chet's addiction.

Halema also called Chet's parents Vera and Chesney, and informed them of their son's problems. She suggested that Chet's father might consider coming to New York to work with his son, acting as an informal tour manager, and that his paternal influence might bring about a change in Chet's lifestyle.

Halema may have been acting with the best of intentions, but was probably not aware of his own addiction problems with alcohol, which hardly left him well placed to act as his son's guardian. It wasn't long before the two men clashed. Bob Zieff remembers playing as Chet's pianist at a gig in Philadelphia when an argument broke out, and Chesney threatened to drive one of the two cars the band were using back to California. "If you take that car, I'm gonna call the police and tell them it's stolen," Chet shouted. The two men circled the room, fists raised, before Zieff stepped in to relieve the tension. "Does this have to happen?" he asked.

Zieff noticed many of Chet's character traits seemed to stem from his father. "Chet started calling him Daddy all the time," he recalled. "It was the two of them against the rest of us, and the rest of the world was evil. Everybody was trying to misuse them."[7]

A few weeks later, Chet landed a gig with alto saxophonist Phil Wood at the Cork 'n' Bib on Long Island, where Chet had been asked to play as a special guest. "Chet was there with his father, who was trying to keep Chet straight," recalled pianist Hod O'Brien. "They were staying upstairs at the Cork 'n' Bib. Charlie Graziano, the owner, had offered to put them up. But Chet's father was an alcoholic, and needed looking after himself. It was kind of like the blind leading the blind."[8]

On the bandstand, at least, Chet could still get his act together, and Hod O'Brien remembers the club was packed when it was announced that Chet would join Phil Woods. "I worked there regularly for a few months. It was a big room, and usually they'd get half the room filled," he recalled. "But when Chet came, the whole room filled; a thousand people could fit in that room. I just thought, 'this guy has charisma'. It was really Phil's gig, with Chet as a guest headliner. The rhythm section was myself, Nick Stabulas on drums and Teddy Kotick on bass. 'Philly' Joe Jones was hanging with Chet that night, and sat in for a few numbers on one set. That was like water-skiing on a totally smooth lake, such a slick ride to play with 'Philly' Joe; that was one of my most thrilling experiences."[9]

Soon after the Long Island gig, Chesney had to return to California, and without the distraction of his father's presence, Chet soon slipped back into his old ways. Zieff accompanied Chet on a two-week stint at a nightclub in Minneapolis, and found himself having to revive the trumpet player, who would regularly pass out on the floor of the motel bathroom. "We'd be three or four hours late for the gig," Zieff later recalled.

Chet was still under contract with Dick Bock's Pacific Records, although he had not recorded an album under his own name since *The James Dean Story*, six months earlier. Dick Bock travelled to New York in early December to supervise the recording of a number of sessions with Gerry Mulligan. Hearing of Chet's problems, Bock was glad to lend a helping hand. He suggested that Chet talk with another Pacific Jazz artist, David Allyn, a singer and former heroin addict, in an attempt to cure him of his addiction. He also proposed a number of recording sessions, including a potentially lucrative reunion with Gerry Mulligan.

Chet asked Dick Bock if it were possible to record a number of Bob Zieff's compositions. Bock had reservations about the commercial appeal of Zieff's work, and reluctantly booked a recording studio for December 9th. "Bock was scared by my music, as usual," Zieff recalled. "It wasn't up to his usual sweet Southern Californian expectation once again! As I remember he asked why it wasn't like what I had done before—he didn't seem to remember that that music bothered him at the time. It got good reviews and sold fairly well—I think—which also probably bothered him, in as much as he liked money."[10]

Indeed, the new compositions were quite different to those that appeared on *Rondette*, featuring Dick Twardzik, or on *Chet Baker and Crew*, recorded the following year after Chet had returned to the United States. Zieff had arranged for Chet to record with a small chamber orchestra, with musicians hand-picked by Zieff for the occasion, including Jimmy Buffington on French horn, Gene Allen on bass clarinet and Bob Tricarico on bassoon. "Chet asked me to go ahead with something so I chose the instrumentation and the players—for once!" said Zieff. "When Bock got the word he called me to let me know that we could get Herbie Mann on flute; I was happy to say there was no flute! Not one of my favorite instruments—or players!"[11]

Dick Bock was uneasy about the recording session, and matters were not helped when Chet turned up late. "Chet was living with me at the time; he was there for some weeks, maybe a couple of months. He hadn't been around for a couple of days as I recall," said Zieff. "He got to the date about an hour and a half late—which would make any date difficult. I would guess that he was spending time at the apartment warming up."[12]

Whilst Chet had no problems navigating the complex charts, it still took valuable recording time to finesse the ensemble arrangements; listen to the unusual structure of 'Twenties Late', for example, with its unexpected pauses and use of space, and consider the rehearsal that must have been required. After about three hours of recording, Bock only had enough material for about half an LP; four tunes, or about nineteen minutes of music.

The musicians saw Bock talking with Gerry Mulligan in the recording booth, and the next thing they knew, the recording session was put on hold. At that point, Zieff assumed the recording would continue next day. He only learned the truth a few days later. "The bassist (Russ Saunders) was in the same studio a day or so after this and asked the engineer what went on," he said. "Mulligan came to the date and Bock conferred with him, and Gerry suggested that the other dates be cancelled. After all Gerry was still under contract to Bock and wanted to help allay his fears."[13]

Despite his own skill as an arranger, Gerry Mulligan may have had some concerns over the complexities of the compositions. Bob Zieff himself recalls being asked to contribute arrangements to a short-lived band co-headed by Gerry Mulligan and Lee Konitz. "A while before this I had composed the basic book (Gerry contributed one piece also) for Gerry's quintet with Lee Konitz; the two of them lasted just about no time, and the group never appeared. Gerry said the things would be recorded for Granz. That never came about either. Gerry was the player having the most difficulty with the music, gifted though he was."[14]

Of the four Zieff compositions recorded that day, only one—'Twenties Late'—was released at the time, only appearing on a Playboy jazz compilation in 1959. The remainder were unreleased until 1993, some five years after Chet's death, when they appeared on a four-CD compilation, *Chet Baker: The Pacific Jazz Years*. The four tunes have also subsequently been added to recent reissues of *Sextet*, Chet's 1954 recording.

The potential significance of these recordings was noted by none other than Gil Evans, the arranger who worked so closely with Miles Davis on such landmark recordings as *Miles Ahead*, *Porgy and Bess* and *Sketches of Spain*. "They should have put these right out," he said. "It would have helped us all."[15]

Ironically, Zieff's bold compositions were later reappraised by Gerry Mulligan. Chet was scheduled to appear at the Randall's Island Jazz Festival in the summer of 1958, and his regular pianist, Bobby Timmons, had fallen ill. He asked Bob Zieff to sit in on piano. "We went on and did those two pieces ('Slightly Above Moderate' and 'Medium Rock') only," the composer recalled. "Charlie Mingus and Gerry Mulligan came up to the stand afterward and were very congratulatory. Charlie said to Chet that he was so surprised to hear that coming from something Chet was involved in! Chet told me that Bobby couldn't get to the gig—perhaps Chet told him to take that day off so Chet could play my pieces under better circumstances."[16]

Given such weighty critical approval, one wonders what would have happened if Dick Bock had had the foresight to release an album of such material at the time. Whilst it might have improved Chet's standing amongst certain jazz musicians, some of whom were critical of his more commercial projects, particularly the vocal recordings, it probably would have done little to stem the slide in Chet's commercial appeal in the late 1950s. Zieff's arrangements did not simply provide a voluptuous showcase for Chet's trumpet, as Gil Evans had done for Miles Davis on *Miles Ahead,* but challenged the listener in a manner not dissimilar to such abstract musicians as Paul Bley and Jimmy Giuffre. Even with the backing of a major label, as Miles enjoyed with Columbia, it is doubtful that such a record would have sold in vast quantities. Equally importantly, Chet was in no fit state to promote such a recording; his addiction left him unreliable, and club owners were increasingly reluctant to risk booking him.

Perhaps if Bock had promoted the Twardzik recordings, or recorded an album of Zieff's arrangements on Chet's return to the US in 1956, before his addiction took hold, it would have been a different story—both for Chet, and the 'underground composer' himself, Bob Zieff.

Perhaps inspired by the success of Julie London's *Julie is Her Name*, recorded two years previously, Bock suggested the guitarist and bass player stay on in the studio and record a vocal session with Chet. The resulting recording was a distinctly lacklustre affair, marred by a weary edge to Chet's singing. Gershwin's 'They All Laughed', in particular, has rarely sounded so joyless. Whether his tone is down to the late hour—he was late for the original session—or Chet's lifestyle at that time, is not clear. It may be that he was not particularly enamoured of the material suggested by Bock; he never again recorded 'The Night We Called it A Day', 'They All Laughed' or 'There's a Lull in My Life'.

The session has its moments, most notably Chet's playing—especially on 'Little Girl Blue'—and that of the guitarist, David 'Buck' Wheat. In the event, Dick Bock thought that the results were too depressing, and the session stayed in the vaults, unreleased bar one track, for over forty years.[17]

Dick Bock was more excited about the prospect of Chet Baker reuniting with Gerry Mulligan, recording together for the first time in almost five years. Mulligan's band was excited to be playing with the legendary trumpet player, with bass player Henry Grimes recalling Chet as a naturally gifted player with "a consistent unity between him and the music".[18]

Mulligan himself was concerned about Chet's condition, and when his former partner turned up late for the first recording session, his eyes hidden behind dark glasses, his worst fears were confirmed. "Music requires discipline, and he once had it," Mulligan later remarked. "He was serious about it, and he worked hard. And heroin is the opposite of that. Heroin is giving yourself up to whim, immediate sensation, immediate gratification."

Chet's playing does lack focus on certain tracks, whilst Mulligan himself sounds somewhat detached; that said, there are moments when the old chemistry comes through. 'Ornithology' sounds as fresh as the original quartet recordings, whilst 'All The Things You Are', which was not even included on the original LP, is superb.

Having finished recording material for the *Reunion* LP, Dick Bock asked the band, including Chet, to stay on in the recording studio to make an album with the jazz singer Annie Ross, who had just recorded the seminal *Sing a Song of Basie* as part of Lambert, Hendricks and Ross. Unfortunately, Chet disappeared halfway through the recording session for some 'immediate gratification' and failed to reappear. "Chet just went to the bathroom and never came back; that's why we had to get Art Farmer," the singer later recalled. "Then he rang me up some days later and said, 'I need money to get the transmission of my car fixed'. I don't drive and didn't know what he was talking about. But I knew he was trying to ask me for money, and said, 'No'. Dick Bock was trying to help him; he was a very kind man."[19]

Annie Ross, Chet Baker and Gerry Mulligan at the Annie Ross 'Sing A Song ...' recording session, December 17th 1957. Photograph by Carol Reiff.

Gerry Mulligan was under contract with Norman Granz's Verve Records at the time of these recordings, and in return for allowing Mulligan to record with Pacific Jazz in December 1957, Dick Bock agreed that Chet be allowed to record one session with Verve Records. In the event, Bock got the better deal.

Norman Granz chose to pair Chet with fellow West Coast musician Stan Getz for what was to be their only studio session. Getz was on his way back from San Francisco, and met Chet in Chicago in mid-February, where he was playing a gig at the Midway Lounge. Granz paired them with a local rhythm section, and with no time to rehearse, they agreed on a handful of songs. Getz played well, but Baker was in no fit state to record. On the opening track, 'I'll Remember April', one of only two tunes they play together, Baker had to be woken from the sofa to take his solo. On a solo feature, 'Autumn in New York', the trumpeter drops a huge clam in the opening bar; bizarrely, there was no second take.

The resulting album, *Stan Meets Chet*, met a reception as chilly as the Chicago winter in which it had been recorded. "When it isn't downright fumbling, most of Chet's playing on this record sounds like a man almost stalling until his solo time is up," said *DownBeat* magazine. *Metronome* was equally scathing, labelling the recording 'a fiasco', and awarding it just one star.[20]

After finishing the gig in Chicago, Chet drove to Milwaukee for another gig, stopping along the way to score. One of the windows in his Jaguar had been smashed, and as he drove through Waukegan, Illinois, he was pulled over by the police. Stoned, and unable to produce his driver's licence, the cop searched the car and found heroin stashed under the front seat. One of Chet's passengers had apparently just been released from prison after serving a five-year sentence, so Chet took the rap for possession and let his friends walk free. "I cut them loose and spent a terrible four days in the Waukegan jail before Halema got me out on bail."[21]

A trial date was provisionally set for August 1958. Chet showed no signs of moderating his behaviour, however, and was arrested again days later in Harlem, New York. With two arrests in such a short period of time, Chet was convinced he'd be forced to serve time. Taking advice from a junkie friend, Chet made the decision to check himself into the US Public Health Service Hospital at Lexington, Kentucky. There he was placed on methadone, a synthetic opiate, for three days, before being moved to an isolated ward referred to as 'skid row' by the fellow inmates. The hospital authorities watched inmates of 'skid row' closely, to make sure they did not suffer too badly from withdrawal symptoms, before moving them to the 'population', where inmates could learn to live normally, and prepare to re-enter society.

The success rate of the Lexington programme seems to have been limited, at best. It was a hospital, not a prison, and visitors found it relatively easy to smuggle drugs to the inmates of the 'population'. Moreover, the hospital was free, and numerous junkies took advantage of the system in return for periodic free accommodation. A study by Professor John Ball, a psychiatrist at Temple University, showed that almost half of the former inmates sampled died young, or were subsequently sentenced to long prison sentences. Of the remaining half that could be interviewed, two thirds were either continually addicted for three years prior to the interview, or else in prison, with no access to drugs. Less than ten percent of the sample appears to have been 'cured', having refrained from drug use for three consecutive years.[22]

Such statistics mattered little to Chet; upon checking into Lexington he wrote a letter to the judge in Waukegan, informing him that he had taken steps to cure his addiction—within weeks, all charges had been dropped.

After a few days on 'skid row', Chet was moved into the 'population'. He initially stayed in the hospital hall, where he got virtually no sleep, but was eventually moving into a private room. He encountered numerous jazz musicians amongst the patients being treated at the hospital; Tadd Dameron, the bebop composer responsible for tunes such as 'If You Could See Me Now', ran the hospital orchestra and the band included pianist Kenny Drew, who would play on Chet's subsequent album, *It Could Happen To You.*

Chet also ran into Mike, one of his former dealers from San Francisco. A repeat offender and long-term inmate at Lexington, Mike was one of the few patients who reportedly had access to the women's section of the hospital. He passed on a message from Joyce, a woman who had met Chet at the Rouge Lounge in Detroit earlier that year. They arranged to meet at the musical rehearsals for the Christmas Show, where she told Chet that she had only checked into the hospital to be with him.

Joyce promised to take care of Chet if he came to live with her in New York, and told him that she had an apartment on 57th Street and had saved a reasonable sum of money that would tide them over until Chet found regular work. With no thought for Halema, who had tried so hard to help him and had bailed him out of prison in Illinois, and no regard for his young son, Chet arranged to check out of hospital with Joyce a fortnight later, and moved back to New York. Chet left the hospital less than six weeks into the recommended four-month treatment.

The romance with Joyce was to prove short-lived, however, and probably a little one-sided. "After two weeks I began to tire of the situation," he later recalled. "Besides, we'd gone through every cent of her fifteen hundred dollars.[23]

Worse was to follow. According to the same tabloid article, Chet shared an apartment with Pixie, a prostitute, and her pimp, Bob, who he described as a "sharp hustler". Bob eventually moved out of the apartment, and returned to his wife, leaving Baker to live off Pixie's ill-gotten gains. Whilst this story may have been exaggerated for the benefit of the tabloid readers, and was not repeated in Chet's sketchy memoirs *As Though I Had Wings*, it does fit in with his pattern of behaviour at this time; Chet did admit to "running around up in Harlem" every day, and regularly turned to crime to support his ongoing heroin addiction.

In many respects, the first five years of Chet's long struggle with drug addiction were his most troubled. This is not intended to trivialise his later problems, which included his struggle to stay on methadone in the 1970s, or his experiments with drug cocktails, such as 'speedballs'. Nor should it diminish the efforts of those closest to him in his later years, such as Ruth Young and Diane Vavra, who to varying degrees tried to keep Chet's problems under control. But in the early years of his heroin addiction, he struggled to live within the confines of society.

Narcotics were harder to obtain in the United States than in parts of Europe; in the UK, for example, heroin and cocaine were available to addicts on prescription, as Chet detailed in his memoirs. In addition, American society was more inclined to disapprove of and disown a celebrity that was addicted to drugs, particularly a white celebrity. This is a view shared by an old family friend, Jim Coleman. "If he was a black guy using drugs, no one gave a shit. But this was a white guy who had looked like James Dean, who became a total anathema to the white capitalist world by saying 'Fuck you, fuck Hollywood, fuck money; I'm going to be a junkie, and do what I want to do'. This did not give him favourable press; it managed to get him barred and blackballed from many places. Remember how they treated Lenny Bruce at that time."[24]

Such factors contributed to Chet's decision to move from the United States to Europe in 1959, and again in the mid-1970s. They also help to explain, in part at least, his turning to crime to support his addiction. In later years, by contrast, he learned how to live his life within 'the system', particularly within Europe; earning enough money to support his lifestyle, and not feel that he was being persecuted for his lifestyle 'choice'.

Of course, it is a matter of considerable debate as to whether anyone would 'choose' such a lifestyle, and this is a topic we will return to later in the book, when we analyse Chet's legacy.

But it is also important to put Chet's condition into a broader context; he was certainly not alone in turning to crime to finance his habit. Again, the 1969 study by Professor John Ball of Temple University suggested that of the drug addicts surveyed, all of whom had embarked on the so-called Lexington 'cure', arrest occurred on average once every four years post-release. By contrast, arrest was rare amongst those that were 'cured', and abstained from drug use post-release. The study concludes:

It appears, then, that two major patterns exist with respect to the life course of opiate addiction in the United States. In one instance, the addict becomes increasingly enmeshed in a non-productive or criminal career as his dependence upon opiates progresses into his adult years. In the second case, the addict terminates his drug-centered way of life and assumes, or re-establishes, a legitimate role in society.

In the summer of 1958, Chet's old manager, Joe Napoli, approached Chet Baker and Bob Zieff with the idea of recording a movie soundtrack. Richard Fleischer had been hired to direct a movie called *Compulsion*, based on the best-selling 1956 novel by Meyer Levin. The plot concerned the killing of a schoolboy by two college students, and their subsequent trial. The movie starred Orson Welles as the defence lawyer, and was a considerable success on its release in 1959. In the event, the plans fell through. "Joe Napoli had no idea of my thinking of course," said Zieff. "I don't know that I would have done it if it had come through."

In July 1958, Bill Grauer of Riverside Records, the New York-based record company he co-headed with Orrin Keepnews, heard of Chet's 'release' from hospital, and contacted Pacific Jazz to enquire as to whether they might be able to record Chet. Given Chet's problems over the previous year, this was a bold move. "My partner, Bill Grauer, who was never a man to admit having been outmanoeuvered, surely could recognise the dangers in a drug-dominated situation, but apparently felt that Chet's sales potential made him a chance worth taking," Keepnews later recalled. "So, without our even having discussed the situation, he informed me that he had put one over on Dick Bock, the Los Angeles-based owner of Pacific Jazz Records, by arranging to take over the four-albums-remaining balance of their contract with Baker. In return, we only had two requirements: to credit Pacific Jazz on the liner of each album, and to let Chet realise that he could no longer call on Bock for advances. All remaining payments would be coming from Riverside!"[25]

Before Chet had recorded a single note for his new label, Keepnews was given a late-night reminder of what his partner had let them in for. "I vividly recall the first middle-of-the-night phone call … Chet needed some cash, and I told him that unfortunately the apartment building's nighttime elevator operator went off duty at midnight, and the front door was then locked until morning. No problem, he informed me; the coffee shop at my corner was open all night; I could just leave an envelope with the cashier."[26]

The following month, Chet was invited to record his first album for Riverside, entitled *It Could Happen To You*. Orrin Keepnews had never been a fan of Chet's voice, but accepted Bill Grauer's argument that Chet's vocal recordings for Pacific Jazz had been his best selling albums. Chet suggested using Kenny Drew, the pianist he had met at the hospital in Lexington; with his broad repertoire, and considerable skills as an arranger. Grauer and Keepnews agreed that this made good sense. They in turn suggested Chet's old friend 'Philly' Joe Jones on drums and Sam Jones on bass.

"In accordance with my partner's high hopes, we began with a vocal album," Keepnews remembered. "I really did give it my best shot to begin with, coming up with an overlooked Rodgers and Hart number titled 'Do it the Hard Way' (from the excellent score to the Broadway hit *Pal Joey* that had established Gene Kelly), which I thought Baker might be able to do something with. But he really didn't have much of a voice at this time, and the personnel, in part selected by each of us, didn't always mesh."[27]

The problems with Chet's vocal were exacerbated by the fact that he turned up stoned for the first session, which was abandoned after two songs, including a slurred version of 'Old Devil Moon'. "After trying hard for a couple of dates, I took the cowardly way out and refused to continue, literally telling Bill that, since all this had been his idea, if he really wanted it he could finish it by himself," said Keepnews.

Later sessions were more fruitful, but Chet's pitch is often wayward; whether this reflects a lack of rehearsal, or a choice of songs that was overambitious for his limited range, it is hard to say. Either way, the reviews suggested Chet's reputation was starting to catch up with him. Martin Williams in *DownBeat* gave the record just one star.

Can you carry a tune? Is your time all right? Sing! If your voice has hardly any range, hardly any volume, shaky pitch, no body or bottom, no matter. If it quavers a bit and if you project a certain tarnished, boyish (not exactly adolescent, almost childish) pleading, you'll make it. A certain kind of girl with strong maternal instincts but no one to mother will love you. The way you make it may have little to do with music, but that happens all the time anyway.

And if the whole thing frustrates, there's the trumpet. If you have a talent for lyric variations, use it a bit … And if you can borrow someone else's style. Of course, you may not develop your own talent or even discover what it's like, but that goes on all the time too. Anyway, you've got a large following and you've won a lot of polls, so who needs to develop his talent.[28]

The jazz singer Dinah Washington was equally scathing in a *DownBeat* blindfold test just three months later. "Is that a singer or someone just kidding?" she asked. "I don't know who it is, but the diction is terrible. At the end it sounded like he said, 'That old bubble moon … '. It sounds like he had a mouthful of mush … I can't rate this. I thought it was the Velvet Fog [Mel Tormé] for a minute, but I can't imagine who it was, unless it was Chet Baker."[29]

Bill Grauer was not easily deterred, and invited Chet back to the studio for a second recording session the following month. "A major goal at Riverside was to create supportive settings in which a strong group of talented and musically sympathetic colleagues could provide him with some of the best and most creative support he ever had," Keepnews explained. Given the problems recording Chet's vocal, Keepnews and Grauer agreed to record an instrumental album that highlighted the lyrical nature of his trumpet playing. "The one that focused on the concept of *Chet Baker in New York* allowed Chet to pursue his personal variation on the melodic side of his principle horn influence, Miles Davis, and also put him in juxtaposition with a swinging and not-really-approving hard bop player, Johnny Griffin," he said.

Keepnews also hired two of Miles Davis's sidemen for the rhythm section: Paul Chambers on bass, and 'Philly' Joe Jones on drums. Chet was certainly not intimidated by the hard bop line-up, and makes a mockery of the so-called East/West divide. 'In New York' is usually held to be the pinnacle of Chet's brief stay with Riverside, but in truth, it's fairly standard bop, with little to distinguish it from many other records released at the time. Whilst Chet sounded comfortable playing with Miles' sidemen, Miles himself had moved on, recording the groundbreaking *Milestones* and *Porgy and Bess* earlier that year. Nor did Chet's playing burn as brightly as that of Lee Morgan, the twenty-year-old Philadelphia trumpeter who had just recorded *Candy* for Blue Note records.

Between recording sessions, Chet spent most of his time in Harlem, hanging around with a former dealer who went by the name of 'Dirty Nick'. In his memoirs, Chet recalls nodding off after injecting himself with heroin in Nick's apartment on 143rd Street, near Lennox Avenue, and waking up with cockroaches crawling all over him.

When he was running short of cash, he simply called Riverside Records, and when he failed to reach either Bill Grauer or Orrin Keepnews, he called them at home. "Before long he had achieved the distinction of forcing me to switch my home phone to an unlisted number," said Keepnews.

When Keepnews ignored him, Chet tried stealing money from Riverside Records using increasingly underhand methods. First he managed to obtain blank cheques from the offices, forged Bill Grauer's signature, and presented the cheque at the Garden Pharmacy on 52nd Street. Unfortunately for Chet, other artists had tried this manoeuvre, and staff had been made aware that it was Keepnews who signed the company cheques.

Chet would have been aware that some Riverside artists, desperate for drug money, earned extra cash by working in the warehouse during their spare time. Stealing records, then selling them on the street, was a common practice. Chet decided to take this to the next level, and break into the warehouse at night. "One evening my wife and I were terrified to see my father—who was our baby sitter that night—frantically looking for us in a theatre lobby at intermission. The story stemmed from the fact that Riverside's night alarm service had my phone number on file, and was reporting a break-in at our record storage area. That one was a classic tale that included Chet's abilities as a second-storey man—scaling a rear wall, entering through an office window left open, having a truck and some associates in the street."[30]

Chet didn't just steal records from his own record company; he even stole them from music stores. He showed the original draft of his memoirs to Giampiero Giusti in Florence in the late 1970s, which included plenty of material that never made the published version. "One story that came out was that near Birdland in New York was a very big music store, named Colony's. Whenever Chet had no money, he used to break into Colony's; the basement was huge, and used to have small windows that opened on to the street level. They sold records in the basement, and he used to steal his own records, climb out of the window. Later he would autograph the albums, and sell them in the street. One night he broke into the store, and ran into another famous jazz musician—a well-known jazz trombonist—doing exactly the same thing."[31]

Another story concerned Chet's impersonating a law official to confiscate drugs from a dealer, a story that emerged with additional flourishes in his published memoirs. "While he was in New York, Chet managed to get hold of a cop's uniform," Giusti recalled. "At night he would go to Harlem, where he knew there would be many drug dealers. He would approach dealers in his uniform, and wait for them to duck inside their apartment; he would follow them in, and challenge them. The dealer might say, 'Don't arrest me, man, I have a wife and children!' Chet would say, 'OK, but this is the last time. I'm gonna let you go, but I'm going to have to confiscate the drugs'."[32]

Late December saw Chet return to the recording studios with a nightclub singer, Johnny Pace. Pace was an Italian-Irish singer, raised in New Jersey, and working the club circuit, where he occasionally got the chance to work with touring jazz musicians. Chet Baker met him in a small Pittsburgh nightclub, and persuaded Bill Grauer to give him his big break. Given Chet's increasingly strained relationship with his record company, it's a wonder this project ever got off the ground. Pace's tone is pleasant on the ear, but his phrasing sounds like that of a nightclub, rather than a jazz, singer. Chet's playing is good throughout, offering delicate support on 'This Is Always', one of the few standout tracks on this unremarkable record. Keepnews wondered what his partner was doing, recording this "cockamamie singer", and was not surprised when the record sank without trace.

Next day, Keepnews and Grauer assembled a more distinguished line up to record an album of ballads, eventually released as *Chet*. The line-up may have been determined in part by the Johnny Pace sessions; perhaps Keepnews was hoping to salvage something worthwhile from the sessions, and persuaded Chet and flute player Herbie Mann to stay on and make an album of ballads with the label's rising star, pianist Bill Evans.

The ballad format was quite deliberate, according to Keepnews, "this being the pace at which the trumpeter was most likely to keep things under control." Pianist Bill Evans and bass player Paul Chambers were working with Miles Davis at the time, and there are hints of the 'modal' playing heard on *Milestones*, and more prominently on *Kind of Blue*, which was recorded just three months later. The smoky baritone of Pepper Adams is heard to good effect on several tracks, whilst Kenny Burrell makes telling contributions throughout. Critics have pointed to the slow, 'junkie' beat that pervades the sessions, but Mann remembered Chet as being on good form.

The result was a late-night classic to rival Burrell's own *Midnight Blue*. Keepnews himself was pleased with the results. "I do continue to consider this by far his most effective series of performances on Riverside," he wrote in the liner notes to the 2007 CD reissue. "It compares quite favourably with any other body of instrumental work he recorded."

The critics seemed to agree; the album received good reviews, and even *DownBeat* softened its anti-Chet stance somewhat. "Baker picks his way here with less certainty than he once did, but the sensuous personal tone and carefully wrought countermelodies are still in evidence and worth hearing."[33]

Having hit upon a potentially winning formula at the third attempt, Riverside looked set to make a modest return on the investment they had made. Sadly it was not to be. In the early hours of February 20th 1959, Chet was arrested in a courtyard at 210 West 147th Street, smoking a joint while he was waiting for his connection.

Orrin Keepnews, for one, was not shocked by the news. "Why was I not particularly surprised to learn that he had been observed trying to make a purchase in East Harlem, in a scene where he was described as the only person of his complexion on the street."

Bill Grauer generously paid bail, but within days, Chet was trying to score at the same scene, this time using money he'd borrowed from his old friend Jack Sheldon. "I was with Stan Kenton in New York and he took my whole pay cheque; borrowed it," Sheldon recalled. "We left town, and I never saw him again for several years. He took me some place up in Harlem; it scared me to death. He said, 'Listen, I just got busted last night'. He was just nutty, you know!"[34]

Chet's careless behaviour led to a second arrest, just two weeks after the first, and when the case came up that spring, the judge ignored his plea of 'Not Guilty'. Noting the trumpet player's eight previous arrests, he sentenced Chet to six months at Riker's Island, the prison on the other side of Manhattan's East River.

Chet spent almost two weeks in the infirmary, undergoing brutal cold turkey, before being let into the 'population'. There he encountered numerous old friends, ranging from musicians, such as Howard McGhee, to old dope connections, like dealer Donald Frankos. He was assigned a job as one of the prison music instructors, and later claimed he spent all day in the gym, either rehearsing or playing basketball. Nighttime could have proved more difficult, but Chet fell in with a crowd who enjoyed playing poker, chess and bridge. Inmates were periodically entertained by the tap dancer Baby Laurence, who used to dancc with a fellow inmate.

Chet was released from jail two months early for good behaviour. His cabaret card had been revoked following his sentence, which meant that he could no longer perform in New York, so he made plans to leave for Europe with Halema and his young son, Chettie.

Before leaving, he had to fulfill his contract with Riverside, and recorded a tribute to Lerner and Loewe, the composers of *My Fair Lady* and *Brigadoon*. It seemed an unlikely project for Chet, who had only previously recorded two of their tunes; he recorded 'Almost Like Being In Love' with Mulligan, and 'I've Grown Accustomed to Her Face' with the singer Annie Ross. It is noteworthy that most of the songs featured were never recorded by Chet subsequently, suggesting his heart was never really in it. Despite a strong line-up, with Keepnews trying to replicate the feel of the moderately successful *Chet* LP, the session failed to gel. A couple of the tunes, 'I Could Have Danced All Night' and 'Show Me', don't work well as jazz standards. Their cause not helped by cloying arrangements from Herbie Mann. Highlights include a duet with Pepper Adams on 'On the Street Where You Live', and the delicate ballad 'I Talk To The Trees', which would not have sounded out of place on the *Chet* album. For the most part Chet sounds detached from the material, with *Metronome* magazine later noting his 'lackluster' playing.

Two days later, Chet was on his way over to Europe. Four years earlier, he'd left on a high, topping the polls in the leading jazz magazines, cheerfully waving as he boarded a Pan Am flight for Paris. No one was present to photograph his departure second time around. His descent into drug addiction was as rapid as his ascent, and mirrored by a steady decline in popularity with both the jazz critics and the general public. One year after his departure, Jack McKinney of *Metronome* magazine wrote a damning full-page article entitled 'Chet Baker: A Major Talent Diminished'.

Chapter Nine

CHET BAKER WITH FIFTY ITALIAN STRINGS 1959–1961

"She was dressed in a dark green sequined evening dress and she looked beautiful ... "—Chet Baker on Carol Jackson[1]

Within six months of Chet's arrival in Italy he was a tabloid figure, his chiselled good looks gracing the cover of glossy magazines such as Epoca, offering a taste of 'La Dolce Vita A Milano' ('the sweet life of Milan').[2] Sadly, the tabloid press had little interest in Chet as a musician. "They didn't give a damn about jazz," said Amadeo Tommasi, the legendary Italian jazz pianist. "The reason they were interested in Chet Baker is that he was handsome and a drug addict."

Tenor saxophonist Gianni Basso agreed. "Jazz was not that popular in Italy at that time, especially compared with cities like Paris, where many American musicians were living," he said. "There was more of a jazz tradition there—in London, in Sweden, in Copenhagen, even in Germany, where jazz musicians played to the US forces. When Chet first came to Italy with Francy Boland, for example, people wanted to dance the waltz or the tango; there were virtually no jazz clubs. Even by 1959, there were only three jazz clubs in the whole of Milan."[3]

Chet had been invited to play in Italy by Amadeo Tommasi himself, who worked with two partners to organise jazz and classical concerts in Italy by overseas artists. "I was a jazz fan, and organised the first visit to Italy by the Modern Jazz Quartet," he recalled. "They did a big tour in Italy, and also played in other parts of Europe. We searched for other jazz musicians, looking for good names that weren't too expensive, because jazz was not yet that popular in Italy. I thought of Chet Baker, and contacted him."[4]

Amadeo Tommasi met Chet and Halema, and their young son Chesney Jr, at Milan train station. He had arranged for him to play a concert in Fiesole, near Florence, with the Quintetto di Lucca. The band had been founded in early 1958, and consisted of Giovanni Tommaso on bass, his brother Vito Tommaso on piano, Antonello Vannucchi on vibraphone, Gaetano Mariani on guitar and Giampiero Giusti on drums. "They led a double life," recalled local photographer Francesco 'Cecco' Maino. "Under the name of 'I Cinque di Lucca' they played in dancing halls and on the transatlantic liners from Genova, Italy to New York, earning the money to keep going and visit the USA (and buy better instruments)."[5]

The concert was scheduled to take place on 25th July at an open air Roman theatre in Fiesole. The Quintetto di Lucca had never played with Chet, and waited nervously for him to arrive. "They had great admiration for Chet, but wanted to know what tunes he wanted to play," recalled Cecco Maino, who had met Chet on his first tour of Italy, and offered to translate for the band.[6]

He arrived late, and there was immediate confusion as to who would be playing piano that evening. "I had told my partner that I would like to play with Chet Baker, in place of the original pianist of the band, Vito Tommaso. I was a very good friend of Giovanni Tommaso, the bass player," Amadeo Tommasi explained. "I was not such a big fan of Vito Tommaso's playing, and my friend said it would be fine for me to take his place. I said to the pianist, 'I am sorry, but I have arranged to play with Chet Baker tonight'. He said, 'No, I am the pianist with this band, and I will be playing'. My partner had told me nothing about this. After that, I decided to leave the partnership with these two other people."[7]

The show opened with Maxime Saury and his New Orleans Sound, playing an Ellington-influenced set, including versions of 'Solitude' and 'Creole Love Call'. They were followed by the Italian actress-turned-singer Cosetta Greco, playing with pianist Mario Cantini, trying her best to sing like Julie London. Finally the Quintetto di Lucca took the stage, initially without Chet, playing a brief set in the style of the Modern Jazz Quartet.

After a few songs, a pale, nervous-looking Chet Baker joined them onstage, wearing an elegant, dark blue, double-breasted suit. Without a word of greeting, he started to play a sublime, slow version of 'Walkin', recorded by Miles Davis five years earlier. This was followed by 'All The Things You Are', a tune that was not familiar to all the members of the quintet. "There had been no rehearsal," recalled bass player Giovanni Tommaso, "and none of us knew many standards at that time. Sometimes he would call tunes we were not familiar with, and sometimes he would not even call the tune. It wasn't comfortable."[8]

His brother, Vito Tommaso, found the lack of communication particularly difficult to deal with. "The pianist knew the chords of 'My Funny Valentine', but this meant nothing to Chet," said drummer Giampiero Giusti. "Sometimes he would start in a different chord. At other times he would begin by counting in the beat, and then surprising the pianist by playing in a different chord."[9]

The audience did not seem to pick up on the confusion within the band, and when they finished playing 'I'll Remember April', they roared their approval. Chet was tired from the flight, and the long drive from Milan, and said, "Maybe some other time." Thinking this was the name of the next song, there was another burst of applause, but Chet was gone.

Later that day a local musician, Francesco Forti, interviewed Chet for the jazz magazine *Jazz Di Ieri e Di Oggi*. He was accompanied by Cecco Maino, who photographed Chet. The interview took place at the Hotel Mediterraneo in central Florence, where Chet was staying with his family.

Cecco Maino had heard rumours that Chet was taking drugs, but found them hard to believe. "When a famous journalist from the north of Italy hinted in his article that Chet was using, he was attacked and ridiculed by the 'eminenze grigie del jazz Italiano'. This was happening after six years of our listening to the Gerry Mulligan Quartet records, so it was quite a shock for me, for my friends, and very difficult to accept."[10]

But when Chet showed up for the interview, pale, nervous, biting his fingernails and smoking incessantly, Cecco began to have his suspicions. At one point, he was asked what he enjoyed most in life, and he repeated an old joke he had once made to William Claxton, suggesting that he loved his Alfa Romeo, his trumpet, his dog, neglecting to mention his wife, Halema. When his wife tried to intervene, he sent her away in tears. Francesco Forti and Cecco Maino were shocked by his behaviour, and had their worst fears confirmed when Chet's manager, Joe Napoli, mimicked the use of a syringe behind Chet's back. "Our eyes were wide open with surprise. It was more eloquent than a whole novel," recalled the photographer. "We adjusted … in time."

Chet Baker being interviewed by Francesco Forti for the jazz magazine Jazz Di Ieri e Di Oggi, *July 1959.*
Photograph courtesy of Francesco Maino.

During the interview, Chet mentioned the composer Bob Zieff, whose work he had recorded on a number of occasions. "He writes music that is so advanced that nobody wants to buy it. Some time ago in Paris I recorded some of his compositions for *Blue Star* … in that LP the pianist was Dick Twardzik, who died shortly afterward. The music on that album can give you an idea of my actual tendencies and what I intend to do in the near future. I have this music at heart; it is very different to anything that has been played up to now."[11]

Chet went on to explain that he had lost numerous arrangements by Zieff shortly before leaving for Europe.

FF: Perhaps during your concerts you could play something written by him, maybe only one at a time?

CB: Just before I left New York I lost approximately twenty of his arrangements—music worth three thousand dollars. I left these in a taxicab and it is not possible now to write them again.

FF: Didn't you keep a copy?

CB: No, unfortunately. He does not make the score—just writes directly on the different parts. He naturally remembers them but how is it possible to write them again—18 or 20 arrangements. And then I would have to pay him again.

FF: Didn't you write a name, an address? Perhaps somebody will take them back.

CB: That they are brought back or not depends on the cab driver.

FF: To him they are worth nothing.

CB: To him also bringing them back is worth nothing.

Bob Zieff was asked about this incident for the liner notes to *Chet Baker in Paris: The Complete 1955–56 Barclay Sessions*, the excellent box set issued in 2007. He suggests that Chet must have been referring to the charts for the aborted December 1957 recording session for Pacific Jazz. "We only recorded the four pieces for Chet with a chamber ensemble," he recalled. "Those were the pieces he lost." Nevertheless, the incident is an important reminder of the high regard Chet had for Bob Zieff's work, and it is unfortunate that Chet failed to develop his music along the lines he suggests in this interview.

Next day, Chet left Florence for Rome with the drummer of the Quintetto di Lucca, Giampiero Giusti. That evening he headlined at the Festival Nazionale del Jazz, performing a short set starting with 'My Funny Valentine'.

A couple of days later, Chet left Italy for Paris. He left his young family to stay in Paris at the home of Peter Broome, an American sculptor whose brother, Ray, had been at high school with Chet. He travelled alone to Belgium, where he was supposed to headline at the first Festival International du Jazz on August 2nd 1959.

The festival took place at Comblain-la-Tour, a tiny village in the Belgian countryside, organised by Chet's manager, Joe Napoli. Napoli had been wounded in the Battle of the Bulge in December 1944, and was rescued and treated by the people of the village, who kept him hidden from General Gerd von Runstedt's Sixth Panzer Division. Out of gratitude, Napoli returned to the Belgian village after the war, and later organised the jazz festival in conjunction with the local mayor, Monsieur Daniel, and two local newspapers, *La Meuse* and *La Lanterne*.

A large, Newport-style stage had been erected on the local football pitch, constructed from scaffolding pipes, and an estimated twenty thousand jazz fans braved the pouring rain to attend the event. The line-up included

Maxime Saury and his New Orleans Sound, drummer Kenny Clarke, who was living in Paris, and local saxophonist Jacques Pelzer.

"Chet est arrivé!" (Chet has arrived!), proclaimed *La Meuse*, but they were getting ahead of themselves. Chet arrived late, and by the time he showed up backstage, he looked pale and nervous. Francis Thorne, a pianist from Long Island, New York recalled: "We were all biting our nails, wondering how he'd get through it."[12]

They needn't have worried. Chet played a short set, and then returned to the stage for the final jam session, his impressive performance stealing the show. "It is obvious that his playing has moved on to a new level," wrote Roberto Capasso in *Jazz Di Ieri e Di Oggi*. "His playing was so sweet that it won over all of the fans. The force of his playing has increased in comparison to his days with Mulligan. He arrived late, but in time to join the Comblain Festival Parade; he was joined by Christian Callens on trombone, Jacques Pelzer on alto sax, Albert Magnusdorf on trombone, George Grunz on piano, Eric Peter on bass and Pierre Favre on drums. It was the fourteenth hour of jazz, and we were feeling almost 'drunk' by this stage; but the performance by Chet Baker and his friends lifted the fog from our brains, and gave us the pleasure of listening to good music."[13]

After the festival performance, Chet got talking with the Belgian saxophonist Jacques Pelzer. Pelzer used drugs himself, and immediately recognised the trumpet player's condition. He invited Chet to his home in Liège, where he owned a small pharmacy that was well known to many jazz musicians in Europe. There he introduced Chet to Palfium 875, a powerful opioid analgesic that had been developed in Belgium originally to treat pain, but also used to treat heroin addicts. He showed Chet how to crush Palfium tablets into a powder, dissolve it in water, filter the liquid through a gauze, or handkerchief, and then inject the contents with a syringe. The effect was similar to that of heroin, and whilst Palfium was eventually made available on prescription only, Pelzer explained that it was available over the counter in Germany, where it was sold as Jetrium.

Chet returned to Italy with Halema and Chesney, and embarked on a brief tour of Italy with the Quintetto di Lucca. They were joined on the tour bus by Maxime Saury and his band, and the singer Cosetta Greco. "Chet was very introverted, and looked pretty wasted," recalled Giovanni Tommaso. "He sat behind us on the bus with his wife, Halema. I had the impression he wanted to be left alone. Besides, my English was so poor."[14]

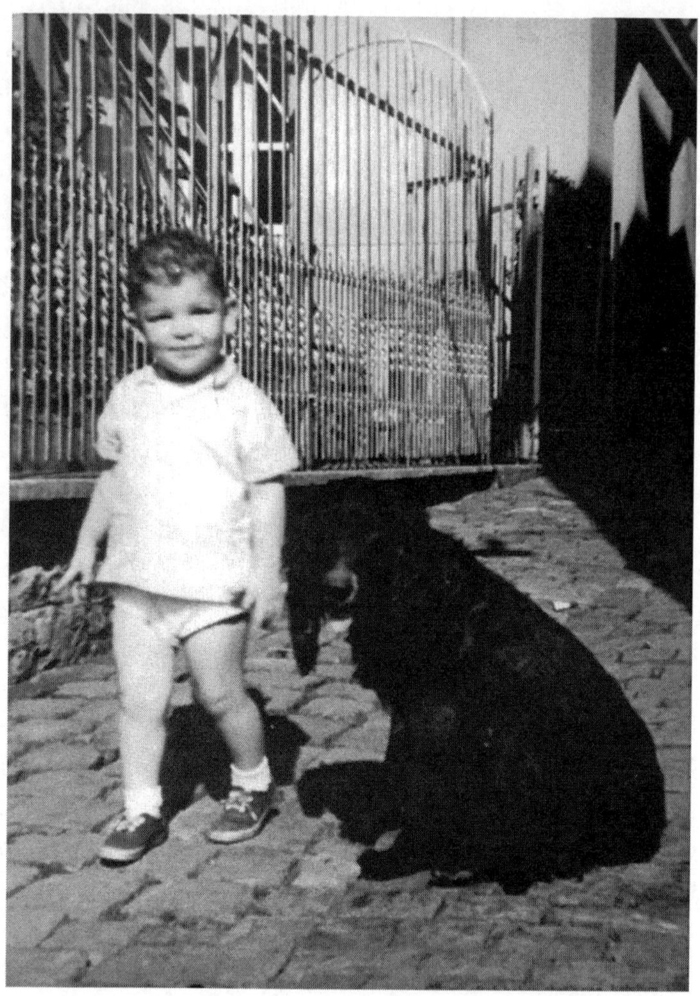

Chet's son, Chesney Aftab Baker, Belgium 1959.
Photographer unknown

Every night, the routine was the same. The Quintetto di Lucca would play two or three songs without Chet, before he would join them onstage. Whilst the band soon became accustomed to Chet's repertoire, there was an underlying tension stemming from Chet's drug use. "Whenever we stopped in places like Rome, Chet hooked up with people who I knew were involved with drugs," said Giovanni Tommaso, "so I assumed he was still using. He always played very well, but I was always nervous about playing with him, so the atmosphere was always pretty tense."

The atmosphere between Chet and Halema had also become strained, and after a week or so of travelling with his family, Halema decided to stay in Rome with their son. Chet had a good relationship with the drummer of the quintet, Giampiero Giusti, in part because he drove his own Alfa Romeo between concerts, rather than travel by bus. "One day he asked me if he could travel in my car, rather than on the bus with the other musicians," he later recalled. "I said, 'Sure!' So we had the opportunity to talk, and built up a good rapport. The first day Chet travelled in my car, Chet was wearing a short-sleeved shirt; it was terrible; the crook of his arm was black with needle marks. 'Peter, all the money I have goes into my arm; I no longer have an apartment, my Chevrolet Impala has gone'. It was terrible. On many occasions he told me he would stop; in Bologna, in Rimini, he did not buy drugs; but before the concert started, dealers would come up to him and say, 'Chet, do you want some drugs, gratis!' This happened all his life."

The tour came to an end after three weeks, and Chet returned to Rome to reunite with his family. In late August, Joe Napoli found work for Chet at a small jazz club, Le Grotte del Piccione (the Cave of the Pigeons), where trumpet player Cicci Santucci played with his band. "It was a nice club in the centre of Rome," remembered Santucci. "We were a little worried, because we were young musicians, so I asked the agent, Joe Napoli, 'Which songs will Chet play with us?' 'Don't worry,' he replied, 'Just follow him!' 'We can follow him, but we'd still like to know what tunes he's going to play'. Anyway, he played only standards."[15]

Cicci Santucci used to pick Chet up at his hotel, and drive him to the club. "I had a quintet, which included the tenor saxophonist Enzo Scoppa," he said. "We would start with two or three numbers, and then I would introduce Chet Baker as a guest, and he would play with the rhythm section. Every time I heard him play it was a lesson in taste and feeling. It was amazing; he used to leave his trumpet on the piano, but he never needed to warm his lips, he simply picked up the trumpet and started to play. Chet played with us for almost two weeks."[16]

One regular visitor to the club was the Austrian actor Lars Bloch, who was living in Rome at this time. He had spent part of that summer working on *La Dolce Vita*, in which he had a bit part role. "I was filming for a couple of weeks, just for the party scenes," he recalled. "That was a good job, paying 10,000 lire a day; you could live for a week on 10,000 lire in those days!"[17]

A copy of the original movie poster for Urlatori alla Sbarra, *1959, used for the DVD.*

Lars introduced Chet and his manager, Joe Napoli, to Lucio Fulci, a young film director who later became known for his low-budget horror movies, such as *Zombi II* (also known as *Zombie Flesh Eaters*) and *City of the Living Dead* (also known as *The Gates of Hell*). He was about to embark on a new movie project, a rock-and-roll movie that was eventually released as *Urlatori alla Sbarra*, which roughly translates as 'Howlers on the Dock' or 'Rock Shouters on Trial'. "We made that film above all to give Chet Baker a hand," Fulci later recalled. "He was in a bad way … he didn't even have the money to live."[18]

Fulci's recollection is something of an exaggeration. Chet had regular work at this time, and his family was living in a hotel in Rome, so he was hardly destitute. But as was the case for much of his life, he spent as much as he earned to fund his addiction, and was constantly asking friends and musicians if he could borrow money. "He always spent more money than he ever made: most of the time before he even earned it," confirmed Cecco Maino. "He kept asking for money everybody on sight: Giampiero, me, Rudy and very few managed to resist, even though we all knew that he would never give it back."[19]

Before filming began, Fulci was warned about Chet's drug addiction. "I remember Joe Napoli told the director, 'Listen, you can't have Chet dressed in short sleeves'. His arm was completely covered in marks," recalled Cicci Santucci.[20]

Urlatori alla Sbarra was essentially a music movie, aimed at the Italian teenagers who had just discovered the thrills of rock 'n' roll. "It was about a bunch of rock and roll kids, out partying," said Lars Bloch. "I played a small part in the movie, one of the guys in the group." The movie helped to launch the careers of two Italian pop singers, Mina and Adriano Celentano, who were close friends with Fulci and his screenwriter, Piero Vivarelli. "Piero wrote many of the songs for Adriano Celantano, including 'Ventiquattro Mila Baci', which I think was his first hit, and came out of the movie," recalled Bloch.

Fulci and Vivarelli didn't really know how to communicate with Chet, and had no idea what they could get out of him. "I was the only one speaking any decent English," said Bloch, "so we hung out. He was playing at night, so he was pretty sleepy and groggy when he came to work on the movie." Chet was given a role as one of the gang members, known only as 'the American'. He was seen sleeping in many of the scenes, an in-joke given that he had often played all night at Le Grotte del Piccione.

In Chet's very first scene, for example, he is sleeping in the bathtub, and wakes up when the telephone rings. He yawns, places the shower handle to his ear, then shouts 'Adriano', calling the singer Adriano Celentano to the real telephone. A little later he is seen sleeping in the elevator where a sign read 'guasto', or 'out of order'; the other gang members are all seen running down the stairs.

Most scenes last for just a few seconds; the only scene of any significance is close to the end of the movie, when the gang members ride on scooters out to a pine forest, where Chet is seen leaning against a tree with a young girl. He tells her that he's tired, and needs to sleep, but then has a change of heart, and kisses her. He then looks down at her and sings 'Arrivederci' in his soft voice, his trumpet appearing out of thin air. This romantic scene seems to impact the other gang members, and other couples are seen flirting with one another. At this moment, at least, Chet looks young and innocent, a far cry from the pale, nervous musician that made his debut with the Quintetto di Lucca.

In many respects, this was the dichotomy that attracted the attention of the Italian tabloid press at the time, and continues to fascinate all these years later; here was a gifted, handsome young musician, whose boyish, innocent looks—for now, at least—betrayed a terrible secret. "They wrote many stories about Chet because he was a junkie American jazz musician, and that's why he was popular—not because of the music," confirmed Giovanni Tommaso.[21]

In mid-September Chet moved from Rome to Milan, where Joe Napoli found him a job at the Santa Tecla, one of a handful of clubs where jazz musicians could play. Photographer Cecco Maino remembers going to the club and watching Chet play with a large number of local jazz musicians, all of who had stopped by to play with him. "I heard him with the 'who's who' of Italian jazz; Masetti, Cerri, Gene Victory, Basso, Sellani, Pezzotta, Libano, Franco Cerri—they all wanted to play with Chet, who was at the best."[22]

Tenor saxophonist Gianni Basso was playing with his own band at the Taverna Messicana, but remembers stopping by to play with Chet on a regular basis. He had the opportunity to play with many American jazz musicians that came through, including Gerry Mulligan, Dizzy Gillespie and Count Basie, but remembers that Chet had a significant influence on his own playing. "In my opinion, the two really great artists were Charlie Parker and Chet Baker," he later recalled. "Dizzy Gillespie was a fantastic player, of course, but for me, he was too fussy. The same with Wynton Marsalis and Michael Brecker; great players, but they play too much. Chet could sometimes play just two notes where others might play ten, but those two notes were important. I used to learn so much from him. He played beautiful melodies, he sang well. Every time he played the same tune he brought new ideas; he was very important."[23]

Chet seemingly found drugs harder to come by in Milan than in Rome, and following the advice of Belgian saxophonist Jacques Pelzer, started travelling to Germany in his spare time to stock up on Jetrium, the over-the-counter analgesic. "I'd fly from Milan to Munich with no baggage," Chet later recalled, "and then fill the pockets of my heavy coat with boxes of injectable Jetrium, then fly back to Italy. It was the closest thing to stuff that I'd ever found … "[24]

He later claimed that his addiction to Jetrium had started earlier, and was exacerbated by the process of filming *Urlatori alla Sbarra* in Rome. In a letter to *Playboy* magazine, he explained how his intake increased from ten 5 mg pills per day to two hundred during his first two months in Italy:

"To make a long story short I began to take more Jetrium. I know I should have stopped working but I like to play, I needed the money and I'd just signed a contract to do a film and club date in Rome. If I'd known what I was letting myself in for in Rome I wouldn't have gone, contract or no. Up at 7 a.m., at the studio from 8 a.m. to 6 p.m. Soundtrack recording from 9 p.m. to 11 p.m., club date from midnight to 3 a.m. By the time I finished that two weeks I was taking 200 pills a day by injection. Seems impossible I know, but thats [sic] how fast my resistance went up."

Halema did not want to raise Chesney Jr in such an environment; Chet was spending money before he'd even earned it, and there was barely enough food to feed his family, let alone pay the hotel bill. She made arrangements to stay with friends in Paris. By this stage "I had left Chet four or five times because of the drugs," she later recalled.

Joe Napoli arranged for Chet to record two LPs on an Italian record label with local musicians, albums that would ironically be distributed by his old label, Riverside, in the United States. The first album, *Chet Baker in Milan*, was recorded over two days in late September, and featured Gianni Basso on tenor saxophone and Glauco Masetti on alto. "After playing at the club one night, Chet asked me if I'd join him on a record, playing arrangements by Giulio Libani with a sextet. I remember we played some tunes we'd never played at the club; on the morning of the session he suddenly decided to play a Sonny Rollins tune ('Pent Up House'). There was no preparation!" remembered Gianni Basso.[25]

The band primarily stuck to bop standards such as Charlie Parker's 'Cheryl Blues' and Tadd Dameron's 'Lady Bird', but also revisited Mulligan's 'Line For Lyons'. For the most part, the results were fairly pedestrian, and lacked any real spark. Baker's tone is not as clean as on his previous European recordings, most likely the result of his drug intake. "Chet played well," Basso recalled, "but was taking too many drugs at this time, and for me, his playing was not at its best. The record he made when he came out of prison, when he was clean, his playing was fantastic. He was more concentrated at this time. It's the same with any substance, including alcohol. I like wine, and when I play after drinking wine, I think I'm playing really well. But when I listen to a recording afterwards, I think again!"[26]

Two days later, Chet was back in the studio to record an album with Len Mercer, (real name Ezio Leoni) and his orchestra. It appears to have been a deliberate attempt to reproduce the Capitol-era Sinatra recordings, even including 'Angel Eyes' and 'Goodbye' from Sinatra's 1958 LP *Sings for Only the Lonely*. The album, initially released as *Chet Baker with Fifty Italian Strings* has its admirers, and has been reissued with different sleeves on numerous occasions. Chet's playing is strong, never overwhelmed by the orchestra, and he is in good voice on the five vocal tracks. The arrangements are extremely heavy-handed, however, and generally inferior to the earlier *With Strings* album recorded for Pacific Jazz. The album failed to meet with critical acclaim at the time, with *DownBeat* referring to the album as 'lethargic'.

Whilst these two albums were hardly on a par with Chet's work for Pacific Jazz, they were to be his last significant recordings for more than two years, as his drug intake escalated out of control, eventually resulting in his imprisonment.

Chet's personal problems resulted in his live performances becoming more erratic. The photographer, Cecco Maino remembers seeing Chet play in Milan on October 1st and 2nd, and being blown away by Chet's playing. "Tony Scott and Lars Gullin played two nights at the Taverna Messicana in Milano with Sellani, Cerri and Prat: some of the best Chet I ever heard," he later wrote.

In October, Joe Napoli arranged for Chet to work with the Italian composer, Armando Trovajoli on the soundtrack to a 1959 movie, *Il Vedovo*. Although no trumpet can be heard on the movie soundtrack, he can be heard—together with a saxophonist that sounds like Lars Gullin—on the CD, which eventually came out on an Italian label. Chet went on to record at least two further sessions with Trovajoli, including the soundtrack to *Il Piaceri del Sabato Notte*, a film directed by Daniele D'Anza (March/April 1960), and *Il Novelliere*, a TV production in which Chet had a small acting part (May/June 1960).[27]

A few weeks later, on November 9th, Chet played a disastrous show at the Teatro della Pergola in Florence, a venue normally used for classical music. The show, entitled *Bussola on Stage*, featured Chet Baker, Romano Mussolini on piano, Lars Gullin on baritone saxophone, Franco Cerri on bass, Gene Victory on drums, plus a number of popular singers, including Chet's old friend Caterina Valente. "(It was) not the right atmosphere for Chet at all," Maino recalled. "He was in a horrible mood, wore a green tuxedo with shiny lapels and sunglasses, played a couple of series of meaningless cascades of notes, then proceeded to shoot up backstage in full view of the service firemen who understood little of what was going on. I photographed the concert. It was the only time I ever talked to Mussolini, a timid person who was very upset for the whole mess, and also resented me taking his photo, although I did it backstage."[28]

Maino believes that the *Bussola on Stage* show was also the scene of the infamous 'Mussolini incident'. Legend has it that Chet was talking to the pianist, Romano Mussolini, and said "Gee, it was a shame about your old man," a story that reinforces the view that he was not best versed in the art of conversation. In later years, Mussolini claimed he had no recollection of the conversation. Chet also downplayed the incident, no doubt frustrated that he was always asked about the event. After all, it was simply an attempt by a stoned American musician to make conversation with a shy Italian pianist, and hardly requires detailed analysis.

Nevertheless, Caterina Valente also claimed to remember the conversation between the two men, which again suggests that the incident took place backstage in Florence, rather than at the airport, as some sources have suggested, or when the two men first met, which was during Chet's first tour of Italy in January 1956.

Chet was floundering without Halema, and contacted her in Paris, begging her to join him in Milan. He had regular work, he told her, and could provide a comfortable living for her and Chettie. It was important for their son to grow up with a father, he told her, promising that drugs would no longer be a part of his life, that it would be different this time.

Halema knew deep down that Chet was never going to change, but wanted to give their relationship one last chance. They found an apartment in the centre of Milan, but it soon became clear that Chet was still dependent on Jetrium, and struggled to function without it. Chet could be very persuasive, and even talked his wife into flying to Germany on his behalf while he was busy with commitments at the Santa Tecla jazz club. It was legal to purchase the drug in Germany, he assured her, neglecting to mention that it was illegal to bring such narcotics into Italy. When Halema refused, he asked his American drummer, Gene Victory—a fellow addict—to procure Jetrium for both of them.

As Chet's resistance to Jetrium built up, he injected himself with greater quantities, taking up to 1,200 mg per day, or the equivalent of 250 pills. "I was in bad shape," Chet later admitted. "Chalky-coloured, not eating, and having terrible, frequent chills." His condition further increased the strain on his marriage, which was on the verge of falling apart. "We lived together, but like two strangers," Halema later admitted.[29]

Chet's addiction was taking its toll on his playing, too, and friends eventually convinced him that he should visit a doctor to seek help. " … I had a physical examination," Chet later wrote. "(The) doctor said I was in perfect health, until my blood test came back. He gave me from three to six months to live if I continued taking Jetrium. Naturally I put myself in a clinic."[30]

Chet Baker in Milan, early 1960: Photograph from Epoca *magazine, February 1960.*

Chet gave notice at the jazz club, and checked into the Villa Turro clinic in Milan on December 4th, persuading Gene Victory to join him. The two musicians were kept unconscious for one week, fed with an intravenous drip, fortified with vitamins and minerals. In the weeks that followed, Chet claimed he felt no discomfort from the withdrawal. The colour had returned to his cheeks, and he started to regain weight. The clinic was reluctant to let him leave, and urged him to see out the entire treatment, which was scheduled to last for two months. Chet was impatient to get back to work, however, and contacted the American consulate, which persuaded the clinic to allow him out in early January, some thirty days ahead of schedule. "I came out clean, felt great, and was determined that this was it, no more drugs. I went back to work," he claimed.[31]

Chet found work back at the Santa Tecla, where he remained a popular draw. One evening he was approached by a local journalist and filmmaker, Enzo Nassa, who suggested making a short movie about his life in Milan, tentatively entitled *Tromba Fredda* (Cold Trumpet), featuring Chet and Halema.

Another regular visitor to the club was a teenage drummer by the name of Laurie Jay, who later played with The Echoes and the Laurie Jay Combo, and went on to manage the British soul singer Billy Ocean. He worked at a variety show at the Teatro Olympia in Milan, headlined by the Welsh singer Shirley Bassey. At the end of each show, Laurie Jay used to encourage his friends to stop by the jazz club to watch Chet play, telling them he was a legendary American jazz star. One evening he was joined by one of the show's announcers, a nineteen-year-old English girl by the name of Carol Jackson.

A striking brunette with large, dark brown eyes, Carol had given up work as a secretary when she won a local beauty contest. On the back of this she landed a bit part in a British movie, a comedy called *Sands of the Desert*, where she played a bikini-clad harem girl. She had travelled to Milan in search of work, and got a job with the Shirley Bassey show on her arrival. "It was my task to announce the different performers, in three different languages," she said. "I don't speak all those languages, but I had memorised the words. I wore glamorous dresses, a different one for each announcement." Stills from the movie *Let's Get Lost* show one such outfit, which consisted of a bikini, high heels and a long flowing headdress, offset by chunky costume jewellery and a gemstone in her navel.

Lonely and homesick, Carol was not enjoying the job, which was not as she had expected it to be. "I didn't go anywhere for the first week but there were other guys there and every night they would say they were going to see Chet Baker," she later revealed, "but I didn't care to go and went back to my room. That went on for a week until one Saturday night they said you're not going home to the hotel, you're coming out tonight whether you like it or not and practically dragged me along. One of the guys had a bunch of records under his arm and going over in the cab they were all talking about Chet Baker and I was hearing all this and I thought God, why would I want to meet him? I didn't even know what he played."[32]

At the end of the set, the club emptied out, and Chet made his way over to Laurie's table to greet him, and sign records for his friends. Chet invited them all to dinner, a gesture that impressed Carol. "At the dinner table, when we went to the restaurant, he was checking me out but I'm thinking well, I'm going home, I'm only here for three weeks and I'll never see him again. No ideas, no thoughts, nothing," she claimed. Halema remembered things quite differently, however, and recalled Carol making eyes at her husband.

Either way, the attraction was mutual, and in the days that followed, Chet pestered Laurie to invite him backstage at the Teatro Olympia, where he hoped to get another glimpse of Carol. "The following week, every night I caught sight of him backstage. He was always talking to somebody and sort of looking my way," Carol remembered. "One night I hear a voice behind me say hello and I turned around and it was him. He says to me, 'Do you remember me?' I said yes and then he asked, 'Did anyone ever tell you that you should be in the movies?' I looked at him and thought this is the old line. I said to him, 'Couldn't you think of a better line than that?' He said, 'It's not a line,' and he got quite indignant about it. I said, 'Oh, it isn't?' He said, 'No, what are you doing tomorrow? I'll prove to you it's not a line'."[33]

Chet told Carol that he knew a movie producer, Mario Fatore, who had seen her at dinner the previous week, and wanted to meet her. Next day, Chet drove her to the studio on the outskirts of Milan where Carol had a 'screen test', after which Fatore handed her a wad of Italian lire for her efforts. It was only at this point Carol became remotely sceptical. "If it hadn't been for that, I wouldn't have been suspicious," she said, "but I had never been paid that way. Your money usually goes to your agent and you get a cheque every so often." Carol accused Chet of staging the whole audition, a claim he vehemently denied. He only came clean in the early 1970s, finally admitting that he been trying to impress her all those years earlier.

Chet started to see Carol after she had finished work, and even used to speed over to the Teatro Olympia in his Alfa Romeo between sets to spend more time with her. One night, he didn't go back home to Halema, calling her next day to tell her the marriage was over. After all he'd put her through, the support she'd given him through his heroin addiction, his spells in hospital and in prison, and his problems with Palfium, it was a cruel way to end things.

Despite their long-standing problems, Halema was heartbroken. On several occasions she confronted Chet and Carol in the Santa Tecla, and in other jazz clubs around town, such as the Taverna Messicana. She begged Chet to come back to her, to look after his son, knowing that without him she was stranded in Italy, four thousand miles from home. The Italian tabloid press soon picked up on the scandal, the cover of *Il Reporter* showing Chet and Carol sitting at a nightclub table, the headline reading 'Il Veleno del Jazz' ('the poison of jazz'). Paparazzi photographers would follow Chet and Carol around the city, taking photos and asking him if he was planning to go back to his wife and child, when he was going to marry Carol. Chet was never comfortable with media attention, even at the height of his West Coast fame, but Carol thrived on the attention, posing for the cameras, enjoying her moment in the spotlight.

Chet persuaded Carol to give up her job at the Teatro Olympia. His contract at the Santa Tecla had come to an end, and he suggested they travel around Italy together. They travelled to Florence, where Chet worked for two weeks, and then down to Rome. Carol has fond memories of the early days; Chet was clean at the time, having stayed off Palfium since his 'sleep cure', and she enjoyed the thrill of exploring the country in Chet's Alfa Romeo Giulietta Sprint. "Chet always used to like to travel late at night when he got off the job because there was no one on the road," she told *Jerry Jazz Musician*. "It was quiet and he thought he could make good time. We did a lot of travelling at night, high speed too! It was nice with the radio on, stopping for a bite to eat, staying at small motels."[34]

News of their exploits was not only splashed over the Italian tabloids, but also reached the UK, where one magazine reported that Chet had kidnapped Carol, and was keeping her against her will by injecting her with heroin. It wasn't long before the press called Carol's father, Albert Jackson, and asked him if there was any truth to the rumours.

With no way of calling their daughter, Albert and Carol Jackson tracked them down to Rome, where Chet was playing at a supper club called Rupe Tarpea. "One look at Carol and they knew everything was cool," Chet wrote in his memoirs. "She was dressed in a dark green sequined evening dress and she looked beautiful. Her father explained to us about all the publicity and crap in the papers. One newspaper even printed a story that Interpol was looking for us."

Others were less impressed by Chet's "cool" demeanour. One of his friends in Rome was a young jazz singer by the name of Lilian Terry. She had first met Chet at the International Jazz Festival at Comblain-la-Tour in August 1959, where she had been performing with Romano Mussolini. They had stayed in touch since then, and had become good friends, even inviting Chet and Halema to dine at her mother's house. "She used to comment on how skinny the poor boy was. 'Surely he doesn't eat enough!'"

Lilian soon learned the truth of the matter, and after a while, stopped lending him money, knowing that it would end up in the pocket of a drug dealer. "Regarding his drug habits, I soon realised that any discussion, advice, prayer or argument, would simply be aimless, like water flowing on a marble slate," she recalled. "He would give me his patient smile and shake his head, and change the subject."[35]

Chet and Carol were staying in a small hotel located behind her house in Rome, and they used to get together in the hotel dining room after lunch, where they would discuss jazz, and even sing their favourite ballads. One day, Chet proposed they record an album of such ballads, assuming they could get permission from their respective record companies.

"Eventually we were given the go-ahead and we met at the hotel to decide with our musicians the definitive list of ballads. That done, we drank to our success. Chet then invited all of us to continue the celebration upstairs where our singing would not disturb the other guests. Entering his room I noticed a black sample suitcase that was open to show its contents. On one side were all kinds of pills, drops and whatever; on the other side were syringes, vials and whatever else was needed to inject. My knees failed me and I sat on the bed as Chet invited me to choose whatever struck my fancy in his pharmacy. I kept shaking my head, speechless, realising that all these years he had never really listened to me. Then came a moment I have never forgotten since then. He told me that if we were to sing together, make a record together, then I had to join the group and do as they did. There was no other way. Still shaking my head in silence I got up, left the room and shut the door on our recording project but, above all, on our friendship as we had known it."[36]

It is hard to rationalise why Chet would have behaved in this way. He did not put pressure on all of his band members to join him; indeed, there were numerous occasions where Chet would actively discourage younger musicians from experimenting with drugs, just as Charlie Parker had sought to protect him. One can only assume that part of Chet was drawn to "innocent" young ladies who liked his "bad boy" image. Halema had fitted that description, and Carol Jackson too. In the years that followed, Chet also fell for Ruth Young, then just twenty-two years old, the daughter of a wealthy Hollywood movie producer. Lilian Terry refused to be drawn into Chet's web, however, and walked away unscathed.

Chet and Carol stayed in Rome for almost one month, and then drove to Bologna, where he was due to begin an engagement at one of the local nightclubs. Arriving in the city with a few days to spare, Chet decided to visit a local dentist to have some work done on his crown, work that he'd been putting off for some months. "I had four teeth gold crowned. If you've ever had any crown work done you know it involves a hell of a lot of novocaine, drilling and grinding. Halfway through my first night's work I began to have a headache. I've had headaches before but this was something else. After work I went to the pharmacy for asperine [sic]. Nothing. I went back to the pharmacy again and bought the strongest painkiller I could get without a prescription; nothing. I didn't sleep that night. The following morning at 9.30 I went back to my dentist. I was desperate. I knew that my resistance to drugs and painkillers was very high because of having been an addict for four years. I explained the situation to my dentist about having taken asperine [sic] and Nisidine with no effect. I asked if Palfium might be prescribed under the circumstances. He wrote me several prescriptions during the following week and advised me to see a specialist in Rome on my return there."[37]

Carol later claimed that she had no idea that Chet had started taking Palfium again, and did not notice that he was using for some time. "Later in this year, he started to take something again, but at first quite sporadically and only with prescription. He kept it hidden from me—I noticed it only after a few months."[38]

Chet had arranged a rehearsal at the club with a number of the local jazz musicians in Bologna. He had no sheet music with him, however, and started to worry when it became clear that a number of the musicians were not that familiar with his repertoire. Luckily the pianist, Amadeo Tommasi, had gone along to the club to witness the rehearsal, and offered to lend a helping hand. "I remember he said, 'Let's play 'Stella by Starlight', and the other musicians did not know the tune," he recalled. "He looked really desperate.

I plucked up courage, went up to the pianist, and said, 'Please let me play'. He was happy to let me take over, and played the right chords to the next tune, 'Polka Dots and Moonbeams'. Chet looked over at me, his gratitude obvious from his eyes. At the end of the rehearsal, Chet came up to me and asked, 'What are you doing this evening? Will you play with me?' I agreed to play, and it was fantastic. At the end of the evening, he told me he had got a job at La Bussola. 'I hope to play with you soon, but I'm not sure when it will be'. I remember he took just L20,000 that evening, the equivalent of just $40–$50. He wasn't making much money."[39]

La Bussola (The Compass) was a glamorous nightclub in Le Focette, situated on the Tuscan coastline. The main room, situated on the first floor, tended to feature stars of light entertainment, such as the popular Italian singer Peppino di Capri, although it is worth noting that Ella Fitzgerald also played at the club that year. Chet had been booked to play a summer season at Il Bussolotto, a smaller lounge at the club, situated on the second floor, starting in June.

Once he had finished his engagement in Bologna, Chet and Carol returned to Rome, where Joe Napoli had arranged a short engagement at a nightclub. Chet was still suffering from intense pain from his dental treatment, and consulted a doctor in Rome, who thought that his condition might be caused by neuralgia. He arranged therapy for him, which included a course of vitamin shots, and prescribed Palfium for the pain.

In late April, Chet found work at a small club in Naples, where his trumpet was allegedly stolen from on top of the piano one night. In his memoirs, Chet claims to have been devastated by the incident. "I was a finished man—I could no longer play, I couldn't earn a living." He suggests he cried all night in Carol's arms. "I had Carol with me, but her words of comfort didn't console me. I had lost my trumpet. I didn't have the money to buy another one."

Chet often reported that his trumpet had been "stolen" in later years, but in most cases he had sold it to fund his drug addiction. On this occasion, Chet reported the theft to Sergio Bernadini, who owned La Busolla, who was kind enough to order an expensive new trumpet for Chet from the United States.

The theft of his trumpet brought the engagement at Naples to a premature end, so Chet and Carol drove back up Tuscany, the opening at Il Bussolotto still three weeks away. They found a place to stay in picturesque seaside town of Marina di Pietrasanta, just outside Le Focette. They moved into a small pensione, Villa Gemma, which was owned by an amateur musician, Giali Giambastiani, who felt honoured to have Chet staying with him, and offered to help him in any way possible.

It was in Tuscany that Chet's addiction to Palfium started to escalate again, quickly spiralling out of control. On 10th May, he tried to obtain Palfium from a local doctor. He claimed to be suffering from severe sinus pains caused by a chronic trigeminal neuralgia, terminology he had picked up from the doctor in Rome. The neuralgia was the result of a major car accident during which he had broken his nose, he explained. The doctor conducted a physical examination of the sinus area, and suggested a course of over-the-counter painkillers. Chet claimed that he had tried such drugs before, and found them to be ineffective. The only drug that he had found to be effective was Palfium. At this point the doctor hesitated, explaining that Palfium was a powerful narcotic, and whilst it was effective as a pain medication, it would not provide a long-term solution to Chet's apparent discomfort. The doctor suggested that Chet consult with a local expert on neuralgia, Professor Niosi, who was based in Pisa. In the meantime, he prescribed Chet with enough Palfium to tide him over until he could see the specialist; a single box of five tablets to be taken once a day.

Chet knew from his experience in Milan that one box was not enough; five tablets crushed and mixed with water were barely enough for a single fix, so he set about searching for other doctors in the surrounding area, soon learning that they could be easily identified by the cross on their car licence plates. He tried his luck with another pharmacist in the same town, and in the days that followed, he started to spread his net a little wider to take in nearby towns such as Forte dei Marmi, Viareggio, Lucca and Pietrasanta. Some doctors probably guessed they were dealing with a drug addict, and turned him away, but others were taken in by his story and supplied him with the Palfium that he craved.

On May 20th, Chet paid his first visit to Dr Roberto Bechelli, a physician from Viareggio, a few miles down the coast from Le Focette. Again, Chet claimed to be suffering from chronic neuralgia, and was prescribed a course of painkillers. When Chet suggested Palfium, Bechelli became suspicious; he had heard of the drug, and was aware of its properties, but had never previously prescribed it to any of his patients. His suspicions were further aroused by the fact that Chet seemed to be extremely familiar with its analgesic faculty. Sensing his hesitation, and taking the doctor's hint that he might be persuaded to write a prescription, Chet slipped him ten thousand lire and walked away with another box of pills. Police later discovered that Chet visited Dr Bechelli a total of twenty-three occasions over the next two months, and was prescribed a total of 775 mg of Palfium, plus a further 50 mg that was prescribed in the name of a friend.

At around the same time as his first visit to Bechelli, Chet made an appointment with Sergio Nottoli, a local paediatrician. After listening to Chet's ailments, and carrying out a physical examination, Dr Nottoli suggested that Chet visit a specialist. Chet replied that a renowned specialist, Professor Niosi, was treating him. As a consequence, the doctor felt that Chet's explanation sounded plausible, and wrote out a prescription for Palfium. Nottoli's suspicions were aroused when Chet returned to his office just three days later, on May 22nd, but Chet claimed that his prescription had been stolen from his car, and produced a police document to support his claim. As a result, the doctor relented, and wrote a second prescription.

When Chet came back again, just three days later, the doctor became alarmed, and suggested that Chet return to Professor Niosi in Pisa for further treatment. Chet complained that he didn't have the money to return to Pisa, and opened his wallet to show that he only had five hundred lire in cash. This time Notolli refused to supply him with Palfium, and Chet walked away empty-handed.

That evening, back at Villa Gemma, Chet explained the problems he had procuring painkillers from the paediatrician to his sympathetic landlord, Giali Giambastiani, who offered to approach Nottoli again on Chet's behalf.

On 28th May, Giambastiani turned up at Nottoli's office and claimed that his tenant, Chet Baker, was lying in bed in the pensione, suffering from excruciating pain. Against his better judgement, Dr Nottoli wrote yet another prescription for Palfium. The doctor was aware that supplying narcotics to a known drug addict was a criminal offence, and on this occasion he tried to cover his own tracks by writing out the script in Giambastiani's name.

As Chet's resistance to Palfium again started to build up, his intake increased. He went back to Nottoli's office again next day, this time on his own. The doctored insisted that the troubled musician return to Professor Niosi in order to continue his therapy. Chet told him that his job at Il Bussolotto had not yet started, and he still didn't have any money. Again the doctor relented, and wrote out another prescription for ten Palfium pills.

Two days later, Chet persuaded his landlord to pay another visit to

Nottoli on his behalf. With Baker waiting outside in the car, Giambastiani again claimed he was in great pain, and pleaded for another prescription. Dr Nottoli agreed, but made it clear that this would be the last occasion he would help Chet in this way. This time he wrote a prescription in the name of Meladiò Aurelio, a friend of Giambastiani.

Chet opened at Il Bussolotto in early June looking pale and washed out, but he was glad to be playing again, and grateful to be earning L25–30,000 per day. He was playing opposite the pianist Romano Mussolini, who was a close friend of the proprietor, Sergio Bernadini. Mussolini's playing did not particularly inspire Chet, as he later revealed in his memoirs. "Everything he played sounded like the blues. He could play 'Stardust' and make it come out somehow sounding like the blues. Hampton Hawes had the same quality, but Romano lacked the fire and imagination of Hawes."[40]

After a few weeks, Chet asked Amadeo Tommasi to take Romano Mussolini's place on piano. "A Dixicland-stylc group was playing thcrc, and the pianist, a friend of mine, asked me to take his place for one month as he had another job," Tommasi recalled. "So I came to La Bussola to play with the Dixieland band. When I arrived in Viareggio, Chet Baker saw me, and said, 'Ah, Amadeo, you can play with me, and Romano can take your place in the other band'."[41]

Although Chet's playing was still strong, Tommasi noticed a change in his behaviour, most likely caused by his narcotic addiction. "In this period, Chet played many Miles Davis tunes, and I used to play some tunes with the same Latin-style that Red Garland used when accompanying Miles," he said. "The drummer didn't pick up on the Latin style, and played with a regular jazz beat. Chet would say, 'Stop! Again', without explaining anything to the rhythm section. We played again, and the drummer made the same mistake again. Chet shouted, 'Stop!' When the drummer repeated the mistake a third time, he said, 'OK, I'm leaving'. I went up to Chet and said, 'Where are you going? The drummer simply doesn't know the intro'. He expected professional musicians to know every tune. Sometimes he could be very hard, not so nice to deal with, and at other times, there were no problems."[42]

This behavioural trait continued to manifest itself over the years, with Chet frequently voicing his displeasure on the bandstand for all to hear. Drummers were his most frequent target, particularly when he found their playing too obtrusive, and contributed to his decision to work with a drummerless trio on a number of occasions in the 1980s.

Cecco Maino also watched Chet playing at Il Bussolotto, and noted that his growing addiction was taking its toll on the music. "For the most part, he played very well," he remembered, "but there were times when he needed drugs, and did not concentrate on the music; as he did at Fiesole, he would just disappear." During this period, Chet was forced to search further afield in search of pharmacists who were willing to supply him with Palfium. The subsequent police investigation revealed that he was able to obtain prescriptions from at least twenty-five doctors in Italy, and one over the border in Switzerland. By now, Carol Jackson was well aware of Chet's problems, with *La Nazione* later reporting that she used to wait in the car while he scored.[43]

In mid-July, Chet and Carol drove to the office of yet another doctor, Enrico Landucci. The doctor was out of the office, and his housemaid, Adua Ghilardi, was not sure when he would return, and suggested Chet come back next morning. Chet claimed he was in incredible pain, and that this was an emergency, and asked if the lady would be kind enough to phone around to see if she could locate the doctor. She went into the next room to make some phone calls, but when she came back, he was gone. In her absence, Chet had stolen a prescription pad from the doctor's office, and run outside to the car.

Next day they drove to Pisa, to visit Dr Maria Vignoli's pharmacy, a place where Chet had successfully obtained Palfium on several previous occasions. On the morning of 15th July, having forged Dr Landucci's signature, Chet walked in with a prescription made out in his name for four tubes of Palfium. The pharmacist's assistant, Anna Maria Tacchi, noticed that the prescription was not dated in the European style, with the day first, then the month, but the other way round. They considered this strange, but went ahead and processed the order. They only had one tube of Palfium left, so they made a note of Chet's name and suggested he come back another time to fill his prescription.

Their suspicions were further aroused when Carol Jackson walked in later that day with a prescription for two tubes of Palfium made out in her name, again on Dr Landucci's pad, again with the date strangely reversed. On this occasion they made a note of Carol's name but refused to serve her, telling her that they had run out of Palfium.

The net was beginning to close in on Chet. Next day, Dr Vignoli called Dr Landucci and asked him about the two prescriptions they had been given. Landucci told them he had never met either patient, and had made out no such prescription. He later learned from his housemaid that a young foreigner had visited his office the previous day. When Chet was eventually arrested, she recognised his photograph in the paper, and was invited by the police to make a statement.

Next day, Chet turned up late at the club late for the first set, and clearly strung out. The club's proprietor, Sergio Bernadini, was concerned by his condition and asked if there was a doctor in the audience. A doctor by the name of Pierluigi 'Lippi' Francesconi stepped forward and offered his services. He was the director of the Santa Zita clinic in Lucca, a clinic that specialised in mental illness. Chet explained the nature of his addiction to the doctor, who suggested that he check into the clinic as a resident. Chet told the doctor that he still needed to work at night, so the doctor agreed that whenever possible he would drive Chet to the club, wait while he played, then drive him back to the clinic.

Chet started his treatment the following morning, with Francesconi explaining that he intended to gradually reduce Chet's daily dose of Palfium whilst simultaneously boosting his immune system through the injection of vitamins and other medications. For the next few days, Chet only saw Carol in the evenings at the club, with the doctor driving him back to the clinic after he had finished his performance.

News that Chet was being treated for Palfium addiction at the Santa Zita clinic soon reached the local police commissioner, as well as the local *medico provinciale* (provincial medical officer), Dr Luigi Cristilli. Cristilli requested that an interim report be drawn up by his department, and based on what he had learnt he decided to interview Chet on July 23rd. Chet was under the impression that this was not a formal investigation, since the police were not involved. He said that he had been living in the area since May 10th, and that in the intervening period he had visited numerous doctors in order to obtain Palfium. He told the medical officer that he had been suffering from acute trigeminal nerve pain as a result of a recent car crash. It was clear to Cristilli that the patient was well aware of the drug's analgesic properties, having been prescribed with the drug on a number of occasions. At this stage, there is no evidence that Cristilli believed that Chet had committed a crime, but presumably he planned to confirm his version of events with some of the pharmacists he claimed to have visited.

The arrangement at the Santa Zita worked well for the first week, but Chet soon tired of staying within the confines of the clinic, and made excuses that he had errands to run. "I couldn't lock him up," Francesconi later admitted, "and when he needed to take care of his business, he used to go out. I wasn't there to be his full-time chauffeur."

Chet was aware that Francesconi was well connected in the local area, and on July 27th he asked a close friend, a lawyer by the name of Joseph Carani, to procure Palfium on his behalf. Carani was a thirty-year-old Italian-American lawyer from Chicago, visiting Tuscany to spend time with his ailing father. Carani was a huge jazz fan, and had met Chet in the United States. When he found out that Chet was playing in the area, he reacquainted himself with his hero, and offered to help him in any way that he could. Scoring drugs was not what he had in mind, but he reluctantly agreed, and drove with Chet and Carol to the office of Dr Bechelli in Viareggio. Yet again, Bechelli was susceptible to a bribe, and made out a prescription for 50 mg of Palfium to Carani, which he duly handed over to Chet.

Four days later, on July 31st, Chet again told Francesconi that he needed to run some errands. The doctor was unavailable that morning, so Chet asked Amadeo Tommasi if he could borrow his car, a Fiat 500. Chet later recalled that he had to go to Viareggio for business purposes, possibly to have his photograph taken, potentially for his next engagement at the Paradise Club in Rimini, starting in late August. "My doctor gave me the Palfium I would need to get me through the day and I set off for Viareggio," he later recalled. "As I approached the entrance to the autostrada I began to feel the need of a fix so I stopped (by) the entrance at a Shell gas station and went in the can (bathroom)."[44]

What happened next is open to some debate. The owner of the San Concordio Contrada gas station, Mr Tolari, evidently became concerned that Chet had spent too long in the bathroom, and went to investigate. He heard muttering from behind the locked door, but when the man failed to emerge after one-and-a-half hours, he decided to call the police. Chet denied that he was in the bathroom for such a long period; in a letter from his prison cell to *Playboy* magazine, he claimed that his veins were hard, and the process took around thirty minutes, whilst in his memoirs he suggested he was there for forty-five minutes, and had just finished cleaning up when he heard a knock on the door.

The policeman who knocked on the bathroom door was Vice Sergeant Milite Ciro, who later reported that he found Chet covered in blood, his legs shaking as he emerged." Chet was arrested, driven to the police station in

Lucca, where his statement was taken and translated. He explained to the police that the drugs were obtained on prescription, not illegally, and that he was undergoing treatment at the Santa Zita clinic, under the care of Dr Lippi Francesconi. A couple of hours later, Francesconi arrived, and Chet was released.

Next day, the local newspaper headline read 'Chet Baker Found in Gas Station Toilet'. The article went on to describe how police had to break the door down, and found Chet unconscious, the bathroom covered in blood. "I wasn't unconscious, they didn't break down the door, nor was there any blood," Chet later complained. "Thats [sic] Italian journalism, but the pity is that most of the simple people over here believe what they read in the papers. Incredible, but true."[45]

There's no doubt that Chet was high when the police found him, but his condition was nowhere near as bad as the newspapers suggested. He returned to the clinic with Dr Francesconi that afternoon, but felt strong enough to drive back into Lucca that same evening. Sergio Bernardini, the owner of La Bussola, had been told of Chet's arrest and asked a friend to drive to Lucca to investigate. Bernadini's friend ran into Chet strolling down Via Fillungo, on his way to the cinema, where he watched the Italian version of the American film *The Last Voyage*.

Despite the misleading press reports, Chet was not over-concerned by his arrest. His prescription was legal, and Dr Francesconi was highly regarded in the medical community.

It wasn't long before the ripple effect of his arrest began to be felt, however. Chet had been driving Amadeo Tommasi's car when he had been arrested. "My parents were professional dentists, very well known in Trieste," the pianist later recalled. "The local chief of police called my mother and said, 'Your son may be involved in drugs'. I told my mother I had nothing to do with drugs, and it was only because he had borrowed my car."[46]

Two weeks later, a report was filed by the ambitious young Public Prosecutor of Lucca, Fabio Romiti, stating that Chet had committed a crime under article 728 of the penal code, having been caught in a public place "in a state of very grave psychological alteration caused by drug abuse". Romiti was concerned about the growing evidence of narcotics abuse in Italy; two addicts had recently been tried, and shortly before Chet's arrest, two dead bodies had been found in Rome, an overdose reported as the most likely cause.

Romiti worked closely with the local *medico provinciale*, Dr Luigi Cristilli, who had published his own report after interviewing Chet in late July. Together they identified a network of doctors and pharmacists who had supplied him with Palfium, examining their prescription records, taking statements from eyewitnesses, painstakingly building a case to prosecute the American jazz musician, and key accomplices deemed to have breached the law.

Chet was unaware of Romiti's investigation. He nominally stayed under the care of Dr Francesconi, although he occasionally procured Palfium without his knowledge. On one occasion, he left the clinic for three days to attend a jazz festival in Belgium with his friend Jacques Pelzer. Francesconi gave him enough Palfium to last for three days, and entrusted it to Carol Jackson and Joseph Carani, who accompanied him on the tour. Once he had arrived, however, Chet made his way to Germany and procured Palfium over the counter to bring back to Italy.

On his return, he started to make preparations for his next engagement, asking Amadeo Tommasi, the pianist who had accompanied him for much of the time at Il Bussolotto, to join him. "Towards the end of the engagement, Chet said to me, 'I will be playing next month at the Paradise Club in Rimini with Jacques Pelzer, my friend. Let's meet there'. It was a nice club—I had played there some three years earlier."[47]

After completing his contract at the nightclub, Chet was released from the care of Dr Francesconi and allowed to return to Villa Gemma. The doctor warned him that he would need to continue the treatment in Rimini, and wrote a letter to the Rimini Sanitary Authority to the same effect.

But Chet never made it to Rimini. On August 22nd 1960, a warrant was issued for his arrest, charging him with "procuring and administering large quantities of the pharmaceutical drug 'Palfium', which belongs to the list of narcotics revised by the High Commission for Public Hygiene and Sanitation". Carol burst into tears as they handcuffed him, shouting, "You can't do it! Don't take him!"[48]

Next day, a warrant was issued for the arrest of Joseph Carani, charging him with procuring three tubes of Palfium for Baker. Dr Roberto Bechelli and Dr Sergio Nottoli were also arrested, charged with writing prescriptions aimed not at curing him of his addiction, but encouraging it, as well as a number of minor offences. Chet's landlord at Villa Gemma, Giali Giambastiani, was also charged with aiding a drug addict. Perhaps more surprisingly, the police also arrested Dr 'Lippi' Francesconi, who was charged with administering a far higher dosage of Palfium than was necessary, a charge that never looked likely to stick.

Criminal proceedings were also initiated against the majority of the other doctors that had been investigated, plus two further doctors in Pisa, Camillo Niosi and Giuseppe Niosi, who were also found to have prescribed Palfium to Chet. They were charged with failing to report that they had aided a patient suffering from chronic intoxication resulting from narcotic abuse to the *medico provinciale*. Some were also charged with failing to prescribe the correct dosage of the drug, or having failed to obtain the correct documentation to ascertain the patient's identity. All of them opted to pay a fine and settle out of court, rather than face the additional embarrassment of going to trial.

After being taking into custody, Chet was put in the infirmary for ten days, after which he was moved to a segregated room. In an interview with *L'Europeo* Chet later complained about his treatment during this period. "I'm always alone, unable to exchange a word except with the guards," he said. "Carani and the doctors are in the same cell. They can speak, have company, console one another."

Whilst in solitary confinement, Chet was subject to endless questioning by the public prosecutor, Fabio Romiti. Chet recounted the circumstances under which he had first started taking heroin, and how a pharmacist, Jacques Pelzer, had suggested he take Palfium, which he had explained was used to treat heroin addicts. He went on to explain how he had become addicted to Palfium, a condition that worsened as a result of his dental treatment.

He confessed to Romiti that he imported Palfium from Germany together with his friend Gene Victory. He also admitted that, on occasion, he had asked his wife Halema to import Palfium on his behalf. He was clearly under the impression that Halema had not committed a crime; she was his wife, and was simply doing what her husband told her to do.

Gene Victory escaped prosecution, selling his drum kit to pay for a ticket back home to the States. Halema was not so fortunate; Romiti discovered that she was still living in Milan and using a provisional warrant, brought her to Lucca for questioning. Under interrogation, she admitted that she had imported Palfium on Chet's behalf, maintaining that she had no idea she had broken the law. Romiti was unmoved, issued a formal warrant for her arrest, and threw her into a cell in the same penitentiary. "At night I could hear Halema, across the courtyard, crying and crying," Chet wrote in his memoirs.[49]

In November 1960, Dr 'Lippi' Francesconi was released, as the evidence suggested his behaviour did not constitute an offence. He had maintained his innocence throughout the interrogation, explaining that under his supervision, Baker had started a treatment to wean him off the drug, and that the amount he prescribed declined over time. The other six defendants were maintained in custody, with a trial date set for April 1961.

Carol Jackson remained in Italy for most of this period, writing to Chet on almost a daily basis, even sending him clippings from *Playboy* magazine. "Carol was very loyal to Chet," recalled Lars Bloch, who had worked with Chet on *Urlatori alla Sbarra*. "We saw her in Rome a few times, as she used to travel back and forth between Lucca and Rome."[50]

The "processo delle vipere" ("trial of the vipers") finally began on April 11th 1961, some eight months after Chet had been taken into custody. Chet was being represented by one of Lucca's most prominent lawyers, Mario Frezza, who was aware of the enormous publicity the case would generate, and offered to defend his client free of charge. Chet stood accused of three charges: possessing an illegal narcotic, stealing prescription forms from a doctor's office, and forging them to obtain Palfium. The public prosecutor regarded the case as something of a formality, since Chet had effectively confessed to the crimes whilst under interrogation. For his own part, Mario Frezza encouraged his client to play for the sympathy of the courthouse, urging him to maintain his air of innocence, the American musician who had committed no crime, simply fallen on hard times.[51]

The trial captured the imagination of the Italian media, who swarmed to Lucca in their droves. A barrage of flashbulbs greeted the arrival of the defendants. Chet looked elegant in a beige jacket, dark tie, a crisp white shirt and dark trousers. He had gained weight in the penitentiary, and without Palfium, the colour had returned to his cheeks; the dirt under his fingernails was the only evidence of the unsanitary conditions in which he'd been kept. He smiled when he saw the cameras, bemused as to why his court appearance should generate so much attention.

The contrast between Halema, who was still married to Chet, and his girlfriend Carol Jackson, who had not been detained, could not have been clearer. Halema clearly felt humiliated by the attention, and kept her head down, hiding her face beneath a shawl and dark glasses. Carol, by contrast, waved at the assembled throng, her hair carefully sculpted into a beehive, white pearls offsetting her new black dress.

The scene inside the courthouse was equally chaotic. "It was kind of weird. There were so many people in the trial, with journalists from all over the country," recalled bass player Giovanni Tommaso. "It was packed, and I had to stand."[52]

Under Italian law there was no jury. The proceedings were chaired by Judge Loria, who was the president of the *tribunale*, and two assistant judges. After the opening formalities, Chet was questioned by the public prosecutor, the two men sitting opposite one another in simple wooden chairs. Speaking through an interpreter, Chet explained that he had been using narcotics since an early age, and continued to do so as a professional musician, despite measures taken by the police, including imprisonment. In this respect, Chet's story was supported by an Interpol report that had been sent to the Italian police in September 1960.

Chet told the courtroom how he substituted Palfium for heroin after he had arrived in Europe, taking the advice of a Belgian pharmacist, who explained that the new product would help wean him off the more harmful narcotics he might otherwise be using. He became addicted to Palfium, however, but overcame this after treatment at a clinic in Milan. His real problems started in March and April of 1960, he explained, when he took Palfium to ease the pain from extensive dental treatment. Playing for the crowd, and trying to elicit their sympathy, he explained how the addiction had intensified as a result of the emotional stress caused by the theft of his trumpet in Naples.

"Tell me, Mr Baker, why are you so desperate for a stolen trumpet?" asked Judge Loria. "You could not buy another? Italy is full of trumpets."

"But it was a special trumpet, your honour," Chet explained. "A three-hundred-dollar trumpet. I bought another, your honour, but the sound came out all wrong."

The court records show the judges had some sympathy with Chet's predicament; in his state of mind he may have been unable to resist the temptation to return to the 'fictive wellbeing' he experienced through narcotics.

Any sympathy the courtroom may have felt vanished when Chet was grilled about how he was able to procure Palfium from a range of doctors in Italy, including those standing trial, Dr Roberto Bechelli and Dr Sergio Nottoli. "During the morning session we knew for sure that he had ratted on all his friends," recalled Cecco Maino, who attended the trial, "and that more than fifty decent, honest people had had trouble with the law due to his ratting."[53]

There can be little doubt that Chet was too open whilst being interrogated by the public prosecutor before his trial. Would the police have learned about Gene Victory's involvement, for example, were it not for Chet's confession? This example aside, however, there is little evidence that Chet 'ratted' on friends; the term implies that he hoped to benefit by helping the police with their enquiries. On the contrary, Chet genuinely believed he had done little wrong, and likewise believed the physicians had simply prescribed him with the drugs he had requested. One wonders how many of these facts would have come to light had Chet been interrogated in the presence of his lawyer?

Before we judge Chet too harshly, it is also important to note that many of the details emerged as a result of the police enquiry, rather than through the interrogation itself. According to the court transcriptions, "the information given by Baker, and *above all* through the numerous prescriptions seized by the police in many pharmacies in Viareggio and Lucca, it was possible to identify many of the doctors from whom Baker had received these prescriptions of Palfium".[54]

The public prosecutor went on to present important evidence to suggest that Chet was not really suffering from trigeminal neuralgia. One suspicious doctor had sent Chet for an examination, but no signs of injury were observed from x-rays carried out by Professor Roberto Boni, director of the Institute of Radiology at the Barbanti Clinic in Viareggio. Moreover, Chet was repeatedly advised to seek a cure for his suffering, but he was only interested in taking Palfium, which only treated the symptoms.

Chet was also cross-examined about whether he imported Palfium from Germany. The court heard that Jetrium, which was the equivalent of Palfium, was available over the counter in Germany. Chet had admitted to smuggling an estimated ten thousand pills under interrogation, but he denied this claim in the courtroom. "I never mentioned a figure like that," he claimed.[55] He did admit that he had asked his wife to carry pills on his behalf, but that she hadn't known what they were. "She's my wife, and she does what I tell her to do," he said.[56]

Finally, Chet was asked about whether he had stolen prescription forms from Dr Landucci, a confession he had apparently retracted. Chet told the court that had made up that version of events to protect his friend, the drummer Gene Victory. One morning he woke up at Villa Gemma to find the prescription forms had been slid beneath the front door, a 'gift' from the drummer. The court records show the judges found Chet's account "highly suspicious and implausible", although they did accept the argument of his lawyer, Mario Frezza, that the forms had no economic value.

Next day, Carol Jackson took to the stand. During her testimony she repeatedly contradicted statements made in a previous deposition. The judges requested that her previous deposition be read back so that she could verify the key facts. "I don't remember," Carol claimed repeatedly, testing the patience of the courtroom. Judge Loria finally snapped when Carol kept referring to Chet as her husband, threatening to charge her with perjury.

The Italian press also sided with Halema, rather than Carol Jackson. Whilst Carol shamelessly kissed Chet on the lips in full view of the courtroom, just yards from where Halema was sitting, Halema preferred to keep her look away, keeping her head down, writing on a notepad. "She's clearly the victim in this situation," wrote Segio Frosali in *La Nazione*.

Chet's wife Halema was "clearly the victim of the situation", according to La Nazione. Photograph by F. Ercolini, courtesy of Francesco Maino.

In closing, Fabio Romiti, the public prosecutor, claimed that Chet had the "face of an angel, but the heart of a demon", demanding a seven-year sentence. Chet's lawyer, Mario Freza, requested a full acquittal. He told the court how

Chet had been devastated by the death of his pianist, Dick Twardzik, and had fallen into a life of addiction. Whilst he had become addicted to Palfium whilst living in Italy, there was nothing to suggest he had imported the drug from Germany, he claimed. Whilst there was evidence pointing to his client bribing certain doctors, his judgement was clouded by his narcotic addiction, and he could not be held accountable for his actions.

On the morning of April 15th, the fifth day of the trial, the judges retired to deliberate. The crowds gathered at the courthouse that afternoon, eagerly awaiting the outcome. At 5 p.m. Judge Loria finally called the defendants to the stand, and announced their verdicts.

Chet Baker was found guilty of possessing an illegal narcotic, the crime he had been arrested for. Whilst the court accepted that his psychological condition was a mitigating circumstance, they argued "He was partially aware of his actions (even if his will was heavily influenced by his drug abuse)." He was acquitted of stealing prescription forms, despite the dubious nature of his account, but found guilty of forging the signature of Dr Landucci. In his defence, the court noted, "it is important to take in account his young age and therefore the time he still has left to redeem himself, the fact that he is a foreigner and therefore is not acquainted with the Italian penal system and laws, and finally the fact that he is a musician and therefore often comes into contact with corrupting environments." Taking into account the fact the mitigating circumstances, but also the fact that Chet repeatedly tried to obtain Palfium, he was sentenced to one year, seven months and ten days in detention, and a total fine of 140,000 lire.[57]

In Halema's deposition, she had admitted to being aware of Chet's addiction, but stated that she was constantly encouraging him to quit. Whilst the court recognised that she had imported drugs from Germany, they accepted her defence that she was not aware that Jetrium was a narcotic. There were also questions raised as to how many times she had made such a journey. Under the circumstances, the court concluded they did not have enough evidence to proceed and absolved her of all charges, setting her free with immediate effect. Considering she had spent eight months locked up in the San Giorgio penitentiary, despite precious little evidence of her guilt, she had already suffered a harsh punishment for her involvement with Chet. As she left the building, she told journalist Dino Grilli that she felt "very sorry for Chet", but that there was no chance of reconciliation. Soon after she returned to the United States, bringing their son Chettie with her.

Chet's friend Joseph Carani had protested his innocence throughout the trial. Whilst he admitted accompanying Chet and Carol to see Dr Bechelli, he claimed he had no knowledge of the prescription being made out in his name, or that Palfium was being used to feed Chet's addiction. On the contrary, he argued, he was doing everything he could to help his friend stay away from drugs. The court found it difficult to assess Carani's precise role in the proceedings, but concluded he was not guilty of the charges brought against him.

The landlord of Villa Gemma, Giali Giambastiani, was found guilty of being an accessory to Chet's crimes, and also of a second, lesser charge of failing to register the arrival of Baker and Jackson at his *pensione*. Nevertheless, the court took into account that he was not a doctor, and was therefore not aware of the nature of Palfium, and the fact that he had no previous convictions. As a consequence, he was fined a total of 26,000 lire and set free with immediate effect.

The court noted that Sergio Nottoli had written a number of prescriptions for Chet, but that as a paediatrician, he was not an expert in this field, and that the prescriptions had been small. In addition, he had urged Chet to further consult a specialist. He was found not guilty of encouraging Chet's drug abuse, but convicted of the lesser charge of falsifying names on two prescriptions, and fined a total of 20,000 lire.

Roberto Bechelli was not so fortunate, and was found guilty of accepting a bribe from a drug addict. He was sentenced to two years in prison, ordered to pay a substantial fine of over 200,000 lire, and had his medical licence temporarily revoked. "The Court has no reason to doubt Baker's statement which repeatedly claimed that on one occasion, and on four or five subsequent occasions, the doctor accepted the sum of 10,000 lire, whereas before that date he had always accepted the standard fee charged for a normal appointment (2000 lire). Dr Bechelli has to be considered fully aware of his contribution in encouraging Baker's addiction of narcotics, as he tacitly responded to Baker's pressure which included high sums of money and other factors (it seems that he had quite an interest in Baker's young friend, Ms Ann Carol Jackson, who would often go with him to see the doctor). All these elements are enough to doubt Dr Bechelli's good intentions and his awareness of feeding Baker's addiction."[58]

A total of seventeen doctors settled out of court, and as a result, no further charges were pressed. Four further doctors were absolved of all charges brought against them, since they did not constitute a crime.

As Chet was led back to the San Giorgio penitentiary, he reportedly expressed remorse for what had happened to Halema, telling one reporter, "I won't divorce Halema. Halema is a wonderful woman. She's a great wife." Carol Jackson seemed to have other ideas, telling Renzo Battaglia of *Giornale del Mattino* that she and Chet would marry as soon as he left prison.

After the trial, Chet was apparently given special treatment by the guards, who allowed him to work with one other foreign inmate, a Yugoslavian mercenary, in the bookbinding shop. The Yugoslavian had passed himself off as an Army officer in several countries, illegally procuring ammunition and firearms from military bases across Europe. According to Chet, he had been held for forty-four months without trial. With precious few books to repair, the two men conversed and played chess by day, cooking spaghetti on an illegal hotplate by night.

Most of the prison guards spoke little English, but Chet built up a good relationship with them over time, graciously agreeing to play their favourite tunes on his trumpet, including endless requests for 'Cherry Pink and Apple Blossom White'. As the months went by, Chet learned to speak reasonable Italian; he was never fluent, as he later claimed, but his accent was extremely good, friends later claimed.

Carol Jackson returned to England after the trial, but continued to write to him almost every day, regularly sending him paperback books and copies of *Playboy* magazine. Even so, conditions were hardly ideal for reading in the dingy light of the historic old prison. "All I had for light was a five-watt bulb in my cell," Chet later recalled, "but I read a lot and almost went blind. It was so cold when one hand turned blue, I'd put it under the covers and change the book into the other hand until that turned blue."

Carol did return to Lucca to visit as often as she could. One prison guard, Mr Peccora, was even kind enough to allow Chet and Carol some private time in the visiting room. "That was nice," Chet later wrote. "I doubt if anyone can appreciate what a little sex can mean until they've been locked up for a few months."[59]

Chet received regular communication from the musicians he had worked with in Italy, especially the Quintetto di Lucca. Amadeo Tommasi, the pianist who had worked with Chet at Il Bussolotto, also wrote to Chet. "I told him I would like to manage him after he came out. He wrote back, and told me that he had a manager, but would like to work with me again," he said.[60]

Chet was also approached by the Italian movie producer Dino De

Laurentiis, who had worked with Fellini on classics such as *La Strada*, and went on to find fame in Hollywood, producing movies such as *Serpico* in the early 1970s. De Laurentiis was interested in making a movie based on Chet's life, with the trumpeter writing the soundtrack and playing himself upon his release. Chet received an advance of three thousand dollars, and started to work on a soundtrack. He later claimed to have written twenty-four tunes in prison, many of them reflecting his loneliness without Carol and his son Chettie, with titles such as 'A Fool In Love' and 'Blue Carol'. Chet could never write music, of course, and on his release he asked Amedeo Tommasi to help him arrange the tunes.

This anecdote may have sparked one of the more peculiar rumours about Chet's time in the San Giorgio prison. A Chet Baker biographer claimed that the owner of a local music shop heard the sound of Chet's trumpet from outside the prison walls, and created a bootleg recording of his playing, "an echoey 45-rpm disc entitled *Chet Baker—Dentro Le Mura* (Inside the Walls). The sleeve bore a crude brown-on-white illustration of a grating in a stone wall ... "

The sketch does indeed exist, but the recording almost certainly does not. The prison walls were approximately twelve meters high, and Chet's cellblock was a considerable distance beyond this, well over one hundred meters back from the street. Even with a prevailing wind, it is doubtful whether Chet's trumpet could be heard, let alone recorded. It is possible that someone was given access to record him inside the prison, but no details have ever emerged.

One of the magazines sent to Chet by Carol was a copy of *Confidential*, which included an article about his arrest, written by a journalist by the name of Mr Bell. Chet was incensed by the contents of the article, and wrote a long letter to *Playboy* magazine, dated Monday, August 14th 1961. The letter begins:

"I could definitely use some legal advice; not in reference to what happened to me here in Italy, but in reference to what I should do about this article about me that came out recently in *Confidential* magazine. I assure you there isn't a word of truth in that whole article. I was never interviewed by any journalist from *Confidential* and would have never consented to an interview if I had been approached by them. If I had been interviewed by them, there would have been no reason for giving my wife's age as 33 when she is only 26. Carol Jackson is 21, not 23 … "

He went on to clarify several issues regarding his addiction, and his arrest, before concluding:

"Mr Bell says that I've spent $300,000 for drugs. What a dreamer. In ten years as a professional musician I haven't earned $100,000. What I'd like to know is; can *Confidential* and Mr Bell get away with writing that story of lies? I seem to recall that they have been sued before. I'm wondering if perhaps I shouldn't have the who(le) bunch hauled into court. I'm sorry to burden you with this mess but I really am quite upset about it. Ciao—Chet."[61]

One month later, on September 8th 1961, Chet Baker and Roberto Bechelli stood in front of the Court of Appeal in Florence. Chet's friend Joseph Carani, a lawyer himself, explained that Chet had conquered his addictions. A number of Italian bands wanted to work with Chet, he revealed, and the well-known movie producer Dino De Laurentiis had signed a contract with a view to filming a biography, a movie that never materialised. The court was lenient to both men, releasing Bechelli, and shortening Baker's sentence by three months and five days, and halving his fine.

Chet's friends were unsure as to the exact date he would be released. In the event, the prison authorities allowed him to leave one week earlier than planned, on 15th December, so that he could be free for Christmas. He reunited with Carol Jackson, spending a few precious days with her at the nearby Hotel Universo in the Piazza del Giglio. A couple of days later he was summoned to the police station where he learned that he had just five days to leave the country, the result of an order from the Ministry of the Interior in Rome. When Mario Frezza learned of his imminent deportation, however, he took out a court order and had the ruling revoked.

In an interview that took place at around the time of his appeal, Chet complained that most of the local musicians had not supported him during his time in prison. "I don't have any friends in Lucca other than my lawyer Frezza and Dr Francesconi," he said.[62]

Such self-pitying nonsense upset many of the friends who had stood by him, and illustrated how Chet's character had changed for the worse since his first trip to Italy in early 1956, before his drug addiction took its toll. Going forward, Cecco Maino revealed, his Italian friends had to face up to the fact that there were two sides to Chet Baker. "Chet looked angelic and played beautiful music when we first met him in 1956," he recalled, "but slowly we found what he really was—a terrible, dangerous, deceitful individual. Like Caravaggio, Rimbaud, Filippino Lippi and many other artists, his works were entirely different from the man. Which did not diminish in the least our approval and admiration for the quality of his music, and made us think that the beauty of what he played and sang was all the more admirable because of the *vita horribilis* that he was living, not despite it. Genius is above normality, and so it has been always."

Chapter Ten

CHET IS BACK!
1962–1964

"When I left England for France, I knew something had changed. I could feel it in my bones, but I refused to believe it, I was so terrified of getting hooked again."—Chet Baker[1]

"Chet is back!" exclaimed the cover of his new album, recorded for RCA in Italy. It had been more than two years since his last proper studio recordings—*Chet Baker in Milan* and *Chet Baker with Fifty Italian Strings*—but both records had effectively sunk without trace in the United States. They were recorded on the Jazzland label, which was distributed by Riverside, but the company spent little time or money on promotion, given the problems they had experienced with Chet while he was under contract. The critics were not impressed either, with *DownBeat* describing the latter LP as 'lethargic'.[2]

Indeed, one would have to go back to *Chet*, recorded in December 1958—a full three years earlier—to find the last time he had recorded a first-rate album, with Chet playing close to the best of his abilities, recording appropriate material, supported by fine, like-minded musicians.

As a result, Chet had fallen off the radar screen as far as the US jazz market was concerned. By the time he left for Europe he had fallen well below Miles Davis in the *DownBeat* Readers' Poll, and had tarnished his reputation with the jazz critics after a series of lacklustre albums. In 1960, *Metronome* went as far as to publish an article entitled 'Chet Baker: A Major Talent Diminished', in which the journalist Jack McKinney described his recent recordings as 'stillborn'.[3]

It was not as though time had stood still while Chet Baker was in Italy, playing in small nightclubs, drifting in a haze of Palfium, frittering away more than a year of his life in a dark, dirty Italian prison. In the three years since *Chet*, his rival Miles Davis had recorded his masterpiece *Kind of*

Blue, reunited with Gil Evans to make *Sketches of Spain*, and released *Some Day My Prince Will Come* with John Coltrane and Hank Mobley. He had also found time to record two official live albums, *At The Blackhawk* and *At Carnegie Hall* (both 1961).

New trumpet stars were starting to make their presence felt. Lee Morgan had emerged from Art Blakey's Jazz Messengers as a star in his own right, releasing a series of fine recordings under his own name on Blue Note records, which eventually culminated in *The Sidewinder* (December 1963). Freddie Hubbard was another new arrival on the scene, arriving in New York in 1958, and eventually replacing Morgan in the Jazz Messengers in 1961. He had started a parallel solo career with Blue Note, announcing his arrival with *Open Sesame* in 1960, and releasing the excellent *Goin' Up* later that same year.

Others had come and gone while Chet was away. Booker Little had gained experience playing with Max Roach in the late 1950s, and was probably the most gifted trumpet player that had emerged since the premature passing of Clifford Brown. Working in parallel with his close friend Eric Dolphy, he had developed a sound of his own, best heard on Dolphy's *Five Spot* recording or his own solo record *Out Front*. Sadly, his life was also cut short, and he died of uraemia in October 1961, aged just twenty-three.

Whilst it was always excessively simplistic to think of 1950s jazz in terms of East Coast versus West Coast, traditional versus modern, it is clear that jazz was fragmenting into a variety of different styles by the turn of the 1960s.

Miles Davis himself was exploring modal-based improvisation, which used scales as the platform for solos, rather than the busy chord progressions that had defined jazz in the bebop and hard bop eras. He had started to experiment with modal improvisation on the title track of *Milestones*, but took it to the next level on *Kind of Blue*. The effect was liberalising in some respects, but it also encouraged a degree of austerity that was almost frowned upon in the bop era. In the liners notes to *Kind of Blue*, pianist Bill Evans eloquently compared such improvisation to Japanese lithography. "The resulting pictures lack the complex composition and textures of ordinary painting," he wrote, "but it is said that those who see will find something captured that escapes explanation."

'Soul jazz' was beginning to emerge as a style within jazz, too, a sound that blended rhythm 'n' blues, the bluesy wail of the 'Texas tenors', such as

Illinois Jacquet, even elements of gospel music. Examples of 'soul jazz' could be heard on records such as Horace Silver's *Blowin' the Blues Away* (1959), Jimmy Smith's *Back at the Chicken Shack* (1960) and Stanley Turrentine's *Up At Minton's* (1961), to name but a few, and influenced the likes of trumpet player Lee Morgan.

Arguably the most important development, however, was the emergence of 'free jazz', a movement that in many respects mirrored the civil rights movement of the late 1950s and early 1960s; its practitioners promoted freedom from traditional harmonic and song structures, and wanted to escape from the shackles of hard bop.

Ornette Coleman made his recording debut in 1958, recording with Contemporary Records in Los Angeles, but it was his move to New York in late 1959 that shook the world of jazz. In October 1959 he recorded *The Shape of Jazz to Come* and *Change of the Century*, claiming he wanted to "break through to a new, freer conception of jazz, one that departs from all that is 'standard' and cliché in 'modern' jazz."[4] The following month he opened at the Five Spot, the music dividing musicians and critics alike. "Hell, just listen to what he writes and how he plays," Miles Davis sniped. "The man is all screwed up inside."[5]

Pianist Cecil Taylor emerged in the mid-1950s, his style in marked contrast to that of Ornette Coleman, frequently employing single-note melodies and disjointed rhythms in his playing, trying to "imitate on the piano the leaps in space a dancer makes," as he once claimed. *Jazz Advance*, released in 1956, remains a remarkable debut, but his recordings for the Candid label in 1960 and 1961 saw him reach a new level of maturity and critical acclaim, with *DownBeat* awarding him its 'New Star' award in 1962.

Despite the mixed reaction to 'free' jazz, its influence soon made itself felt. Sonny Rollins 'retired' from the music scene for two years to practice and further develop his style, and when he re-emerged in late 1961, he soon hired a number of Coleman's former sidemen. John Coltrane embraced the changes more readily, recording *The Avant-Garde* with Coleman's band in the summer of 1960, and working with another 'free jazz' pioneer, Eric Dolphy, in 1961. Even Miles Davis eventually succumbed, his quintet with Wayne Shorter clearly influenced by the pioneering work of Ornette Coleman and Don Cherry.

While Sonny Rollins was trying out new ideas on the Williamsburg Bridge, Chet Baker was four thousand miles away, effectively isolated from the important musical developments that were taking place. RCA Italiana paid him an advance of ten thousand dollars for a one-year contract.

Before he had the chance to enter the recording studio, however, the Quartetto di Lucca had arranged a concert on his behalf at the Teatro del Giglio. All proceeds from the ticket sales went to Chet, making nonsense of his claim that he had no friends in the town.

The concert took place on December 23rd, eight days after his release from prison. The quartet rehearsed that afternoon in the apartment of Antonello Vanucchi, the band's vibes player. The theatre was packed, the town eager to get a glimpse of their local celebrity, who was giving his first performance since August 22nd 1960. The show opened with the Riverside Jazz Band, who played a short set of 'traditional' style jazz, before the Quartetto di Lucca played three songs on their own. Chet then took the stage to rapturous applause and played a lengthy set, including 'Summertime', 'Dear Old Stockholm' and 'Blues for Carol', as well as vocal renditions of 'Just Friends' and 'Forgetful'. Chet was nervous, recalled bass player Giovanni Tommaso, but "let me tell you, he had some chops. He was physically healthy, in good spirits, and musically in the best shape I ever heard him."[6]

That evening, the Quartetto di Lucca invited Chet to join them for dinner at a small restaurant just up from the theatre. "We gave him a really warm welcome back to life," recalled Giovanni Tommaso. "Chet was very thankful that we organised the tribute concert, and impressed by the reaction, with so many people turning out to see him. He actually asked the whole of the band if they would join him for a tour, but only the vibraphonist and I accepted the gig."[7]

Before the tour could begin, Chet had recording commitments to complete. The recording session for *Chet Is Back!* took place in Rome on January 5th 1962. It saw Chet reunited with the pianist Amadeo Tommasi, who had last played with him at Il Bussolotto, and three Belgian musicians that Chet had met on his first European tour—bass player Benoît Quersin, guitarist René Thomas and tenor saxophonist and flautist Bobby Jaspar. The sextet was completed by the Swiss drummer Daniel Humair, who had witnessed that same tour as a schoolboy six years earlier.

There was no rehearsal, and the group decided what to play in the studio. "We selected tunes that were easy to play, a mixture of standards, easy bebop, some Monk tunes," Daniel Humair remembered. "It went very smoothly. Musically we got along very well."[8]

Amadeo Tommasi proposed recording one of his own tunes, 'Ballate in Forma di Blues'. "I taught him how to play the tune, which was in D-flat, a very difficult key for the trumpet," he said. "Chet said, 'Ok, let's record'. After the tune, he said, 'Again', and we played it a second time. When he finished, he said, 'Again!' After we played the tune a third time, I asked him, 'Did you like that version?' 'Yes,' he replied. 'But tell me, what key is this tune in?'"[9]

Chet was in good shape for the recording session. He was completely clean after his spell in prison, and his chops were in good shape, having played regularly in his cell. "He was completely clean, and played very strongly, like Dizzy Gillespie," Tommasi recalled. The same could not be said of the Belgian musicians, who were still grappling with drug problems of their own. "Bobby Jaspar was in very, very bad shape, but he could play," said Humair. "René Thomas wasn't much better, but they were great musicians, so they managed to get to a certain level."[10]

Chet had received considerable attention after his release from prison in Lucca, and the young Swiss drummer noted that it had left the trumpet player with something of an attitude problem. "As a person, he was acting kind of weird at that time," he said. "I am a simple guy when I work. I know what I want, I'll do my job. We had some arguments about the money, because he didn't want to pay us, but this is the usual jazz stuff." It resulted in Chet throwing the cash at the drummer, the notes falling to the ground. "You're going to pick that up," I told him." Sensing that the drummer was ready to punch him, Chet did so, but there was always a tense atmosphere between them thereafter.[11]

"After the recording, I decided I didn't much want to work with Chet," said Humair. "I didn't want to be with junkies, or get into any trouble at the border," he said. "Once you get into trouble at the border, you have problems forever."

As the title of the album suggested, Chet was keen to make a strong statement, and his playing on the opening track sees him playing with a renewed vigour, his tone almost unrecognisable from his troubled period on Riverside. He seemed determined not to drift back into his old ways, taking the pianist to one side after the recording session, and saying, "Amadeo, stay with me, and make sure I don't get back into drugs."[12]

Chet claims to have written twenty-four tunes while he was in prison, and asked for Amadeo Tommasi's help in arranging some of the tunes for him. Lyrics were added to four of the tunes by Allesandro Maffei, a local poet. Maffei also worked as the local court registrar, but did not participate in Chet's trial. RCA Italiana saw the commercial appeal of these songs, and arranged for Chet to record two singles with an orchestra. The arrangements were rewritten by Ennio Morricone, who also conducted the orchestra. Morricone later became a notable composer in his own right, best known for writing the soundtracks to 'spaghetti westerns' such as *The Good, the Bad and the Ugly*. A fan of jazz, he was thrilled to be recording with Chet Baker, according to Tommasi, who played on the session himself.

Chet sung in Italian on the four songs, which included 'Chetty's Lullaby', a tune written for his son, who had returned to the United States with Halema, Chet's wife. "Chet had learned [Italian] by ear in a wonderful way," noted his friend, the photographer Cecco Maino. "He used to make continuous errors of words, phrase construction and so on, but I have never heard a foreigner, especially a North American, sound as Italian as he did."[13]

Having been given the ticket money for the concert in Lucca, and paid an advance on his new recording, Chet had money to burn. "Over the next few weeks, we performed a number of concerts, and he earned more. As soon as he had enough money, he bought himself a different version of the Alfa Romeo Spider to the one I owned!" recalled Giampiero Giusti, laughing. "The story was always the same!"[14]

Chet and Carol stayed on in Rome for another two weeks after the recording session was complete, waiting to hear whether anything would materialise regarding the movie proposed by Dino De Laurentiis. It soon became apparent that the screenplay had not been written, so Chet made plans to go on tour in Italy. The pianist Amadeo Tommasi and the drummer Franco Mondini signed up for the tour, joining Giovanni Tommaso and Antonello Vanucchi, who had been recruited from the Quartetto di Lucca.

The tour itself was somewhat chaotic, the musicians trying to secure bookings as they went along. "We had long periods of free time, and in those days, we had to pay for our own hotels," recalled Giovanni Tommaso. "But I didn't mind; I was enjoying the music and the company."[15]

The quintet spent most of the next few weeks in the larger cities, staying in Rome, Milan and Florence. "In Rome we stayed at the Hotel Livoli, a very nice little hotel," said the bass player. "I remember playing cards, mostly poker, talking about different bands, and Chet taught me how to play bowling. Carol was a lot of fun too, very nice, always laughing, a very 'up' person. It was a nice period."

Chet managed to stay clean for the next few weeks, and as a consequence, his playing was strong, just as it had been on the recording session in January. "The best time I had with Chet was when he came out of prison, when he was clean," Tommaso later claimed. "He was playing fantastic, and we had a close, intense relationship. He was sober, a good friend, and we had a ball. To the best of my knowledge, he played as never again."[16]

During this period, the band played one night at the Olympia in Milan, the venue in which Carol Jackson had been working when they first met. After the show, Chet was talking to the promoter, Nando Latanzzi, and told him that someday he'd like to own a jazz club of his own. "He took me to a small, very elegant room that was not in use. It had a small service bar, a raised bandstand with beautiful velvet drapes, coloured lights, marble-top tables, and plush blue-velvet armchairs with matching carpet throughout," Chet later wrote in his memoirs. Latanzzi ordered a neon sign that read 'The Chet Baker Club', and started to make arrangements for a grand opening a couple of months later.[17]

The friction only really started in March, with drugs inevitably the root of the problem. "After a while he started to smoke marijuana," said Amadeo Tommasi. "I said to him, 'Why do you smoke this stuff? When you do, you don't play so well'. He got very angry with me."[18]

Soon after, the pianist also started to clash with Carol Jackson, which didn't help his relationship with Chet. Looking back, Tommasi can't recall the precise cause of the problem, but remembered that Carol didn't like his music. "She only liked Elvis Presley," he noted bitterly, "which didn't help matters."

The problems came to a head in the port city of Livorno on March 21st. A concert had been organised by the Associazione Riunite Concerti at the Teatro La Gran Guardia. At the soundcheck, René Thomas and Bobby Jaspar showed up unexpectedly. The opening set was played by the new-look Quartetto di Lucca, without Chet, as was standard practice for much of the tour. At the interval, Chet suggested that the two Belgian musicians join them onstage for the second set, and they eventually came onstage for the third or fourth song.

In hindsight, Giovanni Tommaso suspects that the problems started earlier that evening, while the Quartetto di Lucca was onstage, although he has no evidence to prove it. "All I know is that later that evening he knocked on my door, and said, 'I need help'. I didn't know what he wanted, and went back to his room. He said, 'I need to you to tighten my belt around my arm'. I said, 'You've got to be joking!' I was embarrassed; I really didn't want to, and tried to talk him out of it, but he begged me. So I helped him out. Afterwards he lay down on the bed, closed his eyes, and didn't say anything for about an hour. I just sat there in shock."[19]

Giovanni Tommaso hoped that Chet's lapse was just temporary, but suspected the worst. The next day, the band travelled to Lugano in Switzerland, and it was clear from the outset that Chet's state of mind had been impacted by the events of the previous evening. "I arrived twenty minutes late for the concert," recalled Amadeo Tommasi, "and Chet started to play without piano. That was the last concert I did with him."[20]

Worse was to come. After the show, a doctor who had been in the audience invited the musicians to a private party at his house. "At one point, he opened a closet that was full of drugs, and told the musicians to help themselves to whatever they wanted," said Giovanni Tommaso. "Carol walked in at this point, and quickly understood what was going on. I liked Carol very much, and when Chet slapped her face in front of me, I got angry, and said, 'Don't you dare do that again'. He said, 'Mind your own business'. Maybe I overdid it, but I wanted to help some way."[21]

Carol screamed at Chet, pleading him not to go back to drugs. He promised her he would try to stay clean, and the band returned to Milan, where the Chet Baker Club was scheduled to open. "We began rehearsing there every night," Chet later recalled. "Each night, after rehearsal, Nando would lay out a spaghetti dinner for us all; the waiters, bartenders, musicians, everyone. We'd push four or five tables together, eat, and then, after the dishes were removed, play poker or blackjack. I'd go back to the Hotel Virgilio with my pockets stuffed with those big old ten thousand lire notes."[22]

Word soon got around that Chet was in town, and after a few weeks, he received some unexpected visitors at the club. Three African–American men walked in, the tallest of them introducing himself as a drummer by the name of Donald Brown. They had just come from Beirut, he explained, where dope was easy to score. They had no connections in Milan, and wondered if Chet could point them in the right direction. In his memoirs Chet claimed to have sent them away, explaining that he was clean, but they turned up again next night, begging for his help. This time he agreed to help, driving them to Chiasso, just over the border in Switzerland, pointing them in the direction of a doctor that had supplied him with Palfium in the past. "I told them where to go and what to say," Chet later admitted. "Within minutes one of them, Donald Brown, came back with a bottle of Palfium tablets. All in all, a successful outing."[23]

In the weeks that followed, Donald Brown became Chet's permanent companion, much to the dismay of the Italian musicians who had done so much to help Chet get back on track. "After that, it was done, practically," said Giovanni Tommaso. "We lost him. We were supposed to go to Germany, and I refused; I'm sure I did the right thing, because he was busted in Germany."[24]

The ill-fated trip to Germany took place in early June. Chet had been asked to play at a prestigious musical event at the Kongress-Saal, a concert hall in Munich. The German bandleader Werner Müller, who led the Tanzorchestra for RIAS (Radio in the American Sector), planned a special concert on June 2nd, and made tentative enquiries about hiring a jazz musician to accompany the orchestra, thinking it would create additional publicity. Edward Alexander, a US diplomat in charge of music at RIAS, suggested Chet Baker. He had heard that the trumpet player was clean after his well-publicised problems, and figured that he would be relatively easy to hire, given that he was based in Italy. Müller agreed, and Alexander booked him for the concert.

Chet and Carol left for Munich a few days before the official opening of the Chet Baker Club in Milan. To Carol's dismay they were accompanied by Chet's new friend Donald Brown. Upon arrival in Germany they soon discovered that Jetrium was no longer available over the counter, and had been placed on a list of restricted drugs. By the time they reached Munich on the morning of the concert, Chet was a pale, nervous wreck, his intake of Palfium having skyrocketed in the preceding weeks.

Edward Alexander feared the worst, and was therefore pleasantly surprised when Chet showed up on time, wearing a clean shirt and looking fairly respectable. Chet had an attack of nerves before the show, presumably suffering from withdrawal symptoms, but was sufficiently reassured by the organisers that he took his place on the stage, his arrival met with rapturous applause. Against the odds, his performance was a resounding success. He delivered a haunting version of 'When I Fall In Love', and on faster tunes such as 'But Not For Me' and 'Airegin', played with the same strong, confident tone he had exhibited on *Chet is Back!*

After the concert, Müller waited backstage to talk with Chet and to discuss possible plans to work together in the future. Chet had other ideas. He had received his $400 fee from Alexander, and set about searching the city for a late-night drugstore. "I had no connections in Germany," he later noted, "and if I wanted my daily dose of Palfium this meant a wild race around Munich. Instead I stole a bunch of blank prescriptions from a doctor's office. I went straight back to my hotel and filled them in. Not knowing German I had to tell the druggist a cock-and-bull story about my being American and that for this reason the doctor had made out the prescription in English."[25]

The pharmacist asked Chet to wait for a minute, went into his office, and called the police. Within minutes, a police car had arrived, and Chet was arrested. Next morning, Edward Alexander was summoned to the police station, only to be informed that Chet had requested that he represent him, and act as a translator. With newspaper headlines labelling Chet a junkie and a thief, Alexander found himself in a difficult situation. He reluctantly agreed to help Chet, and argued in court that Chet belonged in a hospital, rather than in jail. His defence was successful. Charges were dropped, and Chet was sent to the Harr Psychiatric Clinic in Munich. He was soon joined by his friend Donald Brown, who was busted for possession on June 14th.

Carol Jackson was interviewed by one German newspaper at this time. "I'm not leaving them," she informed the journalist. "When he gets out of the clinic, we intend to go to Switzerland together." Chet Baker and Donald Brown were released on June 27th and deported from the country, escorted to the Swiss border by the German police. "The great trumpeter had ruined his chance at a comeback," reported one newspaper. "Promoters will never again book him after what he has done." He was barred from entering the country for two years.

Chet Baker leaves the Haar clinic in Munich on June 27th 1962, accompanied by his pregnant girlfriend Carol Jackson. Photoreporters.

Chet, Carol and Donald Brown stayed at a friend's apartment in Zurich for the next week, but with Palfium more readily available over the counter, it wasn't long before Chet got into trouble. He was arrested on July 4th, again for forging a prescription, and spent two weeks in a sanatorium. On July 18th he was deported from Switzerland, and made his way back to the Italian border, where to his surprise, he was refused entry. "I sent Carol to Milan, since she was okay with the authorities, and she managed to borrow 150,000 lire from Mario Fatori, an acquaintance of ours who owned a big studio where he made commercials for movie houses and TV … I really hated leaving the club—and my Alfa—behind, and Carol and I both had to leave a lot of clothes and stuff."[26]

Shortly before arriving in Germany, Carol Jackson had told Chet that she was expecting her first child. The subsequent events suggested that Chet was still not cut out for fatherhood, just as when Halema announced that she was expecting back in early 1957.

Carol Jackson had been pressing Chet to marry him for some time. Even as he was being led to prison in Italy, after being sentenced, a smiling Carol proudly told a reporter, "He also wants to get married."[27]

Chet later claimed to have sent money to Halema after his release, but that she never went through with the divorce. "Once again, I don't blame her," he said. "I was always short of money and she was getting mighty little from me. No wonder she had used that divorce money for housekeeping."[28]

Halema told James Gavin, author of *Deep in a Dream*, a slightly different version of events. She had returned to the United States following her release from prison, initially staying with Chet's parents in Inglewood, California. She had eventually found a home of her own, but had trouble tracking down Chet in Europe to finalise the divorce. After a while, she gave up. "I couldn't have afforded it anyway," she revealed. "I had other things to do. I was raising my child. But anytime Chet wanted a divorce, he could have had one."[29]

With the baby due in December, Carol kept reminding Chet to push Halema for a divorce, but Chet claimed there was nothing more that he could do; after all, they needed what little money they had for the baby. By now, Chet was barred from entering Germany, Switzerland and Italy, so they decided to travel to England, with Chet's drug buddy Donald Brown still in tow. "Carol was expecting a baby and naturally she wanted to have it at home," he later told a UK journalist. "In my own case I thought it would be a good idea to start all over again in a new country. I was off junk and I wanted to go steady, and I was certain I would be signed for different engagements in London."[30]

* * * *

Aside from appeasing Carol Jackson, there were other reasons to consider moving to England. He had been approached about taking a bit part in a movie called *Stolen Hours*, starring Susan Hayward, which would entitle him to a short-term work permit.

But the fact that Donald Brown accompanied him suggests that Chet had ulterior motives all along. Jacques Pelzer and others had told him about the 'British system', under which hard drugs were available on prescription to licensed drug addicts.

A book published in the UK, *Heroin Addiction Care and Control: the British System 1916–1984*, explains how the 'system' dated back to the 1920s. "The fundamental ethos of that approach has always been that it is for doctors, not governments or bureaucrats, to decide how patients, whether terminally ill or addicted, should be treated and to determine which drugs to use in the course of that treatment," the book claims. "This is why, in the UK, heroin has always been 'legal' if prescribed by a doctor and why all attempts to prohibit its therapeutic use have encountered strong and successful opposition from the medical profession." It was a system that differed markedly from the US, and it is not surprising to find that a 1967 investigation revealed that several international jazz musicians had been treated as 'patients' in the UK.[31]

Upon their arrival in England, Chet and Carol made their way to Surrey, just outside London, to live with her parents, Albert and Gladys. Gladys was a housewife, but Albert, an engineer without a degree, dreamed of becoming a famous inventor. He had devised a new type of propeller which he claimed improved efficiency, but whilst the device attracted interest from a number of companies, they could never reach an agreement over patent ownership. As a result, he worked as a handyman by day, taking jobs as a carpenter or electrician, and worked on projects of his own in his workshop by night.

Their slightly offbeat suburban English lifestyle, which sounds as though it might have been dreamed up by Ray Davies of The Kinks, was disturbed by the arrival of Chet Baker with their daughter Carol, now expecting a child out of wedlock. They had been prepared to give Chet the benefit of the doubt two years earlier, when they met in Rome, but now their worst fears had been realised. "Her father was a little cockney guy who had never seen a dope fiend in his life," Chet later wrote. "I gave him a fit."[32]

Despite telling Carol and her parents that he intended to stay clean, temptation soon got the better of Chet, and within days he had hooked up with Donald Brown to go in search of the prescription hard drugs they had heard so much about. They made their way to the office of Lady Isabella MacDougal Frankau, located on Wimpole Street in central London. An elderly doctor, specialising in the treatment of alcohol and drug addiction, she was married to a leading surgeon, Sir Claude Frankau, who worked at St. George's Hospital. She was also one of only twelve doctors in the country with the authority to prescribe heroin.

"She was about seventy-five years old, white-haired, and very business-like. She didn't ask me for much information about myself. She had already heard of my antics all over Europe. She simply asked me my name, my address, and how much cocaine and heroin I wanted per day. I started with ten grams of each, having had little experience buying cocaine or heroin at the corner drugstore. Ten grams of heroin in 1/6 gram tablets turned out to be sixty tablets that were the same size as standard diluted tabs. The coke was about what you'd get for five hundred dollars in New York, but pure. The whole script only cost about three-and-a-half dollars. After my first day, my scripts were all for twenty grams of each, and I was off and running under that old English drug system."[33]

A few days later, Chet started work on the movie *Stolen Hours*, which was being filmed at Shepperton Studios. It was the remake of a 1939 Bette Davis movie, *Dark Victory*, updated to give the film more of a 1960s flavour.

Susan Hayward plays Laura, a rich, neurotic socialite. Mike, an ex-boyfriend and famous racing driver, worries that Laura may be ill, and tricks her into a medical examination. She discovers she has a brain tumour, and an operation is performed. The procedure appears to be a success, and her symptoms disappear. Laura falls in love with the doctor that performed the operation, only to discover the tumour has returned. At this point, she renounces her new love and goes back to her old 'jet-set' ways, wasting the little time she has left. Only when she witnesses a racing accident does she realise the importance of making the most of her life.

Chet only appears on screen for a split second, playing trumpet with his band at one of her lavish parties. He also composed the movie soundtrack in conjunction with Melih Gurel, a Turkish–French horn player he had met in Paris. "I came in from Paris last week, and made the soundtrack with Tubby Hayes and the guys," Chet told Max Jones of *Melody Maker*. The other musicians performing on the set were Stan Tracey on piano, Jeff Clyne on bass and Don Brown on drums. "A fine musician, Tubby," Chet claimed, with both he and Melih Gurel agreeing that he was by far the best jazz musician they'd heard in Britain.[34]

Although his presence was required on the set for only a few days, Chet was given a small trailer. The early starts made it difficult for Baker and Brown to visit their new 'supplier'. Pretty soon, Chet found a way around the problem, placing a call to Dr Frankau's office, and arranging for the prescription to be delivered to a pharmacist close to the studio in Middlesex, west of London.

"The pharmacist would make up my package, call a taxi, and have it brought to me at Shepperton," Chet wrote. "I would disappear into my trailer on the lot and fix speedballs until someone called for me." No doubt this helps to explain his stoned appearance in the movie, his eyes carefully shielded by his dark sunglasses.[35]

Once the shooting was complete, Chet hoped to find work as a musician. He soon discovered that the draconian rules that governed the British Musicians' Union prevented foreign musicians from working in the country until they had been resident for one year. "If it hadn't been for Carol being English and expecting the baby, I would have told them to stick their country," Chet later complained to a journalist.[36]

Despite the impending birth of his child, Chet tried to spend as much time as possible away from the Surrey house, spending much of his time "just hanging out and getting high with other people just as screwed up as me." Even so, Chet was too self-absorbed at this time to prevent his drug culture from further impinging on the Jackson household. In his memoirs, Chet recalls being befriended by a London minicab driver, a fellow addict, who managed to give himself a fix whilst driving Chet back to Surrey. Chet invited the driver into the house, so that they could share another hit. After a while, the cab driver started to hallucinate, claiming that someone on the roof of the house was trying to take his photograph, before climbing out of the window, into the cold afternoon air, and on to the roof of the house. "He was there when Carol's father came home. I heard Al yelling, 'What the hell are you doing up there?' at this fool. He jumped down and ran, in a complete panic, for his car. I never saw him again."[37]

That incident, and others like it, led to heated arguments, both with Carol and her father, and Chet reluctantly agreed to spend more time at home. The birth of their first child was just weeks away, and with no steady income, Chet's funds were running low. This did not mean that he was prepared to give up his daily 'prescription', and the same pharmacist arranged a taxi to make regular deliveries to the Jackson household, with Carol's father occasionally left to pay the driver.

In *As Though I Had Wings* Chet claimed it was the coldest winter in England in one hundred years, and for once, he wasn't exaggerating. Terrible fog over London and the South East of England gave way to heavy snow, just before Carol went into labour on Christmas Eve. She gave birth next day to a baby boy, nicknamed 'Red' by the local nurses, as he was the first child born on Christmas morning.

Leaving aside their differences for a few hours, Chet and Al Jackson walked two miles to the hospital to visit Carol, the roads pretty much impassable by this stage. Chet later recalled the snow had drifted to depths of two feet nearer the hospital, pretty much unheard of in the South of England, which was to remain snowbound until early March. Carol named their son Dean Albert Baker, taking the name from James Dean, who Chet still resembled, and her own father.

Carol returned home in early January. She quickly became embroiled in another family argument about Chet's drug use, but doggedly stood by him, in the mistaken belief that fatherhood would make him more responsible. With limited cash, and reluctant to impose any further on her parents, Carol and Chet agreed that it made sense for him to sell his story to a tabloid magazine. As a result, a journalist from *Today* magazine visited the Jackson house in mid-January, and conducted a lengthy interview with Chet. In early February, the first of three articles was published under the provocative headline '30,000 Hell-Holes in My Arm'.

"My arms have been punctured by more than 30,000 times to get morphine and heroin into my veins. The hands with which I make music are scored, scratched and pitted—unmistakeable signs of the chronic mainliner."[38]

Chet also sheds some light on why he started experimenting with drugs in the early 1950s:

"In the first place, I had taken marijuana to kid myself that I was a genius. I was able to say to myself: I did it for my music. I had a message for the world. I had plenty of talent. But I wanted to express myself better, and faster … Drugs enabled me to feel things more quickly, more deeply. I was certain that they were a shortcut to musical fulfilment. Hadn't Charlie "Bird" Parker, one of the greatest jazz talents America had ever produced, been an addict? Couldn't I, too, be a genius with the intravenal aid of narcotics?"[39]

A follow-up article, this time entitled 'All That Jazz, All Those Girls, All That Dope! This was the sorrow in my trumpet', appeared in the March

30th edition, and the third and final instalment in April.

The articles try to paint a cautionary tale, suggesting that he is sick of his addiction, recognising that he risks everything he lived and worked for, and that dope "destroyed any chance I had for a happily married life." There are grains of truth hidden in these lurid tabloid exposes, but the overwhelming impression is that Chet is simply telling the journalist what they want to hear, prostituting himself and his art for a few quick bucks.

Unfortunately, this behaviour also proved to be addictive. The following year saw the publication of a similar article, 'The Trumpet and the Spike', this time going as far as including sordid photographs of Chet shooting up, while his return to the US in 1964 saw the publication of an article in *DownBeat*, 'Chet's Tale of Woe'. Carol also got in on the act, with *Today* magazine splashing out more cash to hear her talk about her "love for Chet Baker". Depressingly, all that really emerges is that tabloids have barely changed in forty years, and that sleaze sells.

Having been paid by the tabloid magazine, it wasn't long before Chet left Carol and Dean at home, and started to revisit his old haunts in London and "acting crazy". Picking up his prescription one weekend, when Lady Frankau usually returned to her house in the countryside, Chet was greeted by a new, younger pharmacist, who evidently recognised him. The man suggested they meet for lunch, and offered to 'help' him. Chet was evidently suspicious, and refused the offer. His will power didn't last long, however, and when the same pharmacist served Chet the following Monday, they agreed to meet in a nearby bookstore. There the man handed Chet a small package containing a vial of cocaine.

Chet consumed the cocaine with friends that same afternoon, but worried that the young man would get caught, since each pharmacy was obliged to keep detailed records. The theft was soon discovered, and under interrogation from the police, the young pharmacist revealed that he had supplied a musician by the name of Chet Baker. He was arrested at the Jackson house the following Friday, and taken to the police station to be questioned. He revealed that he was receiving treatment from Lady Frankau, who confirmed his story to the police. Within hours, she had arranged for a package of heroin to be delivered to the police station, enough to tide him over until his court appearance on Monday morning.

Albert Jackson was in court with his daughter on the Monday morning. The police did not have a strong case against Chet, who had not been caught in possession of the drug. The court agreed to release him on bail into Albert Jackson's custody, and they returned to Surrey together, where Carol's father lectured Chet on the need to be more responsible now that he was a father.

Chet agreed to check himself into a private clinic that Lady Frankau had recommended, but the treatment was voluntary, and a few days later, Chet was procuring dope from street junkies. He picked up an infection, contracting severe blood poisoning, and was rushed to hospital, where he was put on a course of penicillin.

While he was in the hospital he received a surprise visit from the Italian bass player Giovanni Tommaso, who was in London for his engagement party. "I had some money for him from RCA, some royalty payments, because they had no way of contacting him," he said. "When I got there, Chet was in the hospital. Someone obviously followed me, because they saw me giving Chet an envelope, and thought I was giving him drugs. The police followed me home to the family house of my fiancé, and started asking questions to my future mother-in-law. It was very embarrassing for me. They were a wealthy, conservative family; they weren't too happy that their daughter was involved with an Italian, but the fact that he was a jazz musician and there were drugs involved, it made things very difficult. The police even came to my folk's house in Florence. The situation eventually dissolved, but the first couple of weeks were tough."[40]

Once his fever had eased, Chet checked himself out of the hospital, against the will of the medical staff. When police asked Albert Jackson about the alleged drug deal that took place in the hospital, he cracked, and withdrew his bail.

The police rearrested Chet, and threw him into a regular cell. He soon started to suffer from severe withdrawal symptoms, and started to yell, pounding on the door of his cell with the heel of his shoe. As a result, he was taken to the infirmary, where despite the icy winter conditions, guards stripped him of his clothes and dumped him in a padded isolation cell. "Maybe that was part of their psychology," Chet later mused, "to keep you so worried about freezing that you wouldn't have the chance to think about how sick you were."

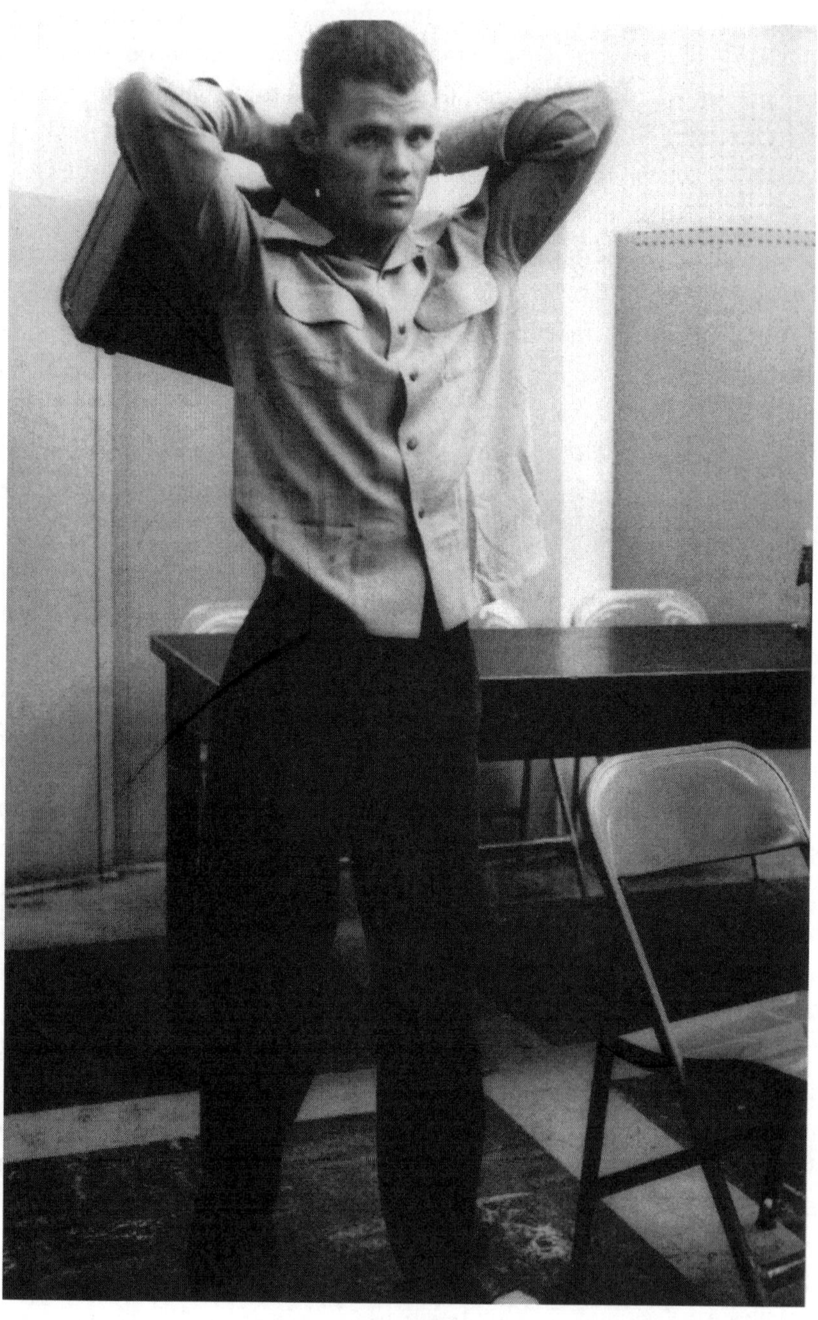

Chet Baker leaves Pentonville Prison, London, March 1963.
Photographer unknown.

Next day he was transferred by prison van to Pentonville Prison in North London where he was held for two weeks. His trial took place on February 15th 1963, in which he stood accused of narcotics violation. "I really couldn't take the whole thing very seriously," he later recalled. "All those seemingly pompous fools with their white wigs."[41]

Despite the lack of evidence to prove he had asked the pharmacist to steal the cocaine, or paid him for it, Chet was found guilty, and sentenced to deportation to the country of his choice. He was sent back to Pentonville until the end of the month, and then transferred to a further prison for illegal aliens. During this time, Carol arranged for them to move to Paris, one of the few countries with a thriving jazz scene that would still accept him. On March 27th, the police escorted Chet and his young family to the ferry in Dover, where they set sail for France in yet another attempt to make a fresh start.

* * * *

Whether it was the impact of undergoing cold turkey at Her Majesty's request, the effect of the cool sea breeze as they crossed the channel to Calais, or the change in the weather after they arrived, is unclear, but Chet arrived in Paris in an unusually eloquent frame of mind. "We got there just as they were sandblasting the grime off all the old buildings in the city. Man, when the sun comes up there, and all those buildings are gleaming orange, gold, mauve—a hundred fantastic colours—Paris is really beautiful."

Despite the problems that had plagued his time in Europe, he was also optimistic about the future, confident that he could stay off junk for the time being. "When I left England for France, I knew something had changed. I could feel it in my bones, but I refused to believe it, I was so terrified of getting hooked again," he later revealed. "A change had come over me, don't ask me why. Months had gone since I'd taken hard stuff and I hadn't the slightest desire to start off again."[42]

Sadly, Chet's words have a hollow ring to them, the desperate promise an addict makes that things will be different this time. After all, it had been just ten weeks since he made a similar claim to Carol's father, Albert Jackson. He had only been clean for two months, but within weeks he'd be using again, reunited with his old junkie friend from Boston, Peter Littman.

From a musical standpoint, he had effectively fallen off the radar screen as far as the US market was concerned. It had been more than one year since the release of his 'comeback' album *Chet is Back!,* and with no recording contract in France, there was little prospect of an imminent release. Still, Chet cared little about such matters. He had never had much time for the workings of the music industry, even at the height of his fame on the West Coast. Although there was a perception that he was living the 'American dream'—with his talent, his good looks, the awards, the movie offers—he had taken a conscious decision to turn his back on this. He felt as though he was being persecuted for using drugs in America, and was unable to live his life the way he chose. Whilst things hadn't worked out the way he planned in either Italy or England, France had a more established jazz scene, and he was confident he could find regular work.

Indeed, jazz was booming in Paris in the early 1960s. A number of prominent American jazz musicians had chosen to leave New York and settle in Paris, including Dexter Gordon, Jackie McLean, Kenny Drew, Kenny Clarke, Art Taylor and Johnny Griffin. There were numerous attractions to relocating from the US to Europe, as Johnny Griffin later revealed. "Coming back to New York I had family problems, government problems, tax problems," he recalled. "And the way that the supposed jazz critics were promulgating the avant-garde or 'free jazz', I thought it was a bad joke. I thought it was a pity. I liked some of the musicians, but the playing was making me sick. I had the chance to go back to Europe and be free without the pressures here, people telling me what I could do and what I couldn't do, the agents in New York. And racism. There was such a big difference."[43]

Chet Baker and his son, Dean, Paris 1963. Photographer unknown.

Paris had also developed a unique atmosphere of its own, quite distinct from other jazz markets within Europe. "There was always something happening in Stockholm, a lot was happening in Copenhagen, where Horace Parlan and others had settled, but Paris was the centre, Paris was happening," said Griffin, who eventually settled in the French countryside. "It had a very different atmosphere to New York. The music came from New York, and places like Chicago, where I'm from, New Orleans, Kansas City, or the West Coast. But Paris had a good feeling, and a lot of people went there to have fun."[44]

Before Chet had the chance to find work in Paris, he was picked up by the police in a drug raid. They had been investigating the local drug scene for a few months, and in the space of a few days picked up 150 suspected addicts, among them pianist Kenny Drew and a saxophonist that worked with Ray Charles, David "Fathead" Newman. Baker was still clean at this time, but given his exploits in England and Italy, was considered a likely suspect. "As I'm maybe the best known junkie or should I say, ex-junkie, among all the cats in Europe, the coppers came rushing up the stairs and hammering on my door," he later complained. "They figured they might as well rope me in with the others."[45]

The police took Chet, Carol and Dean into custody. One by one the suspects were questioned, sometimes for hours at a time. Chet later recalled the scene to Ira Gitler. "I was there twenty-four hours, and everybody was getting sick—they give you a fix in the police stations until they get all the papers typed up and signed, sealed; they give you a fix every three hours—and I never asked for anything the whole time."

With three-month-old Dean crying, Chet pleaded with the police that he was innocent. He was eventually tested, found to be clean, and released. "Understand me, man, there were some sad faces among the cops," he said.[46]

Chet and Carol had very little money at first, and took a small place in Montmartre. The judge in charge of the case had granted Chet a temporary work permit, subject to regular urine checks to ensure that he stayed clean. "He called me back every two weeks, found me clean, and still he didn't lighten up on me."

After a couple of weeks, Chet found work at the Blue Note in Paris, where Bud Powell was headlining. "The Blue Note was the happening club in the early 1960s," recalled Johnny Griffin, who played at the club a couple of nights a week. "Ben Benjamin ran the club, knew all the musicians and they knew him. His wife looked after the money, and looked after the finances, but I always dealt with Ben."[47]

Ben Benjamin was a former American GI, who had settled in Paris after the war. Openly gay, he dreamed of opening his own nightclub, so he entered a marriage of convenience with a French lady by the name of Etla, who ran the business side of things. Etla Benjamin had the reputation as being a hard-nosed, unpleasant woman, and it should come as no surprise to find that Chet found her difficult to deal with. As an interesting aside, Chet's old girlfriend, Liliane Cukier, played her part in the movie *Round Midnight* in 1986, with Chet himself recording one song for the soundtrack.

Chet was only hired to play one or two nights a week, and never had the chance to play with Bud Powell, who performed with his trio. "Of course, by that time Bud was already a little bit strange," Chet later recalled. "Sometimes he'd play beautifully, and then in the middle of a tune he'd stop, stand up, look round, laugh, sit down and play again … it was very strange. Must've been difficult for people who didn't know who or what he was."[48]

While Chet was playing at the Blue Note, he was introduced to Bobbi Parker, a young, black jazz singer who occasionally performed at the club. "She was very sexy-looking; tall and beautiful," recalled Johnny Griffin. With Carol looking after Dean at the apartment in Montmartre, Chet began a brief but passionate affair with her, overlooking the fact that Carol had stood by him during his problems with addiction.

Chet's band at the Blue Note consisted of Luis Fuentes on trombone, Luigi Trussardi on bass and Giorgio Solano on drums. When the band started the engagement, Etla Benjamin was on vacation, leaving her husband Ben in sole charge of the running of the club.

"Chet and Luis Fuentes used to play sitting down," recalled Luigi Trussardi. "One night we were playing when she returned to Paris; she whispered something in the ear of her husband, and he came up to Chet and said, 'Chet, you'd better stand up when you play'. Chet ignored this, and kept playing. Ben went back to his wife, but she insisted that the band play standing. Ben issued Chet an ultimatum: 'Either you play standing up, or you leave'. At that point, Chet shouted, 'Stop!' He left the club, and we all followed, Giorgio Solano taking his cymbals with him. As we left, Etla shouted, 'You'll never play again at the Blue Note!' Chet was very surprised we followed him out of the club, and when I met him again the following year, he said he'd always remember me. He was very upset at the time. It was so stupid—Chet was playing so well."[49]

A few days later, Chet started work at a rival club, Le Chat Qui Pêche (The Fishing Cat), a small basement club situated on the Left Bank. "The club was unique," recalled Hans Kennel a Swiss trumpet player who had been recruited to play at the club, and opened for Chet. "It was a small cellar sitting about fifty–sixty people at small tables with small wooden stools, and a bench that went all around the walls. The stage was tiny and there was one of these stools on the stage, as Chet had started to play sitting down at that time."[50]

The club was owned by Madame Ricard, a former member of the French Resistance. A small, red-haired, chain-smoking woman, she looked after the musicians, allowing Chet and Carol to stay in the apartment above the club. "She was a charming woman, and almost a mother to us," laughed Kennel. "She would always tease me about my Swiss accent, but I couldn't blame her."

Alex Bally, who played drums with Hans Kennel at this time, remembers that she occasionally received visitors who remembered her from the war. "Sometimes old parachutists would come into the club to talk with her, but others were less friendly, and used to threaten her," he said. "During the Algerian dispute, one Algerian grabbed her, pulled her over the bar, and threatened to cut her throat with a flick knife. She still had the scars from that event. She was a remarkable lady, and always had some amazing stories to tell."[51]

Chet's original quartet at Le Chat Qui Pêche was the same band he had used at the Blue Note, but with Peter Littman replacing Giorgio Solano on drums. Chet had always had a stormy relationship with Peter Littman, and this occasion was no exception. After just two or three weeks, the two of them had a heated row in the kitchen of the club, which resulted in Littman being fired. Hans Kennel speculated that the argument might have been about drugs. "He was certainly a worse junkie than Chet," he noted.

He was also prone to making inappropriate comments, both on and off the stage, which didn't endear him to many of the other jazz musicians. On one occasion, Kenny Clarke came into the club and introduced the seventeen-year-old Tony Williams, who had just started playing drums with Miles Davis. "Littman said he knew Tony from Boston as a kid, but thought he couldn't keep time," recalled Hans Kennel. "It still rings in my ears. We were all standing very close together."[52]

Alex Bally thought the dispute might have been over Peter's drumming. "He was a very individual cat, with a strange way of using the cymbals. He used very thick cymbals that sounded horrible, really horrible," he recalled. "Chet loved to play with me because I had some good Zildjian cymbals that sounded really bright. I asked Peter once, 'Why do you play these cymbals?' He said, 'You know, Alex, anyone can play on a soft cymbal because you can't hear the single strokes; the strokes are muffled. That's why I use a hard cymbal because you can hear every beat, and you can't fake it'. It used to sound like a bell."[53]

Either way, Chet asked Giorgio Solano to rejoin the band. Chet was still in relatively good shape at this time, his playing bright and strong. "I've never played better," he later claimed. "When I played some of my old successes like 'Bye-Bye Blackbird' and 'Summertime', I brought the house down."[54]

Hans Kennel also remembers the venue being full for the most part, the notable exception being the August holiday period. "The place was often really packed with people even standing all the way up the stairs, glasses in hand, listening," he recalled. "To name a few 'drop-bys' I clearly remember Kenny Clarke, Tony Williams, Herbie Hancock, Ron Jefferson and Johnny Griffin. Those come to my mind now, but there were many more."[55]

Another visitor to the club was a American playwright by the name of Ken Dewey, who had previously worked with Anna Halprin in the United States. Halprin pioneered what later became known as 'postmodern dance', and encouraged the breaking down of barriers between theatre, dance, music and performance art. Dewey had recently written a play called *The Gift*, and wanted to use this as the basis of a piece of performance art which had been commissioned by the Théâtre des Nations in Paris.

Dewey contacted an old acquaintance by the name of Terry Riley to act as musical director for the play. Riley had a grounding in jazz piano, but also had a keen interest in experimental music, having collaborated with the minimalist composer LaMonte Young to produce music for Anna Halprin's Dancers' Workshop productions. Riley had relocated from the US to Paris in 1962, and was making a living playing jazz piano in the bars of Pigalle, and accompanying floorshow acts in the servicemen's clubs on the NATO bases. "One day I walked into the pool room on Rue Pigalle where we would hang out waiting for the booking agents to come and give us our next assignment," Riley later recalled. "Chet was there playing pool. I was very excited because he was a hero of mine."[56]

On the back of this chance encounter, Riley suggested that Dewey approach Chet, and ask if he would like to participate. Although he understood little about the project on which they were about to embark, Chet tentatively agreed that his band would appear as both actors and musicians.

The rehearsals for the play took place in the ruins of the Vieux Chateau in Valmondois, just outside Paris. In the meantime, Terry Riley, Chet Baker and his quartet and an actor by the name of John Graham met at the RTF Studios in the Florence Bernhart Theatre in Paris to begin work on the soundtrack. "I asked them to play something. I didn't even say what to play," said Riley. "The first thing that Chet did was play a blues duet—bass and trumpet. We recorded that and then I might have suggested they play 'So What' … I had heard him play it at Le Chat Qui Pêche. I asked them to record it with the group and improvise on it just as they did at [the club]. Then I had them all play it solo, with each one improvising on it, so that I had both the group and individual instruments."[57]

Terry Riley explained to his engineer that he wanted to create a long, repeated loop, a process that resulted in what he later referred to as 'the accumulation technique', which was influential in the development of ambient and electronic music. "We started cutting it up into loops and reorchestrating it," he explained, "putting all these loops together. Then I added John Graham's voice using one of the lines from the play. That was cut up and added to it as well as a couple of the sounds that were out of the 'Mescaline Mix' (recorded 1960–62 in San Francisco). One sound is like someone being hit by an arrow. It's almost a human scream. There were many elements. The idea was that it was built into layers of sound that they could improvise within the play."[58]

In the evening, Riley would bring the tapes that he had been working on to the Chateau, where the actors were rehearsing in a barn. "We'd listen to them and the actors would try to get a sense of how to relate to the music," he said. "Occasionally Chet and the band would come out to the chateau and we'd have a full rehearsal with everybody. Ken would watch the whole thing and would try to get the actors to interact more with the musicians and try to get the musicians to be more involved with the action."

The play was rehearsed and later performed on a large metal sculpture that was designed by Jerry Walter. The sculpture was suspended from the ceiling, and used to swing precipitously whenever the actors moved around. The plot, such as it was, involved one actor giving a 'gift' to another actor, and passing on a few words of dialogue, before the gift was passed on to the next person. At the same time, the taped music could be incorporated into the play. The musicians were encouraged to improvise, too, either playing along with the tape, or on their own. "Chet had never experienced anything like this and I remember one day him being very upset," Riley remembered. "Ken talked to him and explained what this kind of theatre was about and later he got more into it."[59]

The Gift played for three nights at the Théâtre Récamier, part of the Théâtre des Nations, starting on July 8th. Chet didn't show up on the first night, so Terry Riley took his place, pretending to play the trumpet by 'blowing' on part of the metal sculpture. The play divided critics and theatregoers alike, but certainly made for a unique spectacle. "It was really happening; there was no written music, so it was different every night," recalled Luigi Trussardi. "We started off playing outside, as people entered the theatre. During the play, it was as though we were playing live music for a movie picture. But we were acting, too, improvising according to certain directions. It was very free!"[60]

Back at Le Chat Qui Pêche, Hans Kennel and his band were still supporting Chet's quartet. "One day in late June, after finishing my second set at 1 a.m., I went to Chet to tell him I could not stay for his last set, because I had to get up very early. When he asked why, I told him I was going to the French Grand Prix car race in Reims," said Kennel. "He absolutely insisted to go with me and I could almost not believe my eyes, when I saw him waiting for us at 7 a.m. in front of the club! We had a great time that day doing something completely different, and by the time we got back for the evening gig, we were a bit more tired than usual."[61]

A couple of weeks later the Norwegian jazz writer Randi Hultin came to Paris on her way to the jazz festival at Juan-les-Pins. She caught up with her old friend Bud Powell, who was still playing at the Blue Note, and noted that he "seemed musically inspired, there was humour in his playing, but he was frail and did not look well." A few days later she made her way to Le Chat Qui Pêche, where she got the chance to listen to Chet.

Between sets, Chet explained to her that he was playing on a borrowed trumpet "I'm playing Kennel's trumpet," he said, "because mine got stolen during a break." She was amazed that anyone would steal a musician's instrument from the club, but later learned that Chet had pulled this stunt on numerous occasions, hocking his horn for drug money. This incident clearly suggests that Chet was using heroin again by this time, and that he was no longer being asked to submit to regular testing by the police in Paris.[62]

The musicians normally kept their street clothes and instrument cases in the kitchen, which was located on the ground floor, above the club itself. One evening, Chet claimed his trumpet had been stolen, and asked Hans Kennel if he could borrow his Martin trumpet. "What a question! I was sitting in front of him playing, my ear at the bell of my instrument, and I didn't miss a note, for sure. I was carried away!" It only occurred to him later that it was strange that Chet had managed to keep his own mouthpiece. "That was when I was told by other French musicians that this was not the first time this had happened, and maybe not the last time," he said.[63]

Around this time, Kennel returned to Switzerland, although his drummer, Alex Bally, stayed on at the club. Chet borrowed a flugelhorn from a local musician by the name of Babar Vittet. On his return to the US he told *DownBeat*'s Ira Gitler of the difficulty he had mastering the new horn. "It's so hard to play, you wouldn't believe it. Nobody would, unless it was somebody who plays one. The mouthpiece is deeper and wider, and it takes so much air to fill out this horn."[64]

In late July, Chet's band was booked to play at Club Three as part of the Juan-les-Pins jazz festival. Chet missed the first two nights of the engagement, as he was waiting for Carol Jackson to return from England. The owner of the club was understandably upset, and called Madame Ricard at Le Chat Qui Pêche to enquire of his whereabouts. "Everyone is waiting for him," he explained. Unfortunately, there was a major misunderstanding on the telephone. Madame Ricard told him that Chet's girlfriend was still in London, or "à Londres", but the club owner misheard, and thought that Carol was "à l'ombre", which literally translates as 'in the shadow', implying she was in prison. The following night, the club owner apparently told the audience that Chet was unable to play that evening because his wife was in prison.

"Carol returned to Paris that day, and we drove down to Juan-les-Pins," recalled bass player Luigi Trussardi. "When we arrived that afternoon, someone came up to Chet and asked if he was OK. 'I heard your wife was in jail', he explained. Chet asked him where he'd heard this story, and the man explained that the club owner had told the audience the previous night. When Chet heard this news, he went looking for the club owner, and punched him in the face. As a result, the gig was cancelled, and we were stranded in the south of France with no money."

Luigi Trussardi believes that the band never played in Juan-les-Pins. He remembers that the French actress, Micheline Prelle, invited them to a party. "We spent the night at her villa in Toulon, and next day, we drove back to Liege," he said. Others recall a slightly different version of events. Randi Hultin recalls Chet showing up Club Three at 3 a.m. with his child in his arms, suggesting that he had healed his rift with the club owner.

The Italian pianist Amadeo Tommasi was playing at the festival with his own trio, and clearly remembers playing with Chet one evening. "My trio with Giovanni Tommaso and Franco Mondini was the first black-style trio, like the Red Garland Trio," he said. "Giovanni Tommaso was playing very like Paul Chambers, and I was playing like Red Garland. I liked Red Garland, Bill Evans obviously, and McCoy Tyner. These were my three favourite pianists. I was without a bass player that day because Giovanni was not free, and Franco D'Andrea, the pianist, volunteered to play bass."[65]

Miles Davis was also playing at the festival that year with George Coleman on tenor saxophone, a concert that was captured on the album *Miles Davis in Europe*. "At the same festival, Chet Baker was playing in a club," the pianist recalled. "After playing I went along to watch him play. It was 2 a.m., and Chet was having an interval between sets, and had a young baby with him. He said, 'Amadeo, come here, tell me what you've been doing'. After a while, Miles Davis came into the club, and Chet said, 'Amadeo, you should play with me. I want to show off my music to Miles Davis'. 'But what about your pianist? You already have a pianist', I said. 'No, I want to do a good show, and I'd love you to play'. So I sat in with him. After the set, he sat down with Miles Davis. My friend Alberto Berti, who was working with Miles Davis, told me that Chet asked Miles, 'How did I play?' 'You played like shit', said Miles. 'Even if I was drunk and on drugs I could play better than you'."

Miles Davis had never come to terms with Chet's early success, and tried to put him down at every opportunity. The story also shows that Chet continued to look up to Miles as a musician. He included recent recordings by Miles in his own set list, such as 'So What' from *Kind of Blue*, and desperately sought his approval each time they met.

Chet returned to Paris in August, but the crowds were notably thinner during the holiday season. Chet appeared at the Comblain-la-Tour jazz festival in early August, where he is thought to have played with Bud Shank. It was probably around this time that Chet appeared on a Belgian TV programme, although it has been difficult to pin down the precise date. The band featured Chet's old friend Jacques Pelzer on alto saxophone and flute, René Urtreger on piano, Luigi Trussardi on bass and Franco Manzecchi on drums. The music recorded that day was later issued on CD as *Chet Baker Quintet: Brussels 1964*, giving the recording date as May 2nd 1964. That date is clearly wrong, as Chet was back in the US by that time. It is more likely to have been recorded in July or August, since Chet plays flugelhorn on the recording rather than his own trumpet. "René Urtreger called me to tell me about the record, and I went out to buy a copy," said Luigi Trussardi. "They hadn't paid any of the musicians, so we sued the record company through the Musicians' Union; it went to trial, and we won. They paid Carol, Chet's wife, and the other musicians. The record is no longer available, as they had no right to sell the recording."[66]

The Belgian recording is now available legally, issued on DVD as *Chet Baker: Live in '64 and '79*, as part of the *Jazz Icons* series. Unfortunately, nobody took the trouble to correct the title, which still has the wrong year, despite the fact that the liner notes correctly identify the recording as taking place in 1963.

Giorgio Solano seems to have left Chet's band over the summer, and was replaced by the American drummer Eddie Jefferson, who was living in Paris at the time. "Chet didn't really like his cymbal beat, and asked me if I could play with him," Alex Bally later recalled. "By that time, Madame Ricard was also pissed off with Eddie, and she fired him, so I got the job. At that time it was me, Luigi Trussardi; we rarely used a piano down there because it was too humid. We played as a trio (or quartet) there until the end of the year. After that, at the end of 1963, I left to play in Spain."

Chet continued to use heroin over this period, occasionally asking the other band members to look after his son Dean, while he went out to score. "Once he asked me to take care of his son in the afternoon," Alex Bally remembered. "It was nice weather, so I took him to the coffee shop next door. He had so much energy, Chet gave me a long cord and told me to attach him to the chair; his son had a 'stroller', and used to scramble between the chairs in the coffee shop. I had to regularly untangle him. He was constantly active!"[67]

Despite his addiction, Chet was in relatively good shape physically at that time. "Sometimes he used to drink two or three litres of orange juice a day, to compensate for his drug use," said Bally. "He had an amazing physique at that time, with not an ounce of body fat. He was very strong. A lot of musicians would not have survived his drug intake."[68]

His addiction doubtless led to chemical imbalances within his body, which may well have contributed to his unpredictable behaviour, both on and off the stage. One time, Carol popped out to the shops to get some groceries, recalled bass player, Luigi Trussardi. "When she came back, she told Chet that a man had been disrespectful to her when she had sat down in a nearby café. 'What did he do?' Chet asked. 'He put his hand on my bottom', Carol told him. Chet had a very small gun, put it in his pocket, and said to me, 'Follow me!' It was like a Western! He went up the stairs, and I followed him, and straight to the café that Carol had described. Chet spotted the guy that she had described, went up to him, put the gun to his head, and said, 'Next time you disrespect my wife, I'll kill you, motherfucker!' And with that, he returned to the club."[69]

On another occasion, the trio left Paris for a one-off concert in Spain. "We drove down in three cars, with Luigi driving in front, me behind," said Alex Bally. "After the concert, Chet gave us his bags and told us to be careful with his luggage. We crossed the border at around three in the morning; it was very cold. We had no problems with the customs officials, and got back to the club in time to play 11 p.m. next evening. But when we got there, there was no sign of Chet. I went upstairs, but Carol had no idea where he was. Next day he showed up with a big smile on his face. 'I got stopped at the border', he explained, 'but they found nothing on me. Lucky you were carrying all the stuff in your luggage!' It turns out he had bought himself some shit! It was a good thing we didn't know; we would have been far more cautious crossing the border."[70]

Onstage, Chet played well for the most part, his tone bright and strong, as heard on the television show recorded in Brussels. On a couple of occasions, however, his drug intake took its toll. "He would ask me to step down from the drums, and would take my place, playing for half an hour, or so, and the whole audience would leave!" laughed Alex Bally. "I asked him, 'So, do you like playing the drums?' He said, 'Well, I like to have a change from time to time. I don't want to always play the fucking trumpet, every single night!'"[71]

Another time, he even tried to give lessons to his drummer. "He told me how to play the cymbal beat like Elvin Jones on certain tunes, and explained the difference in the beat produced by Kenny Clarke and Elvin Jones. Guys like Kenny would play straightforward sixteenths instead of triplets, which is right, actually, but at the time I didn't get it at all. Adding a sixteenth note, and holding the quarter notes, makes the quarter notes even; such playing had a different groove, you know, and on certain tunes Chet wanted me to play like that. For the most part, Chet's drumming sounded pretty horrible! He would just play the beat, no counterpoint, no accents. Luigi Trussardi used to get pretty pissed off having to play with him!"

Despite the occasional drug-related incident, Luigi Trussardi and Alex Bally enjoyed their time with Chet, and learned some important lessons about jazz. "Chet always told me, 'When you play, look for the golden notes, not the blue notes'," recalled the bass player. "Chet may have been a junkie, but he always wanted to play, to be in that universe of beauty." For Alex Bally it had been a steep learning curve, but one which stood him in good stead for the rest of his career. "Although it was a heavy time, it was a great experience for me, allowing me the chance to play with so many of the greats in Paris," he recalled. "I really paid my dues there; I learned a lot from Chet, who had such a great repertoire."

Chet finished his contract at Le Chat Qui Pêche in late November, just after the assassination of John F. Kennedy. "They say everybody remembers what they were doing when Jack Kennedy was killed," Trussardi recalled. "Well, I was with Chet Baker. We were together at the club when we heard the news on the radio."[72]

* * * *

Chet left France for Spain, where he had signed a contract to play for one month at the Club Jamboree in Barcelona. Whilst Spain was something of a backwater as far as jazz was concerned, the money was good, the contract included a small apartment, and he welcomed the warmer weather, particularly after the ice-cold winter he had spent in England.

The club had been presenting jazz artists for a year or so, although many of the locals preferred the room upstairs, which featured local Spanish music and flamenco dancers. Chet also inherited a "pitiful rhythm section", that was unfamiliar with most of his repertoire. "Kenny Drew had been there just before me, and he had walked out on the job and told them they shouldn't even been playing," he later recalled. "He gave them a terrible complex, so when I got there they were really scared to death."[73]

Heroin was less readily available than it had been in Paris. Addicts could register and receive controlled quantities of narcotics, just as they could in England, but the system was closely monitored. Chet soon discovered that Palfium was available, and within days he was back to his old tricks, faking ailments and stealing prescription pads. "During the engagement I met a very prominent and well-connected family and, through them, a doctor with his own new and ultramodern clinics and operating room … I was soon obtaining scripts from him, and it all began once again."[74]

Chet and Carol, together with their son Dean, returned to Paris in early January 1964. In the one month he had been playing in Barcelona, he had lost his craving for heroin, but became completely addicted to Palfium. His addiction was such that he couldn't even drive straight through to Paris; he stopped in Toulouse, put Carol and Dean on the train to Paris, and said he would catch up with them next day.

He proceeded to trawl the streets of Toulouse, desperately searching for a pharmacy that stocked Palfium. When he found one, he handed the pharmacist a prescription stolen from a doctor in Barcelona. The man hesitated, aware that he was almost certainly dealing with an addict, and then reached for a box of Palfium on the shelf behind him. Chet noticed several remaining boxes on the shelf, and when he checked into his hotel that evening, found that he couldn't sleep. He later told his prospective biographer, Lisa Galt Bond, that he returned to the drugstore after midnight, smashed open the glass door, and stole the remaining boxes, returning to Paris next morning.

January 1964 brought the offer of work in Germany. The ban on Chet entering the country had evidently been lifted early, as Chet was booked to play at the Blue Note in Berlin, the city's premier jazz club. The rhythm section consisted of Tete Montoliu, the blind Spanish pianist, together with two local musicians, Peter Trunk on bass and Joe Nay on drums.

As Chet made his way through the packed audience, there was a sense of anticipation in the air. Nobody knew quite what to expect—the West Coast jazz star they had heard on the Pacific Jazz recordings, or the troubled young man they had read about in the press, who had been imprisoned in both Italy and England. In the event, the degree to which his playing had developed surprised both musicians and audience alike. The concert was witnessed by Lothar Lewien, a young German music fan, who later described the impact Chet's playing had left on him.

"He did not announce anything, turned to the piano player, counted a very fast rhythm and started to play: Milestones. It was like his credo at that time: The fast staccato lines of the beginning, the sustained notes of the bridge, the staccato repeat, and his solo: He played long, long lines, fast and really burning. After they had finished he welcomed everybody, saying, "That was something to warm up." To me, this was a very unusual Chet. Then, I only knew the music he played with Gerry Mulligan, Russ Freeman ... I mean the Pacific Jazz recordings. But the Chet then was a hard-driving trumpeter, of course very melodic and his sound was there, but his style was more aggressive in a way. Made a big impression on me. That was not the innocent young boy who improvised like whistling nice melodies. He was blowing the trumpet with fire. But even the fastest attacks always with taste and melodic approach. The expression "bitter-sweet" came to my mind.

"He also sung that night. I remember his closed eyes, while he haunted 'You Don't Know What Love Is'. He did hold the mike as if he needed support. The audience was completely silent and caught by pure emotions floating from the bandstand. But the main impression was the hard-driving trumpeter, because this was a surprise and new to me. He played even 'Solar', a composition by Miles Davis, in an unusual way, very, very fast. The piano player was almost frightened, shook his head, laughed, but followed Chet, who was flying through the tune."[75]

After the first set, Chet disappeared into the night, only returning much later, his hair wet from the cold night air. The band had already started playing when he took to the stage, but he sounded none the worse for wear, soloing as powerfully as he had in the first set. As he left the club that evening, he told Lewien that he hadn't felt well that evening. "Come tomorrow night," he said. "I'll prove to you I can play better."

Sadly, it was not to be. Chet was arrested when he returned to his hotel. Since his arrival in Germany earlier that day he had tried to obtain Jetrium from six different doctors, faking a kidney ailment. His downfall came when he tried to take his prescriptions to a pharmacy; in his rush to get back to the club, he evidently brought prescriptions from two different doctors to the same store. The pharmacist reported the issue to the police, who arrested him in the early hours of January 22nd 1964.

Chet spent a few days in prison, before a judge declared him 'unstable', and recommended he be transferred to a sanatorium in Wittenau until his addiction was cured. The local newspapers made a big deal of the case. "The career of the main with a golden trumpet has come to an end in Berlin," suggested one journalist, while others were more sympathetic, showing photographs of Carol and Dean visiting Chet in hospital. Carol supported herself by finding occasional work as a babysitter, and later told the Dutch magazine 'Televizer' that she "hopes that one day he will be free of his addiction and then will marry me." The press coverage soon reached the attention of US officials in Berlin, who arranged for Chet to leave the hospital after forty days so that he could be deported to the United States.

Chet had left the US in the summer of 1959, upset at the way his addiction was treated by the authorities. "I have a great deal of disrespect for the police department and the correctional people and the way they handle drug addiction," he complained to Ira Gitler on his return, "and I've suffered greatly at their hands."

Yet in the five years he had spent in Europe, he had been deported from Italy, Germany on two occasions, Switzerland and England. Despite this, he refused to accept any responsibility for his behaviour. "It just seemed like a field day for the police department whenever Chet Baker came to town," he said bitterly. "It seemed to be a tie-up between the police department and the newspapers—the publicity bit—because I was always very cool. I never bothered anybody. Everything I did was for myself."[76]

It would take a tragic event, once again entirely of his own making, to shake him free of his dependency, and face up to the reality that change had to come from within. It was an incident that could easily have left him unable to play again—the one thing in life he loved more than heroin.

Chapter Eleven

BABY BREEZE
NEW YORK, 1964–1965

"What (John Coltrane and Ornette Coleman) play seems to have a certain commercial value. But I don't think they'll ever get a gold record. It would be nice, but I just don't think that there are that many musicians that understand the musicians who are considered the avant-garde. To me, reaching people is the most important thing. Otherwise you just lock yourself away in a room and play for yourself—that's all."—Chet Baker[1]

On March 4th 1964, Chet flew into John F. Kennedy International Airport alone. Carol Jackson had been denied a US visa and returned to England with their son Dean, where she stayed with her parents. "When I arrived, the Feds were waiting for me," Chet told the *New York Post*. "They searched me up and down, and when they found I was clean, they let me through. One of them, when he found out I was flat broke, even gave me a ride into New York City." As Chet made his was through the airport, another journalist asked him whether he was still taking drugs. "No, I haven't had anything for forty days," he replied. "I'm cured."[2]

Chet later claimed he arrived in New York with $1.25 in his pocket. He called his old friend Gerry Mulligan to ask for a loan, but the saxophonist refused to help. Another acquaintance suggested he leave New York and live on his farm in Tonka Falls, Minnesota, where he could play in a new Minneapolis club. The plans fell through, however, apparently because the terms of the contract were too one-sided. "He wasn't promising me anything; I was promising him everything," he told *DownBeat* magazine. "He was just acting as a collection agency for all my money."[3]

Having been away from the New York jazz scene for almost five years, Chet felt out of touch, and made a collect call to his old friend Phil Urso, who wired some money to New York. Chet spent the next few weeks in Denver,

Colorado, working his way through the phone book, desperately looking for gigs.

He soon discovered that the tabloid interviews that had taken place in England with *Today* magazine had effectively cost him his cabaret card. A similar style US magazine, *Hush Hush*, had recycled some of juiciest quotes in an article entitled 'The Tragedy of Chet Baker: From Top Jazz Man to Number One Junkie!' As a result of this negative publicity, his application for a cabaret card was eventually denied, which effectively barred him from working in Manhattan. A potentially lucrative engagement at the Village Vanguard was cancelled, leaving him with limited options.

Time magazine, which had once sung his praises, picked up on his predicament in an article entitled 'Back from the Dark Side'. "Ten years ago, when Chet was clean, neat and 24, he was the most popular trumpet player in jazz. Since then, he has traversed the dark side, and it has made him a different and deeper player than he was in the golden days. Now Chet Baker is down and out."[4]

The composer and arranger Tadd Dameron offered to help Chet, and allowed him to sleep on the sofa of his West 72nd Street apartment. The two musicians had met at the Lexington Federal Narcotics Hospital in 1959, where Dameron had run the house band.

Dameron was a veteran of the big band era, known for his work with Coleman Hawkins, Sarah Vaughan and Dizzy Gillespie, to name but a few. Since his release from hospital in 1960, he had scraped a living writing arrangements for Milt Jackson, Benny Goodman, 'Blue' Mitchell and Sonny Stitt.

Both Baker and Dameron were regarded as veterans in the fast-changing New York jazz scene. In Chet's absence, 'free jazz' musicians such as Ornette Coleman and Cecil Taylor had thrown down the gauntlet to musicians of the bebop era; some had responded by adapting their own playing style, such as Sonny Rollins and Miles Davis. Others opted to leave New York for Europe, including Dexter Gordon, Johnny Griffin and Art Taylor.

Having planted the seeds of the new movement, Ornette Coleman had disappeared from public view for two years, opting to learn how to play a range of other instruments, including trumpet and violin. In his place, John Coltrane had emerged as the leading light of the avant-garde, his formidable quartet enjoying an acclaimed stint at Birdland in October 1963, before recording both *Crescent* and his masterpiece, *A Love Supreme*, in 1964.

A few weeks after his return to New York, *DownBeat*'s Ira Gitler asked Chet whether he had heard any of the 'new thingers' that had emerged in his absence. Chet admitted that he hadn't yet heard Ornette Coleman, and that he'd only heard John Coltrane on the turntable. He knew of Coltrane by reputation, however, and was not impressed by his lengthy solos. "Forty-five minutes is a long time to be blowing," he explained. "A lot of people get bugged. He gets hung up playing a little rhythmic figure, keeps on playing the same thing, just breaks up the time differently. I'd rather listen to Stan Getz or Al Cohn myself. But I've heard him play some things which are really beautiful."[5]

Chet also dropped in to see Charles Mingus play at the Five Spot in New York. "I went down there and wasn't impressed at all by what was happening," he said. "On the ensembles the things were ragged. Maybe it was because of the constant changing of things in the group. And Mingus was continually saying things and screaming at different personnel in the band."

He also felt that there was no real need to modify his playing style. "I think there's still a lot to be said within the framework of the standard tunes and standard progressions," he explained. "I don't say you shouldn't blow in those modal veins—they're interesting too—but I don't think you should do it hour after hour, every night." Even if he had dropped out of the *DownBeat* and *Metronome* critics' polls, Chet was convinced that his playing had improved during his stint in Europe. "I know I'm playing ten times better now," he said.[6]

Chet's first opportunity to prove his point came on the weekend of April 11th, when he landed a gig at the Cork 'n' Bib, a club on Long Island. The mother of Jim Coleman, an old family friend, was manager and part-owner of the club. "It was basically an Italian restaurant that had name jazz at the weekends," Jim Coleman recalled. "It was twenty-five miles from Manhattan and it was right on the Long Island railroad. The reason it existed was because of the stringent cabaret laws in New York that did not allow anyone with a drug conviction to work in any venue that was licensed, which was every jazz club and restaurant, of course. That meant that people like Billie Holiday, Chet Baker, played at the Cork 'n' Bib. Everybody and their uncle came out from New York City to see him."[7]

Maynard Ferguson had been playing at the club, and the owners made arrangements for his rhythm section to stay on at the club and support Chet.

Unfortunately, there was no time for a rehearsal. Pianist Mike Abene, bass player Ron McClure and drummer Tony Inzalco were all in their early twenties, and were not that familiar with Chet's repertoire. "He would call tunes we didn't know, and he wasn't easy to follow, because he didn't play very much," recalled McClure. "Mike Abene didn't know the changes to some of his tunes, so Chet would stop in the middle of a tune, sit at the piano, and point to some of the chords. He didn't really play piano, so when he sat down to play chords, it was a joke. He just knew that what Mike was playing wasn't what he wanted to hear. He was angry. It was a pretty painful weekend for us."[8]

Chet also had some problems of his own, particularly on the up-tempo numbers. "The closer was Parker's 'Now's The Time', taken way up," wrote Ira Gitler in *DownBeat* magazine. "The tempo again gave Baker trouble. Perhaps some of the difficulty was the result of playing a borrowed horn with a mouthpiece several sizes away from what he has been playing."[9]

Despite these difficulties, Ira Gitler reviewed Chet's comeback quite favourably. "He is less like Miles Davis than ever before, even though Davis traces crop up from time to time," he said. "Baker is also a much more virile, masculine player then he was before his European sojourn." He also noted the improvement in Chet's singing. "His vocal was soft but not as whispery as of old, with that good phrasing characteristic of instrumentalists who also sing."

Time magazine also gave the concert a good review, expressing optimism that Chet could overcome his problems. "The welcome Chet won was as enthusiastic as it was deserved. He looked pained when he played and downright wounded when he sang, but his music had a bright, aggressive gusto that made it better jazz than the music his fans remembered. Having marinated his art in misery, he seemed at last on a better road than the one he lost."[10]

The optimism proved to be misplaced, as Chet returned to a life of addiction in New York City. Tadd Dameron had started using again, and before long, Chet had joined him. "The next thing we knew, he was off to the pawnbroker to pawn his flugelhorn," recalled Dameron's wife, Mabel.

Chet persuaded Phil Urso, a fellow addict, to return to New York with a view to forming a new band. The saxophonist hired an up-and-coming pianist by the name of Chick Corea on piano. "We played the Cadillac Lounge (in Philadelphia) for two weeks," Urso later recalled. "At the club, two plain-clothes policemen beckoned Chet over to them, went to a dark corner of the room and put a flash light on his arms, so see if there were any marks on his arm. Finding none, they let him finish the night, but they were always asking Chet to step outside and have a talk with him … I call it blatant harassment."[11]

Such harassment helps to explain Chet's attitude towards the US authorities, and why he generally preferred to live in Europe, where he did not feel as though he was being persecuted. Even so, he felt determined not to let the police break his spirit. "Well, that's really the one thing they can't touch," he told Ira Gitler. "I made up my mind not to let it affect my playing in any way because, after all, that's the only thing I know how to do."[12]

It's not clear what rhythm section was used for the Philadelphia gig. Most likely it was bass player Jymie Merritt, best known for his stint with Art Blakey's Jazz Messengers, and drummer Charlie Rice; both were natives of Philadelphia, and part of the house band at the Cadillac Lounge. At the end of the engagement, Chet appears to have asked Charlie Rice to join them on the road. "He was on the first [sic] job I worked in the States when I came back—in Philadelphia," Chet wrote in the liner notes to an album recorded later that year. "When I formed my own band I hired him because I think he plays beautiful drums. He plays more like Kenny Clarke than any drummer I've ever heard. In fact, I think he plays as good as Kenny. He is one hell of a drummer and a real professional—he can do anything."[13]

He almost certainly asked Jymie Merritt to join the band, too. Unfortunately, Chick Corea was unable to join with Chet, presumably because of recording commitments in New York; he made an album with the Dave Pike Nonet on March 31st. "Chick only played for two weeks with us," Urso later confirmed.[14]

Throughout their two weeks in Philadelphia, Chet and Phil stayed in New York City. By that stage, Chet had found a room of his own in a housing project on 97th Street and Central Park West. "If we wanted to get a room and stay in Philadelphia, it was pretty expensive," said Urso. "So Chet says, 'Let's drive, it's only seventy miles'. So we drove back, and Chet stayed in his room. We left at about three in the afternoon each day to get back to Philadelphia, so we could have a little bite. That was a lot of fun."[15]

Chet was renting the apartment from Richard Carpenter, Tadd Dameron's manager. An imposing, overweight African–American with the mannerisms and street talk of a gangster, Carpenter had managed the careers of a number of prominent East Coast jazz musicians, including Lester Young, Sonny Stitt, Gene Ammons, Howard McGhee and Elmo Hope. Most of his clients were addicts, and he took advantage of many of them, who signed away their rights to royalties and compositions for a nominal cash payment.

The most famous case involved Jimmy Mundy, a tenor saxophonist and composer best known for his arrangements with Count Basie and Benny Goodman. Mundy had composed a tune called 'Gravy', the copyright of which was filed with the Library of Congress. Some years after his death, it was discovered that Carpenter had altered the copyright certificate, changing the name of the tune to 'Walkin'', and inserting his own name as composer. The tune became a jazz standard, and Carpenter, not Mundy, received all of the royalties.

More recently he had persuaded Dameron to sign over the royalties to all of his compositions as part of a management agreement, just days after Dameron's wedding ceremony. "We were signing stuff that we didn't understand," his wife later admitted.

On March 16th, he persuaded Chet to sign a similar contract. For the fee of just one dollar, Chet signed away his future royalties, with Carpenter promising him a new record deal. "Chet has a unique singing quality and we fully intend to expose this side of his talent so as to invade the pop field," he told *Melody Maker* of the UK. "There is no doubt in my mind that he can hit it big."

At first, Chet was quite happy with the arrangement. The apartment was big enough for Carol and Dean to join him in the United States, and Carpenter took care of the rent payments, giving him a daily cash allowance for drugs and food for his family. It was only after he started recording again, when he received no royalty payments, that he realised the mess he was in. "Richard Carpenter burned Sonny Stitt, he burned Gene Ammons, Sonny Rollins—he was burning everybody," recalled Phil Urso. "He wanted them to record, but he wanted a cut every time they recorded, because he made the connection for them. He was a crook, a class-A crook. He let Chet stay one floor below him so he could keep him near."[16]

Chet's new pianist, Hal Galper, quickly reached the same conclusion. "He was a bastard—one of the most rotten people in the business. He kept all of Chet's money, and kept Chet on a stipend," he said.

Chet appears to have played some gigs in the mid-West with Claude Thornhill around this time, playing with Phil Urso on tenor saxophone,

Kenny Lowe on piano, Jymie Merritt on bass and Charlie Rice on drums. Kenny Lowe only appears to have stayed for a short period, and by the time the band reached Boston in mid-May, they were looking for a new pianist.

"I was living in Boston at that time," Hal Galper remembered. "A friend of mine, Charlie LaChappelle, lived in Providence, Rhode Island, about an hour and fifteen minutes south of Boston. Chet was playing there at the Kings and Queens club. My friend called me and said that Chet's coming to Boston next week, and he's looking for a piano player. So I got every Chet Baker record I could find and learned his repertoire, and the first night he came into town, I was there first set. I said, 'I hear you're looking for a piano player'. He asked me to play and said, 'What tune do you want to play?' I said, 'Call any of them'. He really liked that, because he knew I'd done my research. I joined the band on the road. That was my first big-time gig."[17]

Chet was suitably impressed, and asked Galper to join the band. They had a recording session booked in New York, and a number of gigs booked across the country over the summer and beyond. Galper soon discovered the full extent of Chet's addiction when he spent a few days at Chet's apartment. "When I first got to New York, I stayed at his place," he later recalled. "I'd get up in the morning, walk into the kitchen, and he'd be standing there in pools of blood trying to find veins that hadn't collapsed yet to inject himself. That would be the first thing I'd see in the morning. I didn't stay there very long."[18]

A few days later, the band entered the recording studio to record Chet's 'comeback' album for the Colpix record label. The band primarily recorded Tadd Dameron tunes, including 'Soultrane'. This was not a blatant attempt to ride the coattails of John Coltrane, whose star had risen so dramatically in Chet's absence, nor was it an attempt to repay Tadd Dameron for his kind hospitality. It simply reflected the fact that the strings were being pulled by Richard Carpenter, who now 'owned' all the rights to Dameron's tunes. Carpenter is also dubiously credited with composing two tunes of his own, including 'Walkin''.

The highlights of the album are two originals by Hal Galper, 'Retsim B' ('Mister B') and 'Margerine'. Looking back, the pianist is not particularly happy with his own performance on the album. "I hated the way I played on that album—I was playing so far behind the beat," he said. "But the tunes I wrote, Chet played all though his life, for the rest of his career. He must have recorded those tunes fifty times for me, which was really nice. At one point

I was playing with him at an outdoor festival in Italy; it was a trio with me, Chet and Jacques Pelzer on flute—how weird that was. Chet's sitting behind me on this chair, and he announces we're going to play 'Margerine'. In *sotto voce* I leaned over and said, 'Yeah, in Oleo! (Another word for oil, also the title of a famous composition by Sonny Rollins).' Chet turned around to me and said, 'Gee, I never got that!' Thirty years of playing it, and he never got it was a pun."[19]

The record label was not clear whether the album would be released that year, or in early 1965, so Richard Carpenter gave it the preposterous title of *The Most Important Jazz Album of 1964/65*. That title arguably belonged to John Coltrane's *A Love Supreme*, recorded in December 1964. But other important changes were taking place with jazz at this time, most notably the growing popularity of bossa nova, thanks in large part to the recordings of Chet's old West Coast rival, Stan Getz.

Even within the confines of jazz trumpet, there were far more significant releases at that time: Lee Morgan had just unveiled his soul-jazz classic *The Sidewinder*, whilst Freddie Hubbard was beginning to flirt with the avant-garde on *Breaking Point*, inspired by his collaboration with Eric Dolphy on *Out to Lunch* in February 1964. Miles Davis wasn't to be left out, either; having experimented with a variety of musicians in the preceding two years, he was on the verge of unveiling his new quintet, featuring Wayne Shorter on tenor saxophone and Herbie Hancock on piano.

Such developments left Chet's new album sounding distinctly old-fashioned, a point not lost on the jazz critics. "It's difficult to get excited over the Baker crew's rewarming of old hash," wrote Pete Welding in *DownBeat* magazine. "What Baker and colleagues are saying here has been said countless times before, with far greater force and conviction."[20]

After the completion of the album, the band went away on tour, starting with a two-week stint at the Jazz Workshop in San Francisco, starting on 2nd June. Pianist Hal Galper, the youngest member of the band, remembers the tour provided him with a steep learning curve. "I learned so much from playing with Chet," he recalled. "He was quite the task-master. And thank goodness he was, because I learned how to swing hot and play light from him. He was the master of that. And how to use self-control. I learned so much from his, it was ridiculous; and yet he didn't know the name of a single note, he was a totally intuitive musician. That's how you learn; you play with these guys night after night, and they tell you, 'No, no, no!' until you get it."[21]

Galper learned the hard way how to play softly behind Chet. "I think it was Chicago," he said. "I was playing with Chet and he was singing a ballad. The place was really packed and everyone was quiet. You know Chet's into soft, so I'm comping with my foot on the soft pedal, hardly hitting the keys at all. Everything was fine until I hit one chord a little bit too loud. Then Chet just stopped. He turned around and screamed, 'You got it!' I mean you either learned how to play soft, or he was going to embarrass you to death."[22]

In early July, Richard Carpenter appears to have arranged for Chet to play at the Newport Jazz Festival, where he appeared as a guest of Stan Getz. Whilst Chet was struggling to re-establish himself back in the United States, Getz was on a roll, having recorded a series of hugely popular bossa nova albums including *Jazz Samba* (1962), *Big Band Bossa Nova* (1962), *Jazz Samba Encore* (1963) and *Getz/Gilberto* (1963). The last of these recordings featured the smash hit 'The Girl from Ipanema', sung by Astrud Gilberto, the young wife of the Brazilian guitarist and singer João Gilberto.

The vibraphonist Gary Burton was in Stan Getz's band at this time, and remembers Chet as a quiet, unassuming man. "He didn't say much, just played and was kind of shy in the presence of Stan who had become a major star in jazz at that time," he said.[23]

This was Chet's first festival appearance in his home country for many years, and he was understandably nervous before the show. In the event, he played well, and his appearance was warmly received by both the crowd and the jazz critics. "He came onstage hesitantly, looking gaunt, anxious and much too pale, stepped up to the mike and nervously placed his flugelhorn to his lips," wrote *Jazz Journal*. "But when he started to play there was nothing hesitant about his music. Despite many years absence and his various troubles, Baker if possible sounded better than ever. His tone is mature and definite and he more than lived up to the expectations of the audience. He also sang a chorus in that delightfully off-beat voice of his. Although dressed in a rather dashing pair of bright red slacks and navy blazer, Chet still looked like a little boy lost when he stepped back from the microphone and acknowledged the applause with a slight inclination of his head before he quietly walked off stage."[24]

Back in New York, the relationship between Chet and Carol Jackson had become somewhat strained. Despite regular hints that she wanted to get married, Chet had made no effort to track down his second wife, Halema, to secure a divorce. It didn't help that Chet still attracted a large number of female admirers. "I remember one gig in Chicago, one girl came in front of the bandstand and lifted her dress up in front of Chet," recalled Hal Galper. "Carol always used to be so jealous. She didn't need to be, because he was so full of heroin, he couldn't get a hard on if he tried. The last thing he was interested in was women. He didn't screw her either!"[25]

Matters were made worse by the fact that Phil Urso had moved into their 97th Street apartment. "I had my own sofa—that was my bed—and Chet and Carol had their own room," he recalled. "I could shower any time I needed, but I had to go out to be by myself, and to take care of myself. Carol did a little cooking, but she cooked mostly for Chet. It's not that she didn't want me there; I ate with them a lot of times. Carol treated me very well, she liked me."[26]

Still, there were times when Chet and Carol would have preferred some privacy. "Phil would think nothing of throwing open our bedroom door at 4 o'clock in the morning to play something he had just written," Carol said. "Once Chet told him he would 'kick his fucking ass' if he knocked again. Chet loved Phil, but he also loved to sleep."[27]

Sleep was the least of the problems with their domestic arrangements. Chet and Phil were both addicts, and according to Hal Galper, they used to pool their funds to buy heroin, leaving Carol struggling to support the family. Richard Carpenter also made Chet's life a misery at this time, taking pleasure from watching Chet and Phil beg for their weekly allowance, meanwhile keeping the bulk of the royalties from their recent recording for himself.

When Chet's old friend from the West Coast, Hersh Hamel, paid a visit to New York, he noticed that Chet was struggling to make ends meet, even with regular gigs across the country. "Carol was having a terrible time," he recalled, "moaning and groaning about not having enough money."[28]

Times were tough for Chet's parents back in California, too. A letter sent from Vera to Chet at this time revealed that Chesney Sr had just lost his job. "I doubt if he will have another job, he is 58 (and) it's pretty hard to find anything at that age, so will [sic] have to try to get by on my salary."[29]

She also warned Chet that the FBI had visited her on two occasions, asking about the article that had appeared in the magazine *Hush Hush*. She does not seem to have been aware that the allegations in the story had been about Chet's drug use. "He didn't tell us what it was about, but I thought you had said something about earning so much money and maybe he was investigating income tax."[30]

Vera also played on Chet's feelings of guilt over his first child. Halema had stayed with Chet's parents after leaving Chet, and Chesney Aftab visited them on a regular basis. "He is a sweet boy. He has terrible mood swings, tho', he can be happy one minute, the next he is mad. He misses having a daddy, after talking to you he probably tells all his boy friends about talking to you." She also adds, quite pointedly, "He doesn't have a watch."[31]

September 1964 brought a possible solution to their financial woes when somebody—possibly Dick Bock—proposed a reunion of the Gerry Mulligan Quartet. The reunion was expected to be a major concert draw, and the Hollywood Bowl was booked for 4th September, with the Miles Davis Quintet also booked for the occasion. A television appearance was also scheduled for the Steve Allen Show on 17th September, although the band may have been taped before the programme was shown.

In the event, the planned reunion never took place, apparently because of a dispute over money. Art Farmer ended up taking Chet's place, both for the concert and the TV appearance, and no further attempts were made to reunite the quartet for another ten years.

With no gigs for a few weeks, Merritt and Rice left the band at this time. Pianist Hal Galper seized this opportunity to ask Chet if he could hire more modern-sounding musicians. "When I first joined the band he had Jymie Merritt and Charlie Rice as a rhythm section," he recalled. "A very bebop, laid-back-groove rhythm section. While Chet was away, on-top-of-the-beat playing had come into fashion. I couldn't play dotted-eighth-sixteenth so I convinced him to let me get a young rhythm section. I got Steve Ellington and Mike Fleming. We were kicking ass, let me tell you."

New recruit Michael Fleming was given a baptism by fire as Chet announced they would drive from Boston to Los Angeles in three days, with Chet scheduled to open at Shelly's Manne-Hole on 8th October. "Three days is unheard of for that trip," he laughed. "No ordinary person would have tried it."

Chet drove at breakneck speeds the entire journey, never afraid to overtake, even with a hill or bend approaching. "At the end of the road would be a hill, and a line of about twelve cars," the bass player recalled. "We're number thirteen. Now we're number six, number five. There might be something coming over the hill, you can't see. Sure enough, here comes a car. You're saying, this isn't happening!"[32]

Fleming has suggested that Chet was becoming unreliable by this time, occasionally nodding out from heroin on the bandstand. For the most part, however, his playing was still superb. "He played great live, just unbelievable," said Hal Galper. "Even when he played bad he was playing great! He never repeated—he was a true improviser. He was a real natural."[33]

Mid-October saw the band return to San Francisco, where they took over from Stan Getz at the Jazz Workshop. The tour was originally supposed to have featured João Gilberto, but he had dropped out at the last moment, citing cramp in his playing arm. According to *Time* magazine, "Astrud replaced him and suddenly found herself a star. Astrud is herself a girl from Ipanema, a section of Rio de Janeiro's sparkling beach front, who came to the U.S. two years ago with João. Last week, with the single edition of 'The Girl from Ipanema' burning up the teen-age record market, Astrud Gilberto was trying to get used to her new billing—at least to the extent of trying to add to her six-song repertory."[34]

Astrud Gilberto had a couple of days off before the band's next engagement, and decided to stay on in San Francisco for one extra night to catch a glimpse of Chet Baker, her idol from her teenage years. She tells the story on her website:

"I sat by myself, at a very discreet table towards the back of the room. At some point, Chet made an announcement. 'I'd like to acknowledge the presence here of a celebrity, a very special young lady' … I, along with everybody else in the audience, started to look around to see who was this celebrity. Then Chet says, 'Ms. Gilberto, would you care to join us for a song?' What??? ME? LITTLE ME? Oh, my God! I thought my knees were going to let me down. I was terrified and, as much as I was flattered, would have given anything to be able to run away and hide … But, that would have been impolite and unacceptable … So, I walked on stage. Quickly, it went through my mind: 'what could I possible sing? Of course they are not going to know any of my Brazilian repertoire …'

"So, real quickly, God inspired me: 'I know what! I'll say "Fly Me To The Moon"; I know the lyrics and I'm sure they'll know the music.' So, I said, meekly, to Chet, 'Can we do "Fly me to the Moon"?' He said, 'Sure!' I said, 'Can we do it in bossa nova?' He consulted with the drummer, then said, 'Yes.' So, we did it! Only God knows what came out, as I was overwhelmed with nervousness, stemming not only from the already familiar 'regular' stage fright, but also from the ultimate intimidation—to sing with my long time idol!!!"[35]

According to Gary Burton, who was also in the audience that evening, it was Astrud Gilberto that asked Chet if she could join him on stage, rather than a surprise announcement. "Chet was playing well and the group was nice. The evening was marred by Astrud Gilberto asking if she could sit in and sing a few tunes. Chet reluctantly agreed and it was disastrous. Astrud had no clue about how to sing in a jazz setting, knew almost no tunes, and expected Chet and his group to essentially accompany her doing the few songs she knew. Most people don't know that when Astrud started singing, she knew no repertoire. For the six months she toured with Stan, she had learned three tunes, which she sang each night. A real beginner. Anyway, it was painful to watch and I was embarrassed to even know her. She didn't know I was in the audience, and I slumped in my chair in the back to remain anonymous. Chet was patient and after a couple of awful, strained efforts to get through some pieces without losing it, he got her off the stage and they resumed their set."[36]

After the Jazz Workshop gig, Chet fired the drummer Steve Ellington, having struggled to adjust to his style of playing. "Steve Ellington played on top of the beat," recalled Hal Galper, "but Chet was from the old school, behind the beat, that laid-back groove thing." In his place he rehired Charlie Rice.

On the way back to New York, Chet and Carol finally got married. She was keen to have more children, and had been pushing Chet for months to finalise his divorce from Halema, and make things legal. They stopped off in Reno and exchanged vows in front of a Justice of the Peace on October 28th 1964, with Phil Urso acting as best man. Unfortunately, they later discovered that Chet's divorce had not yet been finalised, and had to repeat the ceremony in Las Vegas the following year, this time with Chet's father as best man. By that stage, Carol was heavily pregnant with their second child.

There was no time for a honeymoon. Chet returned to New York, where Richard Carpenter had lined up another recording session, this time for the Limelight record label, a new division of Mercury Records. Alto saxophonist Frank Strozier was added to the quintet for the recording, having previously worked with Roy Haynes' quartet.

Richard Carpenter insisted on more emphasis being placed on Chet's singing this time around. He enlisted the help of Bobby Scott, a pianist and singer who had worked with Louis Prima, Gene Krupa and Tony Scott, as well as leading his own group in New York. Outside of jazz he had also enjoyed success in the pop charts, recording a version of 'Chain Gang' in 1956. Scott was also a composer and arranger, having won a Grammy award for Best Instrumental Composition for a song called 'A Taste of Honey', which was used in a Broadway production of the same name; the song had also appeared on the debut album by The Beatles. Carpenter suggested that Chet record the song, implying he still believed he could crack the 'crossover' market, just as Stan Getz had done with his bossa nova recordings.

As with Chet's previous album, *The Most Important Jazz Album of 1964/65*, Carpenter also had his eye on the royalty cheques. Carpenter is credited with composing two tracks on the album, 'Baby Breeze' and 'Comin' Down'; in both cases, the songs were arranged by Phil Urso, suggesting that the saxophonist may well have composed the tunes himself, and allowed Carpenter to claim credit in return for a cash payment. Another track, 'Ev'rything Depends on You' was co-written by Carpenter's brother Charlie, apparently in conjunction with Louis Dunlap and the pianist Earl Hines.

Three of Hal Galper's compositions were included on the album, including 'This Is The Thing' and 'One With One'. He was happier with his own playing on this album. "I played better on *Baby Breeze*, I thought. By then, my chops were in pretty good shape, having been on the road and played with the band, and everything." He does recall arguing with Phil Urso during the making of the album, however. "Phil stole a bunch of stuff from me!" he claimed. "On the *Baby Breeze* album there's a tune called 'This Is the Thing,' and it was based on the changes to 'What Is This Thing Called Love'. There's a certain kind of triadic motion that Phil had not been used to. I had an exercise that I used to work on to get through the tune. He heard me working on that one night, and asked me what it was, so I showed it to him. When we got to the record date, of course the tenor player solos before the piano player. I'll be damned if he doesn't use it on his solo, so I couldn't use it!"[37]

Hal Galper only plays on half of the album, with Chet opting to use Bobby Scott or Bob James on a number of tunes, predominantly the vocal recordings. As Chet wrote in the liner notes to the album, "I like the way he (Galper) plays and I like the way he writes. But we had certain difficulties when it came to vocal accompaniments, which is something different altogether."

Hal Galper left the band shortly after the album was finished, suggesting he was upset over the incident. Looking back, however, he felt he learned a great deal from the experience. "Chet didn't think I could comp for him good—so he did the vocals with Bob James," he said. "But I'll tell you what, I learned how to comp with Chet." Although the two musicians had little in common off the bandstand, they maintained a mutual respect, and continued to work together on an occasional basis. "Chet Baker stands out as one of the greats," Galper said, looking back. "He was a true jazz musician. He really could play. He was better than everyone else. He wasn't that great a technician, but who cares. Miles wasn't that great a technician, either. Chet was a romantic player, even if there wasn't a romantic bone in his body!"[38]

The album was released as *Baby Breeze* in the spring of 1965. The album received more favourable reviews than its predecessor, with *DownBeat* awarding the album three-and-a-half stars, and highlighting Chet's "lyrics and lyricism" as the distinguishing features of the album. "Taking the instrumentals first, Baker uses flugelhorn exclusively, and the depth of its tone equals the depth of Baker's conception." Chet also sings with greater confidence than on his earlier Pacific Jazz recordings, as his vocal on 'Born to be Blue' and 'You're Mine, You' clearly illustrate. "As for Baker's vocals, this album is worth adding to one's collection just to hear how he lavishes loving care on word and phrasing," wrote Harvey Siders. "Baker's critics still complain about the lack of virility in his singing. What they overlook too easily is the wealth of feeling he projects."[39]

Whilst *Baby Breeze* is a fine album in its own right, it was hard for critics and radio stations to categorise the album. It was clearly not cutting-edge, like the music of John Coltrane, who recorded *A Love Supreme* just one month later, in December 1964. And despite the best efforts of Richard Carpenter and Bobby Scott, the album was not a hit with the fans of pop music; it lacked the cool sophistication associated with bossa nova, or the funky, danceable sound that characterised soul jazz hits such as Lee Morgan's 'The Sidewinder'. As a consequence, the album did not sell particularly well, and the label suggested a change of format for his next recording.

Phil Urso took the decision to leave the group in early 1965. According to the sleevenotes to *Baby Breeze*, he returned to live in Denver, Colorado. In a lengthy interview with Denver Westword, published in 1999, he claimed that he left the band because of Chet's drug use was getting out of hand. "I knew what was gonna happen," Urso said. "They were all gonna get high. Chet started to self-destruct. I didn't want to try and keep up with him."[40]

Alto saxophonist Frank Strozier replaced Phil Urso in the band. They may also have been joined by Chet's old friend from Belgium, Jacques Pelzer, who apparently toured with Chet for several weeks in the spring of 1965. The only confirmed date, however, was that he played at the Plugged Nickel in Chicago from 24th March to the 4th April. The lack of concert listings suggest that work was beginning to dry up for Chet; this was partly a function of the decline in popularity of jazz, with younger listeners increasingly drawn to popular music. Chet may also have missed Phil Urso's organisational skills, since he was most likely responsible for a number of the band's booking the previous year. Comments by Mike Fleming and Phil Urso himself suggest that Chet's reputation may also have been a factor, with club owners unwilling to take a risk on a musician that was considered unreliable.

By the time the band returned to New York in April 1965, they had fallen apart. Richard Carpenter had negotiated another album with Limelight Records, proposing that Chet record an album of Billie Holiday songs. Whilst Chet professes his admiration for Lady Day's unique and intimate vocal style in the sleevenotes, one cannot help but feel that this was not a project close to his heart. Rather, it had all the hallmarks of a Richard Carpenter production; a 'big band' that was relatively small in scale, in order to keep the costs down, and arrangements by one of his regular collaborators, Jimmy Mundy, who was no doubt also kept on a stipend.

Chet Baker, during the recording of Baker's Holiday, *April 1965.*

Baker's Holiday was released in November 1965 to mixed reviews. *DownBeat*'s Don Nelson praised Chet for the "delicacy with which he interprets melody. He is more sensitive to the lyrical, to the tender sad-eyed connotations of a ballad. He is the best kind of romantic." Still, the album did nothing to alter the perception that Chet's best days were behind him, and by the time of its release, Carpenter had given up on Chet re-establishing himself as a major star, and he stopped paying rent on his 97th Street apartment.

Even before the release of *Baker's Holiday*, Limelight had expressed reservations about recording another album with Chet Baker. With precious little money coming in from royalty payments, and still being pestered on a near daily basis for drug money, Carpenter made a decision to squeeze as much material from his employee as possible, before dropping him altogether as a client.

Carpenter booked the recording studio at Englewood Cliffs in New Jersey for three days, and booked the Detroit-based rhythm section of Roy Brooks on drums and Herman Wright on bass. Roy Brooks suggested he hire Kirk Lightsey, an old friend of his from Detroit, on piano. "I was conducting for Damita Joe, who was playing at Club Harlem in Atlantic City," Lightsey remembers. "Because of an accident to the drummer, Roy Brooks was filling in. He and I were travelling from Atlantic City to New York every day. After we'd get off from work in Atlantic City, we'd get some sleep, get up early in the morning, ride a bus to New York, get to the studio, and go back to sleep. And then we'd have some food and start the session."

Tenor saxophonist George Coleman completed the line-up. Coleman had been playing with Miles Davis until mid-1964, and eventually left claiming a shortage of regular work and late wage payments by the bandleader. In all likelihood, Coleman was also uncomfortable with the more experimental direction the band was taking. Since leaving the band, Coleman had remained active, having just recorded 'Maiden Voyage' with his former colleague Herbie Hancock.

Chet clearly had no idea of Richard Carpenter's plans to drop him as an artist. He seemed more enthused over this project, which surrounded him with a driving, hard bop-oriented band, than he had been over the big-band-oriented Billie Holiday tribute. As Kirk Lightsey later recalled, he even got the studio early most days to warm up, something that he rarely did, even in the early years. "He was in good shape," he said. "You couldn't tell there was anything wrong at all. Like Dexter Gordon would say when he was asked how he could play when he was so drunk, or so high: "Well, I practice like that!"[41]

On paper, Chet Baker and George Coleman made an unlikely pairing, but as noted previously, Chet's playing had acquired a lustier tone since his European travels, and they adapted well to each other's styles. Although they'd never previously met, Lightsey remembers the two of them hitting it off quite quickly. "George and Chet played together like they'd been married for years and years," he said. "They brought out the best in one another. It was a really good date." Coleman later admitted that he primarily knew of Chet as a ballad singer before the session. "I had no idea he could play like that," he said. "His placement of notes—I was very excited about that. And when he had to go up high, he could do that too—not extremely high, but higher than you would expect from a guy who played like he did, in the middle register."

The sessions were fairly disorganised, according to Kirk Lightsey. "We didn't know what was coming up," he said. "There was no real rehearsal; we would run it down one time, then we'd tape it. During that time, the composer of the songs was in the control booth, writing the next song while we were recording the song before." The composer was Carpenter cohort, Jimmy Mundy, although many of the tunes were later credited, or co-credited, to Carpenter himself.

The young rhythm section was not aware of Carpenter's reputation at that time, although in retrospect they felt they were paid very little for the vast number of tunes recorded—a total of five albums worth of material recorded over just three days. "The word is that Chet didn't get paid in money for these dates; Richard Carpenter had a deal with Chet, I guess," said Lightsey. "Carpenter was there every day. He was OK in the studio; he didn't get in anybody's way, he didn't take money from any of us. He did what he said he was going to do; we made a deal, and he came up with it."[42]

After recording these albums, Richard Carpenter appears to have lost interest in Chet Baker altogether, giving up on his dream of achieving pop success. Some weeks later he apparently stopped paying the rent on Chet's apartment.

On November 11th, Carol Baker gave birth to a dark-haired baby boy, Paul Baker. Two weeks later, Chet left New York for Los Angeles, packing his family and their meagre possessions into his Dodge station wagon to start a new life. In later years, he would tell interviewers that he was desperate to escape 'bean counters' like Carpenter, and that the final straw came when he saw a copy of one of his new albums, released without his knowledge, in a record store window.

The reality is that Chet was finally evicted from his apartment. Frantic phone calls to Richard Carpenter went unanswered, and Chet finally realised the full extent of his problems. He had no more cash than when he had returned to New York, eighteen months earlier. He had a young family to support, but work was drying up, and his manager was no longer paying his rent or allowance. “If I hadn’t been sick at the time, it never would have happened,” he later claimed.[43]

Richard Carpenter sold the master tapes of the August 1965 recording sessions to Prestige Records. The five albums were released over the subsequent two years, with precious little publicity. The albums were given names like *Smokin'*, *Groovin'* and *Boppin'*, clearly aimed at reminding jazz fans of the legendary Miles Davis sessions recorded for the same label in 1956.

The records deserved a better fate than this, although it’s fair to note that the material is spread a little thin; less greed from both Richard Carpenter and Prestige Records, together with more judicious editing, would have resulted in two or three excellent records, rather than the five good, but patchy, LPs that were released. Sadly, they were to be Chet’s last worthwhile studio recordings for several years.

Rather than being back from the ‘dark side’, as *Time* magazine had suggested, he found himself driving towards it, at high speed.

Chapter Twelve

BLOOD, CHET AND TEARS
1965–1972

"When I left England for France, I knew something had changed. I could feel it in my bones, but I refused to believe it, I was so terrified of getting hooked again."—Chet Baker[1]

Los Angeles had changed considerably from the city Chet had left eight years earlier. The airwaves were now dominated by rock and roll, rather than jazz, and the West Coast sound was now considered to be the Beach Boys, who had enjoyed smash hits that year with singles such as 'Help Me, Rhonda' and 'California Girls'. The jazz scene had been in gradual decline for a number of years. Many of the old clubs had changed hands or closed down, and whilst venues as The Lighthouse were still in existence, the Lighthouse All-Stars no longer attracted the big names, and crowds no longer flocked from the beach to hear the Sunday afternoon jam sessions.

In the words of Ted Gioia, author of *West Coast Jazz*, "the West Coast experiment that finally ran out of steam in the early sixties did not die for any lack of musical paths left to explore. Nor was it the hostile critics who killed the music. Economics and rock and roll, television sets and closing nightclubs, layoffs in the Los Angeles aerospace industry, the increase in attractive studio music jobs, the rising costs of providing live music, the growth of a Las Vegas entertainment establishment that lured audiences and artists away from California while bidding up the fees paid for major acts—these are what did in West Coast jazz."

The economic changes that Gioia refers to had their toll on Chet's family. Chet's father, Chesney Sr, had struggled to hang on to a job for a number of years since losing his job in the aerospace industry. Around the time that his son returned to Los Angeles, he had just found night work as a security guard for a construction company. Vera, his wife, continued to work at

W.T. Grants, but was wondering how they could survive in California after she had stopped working.

Vera's relationship with Chet had become increasingly strained over the years. For many years she had lived her life vicariously through her son, and when he strayed from the path that she had mapped out for him, she held him accountable. "It's hard for me to write what I feel, but I have been a very unhappy person the last seven years. Yet I had to go on every day to work and smile to the people like I was a happy person, when on the inside my heart was breaking … " She even goes as far as to suggest Chet no longer called her while she was at work, in case anyone associated the two of them. "Chettie, I wanted to explain why I can't take your calls at the store. For one thing I am afraid someone in the office might be listening in, and besides I get so scared I just start shaking … I would rather no-one at the store know any of my business."[2]

Her letters are cold and calculating, and it is clear that Chet never had the benefit of a warm, loving relationship with either of his parents. It may also help to explain why Chet found it difficult to form a close relationship with his own children; not only was his lifestyle inconducive to fatherhood, but also he had never known his own parents to set a good example. After all, what mother signs off a letter to her son, hoping that he is "fine, healthy, and wiser"?

The manipulative nature of her tone also suggests that Chet inherited elements of his own behaviour, particularly when it came to procuring drugs, from his own mother.

The atmosphere must have been tense when Chet and his young family moved into his parents' house at 129 West Hillcrest Boulevard in Inglewood. Chesney Sr was at home during the day, but was drinking heavily, and when Vera returned home from work, she nagged her son, asking him why he wasn't working, and pushing him to find a place of his own.

Chet called his old friend Dick Bock, from Pacific Jazz, and asked him if he had any studio work. Bock had renamed the label World Pacific in 1958, in an attempt to broaden its appeal, but with sales dwindling, he finally agreed to sell the label to Liberty Records earlier that year. He continued to run the label on behalf of the parent company, but was desperately searching for ways to boost sales. He had enjoyed modest success tapping into the bossa nova scene, recording a number of samba-influenced albums with artists such as Bud Shank, including *Brasamba!*

(1963). More recently he had hit upon the notion of targeting the growing popularity of 'muzak' or 'easy listening'—bland, instrumental versions of popular songs, often overlaid with heavy-handed string arrangements.

One such album was Bud Shank's *Michelle*, which consisted of recent pop hits by the likes of the The Beatles, The Byrds, and The Mamas and the Papas, arranged by conductor Bob Florence. Drenched in saccharine strings and given a choral backing, it proved to be a surprise hit, reaching #54 on the US album charts. Bock invited Chet to take part in the recording session in December 1965 in return for a small cash payment. "Chet showed up late, and wanted to borrow twenty dollars," Shank later recalled. "Past that, everything was all right. He did exactly what he had to do and did it well."

Around the same time, Bock also asked Chet to contribute to a similar style album by the jazz guitarist Joe Pass, entitled *A Sign of the Times*. Once again, the album was arranged by Bob Florence, and included recent hits by The Beatles ('Nowhere Man') and Frank Sinatra ('It Was a Very Good Year').

Bock was encouraged that Chet had not lost his chops, and invited him to sign a new recording contract. He was hoping to cash in on the success of Mexican-style pop of Herb Alpert's Tijuana Brass, whose fourth LP, *Whipped Cream and Other Delights*, had sold over six million copies that year. Ironically, one of the hit singles from the album was a version of 'A Taste of Honey', which had appeared on Baker's own album *Baby Breeze*.

His plan was to ask Chet to front a Mexican-style band of his own, named The Mariachi Brass. He asked his colleague, Bud Dain, to assemble a studio band, and Dain approached the arranger Jack Nitzsche to ask for his help. Nitzsche, who had worked with the likes of Phil Spector and Jackie DeShannon, knew many of the finest local studio musicians, and was able to assemble a strong line up, including guitarist Al Casey, bass player Lyle Ritz, drummer Frank Capp and a horn section consisting of Roy Caton, Lou Blackburn and Lew McCreary. The team played safe with their choice of material, picking well-known recent pop hits that fitted the jaunty, upbeat concept. Bock, Dain and Nitzsche decided to record a mixture of recent pop hits, including 'The Champs' 'Tequila' and Gene Pitney's 'Twenty Four Hours from Tulsa', which were given a latin-style makeover, together with Mexican-style tunes such as 'Speedy Gonzales' and 'La Bamba'.

The resulting album, *A Taste of Tequila*, was derided by the jazz press, with *DownBeat* accusing Baker of "sounding as if he's on the point of collapse". It's no jazz album, certainly, but as easy listening records go, it has its moments; Nitzsche's arrangements give the recording a less anaemic feel than many of the Tijuana Brass albums, and it's interesting to note that it received quite warm reviews when it was finally released on CD in 2006.[3]

It was certainly a sign of the times that some of the finest names in West Coast jazz were reduced to recording easy-listening style albums by the mid-1960s, just ten years on from the peak of its popularity, when Gerry Mulligan, Chet Baker and Dave Brubeck were the subject of articles in *Time* magazine. Looking back, Bud Shank passionately defended his studio work at this time. "You have to eat. You have to survive," he told Roger Cotterrell. "When I became a full-time studio musician, I had been unemployed for a long time since jazz music left us in 1962–63 or whenever. At that time, I don't think any of us realised what was going on, but some American jazz musicians ended up in Europe, some gave up playing altogether, some went off into never-never land by whatever chemical they could find, and then there were some others who went into another business. That's what I did. I went into another business using the tools I had, which was playing the flute and the saxophone. Consider that a copout? No I don't."[4]

Chet was in a similar position, although he had a habit to feed as well as his family. Going back to Europe was not an option for him at this time as he was still barred from entering a number of countries, including Germany, Italy and Switzerland. In the meantime he had to scrape a living any way he could, even if that meant recording albums he was not proud of.

Chet's old friend, the drummer Shelly Manne, offered him a gig at Shelly's Manne-Hole, the club he had opened in Hollywood in 1960. Chet played there for three nights before Christmas in December 1965 as part of a quartet, although the other members of the band are unknown.

A fourth date was scheduled for 3rd January, although it is not clear whether Chet appeared. On December 27th, just a few weeks after his return to Los Angeles, he was arrested in Hermosa Beach for forging a prescription. He was given three years' probation, despite his previous drug-related offences.

Chet managed to put enough money aside from the studio work to move out of his parents' house in Inglewood to rent a small house in Spreckles Lane in Redondo Beach. Within a couple of weeks he was arrested a second time for forging prescriptions, this time in Culver City. Carol did not have enough cash to pay for Chet's bail, and desperately called a number of Chet's old friends, asking for help.

Help came from an unlikely source—the bass player Bob Whitlock, who had last played with Chet back in 1955. Since they had last played together, Whitlock had worked for more than five years with pianist George Shearing. He continued to struggle with heroin addiction, however, which eventually cost him his job. "After that, I had gotten out of the jazz mainstream, but I was comfortable, making a good living," he recalled. "I got a call one day from Carol, his wife, and she informed me that he was being held in the Los Angeles County Jail, and wondered if I could help. So I drove over to see her. She had these two little kids, and I felt really sorry for her."[5]

Bail was set at several hundred dollars, a sum that Whitlock could ill afford. He drove to Hollywood, and went to Shelly Manne's club to ask if he could help. "Shelly was a beautiful guy, a prince," said Whitlock. "I told Shelly that Chet needed to get bailed out, that he was miserable and really sick. Shelly gave me a thousand bucks, and when I left said, 'Don't worry about it, maybe you guys can just come over and play some time'. That's some kind of guy; I had nothing but respect for Shelly."[6]

Bob Whitlock soon discovered why Chet was still forging prescriptions, despite being out on bail. He was not only scoring for himself, but also for his wife. "Carol was hooked at that time, too," he said. "I didn't know that when she called me. Chet had been hooked for years, of course, but I didn't know that she was. She wasn't using as much as he was, but she was most definitely using."

Carol tried to deny this story in later years, but a number of acquaintances were aware of the issue. Micheline Pelzer, daughter of Jacques Pelzer, heard from her father that Carol's addiction dated back to early 1965. "When my father toured with Chet in the spring, she was already hooked," she recalled. Saxophonist Bob Mover also verified the story, claiming that Carol once told him she had a bigger habit than Chet himself.

Sandy Jones, Bill Loughborough's girlfriend in the late 1960s, later claimed that Chet encouraged Carol to take drugs to get her off his back. "Chet told me the reason he turned her on to heroin was because he absolutely could not stand her being a bitch any longer," she said. It is also possible that Carol felt that getting high was the only way she could stay close to Chet, given his ongoing dependency.[7]

After helping him to raise bail money, Bob Whitlock started to spend more time with Chet. "We started going to doctors' offices, telling them we had trigeminal neuralgia or kidney stones," he recalled. "We'd take a little vial of blood in with us to these places. When they'd leave us alone to take a urine sample, we'd take this little vial and drop a teeny bit of blood into it. Naturally, when the doctor got the results back he'd see the blood, and that would indicate there was a stone. It was almost miraculous the way that would work. Trigeminal neuralgia is a kind of facial neuralgia that's very difficult to diagnose. The treatment for it can be more detrimental than the disease itself; people who have it sometimes have one of the nerves snipped, and their whole face drops. It was a perfect kind of scam, because the pain is notorious, and if the doctor has any indication that this is what you have, he's going to write you some kind of pain medication, and usually that means delodin, morphine or numorphan, or one of those very powerful drugs. We managed very well, seeing a lot of doctors."[8]

Dick Bock still managed to find occasional studio work for Chet at this time. In the spring of 1966, he invited him to record a second Mariachi Brass LP. The first album had been a modest success so the Pacific Jazz A&R team assembled another strong line-up of session musicians, including guitarist Herb Ellis and percussionist Victor Feldman. The resulting album, *Hats Off*, was less successful than its predecessor. This partly reflects the formulaic nature of the sound, but also the fact that the bulk of the arrangements were handled by George Tipton, rather than Jack Nitzsche. Don Nelson in *DownBeat* gave the LP a no-star rating, calling it 'a loser' and 'a wipeout'.[9]

Chet was also invited to contribute to Bud Shank's new album, *California Dreamin'*. As the name suggests, it was another album of easy listening, in the same vein as *Michelle*, again arranged by Bob Florence in his inimitable style.

Still on the lookout for a winning formula for the 'crossover' market, Dick Bock suggested that Chet try his hand at another new format—an album of 'mood' music, or 'muzak', backed by a string section. On the sleeve notes to *Quietly There*, the first of Chet Baker's recordings with the Carmel Strings, *DownBeat* magazine's John Tynan suggests that Chet's romantic style is well-suited to recording with strings, suggesting echoes of his 1953–1954 recording with Pacific Jazz. His colleague, Pete Welding, was rather closer to the mark. "Rarely … has Baker sounded as flaccid as he does against the keening strings and choral ooh-ings and aah-ings of these performances. He's a shade out of tune, too, for added drama."[10]

Chet was not entirely lost to jazz at this time, and was still able to secure the occasional gig. On 20th February, he landed a gig at the Edgewater Marina in Long Beach, with a pick-up rhythm section that included Colin Bailey on drums. Colin Bailey's recording career started in 1962, with Vince Guaraldi's *Jazz Impressions of Black Orpheus*, and in 1965 he recorded *A Charlie Brown Christmas* with the Vince Guaraldi Trio, which was one of the most successful Christmas albums of all time.

"The first gig I played with him was a Sunday afternoon gig; I remember it very well," he later recalled. "The guy who booked the gig hired the rhythm section. The bass player's name was Frank de la Rosa. I don't know who the piano player was, but I got Frank the gig. Chet wasn't in great shape, and he had to sit down to play. But he played so good, it was just beautiful."[11]

Thereafter, Chet formed a band that consisted of Colin Bailey on drums, Monty Budwig on bass and Mike Wofford on piano. The quartet played on an irregular basis, with gigs including San Diego (February 27th), and the Edgewater Marina in Long Beach (April 10th, May 8th and June 5th). Chet's drug use seemed to be under control over this period, according to Bailey. "A couple of times he did drugs, but it never affected him," he said. "I mean he wasn't nasty, and he always showed up to the gigs. I loved playing with him; he was the most wonderful guy to play with. He had such great time, and that wonderful sound."[12]

THE LOS ANGELES COUNTY BOARD OF SUPERVISORS

ERNEST E. DEBS
SUPERVISOR, THIRD DISTRICT

IN COOPERATION WITH

THE DEPARTMENT OF PARKS AND RECREATION
AND
THE COUNTY MUSIC COMMISSION

 PRESENTS 

THE PILGRIMAGE THEATER

MUSIC FESTIVAL

GENERAL MUSICAL AND ARTISTIC DIRECTOR: SPINOZA PAEFF
IN A CLASSIC AND JAZZ PROGRAM: PAEFF QUARTET FOR PIANO AND STRINGS WITH GUEST SOLOISTS - THE CHET BAKER QUARTET
SUNDAY AFTERNOON, JUNE 12 AT FIVE P.M.

PILGRIMAGE OUTDOOR THEATER
2850 CAHUENGA BOULEVARD EAST, OPPOSITE HOLLYWOOD BOWL
FREE ADMISSION INCLUDES PARKING

NEXT CONCERT: BEVERLY HILLS SYMPHONY, SUNDAY JUNE 19 AT 5 P.M.
IN "POPULAR PROGRAM", HERBERT WEISKOPF, CONDUCTOR

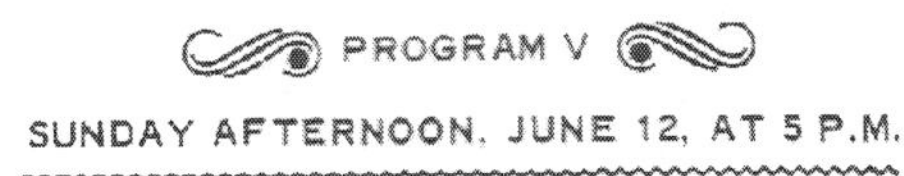
PROGRAM V

SUNDAY AFTERNOON, JUNE 12, AT 5 P.M.

"CLASSICS AND JAZZ"

SPINOZA PAEFF QUARTET FOR PIANO AND STRINGS IN
BEETHOVEN PIANO QUARTET, OPUS 16

SOLOISTS:

SPINOZA PAEFF, VIOLA SOLOIST IN "MORNA" OR LAMENT
Collected by Paeff from native melodies while on the Cape Verde Islands, Portuguese West Africa.

JEROME KASIN, VIOLINIST, "PIECES OF FRITZ KREISLER"

WILLIAM VAN DEN BURG, CELLIST IN "SAINT-SAENS CONCERTO"

ANTHONY BRAND, FLAMENCO GUITARIST IN "POR SOLEA - BULERIAS" AND "ALEGRIAS"

SPINOZA PAEFF QUARTET: GYPSY RONDO BY BRAHMS

Intermission: 15 minutes

THE CHET BAKER QUARTET "IN ORIGINAL MATERIAL"

Chet Baker, Fluegel Horn
Mike Wofford, Piano
Monty Budwig, Bass
Colin Bailey, Drums

Program for the Pilgrimage Theater Music Festival, June 12th 1966. Courtesy of Colin Bailey.

One particularly memorable gig took place at the Pilgrimage Theater, opposite the Hollywood Bowl in Los Angeles. "It was like a mini-Hollywood Bowl," Bailey remembered, "a wonderful place to play". The quartet played two more gigs at the Edgewater Marina in June, before Chet received a prestigious job offer—an offer it was hard to refuse.

Chet had been offered a high-profile gig at the Trident in San Francisco, an elegant high-windowed nightclub by the bay in Sausalito, just past the Golden Gate Bridge. "It was not a typical jazz club; it was classy, it had a restaurant and they served nice food in there," recalled Brazilian bossa nova star, João Donato. "It was not like a jazz workshop; the clientele liked to listen to more mellow, melodic jazz."[13]

Donato had been the sole attraction at the club in June, but around the end of the month, he found himself facing a dilemma. His regular trio had quit, leaving to join a Brazilian guitarist who was offering more money, and he was forced to recruit a new band at short notice. "My friend Lou Ganapoler, who was the manager of the club, suggested we get another musician from the LA, as we still had five or six weeks of the engagement left to run," Donato recalled. "I said, 'How about Chet Baker?' He said, 'That would be great', made a few telephone calls, and got him on the phone with me. I said, 'Would you like to play with me for a few weeks?' He said, 'Yeah!' I asked how much it would cost, and I remember he replied, 'I'm flexible'. So I handed him back to my friend Lou to arrange the details."[14]

Next day, Chet drove up to San Francisco with his family, and checked into a small hotel in Sausalito, just walking distance from the club. By this stage Carol was eight months pregnant with their third child. The band was now advertised as the João Donato Trio, featuring Chet Baker. The two headliners soon developed a repertoire that consisted of both bossa nova tunes and standards. "We played a number of Brazilian tunes, and Chet sang on some of them, too," Donato remembered. "Chet used to sit on his stool, close his eyes, and played very beautifully. Hc didn't communicate much with the audience. He was happy just to play and sing. I loved to hear his playing. Nobody could play like that, nobody could play so sweetly, with so much music, so much melody."[15]

The new-look line-up soon attracted the attention of Ralph Gleason, the influential jazz critic from the *San Francisco Chronicle*, who wrote a positive review of the opening night in an article entitled 'The Best Thing for Chet Baker'. He suggested that the gig was "the best thing that has happened to Baker in years … Although there were the usual first night gremlins and nervousness, it was obvious that the group can, with very little woodshedding, become a lyric jazz attraction of the first magnitude."[16]

In retrospect in seems surprising that Dick Bock had not thought to encourage Chet to record a bossa nova album, rather than the Mexican-style Mariachi Brass albums. After all, the strategy had been immensely successful for Stan Getz. Ironically, Chet had been a far greater influence on the bossa nova movement than Getz himself, even if he was unaware of the fact. "Chet had an important influence on bossa nova, of course," confirmed João Donato. "We listened to Chet Baker play with Russ Freeman. In those days we didn't have many records, and we didn't know how to copy. So João Gilberto and I used to fight over the Chet Baker records. He'd say, 'Let me borrow the record for one day, then I'll give it back to you!' We ended up listening to the records of Chet Baker together, to see how he sang [sic], see how he played." Perhaps Bock took the view that bossa nova was just a passing fad, and would soon decline in popularity.[17]

Chet was oblivious to the positive review they had received, and was often late for the engagement, regularly missing the first set altogether. "Every day I faced the same pressure, with people asking where he is," said Donato. "Chet and Carol were staying in the same hotel as me. I didn't want to disturb them all the time, but a few times I stopped by on my way to the club, around 8 p.m. or 9 p.m., and asked Carol if Chet wanted to join me. She always told me that Chet had left earlier that morning, and hadn't come back. I knew something was wrong, but could never tell what it was."

Carol returned to Redondo Beach in mid-August as she prepared to give birth, leaving Chet alone in San Francisco. She gave birth to a baby girl, whom they named Melissa, on July 22nd 1966. Three days later, on the day she was released from hospital, Chet was involved in an incident that could easily have ended his career as a trumpet player.

The first press report appeared in the *New York Times* on 9th August, by which time Chet had returned to Redondo Beach to recuperate. Chet claimed he had just got out of his car after the show had finished "when five negro youths attacked me". He told the reporter that he had run into the middle of the street, begging for help. "I tried to get into a car with five white guys," he claimed, "but they pushed me back out. There were lots of people on the street, but they didn't help me at all."[18]

This initial account hardly rings true; Chet's hotel was walking distance from the club, and he is unlikely to have taken his car for such a short journey. As always, Chet's junkie mentality meant that the story differed slightly each time, each version refined to elicit as much sympathy as possible for his plight.

Ten days later he told the UK's *Melody Maker* that he had started to walk home from the club. "I was just trying to get a taxi, when five guys surrounded me and tried to beat me up. Ironically, it was two coloured guys who'd saved me after I tried to escape by getting into a car with four of five white kids who first threw me back in the street. The hoodlums beat me some more until these two coloured guys told them to stop and took me to hospital ... They also smashed a part of a tooth off. It was like a nightmare."[19]

DownBeat magazine was treated to an even more elaborate version of events, suggesting that Chet's mouth had healed sufficiently that he was more comfortable talking at length. He claimed he'd been driven to San Francisco's Fillmore district by another member of the band, although the purpose of his visit was left unexplained. As he got out of the car and walked towards a cab stand, five negro men began to walk alongside him, he claimed. "One of them said, 'So you come down here looking for action?'—and with that, he punched me," Baker said. "Then the rest joined in, knocked me down, and kicked me until I was a bloody mess." Chet spotted a car filled with white people and ran toward it. He opened the door, but when he asked for help, he was shoved out the door into the hands of his assailants, he claimed. They beat him about the head until he was nearly unconscious, until a car with two coloured men pulled up. They chased away the attackers and took Baker to a hospital. He was treated there for a cut above his right eye, which required seven stitches, and a smashed upper lip. One of his front teeth was also broken. "The inside of my upper lip was badly cut because of the jagged edge of the chipped tooth," the flugelhornist said. "I probably won't be able to play for at least a month."[20]

This version suggests that Chet was in the wrong part of town when he was beaten, at least implying that the incident may have been drug-related. As years went by, he added further variations. In 1979, he told *Melody Maker* journalist Brian Case that he had got into a dispute with a dealer at his hotel in Sausalito, and that the dealer later arranged the beating by the five hoodlums. In the movie *Let's Get Lost* he claimed to have come across a hoodlum on the staircase on his way to meeting his connection. He put his hand in his pocket, pretending to have a gun, but the man later arranged to have him beaten.

Each time he told the story, Chet portrayed himself as the innocent bystander. Interviews suggest that his wife Carol believed this to be true, but many of his close friends doubt that to be the case. The incident has all the elements of a drug deal gone wrong; it occurred late at night, in the notorious Fillmore district of San Francisco. In all likelihood Chet tried to defraud one of his dealers, and was badly beaten when his deception was discovered. The fact that the attackers targeted his mouth, rather than his ribs, suggested they knew exactly who they were dealing with.

James Gavin, author of the Chet Baker biography *Deep in a Dream*, suggests that the one thread in these stories—the fact that Chet was attacked by the "coloured guys" and rejected by the "white guys"—was an metaphor for the discrimination Chet had felt as a musician. This interpretation ignores the fact that Chet was eventually rescued by two "coloured guys". The fact that he was ignored by a vehicle full of "white guys" probably reflects the fact that they were uncomfortable stopping in the Fillmore district late at night, particularly to rescue a guy who was covered in blood.

It's worth noting that he didn't lose his teeth in the attack, as has been suggested. His teeth were in bad shape before the beating; he had suffered from chronic dental problems for many years, and his heroin addiction had made things worse. Only one tooth was actually broken in the assault, although he subsequently suffered from considerable pain, and eventually had his top teeth removed.

Chet did try to return to work next day, but was unable to complete the engagement. "One day he came in to the kitchen of the club with a bloody handkerchief around his mouth," said João Donato. "I said 'What happened to you?' I got upset, of course—to see this happen to a beautiful person, who I worked with every day. He told me that four guys had hit him in the street, for no apparent reason. Nobody could explain it. He couldn't play the same after that, so I sent him home, and said, 'Take good care of yourself'. Chet returned to Redondo Beach next day, and Lou Ganapoler, the manager of the Trident, arranged for Bud Shank to replace Chet for the remainder of the engagement.[21]

In the meantime, João Donato came across another favourable review of their engagement at the Trident, written by Phillip Elwood of the San *Francisco Chronicle*. He posted the article, entitled 'The Best Thing That Happened to Chet Baker', to Dick Bock at World Pacific in Los Angeles. "Richard called me, and said when you guys get back to LA, let's get together to make a recording," said Donato. "By the time I had finished the engagement, Chet had had his accident, and I asked Richard what he wanted to do. 'Let's do it!' he said. So we got together at my apartment, which was near Sunset and Vine, so we could rehearse for a recording, and get together ideas and tunes. We rehearsed a few things, but I felt he wasn't playing well, and was still having problems with his teeth."[22]

Next day, João Donato and Chet Baker reconvened in the World Pacific recording studio, together with a Brazilian rhythm section. They completed two or three tunes, but Chet was still struggling, and they called it a day. "Richard called me next day and said, 'You should come and hear what the fuck you guys recorded!' Donato recalled. "I went over there to listen, and his playing was not that bad, but it was not that good; it was not the same as when we'd played together at The Trident. Richard Bock told me, 'We cannot do a record like this. You have to find a substitute, another trumpet player, and we'll make a record under your name'. I left the office sad, and never returned. I didn't want to make the record with another trumpet player."[23]

Later that month, Chet was evidently pestering Dick Bock for another loan, and Bock invited him to contribute to a record that he was working on. The album, entitled *Brazil! Brazil! Brazil!*, consisted of previously released recordings by Bud Shank, overdubbed with a string section. "None originally had strings on them," Shank later confirmed. "Dick Bock decided to get on the tail of the success of 'Michelle' and had Julian Lee (a blind pianist writer from Australia) write string parts, and then they were dubbed onto the original tapes. It's my guess—I wasn't present at the string overdub—that Chet once again came by the World Pacific Studio to hit Dick Bock for more money. Dick probably said, 'Here's $20, go play something on this track that they are overdubbing!' I can think of no other reason why this came about. His name is so prominently displayed on the album cover, however!"[24]

Despite the incident in San Francisco, some club owners were still willing to take a chance on hiring Chet Baker. In early October, he landed a gig at the Tropicana Club in Los Angeles, where he played for a total of six nights. "Chet Baker called me for a gig with Terry Trotter, Ray Brown, and Colin Bailey at one of those unattractive little bars near LA airport—the Boom Boom Room [sic], or some such name," recalled saxophonist Pete Christlieb. "It was a strange part of town but people were flocking there to hear the great Chet. There was nothing written, he just called the tunes and we played."[25]

Soon after, Chet invited Christlieb to join him at a gig in Pueblo, Colorado, but things didn't work out, and the saxophonist left after the first week. "If I had been a little older and wiser, I would have asked for the money up front because at the end of the week, I didn't get enough from him to pay the hotel bill, let alone get home. That is what happens when you work for a junkie, so you really have to watch out for yourself. Musically it was the best because he was playing beautifully but everything else was a tragedy! I did some tunes alone with the rhythm section that I wanted him to play and after a couple of times he had them down—he had great ears. Anyway, my wife and I had only been married a couple of months at the time, and here we were in this tiny little hotel in Colorado Springs—eventually we had to wire for money to get home and that was the end of my career with Chet Baker."[26]

Christlieb recalls that his place was taken by Chet's friend Phil Urso. Urso remembers Chet flirting outrageously with the waitress at the club, a restaurant by the name of Gaetano's. "Chet started fooling around with the waitress, but she turned out to be the boss's wife," he said. "So when he got free, he walked up to Chet and punched him right in the mouth. It was a wonder he had any teeth after that."[27]

One night's performance was taped by the drummer, Harry Kevis Jr. "He had a tape reel right by his sock cymbal," Urso recalled. "The recording picked up the sock cymbal more than anything else." The recording was later released as an album, listed under a variety of titles, including *Live at Gaetano's*. It reveals that the chemistry between Chet and Phil Urso remains as strong as ever, and that Chet was is in good voice. The tape also captures the onstage banter between the band members, who sound as though they're having fun. Unfortunately the overall sound quality is poor, as Urso suggests, and the saxophone and piano are barely audible.

In November, Chet was invited back to the recording studio for two more recording sessions under his own name. The first of these was *Into My Life*, the second and thankfully final album recorded with the Carmel Strings. This was followed by *In the Mood*, an incongruous tribute to the bandleader Glenn Miller, done Mariachi-style. The composer Bob Zieff, who had recently moved to Los Angeles, was present for the second recording session, and noted that Chet was in terrible shape. "He couldn't even get through the written parts that were handed to him," he noted.

At the tail end of 1966, Chet dropped in at Donte's, a jazz club in the San Fernando Valley. He had heard that Jimmy Rowles, who taught Chet many of the standards back in the late 1940s, was headlining at the club. Also in the band was drummer Larry Bunker, who had replaced Chico Hamilton in the Gerry Mulligan quartet. "(Chet) looked dreadful and asked if he could sit in," Bunker later recalled. "Jimmy kind of demurred and Chet insisted. This may be apocryphal, but it seemed like he had his horn in a paper bag. He got up on the bandstand and just was absolutely awful. He couldn't begin to play, couldn't put four notes together. He'd let six or eight bars go by while he was figuring out what he wanted to play. I shook my head. It really made me pissed off because of the God-given gift that he had and to have squandered it like that was inexcusable. What a person does with his life is his business. He's a grown man and he can do what he wants, but I knew how brilliant he could have been and I knew how brilliant he was."[28]

James Gavin suggests that Chet was inactive musically for approximately one year from late 1966, because of problems with his teeth. In fact, he performed at drummer Shelly Manne's club, the Manne-Hole, for two weeks in late February, 1967—a gig that featured Dave Mackay on piano, Monty Budwig on bass and Colin Bailey on drums. "Chet was playing good as far as I was concerned, but Leonard Feather published a really unkind review," Bailey later recalled. "He described Chet's playing as being 'as exciting as a women's cook off contest'. It was so unkind—he knew exactly what Chet was going through. I had to leave in the middle of the two-week gig, because I had landed a job with George Shearing—in fact it was the last time I played with Chet. He paid me on my last night, and said, 'You're a wonderful musician, man, I love playing with you'. I felt very honoured to receive that compliment from him."[29]

Chet's teeth were still giving him problems, and in the spring of 1967 he sought the help of Dick Bock. Bock recommended a good dentist, and when it became apparent that his top teeth were damaged beyond repair, paid for dentures to be fitted. "He looked fine," Carol later recalled, "but when he picked up his horn to play he couldn't make a sound. All you could hear coming out of the end of his horn was air."[30]

In the weeks that followed, Chet continued to practice on a regular basis, but still struggled to generate much of a sound. "He finally put the horn down and with tears in his eyes said, 'Carol, I can't make a sound. What am I going to do if I can't play any more?' He tried to look on the brighter side by saying perhaps he could 'just sing'. We both knew that that wouldn't be enough for him, but we held on to that idea because we had to."[31]

In the meantime, Chet faced up to the fact there was no way he could make a living out of music, and applied for welfare. He received $320 per month in basic support, plus a further $130 in food stamps. He eventually started work at a gas station, and in later years suggested he did this for a prolonged period. "I got a denture, and when I tried to play again, I could get no sound out my trumpet," he told *Jazz Hot* magazine. "So I gave it up. I worked almost two years in a gas station, sixteen hours a day."[32]

This was yet another example of Chet's junkie mentality, playing for sympathy at every available opportunity. Carol laughed at such suggestions. "Did Chet have a job at a gas station? Yes, one evening, no more," she said. "It was his idea. I thought it was nice of him, but he said 'Forget about it'. He could not stand that kind of work anyway. He would go nuts."[33]

In the meantime, Carol tried to stay positive. "I encouraged him by telling him that if he kept practicing he would play again," she said. "Not being a musician and understanding the severity of that kind of damage to a horn player I truly believed that that was the answer. It was mere ignorance on my part, but perhaps it was just as well that I didn't understand or I might not have been as positive as I was. I never had any doubts that he would play again, but Chet did."[34]

That summer, Chet ran into Artt Frank, a bebop drummer he had first met in Boston in 1954. "I first heard him on the Armed Service radio in 1951 or 1952," he recalled, "and it blew me away 'cos this guy was smoking—but he was doing it with a subtlety, you know, it wasn't harsh. I remember coming home, and thinking I'd like to meet him. I was living in Maine at the time. I went down to Boston where he was appearing at the Storyville. This guy was so good looking, and he had a bunch of people around him, so I walked over to him and introduced myself. I said, 'Man, I've heard you on the radio, I think you're one of the greatest trumpet players of all time. I'd like to work with you some time'. And he looked at me and said with a soft voice, with a kind of boyish grin, "Well, one never knows."[35]

Artt had relocated to Hollywood in the summer of 1967 with his then wife Earla, an aspiring jazz singer. Like many jazz musicians, he had struggled to earn a living from music, and took on a variety of odd jobs. He had tried his hand at scriptwriting, house-painting, even boxing. "I was kind of a rough guy," he admitted.

Despite the fact that he was on welfare himself, Artt tried to take Chet under his wing. He invited Chet, Carol and the children over to his house in

Culver City. "He had a flugelhorn wrapped in a blue towel," he remembered. "We had a steak dinner and after that I said, 'Chet, do you think you can play something?' He said, 'Well, my chops are really all gone'. He had kind of a half-plate bridge, and it wasn't worth shit, it would just keep falling out of his mouth. And when he started to play, and I noticed he was grimacing, he had a lot of pain in his jaw. He was scared shitless. He didn't think he'd ever be able to play again, and if he couldn't play again, his whole concern was supporting his family. They had the barest of necessities, but they had each other."[36]

This would appear to imply that the beating, and the subsequent fitting of the denture in place of his upper teeth, had finally changed Chet's outlook on life. Unfortunately, the evidence suggests to the contrary. Chet was arrested on four separate occasions in 1967, including once for burglary.

To some extent, Carol blamed Bob Whitlock for Chet's behaviour at this time, increasingly regarding him as a bad influence on her husband. Having been in a relationship with Chet for more than seven years at this stage, one would have thought she would have learned that he hardly needed any encouragement; in any case, his crimes were to support her habit, as well as his own.

Chet Baker and Bob Whitlock had progressed from faking neuralgia and kidney stones to stealing prescription pads from doctors, a trick that Chet had clearly taught his old friend. "At night time we'd sometimes get desperate because there was no doctors' offices open; there was nothing else to do, we had no money, and we were sick. So we'd burglarise doctors' offices, steal their prescription pads, write our own prescriptions and take our chances. Sometimes we'd even sell the stuff on the street, and buy street junk with the money. At this point we were real low-lives; it was nothing to be proud of, but it's a fact."[37]

On one occasion Chet was arrested on suspicion of forging prescriptions, only to be found innocent of all charges. "There were three of us—Shannon, Chet and I—we stopped in this mens store on the fringe of Beverly Hills," recalled Bob Whitlock. "We were just horsing around—meaning if we could have stolen something, we probably would have. The people in the store thought we looked suspicious and called the police, and within minutes they were there. They pulled us aside, searched us, and within minutes they'd found some prescriptions on Chet. They took us all downtown to the main booking office. I was able to bail out by late that evening, and the really lousy part about it was that when I got back to pick up my car—I had a beautiful

1965 Porsche—it was stolen. When I bailed out, Chet said, 'Make sure you get me out, man'. When I called back later, he had already been bailed out. Miraculously all three prescription bottles were legitimate—they weren't prescriptions we'd forged—so we were released without charges, but I lost my car in the process. The irony was that I found my car almost exactly one month later, parked in the same spot as it was stolen! I got the car back, but it wasn't in such good shape as I had left it. There were a few scrapes, and the upholstery was torn."[38]

Bob Whitlock may have got his car back, but it wasn't long before Chet ruined the car through his own driving. "He drove like a maniac," he recalled. "He took the car one day and the whole of one side was dented in. He returned and parked the car as though there was nothing wrong—no apology, no nothing, he just handed me the keys. When I saw the state of it I asked, 'What the hell happened to the car?' 'Well, some maniac hit me!' He didn't even tell me, I had to go out and discover it for myself. Chet was getting pretty weird at this point. I'm not just pointing the finger at him—I was no better than he was. Eventually that car got stolen again, and I never did get it back."[39]

On July 6th 1967, Chet received a phone call from his mother informing him that his father had died of a heart attack, aged sixty-one. He had lost his job as a security guard earlier that year, and spent most of his remaining days drinking heavily, trying to forget the fact that he had struggled to hang on to a proper job for any length of time; the parallels with his son, who had blown several good opportunities since his return to the West Coast, were all too apparent. According to Artt Frank, Chet showed little reaction to his father's death. "Chet was the kind of guy who took things in his stride," he said. "He was very introspective, and he kept his sorrows inside."

In the meantime, Chet continued to practice his playing at home, modifying the way in which he played until he could play a few notes. "As time went by, he was able to play the scale," recalled Carol. "That's all I heard for a long time until he asked me to listen to a simple tune that he had been working on. He played and I listened. It didn't sound too bad, but he still had a lot of work ahead of him."[40]

It was clear that he was still not ready to play in clubs, so Artt Frank helped out where possible, asking Chet to join him on the occasional odd jobs. "I was painting houses, and Chet would come to work with me," he recalled. "I was breaking down a wall one time, it was about forty-five feet long, about four feet high. We were hired to break the wall down, and Chet took a nine-pound sledgehammer, and we broke this wall down in about four hours, non-stop. Chet worked like a fiend."[41]

By late 1967, Chet felt he was finally ready to play in public, and called Dick Bock at Pacific Jazz Records. Bock invited him to play on a new Bud Shank LP, *Magical Mystery*. Chet's playing still sounds extremely tentative at times—the first few bars of his playing on 'Hello Goodbye' find him struggling to hold a note—and it is probably for this reason that a second recording session was arranged with a new band, this time featuring Gary Barone on flugelhorn. The arrangements, still by Bob Florence, are slightly more interesting than on Bud Shank's previous 'pop' albums, suggesting a move away from the 'easy listening' market to a more current, 'psychedelic' sound.

Even after making this record, Chet still struggled to find work at the major jazz clubs around town. Artt Frank felt that his reputation had finally caught up with him. "I tried for the next few months to get him a gig," he recalled. "Nobody, but nobody, would take a chance on hiring him. I think it was because of the drugs. He had a bad reputation, and no one wanted to take a chance on him. I went to Shelly Manne. 'Artt', he said, 'I love Chet. When Chet's right there's nobody on earth any better. But I just can't take a gamble'. He was afraid, as everyone else was afraid, that Chet would not show up because he was an addict, and that he was going to take the money and stiff him, and just get himself fixed. I tried on the phone, I called record producers, called clubs, but they wouldn't want a thing to do with him."[42]

Chet and Carol were struggling to get by on his welfare payments; with three children to support, as well as their addiction, it was hard to make ends meet, and by late 1967, the telephone had been cut off at Spreckles Lane. Carol remembers Chet playing in coffee shops at this time, sitting in with unknown bands, just to get his chops back into shape. "We would go in and Chet would find a table way back in the club—almost as though he didn't want to be seen. Fortunately there was always someone who recognised him and would inform the band leader that Chet was in the club and he would be invited to play. He always started out by apologising that he had no 'chops' but would try. Of course, it wasn't always like that. There were times when he wasn't invited to play. On those occasions he would quietly leave after a couple of sets. In time he began playing better and better."[43]

In the spring of 1968, Chet wrote a letter to his old friend, the drummer

Harry Kevis, asking him if he had a possible job in the auto industry. Kevis had started a new company, United States Automotive Inc. His partner had evidently developed a new battery chemical, and Kevis had been given the responsibility of handling sales and promotion. The product had evidently been well received, with Kevis claiming that progress "has been rapid".

"You don't say too much about this battery chemical, but it sounds very interesting," Chet wrote. "I don't suppose you could use a West Coast Distributorship?" (naturally with old Chet as chief in command). "Seriously I could probably handle it if you would give me a chance. I'd really like to have something to fall back on."[44]

Chet explained that he was struggling to find much work; as usual, he placed the blame with everyone but himself. "As you see, I'm not phoning; my phone is disconnected. I have been here all the time. I hardly ever work. I've attributed it to a great fear on the part of would-be brokers or club owners; sad, but true, anyway." On a brighter note, Chet went on to explain that he had just landed a job; it wasn't a long-term gig, but it was a start. "Of course, I'm still playing. I have the first two Thursdays in April at Donte's restaurant in N. Hollywood, so if it turns out you'll be in this area during that time, let me know, and you can probably take Nick's spot, as yet I haven't let him in on it."[45]

One person who was happy to lend a helping hand was the television star Steve Allen, who invited Chet to appear on his show on June 5th 1968. Allen introduced him as "one of the men who's done an awful lot for the trumpet", and held up copies of his recent albums, most of which had sunk without trace.

Chet emerged looking like a man out of touch with the times, his slicked-back hair looking somewhat incongruous with the powder-blue jacket. Jim Hughart, who played bass with the house band, was somewhat dubious about Allen's motives for inviting Chet on to the show. "Steve was something of a Chet Baker fan, but I don't think he could even begin to tell you why. I think he simply *heard* some people rave about him and figured that he'd better go along with that," he recalled. "He had the unmitigated gall to pick up a trumpet and try to play alongside Chet on his TV show! He also had the nerve to have a second piano wheeled out onto the stage of his show and attempt to play alongside Oscar Peterson! To his credit, Steve seemed to understand that Chet needed some income and put him on the show a number of times."[46]

Chet played 'My Foolish Things', a song he was very familiar with, but his playing was still a shadow of what it used to be. Backstage, Chet pestered the other musicians to lend him money. Paul Smith, the pianist, recalled Chet grasping him by the shoulder and saying, "Hey, they're gonna shut my electricity off if I don't come up with some money for the bill", which was probably closer to the truth than many of them realised. "The Chet I knew was a caricature of a junkie," said Jim Hughart. "He owed me money, too—it was hard to say no to him. We were all in awe of his musical gift and wanted so much to be able to turn back the clock and point him in the right direction."[47]

Next month, Steve Allen invited Chet back on to the show where he performed 'Forgetful'. After the show, he asked Allen for a loan of $500, money he knew he'd never see again. Rather than simply hand him the money, Allen proposed that Chet record an album of his own compositions. Allen was a prolific composer, writing more than ten thousand tunes. On one occasion, he made a bet with the singer-songwriter Frankie Laine that he could compose more than fifty songs a day over the course of a week; he not only won the bet, but one of the songs, 'Let's Go To Church Next Sunday', was recorded by both Perry Como and Margaret Whiting. The vast majority of his tunes were far from memorable, although it is worth noting that he did win a Grammy award in 1963 for 'The Gravy Waltz'.

The recording session is thought to have taken place some weeks later at the Bob Ross Studio, a small storefront studio a couple of blocks from where the TV shows was taped. Steve Allen later recalled that Chet turned up for the recording session stoned and unfamiliar with the tunes, despite being sent the music some weeks earlier. As a result, Allen and Paul Smith walked him through the tunes. "I only have hazy memories of the session," said Jim Hughart, "but I seem to recall Chet being relatively OK—for Chet—and that he was more 'into it' than I expected him to be. Generating any enthusiasm for trying to make something out of a bunch of Steve Allen tunes was a monumental task!"[48]

The album, *Albert's House*, was grim beyond belief. Chet sleepwalks his way through the session, his playing more confident than on *Magical Mystery*, but still weak. It can't have been easy for him to summon much enthusiasm for Allen's bland, soulless compositions. The cheap-sounding organ that appears on several tracks doesn't help matters, nor does the poor quality overdubbing. "I know that Chet, if he had been in control of his life, would never waste time on crap such as this," said Jim Hughart. "He needed money and that's the reason he did this album. And he was trying very hard not to bite the hand that was feeding him. I hated seeing him in a situation like this."

Chet also appears to have recorded an album with Jack Sheldon around this time. Tapes of the recording do exist, but the album was never released. "We did an album with Dave Frishberg on piano and Mick Sorelli on drums—I don't remember the bass player," Sheldon recalled. "We went out with Jack Marshall, who plays guitar, and was a real close friend of mine. He had a recording studio in Balboa. Chettie was staying with me at the time; he was just getting his mouth back into shape after having his teeth knocked out. I was living up on Mulholland Avenue. I had worked in the movies a lot by that time, and had earned a lot of money, and bought a great big mansion. We made an album that never got released, and appeared at a school my son was going to called Harvard Boys School, which was a military school at the time. I moved into that house around 1967, so it was after that—between then and 1970."[49]

Chet made no secret of his drug addiction, but tried to keep his 'non-social' behaviour from spilling over into the music. There had been a number of occasions where this had happened, of course; sometimes he would play well, and it would be difficult to tell whether he was high, but there were occasions where it would impact his singing or playing, such as on *Embraceable You* (1957) or *Stan Meets Chet* (1958). For the most part, however, Chet regarded the music as being the most important thing in his life.

This period in the late 1960s was the first occasion in which he had really let himself go, however, failing to keep his chops in shape between gigs and recording sessions. It would happen again in later years, most notably in the 1980s, but for many observers, it was shocking to see him waste his natural abilities in this way. "We weren't working much at that time; we'd get a gig here and there—maybe a night in San Diego, a night in Santa Ana, playing various bars, but nothing of any consequence," recalled Bob Whitlock. "There was no way we could have made a living from that. Chet would get the occasional spot on TV shows, but they were all such failures. He'd be drugged out to the max, and could hardly handle himself. He was in no shape; he'd be playing a gig every three or four weeks, and never even bother to practice. For such a brilliant musician, such a talented guy, he practiced a lot of self-deception. I don't care who you are, you can't go out and play every now and then and impress people. You're going to fluff a lot of notes. There were nights when I heard him play like an amateur, he was so out of shape. The last time I heard him, he sounded like shit, frankly. He did himself in; for such a marvellously talented guy to appear like that was kind of self-destructive. I was so delighted when I heard that stuff he did in Europe; you could tell he was playing regularly again."[50]

Later that year, Chet was arrested again, initially for driving under the influence. As far as Artt Frank remembered, Chet was arrested twice on the same day in quite bizarre circumstances. "Chet had been arrested for drunk-driving (actually driving under the influence of narcotics). His mother had just bought him a Cadillac, a big brown Cadillac, it wasn't a new one, but it was something he could get around with," he recalled. "He was driving in Gardenia when he side-swiped a parked car. I could have done more damage with my fist than he did with the car. He kept on driving, and some asshole said he left the scene of the accident, so they arrested him. We got him out later that day, and then found Chet had left his wallet inside the jail. We went back to get it, and the officer had just changed shifts. Chet said, 'I left my wallet here'. The guy said, 'What's your name?' He said, 'Chesney Baker'. He said, 'Are you Chet Baker?' And they re-arrested him! He looked at me like a deer caught in the headlights. I forget the charge."[51]

The outstanding warrant was most likely for forging prescriptions. Chet was only held for three days, which was probably fortunate, given his track record. While he was being held, he met the saxophonist Christopher Mason, who was just eighteen years old at this time. He had been arrested for shoplifting and ran into Chet in the holding cell for the LA County Jail. "I was in the holding cell, a huge concrete room with weird acoustics, and I was whistling a tune I'd frequently heard. One of the winos/drunks gets up and makes his way over to me and says, 'That's a nice tune, did you write it?' So I said, 'What, are you kidding? No, it's called "Here's That Rainy Day", and I heard Stan Getz play it.' He says, 'It's a really nice tune'. And I said, 'Yeah, I'll be glad to get out of here so I can play my horn'.

"'Oh, you play a horn, so do I'.

"'Yeah, I play sax'.

"So being a jerk, I say, 'Oh yeah, who are you, Chet Baker?'

"'Yeah, have you heard of me?'

"'If you're Chet Baker, I'm president of the United States!'

"So he shows me the wrist band you have in those places for quick ID, and it says 'Chesney Baker'.

"'Oh great, you're one of those guys with names something like someone famous and goes around trying to cash in on it?'

"'No, Chet is short for Chesney'.

"'Yeah, well, what school did you go to, man?'

"'Glendale High'.

"'Wow, you really are Chet Baker!'"[52]

Over the next few days, Mason offered Chet cigarettes, and they talked about music. They became friends, meeting on several occasions over the years, and Mason eventually invited Chet to record a Christmas jazz album with him in 1986.

Chet's behaviour was placing a considerable strain on his marriage. Carol complained that Chet spent too much time with his junkie friends, rather than trying to find work. Chet also loathed being stuck inside the small house with his family, and was glad to escape at every available opportunity. "Carol was really in love with Chet, but often times he treated her bad," said Bob Whitlock, who continued to hang around with Chet at this time. "He could be insensitive and mean. He was a little more careful with the children, especially with Missy, who was just a little kid. For the most part he was tender with her. But for the most part, Chet was about Chet; he was very self-centred and egotistical, and you had to take the good with the bad. I knew him to be a very fascinating human being. He could be a good friend—warm, sympathetic and understanding—all these wonderful qualities. And he had some of the worst qualities, too. You had to take the good with the bad, and I thought it was worth it."[53]

Chet and Bob Whitlock continued to steal prescription pads from local doctors at every available opportunity. "Here in California they had State Narcotics Control, where you had to have a special prescription to get controlled substances," Whitlock explained. "A regular prescription would not get you morphine, for example, or any of the drugs we wanted." On occasion, Chet went round to visit Bob, and told him he'd experienced a potential problem cashing his script at one particular drugstore that he'd used on three or four previous occasions. "On the last occasion," he told me, "I had a funny feeling. I went back, poured gas on the place, and lit it." I see no reason why he would say that just to impress me. I certainly wouldn't put it past him. I thought he was crazy; I mean, if you got caught for arson, you could go to prison for years."[54]

Towards the end of 1968, Chet visited a doctor in Bellflower, just outside Long Beach, apparently with a legitimate medical condition. A few days later he told Bob Whitlock that he saw where the doctor kept his prescription pads. That night they broke into his office, climbing in through the window, and took the pad. "We gave a lot of scripts out to other guys," said Whitlock. "They would cash them, and we would take the lion's share, giving them something for taking the risk of cashing it. After a few weeks, Chet and I were loaded, and started to antagonise one another. I said, 'Look, let's divide up the script pad'. I went out to the car, and got the pad, which I kept under the floor pad. I counted them out, divided the pad in half. 'That's not fair', Chet said. 'What about Carol?' 'What do you mean, what about Carol?' 'Well I think I should get two-thirds of them, because I've got to support her habit'. I said, 'Well, think again'."

Whitlock divided the pad in half, and started walking towards the door. Suddenly, without a word of warning, Chet punched him on the side of the head. "My God, it hurt! I'd never been hit that hard," he said. "I can only think there was a lot of pent-up anger over that affair with Charlaine all those years earlier. We fought like cats and dogs; I mean, I was fighting for my life. He was a tough little guy, I tell you. Carol came out and said, 'Get the hell out of here. You're gonna have the cops here in minutes!' In seconds, we realised that was probably true, so I jumped in my car and took off. And that was the last time I ever saw him."[55]

A week later, Whitlock was in a drugstore, trying to cash one of the scripts, and sensed the pharmacist was taking too long. He made his way back down the aisle, hoping to slip out of the store unnoticed. As he reached the door, he was grabbed by two uniformed cops, who arrested him. He was charged with burglary and forgery. The burglary charge was later dropped, but he was sentenced to three months in jail and five years' probation.

Arrt Frank had been trying to find work for Chet for several months, without success. His perseverance finally paid off in February 1969, when he landed him a gig at the Melody Room on Sunset Strip. The club had fallen on hard times, overshadowed by the club across the street, the Whiskey A Go Go, where The Doors had once worked as the house band.

On the opening night, Chet was nervous, and overdosed shortly before the show was due to begin. Artt Frank helped Carol to strip him naked, and plunge him into an ice cold bath, which soon revived him. Frank then helped to shave him, while he was still barely conscious, before driving him to the club. "But when he got up on stage, sat down, and the music started, it was like God almighty reached down and touched him," he recalled. "I still don't know how he did it. He picked up that horn and it was wonderful."[56]

Chet was accompanied by Artt Frank himself on drums, Frank Strazzeri on piano and David Dyson on bass. On the second evening, however, Frank de la Rosa took over on bass. The legendary jazz critic Leonard Feather came along for the second performance with his wife. "Before the second set he asked me, 'Do you think you can ask Chet to play that old Tadd Dameron tune, "If You Could See Me Now"?'" Artt Frank recalled. "He played the most beautiful, poignant rendition of the tune. Leonard gave him a wonderful review in the following day's *LA Times*."

"What went on at the Melody Room was just the basic blowing—theme, ad lib choruses, theme," Feather wrote. "At times Baker seemed to falter or lose the melodic line, but for the most part he was a sensitively self-expressive as ever. 'If You Could See Me Now', a perfect ballad medium for him, was played in a spare, elliptical style, intensely melodic, with a coda in the lower register that has always been Baker's most personal area."[57]

Artt Frank refers to the Melody Room gig as Chet's 'real' comeback, as opposed to his engagement at the Half Note in 1973. Part of the problem was that Chet was still in no fit state for a 'comeback'; he valued getting high as much, if not more, than his music. Only after he had quit heroin did his values start to change.

Unfortunately, the Melody Room gig only lasted a few days, and work dried up once again. Chet briefly considered returning to Europe at this time, and wrote a letter to the Italian bass player Giovanni Tommaso, asking him whether work would be any easier to come by in Italy. "Chet tried to contact me from the US asking me if I could do anything for him," said Tommaso. "I had moved to Rome by then, and said I would put the word around, but explained that I wasn't so influential that I could necessarily help him out."[58]

Artt Frank continued to do everything he could to help his friend, and eventually found work for the pair of them at his cousin's restaurant, Stefanino's, on Sunset Strip. "The restaurant was co-owned by Steve Crane, who was Lana Turner's ex-husband," he explained. "He owned many restaurants, and was in partnership with Nicky Blair. I brought Chet up to meet Nicky, and Nicky treated him very well. Nicky gave him some clothes and some money. Chet didn't work around the restaurant, but Nicky gave us odd jobs to do from time to time."[59]

Chet continued to raid doctors' offices around Los Angeles, just as he had in Tuscany in 1960. His luck finally ran out on August 29th 1969, when he was again arrested for forging a prescription. Given his previous convictions for the same offence, his lawyer informed him that he could be sentenced for up to five years. Fortunately for Chet, the judge was a former college trumpet player himself. He decided that Chet needed treatment rather than punishment, and on September 10th, sentenced him to ninety days in the Chino Institute for Men, a rehabilitation centre in California.

Art Pepper had also spent time in the Chino Institute, and clearly regarded it as a much easier option than spending time in prison. "They keep you in barracks instead of cells," he recalled, "and you were entitled to lengthy visits with your family, including picnic lunches." He was fairly scathing about the treatment that was offered, however. "We were all getting counselling. There'd be a social worker or a parole officer, and he'd have a 'group'. The whole idea was to get people to rat on each other, to try to expose people so they'd 'learn' and do better. I'd never seen anything like it … I realised that the only way to make it was to say as little as possible and to try to con the people as much as possible to get out."[60]

Artt Frank one of the few people to visit Chet at Chino outside of his own family. "I had to talk on the telephone between the glass," he recalled. "I said, 'You're going on 40, you've got to turn your life around'. At that point he said, 'You're absolutely right'."[61]

Chet left Chino in early December, determined to live a normal life. He reunited with his family, who had moved in with Chet's mother. Vera had relocated from Los Angeles to Milpitas, a small town near San Jose. As when he had moved in with his parents four years earlier, the atmosphere was tense. The house was small, and not really built to accommodate a large family. She was also obsessive about keeping the place neat and tidy, which was near impossible with three small children. She took her frustration out on Carol, complaining that she should look for work, rather than rely on her husband.

Chet's relationship with Carol had become increasingly strained at this time. She made it clear that she was unhappy living in the same house as Chet's mother, and wanted a place of her own. She was adamant that as a famous musician, he should be able to find regular work. Chet also began to resent his wife's own drug use, telling friends that Carol now had a bigger habit than him.

Chet was desperate to get out of the house, and drove into San Francisco at every available opportunity. He eventually got a gig at a small club in the city, just up the road from a theatre where his old friend, the percussionist Bill Loughborough, was working with a comedy group, 'The Committee'. "People dismiss the music from this era, but when I heard him play, the brilliance still shined through," he noted. "On a bad night, it was still worth going to see Chet Baker, as far as I was concerned."[62]

Loughborough was no longer active in the music industry. "I was heavily involved with multiple careers in that era," he said. "Medical research, satirical improvisational theatre, and a factory making Fresnel lenses." He lived something of a hippy lifestyle, sharing an apartment with his wife Sandi Love, the mother of his young son, Fillmore Love. Loughborough was experimenting with hallucinogenic drugs, including LSD. His wife, meanwhile, was a heroin addict, and when Chet came knocking at the door, begging for cash, it wasn't long before the two of them started using together.

Loughborough admits that he had a 'stormy' relationship with his wife, and was not altogether surprised when Chet embarked on an affair with her. "Chet seemed bitter," Love later recalled, over the problems with his teeth and his struggle to find work, and he was glad to lose himself in a haze of heroin and barbiturates. Over the course of the next few months, the affair became increasingly sordid. One particularly pure batch of heroin led to Love overdosing, and the shared use of a single needle by a number of addicts eventually resulted in her contracting hepatitis.

Junkies would do anything for cash, Loughborough noted. Several items disappeared from his apartment at this time, presumably hocked by Chet or Love to fund their habit. Chet also found work as a getaway driver for a bank robber at this time. "There was a stripper called Jada Conforto, who worked for Jack Ruby in Dallas one time, so her name got into the paper," he said. "She was kind of out there, notorious—she would go in and rob banks while Chet was in the car. I don't know whether he did it for the money, or was just hanging out, and thought it would be fun. He had some strange times, that's for sure!"[63]

In the spring of 1970, Chet wandered in to Riccardo's, a pizza restaurant in San Jose that hosted a Monday night jam session with its house band. Chet introduced himself to the band's leader, Don McCaslin, who played electric piano, and asked if he could sit in.

Chet's arrival went unnoticed by most of the diners, most of whom had little interest in jazz. The band's drummer, a woman by the name of Diane Vavra, recognised him instantly, however. "He looked like a Greek god to me, and I fell in love with him immediately," she later recalled. "He was very gentle, very sweet, very charming. I guess that's what it was. And the mystery about him, the Dr. Jekyll and Mr Hyde kind of scenario."[64]

To most observers, Chet was anything but a Greek god by this stage. His addiction had done little to change his wiry physique, but in other respects, he looked as though he had seen better days. He had allowed his hair to grow longer at the back, and had grown his sideburns, which made him look like an ageing hippy. He had also grown a thin moustache, which hardly added to his appeal. His eyes had become more lined over the years, just like his father, and his mouth had started to pucker prematurely, like an old man, where his denture had been fitted.

Diane Vavra was twenty-nine years old, and had recently separated from her husband, a part-time musician. She lived with her seven-year-old son, Ronny, who was the same age as Dean. She had long, brown wavy hair but her features were far from striking, her face unadorned by make-up, and her lips thin, giving her mouth a slightly hard edge. She looked quite different to Liliane, Halema and Carol, all of whom had been dark-haired, somewhat dusky, and glamorous.

Diane claimed to have fallen for Chet after listening to *Baby Breeze*, five years earlier. "I loved Chet way before I met him because for me he personifies the very thing that gives meaning to my life, and that is jazz," she later told Bruce Weber. When Chet introduced himself to her that evening, she was surprised by the gentle tone of his voice, which seemed in sharp contrast to the stories she had heard about his problems.

At the end of the evening, Chet offered to help her pack her drum kit and escort her home, much to Diane's delight. They soon discovered they had a great deal in common. She was an accomplished musician; as well as playing drums, she had studied saxophone and clarinet. Like Chet, she had a good ear for music, and could annotate a solo, note for note. Her father had also been a musician, but like Chesney Sr he was an alcoholic and had never fulfilled his potential. Chet finally felt as though he had found a soulmate, someone who understood the frustrations he was feeling.

Over the course of the next few weeks, Chet tried his luck at a number of clubs in the Bay area, hoping to find places where he could sit in, and get his chops back into shape. One such club was The Cats, which was located on Highway 17 at Los Gatos, just fifteen miles from his mother's house in Milpitas. It was an elegant club, complete with a restaurant and large bar, and used to attract a number of the local jazz musicians. It was there that he ran into the bass player Ron Crotty, one of the original members of the Dave Brubeck Quartet. They had first met one another back in November 1953, when Chet Baker joined Charlie Parker and Dave Brubeck for a ten-day tour of the West Coast. They had also played together on one occasion at the Officer's Club in the Presidio in mid-1951, shortly before Chet was transferred to Fort Huachuca. "He was just getting back on the scene, and was searching for places to play," Crotty later recalled. "He had changed the way he played, because of the problems with his teeth, but he still had that distinctive sound."[65]

In early May, Chet was introduced to a young pianist by the name of Brian Cooke, who also sat in at the club one evening, joining bass player Ron Crotty and drummer Danny Barnett. "Danny's drums were slipping all over the stage," the pianist remembered, "but Chet's playing was unbelievable that night—these long phrases just kept pouring out."[66]

In the weeks that followed, Chet began to put together a group of his own. "It was rather a funky group," said Cooke. "We had a bassist called Robb Fisher, who has become one of the finest bass players in the area, and a drummer called Michael Eichenholtz. Robb, Michael and I had played together before." Chet introduced them to a tenor saxophonist by the name of Michael McCormick, whom they later realised was one of Chet's drug buddies.

The group started playing at The Cats every Monday night. "It was obvious that Chet was very talented," recalled bass player Robb Fisher, "but also that he was suffering, having a hard time with his chops." The band was still in the process of building up a repertoire when they landed their first real gig at a club called the New Orleans House in Berkeley. In retrospect, it was obvious that they had not had enough time to rehearse. "It was a rather dismal performance," admitted Brian Cooke. "We were all very self-conscious, and didn't really talk to one another."[67]

The gig was sparsely attended, and it was unfortunate for all concerned that one of the paying customers was the influential jazz critic Ralph Gleason. "There was a drummer, young, wild-haired and sometimes unfamiliar with the 1950's bop literature," Gleason noted, "a bassist with long hair hanging from the sides of a huge bald spot and a shining, fair-cheeked pianist who really played … After each tune they sat there motionless for a moment. Sometimes they would confer and sometimes even during the tune they seemed undecided.

"At 9.30 there was only one table of guests and a couple of people at the bar," Gleason continued. "The small audience (it grew by half a dozen before the set ended) applauded tentatively … When it was over, or rather to signal that it WAS over, Baker played a couple of quick figures on the trumpet, pointing it down to the floor and not looking at anybody. He took the horn from his lips and said to the band, 'That was Bird's theme'. Somehow that seems to characterise the evening. Chet played Bird's theme and nobody knew. It was like a bad dream in which something went wrong in 1952 and can't get straightened out, ever. A musical play by Kafka. A musical tragedy."[68]

Published under the headline 'A Few Came To Hear Chet Baker', Gleason's review had a devastating effect. Chet went back to his mother's house and smashed a number of the windows. He then drove over to see Diane, who tried in vain to console him.

Drummer Artt Frank was still trying his hardest to rouse Chet from his bad dream. In early July, he was able to arrange a record deal for Chet with MGM. "I was friendly with a few people in Hollywood because I was an occasional actor myself," he said. "I was friends with the new President of MGM pictures who later hired Mike Herb, who became the head of MGM's record company. So I talked to Michael about getting Chet a recording contract. I figured if I could get him back in the recording studio, it would break the ice and people would be able to help him. Mike agreed, but said that it wouldn't be strictly a jazz album. I said, "What are you talking about?" He said, "Well, if we have to re-launch him he can play the same material as Blood, Sweat and Tears. I took it to Chet, and he said, 'Well…it's a shot'."[69]

Blood, Sweat and Tears were a jazz-rock band, formed in 1967, which attempted to fuse elements of rock, R'n'B and jazz. Their second album, recorded in 1969, was more pop-oriented and won the Grammy award for best album. Chet's own recording comes across as a poor man's Blood, Sweat and Tears, and is the closest he came to making a straight-ahead pop album. It consists of hit singles by Blood, Sweat and Tears themselves, including 'Spinning Wheel', and contemporary pop songs such as 'Sugar, Sugar', which had been a number one hit for The Archies. It was given the working title *Blood, Sweat and Chet*, but was renamed *Blood, Chet and Tears*.

Jazz fans shunned the album; after all, it was recorded just three months after Miles Davis had released his groundbreaking 'fusion' album *Bitches Brew*, which tried to fuse elements of rock and jazz. It's easy to dismiss the album, but it is important to remember that the vast majority of jazz musicians were struggling to make a living from jazz at this time. Chet's old friend from the West Coast, Bill Holman, had resorted to writing arrangements for the pop group The Fifth Dimension, whilst Dizzy Gillespie had just released a 'crossover' album of his own entitled *It's My Way*, which featured the great bebop trumpeter playing covers of Jimmy Webb's 'Galveston' and a medley of songs from the musical *Hair*.

"After we did *Blood, Chet and Tears*, I took to him to Stefanino's restaurant in Hollywood," claimed Artt Frank. "On the way home, Chet asked me to pull over, and I pulled over the side of the kerb, and he vomited. He told me he was so down on himself for prostituting himself to play that kind of music—that *Blood, Sweat and Tears* shit, that it just upset him. I talked to him, and told him that's not the idea. 'You were being yourself, and besides it launched your recording career again'."[70]

Back in San Francisco, Chet's group began to develop a broader repertoire. Pianist Brian Cooke worked on the arrangements, and was encouraged that Chet was extremely receptive to trying out new ideas. "I remember I brought in 'Beatrice', that beautiful song by Sam Rivers, 'Azule Serape', the tune by Victor Feldman, 'Blue Daniel' the waltz by Frank Rosolino, 'Miyako' by Wayne Shorter, 'Love Number One', a beautiful ballad written by Keith Jarrett and 'Dolphin', an expressive piece by the Brazilian musician, Luiz Eca," he recalled. "We also played material that he had been performing for many years—songs like 'Just Friends', 'But Not For Me' and 'My Funny Valentine'. Even when he was stoned, he knew he could fall back on those tunes. He was beautiful at them."[71]

The band rehearsed at Chet's mother's house in Milpitas, playing in the garage, where Chet kept an old upright piano. "Chet's mother seemed to adore him," Cooke noted. "He was her little boy, and he could do no wrong." After a few weeks of rehearsal, the band was in better shape. In late June, they landed one night a week at a small club called Monk's, in Santa Cruz, and in mid-July, a more prestigious gig at El Matador, one of the leading clubs in San Francisco.

Brian Cooke was nervous about the opening at El Matador, but the hard work had paid off. After the first gig, John Wasserman of the *San Francisco Chronicle* wrote that Chet sounded "excellent". He noted that the band sounded dated by the standards of modern jazz, however, describing them as "stopped in time, and the time is not today ... As the band gets together and Baker's physical problems dissolve, it will be interesting to see what evolves." The tone of the article was generally positive, however, and helped to erase the memory of Ralph Gleason's scathing review less than two months earlier. It also helped to secure a follow-up engagement at the same club in mid-September.[72]

The quality of Chet's playing varied wildly from night to night, depending on his physical condition and the state of his chops. "For us it was something of a 'Jekyll and Hyde' experience," admitted Brian Cooke. "When he was alert, it was great musically, but on other nights, it could be a horror show. But through all of that, he was the exciting Chet—the inspiring soloist who played these beautiful lines. He wasn't always good, but when he was really good, it was exhilarating, and made all of the difficulties seem minor by comparison."[73]

The band members saw very little of Chet's wife Carol, or the three children, over the summer of 1970. Carol never came along to the clubs to listen to her husband playing with his new band. Diane Vavra was regularly in attendance, however, watching adoringly as he played. "We saw a lot of Diane, she was very much on the scene," the pianist confirmed. "She absolutely adored Chet."

The return gig at El Matador took place in mid-September. Brian Cooke was again nervous about the opening night, particularly over the condition of Chet and Michael McCormick, both of who were using heavily. "I remember Mike McCormick's girlfriend saying, 'What Brian needs is to get stoned and get fucked'," he laughed. His anxiety took its toll on his health, and he missed two nights of the engagement with what he later described as a case of "psychosomatic mumps". On the first night Mike Nock replaced him, but on the second night his bandmates were excited to learn that Chick Corea would fill in. Chick Corea and Dave Holland had just left the Miles Davis group and had formed a new avant-garde quartet called Circle, with saxophonist Anthony Braxton and drummer Barry Altschul.

Brian Cooke cannot be certain, but he recalls that the second gig at El Matador ended prematurely, with Chet falling out with the club's management. The gig also ended on a sour note for the other band members, who were only paid half of what they had been promised. "The closest I came to having a run in with Chet was over the money," he said. "I called him and said, 'Hey Chet, can we go over these figures?' I got an elaborate explanation—he claimed that he didn't remember, or that he'd had to pay union dues. I guess addicts are used to giving explanations like that. We ended up sitting down with people from the Musicians' Union, trying to get to the bottom of it. In the end, we just gave up."[74]

The band fell apart after this incident. Despite Chet's erratic behaviour, both Brian Cooke and Robb Fisher look back on their experience fondly. "I liked him a lot as a person," said Fisher, "but you couldn't trust him with the money." As if to illustrate this point, Chet called the pianist out of the blue about one month later. "'Hey Brian, I'm coming up to San Francisco—can I borrow $20 from you?' He drove all the way up the Berkeley, where I was living, chatted for about five minutes, then drove into the city."[75]

Although Chet remained in the San Francisco area for the next two years, Brian Cooke cannot remember him landing any prominent gigs. "To the best of my knowledge, he didn't play at all in the months that followed. If he had done, I'm sure I would have heard. I can only speculate that he'd worn out his welcome at the main clubs by that time."

By late 1970, Chet was becoming more open about his friendship with Diane Vavra, even hiring her as a babysitter to look after the children. She witnessed Chet's verbal abuse of his children, a pattern of behaviour he seems to have inherited from his father. She also learned that Chet could be physically abusive, and once saw Carol sporting a black eye.

Diane found Chet to be extremely self-centred, blaming his drug addiction, his verbal and physical abuse, on his intense frustration. He struggled to come to terms with the fact that he could barely make a living from music, as he had nothing else to fall back on. In addition, he could not understand the growing popularity of fusion. "Some of these tunes, I can't hear them," he told her. "I don't know where they're going." He also felt trapped in an increasingly loveless marriage to Carol, but was reluctant to leave her given her dependence on him, both in terms of heroin and financial support for their three children. But there was a more tender side to him, too—a childlike enthusiasm when all was well with the world, a man who would sometimes cry when they made love, grateful for the release from his struggles.

She witnessed the more tender side of Chet in 1971, when he landed a gig at Boise, Idaho. He drove to the gig alone, but shortly after his arrival, arranged for a plane ticket to be sent to Diane. She stayed for the remainder of the week, after which they drove back to San Francisco together. Carol later discovered the ticket stub in Chet's jacket pocket, and challenged him about the affair. When Chet admitted that he had been seeing Diane, Carol flew into a rage, telephoned her and ended up confronting Diane's mother. The incident placed a considerable strain on their relationship, but they continued to see one another for the next eighteen months until Chet moved to New York.

The next two years were fairly barren from a musical perspective. Chet is rumoured to have recorded an album of material written by Dutch painter and sculptor, Karel Appel. The album was apparently recorded in San Francisco, but no tapes had surfaced by the time of Appel's death in 2006.

Chet was arrested on two occasions while living in Milpitas, on both occasions charged with driving under the influence of narcotics. The second arrest, which took place in 1972, may have finally prompted Chet to join the Methadone Maintenance Program; whether he was encouraged to sign up by a judge has never been made clear.

Chet would have been familiar with methadone from the three months he spent at the Chino Institute for Men in 1969. According to a recent White House drug policy document "Heroin releases an excess of dopamine in the body and causes users to need an opiate continuously occupying the opioid receptor in the brain. Methadone occupies this receptor and is the stabilizing factor that permits addicts on methadone to change their behaviour and to discontinue heroin use. Taken orally once a day, methadone suppresses narcotic withdrawal for between 24 and 36 hours. Because methadone is effective in eliminating withdrawal symptoms, it is used in detoxifying opiate addicts ... Methadone reduces the cravings associated with heroin use and blocks the high from heroin, but it does not provide the euphoric rush. Consequently, methadone patients do not experience the extreme highs and lows that result from the waxing and waning of heroin in blood levels. Ultimately, the patient remains physically dependent on the opioid, but is freed from the uncontrolled, compulsive, and disruptive behaviour seen in heroin addicts."[76]

Carol also signed up for the methadone programme, and for the next few years, Dean, Paul and Missy grew accustomed to the site of a tray containing jars of clear liquid sitting on one shelf of the refrigerator. "I grew up with methadone in the fridge," Paul later recalled. "I didn't know what it was." At that time the children were blissfully unaware that both parents were recovering drug addicts.[77]

Chet may simply have been obeying a court order at the time, and was probably unaware of the significance of the step he had taken. In time, it would provide him with his first step back into the jazz mainstream, and a way out of his relationship with Carol.

Chapter Thirteen

SHE WAS TOO GOOD TO ME
1973–1975

"Ruth—a new beginning."—Chet Baker

Carol Baker has claimed that Chet was clean from the moment he enrolled on the methadone programme in 1972. "From 1969 [sic] to 1975, Chet was clean," she said. "The whole time he took nothing but methadone, nothing else, believe me. He became a real family man. He loved his kids, he really cared about his kids."[1]

In fact, Chet was still grappling with a number of issues at this time. He was struggling to stay clean, finding that methadone did not provide him with the same kind of high as heroin. He also had trouble finding regular work, having played only sporadically over the preceding two years. Finally, he was facing up the fact that his marriage was all but over; rather than becoming a family man, as Carol suggested, he had continued his love affair with Diane Vavra, and was considering whether to move to New York with her.

March of 1973 brought a sharp reminder of what might have been when one of the former stars of West Coast jazz returned to California for a triumphant tour. After a number of years in which he had not been particularly active in music, Maynard Ferguson had assembled a new band and was touring nationwide. By the time he reached the Great American Music Hall in San Francisco there was friction within the band, with trombone player Ed Byrne confronting Ferguson over the fact that he had little opportunity to solo. "We would play two gigs a day, but he would only let me take one solo," Byrne recalled. "He had two players who could play on the bill—me and a trumpet played called Bob Summers, and he wanted the audience to know he possessed two really good soloists, but like Gerry Mulligan, he always wanted to follow a bad player."[2]

As the two of them argued, Chet made his way over to talk to Ferguson. He was barely recognisable from the old days, and Bob Summers was the first to recognise him. "Maynard starting bragging to Chet, who was strung out, and Chet went for his throat," said Byrne. "Maynard's bouncer had to drag him off. At that time, Chet was completely strung out, almost destitute. He used to show up to gig after gig, never saying anything to anybody."[3]

A couple of months later, and Chet was in far better shape, playing a small gig at the Sundown club. Steve Houben, a cousin of Chet's friend Jacques Pelzer, attended the gig and introduced himself. "There weren't that many people in the club, probably because not many people knew he was back playing," he recalled. "I talked to him, and told him that I was related to Jacques Pelzer. He told me that they were good friends. Chet mentioned Jean-Louis Chautemps, who he had played with in the 1950s. I told him that I also knew him. When he found out I was a musician, he looked me, and said, 'Are you good enough to play with me?' I couldn't really answer that question. He invited me for the next set, and I played a set with him. I was really scared. He liked my flute playing, because at that time, in 1973, I wasn't really playing saxophone—I'd been playing flute since I was seven. We played a few tunes. He asked me if I'd play more, but I didn't want to spoil it. His playing sounded beautiful to me; he didn't seem to be having any teeth problems at that time."[4]

By early June, Chet had decided that he needed a fresh start. He thought he would try his luck in New York, and drove to Denver, hoping to persuade his friend Phil Urso to join him. If everything worked out, he hoped that he could persuade Diane Vavra to join him, leaving Carol and the children behind in San Francisco.

Phil Urso had also cleaned up his act by this stage, and was working as a music teacher for the Denver Department of Education. He had married an Italian lady in 1969, and by the time Chet arrived, they were expecting their first child. One evening they went to the Warehouse Club to watch Dizzy Gillespie play; Dizzy recognised the two musicians, and took the trouble to introduce them to the audience. "After he got through Dizzy said, 'Why don't you guys come up to my room at the Ramada, and I'll show you my brand new orange juice squeezer!'"[5]

It may not have sounded like the most enticing of invitations, but it turned out to be an event that changed Chet Baker's life, and put his career as a musician back on track. When they reached Dizzy's room, he sent drummer

Mickey Roker down to the lobby to get thirty bucks' worth of quarters. "Dizzy says, 'Let's play a bit of poker!'" recalled Phil Urso. "'By the way, what are you guys doing out here in Denver, Colorado?' Chet says, 'I came from California. There's nothing going on, so I'm on my way to New York, and I think I'm gonna take Phil with me'. Dizzy said, 'So in other words, you guys are out of work?' I said, 'Once in a while, I get one or two nights a week'. Dizzy said, 'Just a minute', and reached over for the phone, and got Rosemary Canterino, who owned the Half Note in New York." Within a few minutes, the first gig of Chet's 'comeback' was confirmed.[6]

The Half Note was originally situated in Greenwich Village, where it had established a reputation for contemporary jazz, showcasing names like Lennie Tristano and John Coltrane. It was run by three siblings—Rosemary Canterino and her two brothers, Mike and Sonny. "It was a homey, kind of Italian restaurant," recalled the pianist Harold Danko. "It was very funky, and well-worn." In October 1972, the club moved to larger premises at 149 West 54th Street, across the street from Jimmy Ryan's. "When they moved uptown they started dressing in tuxedos and charging cover at the door, and had to provide more of a show," said Danko. "Some of the people who liked the old place were not so happy with the way it felt uptown." In fact, the club only lasted for two years in the new location, closing in late 1974.[7]

Chet was initially booked to play for two weeks, starting on July 2nd. The opening was still three weeks away, so Chet called Diane, asking her to join him in Denver. When she arrived, he told her about the engagement in New York. He explained that it could be a fresh start for him, and potentially for her, too—they could rent an apartment together, and find a school for her son, Ronny. Every time they had discussed this previously, Diane had sounded excited, but all of a sudden, she sounded hesitant. "I want to provide a stable home for my little boy," she explained. She had also watched Chet battle to stay on methadone, and knew it would be hard for him to stay clean in New York. They got into a heated argument, and Chet turned physical, breaking one of her ribs. She knew that Chet had hit Carol, but it was the first time she had witnessed his violence first-hand. She returned home alone, convinced that she had made the right decision.

Phil Urso told Chet that if he was going to headline in New York, he was going to have to smarten his appearance. "Chet didn't look very good then," he explained. "I gave him one of my dark suits to try and make him look better. He tried it on, and it looked pretty good. But his face was sunk in from using."

In late June, about a week before they were due to open, they left for New York. "He drove, and I took a 747. I was the only passenger; I could have been the President of the United States!" said Urso. "I landed, took a cab, and went to the Bryant Hotel. I got a room, and sure enough, about three or fours hours later, Chet arrived. He must have been driving awful fast to make it from Denver in the time that he did. He drove very fast, and very good. He had eyes like a hawk."[8]

A saxophonist by the name of Turk Mauro was headlining the week before Chet opened. Chet and Phil went along to the club one evening, and Chet sat in with the band. "He made casual conversation, but looked kind of tired, having driven from Colorado," recalled the band's pianist Harold Danko.[9]

Later that evening, the band's drummer, Mel Lewis, approached Phil Urso and asked him whether they needed a rhythm section. "As far as I'm concerned you're hired, but I have to double-check with Chet," he said. Urso asked Chet, who replied, "Get them, get them!"[10]

The band opened the following Monday. The opening act consisted of Jackie Cain and Roy Kral, a vocal duo who had a recording contract with Creed Taylor's CTI label at that time. Jackie and Roy had been recording since the late 1940s, but had enjoyed something of a revival in the early 1970s, recording *Time and Love* with producer Don Sebesky in 1972.

Chet had evidently forgotten the dark suit that Phil Urso had given him, and turned up wearing burgundy trousers with a pair of cowboy boots—hardly in keeping with the supper club environment the Canterinos were looking for. Rosemary took Chet and Phil to one side before they took to the stage. "She had to tell us to put jackets on, because Chet was very thin, and I had a big pot belly from eating too much," laughed Urso. "We didn't want to show the audience that I had my stomach sticking out!"

Chet was completely oblivious to the fact that his red jacket clashed badly with his burgundy trousers, and apparently saw it as a winning combination. "He looked like a bit like an Oklahoma cowboy who hadn't eaten for a while," Danko later recalled.[11]

The pianist admits that he was both excited and nervous supporting Chet for the first time. "I'd played with Woody Herman before," he recalled, "but I wasn't that seasoned a player." Chet did his best to make the band feel welcome, but Phil Urso was particularly helpful. "He had gotten some of the music together, and had written out parts for the piano—some of the tunes that I didn't know. If Chet didn't seem too happy, he'd usually say something like, 'It's not right!' Then a dark pall would come over the place. Phil would come over and whisper, 'Chet usually likes this chord here'. Phil really knew what Chet's musical preferences were if I wasn't doing the right thing."[12]

Chet had problems with his teeth, particularly in the first week of the engagement. His dentures kept coming loose, and his embouchure would go to pieces. He'd curse under his breath, and try to adjust his teeth, or go backstage between songs to re-glue them. His problems were witnessed by a number of jazz critics, with Richard Williams of the *Melody Maker* remarking that some of the notes he tried to play came out as "empty, whistling air".[13]

One evening Stan Getz walked into the club wearing a white suit, his Swedish girlfriend by his side. Getz had found it easier to adapt to the growing popularity of fusion. He had worked with Chick Corea, who had played with Miles Davis on *In a Silent Way* and *Bitches Brew* back in 1967, when he recorded *Sweet Rain.* He invited the dynamic pianist to play with him again in late 1971, a collaboration that resulted in an album by the name of *Captain Marvel*. The record also featured the electric bass player Stanley Clarke, who went on to play with Corea in *Return To Forever*, and former Miles Davis percussionists Tony Williams and Airto Moreira. Released in 1972, the album had received rave reviews, and is regarded as one of Getz's finest albums of the decade.

Chet and Stan had never been close, and when the saxophonist asked if he could sit in, Chet reluctantly agreed. At one point, Chet suggested they play 'This is Always', but Stan was not familiar with the tune. He walked over to Phil Urso and said, "Sing it to me, Phil, sing it to me."

"He could hear the chords, he knew what to do, but he wanted me to sing the melody," recalled Urso. "Then Chet whispered to me, 'Don't help him, Phil, don't help him!' They didn't like each other, and Chet only let him sit in because he had such a big name."[14]

The New York press soon picked up on Chet's comeback, portraying him as a man who had come back from the dark side. On July 8th, the syndicated columnist Rex Reed wrote an article entitled 'Jazzman Chet Baker is back from his bad trip'. "The story of Chet Baker is an American tragedy," he wrote, "so sordid and sad it makes Billie Holiday's life and *Young Man with a Horn* seem like Disney cartoons."[15]

Two weeks later, Bob Micklin of *New York Newsday* conducted an interview of his own, in which Chet once again recounted his tales of woe. "After I paid my hotel bill last week, I had only $8 left in my pocket," he claimed. "I can't even get enough money to bring my wife and kids here from California."[16]

Many musicians would have been upset to be portrayed in such a way, but Chet was delighted to be back in New York after several years in the wilderness. He also believed that any publicity would help to bring in the crowds. The Canterinos were certainly pleased; despite Chet's initial teething problems, the club had been full most nights, and they invited the band to return for a third week starting on July 23rd.

One Friday evening, a young blonde lady made her way into the club, her eyes damp with tears. Ruth Young, born Ruth Youngstein, was the twenty-one-year-old adopted daughter of the Hollywood film mogul, Max Youngstein. She had recently learned that her parents were getting a divorce, and had just met her father in a nearby hotel. "I wanted to find out what my father had to say to me, to put some perspective on the human ingredients of the divorce," she said. "As a result of our conversation I was so overwhelmed and devastated, unable to figure out what to do, that I walked up the block to the corner of 6th Avenue. I continued to walk, and came across the new Half Note club, which was almost opposite Carnegie Hall. As I approached the club, I saw these posters advertising Chet Baker in the window, and couldn't believe it. I stood there for a few minutes, still upset, before going in."[17]

Ruth was an aspiring jazz singer, and was a fan of artists like Anita O'Day and Julie London. She had sung in a couple of New York clubs in the early 1970s under the stage name of Jessica Shayne, but was plagued by a lack of self-confidence. Chet Baker was another of her childhood idols, and she was surprised to see that he was still playing.

She recognised the barman from the old Half Note, and went over to talk with him for a few minutes, then sat at the bar to watch Chet play. "I watched him throughout his performance, and he was gaunt, and he looked terrible and he was wearing that red and burgundy combination that he thought was such a big hit, which was wild, with a pair of cowboy boots," she said. "He looked absolutely horrible."[18]

Towards the end of the set, he glanced over towards the bar, and made eye contact with Ruth, who sat on a stool by the bar. She looked glamorous and sophisticated, a tall, willowy figure in a red dress, her long blonde hair hanging down in curls, smoking a cigarette. "I believe to this day that that glance established a connection between us," she recalls.[19]

A few minutes later, Chet walked over to the bar. Ruth greeted him by saying, "Hey, I got to tell you, it's great to see you. I think you're doing a hell of a job." Chet was soon drawn to her warm smile and vivacious personality. "He said some kind, simplistic things, which came across as very invitational to me, and eventually said, 'Well, don't be a stranger'," she said. "He probably did not mean that the way I heard it, but I was naïve, and something led me back to the club the following night."

Ruth did not feel she had met a "Greek god", as Diane Vavra had claimed, three years earlier. "Whatever happened after that had nothing to do with love or romance—we connected as human beings," she said. "The fact that he was able to be there looking like he did, and sounding as he did, was amazing; the fact that he could do that told me he had the defiance to believe in what he was. He sounded like hell, looked like hell—but as I found out in the years that followed, he was entitled to that."[20]

Chet soon learned that Ruth came from a privileged background, and in the years that followed he abused this, frittering away her trust fund and selling off a number of her prized possessions.

Ruth was one of three adopted children raised by Max Youngstein, a partner and vice president of United Artists, and his wife, Mae. Youngstein had played a major part in the rescue of United Artists in 1951, when it faced financial difficulties. During his years at the company, he oversaw the production of such classics as *The African Queen* (1951), *High Noon* (1952), *The Night of the Hunter* (1955), *Witness for the Prosecution* (1958), *Some Like It Hot* (1959), *The Alamo* (1960), *The Magnificent Seven* (1960), *The Misfits* (1961), *Dr No* (1962), and *The Great Escape* (1963). He left United Artists in 1963 to form his own production company, producing films such as *Fail Safe* (1964) and *The Money Trap* (1965).

Ruth was brought up in an affluent environment, and remembers meeting Hollywood stars such as Marilyn Monroe and Jane Russell in the living room of their luxury Bel Air house. She remembers her upbringing as unsettled, however, moving house every few years, changing schools and struggling to make new friends. She struggled to form a close bond with her father, who was a workaholic, and by the time she moved to New York, around 1970, she had no real sense of her own identity. Her father made sure she was financially secure, leaving her a "megabucks little trust fund". But as she later explained, she had no idea of her place in the world. "When you grow up with money, you don't understand what anything means," she said. "Until you don't have any."

As fate would have it, Ruth met Chet on Friday 13th—a date that took on even greater significance when Chet died in Amsterdam years later, again on Friday 13th. It is a date that fills her with mixed emotions, even to this day—her "lucky, unlucky day". The next ten years saw the two of them embark on a relationship of co-dependence, in all senses of the word. Chet needed someone to love him, to take care of him. But he also needed someone who could understand him as a musician, something Carol had never grasped. "Chet was like a little baby, in many respects," recalled bass player Jimmy Madison. "Somebody would always wipe his ass for him. Ruth would take care of him. She'd make sure he got to the methadone clinic, she'd make sure he could find his passport, hours before he was due to fly. Things like that happened all the time—there was always some kind of emergency. He was a sweet, lovable guy, but he needed someone to take care of him."[21]

For her own part, Ruth needed a father figure, someone who could see her potential and instill her with the confidence to pursue her dreams as a singer.

Ruth got her first vision of how her life was about to change from Chet's close friend, Phil Urso. She had started to spend more time in the company of the band, both at the Chinese restaurant around the corner from the Bryant Hotel, or back at the hotel itself. "Every time I was in Phil's company, he persisted in telling me that I had to take care of Chet," she said. "I think Phil thought of himself as a watchdog for Chet, in some way or another; he felt a protective urge, in spite of his own drug problems. He was very forthcoming about what he and Chet used to do, and it scared the shit out of me, to be honest. I don't know whether he was still fighting demons of his own at that time, but I appreciated his candour. He explained that I had to keep Chet away from heroin. Thinking about it, I'm not even sure why he came to me; I was overwhelmed, but in the end I was happy to take over the role as Chet's caretaker."[22]

At this stage, Chet had no idea how the relationship with Ruth would develop. He didn't want to be alone in New York, and felt bad about the way things had ended with Diane. In mid-August he wrote a letter to her, addressing it to Diane Vavra-Baker, begging her to come back to him. She eventually agreed to meet with him in Chicago in October, but by that stage,

Chet's relationship with Ruth had developed further, and she was travelling on the road with him. When Diane called his hotel room in Chicago to confirm their plans, Chet's response was cold. "I'm sorry, that's not possible right now."

In the weeks that followed the Half Note engagement, Chet struggled to find another job in New York. "Things got a little slow," Phil Urso later recalled, and he returned to Denver. He had already stayed longer than he had originally intended, and felt the need to get back to his wife. Chet persuaded Harold Danko to stay on, however, and he took over Phil's role in booking the rhythm section. "I had the name of every bass player in town at that point—Richard Davis, Ron Carter. I remember calling around, but these guys were busy, of course. I said, 'I'm the piano player with Chet Baker; can you play Saturday night?' It was a great position for me to be in because they would end up taking down my number. It was a great way for me to make contacts."[23]

In late August, Chet landed a gig playing Saturday nights at a club called the Town Crier at East Islip, a town on Long Island. Harold Danko recruited Harvey Schwartz to play on bass and Stan Gage on drums. Chet found it challenging to play in a quartet, as his chops were still in relatively poor shape. As a result, Danko suggested they hire a friend by the name of Bob Mover to play saxophone. "I took the Long Island railroad out to East Islip," Mover remembered. "I played the gig by ear—he played tunes I never really knew, like 'Dee's Dilemma' and 'Conception'. I managed to get through those tunes. He had a B-flat book, but that didn't help me, because I only played alto at the time, and it was easier to hear it than to try to transpose B-flat into E-flat by looking at it. He liked it, and I got through the night. He was doing Saturday nights, so he said, 'Why don't you come next Saturday?' So I took the train up next Saturday, and after the gig he said, 'Do you want to go to Chicago on Monday?'"[24]

The gig in Chicago took place at the Jazz Showcase, starting on Wednesday 12th September, the band playing for five nights. The gig had obviously been booked in July when Chet was playing at the Half Note, as the posters advertise Phil Urso as appearing with the band. Chicago also appears to have marked the debut of a new rhythm section, with Michael Moore joining on bass and Jimmy Madison on drums. "That was a really fun rhythm section," Danko recalled, "and I hoped that Chet could get enough work to keep us together."

Jimmy Madison lived in the same apartment block as Harold Danko at 808, West End Avenue, just around the corner from Ruth's apartment. "It was a real community," said Madison. "The apartment used to be called the 'Uptown Conservatory', because there were so many musicians living there. It was really close to Manhattan School of Music and Columbia. Over the previous two years I had transformed the living room of my apartment into a little recording studio. By the time I was working with Chet, it was pretty good, and I even started recording little dates for people. We needed a place to rehearse, and we used to play at my house all the time. Harold would come downstairs, Ruth and Chet would come across the street, and we'd have a rehearsal."[25]

The following month, the band was booked to play a week-long gig at Baker's Keyboard Lounge in Detroit. Michael Moore was making his own way to the gig, so Chet agreed to drive Ruth and the other members of the band to the gig in his Mustang convertible. "Chet was supposed to pick us up at 2 p.m., and we were standing around waiting for him," Madison recalled. "It got to 3 p.m., 4 p.m., 5 p.m., 6 p.m., still no sign of him. We were getting really pissed off. It would take hours and hours to drive there, and we were thinking, 'How are we going to do this?' At 10 p.m. he finally shows up. I said, 'What the fuck! Where have you been?' If you know anything about Chet you know that he'd be like, 'Hey, Jimmy, don't worry, everything's cool'. Even when he was upset, he hardly ever raised his voice."

"I remember it was a funky old car, and at least by this time, it smelled like gasoline," Madison continued. "It smelled like there was something leaking. Chet and Ruth chain-smoked all the time, and I was afraid the whole car was going to blow up! This was the late fall, so we drove across I-80, which goes west out of New York, and drove straight through all night, because we had to open next night. Chet and I took turns driving—and when we got out to the middle of Ohio some place, we ran into a blizzard. You couldn't see twenty feet! I happened to be driving when the shit really hit the fan. It was twelve, one o'clock in the morning, and I cannot see the hand in front of my face. All I could see, barely, was the tail lights of a truck that happened to be in front of me and a swirling mass of snow. It was the scariest thing in my life. I was petrified that if I tried to get off the road, I'd wreck, or whoever was behind me would plough into the back of me, and there'd be a three hundred car pile-up. I said, 'Chet, what am I going to do'. In his slow drawl, he said, 'Just keep driving, Jim, keep driving'. 'But Chet, we're going to die!' There was no way he could take over the driving, so he said, 'Just keep going, Jim, you're doing fine'. This whole time Bob was crammed in the back, practically under the drum kit and the luggage!"[26]

Chet's playing was starting to become more consistent by this stage. His chops had become stronger because he was playing on a more regular basis, and he seems to have found more reliable glue for his dentures, which were not coming loose on such a regular basis. "If his chops weren't so good on a certain day, he'd simply sing more, or scat-sing," said Danko. "He would sing what he might have played on the trumpet."

Chet managed to stay away from heroin while he was on the road, making a pilgrimage to the local methadone clinic on a daily basis. He continued to smoke a little pot, however, and almost got busted when smoking in his car between sets outside Baker's Keyboard Lounge. "What looked like a cop car pulled in behind us," Madison recalled. "It had a light on—it wasn't flashing, but it looked like a police car. We thought, 'Oh my god, we're going to get busted'. So we all took whatever we had, and just ate it, gulping it down. We waited for the police to come by, and nothing happened. We waited, and eventually got out of the car, and it turned out it was a fire inspection vehicle that had come to check the club out. We were ripped, because we had eaten everything that we had. Then we broke into nervous laughter, relieved that we hadn't been caught!"[27]

When the band returned to New York in late October, Chet dropped a bombshell, quietly admitting that his wife was going to be moving to New York the following month. "My jaw just dropped," Ruth recalled. "It was a devastating announcement, and something he'd kept very well hidden. Initially I didn't say much, and told him that I didn't think it was going to work out. He tried to coerce me into staying, telling me that he was not happy with his family situation; he was not in love with Carol, he had not been involved with her intimately for many years, and did not know what to do. He was terrified of divorcing her, because he didn't know what legal implications he could suffer. She'd threatened him with the tax thing. 'If you ever leave, I'll go straight to the tax authorities; you won't have to worry about it, I'll do it for you. I'll ruin you'."[28]

Chet felt conflicted and confused, and asked Ruth to give him more time to sort things out with Carol. In the interim, he suggested Ruth pretend that she was his manager. Carol arrived in New York in early November. On the first night of the new engagement, Chet asked Ruth if she could collect Carol from the Bryant Hotel and escort her to the club. Ruth knocked on the door of her hotel room, and was amazed to see a Liz Taylor lookalike standing before her in a white slip. "She'd broken the zipper on her dress and reached for something else to put on," she recalled. "She must have spent a good four hours painting on a face like that."[29]

While she changed, Carol opened up to Ruth as though she was her best friend. "She started talking to me like a confidante, and made some very interesting revelations," revealed Ruth. "She told me about Richard Carpenter, and how she blamed him for her and Chet being hooked on this shit—meaning the heroin and the methadone. She told me she had migraine headaches, and Chet suggested she try it. She denied it in the *Let's Get Lost* movie, but I remember her telling me, and later saw a methadone bottle in Chet's suit jacket with her name on it. Eventually I said, 'We'd better leave, 'cos it's getting late'. So we hopped in a cab, and she's still talking her face off. I got a big kick out of it! Of course it was devastating, I was not very comfortable, but it was very helpful information."[30]

Ruth brought Carol to the club, and between sets they sat at the same table. Chet told Carol that Ruth was working as his manager, and had helped him secure a number of bookings around New York and in the mid-West. "Carol was none the wiser," recalls Ruth. "I felt very sorry for her, had one moment of pity for her that night. After that, forget it—I saw just who she was, what she was. My anger was with him, at that moment, for putting us through this."

Over the next few months, Chet tried to spend as much time as possible in New York, gradually building up his contacts amongst musicians and club-owners. One such new contact was Jack Tafoya, a promoter and jazz enthusiast who ran a non-profit organization called Jazz Adventures. He would arrange jazz luncheons most Fridays, organised occasional concerts, and even hosted a television programme, *Jazz Adventures*, which aired on a public station in New York City between 1970 and 1976.

He also led a nine- or ten-piece band of his own, the Jazz Adventures Orchestra. "He had a small band, and he liked to sing a few tunes here and there—while reading the lyrics on the stand!" recalled vibraphonist Warren Chiasson. "He provided employment for certain musicians. Even Chet played with that little band—and dutifully, just playing in the trumpet section." Jack Tafoya's son, an artist by the name of Patrick Tafoya, joked that a thousand members played with the band every year. "Jazz was my father's passion," he recalled. "I remember coming home from school," he said, "and being told that Dizzie [sic] Gillespie would be joining us for dinner at my father's apartment. That was a special memory for me."[31]

It was through the Jazz Adventures Orchestra that Chet became re-acquainted with the trombone player Ed Byrne, who he had met in San Francisco earlier that year. "Within a few days of arriving back in New York, some people I knew told me there was this nine-piece band featuring Chet that Jack Tafoya had, called the Jazz Adventures Orchestra," he said "They wanted me to be the musical director of that group. They had this guy, Gene Roland, writing the arrangements but they were terrible; he was a big band arranger who had written some things for Stan Kenton that weren't bad, but his five-horn arrangements were awful. They wanted me to bring in my tunes and write some arrangements for the band. Jack Wilkins and Frank Vicari were in the band, and a lot of prominent studio players."[32]

The first gig that Byrne was involved in was a New Year's Eve show just outside New York City. Harold Danko had been invited to go on tour with Woody Herman, and Chet's pianist from 1964–65, Hal Galper, had taken his place in the interim. "Hal had this crazy woman he was living with. She was like a weeper! We were playing up on stage with the Jazz Adventures band—a nine-piece group—and she sat in front of the band stand, crying her eyes out the whole time, shaking her head. Like, 'How did it ever come to this?' She ruined the gig for everybody," laughed Byrne.[33]

Chet played with Jack Tafoya's band periodically through the spring of 1974, mostly in low-key venues, but occasionally at New York clubs such as the Half Note. Ruth Young also started to make bookings for Chet at this time. "I didn't go running off to William Morris, or somebody, and say you've got to take care of this guy. I didn't have that instinct," she recalls. "He was happy for me to do what I could, and give me a small percentage on top. We did very nominal jobs—places like the Town Crier on Long Island, the Ballroom in Baltimore. I used to get up and sing from time to time. Although he was playing in little dives, I took great pride in helping out, and felt like I was climbing the ladder with him. The guys in the band—Harold Danko, Dave Shapiro and Jimmy Madison—were always helpful; 'Why don't you have Ruth call this place, or that place?' There was nothing big time, and it stayed that way until after he started recording again."[34]

Jack Tafoya also introduced Chet to a number of useful contacts in New York. One evening in March 1974, he took him to a club to meet Warren

Chiasson. "Jack knew I had all of Chet's albums, and brought him down to Tribeca; there was a little place I was playing with my trio, called the Merchant's Tavern," said Chiasson. "I had Cecil McBee on the bass, I had Beaver Harris on the drums. I was doing some of my electronic stuff with the vibes, as well as playing acoustically."[35]

In fact, Chet had first met Warren Chiasson back in 1955, on his first tour of Europe. The young vibraphonist was playing with the Royal Artillery Band from Nova Scotia, which was stationed in Germany at that time. They enjoyed a brief vacation that summer and travelled to Amsterdam. "I met Chet at the train station, in between gigs," he recalled. "We shook hands, and I told Chet I had all his albums. He was really nice, and said, 'Good luck to you—maybe we'll hook up some time in the States."

When they did finally hook up at the Merchant's Tavern, Chet was impressed with Chiasson's playing, and suggested they get together. "We played at the Half Note, and I got him Charlie Haden on bass and Beaver Harris on drums," recalled Chiasson. "I alternated between playing the vibes and playing the piano, because he liked my feel on the piano." On one memorable evening, the band was joined by Lee Konitz on alto saxophone. That gig appears to have been witnessed by Jack Tafoya, who invited Chet Baker and Lee Konitz to play on his TV programme, *Jazz Adventures*, with the pianist Keith Jarrett. The subsequent recording was later released as an unofficial LP entitled *Chet Baker—Lee Konitz—Keith Jarrett*.[36]

The band with Chiasson only played for two weekends at the Half Note before going their separate ways. Charlie Haden was playing with Keith Jarrett, drummer Beaver Harris had his own band, the '360 Degree Experience', whilst Chiasson was also working with George Shearing, in addition to leading a group of his own.

In April 1974, Lee Konitz suggested to Chet that they form a band of their own. Chet had been playing regularly with Bob Mover for a number of months, but Mover had left to travel to Brazil, and stayed there through the end of the year. They recruited Michael Moore on bass and Beaver Harris on drums, and played one concert at Ornette Coleman's Loft, a spacious loft-style venue on Prince Street. The concert was recorded by India Navigation, and later released as an album, *Chet Baker—Lee Konitz in Concert*. The saxophonist later suggested the album did not give a good impression of Chet's playing at this time. "Chet didn't feel so good that day," he recalled. "It was obvious that he had no desire to play."[37]

The collaboration with Lee Konitz only lasted a short time before breaking up, with the saxophonist later blaming Chet's attitude. "I had the impression that Chet always had a certain ego problem," he claimed. "When we played together, he believed that I wanted to determine the style of music. That I wanted to be the leader. That wasn't the case at all, but it hurt our collaboration. So I think there was something unmusical going on between us."[38]

Bud Shank also met Chet at this time, and believes that his behaviour was less of an ego problem, but reflected the insecurity he was feeling as a musician at that time. "I think that Chet was unsure of himself then," he said. "The direction of jazz had changed while he was away. I never noticed much of an ego problem myself, but I know that something similar often happens with people who are outwardly very quiet. Chet was like that. He didn't speak much. He was turned in on himself. So he was as a young man, and so he was after his comeback. It was difficult for him to express himself. Every contact, in fact, was a problem for him."[39]

Given his insecurity, he found himself feeling most at home in small venues, where he could get lost in the music. One such venue was Stryker's Pub, situated on 86th Street and Columbus Avenue. Lee Konitz, who lived a few blocks away, had introduced it to Chet. The saxophonist used to play there regularly as a duet with a bass player, and Chet used to sit in with them, as captured in *The Hip*. "Snapshots of the wanderer. In Stryker's Bar, New York City, Lee Konitz and Wilbur Little have pulled a house of about twelve cats for their duet. Nobody bothered to open the back of the bar where the tables are. Suddenly, a third instrument nudges shyly into the unraveling lines. Konitz's eyes blinked open and closed again. He knew who it was from the sound, long before the light caught on the trumpet player with the big African amethyst ring on his little finger. Nobody had seen him come on, and he was sitting there in gloom, feet on the chair, head bowed, playing. 'Hey baby', murmured the bartender, 'It's Mister Chet'."

The owner, Olivia, asked Chet was asked if he wanted to play with his own band, and offered him Monday and Tuesday nights. She only had a limited budget, so Chet started out with a trio, with Harold Danko playing the club's electric piano, and Ed Byrne playing trombone. Occasionally Dave Shapiro joined them on bass, but they rarely played with a drummer in the first few months. "Dave Shapiro didn't play that well back then, but he plays very well now," said Ed Byrne. "His choice of notes wasn't good then, but his time was good."[40]

For his own part, Chet's playing had continued to improve. "He was playing great," the trombonist recalled. "He was inspirational—one of the best players I have ever played with for any length of time, and I've played with a lot of people, including Herbie Hancock. I had great respect for him. He was very melodic. Sometimes his teeth caused him problems, and he couldn't get his lips to work. But then he'd put down his trumpet and sing his solo. And that was interesting—he was the best scat singer I ever heard, because he sang the notes an instrumentalist would sing; not just clichés, like most singers."[41]

Although Carol and the children were now living in New York at the Bryant Hotel, Chet continued to see Ruth at every opportunity. "It was hard for him, but he did live up to what he said he would do—he stayed loyal to me," said Ruth. "He spent every occasion he could with me, and by the time she found out, we were fairly inseparable."

After a few months, Carol began to have her suspicions about Ruth, realising that she was more than just his manager. "One day she started to give me a sense that she knew what was really going on," said Ruth. "At one point she told me, 'You know, Chet has no women friends, and I have no men friends, and that's the way it is'. Eventually I reacted to that remark by wearing a very strong perfume for a while and Carol soon got the message. Chet would complain to me, 'Oh great, now Carol's smelt your fucking perfume'. He was suggesting that I was the one causing problems with his wife."[42]

Chet tried to allay Carol's fears by inviting her to come along to Stryker's one night every week, inviting Ruth the other night. This plan backfired, however, as Ruth became jealous. "The night that Ruth wasn't there she would get fucked up and keep calling the club," recalled Ed Byrne. "The Puerto Rican bartender, knowing that it was her, would not answer the phone all night. It used to ring off the hook, all night long. She would just ruin the music."[43]

The reasons for Ruth's anxiety soon became clear. The band was playing a gig in Boston, and Ruth was enjoying the summer heat. "I was running around in a bikini in this hotel, and noticed my boobs had got bigger," she said. "I found out I was ten weeks pregnant. When I told Chet he just said, 'If that's what you want, sure. I'll help you as much as I can'. Like the way he helped out with Carol. That was devastating. I really wanted a baby, but only for the right reasons." Ruth didn't want to make the same mistake as Carol, and terminated the pregnancy.

In the years that followed, Ruth became pregnant on two further occasions, despite her attention to birth control. "Second time around, I only waited seven weeks. But the first one still haunts me," she recalled, her eyes filling with tears. "But that's what I loved about him, too—he didn't pull any punches."[44]

Back in New York, a young record producer by the name of John Snyder made his way to Stryker's to listen to Chet play. Snyder worked for Creed Taylor, who had worked as a producer at Verve records for a number of years, before founding Impulse! Records in 1960. Seven years later he formed CTI, which soon developed a reputation for jazz fusion, and was home to artists such as George Benson and Freddie Hubbard. A lawyer by training, Snyder was hired to run the publishing company, but was eventually responsible for legal and business affairs, publishing, manufacturing and distribution. "I was just a junior guy, I was twenty-five years old. By the time I left there at twenty-seven, I'd been in charge of every department. It was because the business decisions were so bad, Creed had to keep firing people. So as the department heads got fired, he just put me in their job. I was smart, and I worked twenty hours a day, and I had no political agenda, so he trusted me. I was in charge of the contracts, and I got put in charge of A&R at one point, because he asked me to find songs for Hank Crawford, and I found ten songs. He thought that was really good, and kept giving me more stuff."[45]

John Snyder was a trumpet player himself, and had long idolised Chet. He had tracked his comeback with considerable interest, and when a fan sent him cassette tapes of Chet playing in a New Jersey club, he played them to Creed Taylor, hoping he would agree to sign him to the label. "My boss heard the tapes and said, 'He can't play any more'. I said, 'Well, he's been fighting a lot of battles'. But he said, 'No'."[46]

Several months later, Creed Taylor had a change of heart, and signed him. "A woman at a cocktail party asked Creed, 'What's happened to Chet Baker?' Creed called me and said, 'Get me Chet Baker'. What I couldn't do in five months, she did in one night."[47]

Chet's latest 'comeback' album, *She Was Too Good To Me* was recorded over two sessions; the first took place on July 17th 1974, the second session a few months later in late October and early November. The album was recorded at Rudy Van Gelder's studio in New Jersey, and was recorded with a stellar line-up, including Bob James on keyboards, Ron Carter on bass and Steve Gadd on drums. "The musicians on that date were almost like a house band for us at that time," recalled the arranger, Don Sebesky. "Looking back now, it was a golden time for us then; that was our daily bread, and we didn't give it a second thought. As the jazz recording business changed, and CTI eventually went out of business, we realised how lucky we were to have the label for that tenure."[48]

Chet Baker is back.
Back after knocking 50s jazz fans out with a trumpet style so lyrical, so original, that he was said by critics to have revolutionized popular music.
Back with a new album—"She was Too Good to Me"—exclusively on CTI records and tapes.
Back with his friends Hubert Laws, Bob James, Ron Carter, Paul Desmond ...and with Don Sebesky putting it all together.
Chet Baker, welcome back.

CTI
The Artist's Choice
Distributed by Motown Records

Promotional ad for 'She Was Too Good To Me',
DownBeat *magazine.*

The album also paired Chet with the lyrical alto saxophonist Paul Desmond, who had made his name with the Dave Brubeck Quartet, and had known Chet since his early days on the West Coast. "Paul was on the label as well, so he was a natural counterpart to Chet, because his approach was so similar—his lyrical, song-like approach," said Sebesky. "Everyone thought it would be a good idea for them to play together."

Sebesky himself had been a big fan of Chet's playing since his early recordings for Pacific Jazz, and was surprised and delighted to see that he was still playing so well. "He was not playing as hard as he did in earlier years, but he was still very lyrical and we picked material that we thought would be consistent with his approach." Creed Taylor and Don Sebesky proposed most of the material. The arranger apparently came up with the idea of recording the title track, an obscure Rogers and Hart song written for the Broadway musical *Simple Simon*. John Snyder believes that 'Funk in a Deep Freeze,' written by Hank Mobley, was the only number Chet selected for the recording.

Don Sebesky and Creed Taylor tried to capture Chet's natural lyricism, rather than push him towards a more fusion-oriented sound. The lush strings, which were added later, were aimed at complementing Chet's soft tone. "I don't think there was any conscious effort to cushion Chet," Sebesky claimed. Chet sounds in good shape on the opening track, 'Autumn Leaves', his soft tone and melodicism intact. 'She Was Too Good To Me' reveals Chet to be in fine voice, too, his singing a fraction deeper than on his mid-1960s recordings. Flautist Hubert Laws replaces Desmond for a delightful version of 'Funk in a Deep Freeze', but the highlight of the album is an exquisite reading of Johnny Mercer's 'Tangerine', Baker and Desmond playing off one another effortlessly.

The album was released in late 1974, and received mixed reviews. "He has almost no voice—it's all silences, slides, whispers, yearnings in its purest form," wrote Paul Nelson in the Village Voice, "but his phrasing can be superb, the romantic impact devastating." At the time the album was released, the jazz market was dominated by fusion, and sales were modest. The big hits of that year included *Thrust* by Herbie Hancock, which reached No. 13 in the Billboard Top 200, and Weather Report's *Mysterious Traveller*, both of which featured ex-Miles Davis alumni.

Chet had lovingly dedicated the first rough copy of his new album to Ruth Young, who had attended the recording sessions. He used his first cheque from CTI to make a down payment on a small house in Dobbs Ferry in Westchester County, about twenty miles north of New York City. For Carol, it was the house of her dreams; they could finally move out of the seedy Bryant Hotel and the children could start to live a normal life. For Chet, it was an excuse to spend more time with Ruth, and he spent more time staying over at her apartment at 817, West End Avenue. He saw it as the first step towards leaving Carol, and told Ruth he would leave her permanently once she had stopped taking methadone. He was still afraid to push for a divorce, however, as Carol continued to threaten to report him to the IRS for unpaid taxes.

Throughout the autumn of 1974, Chet continued to play at Stryker's Pub for two nights a week, supported by Harold Danko, Ed Byrne and Dave Shapiro. Occasionally Warren Chiasson or Hal Galper would sit in for Danko, or Jimmy Madison would sit in on drums, but Chet was happy to keep a low profile. "Olivia, the owner of the place, wanted her jazz club to be pure—you're going to go in there, pay your price, and listen to these jazz masters," recalled Warren Chiasson. "She loved Chet, she thought his music was so fabulous. There were excellent acoustics, and he played the club very well. Chet could just concentrate on playing his trumpet, shutting out the whole world."[49]

Occasionally, an unwelcome guest would come by the club. One evening a jazz musician by the name of Don Elliott dropped in. He played the mellophone, a brass instrument sometimes used in marching bands, and also sang, lending his vocals to the soundtrack of the Steve McQueen movie *The Getaway* (1972). "He played very well, and had made a lot of money as a singer," recalled Ed Byrne. "He wanted to attach himself to Chet, and just showed up, night after night, and sat in, all night long. He followed us for about a month, and finally blew it by asking Chet if he wanted to join up with him, and form the Don Elliot/Chet Baker Quartet. That did it."[50]

The record producer Don Friedman became aware of Chet's comeback at this time, and set about trying to arrange a reunion of some of the biggest names in West Coast jazz at New York's prestigious Carnegie Hall. Gerry Mulligan was amenable to the idea. He had enjoyed considerable success in the early 1960s with his Concert Jazz Band, but had spent several years in the creative wilderness before the release of *The Age Of Steam* on A&M Records in 1971. Like Chet, Mulligan was unrecognisable from his 1950s prime, the short-cropped hair replaced by long, graying hair and a thick beard. His sense of self-importance had changed little over the years, however. "I spent a lot of years building up a place for myself," he later claimed. "I wanted to play in orchestra halls and places that were built for music, with audiences that were dressed and aware. I had no intention of playing sewers, which is what Chet did … No sir, not me."

Creed Taylor wanted to record the event, and asked John Snyder to negotiate a number of the details with Gerry Mulligan and Chet Baker. Gerry Mulligan wanted the two musicians to play separately, rather than try to reform the original quartet. "I didn't know anything about the politics at that point, between Chet and Gerry—that's deep water there," said Snyder. "Gerry was just a pain in the ass, a huge ego. Chet was not; he wasn't deferential, but he knew who was in charge. They were just two totally different people. Gerry was always way outside, looking for the world, and felt the world was his. Chet, by contrast, went deep inside of himself, and had to fight for every straw."[51]

Don Friedman managed to persuade Stan Getz to play on the same bill, but his set went unrecorded, because he had just signed with Columbia. Creed Taylor wanted to use CTI musicians for the concert recording, but both Chet and Gerry arranged for one or two of their regular sidemen to play. The trombonist Ed Byrne joined Chet whilst Gerry was accompanied by vibraphonist Dave Samuels and a new recruit to his working band, guitarist John Scofield. "I had only been playing with him for a few weeks. We'd played a week at a club in Boston, which was my first gig with him, then he called me and said we had another gig in a couple of weeks time, and it's at Carnegie Hall," the guitarist remembered. "I was living in Boston, an ex-Berklee student, driving down to New York for a gig at Carnegie Hall with Chet and Stan. It was just incredible!"[52]

Ruth Young helped out, arranging the booking with Carnegie Hall. In the meantime, John Snyder arranged the rehearsals. Somewhat surprisingly, given the egos involved, the rehearsals went smoothly. "I remember being at rehearsals at Carol's Music with Creed Taylor and Getz and Mulligan, and everybody was there," recalled John Scofield. "I was just so in awe of these big jazz stars, but everything seemed amiable." The fireworks were being saved for the big night.

Gerry Mulligan and Chet Baker rehearsing for the Carnegie Hall concert, 1974.

The concert took place on Sunday, 24th November. There was a considerable tension backstage, in part because the venue was much bigger than many of the musicians were used to playing. "It's like recording with strings," Chet told Doug Ramsey, "you can't help feeling all that weight. I'd just as soon be playing at Stryker's Pub." The fact that the show was being recorded only added to the tension. "I was there to play the guitar, and there was this big hubbub with all these technicians running around, getting ready to make a live recording," John Scofield remembered. "I was just holding my breath, hoping that I didn't mess up completely. I was as nervous as hell!"[53]

Ruth Young was backstage with Chet, suitably dressed for the big occasion in a red, off-the-shoulder dress and a genuine leopard-skin coat. "I was as voluminous and impossible-to-miss as you could possibly be," she laughed. "The way I was garbed, I was quite a striking-looking person." Preparations were interrupted by the sounds of shouting, at which point Chet's wife Carol stormed in, the children in tow. "She had seen the advertisement that he was playing, because it was a well-publicised event, and she was there for money," said Scofield. "They were having a screaming match, just before he played."[54]

Ed Byrne remembers being on stage by this point. "They announced our names, the sidemen first—Ron Carter, Bob James, Harvey Mason and me," he said. "Then they announced the star. We're all standing there, waiting to play, and there's no Chet. There was a ruffle behind the curtain, and you could see that there was something going on."[55]

The organisers hurriedly arranged extra seating at the front of the auditorium for Carol and children, as Chet made his way on to the stage. Chet was still shaken by what had happened, and a few songs into the set, nearly got into a fight on stage. "Creed Taylor was the biggest producer at that time, and at the last minute he started calling tunes that we hadn't played together," Ed Byrne remembered. "Chet, stupidly, would go along with things like that. When Creed suggested we play 'The Thrill Is Gone', Chet counted off the slowest ballad I have ever heard. I'm backing him while he's singing, and I take the first solo. I started paraphrasing the melody, and Bob James started comping chords four times faster, like a bossa nova. I'm looking at the two of them thinking, 'What's going on here?' Chet's on the left hand side of me and leans over and James is on the right side, and Chet yells at James, 'He's trying to play a ballad!' And James was a big-time producer, even then, and shrugged his shoulders as if to say, 'Fuck you, this is what I'm doing.' Chet turned bright red, and started to walk over, and looked like he wanted to punch his face in front of everybody. I blocked him physically while I was playing the solo, and shook my head at him. He backed off, but if it hadn't of been for me, he would have punched Bob James."[56]

The rest of Chet's set passed off without incident, and his solo on 'My Funny Valentine' drew the loudest applause of the evening, an incident that would not have been lost on Gerry Mulligan. The backstage party was another tense affair, with Ruth and Carol doing their best to attract Chet's attention whilst ignoring one another. "It was like a total zoo," said Ruth. "There was a lot of bizarre energy being exchanged."

Two albums worth of material were later released under the name *Carnegie Hall Concert, Volume 1 and Volume 2*. Although it appeared on Chet's record label CTI, Mulligan's name was placed above that of Chet on the record sleeve, and the saxophonist dominates the track listing, and hence the royalties. Chet was clearly upset by the way things had panned out, and made his feelings known in a number of interviews. "It was my record company that made those Carnegie Hall albums—I was the one with the contract," he told Les Tomkins, backstage at the Roundhouse in London. "So Gerry comes along, we work together, they record it. They release the album, and he arranges it; so, of course, the album is in his name, and I'm a sideman. You know, that sort of thing is very important to him—that his name is the biggest one up there, and he gets the royalties, and so forth. Well, I guess that's what they call 'taking care of business', but somehow it just doesn't seem right, with my record company. But it's all music—if people enjoy it, buy the album and they like it, then I'm satisfied."[57]

Despite his concern over the royalty payments, Chet's comeback had been a considerable success. Eighteen months earlier he had been on welfare, struggling to find work; now he was playing on a regular basis, had a recording contract with a major jazz label, and had played to a capacity crowd at Carnegie Hall. Ed Byrne sensed he was struggling to come to terms with the changes mentally, however. "After the Carnegie Hall concert, for which we got paid double-scale, we went back to Stryker's for twenty-five dollars each," said Byrne. "We were sitting there playing to a pretty much empty house and Chet turns around to me, halfway through the first set, and says, 'You know, man, this is where it's at'. I looked at him and said, 'Really?' I mean, we had literally just returned from recording at Carnegie Hall."[58]

Ed Byrne got another glimpse of the self-destructive side of Chet's personality when he participated in a brief tour of New England that Ruth had booked. "We traveled to Baltimore and Cleveland, and to Ohio a couple of times—we did a TV show and a bunch of gigs in Ohio. I put the band together for the tour—I had Duke Jordan on piano, who was Bird's piano player, and Jimmy Garrison on bass. The band was out of sight!"

The problems started in the car, with Chet needing to find methadone, then antagonising Jordan and Garrison with his inadvertent racist remarks. "I was like the referee the whole time," said Byrne. "I'd been in the car with them for ten minutes, and Chet would say something, and Duke and Jimmy would say, 'Say what!'" The music was a success, however, with the band incorporating a couple of Duke Jordan's tunes into the set. "We played one night in Massachusetts, and the audience was wonderful, they loved us. After the gig, some guy who owned a recording studio insisted we come back to his place. I was played out, and felt I'd played everything I wanted to play at the gig. But Chet went along with it, and we recorded tunes that none of us knew, stuff like that. That recording has never surfaced."[59]

The atmosphere remained tense throughout the tour, and by the time they had returned to Stryker's, which was scheduled to be the last night, Chet was in a foul mood. "Chet was doing the sort of stuff he'd do when he was pissed off," Byrne recalled. "He would just start playing obscure tunes by the likes of Bob Zieff or Phil Urso that nobody knew. He wouldn't count the tune—he'd just start playing. Both Duke and Jimmy were sweating bullets. I carried a briefcase of tunes with me, so whenever Chet called a tune I didn't know, I would research it, take sheets with me, and sometimes write arrangements. So I'm throwing sheets at them all night long. By the end of the first set, Jimmy was really pissed and upset, sweat all over him. He left after that set, left his bass on stage, and just took a cab home. He never came back."[60]

In January 1975, the saxophonist Bob Mover returned from his extended stay in Brazil, and reunited with Chet at Stryker's. "Chet had hired a trombone player called Ed Byrne, who was a friend of mine, and I started to sit in with them." Mover was surprised to see the extent to which Chet's chops had developed in his absence. "Harold Danko and I played a lot with Chet over this period, and agreed that if Chet were a baseball player, he would be batting somewhere around .700 and .750, which was awful good," he recalled. "If you played ten nights with Chet, he would play great on five of those nights, he would play quite well on two of those nights, and on three nights he just wouldn't feel like playing. Even on the same material, he would find fresh ideas. He was remarkably consistent for someone with those problems."[61]

A few weeks after Mover's return, Ed Byrne quit the band, citing his strained relationship with Ruth Young. Chet used to encourage Ruth to sing with the band, and overcome her stage fright. She drank heavily to overcome her nerves, or took pills. "She was a terrible, destructive force," said Byrne. "She would sit in and try to sing, but she was awful, and would forget the words she was so drugged out." He expressed his views to Chet on more than one occasion, and eventually Chet asked Bob Mover to take his place in the band.[62]

By this time, other jazz musicians had picked up on Chet's regular Monday and Tuesday night appearances at Stryker's, and used to drop by. "Great musicians lived in the neighbourhood, so people like Joe Farrell would come and sit in with us, and Anita O'Day would join us when she was in town," said Mover.

In February 1975, Chet was offered the chance to play for a further two nights a week at the St James Infirmary, a club in Greenwich Village. The club had been established in November the previous year by the pianist Hod O'Brien and his partner, Roswell Rudd. "It was a basement club in Greenwich Village, several blocks south of the real Village area, on Leroy Street," said O'Brien. "It was about ten blocks south of Sweet Basil on 7th Avenue. It was like a poor man's Village Vanguard; it was smoky, dingy, but it was a funky club, and for a while, it started to take off. On the weekends I would bring in musicians like Zoot Sims or Al Cohn, Pepper Adams one time, Archie Shepp came, Charlie Rouse—different stars who would come in to play with our rhythm section."[63]

Chet started playing at the club every Wednesday and Thursday night, supported by the house rhythm section of Hod O'Brien, bass player Cameron Brown and drummer Beaver Harris. "I noticed during this period that his playing was really coming back," noted the pianist, "and I hope I had something to do with that. It was just a ball to play with him. We had a good relationship while he was working at the club; he was happy with the pay he was getting at that time, which was $65 a night, which was OK in 1975. Chet was the main draw there, together with Archie Shepp."

Chet used to attract other musicians to the club, including the trumpet players Tommy Turrentine and Lonnie Hillyer. Chet was happy to share the stage with them, and occasionally let them play his horn. "It happened so often that they almost took over the gig," O'Brien remembered. "One night I couldn't take it any more and started pounding my fist on the piano. Everyone stopped playing. I said, 'Chet, get over here and play!' I wasn't mad at Chet for not playing, but I thought he was being too nice to these guys, letting them run all over him. I rarely explode, but that was one occasion when I lost my temper."[64]

The only occasion on which Chet had a falling out with Hod O'Brien was in the summer of 1975, shortly before the club closed. The landlord claimed he hadn't been paid for some time, and wanted to talk to O'Brien about the matter. "When I saw the landlord come into the club, I got all uptight and went up to talk to him, before we'd even finished the number," he later recalled. "As I was talking to the landlord, I saw Chet walking out of the club, trumpet in hand. I rushed out to him, as we still had more sets to play that evening. 'Where are you going?' He turned to me and said, 'Don't you ever walk in front of me while I'm performing'. So I learned never to upstage your leader! I begged him to come back, and told him the club was floundering, and he agreed to come back."

In the spring of 1975, Chet's personal life began to unravel once again. As a result of the publicity surrounding the Carnegie Hall concert, Chet's neighbours in Dobb's Ferry discovered that he was a former junkie and jailbird. Carol later claimed that thirty or forty children would cycle past the house every night, and pelt the family with garbage. Carol, like Chet, is prone to exaggeration, but the children were undoubtedly harassed, and afraid to go to school. Chet helped the family to move out in the middle of the night, helped by his friends Bob Mover and Tommy Turrentine. In the movie *Let's Get Lost*, Carol thought she remembered the children inflicting their revenge on the neighbours by freeing a dozen mice that they had kept in a cage.

Chet was reluctant to have Carol move back to New York, and accepted an offer to move in with his old friend Artt Frank, who was now living in Maine with his wife Earla, an aspiring jazz singer. Earlier that year, Artt had written to Chet, proposing that he write a book about him. He suggested that Chet had received no respect as a jazz musician in his home country because he was white.

In fact, nothing could be further from the truth. Now that he had cleaned up his act, his career was flourishing. Chet's contract with CTI was quite generous. "Creed Taylor had given Chet a sweet contract, setting up his family in Dobb's Ferry with a nice house, and giving him regular cheques," noted Ed Byrne. "I was with him when he used to go and pick them up. And he was recording with all the major names, like Jim Hall, plus his own albums, so I thought he had a pretty good deal." He worked for four nights a week in New York City; granted, Stryker's only paid $25 a night, but he received $65 at the St James Infirmary. In addition, he played outside the city most weekends, often at clubs in Connecticut, New Jersey or New Hampshire. On top of this, his profile had risen since his return to New York, and he was now being invited to play at more prestigious venues, such as the reunion with Gerry Mulligan at Carnegie Hall, or the Tribute to the American Song, an event which took place at the Avery Fisher Hall. It was quite a change from the six-plus years he had spent on welfare.[65]

One memorable out-of-town gig took place at Baker's Keyboard Lounge in Detroit, where Chet headlined for ten nights, starting on Friday, 4th April. The club had arranged for the band to stay in an old-fashioned, two-storey motel on the Eight Mile Road, several miles from the club. "I don't think it was a whorehouse—but the whole second storey was full of whores," said Jimmy Madison, laughing. "I don't know whether they did their business up there or not, but during the daytime, their pimps used to hang around up there too. One afternoon I was sitting with the bass player, Dave Shapiro, in his room, writing a postcard. It was about 2 p.m. All of a sudden we hear bang, bang, bang—a gun going off. Three or four shots, and we all hit the floor. We heard glass shattering, and then the screech of a car pulling away."[66]

Within minutes, more than ten police cars had arrived, pulling into the car park from all angles. Madison and Shapiro only learned later exactly what had taken place. "The glass door of the motel lobby was shattered. We went outside and asked one of the staff what happened," said Madison. "Apparently one of the pimps was sitting outside, looked down, and saw another pimp trying to break into his Cadillac. The guy upstairs pulled out his piece and started shooting, shot the door of the hotel out, didn't hit anybody. The guy downstairs ducked, and his big white pimp hat blew off. He then jumped into his car, and drove off. Chet, meanwhile, had been standing in his doorway, and watched the whole thing happen. When the guy speeded out of there, he left the hat lying on the ground. Chet went over, picked it up, and put it in his room. The police finally left after an hour or so, once they had interviewed witnesses. Chet was still standing in the doorway, when a car pulled up, and out jumps the guy who had been shot at. He walks up to Chet and said, 'You didn't happen to see a hat, did you?' Chet walked into his room, grabbed the hat, and said, 'You mean this one?' 'Yeah!' Chet handed him the hat, and the pimp thanked him, got in his car, and drove away. He was an innocent bystander, and barely said two words as the whole thing went down."[67]

Back in New York, Creed Taylor suggested inviting Chet to a recording session he was planning with the guitarist Jim Hall. "He suggested Jim record the *Concierto de Aranjuez*," said Don Sebesky. "I can't remember the reason—perhaps he'd been listening to Miles' *Sketches of Spain*. We had this wonderful band of musicians to choose from. They were all part of the family, and there was no real incompatibility—that's what made it sound so fluid. It was almost like a sports team. Everyone knew each other's characteristics, and responded accordingly. It was the best of all worlds, and made my job so much easier."[68]

Jim Hall initially had some reservations about playing with Chet, and only knew of him by reputation. "I had never played with Chet, in fact I had only met him once before," he wrote in the liner notes. "I was a little apprehensive at first because I didn't even know that Paul and Chet were going to be on some of the tunes together. But we hadn't been in the studio long before I realised it was all falling into place."

Concierto de Aranjuez takes up the whole of one side of the album, and ranks as one of Chet's finest recordings of the 1970s. Remarkably, it was done in just one take. "Everyone said, 'Well, we're not going to get anything better than that, so let's call that a record'," recalled Don Sebesky. "It's hypnotic. The arrangement is minimal on that record, it was just a framework. I just provided guidelines as to when each musician should come in. It wasn't particularly tricky or involved, we just allowed the individual voices of these artists to fill the space without being interfered with; as Dizzy Gillespie said, it's not so much the notes you play, it's the notes you leave out. Everybody was in such a great musical space, and was so compatible. It's such a rare event when everything comes together so organically, you wish it could happen more often."[69]

For a while, Chet divided his time between Ruth's apartment on West End Avenue and Artt Frank's house in Maine. Artt would occasionally drive into New York City with Chet and sit in on drums at Stryker's. "We weren't getting an awful lot of money, but it was never about money to Chet—he lived to play, and he played to live," he recalled. "The place was always packed when Chet was playing." The arrangement only lasted a few weeks, however; Carol became suspicious when Chet failed to return to Maine, and soon insisted on moving back to New York.[70]

By this stage, Carol began to suspect that Ruth was more than just Chet's manager. Ruth sensed the change in Carol's behaviour when she brought her father to watch Chet play at Stryker's one evening. "He had Carol on his arm that night; there were still occasions when he had to," she recalled. "I thought everything was OK, but when we got up to leave, she went up to my father and shook his hand, introducing herself as Chet's wife. I think my father got wind of what was going on."

A few nights later, the problem escalated. Hod O'Brien's club, the St James Infirmary, had finally folded over the summer, and had been auctioned off by the City Marshall. Hod kept the club's heavy electric piano and speakers, and used to carry them over to Stryker's when Harold Danko was unavailable. He was on stage when he witnessed a fight break out between Carol and Ruth. "They were sitting at a table together, back in the corner," he recalled. "The band was doing a trio number, and all of a sudden,

Carol was trying to hit Ruth with a fork, and they were going at each other."[71]

"She was like an animal," Ruth recalled. "She was screaming, 'How dare you do this! That's my husband', and called me a whore." The bartender, Pedro, came to Ruth's rescue and hauled Carol away from her. Chet stormed off the stage and confronted his wife, shouting, "Well, you've finally done it now, bitch!"

Ruth was shaken by the assault, and Hod O'Brien took her back to his place, and let her sleep on his couch. Looking back, Ruth still struggles to comprehend Carol's undignified behaviour. "It was a pitiful scene in a public place; never in my lifetime have I experienced anything like it." She firmly believes the incident effectively brought the marriage to an end, even if Carol refused to accept it. "I'm sure she lived to regret that," she said. "In the end, Chet really didn't like her very much; she played her role so well as a victim, the mother of his kids, but after that, he'd finally had enough." Rather than deal with the problem once and for all, and file for a divorce, Chet arranged for Carol to fly to South Africa to visit her twin sister.[72]

In her absence, he made plans to take Ruth on a tour of Europe, taking in Italy and France. Chet had been approached by an Italian jazz promoter by the name of Alberto Alberti, who had first met Chet back in 1956. Alberti worked for a company called Festival Productions, which was owned by George Wein, the founder of the Newport Jazz Festival back in 1954. He invited Chet to play at two European jazz festivals that summer; one at Pescara, on the Adriatic coast of Italy, and one in Nice, on the French Riviera.

Before leaving for Europe, Chet had been invited to play at a prestigious show, the *Schlitz Salute to Jazz and the American Popular Song*. The event took place on 1st July at the Avery Fisher Hall, part of the Lincoln Centre. The gala event was hosted by the comedienne Phyllis Diller, and was broadcast on National Public Radio. "The idea was that different performers chose different composers," explained alto saxophonist Bob Mover. "For example, Zoot Sims and Jim Hall were doing Gershwin, Margaret Whiting was performing songs by her father, Richard Whiting, and Johnny Hartman was supposed to do Duke Ellington; but it was strange, he sung one Duke Ellington tune and then went into his nightclub act."[73]

Chet elected to perform three songs by Rogers and Hart: 'My Funny Valentine', the song he was most closely associated with, 'With a Song in my Heart' and 'Have You Met Miss Jones?" Two weeks before the show, he borrowed a book from Bob Mover, *The Music of Rogers and Hart*, in an attempt to memorise the lyrics the lyrics to 'Miss Jones', a song he was not that familiar with. By the night of the concert, he had failed to learn all of the words, and asked Margaret Whiting to teach him backstage. He was still worried that he would forget the words in front of such a large crowd, and arranged Mover's songbook on top of a small music stand at the front of the stage. "'Chet, I don't think that book's gonna hold'," Bob Mover warned. "One of Chet's favourite things to say to me, because I'm Jewish, was, 'Man you worry too much!' It was like one of our comedy routines. Chet announced 'Miss Jones', put his glasses on, and started singing. 'Have you met Miss Jones? Someone said as we shook hands, she was just…' And about this time, the book tumbles, and falls into the front row. It was an old book, one I'd had for a few years, and the pages start flying out!"[74]

John S. Wilson, the jazz critic at the *New York Times*, witnessed the concert. "He had never liked Chet very much and always seemed to have it in for him," recalled Mover. "I remember waiting up all night, thinking that apart from that incident, it had been a pretty good concert. I remember getting the paper, and still remember the review verbatim: 'Then the Chet Baker sextet proceeded to turn the airy melodies of Rogers and Hart into boring, instrumental non-entities, while the leader, a singer of painfully limited scope, tried to decipher the lyrics which he had not bothered to learn, written on a sheet of paper set before him'."

Since his comeback had started two years earlier, Chet had struggled to cope with major events; something in his mindset caused him to self-destruct. At the Carnegie Hall concert, he had almost got into a fight on stage. Ed Byrne also remembers a CTI concert at Yale University around this time where Chet almost got into a fight backstage. The gala concert at the Avery Fisher Hall involved a different set of circumstances, but again, he seems to have felt overwhelmed by the occasion. "One of the salient characteristics of Chet Baker was that he had a completely volatile temper," noted Ed Byrne. "My role, as well as being his arranger and his soloist, was that I had the job of keeping him out of trouble."[75]

But what was the root of Chet's violent mood swings, and why did they tend to manifest themselves on the big occasion? "That's probably one of the most difficult questions you're going to be asking anybody," said Ruth Young, who knew Chet better than anybody at this time. "It was a tough thing to get inside the head of Chet, a tough thing to explain. I would say there was a meltdown of a kind, some unraveling, and that was the beginning of the end. He got so aggressive—whatever self-doubt, whatever dislike, whatever contempt—all of the things that had ever been an irritant for him to deal with—were starting to take on a different dimension."[76]

It has been suggested that methadone may have caused a chemical imbalance in Chet's body that intensified his behavioural patterns, but Ruth Young doubted this was the case. "My understanding is that methadone is one of the least damaging drugs in relation to your mental state," she explained. "If anything, it's the most horrendous thing you can take to destroy your body. It would be more humane to do what they used to do in England—Chet used to talk about that. If you were an addict, you used to be able to line-up, get your stuff. In the US they gave you this 'socially acceptable', synthetic crap that will rot your whole body. But I don't believe that methadone *per se* has any impact on one's psychology. Heroin had a far greater effect on your mind; it was like wearing a coat of armour, preventing pain, discord and disharmony. If you were in pain, it felt like you were in a wonderful, peaceful place, which is why it was so popular. It throws a wall up between you and the rest of the world. It's a big myth that heroin can make your artistry come alive. So I don't think methadone had anything to do with Chet's behaviour at that time."[77] Indeed, Chet's violent mood swings pre-dated his use of methadone, as demonstrated by numerous incidents in the mid-late 1960s, such as his fight with Bob Whitlock or his physical abuse of his wife Carol.

Ruth did not deny that drugs could, on occasion, exacerbate Chet's moods. "He was fine with opiates, but was not OK with sedatives like Seconal, Nembutal—forget it. He could not do those, and he did not like psychotics. Chet himself told me that very early on; he said, 'Don't ever get me these things, don't ever have them'. Likewise, when he added coke, it brought out the insane part of him. It was like being allergic. I don't think the drugs he took up until that time caused him any mental instability. I just think he was troubled, and was destined to have difficulty anyway."[78]

Ruth believes that most of the demons Chet was battling at this time dated back to his childhood, and in particular, the high expectations his mother placed on him. In addition, he never appreciated the trappings that came with fame, even in the early years of the Gerry Mulligan Quartet. "He couldn't stand the hype, couldn't stand the promoters, couldn't stand being tagged as the pretty boy—he wasn't interested in all that," she said. "And when the Twardzik thing happened, he didn't have the persona to withstand the pressure. It was too much of a burden, putting this thing on him. He ended up crawling into his needle; he wanted to be pain free. He was no different to any of the kids that fall out today, like River Phoenix—dead at 23. If you want to play around, you've got to know what you're playing with. And that's what Chet was good at; finally, he knew what to mix and what not to mix. Unfortunately he became a very unhappy guy."[79]

As a consequence, Chet tended to feel exposed and uncomfortable when he was presented with the opportunity to perform on the big stage. He felt more at home in the intimacy of a small club, where he could lose himself in the music without having to concern himself with a 'performance'. To some, this made Chet a failure. Gerry Mulligan took pride in the fact that he no longer had to play in nightclubs, and had graduated to the concert hall circuit. Ed Byrne characterised Chet as a born loser. "Like Jaco Pastorius he couldn't deal with success," he claimed. "He kept self-destructing throughout his whole career. People were always lined up to help him, set him up, and fix his life for him. And he would always ruin it, because he understood losing, mistrust and hate. He had a lifestyle he hadn't had in several years. It looked to me like Creed Taylor was great to him. He had regular funds coming in, they got him that house, and set his family up in it. He was totally uncomfortable with winning. And I think that defines his personality, quite frankly."[80]

Most of Chet's contemporaries did not see him in this light, however. Bob Mover, for example, preferred to see him as a man who appreciated intimacy, both as a musician and as a human being. "Chet really liked intimate situations; musically, with women, with friends," he explained. "Chet wasn't the type of guy who liked to go to a party with forty people. He was very good one-on-one, or with like three people talking. He could be a very good companion that way. I had some very good train trips with him, just the two of us; he understood about friendship, and understood about giving a little of yourself, telling you stories that showed some perspective on life. And often his view was pretty negative about a lot of things; but a lot of times, what he told me was unfortunately true, about human nature."[81]

Ruth Young believed that Chet had experienced fame, and no longer wanted to be part of it. "I respected him for that," she said. "He just wanted to play his music, and wanted his music to be heard. That's as far as he wanted to be involved—the rest of it was too much. He didn't take advantage of his reputation, saying, 'You've got to do this for me'. He even joked about that. 'You can't do that, I'm a fucking star!' He didn't want what came with the territory."[82]

When Chet was presented with the opportunity to return to Europe in the summer of 1975, he leapt at the chance. In Europe, he had never felt the burden of expectation that was starting to weigh on him in New York. In addition, he harboured a lingering resentment of America that stemmed from the way he felt he had been mistreated as a drug addict. He told one Italian journalist how his daughter Melissa had been mugged in Dobb's Ferry on her way to school. "A black guy held a knife to her throat and tore a watch off her wrist that I had given her for Christmas," he explained. "It was worth four dollars. But today they go to New York to kill a man for ten dollars."[83]

But there were other, more positive reasons for wanting to return to Europe. It gave him an excuse to leave his wife Carol, and make a fresh start with Ruth—"a new beginning", as he later described it. He also revealed that beneath his fragile, damaged shell, was the heart of an old-fashioned romantic. "Every young girl has to see Europe," he told Ruth, filling her with hope that things were about to change for the better.

Chapter Fourteen

YOU CAN'T GO HOME AGAIN
1975–1977

"The records after 1974 have greater value, much more depth. I play much better because I have all these years of experience behind me. In 1952, '53, I was another novice. I only played since 1947."—Chet Baker[1]

Chet Baker's latest comeback met with a mixed reaction amongst the US press. Some regarded Chet as little more than an historical curiosity, a relic of the bebop years who had fallen on hard times, a man blessed with an incredible natural ability who had turned his back on the American dream. For the most part, jazz critics praised his lyricism, but were uncertain of his relevance in a musical landscape dominated by jazz-fusion. John S. Wilson of the *New York Times* seemed to hold a grudge against him, and was particularly dismissive, describing his reunion with Gerry Mulligan at the Carnegie Hall as little more than a 'nostalgia parade'.[2]

By contrast, the European press welcomed him with open arms, despite his numerous drug-related offences over the years. The Italian journalist Costanzo Constantini was particularly effusive in his praise, describing him as 'the Rimbaud of jazz, often defeated but every time rising … the sweet and fragile boy grown in the slums of New York … a bird whose wings are always broken, the defenseless victim of every violence in the wild city'.[3]

Chet was quick to pick up on this, and when he was interviewed at the Pescara Jazz Festival in mid-July 1975, he made a number of disparaging comments about America. "Texas, Arkansas, Arizona—the people are just stupid," he told journalist Marco Molendini. "There's no culture. The social relationships are awful. Nobody looks you in the eye. Nobody speaks. Even in jail, nobody says a word to each other. It's hard to have friends. At night you can't go out. Everyone's afraid, of the violence, of everything."

Coming from Chet, who had spent several years nursing an antisocial habit of his own, the criticism seems a little rich, but there can be no doubt that he felt a greater sense of freedom in Europe; he was made to feel more welcome, and there was less pressure to conform.

Alberto Alberti, the Italian jazz promoter, had booked Chet to play two festivals that month; one at Pescara, on the Adriatic coast of Italy, and the other at Nice, on the French Riviera. His band consisted of highly regarded American jazz musicians, including pianist Kenny Drew, bass player Larry Ridley, and drummer David Lee.

Whilst Chet was delighted to be back in Italy, there were ominous signs of his fragile temperament. He ran into Charles Mingus and his drummer, Elvin Jones, backstage at the Stadio Adriatica. According to the Italian trumpet player Cicci Santucci, both had been drinking heavily, and then started to trade insults. "I was speaking with Chet, and he suddenly yelled out, 'Shut up!' cursing the two of them. They looked at Chet, stunned, and didn't react, surprised by Chet's outburst."

By the time Chet took to the stage, it had started to rain. The musicians had limited shelter in the open-air stadium, and the sound quality was poor, as the quartet struggled to hear one another. Despite the difficult conditions, Chet played a fine set, including 'Funk in a Deep Freeze', from his new album *She Was Too Good To Me* and 'My Funny Valentine', a guaranteed crowd-pleaser.

Bass player Larry Ridley had grown up in Indianapolis as a contemporary of trumpet player Freddie Hubbard, and the two of them had played along to old Chet Baker Quartet tunes when they were in their teens. "Chet was playing well at Pescara, he sounded good," he later recalled. "He always had such a beautiful concept; part of it came out of the Miles influence. When I first started listening to him, he stuck me as being a disciple of Miles—the way he phrased things, the ranges of the instrument he used. Although he had a signature of his own, you could still pick out the influence."[4]

Later that evening, Chet ran into Elvin Jones at a small club, and proposed the two of them take to the stage together, and play as a duo. "The next thing you know, Chet starts playing with some linear concept, and Elvin joins in," Ruth Young remembered. "It was one of the most brilliant moments I ever heard. Chet liked Elvin very much." The relaxed, informal atmosphere continued back at the Esplanade Hotel, where Chet joined yet another jam session with a number of other musicians who had appeared at the festival, including Canadian saxophonist Pat LaBarbera.[5]

Ruth loved being with Chet in Europe, but any notion that their trip would be some kind of honeymoon, or mark a fresh start, was shattered by the events of the next few days.

On July 17th, they made their way to Nice for La Grande Parade du Jazz, an eleven-day festival that featured Dizzy Gillespie, Milt Jackson, Clark Terry and Benny Carter. Chet's nerves were frayed from the very beginning of the festival. A representative of Festival Productions had apparently promised Chet that methadone would be made available—as it has been in Italy—but on his arrival in Nice, none was to be found. "When he found out, Chet threw his horn in the air, and it smashed into the street," said Ruth. "Then he picked it up and smashed it again."

By the second day of the festival, Chet was beginning to suffer from severe withdrawal symptoms. "Oh boy, your man Chet's got problems," drummer David Lee told one of the other musicians. "He is being completely crazy. Everyone wants to kill him!"

Things were made worse when the band played later that evening. The saxophonist Bob Mover, who had played with Chet back in the United States, had made his own way to the festival, uninvited, hitchhiking his way to the south of France. "He literally walked on the stage, unannounced, and started playing," recalled Ruth. "Chet kicked him in the ass, and booted him off the stage."[6]

Chet was still suffering from withdrawal symptoms next day. That evening, he was scheduled to appear on the Arena Stage, just outside the city, for a televised jam session with saxophonist Zoot Sims, pianist Kenny Drew, bass player Larry Ridley and drummer Ray Mosca. Chet was uncomfortable playing with Sims, complaining that he was an alcoholic. Chet's worst fears were confirmed when the saxophonist handed Ruth Young a bottle of Cutty Sark whisky before he went on stage. "I think you're going to be the keeper of my bottle," he told her.

Chet's temper boiled over as he took to the stage. He opened his trumpet case, and took out some loose sheets of music. "What, are we going to have a rehearsal?" asked a surprised Sims. "Fuck you, man!" said Baker. Surprised by this sudden outburst, Kenny Drew muttered something under his breath. Baker overheard, and made it clear that he had no desire to play with him, either. Zoot Sims and Kenny Drew left the stage together, much to the amazement of the rest of the band, who played on as a trio.

On Tuesday, July 22nd, the musicians had a day off, and were invited to a beach party at Juan-les-Pins, a few miles along the coast. Ruth Young had already experienced Chet's intense jealousy a few days earlier, when she had patted Alberto Alberti's knee over lunch. Returning to the hotel that afternoon he had confronted her, in full view of the other guests. Clearly his experience with Charlaine, who used to provoke him to attract his attention, had left him emotionally scarred, making it difficult for him to enjoy a normal relationship. Still, nothing had prepared Ruth for what was about to follow.

Ruth had gone swimming amongst the sailboats moored off the beach, and when Chet saw her talking to someone in the water, he flew into a rage. "By the time I came back in, doing my best Bo Derek act, he walked across the beach and smacked me across the face, and accused me of two-timing him," said Ruth. "I had supposedly set up some rendezvous out there in the water; it turned out to be some middle-aged woman with a short haircut! But he went out of his mind. That was the very first time he'd hit me. I'd never been in a situation like that, and it took me a while to get over it."[7]

The incident took place in full view of a number of the other jazz musicians, including Dizzy Gillespie and Zoot Sims. Bob Mover came to Ruth's rescue, and offered to take her back by train to the hotel in Nice.

When Chet returned later that afternoon, Ruth threatened to leave him. "First you didn't tell me you were married," she explained, "and now this." Chet broke down in tears, the first time she had ever seen him cry. He tried to rationalise what he had done, explaining how his father had beaten the hell out him when he was a child. "He had evidently acquired the same habits—it was taught behaviour," said Ruth. "He had also hit his own kids—Paul in particular—he made no secret of it."

Ruth was also aware that Chet had beaten his wife Carol, and was petrified the same thing would happen to her if she stayed. "He explained that she had deserved it, given the nature of the things she had done, and told me to forget about it."

Looking back, Ruth is convinced that a large part of his behaviour during the Nice festival was down to his chemical imbalance, having stayed off methadone for several days. "It was a combination of the physical detox, and not knowing what was going to happen next, how he was going to pull anything off without methadone. He was not prepared to go back to the needle at this stage—he still wanted to be methadone-maintained. It was a nightmare situation for him to be facing."

As the night wore on, Chet opened up about the pressures he was facing. He was pleased to be back on European soil, and felt that his career was finally beginning to get back on track. In addition to the pressure of staying away from heroin, he clearly felt conflicted about his family. "There was the albatross of Carol and the kids," explained Ruth. "The relationship was long dead, but he didn't want to deal with the responsibility. At the same time, she was making threats—putting the guilty screws on him. He was absolutely overwhelmed. 'What am I going to do?' he asked. 'Whatever happens, we're both going to get hurt'. It was a torrid moment for both of us, but particularly for him."[8]

For one brief moment, the two of them considered ending their lives, removing the burden of pressures once and for all. "It's a lovely memory, but at the same time, kind of pathetic," Ruth revealed. "We looked at one another, and eventually he said, 'Why don't we kill ourselves?' It became a mini-drama. 'I'll take the methadone, and you jump off the roof', I said. 'No, I'll take the methadone, you take off the roof!' he replied."

It was rare for Chet to open up in this way, to reveal the demons that were plaguing him. Whilst the conversation cleared the air with Ruth, and helped her to understand what she had let herself in for, it did nothing to alter the chemical changes Chet's body was going through.

Next day, Chet played a jam session at the festival with saxophonists Zoot Sims Eddie 'Lockjaw' Davis and Bob Mover, and pianist Gerald Wiggins. Zoot Sims took into upon himself to call the first number, and suggested Dizzy Gillespie's 'Groovin' High'. Chet muttered something about not wanting to play that tune, at which point Sims exploded. "Oh yeah? You don't want to play that? Well, what *do* you want to play, Chet?"

"I wanna play 'Four'," Chet explained.

"You know what? We can play 'Four'. We'll play whatever you wanna play. Because you're a fucking baby, Chet. You were a fucking baby in 1955, and you're still a fucking baby. Now we'll play what the baby wants," Sims said, counting in the tune.

The stunned musicians started playing, but Sims and Baker continued to argue, prompting Chet to storm off the stage. Mover followed him, begging him to come back on. "The local magazines are going to write that you stormed off stage," he explained. "It's not good for your career if you do these things." As the saxophonist pressed him to reconsider, Chet turned around, and for the second time that week, kicked his backside.

Whilst this latest incident took place in front of the festival organiser, George Wein, he kept Chet on the roster for the remaining days of the festival. The day after the closing ceremony, several of the musicians, including Chet's quartet, made their way to Italy where Wein had arranged a handful of one-day jazz festivals. The second of these took place in the historic town of Città di Castello in the northern part of Umbria, close to the edge of Tuscany.

The festival in Nice had been well organised, with each musician given a detailed schedule outlining when and where they were expected to perform. The arrangements in Italy appear to have been somewhat chaotic, however, and after his set, Chet stormed off in search of George Wein. "I said, 'Take this festival and suck it'. Then I grabbed my trumpet and threw it at his head, as hard as I could. A marvellous instrument. It was the first time in my life that I did something like that. But I just couldn't stand the situation. I wanted to play, but it was simply impossible. The festival was disgracefully organised."[9]

There were times in Europe where Ruth got to see another side to Chet's character; when taking his methadone on a regular basis, she would see glimpses of the reticent, quietly-spoken man with the naughty twinkle in his eye that effortlessly charmed the jazz critics when he emerged on the scene in the early 1950s. "Being in the car with Chet could be a wonderful experience. It was natural for us to be lucid and as forthright with one another, in the same way that other people might talk over breakfast. On the longer trips in Europe, I would literally lay on his knee, on his right leg. I would usually be a little bit weary, but would talk and ask him questions. That was how I got to know so much about him. Chet was rarely that intimate with other people—I just had that way! The fact that he found it comfortable to talk openly with me, repeatedly, suggested he'd wanted to do that for God knows how long—maybe since his childhood. He hated having to always be 'on', and welcomed the chance to have someone he could really be himself with."[10]

There were other occasions, particularly in the early years of their relationship, where Chet revealed a romantic, sensitive side to his nature that seemed at odds with the deplorable behaviour he had exhibited in Juan-les-Pins. Ruth remembered one occasion, back in the United States, when he carried her over the threshold of her apartment through to the bedroom, where he had carefully arranged several bunches of flowers around the bed. "He was quite schizophrenic, the way he was put together," Ruth confirmed. "Someone once said that I made him as civilised as he could be, by having him in my company, and I'm sure that's one of the reasons why Chet liked me to be around."

After completing the festival dates in Italy, Chet brought Ruth to Liège in Belgium, to introduce her to his old friend Jacques Pelzer. Pelzer first met Chet in Paris in 1955, on Chet's first European tour. They met again at the Festival International du Jazz at Comblain-la-Tour in 1959, and had been close friends ever since. Chet and Carol stayed with him in 1962, after Chet had been released from prison in Italy, and visited on a regular basis before Chet returned to America in 1964. Chet was grateful for his hospitality, and returned the favour by inviting Jacques to tour with him in the US in the spring of 1965.

Their friendship was based not only on music, but also on drugs. Pelzer had inherited his father's pharmacy in the leafy hilltop suburb of Thier-a-Liège, and had helped to turn Chet on to Palfium as an alternative to heroin in 1959. Drugs had played an important role in Pelzer's own life, too. His wife Andrée, who had been addicted to heroin for ten years, took her own life in 1961. The precise details of her death remain murky, but their daughter, Micheline, believes she swallowed caps of mercury after discovering that Jacques was having an affair. Heroin had also claimed the life of his close friend, the saxophonist Bobby Jaspar, who had died in 1963 at the age of just thirty-seven.

Pelzer felt a lingering guilt over his wife's death, and like Chet, had turned to drugs to bury his pain. His preferred drug was codeine, an opiate known for its analgesic properties. He had developed a red-coloured codeine-based syrup, which also proved popular with visiting jazz musicians, including Stan Getz, Dexter Gordon and Chet himself.

Like Chet, Pelzer's roots were in bebop. "As an alto player, he loved Sonny Stitt and Cannonball, but Bird was the alto player he admired the most," claimed his daughter Micheline. Whilst he had flirted with free jazz in the 1960s, he struggled to cope with the changes that were taking place, and found himself playing less frequently. In 1973, however, he had formed a fusion-oriented band called Open Sky Unit with the American singer and pianist Ron Wilson, his cousin Steve Houben, who also played saxophone and flute, and his daughter Micheline, who played drums.[11]

Chet was joined in Liège by Bob Mover, who had patched up his differences with Chet, and by two other members of his US band—pianist Harold Danko and bass player Dave Shapiro. Chet's old drummer, Beaver Harris, was already in Europe, where he had been playing with Archie Shepp. They had been invited to play a couple of festivals, at Laren in Holland, and Antwerp in Belgium. In addition to the festival appearances, Chet played a couple of gigs in Belgium as the guest of Jacques and Open Sky Unit.

Ruth Young found the atmosphere in the pharmacy somewhat strained. Jacques Pelzer had been close to Chet's third wife, Carol, and their first son, Dean, and believed that Chet's relationship with Ruth was little more than a short-lived affair. "Jack and I had a very intense relationship," confirmed Ruth. "We bumped heads several times at the very beginning. His solidarity seemed to be with Carol and kids, which made it very difficult. But he had no problem telling me he was very fond of me, so I think he felt very conflicted."

The problems were compounded by the fact that Ruth initially had a difficult relationship with Jacques's daughter Micheline. Micheline had been turned on to jazz in 1965, when she watched John Coltrane play 'My Favorite Things' at Comblain-la-Tour. She learned to play the drums, and in 1968, started to accompany saxophonist Barney Wilen in Paris. Her big break came in October 1969, when she was spotted playing at the Festival de Liège by Miles Davis' sideman, saxophonist Wayne Shorter. He invited her to New York, where she appeared on his album *Moto Gross Feio*. While she was in New York, she further developed as a musician, playing with the likes of Chick Corea, Steve Grossman and Woody Shaw.

Back in Europe, she fell in love with a French pianist, Michel Graillier, who went on to play with Chet regularly in the years that followed. Graillier was an alcoholic, and prone to bouts of depression, and it wasn't long before Micheline developed a heroin habit of her own. She had kicked heroin by the time Chet arrived in late July 1975, but was struggling to stay clean. When Ruth caught her raiding the pharmacy one day, Ruth told Jacques what she had witnessed. "She went a bit nuts over that, and I can't blame her in a way," said Ruth. "I was trying to help her, but in retrospect, it's easy to see how she couldn't see that I meant well by it."[12]

With no concerts for a few days, the band spent their days playing in

Jacques' parlour, joined most afternoons by a number of local musicians. To Ruth's obvious frustration, Chet and Bob Mover took advantage of Jacques' hospitality, and started to take morphine suppositories. "The two of them were taking 9 and 20mg torpedoes; Chet was only supposed to be on methadone, but he was being a bad boy."

The week he had spent with Jacques Pelzer took its toll on Chet physically, and by the time he played at the International Jazz Festival in Laren on August 7th, he looked gaunt, his cheeks caved in, framed by his unkempt, long hair, and his dark eyes hidden behind a pair of large sunglasses. His appearance was made worse by the fact that he had chosen to wear a pair of blue velvet trousers he had borrowed from Ruth Young. There was nothing wrong with his playing, however. His chops were in good shape, having practiced every day in Liège, and the band gave an impressive performance. In *DownBeat* magazine, Dan Morgenstern went as far as to suggest that Chet's playing had "the emotional quality we associate with the late Billie Holiday."[13]

After the show, he was interviewed by Maarten Derksen, an employee of the renowned Dutch promoter, Wim Wigt. "He didn't look too well, but he was coherent," he noted. "I get the audience that had earlier been to hear Miles Davis," he told me.[14]

Back in Liège, Chet tried to warn Bob Mover about the dangers of getting hooked on morphine. "If you're going to take this stuff, you can only take so much of it," he explained. "The 20mg tablets are fine, but only take them every two days, not every day, and then you can avoid getting a habit. You can still get the pleasure of it without getting into trouble."

The saxophonist failed to heed Chet's warning, and spent his days getting strung out with Micheline and Michel. One morning he woke up, and complained to Chet that he felt unwell. "Chet said, 'I think I know what it is. It's not stomach flu—you've got a problem. Go get high, and then we'll talk about it'," said Mover. "So I got high, and started feeling better. He says, 'You feel better now, don't you? Much better?' I said, 'Oh, yeah'. 'Well, pretty soon you're not even going to get high; you're going to get normal. All that time you're spending practicing, all that time you put into your music—forget about it. You'll be spending your whole day just coping, wondering where you can get high. If that's the life you really want to live, I can't do anything about it. You really should think about it'."[15]

Mover did listen second time around, and decided he didn't want to return to New York strung out. "I wasn't a junkie—my grandmother didn't bring me up to do that." A couple of days later he took himself down into Jack's basement, and put himself through cold turkey. "When things got really bad, I took a sip of the codeine syrup, to ease the pain," he later recalled. "I got through it. I messed around with Chet a little bit later, but I was never a real junkie."[16]

Once he had recovered, Chet introduced him to Florence Thomas, the daughter of the Belgian guitarist René Thomas. The two of them enjoyed a summer romance, and she eventually moved to the United States with him. They found a small apartment in Greenwich Village, and Chet helped them to paint the place, even giving Bob some extra cash to help them get started.

Another visitor to the pharmacy that summer was Chet's old girlfriend, Liliane Rovère. In the intervening years, she had turned her attention to acting, and was passing through Brussels in August with a theatre troupe. When she heard Chet was back in Europe, and was staying with Jacques Pelzer, she made her way to the house in Liège. Ruth was extremely upset when she heard the news, and refused to go downstairs to meet with her. "There was a sense of jealousy, and perhaps even a sense of resentment because of what I had heard about her," she later explained. "The going story for years was that she was the one who got him started on heroin. I guess I saw her in the same way as Carol portrayed me; the one who really got him started."[17]

In fact, Chet had messed around with heroin long before he met Liliane, and he only became fully addicted after he had split with her, and returned to the United States in 1956. To his credit, Chet defended Liliane in this regard. "He told me it was his own doing, his own failing—that was fairly noble for him," Ruth admitted.

The band returned to New York in late August. Chet had been booked to play at the CTI All-Stars Concert at the Wollman Rink, an outdoor ice-skating facility in Central Park. It was a prestigious event, featuring many of the label's best known stars, including George Benson, Grover Washington, Joe Farrell and Hank Crawford.

Chet was scheduled to appear with his Quintet, but Dave Shapiro and Beaver Harris were evidently unavailable; Cameron Brown stepped in on bass, and Chet's old friend Artt Frank took over on drums. As they walked across Central Park, listening to the soundchecks taking place, Artt Frank sensed that Chet was nervous, and remembered that he preferred playing small, intimate gigs, rather than large festivals.

Once again, Chet struggled to rise to the big occasion. Part of the problem was that he was scheduled to follow George Benson, one of the label's biggest stars. Benson sensed that the audience had come to party, and peppered his set with his biggest hits. It was always going to be a tough act to follow, but Chet made matters worse by starting his set with a little-known Duke Pearson tune, 'Jeannine'. "It was passable, but it wasn't our best thing," said Bob Mover. For the second tune, Chet called 'My Funny Valentine', but counted the band in at the slowest tempo imaginable. "It would have been beautiful at Stryker's, at the right time, but not in front of two thousand people. Or if we'd really brought the house down with the first tune—but we didn't," the saxophonist continued. "People started booing us, and some food was thrown at us, as I recall."

Artt Frank had stayed in touch with Carol Baker while Chet was in Europe, and reminded him of his domestic obligations. The children were missing him, and had not been attending school on a regular basis, he explained. Chet felt conflicted; he had no intention of returning to live with Carol, but wanted to make sure he was providing for his family. He reached the decision to rent an apartment in Ruppert Towers, a brand new high-rise block that had been erected on the site of the Jacob Ruppert Brewery on 3rd Avenue and 90th Street. It was a luxurious condominium, complete with parquet floors and a fitted kitchen, but Chet never paid to furnish the place properly; the family's only real furniture consisted of a few old beds, a table and chairs, a television set, and an aquarium, where Dean kept a collection of tropical fish. Renting such an expensive apartment was "some kind of blind positive thinking on Chet's part", according to the pianist Harold Danko.

Chet made a token effort to bond with his children over the next few weeks, enlisting Dean and Paul's help to paint Bob Mover's new apartment, and slipping the children some cash. His relationship with Carol was more difficult, however. He had never formally announced that he was leaving her, and never asked for a divorce; in all likelihood, he was worried about the size of the potential divorce settlement, or that Carol would carry out her threat, and report him to the Internal Revenue Service.

Instead, Chet told her that he intended to return to Europe. A local promoter had arranged a tour in Italy, and it would probably be best if she stayed in New York to look after the children. According to Artt Frank,

Carol accepted Chet's decision gracefully. "I was not in the least bit surprised when Chet returned to Europe. Neither was Carol, she had three kids, and Vera was not in the best of shape. Chet always wanted Carol and the kids to be with him but Carol knew that that would be an impossibility—the kids not having a solid home or continual schooling, so she talked it over with him, and they agreed that it would be far better for her to stay in America and for him to have the freedom to travel wherever he wanted to and whenever he decided to."[18]

Certainly Carol's subsequent letters to Chet suggest that she expected him to return to the United States and live with her and the children. "I know you are aware of how tired I am of being alone," she complained.[19]

In late September, Chet returned to Europe with his regular pianist, Harold Danko. Dave Shapiro had accepted another job, and opted to stay behind, whilst Bob Mover decided to stay in New York with his girlfriend, Florence Thomas. "We played at occasional festivals, and then went back to Italy for the first time in all those years, which was a well-publicised event," recalled Danko. "He was really well received; when I think back on it, it was like one of those Austin Powers movies! We had a couple of different bass players, but for the most part it was Isla Eckinger, a bass player from Switzerland, on that tour. For me, we went to some interesting places and earned some pretty nice money for the most part."

If there was no gig for a few days, the musicians would return to Jacques Pelzer's pharmacy in Liège, where Danko would spend his days practising at the piano. "Jacques Pelzer was great, he was a funny man. He had a woman friend who had lived with him for a while, and we would have all of our meals prepared. But I stayed out of whatever was going on at the drugstore!"[20]

Chet returned to the US again in late October 1975, bringing Jacques Pelzer with him. A US promoter, encouraged by the sales of *She Was Too Good To Me*, had booked a short tour, starting at the Catamaran in San Diego, where Chet would play opposite Stan Getz.

Chet called Bob Mover, and asked if he wanted to join them on tour. When he accepted, Chet, Ruth, Bob Mover and Jacques Pelzer piled into Chet's old Mustang, bringing Ruth's cat along for good measure. Chet had arranged for Harold Danko to fly to the West Coast, but they decided to keep their costs to a minimum by hiring a local bass player and drummer when they arrived. Along the way, Bob Mover remembered they talked about music almost non-stop. "Between us we must have gone through about three hundred songs," he recalled. "One of us would sing, try to remember the lyrics—he was a good musical hang."[21]

When they finally arrived in San Diego, the scene was fairly chaotic. Stan Getz was staying at the same hotel, and kept knocking on Chet's hotel door, trying to hit on him for drugs. Chet took advantage of the situation, making fun of his old rival. "Stan would say, 'Hey, Chettie, did you just say I could or could not get another bottle of methadone off you?'" recalled Ruth. "While Stan was waiting for a reply, Chet would turn to me, change the subject for a few minutes, and then eventually go back to Stan and say, 'I don't know, check with me in a couple of hours'."[22]

In the meantime, Ruth's nerves were frayed because on the first night Chet had spotted his mother, Vera, sitting in the audience. She had recently moved from Milpitas, near San Jose, to return to Oklahoma, but had somehow got wind of the fact that Chet was playing on the West Coast. "It was a pivotal moment because Chet thought he could introduce me to Mommy," said Ruth. "With my neurotic insecurity, I remember taking a long time to get ready—I wanted to make a good impression. Before I had the chance to meet her, however, she called the room and they had a big argument over the phone. Chet must have told her that he was with me, and she asked, 'Who's that bitch you're with?' In all the years I knew Chet, I never once met her face to face, never spoke to her. It hurt very deeply. I could see her perspective, but I couldn't possibly agree with it."

Tensions were running high on stage at the Catamaran, too. With Bob Mover in the band, Jacques Pelzer stuck to playing his flute, and occasionally a little soprano saxophone. One evening, Bob Mover proposed making some changes to the front line. "I didn't just play the head and play solos like Art Blakey's band in those days—not that there's anything wrong with that," he recalled. "We were trying to be adventurous and take the music to another, more polyphonic, counterpointal type of place. Not unlike the way Gerry Mulligan did it, but in a different manner. It would be more like if you could imagine Chet playing counter-point with Lee Konitz, instead of Gerry Mulligan. That kind of idea, except we played with a piano."

Bob Mover made the mistake of criticising the playing of Pelzer in front of Chet, claiming that his chops were not in the best of shape. Chet took offence at this, and swung a punch at Bob Mover, hitting him on the nose. Chet then fired him from the band, leaving him to return to New

York alone. "See, Chet had a thing with his friends," Mover explained. "In one way it was admirable—he really valued cats that had helped him out, like when he got high, or whatever. He was grateful, and wanted to pay his friends back. Even if he didn't pay them back in money, he had some kind of code. Jacques really saved his life in Europe, keeping him in the pharmacy, keeping him in drugs. They were good friends. And Jacques loved Chet—I think he would have given his life for Chet. I really believe he was capable of that."

The next gig on the tour appears to have fallen through, and Harold Danko remembers asking Chet if it was possible for him to return to New York between gigs to supplement his income with teaching work, indicating that Chet should pay for his return flight. "Chet said, 'The next gig's in Detroit. If I get you back to New York, you've got to get yourself to Detroit'. Chet really respected the fact that I really loved the music, and wanted to be there for that. I was living a really straight lifestyle, and he was like a big brother, looking out for me. There were experienced piano players on the New York scene that he could have worked with, but I think he realised that I really wanted to be doing the gig. I wouldn't bug him about the money, or bug him when a particular gig fell through. He knew that I also supported myself through the teaching, and he respected that."[23]

Bob Mover later heard that the gap in the schedule was later filled with a gig in Los Angeles, and that Hampton Hawes filled in on piano. "That was a gig I'm still kicking myself for," he admitted. "To hear him and Chet together would have been great—I'm sorry I missed that."

Harold Danko rejoined the tour in Detroit, as planned, where the band played at Baker's Keyboard Lounge. Jimmy Madison appears to have rejoined the band on bass for this gig, before they wrapped up the tour in Dayton, Ohio.

With Jacques Pelzer in town, Chet reluctantly spent the holiday season staying at Ruppert Towers with Carol and the children. At this point he informed her of his decision to return to Europe again in January, where another tour of Italy had been arranged. Carol was evidently unhappy with this arrangement, and the subsequent arguments were overheard by their neighbour, Kay Norton, who lived in the apartment upstairs. It so happened that Norton ran the jazz division of United Artists Records, a company founded by Ruth Young's father. "She later told me that this guy was constantly screaming at his wife, and otherwise playing his trumpet in the bathroom," Ruth revealed. "She didn't mind the music, given her job, but couldn't believe the verbal abuse."[24]

Whether it was caused by the influence of Jacques Pelzer, or the deterioration in his relationship with Carol, it is hard to say, but Chet certainly started to take more drugs at this time. He seems to have stopped short of injecting himself with heroin again—that would come later—but does seem to have messed around with different pills. Jacques Pelzer's cousin, Steve Houben, came to the US in early January 1976, intending to study at Boston's Berklee College of Music. He stopped by New York, and remembers visiting the family at Ruppert Towers. "Carol was living there at the time," he recalled, "but there was virtually no furniture. I only stayed a few hours, but it was very messy at that time because Chet was highly under the influence of drugs."

Chet's increased drug use was also a feature of his Italian dates when he returned to Europe with Jacques Pelzer in mid-January 1976. Chet had arrived in Rome without his trumpet—normally a sign that he had pawned his instrument to buy drugs—and called the Italian trumpeter Cicci Santucci, to borrow his horn. Chet then called upon his old friend, the Italian bass player Giovanni Tommaso—one of the original members of the Quintetto di Lucca, who had played with Chet back in 1959.

Tommaso arranged local jazz musicians to join them for the next few nights, including the pianists Enzo Rondisi and Ignacio Garcia, and the drummer Gianni Cavallaro. The atmosphere on stage was tense, however, with Chet openly critical of both the pianist and the drummer. "He never said anything to me because he always liked me as a person," said Tommaso. "But I remember on one of the last concerts, in Bologna, I think, there was a misunderstanding between me and the pianist when we were playing 'My Foolish Heart'. Chet played the tune so slowly it was almost impossible to play. I had the idea that we would be playing it half-tempo, but Chet wanted it even slower. For the first couple of choruses, it didn't happen. After the concert, over dinner, Chet said to me, 'You should know by now that I consider you a dear friend. I could easily have criticised the rhythm section on the bandstand tonight, but I didn't say anything'. I said, 'Chet, I feel like shit, I'm sorry!' 'Don't worry!' he said, which was very sweet, as he was often very tough with other musicians."[25]

At the end of the tour, Chet asked Tommaso if he wanted to join the band for a series of dates across Europe in February and March. "I declined his offer," he said. "In the end, it was a tough decision to make, because he was one of my heroes, but I think I made the right choice. From a technical standpoint, Chet was playing well, but was not as bright as he had been in the early 1960s, because of the problems with his teeth. But he was still a great artist, and his singing had improved. Perhaps because he couldn't do everything he used to with the trumpet, he was more expressive as a singer. Artistically, he was great, but technically, I think his best days were over."[26]

This anecdote is interesting for a number of reasons. Firstly, Tommaso was not alone in believing that Chet's best days were behind him. The pianist Amadeo Tommasi expressed similar sentiments about Chet's playing at this time, whilst saxophonist Herb Geller, who played with Chet in the early days of the Gerry Mulligan Quartet, and again at the end of his life, claimed that he never sounded better than when he played at The Haig.

For his own part, Chet was convinced he was a far better player than in his early years. In 1964, on his return to the United States, he told journalist Ira Gitler that he had not deserved to win the *DownBeat* or *Metronome* polls in the early 1950s. "I know I'm playing ten times better now—and I'm not even mentioned in the polls."[27]

Chet's beating in San Francisco had meant that he had to rebuild his technique from scratch, but for all the technical difficulties associated with playing with dentures, Chet felt he had continued to develop as a musician. "The records after 1974 have greater value, much more depth," he told Jeroen de Valk. "I play much better because I have all these years of experience behind me. In 1952, '53, I was another novice. I only played since 1947—jazz, that is. Now I've played jazz for over forty years."[28]

A number of the musicians who played with Chet in his later years support this view. The Italian bass player, Riccardo Del Fra, felt that Chet's style continued to evolve after his comeback, particularly when he started to experiment with a 'drummerless' trio in the late 1970s. "The way he played the trumpet in his last six or seven years is special and original, and completely different to the way he played when he was young," he explained. "I think he found his own way—he was convinced that playing without a drummer was enjoyable, not just because of his teeth, but because of the sound control."[29]

The American-born musician and journalist, Mike Zwerin, who played with Miles Davis and Gerry Mulligan on the original *Birth of the Cool* sessions, was also convinced that Chet was a better player in later years.

"His playing certainly improved," he wrote in *The Parisian Jazz Chronicles*. "Towards the end, on a good night, he could play jazz just about as well as it has ever been played."[30]

But there was an important qualifier to his statement. "There were not enough good nights," he admitted. And that brings us to the second issue that emerges from Tommaso's recollection. Chet's behaviour was becoming more erratic. He had started to mess around with drugs again, rather than sticking to a strict dosage of methadone, and this contributed to what Tommaso described as a 'heavy' atmosphere on the bandstand. When Chet went back to using heroin on a regular basis, which started in late 1978, he became even more unreliable, which may help to explain why Tommaso felt he had made "the right choice."

Thirdly and finally, Chet's drug use and itinerant lifestyle made it difficult for him to maintain a regular band—a problem that had plagued him ever since the departure of pianist Russ Freeman in 1955. As a sideman, working with Chet meant travelling long distances between gigs, lengthy searches by customs officials, putting up with the bad nights, when Chet was late, or his chops were in poor shape, and getting paid on an irregular basis. There were notable exceptions, of course—his quartet with Markowitz/Rassinfosse/Brillinger in late 1978, his trios with Catherine and Rassinfosse, Graillier and Del Fra—but too often Chet was happy to settle for working with musicians that were adequate, rather than superlative, and his reputation suffered as a result.

In early 1976, at the suggestion of Jacques Pelzer, Chet started to work with the legendary Dutch agent Wim Wigt. Wigt had worked as a promoter since 1972, representing a wide variety of American jazz artists including Dexter Gordon, Ben Webster and Art Blakey. His reputation amongst the jazz community was mixed; drummer Ben Riley complained that he arranged difficult schedules, and paid poorly, whilst saxophonist Branford Marsalis, cutting his teeth with Art Blakey in the early 1980s, was upset that the entire band was being transported across Europe in a single Volkswagen minibus. "Wigt wouldn't have done that to Sting," he noted bitterly.[31]

In fairness, Wim Wigt, together with his wife Ria, were highly supportive of Chet in the years that followed, providing him with regular work, and later assigning him a tour manager in the form of Peter Huijts, who did everything he could to look after Chet's interests. In late 1975, Wim Wigt had made some initial enquiries and found there to be considerable interest in booking him, most notably in Germany, where he had not played for a number of years. "We had booked him to play at several festivals in Germany," Ria Wigt explained. "The first few concerts went reasonably smoothly, but then we found out that he was forbidden from entering the country, even though he had entered on several occasions." They explained the situation to Chet, who was also surprised to hear that the ban was still in place. "I don't think it's right that they should make me stay out of the country for fifteen years," he complained. "I mean, I didn't exactly rob the First Berlin National Bank. All I did was go to two doctors. It's ridiculous."[32]

On March 21st, Chet was booked to play at a festival in the Bavarian town of Burghausen, just over the border from Salzburg in Austria. Wim Wigt thought the ban may not be enforced, and suggested Chet make his way over the border at a quiet checking point before making his own way to the festival. "We had several bands playing at the festival, and later received a phone call from one of the musicians accompanying Dexter Gordon that the police were waiting for Chet," said Ria Wigt. "At that time we didn't have mobile phones, so we couldn't inform Chet."[33]

Chet was arrested on his arrival at the festival, and quickly swallowed a large chunk of hash that he had stashed in his trumpet case. He was imprisoned overnight, and when pianist Harold Danko visited him next morning, Chet still looked a little the worse for wear from the hash. "Everything's okay," he drawled slowly, "I'll see you tomorrow!"

Wim Wigt appealed to the German police to have the ban lifted, but was told that they would have to go through the correct channels. The police did allow Chet to play one final gig at Sinkkasten on March 25th, after which he was ordered out of the country. Some months later, the ban was officially lifted, according to Ria Wigt, and it was possible for him to play in Germany without any restrictions.

Chet spent the next few weeks dividing his time between Italy, where *Musica Jazz* suggested he played a number of gigs, and Belgium, where he stayed with Jacques Pelzer. In May, he returned to the United States where he would have caught up with Carol and the children in New York, and visited his mother in Oklahoma. The only known gig over that period was at the King of France Tavern in Maryland, where he is billed to have played May 11th–16th.[34]

Chet had been offered a lengthy engagement at the Music Inn in Rome, starting in early July. The Music Inn had been established by an Italian playboy by the name of Joseph 'Pepito' Pignatelli. Pignatelli had been born into a wealthy family, but his father had blown a large portion of the family fortune. As a young man he had enjoyed a decadent life, developing a taste for drugs, which briefly saw him imprisoned in the 1950s. He also developed a love of jazz, and even learned to play the drums. The basement club, which was located on Largo dei Fiorentini, close to the Vatican, was opened in 1973. The club had played host to a number of visiting American jazz stars, including Bill Evans and Johnny Griffin, allowing Pignatelli the chance to sit in with his heroes.

Chet had flown to Rome with his old pianist, Hal Galper. Harold Danko had decided to remain in the US, so Chet offered Galper a job for the summer engagement. They were joined by Pignatelli himself, who sat in on drums, and a local Italian bass player. Chet soon grew dissatisfied with Pignatelli's heavy-handed playing, and asked him to step down. The bass player was next to go, as he struggled to keep time in the absence of a drummer. "He kept firing people as time went on because they wouldn't play the way he wanted," the pianist confirmed. "Chet had one bad habit I didn't like—he would talk on the bandstand. He'd critique you while you were playing. That's something I always hated because you're wide open, you have no defences. So when it got down to a duo, it occurred it to me that he couldn't take a crack now—I was his band. One night I was playing outside the tune a little bit, which was kind of fashionable, outside the key and the changes. I heard him say, 'Gee, Hal, every time you do that I don't know what you're doing and I get lost'. I couldn't believe it—he actually had a comment to make!"[35]

Towards the end of July, Pepito and his wife Giulia 'Picchi' Gallarati announced that they were intending to go on holiday to Greece, and asked Chet and Ruth whether they would consider taking over the club for a few weeks. Ruth thought it was a kind gesture, and listened intently as Picchi explained some of the formalities. "It was wild," said Ruth. "I got a taste of what it was like to be a club owner. I was making pasta in the kitchen for the entire crew of people. For the first week or two, we got good crowds."[36]

Whilst Ruth enjoyed the experience, Hal Galper was disappointed. As the weeks progressed, attendance at the club tailed off sharply. "It was a disaster," he said. "Pepito left us in the club for the summer, but didn't tell

Chet that nobody was in Rome in August."

Over the course of the summer, Chet also became reacquainted with the jazz singer Lilian Terry. They had become close friends in 1959 after meeting at the International Jazz festival at Comblain-la-Tour. They had even discussed recording an album of ballads, but Chet had ended the project—and with it, their friendship—by insisting that she had to use drugs if they were going to work together. The two of them were invited to participate in a weekly radio programme, *The ABC of Jazz*, in which they would play and discuss their favourite recordings. The reunion was awkward, however, as they struggled to recreate their old chemistry. "At every meeting we would hug with a sort of mutual embarrassment," she remembered. "I would notice that he was ever more emaciated, looking like an old Chinaman."[37]

Chet and Ruth spent the autumn of 1976 staying with Jacques Pelzer in Liège. Chet kept his chops in shape by playing occasional gigs with Pelzer, and on one such occasion he was introduced to a promising local bass player, the twenty-four-year-old Jean-Louis Rassinfosse, a tall, imposing figure with a thick moustache. His playing made a considerable impression on Chet, who invited him to join the occasional concert. A few weeks later, in October, Chet surprised Rassinfosse by asking him to join the band on a three-week tour of Sicily. "I was astonished," he later recalled. "It was myself, Jacques, at the beginning of the tour, Michel Herr on piano, and then he was replaced by René Utreger. There was also an additional friend of Chet's playing percussion, Alex Serra. He was not really part of the group, but he was a friend of Chet's, and was hanging around."[38]

Rassinfosse enjoyed Chet's playing at this time, and thought the band was very tight. Above all, he was impressed by Chet's considerable stage presence. Even though there was little communication with either the band or the audience, and he sat with his legs crossed, hunched over his trumpet, he managed to convey a unique aura. "He could set an atmosphere without saying anything, without any kind of show or attitude," he later recalled. "He showed so much concentration that everyone had to join him and play his way. He was a master of being able to transmit emotion through an instrument, which is what most musicians aim to achieve—to project something which immediately reaches the audience emotionally … not only technically, or any other way."[39]

Chet returned to the United States to see his family after the tour of

Sicily, but returned to Belgium in December, playing a handful of gigs with a larger band, which may have included Micheline Pelzer on drums, and her husband Michel Graillier on piano. Towards the end of the year, Jean-Louis Rassinfosse explained that he was obliged to join the Belgian army, and would have to leave the band. "That's a pity. I could try writing a letter to the King, maybe," Chet had offered. "I'm not sure that will work," the bass player laughed.

"The day before I went into the army I played a concert with Chet in Liège. Right after this, I went from heaven into hell. It was a big contrast. Chet told me we could play together when I got out, and he called me a few months after I had finished. That was in late 1978."

Chet returned to New York in late December 1976. Any momentum he had started to build after his 'comeback' in 1973 had effectively been lost. He had spent the best part of eighteen months in Europe, and in that time, he played only a handful of gigs in North America, and had not recorded a single album.

As always, Chet cared little about the business aspect, and was happy to resume playing at Stryker's pub, the small basement saloon on 86th Street and Columbus Avenue. One night he met an old friend of Bob Mover, a baritone saxophonist by the name of Roger Rosenberg, who used to live a couple of blocks from the club. "For me it was a fantastic experience," he remembered. "Prior to that I did a lot of Latin gigs, playing with Tito Puente, Mongo Santamaria, Eddie Palmieri, all those guys, and also with Buddy Rich's band, but this was the first real opportunity I got to stretch out and play jazz. I ended up playing with him on and off for about two years."[40]

The record company executive, John Snyder, who had helped to sign Chet during his tenure at CTI. Records, soon got wind of his return. Snyder had resigned from CTI. in 1975, and had joined A&M Records, the label established by Chet's one-time rival Herb Alpert. "When I left CTI, I took Chet with me," Snyder later explained. "There were a few others that I took, including Paul Desmond. I wanted George Benson, but Jerry Moss, the label's co-owner, wouldn't let me sign George because he was too much money. But I knew he would sell a lot of records. I was in charge of sales at CTI, so I knew everybody's sales figures. I knew that George was selling 150,000–200,000 records. He wanted $90,000, which was like nothing, but the boss wouldn't let me do it. George Benson went on to sell ten million records!"[41]

Jerry Moss agreed to take over Chet's contract, but worried that Chet was too 'jazzy' to sell many records. The airwaves were increasingly dominated by adult-oriented rock, or AOR, with Peter Frampton's *Frampton Comes Alive* the best-selling album of the year, closely followed by Greatest Hits albums by the likes of the Eagles and Chicago. From a commercial perspective, jazz was dominated by fusion and jazz-funk, pioneered by the 'disciples' of Miles Davis's groundbreaking *In A Silent Way* band. In 1976, Weather Report, the band co-led by Joe Zawinul and Wayne Shorter, produced their breakthrough album *Heavy Weather*. Around the same time, Chick Corea's band, Return To Forever, recorded *Romantic Warrior*, whilst Herbie Hancock continued to blur the boundaries of jazz and funk, recording *Secrets*, one of his most commercial albums to date.

Moss voiced his concerns to John Snyder, who raised the issue with Chet. Snyder suggested they invite Don Sebesky, who had worked on *She Was Too Good To Me*, to handle the arrangements. Chet had always admired his work for CTI, and was amenable to the idea. "I know if it's going to be Don Sebesky, it's not going to be something too free," he told Gudrun Endress, the editor of Jazz Podium Magazine. "I mean, it's going to be pretty, I'm sure of that, because he has wonderful taste in music. And he's a good arranger."[42]

Between them, John Snyder and Don Sebesky arranged a fine group of musicians. John Snyder recalls inviting the guitarist John Scofield, who had made quite a name for himself since playing with Gerry Mulligan at Carnegie Hall—his first ever recording. He also invited alto saxophonist Paul Desmond, who had also played on *She Was Too Good To Me*. Unfortunately, it proved to be one of Desmond's final recordings. "He was dying of lung cancer," John Snyder recalled. "A few days later he went down to an Art Garfunkel session and recorded one song. I'm not sure it ever came out."

Don Sebesky invited tenor saxophonist Michael Brecker to play on the album. He had enjoyed considerable success with his elder brother Randy as part of the Brecker Brothers, and was presumably brought in to add some credibility to the 'fusion' oriented sound. The rhythm section primarily consisted of CTI regulars, including Ron Carter on bass and Tony Williams on drums.

It sounded like a promising line-up, on paper at least, but the sessions didn't gel particularly well for a variety of reasons. For one thing, Don Sebesky was never fully convinced that the 'fusion' approach would work with Chet's playing style. "I took it as far as I thought it could go with him, and still sound consistent with his nature," he explained, "but it was not my favourite road to travel with Chet. I prefer the earlier recordings with CTI. But I've run into that many times; artists want to sound like someone else, and when they hear the outcome, they're disappointed because they find their attitude is what it is, and it's what their fans expect. So when their fans are disappointed, they feel as though they've tried to appeal to a group of people other than those who have always been faithful to them; so then nobody's happy." As a consequence, the main album that was recorded, *You Can't Go Home Again*, sounds fusion-lite, the prominent electric piano lending the recording a very dated feel.[43]

The atmosphere was not helped by the fact that the main parties involved failed to keep one another informed about who would be playing on the album. Chet does not seem to have been aware that Michael Brecker had been asked to play, and invited baritone saxophonist Roger Rosenberg, one of his regular partners at Stryker's, to join the session. "I was really excited, getting the chance to record with this guy," he later recalled. "So I come down the studio, and there's a band there, and Don Sebesky—it was clear that I wasn't supposed to be there. I was there when they were recording *Un Poco Loco*, and Mike Brecker was there, who was one of my good friends. It was really embarrassing for me, sitting there, and thinking that Chet had overstepped his bounds."[44]

Whilst Chet was uncomfortable with some of the arrangements, John Scofield remembers the session fondly. "Chet was so nice to me; I just remember a real warmth coming from him more than anyone else on the session," he said. "The music was just sort of laid out for him by Don Sebesky; it was almost as if he was a sideman on his own date. But he was on great shape, playing-wise, and didn't seem to be high at all. I listened to it afterwards and listened to my own playing, and thinking it was not so good. Then I listened to the way Chet played, and thinking, 'OK, that's the way to do it'."[45]

The album was recorded over three days, and finished on February 22nd. Don Sebesky was evidently disappointed with the final results, and recorded a string section and additional percussion in mid-May. Chet only got the chance to listen to the final recording when he was back in Belgium in the summer of 1977, and was disappointed with the results. "I think that record was ruined with the extra percussion they added afterward," explained Ruth. "We drove around in the car, listening to the final recording, and could not believe the changes they'd made. I loved the literature reference, too, the whole Thomas Wolfe aspect too, which was touching; Chet didn't pick up any of those references, of course, but could relate to the music."[46]

The album was not released until May 1978, one year after it had been mixed. The delay may have reflected the fact that it was not considered a priority by the record label, A&M; it may also have been held up by the departure of John Snyder, who had left to form his own record label.

The album received mixed reviews. *DownBeat* magazine found the combination of Chet's playing and Don Sebesky's fusion-type arrangements an uncomfortable fit. "The trumpeter's lyric lines are too often tangled and lost among the arranger's pushy backdrops," noted the reviewer, awarding the album three stars. "When the material is right, however, Baker shines. His outstanding performance on the title track 'You Can't Go Home Again' is poignant and restrained. Elsewhere it's Brecker and Scofield who excel. The saxophonist's dramatic sweeps through 'El Morrow' [sic] and the guitarist's electric probe of 'Love For Sale' are especially impressive."[47]

Others were more positive. "'You Can't Go Home Again' indicates that [Chet] has come a long way," claimed *Playboy* magazine. "The arrangements by Don Sebesky help considerably; they're both intelligent and exciting … [Baker's] tone, the only reservation we had about his playing, has put on weight. We like it—and the album—very much."[48]

Sales of the album were modest, and Chet never recorded a follow-up album for A&M, which increasingly focused on pop music in the years that followed. Despite this, *You Can't Go Home Again* did more to spark a revival in Chet's career than his more celebrated recordings made for CTI in the early 1970s. As so often the case with Chet, this had more to with luck than judgement. The album was released in the United States in mid-1978, by which time he had a regular touring band; whilst this might be considered a normal state of affairs for most leading jazz musicians, it was unusual for Chet, given his nomadic lifestyle. By the time he was invited to return to Europe, in the autumn of 1978, he had kept more or less the same band in place for several months. This resulted in a number of fine live recordings—arguably the most consistent body of work he had delivered since the mid-1960s. This in turn attracted the interest of one of the larger European jazz record labels, SteepleChase, who signed him for a number of landmark recordings.

Whilst A&M effectively allowed Chet to leave the label, they were quick to cash in on his death, issuing an album of 'outtakes' from the February 1977 sessions in 1989. The resulting album, *The Best Thing For You*, is free of the strings that were overdubbed on the original recording session, and supports Ruth Young's view that the changes spoiled the music that had originally been recorded.

Soon after, John Snyder left A&M Records to form his own label, Artists House. His dream was to break the mould of the music industry, and establish a label where the artists enjoyed ownership of their own music, in addition to earning a higher royalty fee. The record label effectively leased the music from the artists for a period of five years, after which the artist was free to do whatever they pleased. The royalty fees were almost double those offered by the majors, and were calculated not on records sold, which was the industry norm, but on records manufactured. In addition, the records were beautifully packaged, pressed on virgin vinyl, with gatefold sleeves, and informative liner notes, often running to several pages.

The experiment ultimately failed for a variety of reasons. He assumed that if the records were good, and in most cases they were, that distribution would be easy to come by. "I was naive to the extent of thinking it would be good for everybody at every stage," he later recalled. "We had a producer we could be proud of making and selling, and people had something they could be proud of buying. We had both ends of that equation but not the middle." Another problem was that he had a couple of junkies signed to the label—Chet Baker included—which quickly drained the company's limited resources.[49]

The seeds of Artists House were sown in February 1977, whilst Chet was recording *You Can't Go Home Again*. The New York recording studio, Sounds Ideas, had been booked for a number of days by A&M, but was not being used on February 20th. John Snyder asked if it was possible to use the studio for a project of his own, and was given permission. Like Chet, he felt uncomfortable with the fusion-tinged sound that A&M had requested, and wanted to record a straight-ahead jazz session. He retained Ron Carter on bass, and then placed a call to the drummer Mel Lewis, and asked if he was available. Mel Lewis in turn recommended two members of his band, the Thad Jones/Mel Lewis Jazz Orchestra—saxophonist Gregory Herbert and pianist Harold Danko.

It was ironic that Harold Danko was finally recording a studio album with Chet Baker, more than six months after he had left the band. "I remember Chet did the album with Gerry Mulligan at that time—the Carnegie Hall concert—and Gerry insisted on using his own band," said Danko, looking back. "That was a disappointment to me. There were a couple of tunes came up when I was touring with Chet, and we worked on them as a band, but he wasn't in the position to say, 'No', I'd rather have my own piano player. It was the same with the first album he did with Bob James, *She Was Too Good To Me*; I remember hearing that record, knowing that we'd played some of those tunes. On the one hand it was good, because people wanted to hear Chet, but there wasn't a really good reason I could hear why his working band couldn't have done that record."

With limited studio time available, the recording was a straightforward process. "It was one of those dates where we arrived with some tunes we could play, and just played them," the pianist recalled. "It seems to me that there were only one or two takes of each tune—that was generally the way Chet did recordings." The highlights of the session are a version of Miles Davis/Wayne Shorter's 'ESP', with Chet playing mute, and a lengthy version of 'Once Upon A Summertime', which Chet played regularly in later years. The album was eventually released in 1980, by which time Snyder's fledgling label was already beginning to struggle.

Chet and Ruth were scheduled to return to Europe in early March. An Italian record label had approached John Snyder about recording an album with Chet, and a number of European tour dates had been booked. Before they left New York, Ruth Young made some enquiries with a handful of local musicians, to see if they wanted to join the tour. Harold Danko was happy to stay with Thad and Mel, who offered regular work. She also called pianist Hod O'Brien, who had been working as a shipping clerk for a record company since the closure of his club, the St James Infirmary, in 1975. "I was excited about that," he remembers. "It would have been my first time in Europe, but it never did come through." In the event, Chet seems to have decided to play with local European musicians, which was presumably a cheaper option.[50]

Chet Baker and Ruth Young in Milan, March 1977.
Photograph by Paolo Liaci.

The new album—Chet's fourth of the year—was recorded for Carosello Records at the Cap Studio in Milan. The album saw Chet reunited with the great Italian tenor saxophonist Gianni Basso, who had first played with Chet almost twenty years earlier on *Chet Baker in Milan*. Chet's old friend Jacques Pelzer also appeared, playing alto saxophone and flute. The rhythm section was not as strong, however. The pianist, Bruce Thomas, had apparently been recommended by John Snyder, but lacked the experience needed to play with Chet Baker and Gianni Basso. The drummer, Giancarlo Pillot, was also a little too heavy-handed for Chet's liking.

The resulting album, *The Incredible Chet Baker Sings and Plays*, is an uneven affair, but interesting for two main reasons. First of all, it marked Ruth Young's debut recording. Ruth had sung occasionally on stage with Chet, primarily in the intimate surroundings of a small jazz club, like Stryker's in New York. Despite his efforts to encourage her, she was still plagued with self-doubt about her own abilities. "I was still intimidated by him, musically, and I had no confidence in my own singing," she recalled. "Chet wanted me to be regarded as a professional singer. He eventually backed me into a corner, and convinced me to do it."[51]

Chet and Ruth sang duet on two songs, 'Autumn Leaves' and 'Whatever Possessed Me'. Ruth was asked to sing in Chet's key, however, leaving her feeling uncomfortable with the recording. "To this day, I can't understand how so many people have found that album touching or appealing, but they have," she said. Sadly, the experience did little to improve her fragile confidence, and it would be a full twenty-five years before she attempted a follow-up, despite Chet's words of encouragement.

The other interesting feature of this album is the change in Chet's tone, which sounds frail and airy compared with the recordings made in New York the previous month. Chet was in agony throughout the recording session, suffering from severe stomach pains that he later discovered were the result of kidney stones. "He was trying to play so defensively to avoid that pain. This was the birth of the aerated sound that you hear, that became more prominent on his later recordings," explained Ruth. "Things came to a head a year or so later, when he had to jump off a moving train to get to a hospital. To Chet's credit, he made the most of it, and made it as musical as possible. The emergence of that sound was astounding, and makes for some of the album's other shortcomings."[52]

In the weeks that followed, Chet played a number of dates across Italy that had been booked by a local agent, Rita Amaducci. His band consisted of the same line-up that had appeared on the studio recording, with the exception of Bruce Thomas, who was replaced by Jacques Pelzer's son-in-law, Michel Graillier.

Chet was seemingly in a fragile state on this tour, however. His kidney stones were causing him considerable pain, and he was sleeping badly. Rather than consult a doctor, as Ruth had suggested, he decided he would try to kick methadone, worrying that his body had become too dependent on drugs. This resulted in chemical imbalances in his body, which in turn caused violent mood swings.

On one occasion, Jacques Pelzer was driving his old Peugeot from Milan to Rome, with Chet in the passenger seat, and Ruth Young, Michel Graillier and his wife, Micheline, crammed into the back seat of the car. They were scheduled to play a concert near the Castel Sant'Angelo, a famous old building near the Vatican, but were late leaving Milan. Chet soon grew impatient with his friend's driving. "My father wasn't driving fast enough for Chet, who said, 'Come on, man, let me drive'," recalled Micheline. Eventually Jacques relented, and the two of them swapped places.[53]

"Chet drove like he always used to drive. Eventually my father said, 'Chet, it's an old car, I'm worried it won't last, and I don't have the money for a new one'." Chet ignored the warning, and continued to push the car to its limits in a desperate bid to make up lost time. Jacques Pelzer continued to voice his concern until a fierce argument broke out. Chet slammed on the breaks in the middle of the road and stormed out of the car. "Fuck you all, I'll go to Rome by myself," he shouted. He left the highway, wearing just his old sandals on his feet, and trudged into the wilderness, with no town in sight. Ruth and Micheline both shouted, "Chet, Chet, come back," but it soon became apparent that he had no intention of returning.

They drove on to Rome alone, and by the time they had parked the car, smoke was beginning to emerge from the engine, the electrical system shot to pieces. When they arrived at the venue, the organiser informed them that Chet was in his hotel room; apparently he had been able to find a train, and arrived in Rome before the others.

Shortly before the start of the show, saxophonist Gianni Basso, bass player Lucio Terzano and drummer Giancarlo Pillot arrived at the venue.

Chet still had not showed up, and when Ruth called the hotel, he refused to come down from his room. The Italian musicians thought the band should play anyway, at least putting on a show for the audience. Pianist Michel Graillier refused, explained Micheline. "He said, 'If Chet's not here, I'm not going to play'. My father also refused." Later that evening, Chet summoned the whole band to his hotel room. "You two," he said, pointing to Michel and Jacques. "You stay with me." Then he pointed to the Italian musicians. "You three," he shouted. "You're fired!"[54]

More madness was to follow. The Belgian bass player Benoît Quersin, who had first played with Chet in late 1955, invited him to play a short tour of Zaire, an event that was sponsored by the Belgian consulate. Quersin was working for a museum in the capital city of Kinshasa at this time, researching the music and behavioural characteristics of the pygmies.

Chet and Ruth, accompanied by Jacques Pelzer, Michel Graillier and his wife Micheline, flew from Brussels to Gabon, and then on to Kinshasa. Chet was delighted to find that he could rent a Mustang at the airport, and insisted on driving to the hotel. "Can you imagine Chet in Africa?" asked Micheline. "It was like Tintin in Zaire! He arrived at the hotel in an old Mustang, slammed on the brakes, and the car span three times before it finally stopped!"

It soon became apparent that their host Benoît Quersin had started to lose his mind. He had split from his wife, who was still living in Aix-en-Provence, and was now living with a harem of local girls. Despite this, he would still make a pass at Ruth, who found his behaviour distasteful. Jacques Pelzer found himself drawn towards his friend's lifestyle, however, and in the days that followed he embarked on a passionate affair with a fourteen-year old girl. "Jacques must have been in his fifties at the time—he was a few years older than Chet," recalled Ruth. "The darling little girl named Mami he took up with was just that, a sweet little girl. She found nothing odd about being with a man old enough to be her grandfather, which made it all the easier for Jacques to enjoy their twisted tryst. Unbelievable, I thought. And when Mami first saw me she flung herself into my arms and refused to let go as she checked me out from head to toe. She'd probably never seen a white woman before."[55]

The relationship between Chet and Ruth, and indeed Michel and Micheline, seemed quite normal in contrast to the crazy scenes going on around them. Ruth remembers the trip left a positive impression on her from a musical perspective. "At one point Chet said, 'Let's try this—just me on trumpet, and you singing'. It was 'As Times Go By'. It was one of our more in-depth moments, musically. He suggested I sing that song, and others, on a more regular basis. The whole thing was an amazing experience—even with all of the peculiarities—and I think we all came out of it closer than ever before."[56]

On other occasions Chet could be quite self-absorbed, his anti-social behaviour frequently antagonising the local people. "One morning, the waitresses were making a lot of noise over breakfast," recalled Micheline, "so he took his trumpet and started playing in the restaurant at eight in the morning!" On another occasion he drove to the local market with Ruth and Micheline, who wanted to explore the city. "There were pools of water where it had rained, and he screeched through the water, splashing the local people, who were left glaring at the three white people in a Mustang," said Micheline. "I was scared to death, and said, 'They're going to kill us!' Chet was so crazy."[57]

The first concert, a show arranged for the US Ambassador, was scheduled for the Sunday night. The band opened with jazz standard 'Cherokee', but after playing the theme, Chet's dentures started to come loose. "It was a Sunday, and most of the stores were closed, so Chet took the Mustang, and decided to find a drugstore while the band kept playing," recalled Micheline, who was playing drums. "My father started to panic a little bit, and didn't remember the bridge. We kept playing the theme, over and over again, at a very fast tempo. We played the theme for about twenty minutes, and I was starting to suffer from cramp in my arms. Chet eventually came back, having found a drugstore, and joined us for one last theme. The audience must have wondered who he was, acting like royalty, just playing the theme and then leaving the stage!"[58]

A couple of days after the show, Jacques Pelzer had been out for the day in the Mustang, accompanied by Micheline and Michel. It was early evening, and they were heading back to the hotel, where they were supposed to meet Chet, before going on to a show. They were still outside the city when Jacques lost control of the vehicle, which rolled several times before crashing to a halt at the foot of a steep ravine. Jacques was badly injured in the accident, and was losing a great deal of blood. Micheline went in search of help, looking for a passing car, while her husband Michel probably saved his father-in-law's life, talking to him constantly to prevent him from falling unconscious. Jacques was eventually taken to hospital in the city, where he spent two weeks undergoing treatment. Michel suffered from only minor injuries, but was bitten by a spider in the ravine, and contracted malaria. "Jacques was a mess," recalled Ruth. "Frankly I don't know how any of them survived that crash."

Jacques had suffered a broken leg in the car crash, and spent the summer of 1977 recuperating at his pharmacy in Liège. Ruth Young spent a great deal of time with Jacques in the weeks that followed, helping to nurse him back to health. "We had always had an intense relationship," she later recalled. "His solidarity always seemed to be with Carol and the kids, which made it very difficult. But he had no problem telling me he was very fond of me, so I think he felt very conflicted."[59]

Chet does not seem to have worked much in the weeks that followed. Jacques Pelzer's cousin, Steve Houben, was still studying at Berklee College of Music, in Boston, but came back to Europe for a month in June, where he recorded his first album. Another American trumpet player was supposed to join the recording session, but phoned to say he wouldn't be able to make it. "I still had two more numbers to do," the saxophonist remembered. "Chet was in Liège with Jacques, so I asked him if he'd like to join me. 'The problem is, the studio is booked for nine in the morning'. 'No problem', he replied. 'I'll be there. Just come and pick me up'. He arrived at eight next morning, all dressed up, like he was going to work in an office, waiting with his case. I told him, 'I don't have a lot of money for you to do this'. He said, 'No problem, I don't need money. Let's play!' He played beautifully on two pieces. I didn't pay him anything, but drove him back to the house and thanked him."[60]

Whilst Chet was enjoying a relaxed summer in Liège, his family was struggling to make ends meet back in New York. Carol would write to Chet, asking him to send her money, and whilst he would do so on an occasional basis, more often than not he found it easier to ask John Snyder—who was working at Artists House Records—to send her an advance. At this stage the label had not even released Chet's album *Once Upon A Summertime*, so Snyder was effectively paying for Chet's family out of his own pocket.

"Chet was an asshole, and didn't treat her right at all," said Snyder. "He was not meeting his responsibilities with his children. Occasionally he might try and make an effort, but not in any consistent way. He would tell me to send her money, and I would send her money—that was pretty easy for him to do! I was paying her month-to-month there for a while. It wasn't because I was making money, because I wasn't. I was trying to run a record company, but I was also managing Ornette Coleman at the same time, and Jim Hall, and Gil Evans. I spent my entire time living in the office. It ended up driving me underground, because it was too much."[61]

In return, Carol used to confide in John Snyder, expressing her frustration over Chet's prolonged absence, and her bitterness over his relationship with Ruth Young. "I think she felt Chet was her only hope," he said. "I guess the option would have been to go out and get a job, get an education, get a life. Or take Chet to court. But how could you expect her to metamorphose into some rational being? Were she that, she wouldn't have got herself into that in the first place."[62]

Snyder also tried to help Chet's family in other ways. Dean seemed like a lost soul to him, desperately in need of a father figure, so he employed him at the record label, running odd jobs. He also befriended Chet's daughter Missy, who had just turned eleven years old. "Melissa was like a pen-pal," he recalled. "She would write me letters, and send me her poetry. It was the saddest thing you could possibly imagine. She was a beautiful girl, she was stunning, but had no self-image. Her teeth eventually rotted out. It was sad to see the effect that Chet's absence and Carol's bitterness had on his children—it was devastating."[63]

The neglect became too much to bear in the summer of 1977. The rent and utility bills for the apartment at Ruppert Towers had been unpaid for several months. First the power was cut off, and then the apartment was repossessed. Carol and the children made their way back to Oklahoma, where they stayed with Chet's mother for a few weeks. From there she was able to call Chet in Belgium, and announced that she was going to come over to Europe with the family.

Ruth was extremely upset when Chet told her the news. "I had been with Chet at Jacques' place in Liege, and Chet told me that we'd have to come to some arrangement because Carol was coming over," she said. "This was devastating news; I was stunned. It was like something out of one of the sickest soap opera scenes one could imagine. Chet again agreed to indulge Carol and her smart-assed proposal. He still felt badly for how he had just walked out on his entire family without batting much of an eye, and still wondered if she'd really ever carry out her threat of exposing him to the IRS. He never expected Carol to refuse the fact of their obviously defunct marriage and always hoped she'd one day look for a new life for herself without him. But now the insane plan was that she would stay with Jacques for a while before going on to England where she would visit her parents. Chet was very matter of fact about the entire incident; he was actually passive about it."

Carol arrived in Belgium in August accompanied by Paul, Missy and the family dog; Dean had opted to stay behind in Oklahoma with his grandmother. Chet had arranged for Ruth to stay with Lou McConnell, a young American tenor player, who was living in Liège at that time. "He was a really sweet guy," said Ruth, "but he was going through a crisis of his own with his girlfriend at the time. Chet and I still managed to get together most evenings, and Carol didn't seem to be any the wiser—she just seemed to be in a state of denial."

Carol refused to acknowledge that the marriage was over, and spent the next few weeks re-living her sepia-tinged memories of the early 1960s. "Carol used to sit at the table and say, 'Chet, do you remember when we met, and we went to the beach? We were so in love'," recalled Micheline Pelzer. "Chet snapped back, 'Yes, of course I remember'. It was obvious he was no longer in love at all. He always respected Carol, but the love was over."[64]

Micheline also noted that Carol was still taking methadone at this time, some four years after Chet had effectively left her. "Carol was on heroin for a while, certainly," she confirmed. "I'm not sure whether Chet tried to share his love of heroin with her. Maybe she thought she would try it to be closer to him, I don't know, but she got strung out, little by little. She was still taking methadone when she came to Belgium that year."

Chet soon tired of Carol's constant presence, and made arrangements to move back to North America with Ruth Young, leaving Carol and the children in Belgium. He clearly felt some guilt at leaving her behind, and mailed a cheque to her to help cover her expenses.

A few weeks later, in early October, Carol wrote him a letter complaining that she no longer felt welcome staying with Jacques in Liège, and was considering moving back to England to live with her parents, who were now retired. The letter again confirms that Carol refused to accept that the marriage was over. "I love you, but you've hurt me so much along with the lies and deceit," she wrote. "I could put that behind me if you wanted to make things work between us again—that's the problem, you do things that show me you don't really care, and being alone hurts more than anything—try it sometime."

Chet saw the letter was from Carol, and handed it to Ruth, still unopened. "I can't deal with this shit," he muttered. "You read it."

Army life in Germany: Chet Baker (far left) with friends from the 298th Army Band, 1947: Photograph courtesy of 'Sebby' Papa.

College days: Date unknown, but probably taken whilst Chet was attending El Camino College, 1948. Photographer unknown.

The Gerry Mulligan Quartet: On stage at The Haig, Los Angeles, 1952. From left to right, Chet Baker, Gerry Mulligan, Bob Whitlock and Chico Hamilton. Photograph by William Claxton / Courtesy Demont Photo Management, LLC.

Chet Baker sings: Recording 'The Thrill Is Gone' with Russ Freeman at Radio Recorders Studios, Hollywood on October 27th, 1953. Photograph by William Claxton / Courtesy Demont Photo Management, LLC.

Charlie Parker's protégé: From left to right, Jimmy Rowles, Carson Smith, Chet Baker and Charlie Parker: Los Angeles, November 1953. Photograph by William Claxton / Courtesy Demont Photo Management, LLC.

Chet Baker in Europe: From left to right, Chet Baker, Jimmy Bond, Dick Twardzik, on stage at the Concertgebouw, Amsterdam, September 17th, 1955. Photograph courtesy of Eddy Posthuma de Boer.

Missing tooth: Chet Baker on stage at the Concertgebouw, Amsterdam, September 17th, 1955. Photograph courtesy of Eddy Posthuma de Boer.

Promotion: Chet Baker with his girlfriend Liliane Cukier in London, October 1955. Photographer unknown.

Second marriage: Chet Baker with his new wife, Halema Alli,
Redondo Beach, Los Angeles, summer 1956.
Photograph by William Claxton / Courtesy Demont Photo Management, LLC.

New York: A rare outtake from the 'Chet' photo session, 1959. Original cover produced and designed by Paul Bacon, Ken Brearen and Harris Lewine.

Awaiting trial: Chet behind bars in the Inner Courtyard of the Tribunal of Lucca, April 1961. Photograph by F. Ercolini, courtesy of Francesco Maino.

On trial: Chet Baker facing the town's public prosecutor, Lucca, Italy, April 11th, 1961. Photographer unknown.

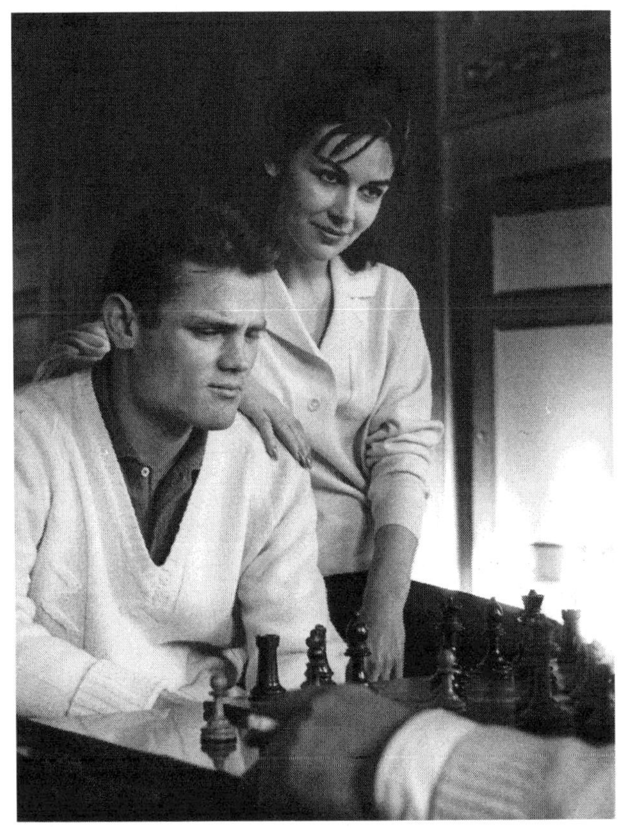

Carol: Chet Baker and his then girlfriend, Carol Jackson, in Lucca, 1961. Photograph courtesy of Graziano Arici.

Release: Chet Baker in the Hotel Universo, Lucca, December 1961, following his release from prison. Photograph courtesy of Graziano Arici.

An early publicity shot for The Mariachi Brass, featuring Chet Baker (second right). Photographer unknown.

Reunion: Gerry Mulligan and Chet Baker rehearse for the Carnegie Hall concert, November 1974. Photograph by Franca R. Mulligan.

A new beginning: Chet Baker with his girlfriend, Ruth Young. Photograph by Lamberto Londi.

Gaunt: Chet Baker in Laren, Holland for the International Jazz Festival on 7th August, 1975. Photograph by Pieter Boersma.

Chet Baker in Italy. Photograph courtesy of Ruth Young.
Photographer unknown.

Ballads for two: Chet Baker recording with Wolfgang Lackerschmid,
Tonstudio Zuckerfabrik, Stuttgart, January 8th, 1979.
Photograph courtesy of Hans Kumpf.

Rehearsal: Chet and Ruth at the Musikpodium, Stuttgart, Germany, January 16th, 1979. Photograph courtesy of Hans Kumpf.

Drummerless trio: Chet Baker with Niels-Henning Ørsted Pedersen and Doug Raney, Montmartre, Copenhagen, October 1979. Photograph by Jorgen Bo.

Return to the drummerless format: Philip Catherine, Jean-Louis Rassinfosse and Chet Baker on stage, date unknown. Photograph courtesy of Porgy en Bess.

Relaxing at Jacques Pelzer's house: Chet Baker in Liège, March 1986. Photograph courtesy of Jacky Lepage.

Last love: Chet with Diane Vavra in Liège, Belgium, March 1986.
Photograph courtesy of Jacky Lepage.

New-look trio: Chet with Philip Catherine (left) and
Riccardo del Fra (centre) at the Bothanique, Brussels, Belgium, April 11th 1986.
Photograph courtesy of Jacky Lepage.

Disastrous: Paul Bley and Chet Baker at the Montreal Jazz Festival, July 3rd, 1986.
Photograph courtesy of Denis Alix.

Sublime: Backstage at Hitomi-Kinen-Kodo, Tokyo, Japan on 14th June, 1987. From left to right Diane Vavra, Chet Baker, Harold Danko, John Engels and Hein van de Geijn.
Photograph courtesy of John Engels.

Chet smokes: Chet Baker with Space Jazz Trio at Corto Maltese, Ostia, Italy in November 1987, featuring John Arnold (drums), Massimo Moriconi (bass) and Enrico Pieranunzi (piano). Photograph © Bertrand Fevre, France.

Alone at the end: Chet at the Teatro alla Giustizia, Mestre, Italy on March 22nd, 1988. Photograph courtesy of Paulo Gant.

Sad scene: Chet Baker at Jazzclub Thelonious, May 7th, 1988.
Photograph courtesy of Hajo Piebenga.

Funeral: Melissa (Missy) Baker places a rose on the coffin of her father,
May 21st, 1988. Photographer unknown.

Chapter Fifteen

SOMEDAY MY PRINCE WILL COME
1978–1979

"It's not a band that sells itself on snappy clothes, modeling today's fashions, and it's not a band that wears funny hats or tries to be funny. We're just up there to play music. And that's all."—Chet Baker.[1]

When Chet returned to the United States in late 1977, he quickly settled into his old routine, playing two nights a week at Stryker's, the bar on 86th Street and Columbus Avenue. His 'comeback' had been moderately successful; albums like *She Was Too Good To Me* and *You Can't Go Home Again* had been fairly well received, and sold in respectable numbers. As a consequence, work was easier to come by, and he was offered fairly regular gigs at venues such as the Village Vanguard and Sweet Basil in New York, Baker's Keyboard Lounge in Detroit and the Keystone Korner in San Francisco.

From a personal perspective, he was also more settled. He had been in a relatively stable relationship with Ruth Young since the summer of 1973, and whilst his wife Carol had never accepted that the marriage was over, Chet had moved on.

His health seemed to reflect this stability; for the most part he stuck to the methadone programme, controlling his drug intake. Occasionally he would fall off the wagon in the company of other addicts, but most of the time he was in reasonably good shape. This view was confirmed by many of the musicians who played with him at that time. "When I first started playing with him, he was on the methadone programme," confirmed drummer Jeff Brillinger. "As far as I'm aware, he didn't do any hard drugs for the whole of that year. He was doing other things—smoking pot, taking pills, that kind of thing, but not the hard stuff. His playing reflects that. He was playing very well, with a lot of fire, which people don't always associate with him."[2]

This period of stability, which lasted for roughly two years—1978 and 1979—was mirrored by his recorded output, which contained some of the best music since his comeback. They include albums such as *Live at Nick's* and *Broken Wing*, both recorded in late 1978, and a series of live recordings for Denmark's SteepleChase Records, including *Someday My Prince Will Come* and *The Touch Of Your Lips*, recorded the following year.

One of the first musicians to hook up with Chet on his return to the US was baritone saxophonist Roger Rosenberg. Rosenberg was an old friend of saxophonist Bob Mover, and had sat in with the band one night in August 1973 at the Town Crier in East Islip, out on Long Island. "And then I used to live around the block from a bar called Stryker's," he recalled. "Chet would play in there, and I used to go along periodically and sit in." He reunited with Chet in November 1977, on his return from Europe. By that stage, Bob Mover was no longer with the band, and Chet invited him to join.

Rosenberg soon picked up on the style Chet was looking for. "I remember one night at Stryker's, a New Year's Eve gig, he asked me to play. I don't remember the rhythm section, and I'm pretty sure there was no drummer. I remember Lee Konitz was playing on the gig. We were playing the ballad, ''Round Midnight'. I was kind of slow, and I hadn't been playing with him that long. As I recall, he'd played the chorus, and it was my turn to play, so I played the chorus, and in the bridge he came in. I stopped playing, because I figured he was coming back in. For some reason he got really angry with me. I could tell he was really upset so I went up to him, and he told me that he wanted me to keep playing while he was playing background. So that became a thing we used to do a lot in the band—we'd play background behind each other, or do a lot of things where we would play off each other."[3]

Another musician who started playing with Chet around this time was a fresh-faced young bass player by the name of Jon Burr. "I came to New York in 1975, and met Chet in 1977," he confirmed. "I joined Buddy Rich's band in the spring of 1976, and then I started making my way around the clubs of New York, sitting in with various people." He sat in with Chet Baker at Stryker's in late 1977, and soon became a permanent fixture.

Burr recruited a studious young pianist by the name of Phil Markowitz. "Jon called me, and said that Chet needed a piano player for that night," said Markowitz. "It was very matter of fact. We played everything at the gig and it went well. Chet was his usual mild-mannered self, counting off tunes, really mellow and playing great." Chet was immediately impressed by Markowitz's playing, and later described him as "one of the most sensitive, lyrical and inventive piano players of all time."[4]

Word soon got out that Chet was back in the United States, and after the modest success of *You Can't Go Home Again*—which had featured the 'fusion' musicians John Scofield and Michael Brecker—Chet was offered a prestigious gig at New York's Village Vanguard in early 1978. At this point he recruited drummer Jeff Brillinger to join the band. Brillinger had sat in with Chet previously at the St James Infirmary in New York, and Chet knew that he was a sensitive player.

At first, the new-look band played a number of songs from Chet's most recent recordings, including charts from *You Can't Go Home Again*. "I think Chet must have really liked Sebesky's arrangements," recalled Phil Markowitz, "and it was a great recording with Paul Desmond. Although his book was huge, we played a lot of stuff from that record—'Un Poco Loco', 'Love For Sale' and 'You Can't Go Home Again'.[5]

In the weeks that followed, the band began to gel, and the musicians found that Chet was quite responsive to ideas they brought to the table. "I think it was good for him because we had a working band there for a while," recalled Jeff Brillinger. "He did so much stuff with pick-up rhythm sections. I think it was good for him to have a bunch of guys that he knew, and felt comfortable with. We were able to develop some original material. We were doing some tunes by Phil Markowitz and Roger Rosenberg, and were getting some of that cohesiveness that you get with a working band. I think we pushed Chet a little bit musically, expanding his repertoire."

After the gig at the Village Vanguard, the new-look band embarked on a short tour that included Dayton, Ohio (Gilly's), Chicago (Jazz Showcase) and Detroit (Baker's Keyboard Lounge). Roger Rosenberg remembered a strange incident after the gig in Detroit. "It was a great gig, and we had a good time. Chet used to love to drive every place; I'd been in the car driving with him, and had some experiences that were a little bit uncomfortable for me. So I decided I wasn't going to drive with him any more, and flew out to this gig with Jeff. We were all staying in this motel by the club. We finished the gig, and Chet decided he was going to drive straight back. I got this call early next morning from the front desk saying that he'd skipped out on the bill. I couldn't figure out what had happened, and talked to them. It was a drive-through, and you could pay your bill as you were driving out. Apparently not too long before, the woman who was working on the desk had been held up, and when Chet drove through, thought that he looked like the person who had held her up, which of course was not true. I don't know what transpired, but Chet drove off. These kinds of things could crop up when you played with Chet! But all of this stuff was worth overlooking just to play with him; the experience was so absolutely incredible."[6]

The band seems to have returned to New York in late January before flying out to the West Coast in early February. The band played for one week at The Lighthouse at Hermosa Beach in Los Angeles, before moving on to the Keystone Korner in Los Angeles. A CD was later released of the final night in San Francisco, entitled *Sings, Plays—Live At The Keystone Korner*. Unfortunately it does not capture the band at its best. The recording was made by the club's owner, Todd Barkan, but the recording quality is poor, and the balances incorrect. Chet's playing was also patchy that night. He fluffs his entrance on 'Secret Love', and seems to disappear part of the way through 'Blues 'n' Boogie', presumably to re-glue his dentures. The notes to the 'Keystone Korner' recording, written by Ira Gitler, suggest that Chet had broken his dentures prior to the concert, but this is incorrect; that incident occurred a few months later at Sweet Basil in New York.

Chet's former lover, Diane Vavra, was in the audience on the opening night at the Keystone Korner. She hadn't seen him in four years, since that fateful night in Denver, when Chet had left her with a broken rib. They met after the show, and finding there was still a spark between them, she invited him back to spend the night. Next day, she suggested they meet up again, but when she attended two of the subsequent shows, he showed no interest in renewing their relationship. Bitterly disappointed, she threw her glass at the wall of the club and drove home alone.

The band returned to New York in mid-February, before travelling to Canada for a gig at the Rising Sun in Montreal in early March. A recording of this gig has also emerged subsequently and offers a better example of how the band was starting to gel. Roger Rosenberg plays gently under Chet's vocal on 'Oh, You Crazy Moon', and the horns play off one another on 'Love For Sale'. Listening to these recordings now, the saxophonist feels that he overplayed on some solos at that time. "I think, 'Why didn't I take advantage of the fact that I was playing with one of the most lyrical trumpet players in the world?' Of course, I was twenty-five or twenty-six, and that's what saxophone players were doing back then."[7]

The band's pianist, Phil Markowitz, left the band in mid-March. He was offered another gig for more money than Chet could offer, and left on good terms. His replacement was Jim McNeely, who had been recommended to Chet by another pianist, Harold Danko. "I knew a couple of other guys that were playing with Chet—Jon Burr and Jeff Brillinger," the pianist told me. "We played in New York, we played in a couple of clubs around the New York area, we also played up in Boston and I remember a gig in Detroit that we played. Chet was very quiet, but he was always very pleasant to me. In terms of his health, he was in pretty good shape. He was playing very strongly; I was surprised sometimes by the energy of his playing. Most people thought of him being laid-back and cool-school, but Chet was playing rather intensively at the time. He was playing great, and it was a lot of fun playing with his band."[8]

By the spring of 1978, Carol Baker and the children had settled into a new apartment in Flushing, Queens. Chet believed that Carol was now drug-free, and felt he could now make their separation more formal. He filled a suitcase with a number of his most treasured possessions, including his *DownBeat* and *Metronome* awards, and moved them to Ruth Young's apartment. He was still reluctant to ask for a divorce, given Carol's previous threats to report Chet to the IRS. For that reason, Chet continued to arrange for post to be delivered to a number of different names and addresses—Ruth Young, his mother's address in Oklahoma, Carol Baker's apartment and even Jacques Pelzer's pharmacy in Liège.

While Chet was packing his belongings, Carol Baker discovered an envelope of nude photographs that Ruth had once given him before he went away on tour. Carol was still living in denial, even after all this time, and revealed what she had found to Chet's mother. Vera, who was now sixty-seven, had retired and moved back to Yale, Oklahoma. She sent Chet a scathing letter, which again revealed her disappointment in the way he had let her down. She was particularly malicious in her reference to the role of Ruth Young, who she described as "acting like a whore". She also accused Chet of spending all of his money on drugs for Ruth—who certainly dabbled, but was not an addict—whilst leaving little for his children. The letter was probably prompted by the fact that the children had expressed an interest in moving in with their father and his new girlfriend.[9]

Ruth Young's new apartment was in a brownstone on 71st Street, just off Central Park West. It was a narrow one-bedroom place—big enough to house her baby grand piano, and their limited possessions. Ruth had decorated one wall with a collage of Chet Baker photos and memorabilia, artfully arranged around a childhood photo of her. Despite the small size of the apartment, Chet told his children they were welcome to move in, and within a few weeks, Chet and Ruth were joined by three children, two cats and a dog.

Despite the cramped living conditions, Ruth did everything she could to make the children feel welcome. Dean was now fifteen years old, and whilst he had a shy demeanour, Ruth remembers witnessing the occasional flash of his father's hot temper, smashing his bicycle helmet on the lid of the piano.

Paul, who was twelve years old, seemed the most troubled of the three children. Chet was verbally and physically abusive towards him, a pattern of behaviour he had clearly inherited from his own father. "Chet's father was an awful drunk, and his beating tirades came out of alcohol," said Ruth. "Chet adored his father, but this didn't seem to get through to him. The same thing happened to Paul. Paul adored Chet, and yet he couldn't get through—instead of being a son and a real person, Chet saw him as a nuisance and a disappointment. Paul was Chet's main target, but he would also beat Missy. He wasn't a nice guy in that way. These things are unsavoury, but they're the truth." As a result, Ruth remembers Paul as being a lost little boy. "He was nowhere, he didn't know what the hell life was about," she recalled.[10]

On the face of it, Missy, the youngest child at eleven, seemed to be relatively well adjusted. Ruth recalls her drawing a sketch of a heart, inside which she had written 'Chet 'n' Roofie 4 ever'. But beneath the surface, she remained deeply troubled.

Over the course of the summer, the band played a number of gigs around the New York area, including Sweet Basil and the Village Vanguard in New York City, Gulliver's in New Jersey, Lulu White's in Boston, and Baker's Keyboard Lounge in Detroit. For the most part, Chet's chops were in good shape. "Chet always claimed that he never read music, which was probably true," recalled the pianist Jim McNeely. "But Chet had these amazing ears; we'd play some rather complicated tunes, harmonically speaking, and he'd play these beautiful lines through them. That was the way he operated; his instincts were so strong. I was pretty amazed by the complexity of some of the material he would play."[11]

One night at Sweet Basil was particularly memorable, according to the band's drummer, Jeff Brillinger. "Stan [Getz] sat in with Chet. To hear those two guys together—that was the best moments I had," he said. "They may have had their problems getting on well, but they sound great together, that's for sure."[12]

Later that same week, Chet had problems with his dentures, and his plate broke before the start of the show. "He wasn't able to play," recalled the saxophonist Roger Rosenberg. "I thought, 'What's going to happen?' But the whole night he sang the trumpet parts, just scatting. And he was really one of the great scat singers; he was one of the few people you'd hear scat singing who would actually scat sing stuff that wasn't gibberish. Anything he could play he could scat. Because he was a great musician, he was able to do that stuff with his voice."[13]

Chet also played the occasional gig with a local pick-up band at this time. One such gig took place at Lulu White's in Boston, where Chet was scheduled to appear with the pianist Ray Santisi and the drummer Alan Dawson. "Unfortunately, as often happened with Chet, he had gotten into a very big argument with them," Jeff Brillinger later recalled. "I'm not sure what happened, probably something over the music, but there was a big scene. All of a sudden we got a call from Chet to come up to Boston at a moment's notice, and we finished the week up there."[14]

Chet made two studio recordings over this period, but neither of them was particularly memorable. The first took place with his regular band, who did a recording session for the Artists House label. "There was a recording that we did in the studio with the producer, John Snyder, but I guess he felt that Chet was not that into the recording, so they never released it," said Roger Rosenberg. "I always suspected that some day that recording would come out, just because he was part of it." John Snyder confirmed the existence of unreleased recordings, but still feels they should remain in the vault. "There's not really enough for a record—it's like forty minutes," he said. "As I recall, there are several versions of several songs."[15]

The second session took place with the singer Astrud Gilberto, who recorded an album by the name of *The Girl From Ipanema* with the producer Don Sebesky. Gilberto had written the melody for a tune by the name of 'Far Away', and Hal Shaper had written lyrics for the tune. "It was a thrill to sing with him as a duet, especially doing one of my own songs," she explained in an interview featured on her website. "Definitely a highlight of my career!"

Don Sebesky did not regard the recording session as particularly successful, however. "It wasn't a very successful record for a number of reasons," he recalled. "We were playing in a very cramped studio, and the sound wasn't good, so Chet wasn't very relaxed. The tune wasn't all that good either. It wasn't like when we were at CTI and we had Rudy van Gelder's wood-lined studio, almost cradling your sound. Chet and Paul used to stand in the middle of the room and smile because when they played, the sound used to come back to them in such a natural way that it made them want to play more."

Chet's pianist, Jim McNeely, left the band late summer. "John Scofield had offered me a job," he later recalled. "John was going to be doing his first tour as a leader in Europe, and that's when I told Chet I'd be leaving. Then Mel [Lewis] called me to join Thad and Mel, and this was a much longer tour, so I ended up doing the Thad and Mel thing." He left on good terms, and was replaced by Phil Markowitz, who was happy to rejoin the band.

Around this time, Chet became acquainted with a car salesman, James Felds, who introduced himself at a gig in Long Island, and offered his services as a manager. Ruth Young, who handled most of Chet's US gigs at that time, was not impressed. "Felds was the next creep to come along. He was a used car salesman with a dead-end life. The concept of "use" came quite naturally to this greedy jerk. I couldn't stand this guy and made no secret of it," she recalled."[16]

Whilst Ruth was right to be suspicious of Felds' motives, he did prove adept at arranging a tour schedule for Chet. "He was new to the music business, and was kind of an alien figure, because he didn't know much about the music," recalled Jeff Brillinger. "But he was kind of a talker, and could get things done, and was on the scene when this European tour came up. Quite frankly, I would have had a lot of trepidations about going to Europe with Chet, but with this manager there, I felt he would take care of business."[17]

Felds worked with Chet's producer, John Snyder, to plan a European tour. He soon discovered that Chet was still banned from entering Germany.

John Snyder worked with a German lawyer, Erich Kremer, to appeal the ban, and convince the German authorities that he was now clean. They were assisted by a German tour agent, Gabriele (Gaby) Kleinschmidt, who allowed her name to be listed along with Chet's at every German border crossing.

The band's bass player, Jon Burr, left the band before they could depart for Europe. He accepted an offer from Stan Getz, much to Chet's dismay. "Stan was saying things like, 'I'm going to produce you'," the bass player later recalled. "Also, Stan had a higher profile in the States at that time, and I perceived it as a better opportunity." He was replaced by a young bass player by the name of Scott Lee, who went on to work with artists such as Lee Konitz, Freddie Hubbard and Joe Lovano.[18]

The saxophonist, Roger Rosenberg, decided to leave the band in October. "He did this European trip that lasted for about seven weeks, and asked me if I wanted to do it," he recalled. "I'd been working with him for almost two years, and I had had enough experience with him to know that you might not get paid exactly what you thought you were going to get paid, he might act a little erratic, things like that. So I talked it over with my wife. At that time I was pretty young, and didn't have a lot of extra money, and I felt really uncomfortable going over to Europe without a substantial amount of my own money, just in case something went wrong."[19]

The European tour started in Germany on November 2nd 1978. Gaby Kleinschmidt had arranged an efficient schedule taking in cities such as Frankfurt (2nd), Wilhelmshaven (3rd), Sittard (5th), Köln (6th and 7th) and Berlin (8th and 9th). Thereafter, the group departed for France, which included gigs in Chateauvallon (10th), Paris (12th) and Avignon (15th). Chet's new manager, James Felds, would appear to have negotiated recording rights with several of the club owners on the trip, and as a result, the tour is extremely well documented. The first gig that was recorded was at the Centre Culturel in Chateauvallon. Unfortunately, Chet's chops were not in the best of shape that night. He scats for much of the opener 'Oh, You Crazy Moon', and his solos are unusually hesitant. It's interesting to note the band's influence on his repertoire, however; 'Love for Sale' is given an upbeat, funky reading, driven by Brillinger and Markowitz, whilst Wayne Shorter's wonderful 'Beautiful Black Eyes' became a regular part of the set list on the tour.

Chet's pianist, Phil Markowitz, later claimed he became more aware of

Chet's legacy once the band started to play in Europe. "There were more festivals and absolutely hushed crowds at the clubs," he later recalled. "They were coming out to see an icon, of course out of love and respect and also to see if he could still do it—which he could of course on a remarkable level."[20]

Chet's old friend Jacques Pelzer joined the band on stage in Luxembourg on 17th November. A tape exists of this performance, and whilst Chet plays well, the sound quality is poor. Thereafter, the band played one gig in northern Italy, before returning to Germany for a series of concerts in late November.

The band was taped once again at Nick Vollebregt's Jazz Café in Laren on November 30th. The recording, which was later purchased by Gerry Teekens of Criss Cross Jazz, and later issued as *Live At Nick's*, ranks as one of Chet's finest recordings of the decade. The album offers conclusive evidence that Chet was starting to gel with his young band. It also marks the first appearance on record of 'Broken Wing', a tune written for Chet by the pianist Richie Beirach, which became a staple part of his repertoire in his final years.

The band's bass player, Scott Lee, had to return to the United States in the middle of the tour. As a consequence, Chet invited the Belgian bass player Jean-Louis Rassinfosse to watch the quartet play in Belgium in early December. "After the gig he explained to me that there were going to be a few changes, with Scott Lee going back to the States. 'Do you want to go on tour with us next month?' I said, 'Yes, of course, I would love to'."[21]

Rassinfosse's first gig with the band was in Stockholm, on December 11th. "Chet was in good shape," the bass player later recalled. "He was well dressed, as though he was trying to regain authority. He was even travelling with an agent [Felds]. It was the only time I can remember Chet travelling with some music. He had some charts, including some of the Don Sebesky arrangements from *You Can't Go Home Again*, which we kept in a big folder. The group was very tight." A tape does exist of the Stockholm concert, and it is regarded as being one of the highlights of the tour; sadly the recordings have not yet been made available.

The group played a few gigs in Norway, including a gig at the Club 7 in Oslo. Unfortunately, one of the band members—presumably Chet himself—left the sheet music on a sidewalk in Oslo as they climbed into a taxi. "From that moment, we had no music written any more," said

Rassinfosse. "When we started looking for replacements in the band in early 1979, there was a big problem. If people didn't know the music, or had no knowledge of the standards, there was no written repertoire that someone could learn in a few days." After that incident, he started to keep his own book of music. "Every time Chet started talking about a tune I didn't know, I tried to find a version so that I had some information about it," he said. "This was very helpful when we started to play with [guitarist] Philip Catherine, who didn't know so much about the standards at that time."[22]

Later that day, the band took a train from Oslo to Trondheim. Chet was still suffering from pains associated with kidney stones—the same pains that impacted his playing on the recording of *The Incredible Chet Baker Plays And Sings* the previous year. "Chet was suffering like hell," Rassinfosse remembered. "We didn't know what it was. Chet got out of the train, and we went on to Trondheim, assuming he would join us later. In the end he was hospitalised for a few days."[23]

Chet had been suffering from excruciating but sporadic pain for the best part of eighteen months. He stubbornly refused to consult a doctor, and was convinced the pain was caused by cancer. "The one time I ever went through his trumpet case, other than to hand him his trumpet, he asked me to get the Fast Teeth powder for his dentures," Ruth Young later recalled. "I couldn't find it easily, and checked under the panel of his trumpet case. I found the adhesive, but also found a piece of paper. Normally I wouldn't take any interest—it's like looking inside a woman's purse—but on this occasion I drew the paper closer to me. It turned out it was a will he'd drawn up himself. 'By probing very closely with my fingers, there can no longer be any doubt; I am dying of stomach cancer. How can I thank all the good people—there have been so many'. It was so pitiful; he was in so much pain, and had self-diagnosed that he was dying."[24]

The hospital quickly diagnosed the problem as kidney stones, much to Chet's relief. Ruth Young was convinced that the problem was caused by Chet's poor diet living with Carol for ten years. The pain associated with his ailment did impact Chet's playing at this time, lending a fragile, airy tone to his playing. It's interesting to note that Chet tried to reproduce this sound in his later years, even once the problem had been diagnosed. That same soft tone can be heard to good effect on many of his recordings from

1983 onwards, including the excellent recordings with Philip Catherine and Jean-Louis Rassinfosse.[25]

The band reconvened in Paris in late December, where a number of gigs had been booked. Chet was approached to record two albums at this time, but as a result of scheduling conflicts, they had to be recorded on the same day. A French record producer, Gilles Gautherin, arranged the first on the afternoon of December 28th. He wanted to record Chet's band, but requested that Rassinfosse be replaced by the more experienced Jean-Francois Jenny-Clark—known as J-F for short. Rassinfosse readily agreed to this condition. "I was a big fan of J-F, so I was very pleased to be in the studio when they were recording the album. He was a much more accomplished bass player than I was at that time; I was just a beginner in some ways, with just a few years of music behind me. It was good for me to meet him, and hear him play."[26]

The resulting album, *Broken Wing*, was arguably Chet's best studio album of the decade, and a suitable monument to a memorable tour. The repertoire is similar to the preceding live shows, opening with a delicate version of 'Broken Wing', with Chet on muted trumpet. 'Black Eyes' follows, and although the studio recording is somewhat inferior to the live version on *Live at Nick's*, where Chet has more time to stretch out, there is compensation in the form of a wonderful solo from Jenny-Clark which leaves you wondering why he did not work with Chet more frequently. 'Oh You Crazy Moon' is let down by an imperfect vocal from Chet, but there's a gentle swing to 'How Deep is the Ocean', which is far superior to the studio recording on *The Best Thing for You*. The album closes with a rare composition from Baker, 'Blue Gilles', a tribute to the French producer; it's little more than a slow studio jam, but it's enjoyable enough.

The band went on to play a gig that evening at La Chappelle des Lombards, a small club near the Opéra Bastille in Paris, which Phil Markowitz remembers as being even better than the studio recording. "Chet was totally burning that night," he remembered. After the show, Gilles Gautherin invited the band to a party to celebrate the studio recording they had made earlier that day. He was unaware that the band had already agreed to make another studio recording after the show. "We had to make excuses, telling him, 'Oh, we're so tired, we need to go back to the hotel'," Rassinfosse laughed. "We did go back to the hotel, but from there, we took a one-hour bus trip to the studio".[27]

Whilst some critics have suggested that the title of the resulting album, *Two A Day* refers to Chet's drug intake at this time, nothing could be further from the truth; it was simply a joke, referring to the fact that it was the second album they had made that day. "*Two A Day* does sound a little tired," Markowitz admits, "which we were, starting the recording at two in the morning." The album kicks off with a rare Chet Baker original composition, named after the record itself, and there's a sprightly version of 'If I Should Lose You'. The tempo begins to sag on 'Blue Room', however, and by the time we get to Chet's vocal on 'This Is Always' it sounds as though he's finally ready to call it a day.[28]

The band spent the next week playing at the La Chapelle des Lombards, which effectively brought the tour to a close. The atmosphere had started to change, however, and the magic of the previous weeks started to fade. Chet had arranged for Ruth Young to fly over from New York, arriving in time for his birthday, and to celebrate the New Year together. Ruth remembers an argument between Chet and his manager at this time. "I can't remember precisely, but I think he stiffed Chet over one of the recordings," she recalled. As a consequence, Felds was fired and returned to the United States. "I remember Chet saying, 'From now on, I don't want an agent'," recalled Jean-Louis Rassinfosse.[29]

On New Year's Eve, Chet and Ruth met up with a few old friends, including Jacques Pelzer and his daughter Micheline. They were joined by a French record producer, and after dinner, the group returned to Chet's hotel room at the Hotel California, situated near the Champs-Elysées. It was here that the Frenchman produced a small bag of heroin, and asked if any of them wanted to join him for a snort. "He gave into temptation, but he used to say he liked that," recalled Micheline, who had also managed to stay off heroin for three years until that point. Asked why Chet gave into temptation at this time, Micheline thought there were probably a variety of factors. "He had more money, maybe that was a factor," she suggested. "He was working regularly, good gigs, and also recording, which was lucrative."[30]

The gig at La Chapelle finished in early January, which was effectively the end of the tour. The band's pianist, Phil Markowitz, returned to the United States at this time, but drummer Jeff Brillinger stayed on, encouraged by Chet's promise of additional gigs in the New Year. "I ended up hanging around Paris for about a week, waiting to hear something," he recalled.

"But I never heard from Chet. He had resumed his heavy drug use, and felt like he was in another world. I didn't even know how to get in touch with him and never really saw him again."[31]

For Brillinger, it was a sad way to end a highly successful tour, but Chet had always found it difficult to stay on the methadone programme, and was always open to temptation—whether it was the cash burning a hole in his pocket, or the presence of old friends who could lure him back into temptation. Either way, he stuck to snorting heroin, rather than injecting—which gave him less of a high, but was also less addictive. Within a few days he was back on the methadone programme, determined once again to prove he was in command—just as he had at the start of his European tour back in November 1978.

Later that month, Chet made his way to Germany for a record date with a young German vibraphonist, Wolfgang Lackerschmid. The two musicians had encountered one another at various European music festivals, and were later introduced by Chet's German tour manager, Gaby Kleinschmidt. She approached Chet's then manager, James Felds, about recording an album, and a studio was booked in Stuttgart. On the face of it, the two musicians had little in common. "The funny thing is that I played mainly free improvised music at those festivals," Lackerschmid recalled. "I was also able to sneak in some of my own tunes. Some passages of the free improvisations turned into some melodic, even romantic moods, but the main concept was powerful 'new' jazz. I guess Chet must have heard or felt my 'romantic side'."[32]

They agreed to record an album of duets, without the support of a rhythm section. At Chet's suggestion they warmed up by playing 'You Don't Know What Love Is', a standard that was familiar to the young German musician. It's interesting to note that Chet's tone again sounds more aerated on this recording; it's not clear whether this is the after-effect of Chet's 'long weekend' in Paris, or whether he was looking to experiment with his 'new' sound. Either way, it sounds very effective in this stripped-back setting.

Chet Baker and Wolfgang Lackerschmid, Stuttgart, Germany, 8th January 1979. Photograph by Hans Kumf.

One of the highlights of the session was a composition by Lackerschmid. "When we recorded it, the piece did not have a title. I'd only just completed it, and had not yet copied out the changes in Bb," the vibraphonist recalled. "I was about to do this when Chet said, 'I don't need changes. I got the melody … '. Of course, that says a lot about him and the music itself. If you have the melody you can also master the form and the harmonies, and you don't have to churn out notes according to the dictates of a bunch of harmonic symbols."[33]

After they had recorded the piece, Chet and Wolfgang's girlfriends sat in the control room, and started to cry. "They were so moved by the recording but a little embarrassed, too, that we had caught them in such a vulnerable state. Whereupon we both said, 'Why shouldn't you cry?' and that became the title."[34]

During a break in the recording sessions, Chet and Wolfgang took a break in a nearby restaurant, enjoying a dessert of vanilla ice cream with warm, fresh raspberries, so good they both ordered a second portion. Their creative juices flowing, Wolfgang proposed they try to improvise a tune "the way the dessert tasted". They agreed a key, and discussed how to begin, and the tune quickly unfolded. One critic later misread the LP's song titles, and described how the duo had captured "the brooding heat and solitude of the 'desert'."

Chet greatly enjoyed the recording sessions, and the sense of space that the 'duet' recordings allowed him. This is probably an underrated album in Chet's long discography; it predates the 'drummerless' recordings he made for SteepleChase Records in late 1979, and the later sessions with Philip Catherine and Jean-Louis Rassinfosse; records that form a vitally important part of Chet's legacy. Lackerschmid remembers being impressed by Chet's playing at this time. "Moreover, he was the only one who interpreted my compositions exactly the way I had imagined them," he said. "He hit the right mood and, during recordings, was very concentrated and serious."[35]

On January 17th, Chet travelled to Stuttgart to take part in a recording session with a big band led by the German conductor Erwin Lehn. The highlight of the session was a version of Michel Legrand's 'Once Upon A Summertime', in which Chet plays a poignant solo, perhaps remembering the summertime of his youth in sunny California.

After the recording session, Chet and Ruth made their way to Italy, where they stayed at the house of Giampiero Giusti in Florence. Giusti had been the drummer with the Quintetto di Lucca, who had played with Chet back in 1959. In the intervening years he had become one of the wealthiest men in the region as a result of his paper factory, established in the late 1960s.

Chet had a handful of bookings over the next few weeks— including the Riverclub in Palazzo Corsini in Rome, the Arcadia, another club in the same street. The band on these gigs consisted of Michel Graillier on piano, Jean-Louis Rassinfosse on bass and Chet's old friend Jacques Pelzer on piano.

"Giampiero Giusti had a beautiful house with a cellar, where he used to hold concerts," recalled the photographer Francesco 'Cecco' Maino. "Chet played more regularly there than he did in the regular theatres in the city." Four of these informal jam sessions were filmed, although only one was dated (February 17th). "Chet was much happier to play there, as he did not have to keep strict hours or follow certain rules," he said.[36]

Most days Giusti went to work in the morning, returning around 8 p.m., at which point he would make a large bowl of spaghetti with tomato sauce, which was Chet's favourite dish. After dinner the music would begin. "He used a special adhesive for his dentures," Giusti remembered. "One night he had run out, and he had to use a local Italian adhesive which didn't work so well, and after two or three songs his teeth came out, and he could no longer play. Ruth sang one or two songs, and then Chet took over and sang scat. It was the first time I had heard him sing scat."[37]

The only thing that occasionally darkened the mood was Chet's temper, which flared up from time to time. "One night Chet was tired, and went to bed, and Ruth and I stayed in the cantina talking," said Giusti. "We spoke about many things; she told me about her family, her relationship with Chet, about many things. At about three o'clock in the morning Chet woke up, and suspected Ruth of sleeping with me. He started shouting at Ruth, and they got into a fight, hitting one another. I can tell you that I never saw Ruth like that, never, because if it is the wife or girlfriend of my friend, I would always respect that."[38]

The silent video footage would appear to support this anecdote; Chet can be seen playing trumpet in the cantina in a jam session. Ruth later joins the musicians, and is seen sitting at the back of the stage next to Giampiero, who has his arm around her, talking. Ruth then starts to sing with musicians, but Chet starts to sulk, and moves from the front of the stage, where he has been sitting, to the back of the stage, behind the piano. Ruth Young remembers the evening well. "I'm a very touchy, feely person, that's what I'm like," she laughed. "It doesn't mean anything, provided your head's in the right place. Chet was way too insecure."[39]

After several weeks in Italy, Chet and Ruth travelled to Paris, where they again met with the French record producer Gilles Gautherin. Gautherin was a friend of the French actor Jean-Paul Belmondo, who was working on a movie called *Flic ou Voyou* (Cop or Hood). He proposed that Chet appear on the soundtrack, which consisted of a number of miniatures composed for the movie by Philippe Sarde. Chet was joined by a number of the other CTI Records regulars, including bass player Ron Carter and flautist Hubert Laws.

"Elvin Jones was supposed to play drums on that record, but he wanted too much money; he wanted more money than they paid Chet," Ruth later recalled. "I ended up sitting on the floor of the booth that Ron Carter was playing in. He looked down at me and said, 'What's this, a little inspiration for me? That's cool!'"[40]

Chet was paid around $8,000 for the soundtrack recording. "Chet never opened a bank account—that would have broken all the rules," recalled Ruth, laughing. "Once he got the money, we had a party, and we were all higher than kites." What followed was a repeat of New Year's Eve, with Chet inviting Gilles Gautherin, Michel and Michelin Graillier to the California Hotel, where they were staying. On this occasion, Ruth joined in the fun, rather than stay on the sidelines. "What we did in Paris was incredible! We had a ball, an absolute ball. That's when I got to be Crazy Lily—my eyes were so relaxed that one eye was going this way, the other eye was going that way. I made the most of never getting hooked."[41]

Ruth Young and Micheline Graillier both have memories of Chet being generous in this respect, although there was still an element of his behaviour that was also inherently selfish, spending money on himself, but neglecting his children. "That's why Carol is so angry and bitter," suggests Ruth. "She missed out on Chet's generosity. He never behaved liked that in her company."

In the weeks that followed, Chet embarked on a European tour, once again put together by Gaby Kleinschmidt. Jean-Louis Rassinfosse stayed with the band on bass. Michel Graillier was replaced by Phil Markowitz who flew in from the United States, and rejoined the band on piano. Drummer Charlie Rice from Philadelphia, who had played with Chet on albums such as *Baby Breeze* in 1964, completed the line-up. "The concerts were very good," recalled Rassinfosse. "Charlie was a nice man, and the sort of drummer that Chet wanted to play with—not too loud, kept good time. He wanted something steady that would help him project his own thing."[42]

The tour primarily took in venues in Germany and Austria—Kleinschmidt's home territory. The quartet played one night at a club by the name of Ankel Pö, in Hamburg. The show was witnessed by a journalist, Rene Magron, who later wrote about the apparent source of the fragile, emotional trumpet sound that Chet produced. The audience was entranced by the "very skinny, sickly-looking man" on the stage. His music "went right in the centre of the audience's hearts," he wrote. "I see it on their faces, everyone is feeling it … It's a broken, lonely, but at the same time endlessly sweet and emotional sound … this is obviously a torn, abused man, someone who has gone through many hells."[43]

Once the organised tour was over, Markowitz and Rice decided to return to North America, rather than stay on with Chet in Europe. "Chet had other work arranged where he did not need us, especially in Italy," explained Phil Markowitz. "He had a long history there and liked playing with those cats, and of course he could make better bread playing with local cats."[44]

Jean-Louis Rassinfosse confirmed that Chet had expressed a desire to work with more local musicians. "Eventually we ended up making more music with people who were around here—including Horace Parlan, Michel Graillier, Joe Gallardo," he said. "This is what Chet was looking for. People who were available on a regular basis, not having to tour every day, as you would with musicians abroad."

Pianist Michel Graillier started to become a more regular fixture in Chet's band around this time. As Rassinfosse explained, there was something about his playing that appealed to Chet, and gave him a sense of space. "There was a lot of respect between Michel and Chet. Michel was a fantastic player that Chet really appreciated; he was a really tasty soloist, and very good at accompanying. There were occasional difficulties because Michel used to drink too much alcohol, which Chet was not into at all. Chet would not worry about what other people were doing, only the consequences on the bandstand. If someone was juiced, and couldn't play, it would be terrible for him. On some occasions they even fought on stage because of this."[45]

In June, Chet invited the young German vibraphonist, Wolfgang Lackerschmid, to join the band for a few dates. Lackerschmid later recalled that he felt "overwhelmed, happy and excited," to be asked by Chet, and readily agreed to play a few dates. Chet had no formal manager at this time, and the travel arrangements were often chaotic. "I remember travelling from the Kongsberg Festival in Norway straight to Felden in Austria by train and ferryboats," laughed Lackerschmid. "I was carrying my vibes all the way on my shoulders." Despite this, he had fond memories of the tour. "Sometimes in the train, he taught me new tunes by just singing them to me, and sneaked back a smile when we played them in the evening," he said. "He must have enjoyed that I was able to work totally ear-based, like he did."[46]

On 20th June, Chet travelled with Jean-Louis Rassinfosse to Copenhagen, where they teamed up with the pianist Horace Parlan, a long-term resident in Denmark, and local drummer Aage Tanggard, for a concert at the Jazzhus Montmartre. Chet was having troubled with his teeth that evening, and by all accounts was in a foul mood. The show was witnessed by Nils Winther, the owner of SteepleChase Records, who suggested making a studio recording next day. He proposed a trio recording with the legendary bass player, Niels-Henning Ørsted Pedersen, and the guitarist Doug Raney, who was the son of Jimmy Raney—who, like Chet, had played with Stan Getz in the early 1950s.

Nils Winther collected Chet from his hotel at 10 a.m. next day, and they met the other musicians at the studio. "The engineer of the studio hadn't showed up yet so we sat outside waiting for him to arrive," recalled Doug Raney. "Chet struck me as a rather quiet person, at any rate he didn't say much."[47]

"The recording session was very easy, and has a very special feel," said Nils Winther, who produced the record. "We stuck to the standards; Niels-Henning suggested some chord changes, and Chet didn't know what he was talking about, so they played it for Chet. He said, 'Fine, that sounds good'. We made a direct-to-two-track, and mixed it on the spot. The only problem we had was that Chet played very close to the microphone; the minute he finished his solo, he'd take the spit out of his horn. If we weren't very quick, you could hear the sound!"[48]

Chet apologised to the producer after the recording session, explaining that his chops were not in the best of shape. "He didn't sound bad," recalled Raney. "Just not as fluent as he was on other occasions."[49]

The recording, which was issued as *The Touch of Your Lips*, was in many ways a landmark recording for Chet in a number of respects. Firstly, it was one of the first 'drummerless' recordings he made, a format that he enjoyed, and used increasingly in his later years. It allowed him to develop long, uncluttered lines, a style that was particularly effective on the ballads that he tended to favour. It required a bass player who was a good timekeeper, like Niels-Henning Ørsted Pedersen, and it is unfortunate that they did not record together more frequently. Second, the album was released on a bigger label, which enjoyed wider distribution; in the sleeve notes, Ira Gitler mentions that Chet's records had not been widely distributed in the US since his CTI days. The SteepleChase records helped to raise Chet's profile once more, at least temporarily.

Chet's girlfriend Ruth Young also regards this record as being one of the pivotal moments in Chet's long career. "Chet's playing became more minimalist at this time," she said. "He'd always held the belief that less is more. And now it was evident that a new sound was emerging due in part to his kidney stone pain, but also because of his dissatisfaction with many of the drummers he'd been playing with. He wanted a more stripped-back sound, less instrumentation. He had turned a new page, and was on a course of his own. He had reached, in my opinion, the most sophisticated musical moment of his career. I thought it was brilliant playing—the mood, the tone, the spirit. Just brilliant."[50]

In the weeks that followed, Chet resumed his tour with Lackerschmid, Graillier and Rassinfosse, which continued through July. The following month, he was offered a two-week gig at the Club St Germain in Paris, and made a conscious decision to return to the trio format of the SteepleChase Recording. He kept Jean-Louis Rassinfosse on bass, and asked guitarist Doug Raney if he would like to join. "The first few days were pretty much like the record date as far as Chet was concerned," recalled Raney. "Then suddenly one night his chops were fine and he played like a whirlwind, fast long lines with that perfect timing he had. It scared me a bit. I remember thinking, 'This guy's a giant!'"[51]

The relationship between the musicians in the new-look trio was somewhat intense. "Chet was kind of up and down with his moods; he'd be in a good mood one day, a really shitty mood the next," said Raney. Rassinfosse also found the guitarist to be somewhat intense. "Doug was a bit like Chet, he was also an introvert, not saying very much," he recalled. "In a way, he was trying to find his own identity, away from his father. He was in a storm. But he was a fantastic musician."[52]

Doug Raney kept pushing Chet to rehearse during the daytime so they could polish certain tunes and improve the timing. "We kept agreeing to rehearse during the daytime but he would never show up," he said. "We'd have these long talks after the gig: 'Let's work on this, let's do that'. I remember going to the club almost every afternoon, but he never came." The guitarist wondered if Chet's drug habit was to blame, but his addiction was under control at this time; the truth is, he hated to rehearse, and preferred to work on new ideas on the stage.[53]

In early September, Chet travelled to London for another studio recording. The session was pulled together by Philippe Gaviglio, who had worked with a number of jazz artists in Europe, including Chet Baker, Barney Kessel and Clark Terry. He proposed pairing Chet with a young singer by the name of Rachel Gould, who had approached him after a show by the Clark Terry Big Band in Germany. "After the concert she gave me a cassette to listen to, probably hoping I could find work for her in the future," he said. "The music was not that good but I was impressed by the quality of her voice, which was crystal clear, warm, soft and capable of some bluesy accents."

Chet was not particularly enthusiastic about Gaviglio's proposal. He had never heard of Rachel Gould, and worried she would not be up to the task. "He said 'I'll do it if you want, but please make sure you choose the right songs to record, I don't want any mistakes on the repertoire'."[54]

Gaviglio made the decision to use Barney Kessel's rhythm section, which consisted of drummer Tony Mann and bass player Jim Richardson. The band was completed by the guitarist Jean-Paul Florens and his brother Henri on piano. Despite some initial tensions, Gaviglio remembers a relaxed recording session. "Everyone did a great job," he recalled. "The spirit was there, the magic was there, it was very intimate. It was a real jazz atmosphere."

The session resulted in two albums—*Rendez-Vous* and *All Blues*. In truth, there was probably enough good material to fill one LP, but it sounds a little thin when spread over two. Chet's playing is excellent, demonstrated to good effect on a lovely reinterpretation of 'My Funny Valentine'. There is some strong interplay between Chet and guitarist Jean-Paul Florens on ''Round Midnight' and the guitarist's own composition, 'Phil's Bossa'.

After the recording session, Chet returned to work with his trio. "I continued working with him for a few months, mostly one-nighters in France, Switzerland, Belgium, Holland and Italy," recalled guitarist Doug Raney. One particularly memorable show took place in Cosenza, Italy, on 30th September. "The gig in Italy was weird, like a scene from a Fellini film," said Raney. "There were all kinds of people hanging from the scaffolding above us. Also there was a guy sitting on a chair on the stage with a beer in his hand throughout the concert. When we were finished, he got up, bowed to the audience, and collapsed."[55]

On another occasion, a funny incident occurred in Italy. "We were at the airport, and there were problems with the bass," explained Raney. "We had a ticket for it, but they wouldn't let us take it on the plane. Finally they asked the captain, who has the final say in such matters. He approached us and suddenly burst out, 'Chet Baker! I have all of your records!' Needless to say, we were allowed to take the bass along. We were given champagne, Chet signed autographs, and we were invited into the cockpit. I thought they were going to let Chet fly the plane!"[56]

But travelling with Chet was not always a laughing matter. "Although I enjoyed playing with him, the tours were by no means picnics," said Raney. "There were always mix-ups, practical problems, etc. I ended up travelling by myself because I knew he had drugs. The trunk of his car was filled with all kinds of pills and stuff. After one incident at the Swiss border I insisted on crossing borders without him."[57]

The trio ended up back in Copenhagen in early October. After the success of their studio recording, *The Touch of Your Lips*, Nils Winther planned to reunite the trio for a live recording at the Jazzhus Montmartre. The day before the show was scheduled to take place, the producer asked Chet if he would be interested in recording an album of Duke Jordan's own compositions. "Duke and Chet knew each other from many years back," said Winther. "They met in the 1950s, and they had both worked with Richard Carpenter in the mid-1960s. He used to publish a lot of Duke Jordan's recordings; they went out under Duke's name, but he never got paid. Duke was living in Copenhagen, and I recorded him on many occasions. There were a number of similarities between the way that Duke and Chet played; they both had a very melancholy and pretty way of playing. I thought they would work well together."[58]

It turned out to be an inspired move; Duke Jordan's lyrical but melancholic style was well suited to Chet's own playing. Chet's chops were also in better shape than on the previous studio session with SteepleChase, and it's interesting to hear him play with a muted trumpet on some tracks. One highlight is the dark, brooding 'Kiss of Spain', which opens with the drums and the bowed bass of NHØP, before Chet enters on muted trumpet, echoing the sound of early Miles Davis. Other tracks recall some of the excellent recordings Chet made with Russ Freeman in the 1950s. 'Sultry Eve' is taken at a slow pace, suggesting a hushed intimacy, whilst there's a playful bounce to the waltz-time 'Glad I Met Pat' that brings to mind the style of Bill Evans.

At the request of Nils Winther, Niels-Henning Ørsted Pedersen stood in for Jean-Louis Rassinfosse on bass for the live recording next day. "Of course, there was no envy from my point of view," said Rassinfosse. "It was wonderful for me to meet Niels-Henning, who for me was a hero on the instrument. I was very happy to watch him play, to see how he was recorded."[59]

The producer was keen to reproduce the 'special sound' of the earlier studio recording. In all likelihood, he also had half an eye on record sales, since Ørsted Pedersen was something of a star at that time. Chet was on fine form that night, his chops in good shape after playing regularly for several weeks. Most of that period had been spent touring with Doug Raney, so there was probably a better understanding with the guitarist second time around. "They played three sets that night, and I think we eventually released everything they played," said Winther. "When great music happens, it happens."[60]

The material recorded that night was sufficient to fill three LPs—*Daybreak*, *This Is Always*, and *Someday My Prince Will Come*. The highlights are almost too numerous to mention, but include a gorgeous reading of Richie Beirach's 'Broken Wing', a lengthy version of 'How Deep Is The Ocean', and Bob Zieff's 'Sad Walk', which he originally recorded with pianist Dick Twardzik back in 1955. These landmark recordings helped to cement Chet's 'comeback'. He seemed to thrive in the 'drummerless' format, which allowed him to explore freely, producing a dazzling display of ideas with the minimum of backing. It was a format that Chet would return to frequently in the years that followed, most notably in the trio with Philip Catherine and Jean-Louis Rassinfosse, but also with Michel Graillier and Riccardo Del Fra. The records were also released on SteepleChase—a major jazz label with strong global distribution, which helped to raise Chet's profile after his years in the jazz wilderness.

After the recordings in Copenhagen, Chet went back on the road with Raney and Rassinfosse. At one gig in Spa, Belgium, Chet's friend Jacques Pelzer introduced him to a young American pianist by the name of Dennis Luxion. Luxion was a native of Springfield, Illinois, who had moved to Belgium that summer. "My wife had introduced me to all the local musicians—people like Jacques Pelzer, Steve Houben," Luxion recalled. "Chet asked me to sit in with them, and I played a set with them. After the show, he asked me if I'd like to start working with them."[61]

The band—now a quartet—played a few gigs in Germany before a mix-up occurred in the travel arrangements, and Chet sent Doug Raney to the wrong town. "The next day I was supposed to meet him in Aachen or Essen; the concert was at the other place," he recalled. "I got to the town for this non-existent concert, but finally gave up and went home. I tried to call him, but by the time I reached him, he thought I'd quit. He was paranoid! I tried to explain what happened, but he didn't call me so much after that."[62]

In the weeks that followed, the band played a number of gigs in Germany, occasionally joined by other musicians—including Jacques Pelzer, saxophonist Lou McConnell and vibraphonist Wolfgang Lackerschmid. "People had told me stories about Chet yelling at certain piano players on the bandstand, even people like Michel Graillier who he had played with for years," said Luxion. "But I never had a problem with Chet on the bandstand. There were times when he might have good reason to! But we got along very well."

In November, Chet made a second recording with Wolfgang Lackerschmid. The guitarist Larry Coryell had heard them perform as a duo, and came backstage after the show to propose they make a recording as a trio. Unfortunately, the German tour manager Gabriele Kleinschmidt became involved in the negotiations, and insisted they recruit a rhythm section. "I told her the duo is great, so we should not abandon this concept," said Lackerschmid. "'Ballads For Three' is all we need. When she still insisted on a rhythm section, I made a joke, saying, 'If that's the case, they both have to be named Williams'. Kleinschmidt evidently missed the joke, and without his knowledge, recruited Miles Davis's old drummer Tony Williams, and bass player Buster Williams. "Of course it was a thrill for me meeting them and to play with them," laughed Lackerschmid. "But I never thought seriously putting them in a line-up like this!"

Unfortunately, the arrangements for the recording session were just as confused as the negotiations over the line-up. "In the end, we only had a couple of hours together," explained Lackerschmid. "Everybody came in on a different flight and the schedules didn't really match." As a consequence, the arrangements sound cluttered and under-rehearsed for the most part, and one can't help but feel that a more stripped-back sound—as originally conceived—would have produced a better record.[63]

In mid-November, Chet made his way to Italy for a short tour with a local band. The tour had been arranged by a local promoter by the name of Paolo Piangiarelli, who went on to form a jazz record label by the name of Philology. Rassinfosse and Luxion were not required for these dates; Rassinfosse decided to stay in Belgium, but Luxion went along for the trip. "I went with him, and kind of hung out," he explained. "We were roommates for a week or two, and had a lot of fun."

Piangiarelli recruited a jazz trio led by the twenty-nine-year-old Italian pianist Enrico Pieranunzi to accompany Chet. Pieranunzi was already a veteran of the Italian jazz scene, having recorded his first album back in 1975. The bass player was twenty-three-year-old Riccardo Del Fra, who had previously played with Art Farmer, whilst Roberto Gatto played drums. The first gig took place at Macerata, a small town three hours north east of Rome. "Chet looked in good shape," recalled the pianist. "He may have been a little tired after a long car trip he had made to reach Macerata. However, he sounded great and the concert went very well."[64]

The gigs that followed had a profound impact on the Italian musicians, who are now some of the most widely-respected musicians in the European jazz scene. "I'll never forget the feeling when we first played together," said Riccardo Del Fra. "Time felt relaxed, even when we played fast; the relationship between time and sound changed; he had the power to send us to another place. It was not just a matter of playing with a charismatic musician; I had played with other famous musicians, even though I was just twenty-three. There was a strong feeling that something different was going on."[65]

Pianist Enrico Pieranunzi plucked up the courage to suggest that they record an album together once the tour had been completed. "Maybe I was a bit shameless in doing that—after all I was only a good young Italian pianist, whereas he was a living jazz legend. But the music during the concert had been so nice, the musical feeling between me and Chet so deep, that all this gave me the heart to ask him. He told me 'OK', and this of course made me happy. I immediately began to compose some new tunes with the sound of his trumpet in mind."[66]

The resulting album, *Soft Journey*, primarily consisted of original compositions by the Italian pianist. "Since the material to record was all new, Chet and I agreed to rehearse it for a while in order to put himself and all the group at ease with the tunes," the pianist explained. "Of course I had prepared all the charts in the proper way, lines and changes, all written down—but Chet told me he was not interested in learning the tunes through the changes. He said, 'Play the melody many times, I'll learn the tune this way'. That was a bit surprising to me, but it somehow revealed a 'secret' side of the magic in his playing—something I would keep forever in my mind—and that is trying to relate to the melody of a tune, because that is the place where the tune's story is."

The album was recorded over two sessions, one month apart—the delay caused by Chet suffering from a bout of flu. Pieranunzi was delighted with the outcome, and the album certainly has its moments. Chet was particularly taken by the pianist's composition 'Night Bird', which became a regular part of Chet's repertoire in the years that followed.

While he was recovering from flu, a letter arrived from Carol Baker. She was struggling to support the family on her own, she claimed, and had taken a job as a secretary in a Manhattan real estate firm. The children were also suffering as a result of their father's neglect, she claimed. Paul had no bed, and slept in a sleeping bag, whilst Melissa's teeth were full of cavities. To make matters worse, eight drunken youths had tried to break into her apartment. Carol still seemed to be clinging to the hope that Chet would eventually return—ignoring the fact that he had been with Ruth for seven years now, and had recently moved his belongings into her New York apartment. Chet had little interest in helping his children, but Ruth felt bad about their plight, and telephoned her mother, arranging with her help the transfer of $500 from her own trust fund to be sent to Carol and the children.[67]

Looking back over the preceding two years, Chet had many reasons to be proud of his achievements. *You Can't Go Home Again* had been a modest success, raising his profile in North America, and bringing his music to the attention of a younger generation of jazz fans. The European tour that followed had been a resounding success, resulting in a number of fine recordings—most notably *Live At Nick's* and *Broken Wing*. The tour further boosted his presence in Europe, resulting in a steady stream of work, and lucrative offers from a high profile label, SteepleChase Records.

His personal life was also more settled. He had stayed relatively clean for most of this period, sticking to the methadone programme. He had occasionally lapsed, treating himself to the odd snort of heroin, but he had not been tempted back to the needle and the addiction that would imply. His relationship with Ruth was also on a steadier footing, particularly now that Carol was effectively out of the picture. With money in his pocket as a result of his recent recording sessions, he briefly considered the idea of buying an apartment in Rome, and living a more settled life.

But there was something in Chet's psyche that always led him away from stability, to push the boundaries; in his younger days it was the sheer cliffs of southern California, at other times it was the thrill of accelerating in his sports car, or the buzz he got from swerving to avoid danger at the last second. "Chet would talk about buying a house, but he wasn't really interested in that," said Dennis Luxion. "He wanted to live on the edge, play on the edge.

That could be good, because when he was playing, he was really playing. You could see it in his driving too; he was a really intense driver. He was a very focused person in some respects, but with no long-term organisation in his life."[68]

It was that same desire to live on the edge that caused him to accept the invitation to the apartment of Giuseppe, a well-known drug addict and dealer who was a regular at the Music Inn in Rome. "I remember Chet picking up the syringe that Giuseppe had prepared, holding it up to his face, and saying 'Gee, I haven't done one of these in a long time'," said Ruth. She started to get hysterical, screaming, and begging Chet not to do it. But it was to no avail.

"After that, he tried to get away with murder," Ruth explained. "He screwed around with the methadone program like a real pro, and was back to his old junkie tricks. He'd get off his methadone for a while, so that when he took his next hit of heroin, he'd be sure to feel it. So it was goodbye methadone and hello heroin one more time." In the end, his relationship with heroin proved to be stronger than his relationship with Ruth.

He was still an addict.

Chapter Sixteen

BROKEN WING
1980–1982

"Soloing is like telling a story to a child; you can't start with a difficult line. You begin by saying, 'Once upon a time, there was a castle, and there was a king that lived in the castle'... "—Chet Baker[1]

After the incident in Giuseppe's apartment, things started to unravel. First of all, Chet became convinced that he could continue to function on heroin, just as well as he could methadone. "Chet oversimplified it all, of course, and felt 'what's the fuss about? I can handle it'," explained Ruth. "And ultimately, that's the attitude I adopted. If this person could create something incredibly unique, and go through all the crap required to do it, then yes, he should be left alone. Granted it was a ridiculous conclusion, but I was losing my grip."[2]

Word of Chet's renewed addiction spread fast. Giuseppe became a daily visitor to Chet's hotel in Rome, the Anglo-American, and became his regular supplier when he was in town. Drug dealers were now waiting in almost every city, eager to lure him at every opportunity. Chet also started to attract a new crowd of hangers-on. They included two former Warhol acolytes, Tom Baker and Joe Dallesandro, who were desperate to extend their fifteen minutes of fame, and Luiz Gasco, who offered to work as Chet's manager in late 1982.

Chet's drug problem also started to affect his music. The quality of his live performances became more erratic. The problem was exacerbated by the fact that Chet did not like to take drugs alone; he started to invite other junkies to join the band—musicians like Leo Mitchell and Sal Nistico—which had the inevitable consequences.

It also had a negative impact on Chet's recordings. On methadone, Chet's drug intake was more regulated. Going forward, he would occasionally do anything for a fix—and that included signing agreements to allow sub-standard live recordings, often without the knowledge of the musicians in his band. As a result, his output was diluted by poor recordings for small, independent labels such as Circle Records and Philology that dented the reputation he had done so much to rebuild.

The fact that Chet was looking for ways to get off methadone, and back on to heroin, also started to eat away at his relationship with Ruth Young. Her initial reaction was to beg him to stop. "You might as well marry Giuseppe," she shouted. "You're not in love with Carol, me, or anybody, you're in love with Giuseppe!"[3]

When that failed, she started to drink more heavily, and even started chipping—or using occasionally—herself. "I was a mess," she admitted. "But I was functional enough to protect his interests at all times, and at all costs."[4]

One musician that met Chet in Rome at this time was a bearded twenty-three-year-old Italian by the name of Nicola Stilo, who could play both the guitar and flute. "I went down to the Music Inn in Rome with some other musicians," he later recalled. "At this time, it was the only serious jazz club we had in the city, and was run by a drummer called Pepito Pignatelli. Chet was playing with some old friends, some very good Italian musicians. At first we just talked, and I tried to get to know him as a friend, and after a few weeks, I started to play with him."[5]

By that stage, Chet had moved out of the city to a town called Palombara. "The first time I played with him was in a beautiful house in the countryside outside of Rome, where he was staying as a guest with some wealthy friends," said Stilo. "Chet had invited me and a few friends, and we stayed there for two days. We brought a piano, double bass, everything! The first time was beautiful."

Stilo had grown up listening to Miles Davis, but when he heard Chet play, he fell in love with his style of playing. "As a musician, I thought Chet was very natural. Even standing behind him, watching him play, you could sense the elegance that he brought to the music. It was like learning a special musical language, a personal language. Each night he put something new in his playing. Even when he was playing with younger musicians, he was always listening carefully to their phrasing. Playing with him was the best musical education. He was very modest, and extremely generous."[6]

But there were others who tried to take advantage of Chet's generosity. Tom Baker was a former protégé of Andy Warhol. His dark hair and good looks won him the lead role in the 1967 movie *I, A Man*, in which he sees six different women in one day in New York—having sex with some, talking with some, fighting with some. He later moved to Los Angeles, where he became a close friend of Jim Morrison of The Doors. When his movie career failed to take off, he turned to drugs and alcohol, and by the time he turned up in Rome in 1980, his looks had faded, and his body had become bloated.

"Tom Baker found out that we were staying in Palombara and invited himself over," said Ruth. "He had been a nice looking guy, but by this stage was reduced to hustling, kind of a male whore. He wanted to get closer to Chet, and pitched the idea of the book project. In return for a sum of money he was given rights to a book deal. I was witness to the contract, using my legal name of Youngstein."[7]

In fact, Chet had started to write his memoirs in late 1978. His then manager, James Felds, convinced Chet he could sell the story to a publisher, or even to Hollywood. "Chet thought he was gonna see some money," explained Ruth. As a result he began to write his life story, scribbling his memories in a notebook in hotel rooms, on train journeys, and at airports. When Felds was fired, he disappeared with at least one of the notebooks.

Chet is known to have kept hold of at least one notebook, however. In January 1979, he showed the manuscript to his old friend Giampiero Giusti, and asked his opinion. "After I read what he had written, I said, 'Chet, you are crazy! You will get yourself killed'," said Giusti. "In the book he mentioned the names of his New York drug dealers, and their bosses. 'My publisher asked for some shocking information, otherwise the book won't sell—and I need the money to keep me in drugs'." To date, this notebook has not been found, and the material has not been published.[8]

Tom Baker had no intention of writing Chet's biography, but wanted to write a screenplay, using his theatrical experience from the early 1970s. Back in New York, he was able to track down James Felds, and obtain a copy of the partial autobiography. He also got in touch with Carol Baker, who decided that she also wanted to be involved in the project. "Carol thought he was wonderful," said Ruth. "She wrote to Chet, and said there's no reason I can't do what Ruth is doing. I told Chet, 'You tell her from me that she didn't have to wait ten years to utter that comment. Now she gives a damn if you work or not! How convenient.'"

After a few months, Tom Baker's initial enthusiasm for the project began to fade, one of many unfinished scripts and documentaries he left behind.

Baker died of an overdose just eighteen months later, aged just forty-two, his body found in a well-known junk den on the Lower East Side in New York City.

While they were staying in Italy, Chet complained to Ruth that his children had stopped writing to him. Ruth encouraged him to reach out to them, and in mid-January he wrote a letter to his son Dean. He started by apologising for missing his seventeenth birthday (Christmas Day 1979), and went on to offer him advice about growing up. Chet suggested he consider joining the Air Force, or get into computers. He also noted that he wouldn't be around to help, because he didn't expect to live much longer.[9]

Chet also started writing to Paul. Given the way he used to treat his son, he evidently found the letter difficult to compose. He began by explaining that whilst Carol had accused him of being a worthless junkie, he found work hard to come by, and it was difficult to send money home. He must have been aware how hollow this sounded, and apologised for not explaining to his children why he had had to leave the United States and go to live in Europe. In a rare moment of self-admission, he confessed that he found it difficult to have an honest conversation with his own children. In the end, however, the letter was never posted, further depriving Paul of the father figure he so desperately needed.

Chet completed the recording of *Soft Journey* with Enrico Pieranunzi on January 4th 1980. After the session, Chet asked all of the musicians—except Pieranunzi—to go on tour with him to Germany in February and March. He told the Italian pianist that he had already hired Dennis Luxion on piano. "I think Chet also thought Enrico was playing too much, playing too many notes," explained the band's bass player, Riccardo Del Fra. "Enrico felt a little hurt, but probably because of this, he started to change. He started to listen to Bill Evans, and experiment with space and silence." There are countless examples of Chet's influence on Pieranunzi's later recordings, but an obvious place to start is the exquisite 'When All Was Chet', from the CD *Ballads*.[10]

Around this time, Chet made two more recordings—one official, one unofficial. The first took place in Belgium, while Chet was staying for a few days with Jacques Pelzer. Jacques's younger cousin, Steve Houben, had returned to live in Belgium. "At the time I was back from the US with a few young cats who were at Berklee with me, and we put a band together," the saxophonist explained. "The band had Kermit Driscoll on bass, Bill

Frisell on guitar and Dennis Luxion on piano. Bill was not that well known at the time, but right after that he went to ECM."[11]

Houben managed to persuade a local businessman, Phillipe Defalle, to finance the recording, and the album was eventually released as *Chet Baker—Steve Houben*. "Chet played beautifully, and Bill on one or two tunes played some gorgeous music," Houben recalled. "Chet liked the record very much. Chet was not talking very much. We got on really well, but we weren't that close—I wasn't into his stuff." The highlights of the record are a good version of 'Beatrice' by Sam Rivers, and a lovely vocal by Chet on 'Deep in a Dream', where the saxophonist plays gently beneath Chet's singing.

The second recording took place during a brief return visit to the United States, just before his lengthy European tour. Chet played a gig at the Backstreet Club in New Haven, Connecticut. The band included his old friend, the drummer Artt Frank, who had stayed in touch with Chet during his long spells in Europe. He had written to Chet on numerous occasions, reminding him that he had visited him in the LA County Jail in 1969, and got him a record contract to record *Blood, Chet and Tears*, when nobody was interested in signing him. Chet could be a loyal friend, and was happy to return the favour. The band that evening included pianist Drew Salperto and bass player Mike Formanek. A bootleg recording, presumably made by Artt Frank himself, was later issued as *Burnin' At Backstreet*.[12]

The recording reveals both the positive and negative aspects of Chet's playing at this time. On the one hand, his playing is strong, and uncharacteristically fiery for this time. Gone is the soft, airy tone heard on the SteepleChase recordings, replaced by a blazing intensity. On the other hand, he was playing with musicians who were not familiar with his repertoire, and had not bothered to rehearse. This resulted in an explosive argument with the pianist during 'Milestones', and a tense atmosphere for the remainder of the show. "After the session at Backstreet," said Artt Frank, "Chet and I were driving to the hotel and I commented on how hard I thought he'd been on Drew and Mike on the stand. I said, half jokingly, 'Man, you're a bastard to work for, Chet'. He turned, looked at me for a minute, then smiled and said softly, 'Why? All I want is perfection.'"[13]

Back in Europe, the tour kicked off with a two-week gig at Le Dreher in Paris. "There really weren't too many drug issues with Chet at this time, when things were really out of control," recalled the band's pianist, Dennis Luxion. "But there were two places where he felt comfortable knowing people, where things could get a little chaotic. One was Rome; we might be in Italy playing a gig, driving back in Chet's Citroen, and before we went back to the hotel he'd stop at his connection's place. The whole band would be waiting in the car; that wasn't a whole lot of fun. Paris was the other place, and Le Dreher was the same scene. I don't remember seeing Chet in Paris that time, except for the gig."[14]

Most nights in Paris, Chet arrived to the gig late, and in poor shape. "We were starting around 11 p.m., and going on to around 3 a.m.," confirmed Luxion. One night was captured by the French movie producer Léon Terjanian, who later released a film of the concert, *An Evening With Chet Baker*. Chet's playing is flat and uninspired for the most part—in sharp contrast to his playing in the United States just two weeks earlier. The highlight of the film is a backstage interview, conducted by Chet's old girlfriend from the early 1950s, Liliane Cukier. By this stage she was an established actress in France, married to the French bass player Gilbert 'Bibi' Rovère. Halfway through their conversation, Liliane spots a syringe sticking out of Chet's shirt pocket. "What is that you've got in your pocket there?" she asked. "That is a syringe I use to, err … oil my trumpet," he laughs. "That's the only use I have for a syringe these days." It's a sad image of the way in which Chet's life was starting to slide now that he was starting to switch from methadone back to heroin.

Tenor saxophonist Maurizio Giammarco left the band after the gig at Le Dreher, and was effectively replaced by the young Italian flautist, Nicola Stilo. "After a month or two I received a phone call from Ruth who said, 'Chet Baker wants you in his band', and that was the beginning of the 'endless tour'. Apart from the year I spent in Brazil, I played with Chet for four, six, even eight months a year. We started with a little tour in Sicily, but after that we played in Germany, in France."[15]

The band's bass player, Riccardo Del Fra, remembers many good nights on this tour, with Chet in relatively good shape, relishing the drummerless format and delivering lengthy, bop-style solos. Unfortunately, the recordings from this era suggest that Chet's playing was starting to become more erratic. The band was recorded live at the Subway Club in Cologne, Germany, and three LPs were later released by Circle Records—*In Your Own Sweet Way*, *Just Friends* and *Down*. The contrast with the three live recordings recorded by SteepleChase five months earlier could not be more pronounced. The concert opens with a twenty-six-minute version of Russ Freeman's 'No Ties', with Baker's opening solo lasting for fourteen minutes; Chet seems to lose his thread part of the way through the solo, and can be heard cursing.

Releases like this helped to spoil the reputation of Chet's later recordings. The concerts were badly recorded compared with the excellent SteepleChase recordings, and the sound quality is poor. *DownBeat* later described the records as "shambling efforts in which Baker, alternately, beguiles one with snatches of excellence, then stultifies with long stretches of aimlessness". It's also worth noting that many of the recordings were made without the permission of the other musicians, who were not paid royalties. Instead, Chet took the cash from the record company and used it to buy drugs.[16]

The same band is heard to much better effect in early April, in a studio recording made in Munich for Intercord Records. *Leaving* features four original compositions by the band's pianist, Dennis Luxion. The most memorable of these is the haunting 'Blues for C.R.'; others, like 'You've Flipped Out', sound somewhat under-rehearsed. The record also features Chet's first studio recording of the title track, written by Richie Beirach, which would be a staple of his repertoire going forward. "It became one of his favourite songs, and we played it for the next ten years," noted the flute player Nicola Stilo.[17]

Chet is honoured at the Arkadia Club in Florence, April 7th 1980. Photograph by Francesco 'Cecco' Maino.

A few days later, Chet travelled to Italy, where he had been invited to attend an award ceremony at the Arkadia Jazz Club in Florence. On April 7th, the local Social Democratic Party presented him with a plaque, engraved with the following: 'Thirty years of body and soul for jazz: to the greatest white trumpeter, Chet Baker, from his Florentine friends'. He was also given two silver cups, one of them ironically "for his help in the fight against drugs". Chet seemed somewhat puzzled by the award, and was photographed by the Italian photographer, Francesco 'Cecco' Maino, holding the cups aloft with a bemused smile on his face.

The tour complete, Chet and Ruth returned to United States in late April. 'Cecco' Maino flew to New York at this time, and visited Chet—who he had known, on-and-off, for almost twenty-five years. "'Cecco', he said. 'Look at the way people treat me here in New York'. We went up the stairs to Artist's House records, and immediately, people in the office started to complain. 'Why do they treat you like that?' I asked him. 'You are a genius'. 'Oh, they don't understand', Chet told me." The Italian later discovered the truth—every time he returned to New York, Chet visited the record company and asked for money, using a different excuse on every occasion. He had even told Carol Baker to telephone the record company and ask for money, on occasion. It's worth remembering that whilst the owner of Artists House, John Snyder, was a loyal friend, Chet had made just one recording for the label—*Once Upon A Summertime*. It was perhaps no wonder that Chet was treated that way by the staff, nor that the record label was struggling to stay afloat.[18]

Later that day, Chet told Maino that he had a photograph on the wall of Ruth's apartment of him playing with Charlie Parker—neglecting to mention that it belonged to Ruth Young. "'I can give it to you', he told me. I did not trust him to send it to me, so I walked all the way back to Central Park (36, West 71st Street). Ruth answered the door, initially thinking I must be a drug dealer; I did not know her personally at that time. The entrance led straight to the dining room, where there was a fireplace, and over the fireplace was the photo he had told me about. I took the photograph, and walked all the way back downtown, through Manhattan, to meet up with Chet. By that stage I realised that the only way to talk to Chet, to be seen as a 'friend' was to give him money. I went to the bank, took out $250, made him sign a receipt, and gave him the cash. Rather than stay with me, he promptly disappeared. I didn't think it was the right way to behave, and after that, we were no longer friends."[19]

'Cecco' elaborated as to the reasons his friendship with Chet had eventually reached breaking point. "The stolen photo was only the conclusion of twenty years of continuous lying and cheating on his part—too many of my friends got in bad trouble just for trying to help him. So finally I decided that I could sit and listen to his music without trying to be his friend. Chet's horrible behaviour never changed my highest opinion of his artistry and his music."

While Chet was in New York, he made one studio recording with his former CTI label mate, bass player Ron Carter. It's not clear how Chet came to be involved in the recording—Carter was always a fan of Chet's playing, and may well have been invited to the recording session by Don Sebesky, who would have known how to reach Chet. The resulting album, *Patrão*, is a slightly lukewarm Latin-tinged set, but Chet does not disappoint, playing well throughout, including a beautiful muted solo on 'Nearly'.

When Chet left for New York, he gave no precise date to his band—pianist Dennis Luxion, flautist Nicola Stilo and bass player Riccardo Del Fra—as to when he would return. "This was before e-mail, so when he was in New York I tried to write him a letter to ask him what was going on, so I could make some plans," explained Luxion. Chet eventually returned to Europe in June, he called Luxion and the other musicians, and informed them that Gaby Kleinschmidt had arranged another lengthy European tour. Dennis Luxion politely declined the offer, and opted to spend more time with his wife.

"There were a couple of issues," the pianist explained. "When I was working with him before, it wasn't like there was a defined tour; we went out for some gigs, and he'd add on gigs all the time. So my wife wasn't really happy about that. There were also the gigs at the Subway—there wasn't an issue at the time, but when the records came out, I never got any money for those. But the main thing was the record in Munich (*Leaving*), for which Chet said we would get paid a certain amount, but we never saw. So when he came back, he gave me no notice and still owed me some money. So when he asked me to go on the road next morning, I said, 'You know, I don't think so'. With Chet away in New York I'd taken a bunch of gigs, and touring would have meant cancelling some pre-arranged gigs. I didn't think Chet was a very organised bandleader. The band could have been better with a musical bandleader, and more rehearsals—it was a little too loose for me.

I did like working with Chet, but leaving then would have meant the end of the relationship with my wife. She was like, 'You leave now, and you don't come back!'"[20]

The Austrian guitarist, Karl Ratzer, effectively replaced Dennis Luxion in the band. The tour opened with another two-week gig at Le Dreher in Paris. Despite Chet's erratic performance there in February, he was still a popular draw at the small, basement club. Some of the less experienced band members seemed to have trouble keeping time in the 'drummerless' format, and Chet suggested they hire a drummer for the remainder of the gig. "At this point, I mentioned that Al Levitt (an American drummer, living in Paris) was in town," recalled bass player Riccardo Del Fra. "This little phrase changed my life, although I didn't know it at the time. When I mentioned Al Levitt, Chet said, 'Al Levitt. When we played together before, everything was so nice'. When I was living in Rome earlier that year, I was playing twice a year, and here we were playing a fifteen-day gig at Le Dreher in Paris. All of a sudden I was living in a Jack Kerouac book with Chet!"[21]

Two nights of the engagement were again recorded by Germany's Circle Records. As with their previous recording in Cologne three months earlier, the quality of the recording is atrocious. Chet's vocal on 'There Will Never Be Another You' is barely audible, and at times the audience is more closely recorded than the musicians.

That said, Chet's voice was in far better shape than on his previous visit, and some of his playing is first-rate. Chet's solo on Russ Freeman's 'No Ties' (from the *Tune Up* LP) is one of his longest on record, and never seems to run out of ideas, and 'Leaving' (also from *Tune Up*) is also superb. "If you listen to these records," said Del Fra, "he plays like a bopper. It's very different to what we did later—records like *Chet Baker Sings Again* or *Chet's Romance*. In those years—I'm sorry to say it—he sounded more romantic, melancholic. He had found another way to play that was more personal, but less implacable. A rhythm like bop is implacable. With a song you can always adjust, and fly around. He moved to a style that allowed more freedom of expression—a more poetic world."[22]

Riccardo Del Fra makes a very good point. Whilst Chet came to fame as part of the West Coast 'cool' jazz, he was at heart a bebop jazz musician—something that Charlie Parker had identified very quickly. Whilst the tone of his playing may have softened by 1980, his bop influence had not—

as records like the SteepleChase live recordings make abundantly clear.

Whilst Chet's roots remained firmly embedded in bebop, which had first emerged in the mid-1940s, his soloing continued to evolve. "He never forgot to develop his own style," noted Del Fra. "The way he played the trumpet in his last six or seven years is special and original, and completely different to the way he played when he was young." Another bass player, Jean-Louis Rassinfosse, noted the same trend. "The evolution was in Chet's soloing, the way he brought emotion out in the music," he explained. "I like the fact that he played the same tunes throughout his career; you can compare the way he was playing in the 1950s, the 1970s and the 1980s. This is interesting for me as an improviser, to see how he developed the idiom of improvising and creating new melodies around fixed material."[23]

Riccardo Del Fra thinks the evolution in Chet's soloing around this time stemmed from the freedom of playing without a drummer for much of the time. "Chet was convinced that playing this way was enjoyable, not just because of his teeth, but because of the control it gave him over the sound," he explained.

The albums recorded at Le Dreher infuriated the drummer Al Levitt. He noted the recording equipment in the club one night, and was assured by Chet that Circle Records only intended to make a test recording. A few months later, Levitt found *Night Bird* in a record store, and wrote an angry letter to both Chet and Rudolf Kreis, the owner of Circle Records, demanding an explanation. Kreis responded with a copy of a contract signed by Chet on June 25th, the date of the recording, in which he promised he would pay the musicians himself. Disputes over money seemed to be more commonplace now that Chet was starting to use heroin again, rather than sticking rigidly with the methadone programme.

One regular visit to Le Dreher that summer was a Brazilian pianist and composer by the name of Rique Pantoja. "I was twenty-four years old and had just left Berklee," he recalled. "I had learned a lot of things, but still didn't have the chops. A friend of mine recommended going to France, and we put together a band, Novos Tempos, which ended up playing seven nights a week at a small basement club, Le Petit Opportun."[24]

A French record producer, Yves Chamberland, was a regular visitor to the club, and offered to produce the band's first record. He suggested they need a guest star to help sell the record, someone who could join the band for one or two songs. "A couple of months later, Chet was playing in town, just two blocks from where we were playing. We used to play three or four sets a night, but I went along to the club on our break. When Chet had a break, I approached him and said, 'I am a pianist and writer from Brazil. I've written a bunch of songs, and I play in a band, Novos Tempos. We also have a bunch of friends in common'. 'Who?' Chet asked. 'Well I know Claudio Roditi, from New York City'. 'Yes, I know Claudio!' 'And I know Bob Mover, who's a phenomenal alto player'. Bob was from Boston, and used to visit the city every other weekend to visit his father. Chet was very friendly, and we talked for a while. I asked him if he'd consider playing a couple of songs on our record. He said, "OK, well I'm going to be here for the whole week. I'll stop by and see the band. Then I'll let you know."[25]

Chet kept his promise, and a couple of days later, made his way down the spiral staircase of the club, trumpet in hand. "I hadn't seen him come in, and we were playing one of my songs," said Pantoja. "All of a sudden he started blowing from the staircase, a sign that he dug what was happening. He sat in with the band—we played Brazilian jazz, some up-tempo sambas. At the end of the evening, he said, 'It sounds good'. I asked him if he'd be able to record a couple of songs with us, and he said, 'I'll let you know. Right now I have to play another gig in another city in France. If everything works out, I'll have someone get in touch with you'."[26]

A few weeks later, Ruth called to arrange a rehearsal, and Pantoja called Yves Chamberland to book some time at his studio, Studios Davout. The recording sessions, which took place over three days in late July, went very smoothly. "Chet was so lyrical," said Pantoja. "The interplay between us was amazing—he would catch one idea, and develop that idea. During the solo on the song '*Salsamba*' there's a phrase that lasts for nine bars where Chet does not even take one breath. I remember thinking, 'Man, when's he going to breathe?' He had such control, it was flawless."

The band's accordion player, Richard Galliano, remembers the whole band learned so much from Chet about the use of space in music. "From then on, everything was changed," he noted. "Tempos, nuances, purposes, breathings … a magical feeling flooded over us. Chet is a tightrope walker playing with space and emptiness."[27]

Chet Baker with Novos Tempos,
featuring Rique Pantoja (centre), July 1980.

The record was later released as *Salsamba by Chet Baker Meets Novos Tempos*. Chet's then girlfriend, Ruth Young, regards the album very highly, and wished that Chet had recorded more bossa nova. "That record was fantastic," she said. "My own music was rooted in the bossa nova, with people like Antonio Carlos Jobim, and the original more contemporary recordings of Herb Alpert's Brazil '66 being major infleuences for me. I adored Brazilian music when I first started singing. I wish Chet had recorded more boss nova, but I don't think it ever really caught his fancy. Chet could have completely cleaned up in Brazil had he have chosen to develop his playing along these lines, and developed a major career in markets like Japan and South Korea."[28]

Earlier that year, Chet had written a letter to his daughter Missy, suggesting she visit him in Italy for her fourteenth birthday. His Italian agent, Rita Amaducci, had booked a six-week tour in late August and September, and Chet promised to send her airline tickets.

Carol Baker was furious at this suggestion, and in mid-June wrote a scathing letter to Chet in which she suggested the vacation must have been Ruth Young's idea, and referring to her as "an interfering bitch". In the weeks that followed, Missy claimed that her mother taunted her constantly, claiming that Chet would never follow through with his promise.[29]

But Chet did deliver on this occasion, and the airline tickets duly arrived in mid-July, in time for her birthday—one of the few occasions on which Chet seems to have remembered. Carol had to relent, but wrote back to Chet and demanded that Missy not be allowed to spend much time with Ruth. Indeed, the letter reveals the depth of the bitterness about the break-up of her marriage, which had effectively ended seven years earlier.

"She (Missy) is quite aware that Ruth worked very hard to destroy her family life and I know this is at the root of all her problems. For instance I don't like the idea of her seeing you hop in and out of bed with that sick bitch. She doesn't see this kind of thing at home and I don't see why she should have to see it while visiting with you. Quite frankly, Ruth is not a healthy person for an adult to be around, let alone a young girl, particularly my daughter. She may be able to pull the wool over your eyes but she doesn't succeed with other people."[30]

In the days before her departure, Carol did everything in her powers to poison her daughter's mind about the influence of Ruth Young, and make the forthcoming vacation as difficult as possible. Ruth later discovered that Carol referred to her as a "whore" who took her clothes off in front of musicians. She also claimed that she was a drug addict, burning through every penny that her father had earned, depriving Missy of the new clothes she really wanted.[31]

As the tour approached, Chet called Rique Pantoja from Italy, and asked him to join. "I have a band here, but it would be good to do something with a Brazilian flavour," Chet explained. "Can you come with the drummer and the bass player? I'll ask Nicola Stilo to join us." In the end, the bass player, Michel Peyratoux, was unable to make the tour, and Chet recruited the Italian bass player Enzo Pietropaoli, who had first met Chet in Italy in late 1979.

The tour kicked off in Rome. From a musical perspective, it was an exciting time for the piano player. "As a young musician and composer, to be playing with someone of Chet's calibre—and have him say that he wanted to play one of my songs, 'Arbour Way'—for me it was a great encouragement," said Pantoja. "It made me think I was doing something right with my writing, because someone like Chet wanted to record and play my songs. It was a dream come true."[32]

Pantoja also learned a great deal about the technique of building a solo on that tour. "As a young player, I realised I wasn't on the same level as Chet; I wasn't insecure; I knew I was there because he loved my style, the rhythm, the percussive style of my playing, but I knew I had to get my act together. I remember asking Chet about improvisation, and asked what approach he took when he started a solo. 'Do you think of patterns, do you think of notes that work, or do you just run with the melody that you have in your ear?' Because part of our brain works like that; we use our intuition, but we also use our knowledge. What he said impacted me forever. 'Soloing is like telling a story to a child; you can't start with a difficult line. You begin by saying, 'Once upon a time, there was a castle, and there was a king that lived in the castle'. He then started scatting a simple line to demonstrate, then took a breath. As a pianist, we don't have to worry about taking a breath, so it's easy to play fast lines without breathing. I said, 'Man, that's incredible'. Because improvisation is instantaneous composition; you're composing on the spot over the chord changes. So his approach was a very lyrical, melodic one. Now I tell my students that they have to build a solo, you've got to tell that story over the same harmony."[33]

From a personal perspective, the relationship between Missy, her father, and Ruth Young, was initially quite harmonious. To make matters easier, Chet rented a house by the beach for a few days. Missy enjoyed swimming most days, and Chet promised to send her money so she could get her teeth fixed when she returned to New York. In a letter to her friend Ronda, Missy wrote that she was having a great time, and wished she could stay in Italy forever.

The bass player Enzo Pietropaoli also noted that Ruth Young exerted a somewhat calming influence on Chet at this time. "Chet was very strong and healthy most of the time on that tour, and it was difficult to tell when he'd taken drugs. I think Ruth had a lot to do with it; he never stopped taking drugs, but when he was with her, I sensed he was more controlled. She could be like a soldier, ordering Chet, 'Don't do this, don't do that!' Maybe Chet didn't always like it, but he was healthy."[34]

The problems only started when they left Rome. Rita Amaducci had booked some concerts in Sicily. There was not enough for everyone in Chet's car, a Citroen, so he opted to fly to Italy, leaving Ruth, Missy, Rique Pantoja, Enzo Pietropaoli and drummer José Boto to cram into the car, and make the long drive south to Sicily. In the searing heat of the Italian summer, it was a recipe for disaster.

The tension between Missy and Ruth started to mount. "She was seven years old when I met her, and liked me a great deal, writing me letters and sending me drawings," explained Ruth. "All of the children enjoyed my support—they didn't have it from anywhere else. But by the time she reached fourteen, she had started scheming with Carol, and things started to change." Pantoja was not aware of the long and involved family history, and felt that Ruth was being mean to Missy. "I remember trying to comfort her, Missy, a few times," he said. "She seemed like a troubled teenager."[35]

By the time the band reached Messina in Sicily, something had to give. When Chet discovered problems with the tour arrangements, he fired his Italian agent Rita Amaducci. "Missy had never liked her, and when Chet broke things off with Rita, I saw Missy in the corridor of the hotel, jumping up and down on her suitcase," said Pietropaoli.[36]

Returning from Sicily, the band played one gig at a castle on Ischia, an island off the coast of Naples. "Mussolini's son sat in and played piano that night," recalled Pantoja, "and another musician played trombone." A few nights later, over on the Adriatic coast, Missy discovered Chet's syringe, wrapped in an elastic band, in the hotel bathroom. "She said, 'Gee, Dad, what's this?' He got angry with her, and shouted, 'What do you think it is?'" said Ruth. "Then he grabbed the works from her hand, stormed into the bedroom, and slammed the door shut. It was absolutely nuts."[37]

The band eventually returned to Rome, where an Italian record producer proposed a recording session. "A producer in Rome, who owned the Manuva club, decided to produce a record with Chet, Rique Pantoja, with a number of local musicians, including Roberto Gatto and myself," explained the bass player Enzo Pietropaoli. "It was a great band, and we had some good arrangements, including some Don Sebesky arrangements. I don't know why it never came out."[38]

The band was staying at a Holiday Inn on the outskirts of Rome. Chet now had easy access to his local dealer, and no longer felt the need to follow Ruth's advice and stay clean in front of his daughter. "He was getting higher, and higher, and higher," said Ruth. "He was out of control." At this point, Rique Pantoja confronted Ruth, and asked her why she put up with his behaviour. "He's one of the few people who openly questioned my relationship with Chet. I don't remember what I answered," said Ruth, who was starting to have doubts of her own.[39]

By now, Chet had spent the money he had earned on the tour, and was starting to run out of cash. At this point, he even resorted to calling one of his long-standing fans in Denmark, and begged him for cash. "Chet called him while we were staying in Rome, and said 'My daughter's here, I'm short on money and she's not eating; do you think you can send me five hundred bucks?'" said Ruth. "He used the excuse of his daughter. By this stage there was a growing amount of con artistry. Sure enough, the guy went to the Western Union, sent it right to the hotel. Chet collected the money, left, and twenty minutes later it was gone."[40]

Ruth knew that Missy was due to fly back next day, and wanted to make sure Chet was clean enough to drive his daughter to the airport. "Chet eventually pulled one of his stunts and said, 'Right, pack your bags, we're leaving tonight'," said Ruth. "'What are you talking about?' I said. 'Just what I said, we're leaving. We're gonna leave down the fire escape, and leave without paying'. He didn't want to part with any money for a hotel when he could otherwise sink it into his veins. Having been raised the way I was, I was completely devastated, and opposed to his pathetic intention. I screeched at him that this was wrong. Chet said, 'Let's just pack this shit! Look, if this son-of-a-bitch could build this motherfucking hotel, he certainly doesn't need my money!' Now this was the best junkie humour I'd ever heard!"

With Missy on the plane and heading back to New York, Ruth had time to question the way in which her relationship with Chet had started to decline, now that he was using heroin on a more regular basis. "I understood what he was going through, and sympathised up to a point," she explained. "I gave it everything I could, but it was getting out of control. It got so ugly that I thought about crawling into it, just to not have to think about it. That raised the issue that if I jumped in, who would take care of anything. That was the beginning of the end for me."

The following month, Chet's German promoter Gaby Kleinschmidt was planning a tour with Wolfgang Lackerschmid, Larry Coryell, Buster Williams and Tony Williams, timed to coincide with the launch of the album they had recorded together the previous year. In the event, the arrangements fell through, and neither Buster Williams nor Tony Williams flew over to Europe. Their places were taken by Frank Tusa on bass and Alphonse Mouzon on drums. The six-week tour took in Germany, Switzerland and Austria, and whilst no official recordings were made, bootlegs suggest that Chet was not in particularly good shape.[41]

One night in Vienna, most likely on that tour, Chet and Ruth were invited to stay at the apartment of an admiring gay couple. They had dinner together, and when Chet explained that he wanted to get high, they referred him to a local drug dealer. Later that night, after the couple had gone to bed, Chet arranged to meet the connection outside on the street. When Chet discovered he was also a junkie, he invited him up to the apartment, and they shot up together. Soon after, the dealer collapsed, dead of an apparent overdose. "You grab his feet," Chet whispered to Ruth. "We've got to get him out of here." They heaved the dead body down the stairs, trying not to disturb the neighbours, and dumped the body behind a bush further down the street. "Nobody can handle the road like you," he told Ruth, by way of thanks.[42]

Chet and Ruth returned to New York in the winter of 1980/81, grateful to have a break from the hectic tour schedule Kleinschmidt had arranged in Europe. Ruth tackled Chet about his worsening behaviour under the influence of heroin. "I remember saying to him at one point, 'If this had been another woman, it would have been nothing, it would have been a piece of cake'. I think Diane and Carol's difficulties with Chet all stemmed partly from his heroin use; but in their case, I think there was an egocentric element—as women, they were going to try to change him."[43]

But Ruth still hoped that she could mend his ways, and arranged an appointment with a drug counsellor in New York. Just before the scheduled appointment, Chet called her from a phone booth outside the clinic and explained that he couldn't go through with it.

Nevertheless, Chet did make a token effort to clean up his act. He got in touch with the vibraphonist he had worked with in the early 1970s, Warren Chiasson. "He used to come over to my place—I live at 38th and 3rd Avenue here in New York," Chiasson recalled. "He'd come over here with his lady friend at the time, Ruth Young, and she used to bake some cookies, while we rehearsed in the afternoon." The band played the occasional gig around New York, including Gulliver's in West Paterson, New Jersey, and Struggles in Edgewater, New Jersey.

"What amazed me about Chet, the place would be packed, wall-to-wall, and they'd be listening to him reverentially—the silence was like a church," said Chiasson. "On the bandstand Chet was all music, it was like he could shut the world off, and just concentrate on what he had to say musically. He played with a phenomenal amount of energy, he would play long sets, especially at Gulliver's; he'd play for an hour and a half, take a break, then come back and play two hours. At Gulliver's he used Anthony Cox on bass, who'd just come in from Minneapolis, I believe, and a black drummer."[44]

The black drummer that Chiasson refers to was thirty-six-year-old Leo Mitchell, a native of Jacksonville, Florida, who had moved to New York some years earlier. He shared an apartment on West 21st Street with his girlfriend Diane, who was a white public-school music teacher. She remembers meeting Chet Baker for the first time at the gig at Struggles in Edgewater, New Jersey. Chet tried to turn on the charm, and told Diane it was a pleasure to meet her, he had heard so much about her—but she saw right through him. "Chet's motivation was to get money to buy drugs."[45]

Her worst fears were confirmed a few nights later, when Ruth Young invited the two of them over for dinner at her apartment. Chet and Leo Mitchell left early evening, explaining they were popping out for cigarettes; they didn't return for a few hours. "Leo Mitchell would have done anything for Chet," explained Ruth, "and that's all he cared about at this time."

By this stage, Ruth was worn down by Chet's increased drug use. She felt that Chet was drifting away from her, closer to drug buddies like Leo Mitchell. She tried to persuade Chet to let her shoot up, but he discouraged her. Eventually he gave in, and allowed Leo Mitchell to shoot her up. She started 'chipping' for a few weeks, but when she started to experience a fever—the first sign of addiction—she forced herself to quit. "No more stuff for me", she wrote in a note to Chet, dated March 22nd 1981.

Around the same time—in the winter of 1981—Ruth discovered a letter Chet had started to write to Carol, promising she could join him on his next European tour. Ruth was livid, and confronted him over the letter. She subsequently discovered that Carol had written to Chet, and threatened to report him to the IRS for unpaid taxes since 1964, when he had returned to the US. Ruth was understandably alarmed by these developments, and explained to Chet that Carol was simply playing games with him. As a consequence, Chet signed a handwritten contract dated February 25th, promising all income from any autobiography or film about his life to Ruth Young.

The topic of an autobiography had been raised once again, this time by a lady by the name of Lisa Galt Bond, a bohemian who lived in the East Village. Bond was attracted to the jazz scene, and gave occasion presentations of her self-composed 'jazz poetry'. She also had further literary pretensions, and interviewed various jazz musicians with a view to eventually writing a book.

She worked in a number of small clubs to make money, including a new jazz club that had opened on East 23rd Street called Jazzmania. She had heard that Chet Baker was back in New York, and spoke to the club's owner about making a possible booking. Aware of his unreliable reputation, the owner agreed to book Chet for just two nights.

Bond telephoned Ruth Young, who explained that Chet's fee for two nights would be $800. Chet then called Bond himself, and requested half of the fee in advance "for music paper", which the club's owner reluctantly agreed to. Bond arranged for Chet to collect the advance from her apartment, rather than the club, with a view to interviewing him. When he showed up next morning, he was wearing his trademark leather sandals, despite the crisp spring weather, because they felt more comfortable on his swollen feet—the effect of injecting himself between his toes.

Grateful for the cash, Chet agreed to talk with her for a few minutes. He discussed his fears of being tracked down by the IRS, the result of the numerous threats made by Carol over the years, and explained that he used several addresses to avoid being caught, including those of Ruth, Jacques Pelzer in Liege, Carol herself, and even jazz clubs that he played in Europe on a regular basis, where he was on good terms with the owner. Bond sensed that Chet was frustrated over the fact that he was struggling to make a living, although she was unaware at the time that Chet regularly signed recording contracts for cash, rather than royalty payments.

Chet recruited a new-look band for the gig at Jazzmania, reuniting with pianist Phil Markowitz, and recruiting Dennis Irwin on bass and Leo Mitchell on drums. Dennis Irwin had recently completed a three-year stint with Art Blakey's Jazz Messengers. He remembered seeing Chet play at Stryker's Pub in 1975, a night that left a profound effect on him. "Bob Mover told Dave Glenn and me that he was playing with Chet at Stryker's," he wrote. "We trekked uptown to 86th and Columbus to hear a quartet without drums—Harold Danko on piano, David Shapiro on bass, Bob and Chet the front line. The first set and a half was a mixture of jazz compositions—Jimmy Heath's 'C.T.A.', George Shearing's 'Conception', as well as vocal renditions of standards like 'Just Friends' and 'But Not For Me'. I was unaccustomed to hearing two horn-players do the kind of backgrounds, sendoffs, and counterpoint which Chet and Bob executed, with Dave and Harold churning and swinging. Near the evening's end, Chet invited Dee Dee Bridgewater to join them. She sang 'Softly As In A

Morning Sunrise', 'Invitation', and 'Green Dolphin Street' with abundant style and joy, to close out an evening still vivid and powerful in my memory. Dave and I floated downtown, inspired and ready to redouble our practice efforts."[46]

The two nights at Jazzmania were a resounding success, packing in the crowds, which included former Andy Warhol stars Joe Dallesandro and Tom Baker. One customer who was rather less welcome was Carol Baker, who refused to buy a ticket and elbowed her way in, announcing to anyone who would listen that she was "*Mrs* Chet Baker". Aware of Ruth's relationship with Chet, Lisa was careful to sit Carol near the back of the club, well away from the stage and Chet's gaze.

It took the new rhythm section a little while to adjust to Chet's requirements. "Once in a while, Leo and I would get carried away, perhaps leaning forward on the time, not so much getting faster as just playing upbeats and anticipations, when Chet preferred steady downbeats," recalled the bass player. "When we got out of hand, he would turn around in his chair and grumble, 'You guys are rushing … '". Chet needed the pulse even and relaxed."[47]

Encouraged by the success of the Jazzmania gig, Lisa Galt Bond called Ruth Young again, and suggested that she write a book of her own, with a view to eventually selling the film rights. She took on the flimsy manuscript from Tom Baker, who had made little progress over the preceding year with his own project, and agreed to interview Chet over the months ahead to fill in the numerous gaps in the narrative. On March 4th 1981, she and Chet signed a contract, prepared by her literary agent, Charles Neighbors, giving her 15% royalties on publication and various other rights, including movie rights. Ruth Young was not impressed by the fact that yet another person was trying to cash in on Chet's name. "In my book, they were all vultures," she said.[48]

Lisa started the project enthusiastically, encouraged by potential interest from Marvin Worth, who previously produced successful movie biographies of both Janis Joplin (*The Rose*) and Lenny Bruce (*Lenny*). She interviewed Chet quite extensively about his upbringing, and by late summer had written a flimsy book of her own, which she submitted to a number of publishing houses. The book met with rejection letters from the major publishers, and the film rights came to nothing. Details of Galt's interviews with Chet eventually came to light in James Gavin's 2002 biography, *Deep in a Dream: The Long Night of Chet Baker*.

Carol Baker later inherited a partial version of Chet's original manuscript—which had made its way from James Felds to Tom Baker, and then to Lisa Galt Bond. The manuscript was published in 1997 under the title *As Though I Had Wings*. No real attempt was made to clean up the timeline, which is blatantly wrong in places, or correct the numerous spelling mistakes. Whilst the *New Yorker* was broadly positive, describing each chapter as being "like a sketch done at the beach on a perfect, drowsy day", others were more critical, pointing out the flimsy nature of the book and the numerous inaccuracies. The New York *Daily News* described it as a "wisp of a book" that "doesn't offer a shred of reflection or self-awareness", perhaps unaware that Baker himself was sorely lacking in self-awareness.[49]

In early March, Chet and Ruth returned to Europe to play a selection of dates arranged by Gaby Kleinschmidt. One of the gigs, in Ludwigshafen in Germany, saw her put together an experimental line-up featuring the French bass player Jean-Francois Jenny-Clark, who had played with Chet on *Broken Wing* in late 1978, with a Belgian guitarist by the name of Philip Catherine, who was known for his jazz fusion playing with Jean-Luc Ponty, and for replacing Jan Akkerman in the Dutch rock group Focus. It sounded an unlikely match on paper, and so it proved to be. When the first night didn't work out, Chet opted to keep Philip Catherine but replace Jenny-Clark with his old friend Jean-Louis Rassinfosse. It was only a one-off gig at that time, but Chet enjoyed the experience, and reunited the trio later that year.

Over the next few months, Chet played with an assortment of musicians rather than with a steady line-up, which seemed to be a regular pattern now that he was using. He had travelled to Europe with a tenor saxophonist by the name of Sal Nistico. Nistico had come to fame with Woody Herman's Herd in the early 1960s, and later played with Count Basie and Dusko Goykovich's Sextet. Whilst Chet respected him as a musician, he was invited more because he was a regular drug buddy in New York, like drummer Leo Mitchell. Ruth Young confirmed this version of events. "This was around the time Chet and Sal Nistico were messing around, trading methadone and heroin," she later recalled.

The line-up for the first few weeks seems to have been Chet Baker and Sal Nistico, German bass player Joachim 'Rocky' Knauer, Costa Lukac on guitar and Lala Kovacev on drums, with Wolfgang Lackerschmid occasionally sitting in on vibraphone. At some point in April, Nistico had to return to the

United States, so Chet placed a call to his old friend Bob Mover, who was now living in Boston. "Chet called me and said, 'You're living in Boston?' I said, 'Yeah. I'm teaching some classes at Berklee, and I got a little band I'm playing with'," Mover explained. "'Teaching at Berklee? Don't you think you're a little young to be out to pasture?' Then he said, 'I've got a little job in Europe which could pay you between one and two thousand dollars a week; do you want to make it?'"

Sal Nistico and Chet Baker, Camden Jazz Festival, London, March 20th 1981. Photograph by Jak Kilby.

Bob Mover was still tempted to do drugs around Chet, just as he had done in the mid-1970s, but he was careful not to get hooked on this occasion. "I remember one night we did a little heroin in Paris when I went back with him to Europe," he said. "I didn't get strung out, but I liked to do heroin with him sometimes, just to get in that state of mind and be with him in that same state. Then I could leave it, and I wouldn't want it next day. There's a certain period in a heroin high, after the nodding and everything, where you get this nice lucidity, and can be very conversational. We would even talk about God. Chet could be very articulate, and when you were high too, he trusted you a little more. It was like being blood brothers, even though I didn't use needles with him. Chet was a little selfish. But when Chet had what he needed, and didn't have to borrow money from people, he was just a really nice cat."[50]

In the middle of the tour, Chet flew back to the United States for a prearranged gig at Fat Tuesday's in New York. Phil Markowitz had agreed to play piano, and lined up a prestigious rhythm section of Ron Carter on bass and Ben Riley, a drummer who'd played with both Sonny Rollins and Thelonious Monk in the 1960s. "The big thrill was having Ron and Chet up to my little apartment to rehearse," said Markowitz. "I was in seventh heaven playing with those cats at my crib."[51]

The first night of the gig was scheduled to be broadcast live on NPR, and was eventually released as a live recording. Unfortunately for Markowitz, Chet ran into his old pianist Hal Galper in the audience, and went outside to smoke a cigarette. "The next thing you know Hal was sitting in on the second tune," Markowitz explained. "Unfortunately he never got back up, and finished the set! As a result, I play on only one tune on the record. I was pissed, and of course I never got paid for the release!"[52]

The show at Fat Tuesday's had the makings of a great gig. The West Coast saxophonist Bud Shank was in New York, and was about to record a television show with the New American Orchestra. He swung by the club, saxophone in hand, and was able to sit in on the first set. Unfortunately, Chet was badly jet-lagged that night and not in the best of shape, sounding weary and uninspired. As a consequence, the show received generally poor reviews. "He grimaced his way through some five tunes with what appeared to be angered resignation," wrote Don Nelsen in the *Daily News*. "He looked like he was forcing every note."[53]

Chet returned to Europe in May, where he welcomed pianist Dennis Luxion back into the band. "I can't remember the exact circumstances, but I ended up working with him again," said Luxion. "I remember I got some postcards—he wrote to me a couple of times saying, 'Let's work things out'."[54]

A few weeks later the band—which included Bob Mover, Jon Eardley on flugelhorn, Rocky Knauer on bass and Burkhart Ruckert on drums—found themselves playing at the Salt Peanuts Club in Cologne, Germany. In a repeat of the events the previous summer, at Le Dreher in Paris, Chet made an arrangement with Rudolf Kreis of Circle Records to make a recording, again failing to inform the other band members. "It was the kind of set up where he was recording but it wasn't clear whether there was a record that was going to be produced, or he was just recording stuff," explained Dennis Luxion. "I'm sure he made arrangements with Chet, or that he made arrangements with Jon, but I never got paid. We would have got paid for the gig, but not the recording."

Once again, Rudolf Kreis recorded enough material for three LPs, later issued as *My Funny Valentine*, *'Round Midnight* and *I Remember You*. Whilst it is unfortunate that the other musicians did not get paid, the fact remains that these are by far the best of the various Circle Records releases of this period. To begin with, the recording quality is of a much higher standard, and from a musical perspective, there's some nice counterpoint between the three horns. "There are also other tracks that I thought were better that were never used," recalled Bob Mover. "There's a tune I wrote called 'Twardzik' which never came out. Chet would always play tunes that I wrote with the band, was always very supportive of cats in the band; he played my tunes, he played Harold Danko's tunes. Stan Getz was like that, too."[55]

While the band were in Cologne, Chet Baker and Bob Mover were invited to host a 'Master Class' in a local music store, an event that was being filmed for German TV. "There were many young German musicians there," the saxophonist explained, "and for the first hour or so of the class, the cats were playing. I'm making comments, and going over the piano, and saying, 'When you negotiate this kind of progression, sometimes you might want to think about this kind of movement'. Chet had not said a word, but was sitting there, paying attention, and smiling, offering his approval. They asked Chet if he had anything to add, explaining that they'd like to get him saying something on the news. Chet got up, and said, 'Well, I think that all that Bob is saying works very well, but the only thing I could tell you is that I've always felt it's very important to try and swing and find the pretty notes'." Chet may have lacked the technical skills to teach a master class, but there was still plenty they could learn from him, as Mover himself was well aware.[56]

The tour lasted for several weeks, and on many nights the band did not get paid. "I began to think, 'Hmm, what's going on here, shall we talk to Chet?'" recalled the pianist Dennis Luxion. "When the tour wrapped up, everything was fine, but I don't think we got paid until the very last gig."[57]

The final gig of the tour was back at Le Dreher in Paris, where Chet was always a big draw. Jon Eardley was unable to make the gig, so Ruth suggested they call Claudio Roditi, who had first played with Chet in Boston back in 1974. "We played ten nights to the Le Dreher club," he recalled. "He had hired two different bass players for that engagement, which I understand was quite a common occurrence! They ended up splitting the gig. One of them was Jean-Louis Rassinfosse, and that was when I met him. It was a terrific experience. Towards the end of the engagement, I started to play with more of a lyrical style, and I noticed that Chet was starting to play with more of a fiery style—he was playing some double-time phrases, and playing with a lot of force. So there was some sort of crossover; you can't escape that when you play with someone. His playing was very good, with lots of fluidity and some beautiful phrases."[58]

Chet returned to the United States in early June, and almost immediately started a two-month tour booked by his agent, Linda Goldstein. The tour took in the Pacific Northwest and Canada, where Chet had not played for a number of years. The tour kicked off with a two-week gig at Bourbon Street in Toronto, and also included the second Edmonton Jazz Festival in mid-August. His band on this occasion included pianist Lou Levy and bass player Monty Budwig.

Chet was interviewed by Maggie Hawthorne of *DownBeat* magazine during the course of this tour, and gave some interesting insights as to why he had started to experiment with a 'drummerless' trio. "It's the difference in volume of the things" he says, "without those cymbals ringing all the time, you know. The whole atmosphere of the thing without drums is much softer. And everything is much clearer. You can hear everything and follow it very easily. Drums cover up stuff." He exhibits a similarly restrained view of the piano, "if they play too much." Baker wants "somebody who doesn't over-play, who plays the right chords at the right time and not too busy; someone who leaves space."[59]

He also explained the new, softer tone he had started to produce on the trumpet; a sound which had started because of the pain he was suffering from kidney stones, but was becoming a more regular feature of his playing. "Baker no longer plays flugelhorn, as he has occasionally in the past, preferring to concentrate on trumpet. 'I don't want to carry a lot of things around with me. One horn is enough when you're running for trains and connections. I want to travel as light as possible. This horn has a large bore and, if the sound system is good, it can get a mellow sound like a flugel'." He enhances and fosters that muffled, mellow tone by jamming his horn up tightly to the microphone, swallowing it with the bell. He rarely uses a mute, preferring to work the electronic and physical characteristics of his tone into a muted timbre. "Mutes muffle the low notes," he explains as he jams in a borrowed mute to illustrate."[60]

Linda Goldstein reportedly told *DownBeat* she found it easy to book Chet Baker's tour, and was planning a ten-city tour of South America in November. That tour never materialised, with Chet again opting to return to Europe. "There's more work there and I think it's a lot better conditions, too, for working," he told Maggie Hawthorne. "For instance, you seldom run into a bad piano or one that's out of tune. And they usually have pretty good sound systems. You see much more curiosity and enthusiasm and whatever you want to call it concerning this music."[61]

In all likelihood, Chet also found it easier to fund his heroin addiction in Europe. Despite working steadily since his return to the United States, Chet pestered Ruth for cash, and she reluctantly gave him five thousand dollars from her trust fund. Once he had burned through that, he took to forging her cheques, cashing them at the Colony Music Store in Times Square. On August 25th, the store manager wrote a letter to Ruth Young, explaining that two of the cheques, totalling $212, had bounced. "I got a letter from Colony Records saying that if these checks aren't paid, we are going to post them for all to see in the store," said Ruth. She eventually repaid the money out of her own pocket.[62]

Chet's spell in Europe in late 1981 has not been particularly well documented, but there is evidence that his drug use was starting to spiral out of control. On one occasion in Italy, Chet invited a tenor saxophonist by the name of Larry Nocella to his hotel room. Ruth Young's resolve to stay away from heroin was being tested by Chet's escalating drug use, and she asked him to inject her. She overdosed, and her body turned blue. Baker and Nocella carried her lifeless body down eighteen flights of stairs and drove her to the nearest hospital. "He figured he'd have to get me there fast, or he'd have another stiff on his hands," Ruth later explained.

Chet's behaviour at this time was also a concern to his German agent, Gaby Kleinschmidt. She had booked him to play a gig in Bremen, Germany, following a gig in Austria. He opted to drive over the border with the other band members, leaving her to take the train. With limited space in his car, he requested that she carry his trumpet case. The train stopped at the border, and was searched by the police, who inspected everybody's passport. Learning that Kleinschmidt was Chet Baker's agent, they asked her to step off the train. The police questioned Kleinschmidt about her relationship with Chet Baker, and trained police 'sniffer' dogs checked her luggage. She was found to be clean, and allowed to board the next train. Shaken by the experience, she opened Chet's trumpet case and discovered seven envelopes of cocaine. The dogs had evidently been trained to search for cannabis, not cocaine. Realising she could easily have been imprisoned, she vowed never to work with Chet again.

In early November, Chet Baker reunited with the Belgian musicians, guitarist Philip Catherine and bass player Jean-Louis Rassinfosse, for a couple of shows. The reunion was the result of a chance encounter at a show in Germany. "I had been attending a Ron Carter concert in Guthausen, and Chet was playing there with another group," said Rassinfosse. "I hadn't booked anywhere to stay at the festival, so Chet said to me, 'Why don't you stay in my room?' The next day we travelled back to Aarau in Switzerland, and Ron Carter was playing on the same bill. It worked out very well, and then we had some more gigs to do in Barcelona. It was a beautiful old hall, and Philip also did some stuff on acoustic guitar for the first time. Chet was in really good shape, playing extensive solos, and playing incredibly fast lines. After that we played in Portugal, just outside Lisbon, at a jazz festival. It was another beautiful concert, taped for Portuguese TV. For years afterwards, the guy kept telling me, 'Yeah, I'll send you a copy, don't worry!' Finally, he died. One day the tape will resurface from beyond the grave!"

In mid-November, Chet started a tour of Italy. The band comprised Nicola Stilo on flute, Dennis Luxion on piano, Riccardo Del Fra on bass, and drummer Leo Mitchell, who had flown in from New York. "I liked Leo—he was a great drummer, and a really nice guy, but too much into the drug thing for his own good," recalled Luxion. Leo and Chet were using regularly on this tour, and they were soon joined by some of the younger musicians. "Nicola Stilo was clean when he first met Chet, but soon joined the party," explained Ruth. "It was difficult to be around Chet if you were not a part of it. Even Riccardo got hooked, and found it difficult to eventually kick his habit."[63]

Once again, Chet's growing dependency made him unreliable from a financial standpoint. "One day Dennis Luxion and I left the band together," revealed Riccardo Del Fra. "It's not that I was very material, otherwise I would not have played with Chet for eight or nine years. But sometimes, even with friends and family, there are certain things you can't accept. One night we found out there was no money again, and Dennis and I took the car from Genoa and drove back to Paris, which was kind of crazy! I remember afterwards, Nicola told me that Chet was throwing the money in the hotel room saying, 'I don't know what Riccardo thinks I've done with the money!' But a couple of weeks later he called me back saying, 'I've got the money for you, come on, we've got things to do'."

In late November, Leo Mitchell's mother died, and he flew back to the United States. His place was temporarily filled by another American, Al Levitt, who had evidently forgiven Chet for not being paid for the recording at Le Dreher in Paris, the previous year. Another American expatriate, living in Europe—Sean Levitt—joined the band for a few gigs. The tour appears to have finished in Spinea, near Venice, on December 23rd, at which point Chet, Ruth, pianist Dennis Luxion and guitarist Sean Levitt returned to the United States for Christmas.

Shortly after his return, Chet landed a weekend gig at Jazzmania—presumably booked by his erstwhile biographer Lisa Galt Bond. Dennis Luxion and Sean Levitt stayed on for this gig, with Dennis Irwin playing bass. Karl Ratzer, the Austrian jazz guitarist, also sat in for some sets. "The drum throne sat unoccupied, but that weekend, every time he wasn't soloing, Chet played great brushes," Irwin later recalled.[64]

Chet was never one to analyse, but if he had taken the time to look back over the previous year, he might just have realised that his addiction was taking its toll on the music. His recorded output had been limited, with no releases on any of the 'major' labels, such as SteepleChase. The band's line-up had also been unsettled, with Chet inviting fellow users to join the band—musicians such as Bob Mover, Sal Nistico and Leo Mitchell. Whilst they were all superb musicians in their own right, 'clean' musicians were perhaps less inclined to join the band. "By this stage, it was an on-again, off-again situation," admitted Dennis Luxion, who had stayed clean. "I was playing with Chet on a more defined basis, for a specific number of gigs. Chet basically lived on the road, and I wasn't really interested in that sort of lifestyle."[65]

Work dried up going into January, and Chet again found himself short of cash. Under normal circumstances he might have called in at his old record label, Artists House, but the label had finally folded. As a result he decided to pay a visit to the founder John Snyder, who was still living in New York.

"When I went out of business in 1981, I was non-functional for a couple of years," Snyder admitted. "My wife had left, took the kids, took the furniture, and I was living in this apartment with no electricity, no furniture, no nothing. I had a rented TV set, a rented lamp, and a long extension cord. I would plug the extension lead in the hall so I could watch TV, or have a lamp to read by. It was a nightmare; it was like the end of my life. I was sleeping on a piece of foam rubber on the floor. I wouldn't bathe for weeks, and I wouldn't go out, ever. This went on for almost a year. Nobody called, as I didn't have a phone. I was just lying there thinking, 'Where the hell did I go wrong, what the hell am I going to do now?'"[66]

John Snyder still lived in a nice apartment building, and was surprised when the doorman called up to tell him Chet Baker was in the lobby. "I hadn't bathed for a few weeks and I had my bathrobe on," Snyder recalled. "I opened the door, and he looked stunned. 'You look worse than I do!' I said, 'Well, Chet, you're not looking too good, either'. He said, 'No, I'm not good. Have you got any money?' I said, 'Chet, I've got fourteen dollars'. He said, 'Can I have half of it?' I said, 'You want seven dollars?' He said, 'Yeah'. I gave him seven dollars, and he turned around and walked away."

Ruth was finding Chet's behaviour increasingly intolerable. He constantly pestered her for money, and when that failed, he even sold some of her possessions. "He tried to get rid of my original copy of *Flic ou Voyou*," said Ruth. "There was some really creepy guy, and Chet had signed it, 'To so and so, all the best, Chet Baker'. The guy was going to give him fifty bucks for it. I said, 'Give me that, you stupid fuck! What are you doing? Who in the hell are you anyway? Just get out of my house!' I did all that I could to keep that recording and still have it to this day!"[67]

Occasionally Chet would stop by Bradley's, a small jazz club on University Place, in Greenwich Village, where his old friend Kirk Lightsey was the resident pianist. "Chet would just sit down, put his paper bag on the table, pull the horn out, and start to play," the pianist recalled. "Oh boy, that would be so thrilling! He would play these touching ballads, and people would start to cry."[68]

Shortly after this, in mid-February, Chet had sunk so low that he even hocked his trumpet. Mathias Winckelman of the German jazz record label Enja Records, had approached Chet about doing a recording with a piano player. Chet evidently felt intimidated by the pianist, so Winckelman proposed he work with a young vibraphonist by the name of David Friedman. "Mathias gave me Chet's number," said Friedman. "At that time he lived on the Upper West Side in New York. I called him up and he was very friendly—he knew who I was, and that we were supposed to be making a record together. He met me that evening wearing a bathrobe. I remember thinking he didn't look great, but he was a wonderful spirit, and really into the music. He had a baby grand piano in the apartment, and said, 'Let's look at your tunes!' I started to show him the tunes and suggested playing them together. 'At the moment, I don't have a trumpet', he told me. So I just played him my tunes, and he said, 'Oh, they're really nice'."[69]

A studio was booked for late February, with Chet Baker and David Friedman scheduled to be accompanied by Buster Williams on bass and Joe Chambers on drums. "He didn't show up for the first session," the vibraphonist recalled. "I hung around with Joe, Buster and Mathias. Mathias tried calling his girlfriend, who had no idea where he was. I remember Joe being very irritated, and wanting to split. But we waited, and the whole day we did nothing."

Chet did show up for the second recording session, however, which took place on February 23rd. "We did the whole recording at the second session, which I felt was a pity," said Friedman. "The music was challenging, and it would have been good if we had time for some alternative takes to try some stuff out. There was one tune called 'Three Plus One Equals Five', which was originally called 'Syzygies'. It was the first time Chet had recorded a piece without a harmonic basis, without chord changes, and it was a big challenge for him. We managed a couple of takes, but I think we could have got even more out of it had we have had a little more time to rehearse. We put the alternate take on the CD; I think it was a little faster."[70]

In addition to recording four of Friedman's own compositions, the vibraphonist selected two standards. "I chose the tunes quite impulsively," he remembered. "We did Horace Silver's 'Peace' and 'The Song Is You', a song I don't even know very well. Chet said, 'Let's do it in B flat.' 'That's great', I said, and all of a sudden, he said, 'No, let's do it in G. Go!' And then we did the take. I remember being quite surprised and quite challenged by that impulsive key change."

Friedman admits that Chet's style at that recording session had a profound impact on his own playing. "Chet is a very interesting player—he reads lines, he reads notes, but I got the impression he wasn't real good at reading chord changes. What he would do, which had a really big influence on me later, he would listen for the harmony, and then he would start to play by ear; then he would wait for the next harmony to come, then he would start to play. He'd do that until he knew the tune well enough to create a flow. I had the feeling that he played harmonically by ear, and wasn't really reading chord changes. Most of his life he played standards—well-known tunes that he'd learned—and he knew them. But when he played these tunes of mine—'For Now', for example, has really difficult changes—he read the melody down fine. But he was playing the changes by ear, listening to the chord changes, and playing it very simply and directly. That really impressed me, and after doing that session with him, I remember trying to do the exact same thing. For a long time, whenever I played a new tune with somebody, when it came time to solo, I wouldn't read the chord changes; I'd wait, listen, and try to play by ear. I got that from Chet. Even for a classically trained musician, interpreting chord changes is not that easy—it's something you've got to get used to. But you really have to develop your ears, that's what it boils down to. Doing the session with him, and observing the way he approached chord changes really influenced me."[71]

Chet told Friedman that he really liked the tunes they had recorded that day, and that he'd be playing in a small jazz club next evening. "He said, 'Let's meet. I'd love to have some more of your tunes'. I believed him, and went to the club at 9 p.m., and there was no sign of him. I wasn't angry, just disappointed. I would like to have played with him again."

The album was later released as *Peace*, and stands out as being Chet's most significant studio recording since the SteepleChase recordings, made three years earlier in late 1979. "I did call Chet's girlfriend [then Diane

Vavra] after the record came out, and we got together for lunch," said Friedman. "She thought it was an important record for his career because it was so different."

Over the spring, Chet landed a gig at the Lush Life jazz club, playing opposite bass player Charlie Haden, pianist Kenny Barron and drummer Ben Riley. Tuba player Howard Johnson and flute player James Newton rounded out the band. After the gig, the band went into the studio for a recording session that was eventually released as 'But Not For Me'. Drummer Ben Riley cannot recall why the record was released until 1994—six year's after Chet's death. "In those days there were all sorts of situations, where it was strange how they handled their business, and who they were handling," he explained. "I think the record company was afraid to deal with Chet."[72]

Chet's reputation was starting to catch up with him, and he found work increasingly hard to come by at this time. Things were made worse by the fact that Carol had financial concerns of her own, and was pressing him for more money. Chet in turn took his frustrations out on his girlfriend, Ruth Young. "Chet was blaming me for all sorts of things, and insanely enough was holding me responsible for his troubles with Carol," she recalled. "Incredible! He became increasingly verbally abusive. At one point he said, 'That's it, I'm going to retire; I don't want to play any music any more'. I think it was becoming evident to him that I was at the end of my rope!"

Despite this, Chet was offered a prestigious gig in June at the Blue Note, a new jazz club that had opened in Greenwich Village. He put together a new-look band for the occasion that consisted of tenor saxophonist Sal Nistico, pianist Phil Markowitz, bass player Dennis Irwin and drummer Leo Mitchell. Pianist Hod O'Brien remembers being invited to sit in on a couple of occasions, and remembers Chet's playing as erratic. "I think it had a lot to do with what kind of shape he was in on a given night," he said. "At times he played astoundingly well, perfection, and then other nights he'd be frantic, just trying to get stuff out, and he'd end up repeating phrases."[73]

The gig was warmly reviewed by the *New York Times*, whose jazz critic had presumably caught Chet on a good night. On the Fourth of July, the final night of the engagement, the club's owner paid Chet in cash. He and Leo Mitchell left between sets to cop, and never returned, leaving the rest of the band to play on without them. In the years that followed, he was never offered a return gig at the Blue Note.

That same summer, Carol filed a complaint against Chet with the Queens

Family Services, alleging non-payment of support. Chet failed to turn up to the hearing. He pleaded with Ruth Young to give him more money from her trust fund, but by this stage, her trust fund was starting to dwindle. "He was causing more and more problems for me," said Ruth. "He even started selling my records downtown on a soapbox—he took my entire Frank Sinatra collection."[74]

When Ruth confronted Chet over his appalling actions, Chet became apologetic, promising that things would go back to 'normal' if they returned to live in Europe. "His way of dealing with everything was to say, 'Don't worry, we'll go back to Italy. We'll have a good time'," said Ruth. "He didn't want to lose me, but he didn't know how to account for his bad behaviour. He didn't know how to deal with it. It was like dealing with an alcoholic. He would never say, 'Give me another chance,' because he wasn't like that."[75]

A couple of weeks later, Ruth Young returned home to her apartment to find that it had been burgled. Several items of jewellery were missing, including an Omega watch, a gold bracelet and three silver rings. The thief had also stolen four of Chet Baker's award plaques, an Oriental scroll and a few items of Ruth's clothing, including a sealskin jacket. Chet was shocked by what had happened, and helped her to make a list of the missing items, with a view to reporting the theft to the police. Ruth had recently had some repair work carried out to the bathroom, and they thought the plumber was the most likely suspect in the robbery.

Ruth only discovered the truth during the screening of Bruce Weber's Chet Baker documentary *Let's Get Lost*, in late 1988, a few months after his death. Chet's daughter, Melissa, had gone to visit her father. When she discovered he was not at home, she peered in through the open window, and then climbed through. She gathered her father's few precious belongings—including the award plaques he had been presented in Italy in April 1980. She also wanted to hurt Ruth, who she now blamed for the poverty the family had endured in Queens, New York. "I also got her back for a few things she'd said to me and done to me too," said Missy. "And I don't feel guilty about a bit of it either." She told Weber she had hocked the jewellery. "All of it," she said with a smirk. "For ninety dollars."[76]

The most shocking thing about this admission was that it was made in front of her whole family, and that Carol Baker looked genuinely proud of what her daughter had achieved.

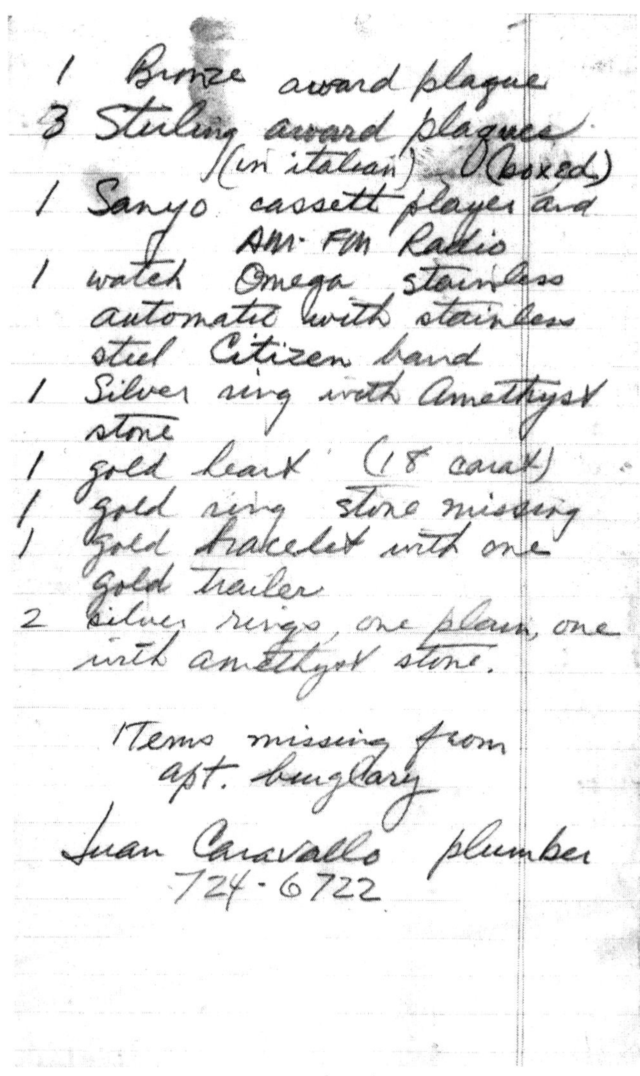

1 Bronze award plaque
3 Sterling award plaques
(in italian) (boxed)
1 Sanyo cassett player and
AM-FM Radio
1 watch Omega stainless
automatic with stainless
steel Citizen band
1 Silver ring with Amethyst
stone
1 gold heart (18 carat)
1 gold ring stone missing
1 gold bracelet with one
gold trailer
2 silver rings, one plain, one
with amethyst stone.

Items missing from
apt. burglary

Juan Caravallo plumber
724-6722

Copy of Chet's handwritten note, identifying some of the stolen items, July 1982.

Looking back, Ruth is convinced that the robbery was carried out by Missy in conjunction with her brother Dean—as there is no way Missy could have carried everything on her own. "My mother had given me this seal jacket," she said, "And my father used to come back from trips with presents for my sister and I. They took everything I ever had from my childhood, from around the globe. Some friends of my parents had been to the Orient years earlier and had brought them a hand-sewn silk screen scroll, which I had hanging on one of the walls."[77]

Chet was informed of the perpetrators during the filming of the documentary in 1987. "Chet even wrote a letter to Carol saying, 'You know the thing [scroll] that Dean took—I want you to give it to Bruce, and give it back to her'," explained Ruth. "He asked Carol to do the right thing, but she just ignored him. When Bruce eventually asked her about it, she said, 'You mean that scroll over there? It's staying right where it is. I mean, what does it look like—that I'm Saks 5th Avenue?' I'll never forget that so long as I live."[78]

Once Bruce Weber found out how upset Ruth was to learn what had happened, he offered to help out. "He was kind enough to send some his people round to all the pawn shops in Queens, where Carol was living, in an effort to get the things back for me," said Ruth.

Asked whether Missy had turned away from Ruth in her teenage years, and back towards Carol, Ruth expressed her doubts. "It's difficult, because I'm trying to be as objective as possible," she explained. "As Tennessee Williams said, you can never understand someone, until you try to see their point of view. In the movie she said, 'I got her back for anything she ever said or did to me', and laughed. Where did that come from? I think the kids think they're special because they're Chet Baker's children; they believe their name is like Hilton. Missy was the most divisive and manipulative of Chet's children—she was absolutely her mother. She was determined to get what she wanted, whatever damage that might cause. She felt as though she had been rejected emotionally. She didn't talk to Chet about these things, saying, 'Dad, why are you doing these things to Mom?' That would have been sane, would have been pertinent."[79]

Shortly after the robbery, Carol Baker and the children relocated from Queens, New York, to Stillwater, Oklahoma, just a few miles from where Chet's mother was living in Yale. She took a job there as secretary to the dean at Oklahoma State University, which helped the family to get by in the absence of support.

Around the same time, Chet and Ruth left for Europe, an ill-fated attempt to patch up the growing cracks in their relationship. They stayed with Chet's old friend Jacques Pelzer in Liège in Belgium. A few days into their trip, Carol tried to telephone Chet at Jacques's house, only to reach Ruth. She informed her that Dean had been involved in a bad car accident in Oklahoma, and was in a serious condition. "Dean's car accident was another one of Carol's failed attempts to play the victim," said Ruth. "In the movie *Let's Get Lost* she claims that Chet was in Europe, and never did call. Although I too was stunned at Chet's alarming apathy, I had informed Chet of Dean's accident immediately and insisted that he call Carol. The sad fact is that he didn't care enough to call and never did. That's unfortunately how Chet chose to deal with it."[80]

The holiday in Europe did little to repair Chet's deteriorating relationship with Ruth. Desperate for drugs upon his return to New York, he again begged Ruth for more money. When she refused, he pointed to a silver plate they'd been given from a town in Belgium, near Brussels, and asked her to hand it over. "He demanded that I give it to him, and said that it was his—which it actually was," said Ruth. "I told him to go and call someone else for a change. 'You got feet—go walk!' But all the while we did this, there was still an 'I love you!' about it."[81]

On other occasions, however, Chet became violent. On one occasion, he lost his temper and tore down the montage of photos and memorabilia that Ruth had lovingly assembled above the fireplace in her apartment. Another time, Ruth reached for the telephone to call the police, only for Chet to grab the cord, and wrap it tightly around her neck. When he eventually calmed down, Ruth refused to accept his explanation that the drugs were to blame for his behaviour. "Don't tell me you can't think through the fucking drugs," she shouted. "Depending on the strength of your character, heroin is no different from any other drug that accentuates who you are to begin with."[82]

One of the few friends who stood by Ruth at this time was Lisa Galt Bond. "She said to me, 'You really don't need this', and really influenced my thinking at this time. I got on Chet's ass when he started messing up to the extent that he did. Chet eventually got wise to this, and said, 'Why don't you go and call Lisa? Just get off my back'."

Chet embarked on a brief tour of Canada at this time, arranged once again by his US agent, Linda Goldstein. Ruth convinced Chet that he needed to dry out, and get the drugs out of his system. She booked a cheap holiday in St Croix in the Virgin Islands, paying just $900 for a ten-day trip, and called him in Alberta to inform him of the arrangements. "Two days before we were due to leave, I tried reaching him, but couldn't find him," said Ruth. "I finally got a message that he wouldn't be able to make it. It was the same old crap, which I really didn't expect this time."

With the flight booked for the next day, Ruth called Lisa Galt Bond, and persuaded her to take Chet's place. "She went with me, but couldn't handle the fact that we were short of money," laughed Ruth. "A bit like when I was on the road with Chet!"[83]

Ruth returned home to New York on September 17th. She had tried phoning him from St Croix, but he had not picked up. Opening the door of her apartment, she could feel his presence. He failed to answer her call, and opening the door of her bathroom, she found him shooting up, quite oblivious to her presence. "I literally put him out on the street, and locked the door," said Ruth. "But a few minutes later he broke back into the apartment through the first floor window. 'Oh, it was a piece of cake'," he told me. 'You just do this'. He was totally consumed with the explanation. "'Just get out! I don't need your explanation about how easy it is to break back into my apartment'."[84]

Chet refused to leave, and Ruth eventually stormed out of the apartment. She walked down Columbus Avenue, crying hysterically, and ducked into the first bar she came across—a small Mexican bar owned by the actor Malachy McCourt and his brother. "There was a twenty-four-year-old bartender there, Michael, who saw the distress I was in and let me stay with him. He was a very kind person, and I trusted him, and stayed over at his place at Washington Heights. I literally had the clothes on my back; I had this sarong I was wearing, and my purse. Eventually he brought me this little Chinese robe, and said, 'If I look at you one more time in those clothes ...'"

She stayed with the young bartender for several days, telephoning her apartment every day, and hanging up the phone when Chet answered. "Michael told me, 'You should talk to him', and he was right, but that's what I was never able to do," explained Ruth, in tears at the memory. "I couldn't confront him. I knew why—if he had said anything, I probably would have gone back. Which I did really didn't want to do ... I really didn't want to do."[85]

One day, Chet failed to pick up, and Ruth tentatively made her way back to the apartment. The scene that met her eyes was devastating. "The piano had gone, and I found a piece of paper saying, 'This is the property of Chesney Henry Baker—a Harman Baby Grand from 36, West 71st'. That's when I finally did lock him out for good," said Ruth. "I eventually called the people he sold it to, and they said, 'Sorry, that's ours now'. That was the price I paid to leave him."[86]

Ruth later discovered that Chet had made two phone calls in her absence. "The first was to Lisa Galt Bond," Ruth explained. "Chet picked up the phone, dialed her number, and said 'Fuck you!' He held her accountable. The other phone call was to a dear musician friend, who did not deserve the phone call that he got. He said, 'Lou, she's all yours'. Click. Chet was devastated by my taking the stance that I did. He never expected that I would leave, and was scarcely prepared for it. It was never a blame game, but he thought he would address the issue with the two people who were close to me, and influenced my decision."

A few days later, she let him in one final time—to collect his belongings, and make one final phone call. Only later did she discover that he used her telephone to call Diane, his old girlfriend from the early 1970s. When Ruth discovered what had happened, she confronted him one last time. "We had a huge row about it," she revealed. "He could not be without a person, he could never be alone. He didn't even want to go back to her."[87]

In an extraordinary development, Diane Vavra actually had the nerve to call Ruth Young a few days later, and ask for some advice. "She said, 'Hi, this is Diane. I know that you and Chet have broken up. Is there anything you can tell me about that I need to know?' It was that peculiar!"

A few months later, around the turn of the year, the buzzer to Ruth's apartment rang, and she opened the door to see the drummer Leo Mitchell standing on the street outside. "I've got something for you," he said, and Chet stepped out from behind him. "He was his usual, meek self," said Ruth. "He looked so sad and lost. He'd just come back to see me, hoping for a reconciliation. Leo knew what was going on, and also knew we really belonged together. It was a terribly difficult moment."[88]

Ruth Young still believes that she fared much better than Chet's wives, Charlaine Souder, Halema Alli and Carol Jackson. She was clearly Chet's soulmate, a fact that many of his friends—including Leo Mitchell—clearly recognised. "I always felt I was indeed secondary to the music and the drugs, but I always believed that I had inched up just ahead of the car!" she laughed.

Looking back, Ruth admits there were many times she could have bailed out, particularly in the later years. "But he desperately needed someone to take care of him," she explained. "In most relationships there is a honeymoon phase, and that phase was clearly over. Chet needed a doctor, or nurse, some kind of entourage, but instead I was all he had to rely on. I still feel as though the moment I stopped looking out for him, he was gone ... "

Chapter Seventeen

MR. B
EUROPE, 1983

"You know, Luis, all that negative publicity about me. Believe it or not, it works for me—the place will be packed."—Chet Baker[1]

In 1982, Chet Baker allowed his renewed addiction to take over his life. He became increasingly unreliable; his playing became more erratic, and he would fail to show up to gigs and recording sessions. In the words of the vibraphonist David Friedman, who recorded with Chet in February of that year, "I don't think he was really in control of his own destiny at that point."[2]

His personal life also began to unravel. His growing drug use meant that he had less cash to send to his family, culminating in a court hearing for non-payment of support. Eventually his wife and children had to leave New York to return to Oklahoma, simply to make ends meet. His addiction also chipped away at his relationship with his long-standing girlfriend Ruth Young, who finally walked away in September 1982. "I didn't leave because I didn't love Chet," she explained. "Hardly. I just didn't know how to cope with things any more and truly believed that great harm would come to one of us if I stayed."[3]

The subsequent revival in Chet's fortunes in 1983 had less to do with Diane Vavra, Ruth's replacement, than it did his new European agent, Wim Wigt, who booked Chet on a high profile tour with Stan Getz in early 1983, and managed many of his later tour arrangements.

Diane Vavra had learned to live with disappointment. Her attempt to reignite the flame with Chet on his West Coast tour in early 1978 had come to nothing, with Chet showing little interest beyond a one-night stand. She had subsequently worked on a master's degree, whilst raising her teenage son, who suffered from drug problems of his own. Now forty-two, she continued to practice both the soprano saxophone and clarinet, but was plagued with self-doubt, and limited her playing to part-time teaching.

Chet's phone call from New York had caused her heart to soar, but she was realistic enough to realise that he did not always deliver on his promises. So it was a pleasant surprise to come home from work one evening in early October and find Chet on her doorstep, a bouquet of flowers in his arms. In the days that followed, they caught up with one another, Vavra surprised to hear how bitter Chet felt about the way he felt he had been treated, particularly in North America.

Diane felt alarmed when Chet asked her troubled son to go out and buy drugs for him. Despite everything that had happened between them, he still felt like a Greek god to her. But there were numerous other warning signs that Chet had not changed his ways.[4]

One evening, Chet was sitting in with a local band in a bar in Palo Alto, just north of San Jose. One of the band members, Terry Henry, introduced Chet to a fellow trumpet player by the name of Luis Gasca. Gasca had studied at the Berklee School of Music, and subsequently played with the likes of Stan Kenton, Count Basie and Mongo Santamaria in the 1960s. In the 1970s he had appeared on a number of rock-oriented albums, playing with the likes of the Jefferson Airplane and the Grateful Dead, before drug addiction took its toll on his playing career.

Luis Gasca recognised a kindred soul, and offered to work as Chet Baker's manager. "I had just come in from Mexico, and I also had drug problems at the time," he explained. "I wanted to get back to playing. I said to Chet, 'Why don't we team up? I'll do the booking'. I took care of Chet when no one else would touch him; and by that time, no one would touch me either. I could understand him, because I had the same problems."

Gasca started by placing calls to various clubs in San Francisco and Los Angeles, but most of them were aware of Chet's reputation, and worried he wouldn't show up. "I used to call clubs and say, 'Give me the door, and I'll deliver Chet Baker. That way if he doesn't show up, I've also got something to lose'. One of the clubs I approached, a club called 'My Place', said they'd never heard of Chet Baker. I said, 'Do you know who Leonard Feather is?' The owner said, 'Yeah, he writes for the *LA Times*'. I said, 'Well, if I get Leonard to call you, will you think about it?' I called Leonard, and asked if he'd do me a favour. He called the club. I asked the club owner, 'How do you want to do this? Let's split the bar and the door'. He said, "No, I can't split the bar'. 'No problem, we'll take the door', I told him."[5]

Gasca also asked Leonard Feather to interview Chet for the *LA Times* to generate some publicity for the forthcoming show. "Although Chet respected Leonard, he wasn't too crazy about him," said Gasca. "I had to give Chet two grams of heroin just to get him there." As a consequence, Chet turned up at Leonard Feather's house strung out. "When the article came out, it was horrible," said Gasca. "It said nothing about the music—it said Chet Baker was this, Chet Baker was that, Chet Baker was a junkie, how he was unreliable and might not show up. I could have killed Leonard. I was pissed off because I needed help."[6]

But Chet was not worried by the negative impression he had created. "'You know, Luis, all that negative publicity about me. Believe it or not, it works for me—the place will be packed'." "And you know what?" said Gasca. "He was right. Herb Alpert was there, Joni Mitchell was there. Everyone wanted to be there because he hadn't played there for seven years. Charlie Haden was there that night. He came up to me and said, 'Luis, I wish you had called me to play bass'. I never thought about calling Charlie Haden to play. At the end of the first night the owner came up to me and said, 'I wish I'd taken half the door!'"[7]

Fuelled by the success of the gig in Los Angeles, Gasca proposed a four-week tour. Diane opted to stay behind, but Chet decided to bring his son Dean. He was feeling guilty that he had not been to see him since his car accident, and arranged for him to fly down and meet them.

"I booked him into some nice places," said Gasca. "After Los Angeles we went to Las Vegas, which was rare for Chet Baker. I mean, Chet Baker in Las Vegas! I'd played there myself with Woody Herman." From Los Angeles, they drove to Denver, where Chet reunited with his old friend, Phil Urso. "We played at a great little Mexican hole-in-the wall. The place was packed, with a lot of his old friends coming over. But after the show, everyone passed out in the room. It was sort of pathetic!"[8]

Chet collected his son Dean from Denver airport, but Gasca remembers their relationship as being incredibly strained. "The son had recently been hit by a car, and was mentally not all there, but he was a wonderful kid," he revealed. "For two weeks, they never spoke to one another. I took care of the son, me and Terry Henry, who was driving on the tour. We gave him money, food to eat."

Terry Henry was also helping Luis Gasca with the tour bookings, many of which were made on the fly. Early in the tour, Henry ran up $1,200 of phone bills trying to secure bookings. When Chet discovered that Gasca was withholding some of the door money, he confronted him angrily. "He thought I was taking money from him, which was far from the truth," said Gasca. "I said, 'Chet, your friend Terry has run up a lot of phone bills—I mean, phoning round, trying to book Chet Baker, this sort of thing doesn't come for free'. He even spoke to Terry Henry to confirm the story. He was pretty street-wise—a bit like Art Pepper, he wore his rough edges like a badge of honour."

After Denver, they drove to Texas, where Chet played in Austin and Dallas. Gasca struggled to book additional gigs, and arranged for Chet to make a presentation at the Houston School of Performing Arts, which seemed like an unlikely match. "I thought this would be a good idea because the schools had come a long way as far as music education was concerned," Gasca explained. "There were a number of colleges teaching jazz appreciation, and things had come a long way from the days where you could not even mention the word 'jazz' in the United States. I booked him to go to the School of Performing Arts during the daytime so Chet could talk to the students about jazz. I thought they would be able to see the serious side of Chet right there. It was tough to do, because Chet was not particularly talkative, and being a junkie is not a very social thing. It was hard for me to convince him that it was a good idea. But Chet was good with the kids; he'd be sitting there, looking like he was nodding out, but then started talking. At one point he asked them, 'Why on earth in the world would you want to go into jazz when there's no job?' It was amazing to me that Chet Baker would look at things in this way. He was not trying to discourage them, but making sure they knew what they were getting into. I think Chet surprised himself that day."

With no more gigs lined up, Gasca booked Chet to do a radio show in Houston. In the end, Chet couldn't make it, because he was ill. "I phoned the radio announcer, and told him that Chet was sick, and he said, 'No problem, I'll tell the listeners that Chet is sick, and will be coming to play tomorrow'. He called me back twenty minutes later, and told me that a doctor had called the radio station, and offered to help. A few minutes later the doctor called and said, 'I heard Chet Baker was sick, and wondered if I could do anything?' I said, 'Well, you can come over and see him'. He came over, and was happy to give Chet anything he wanted. The next thing I know, Chet's moved into his house, and was driving around town in his convertible

Jaguar!" The doctor concerned, Joe Ellis, stayed in touch with Chet in the years that followed, and even helped to arrange a recording session in 1985.

Driving back to Los Angeles, Chet made arrangements for his son Dean to go back to Oklahoma. Chet was happy to put his son on a Greyhound bus, but Gasca insisted they drive him back to Denver, and put him on a plane. "That was a part of Chet I didn't like—he could be a real con man. So we had two con men, him and me," he laughed. "I used him, and he used me."[9]

Chet reunited with Diane Vavra in mid-December, before making preparations to go on tour with Stan Getz in January. He told Vavra that he would make arrangements for her to fly to Europe in the spring of 1983, once the tour was over. In the meantime, he arranged to fly to Oklahoma to meet with his mother and family, and then on to New York, where he would meet with Getz.

Chet also met with Luis Gasca one last time in New York. "I owed him some money, and had $1,200 for him," said Gasca. "I sat down with him, having taken care of his ass for two months, and he virtually ignored me. I went up to the bar, ordered a drink, and said, 'Put it on Chet's tab'. The barman looked at me, and said, 'Are you with Chet?' I said, 'Yes, I've been his manager for the last few months. We're together'. A few friends came along, including Dave Valentine, and we had something to eat and a few drinks. A week later, Chet was given a bill for around $230. He was told it was a bill run up by his manager, to which he replied 'I don't have no fucking manager!' Chet called me, and I said, 'Chet, I just bought you $1,200. I just flew into New York, you act like you don't know who the hell I am. Don't worry about the $230, I'll pay you next week'. He said very softly, 'Luis, if I ever see you again, I'll knock the shit out of you'. 'Well Chet', I replied, 'People are big on the telephone. Let's see what happens if we ever meet again!' The conversation ended with me telling him to go fuck himself, and he told me the same. He never did get his $230!"[10]

In the meantime, Stan Getz and his girlfriend, Jane Walsh, had serious reservations about going on tour with Chet. "I said to Stan, 'This is a precarious thing', said Walsh. 'You're just starting out on your sobriety. You've just begun at the university. You're going to be a professor. Your sobriety is shaky, and Chet is crazy and is going to be drinking and drugging'. So we told Wim Wigt, 'We'll do the tour, but we won't room with this guy. Don't put him on the same plane with us. We don't want to go through customs with him'."[11]

Getz's worst fears were confirmed when he ran into Chet in a jazz club in New York City, just weeks before the tour was scheduled to begin. "I met Stan in New York at the end of 1982," explained Win Wigt. "He said, 'Chet came by last night at Fat Tuesday's and he looked like a bum. I have no desire to go on tour with a guy like that. I've been a junkie, I freed myself from that world, and I don't want to have people like that around me any more. He asked for money, and he looked like a bum. Take Chet or me—or cancel the whole tour'."[12]

Wigt managed to calm Getz down, reminding him that he'd already been paid his advance, and that the tour dates had already been booked. The tour was scheduled to last for six weeks, and took in Holland, Denmark, Sweden, Norway, France, Spain and even Saudi Arabia. The final arrangements were marred by the sudden death of his manager, Jack Whittemore, who died from a brain haemorrhage at the age of just sixty-nine. The funeral took place on February 6th, and Stan Getz flew to Holland next day accompanied by Jane Walsh, and his band.

Stan Getz's band at this time comprised pianist Jim McNeely, bass player George Mraz and drummer Victor Lewis. McNeely was in Australia at this time, touring with the bandleader Mel Lewis, and was replaced for the first nine or ten days by Gil Goldstein, who was working on a project in Switzerland at that time.

The tour kicked off at the Singer Concertzaal in Laren, Holland, on February 10th 1983. Tensions were running high from the very first show. The two stars shared the stage, primarily playing duets. The set included two vocal performances by Chet, including 'My Funny Valentine', and two solo performances by Stan Getz, including 'Lush Life'. "Chet was getting much more applause than Stan," recalled Irv Rochlin, an American pianist who attended the show that night. This version of events was confirmed by the tour manager Wim Wigt. "Stan Getz was like a spoilt child and he was very insecure," he recalled. "He was jealous of the success that Chet was enjoying. So there was a constant conflict."[13]

Getz also had an irrational dislike of the stand-in pianist, Gil Goldstein. "He'd go on to the stage before they started, saying things like, 'Is there a piano player in the house that would like to sit in?'" said Per Husby, a pianist who played with Chet later that year. "Chet was furious about this, and didn't think you should behave like this towards other people". Of course, Chet had a tendency to criticise other musicians on the bandstand, so this was perhaps a case of the pot calling the kettle black.[14]

The problems may have been exacerbated by the fact that his band clearly enjoyed playing with Chet. "He was one of the most soulful musicians I've ever worked with," recalled Victor Lewis. "His pacing was quite unique—he had a very relaxed style. Less was better with him. He didn't play a lot of notes, but he would play all of the so-called 'butter notes', all the most beautiful and effective notes of the chord. That, along with his phrasing and his tone. He played very much like a singer would sing."[15]

Chet was also more friendly backstage, and travelling between shows. "Stan was, for lack of a better term, like 'jazz royalty'," explained Lewis. "There was a slight separation between Stan and the guys in the rest of the band. He stayed at a different hotel. But with Chet there was more camaraderie. We all stayed at the same hotels, hang out on occasion, if we had a little time out. He was a great guy to hang out with. He was also humble in a lot of ways."[16]

A few days into the tour, Getz made the first of several complaints about Chet's behaviour, complaining that he had bought George Mraz a cognac, knowing full well that Getz was trying to moderate the bass player's intake.

Despite the tension, Wigt was confident that Getz would continue with the tour until they reached Stockholm, at least. The Sonet record label had contracted with him to record the concert on February 18th, with a view to broadcasting the show on the radio, and later releasing a live recording.

Pianist Gil Goldstein was scheduled to play in Stockholm, but Getz requested that his regular pianist, Jim McNeely, try to fly over one day earlier. "Which was fine—except that I happened to be in Australia where I was finishing up a tour with Mel Lewis," he said. "I was originally supposed to fly back to New York and then fly to Oslo the following day. Instead I flew from Sydney to Stockholm—a little matter of forty hours with the various changes en route. And I can tell you it was quite a shock to be hanging out on a sunlit beach in Sydney one moment and then facing the rigours of a cold February in Stockholm the next!"[17]

The change of schedule also meant that McNeely had no winter clothes in his suitcase. "The original plan was that I had a day in New York to unpack all my summer stuff, and pack my winter stuff," he explained. "When I arrived in Stockholm, the road manager picked me up, and the first thing we had to do is go shopping. Wim Wigt, the promoter, bought me some winter clothes, and I went back to the hotel, put some of them on, and went to the venue."[18]

Two shows took place that night. Excerpts were originally released as *Line for Lyons* on Sonet records, but the two shows have now been released in their entirety on Verve records as a three-disc CD set, *Stockholm Concerts*. Chet does not seem to have been in particularly good shape for the first show, and one wonders what he had taken before the concert. His vocal on 'Just Friends' and 'My Funny Valentine' is weak, and the video footage shows that Getz was not impressed. The second show was a distinct improvement; Getz plays quietly beneath Chet's vocal on 'Valentine', and there is a spirited 'Line For Lyons', one of a handful of songs that the two leaders play together, where they unite without the aid of the rhythm section.

Jim McNeely was suffering from severe jetlag during the show, and felt that he was playing on autopilot for most of the night. "It was the weirdest feeling to be sitting at the piano for the sound check—I could feel my fingers touching the keys, but somehow there was no connection to my head," he said "But then, as soon as Stan started to play, I felt right at home because I was so used to the sound. He played with such confidence, such authority, that it was tremendously reassuring."[19]

Wim Wigt remembers that Stan Getz was paid a fee of seventeen thousand dollars for the recording, as well as a generous royalty fee. "He was the leader as far as he was concerned," said Wigt, "and so he got the money. Of that, he only gave Chet two thousand dollars. That's Mr. Getz for you. I thought Getz had no class."[20]

The following night, the tour moved on to Baerum, just outside Oslo, in Norway. The concert was broadcast on Norwegian radio, and later issued as a two volume CD, *Quintessence*. Chet's voice is in much better shape on this occasion, and McNeely contributes far more, delivering sparkling solos on the likes of 'We'll Be Together Again'. Even Getz seems to have thawed somewhat, perhaps sensing the improvement in Chet's contribution.

The improved atmosphere did not last for long, however. Chet seems to have missed the first of two concerts in Paris, on 23rd February, prompting Getz to complain to Wim Wigt that he was pulling all the weight.

For the first week of the tour, Getz tried to avoid meeting with Chet at all costs, worried that he would give in to temptation. "Backstage he tried not to even see Chet; he tried to avoid him as much as he could," noted the Victor Lewis. "It was like he didn't even want to meet him halfway." According to Getz's biographer Donald L. Maggin, the strain had started to take its toll, and by the second week the saxophonist was drinking and snorting cocaine.[21]

The next stop was Spain, where Chet arrived late at the designated meeting point. "Stan was quite angry about that," recalled Jim McNeely. "He was looking for a reason to get rid of Chet, and not just make it look like he was firing the guy for no good reason. He would come up to me and Victor and George and say, 'So what's it like playing with Chet?' We'd say, 'It's fine'. And he'd say, 'Well, you guys don't have to do that—I could get him fired off the tour if you want'. And we said, 'No. It's fine, we like Chet'. Because all of us knew him, and liked him, and Stan was just looking for us to be the bad guys. We wouldn't go along with that."[22]

In late February, the musicians returned to Paris. They stayed a couple of hours outside the city centre, before catching a bus to the airport next day for a night flight to Saudi Arabia. They were scheduled to play at a sports palace in Jeddah at the invitation of a cultural committee of Western ambassadors, including the American, Swiss and Norwegian ambassadors.

Chet arranged to meet his connection at the airport, and managed to smuggle a small parcel of heroin on to the plane. For the first time on the tour, the two stars had to take the same aeroplane, given the limited number of flights going to Saudi Arabia. "On the plane, Chet ran into George [Mraz] who by this time was pretty toasted—he'd had a few drinks," explained Victor Lewis. "So George didn't know whether he was coming or going at the time. Chet said, 'George, do you want some of this?' George was so drunk at the time, he couldn't tell the difference between coke and heroin. When he comes out, he runs into Stan, and says, 'Stan, do you want some of this?' Stan said, 'OK', went into the bathroom, and quickly saw that it wasn't coke. Stan got an attitude, and flushed the packet down the toilet. Later, Chet runs into George, and says, 'George, have you got my thing?' George said, 'Oh, I gave it to Stan'. Chet says, 'Oh yeah?' with this 'uh-oh' voice. He goes to Stan and says, 'George said he gave you my thing'. Stan said, 'Yeah, and I saw what it was, and flushed it down the toilet'. The look on Chet's face of hurt and disappointment was so endearing; I really felt for him!"[23]

Tensions rose still further when the plane arrived late, at around 3 a.m., and Getz discovered he had left his saxophone on the plane. "The next day they had to put out a call, looking for a Selmer tenor saxophone," said McNeely. "Two people showed up with instruments. I remember one of them had a big, red plastic mouthpiece, and that was the one he used. Luckily we were there for two or three days, and next day, the plane came back to Jeddah, and they were able to deliver the saxophone in time for the second night."[24]

Getz and his girlfriend were not married, and were not permitted to share a hotel room. As a result, they had been invited to stay at the house of the U.S. Ambassador. The ambassador invited Stan Getz and Chet Baker to dinner the next evening. "The ambassador's home is a phenomenal place, Malaysian servants all over," recalled Getz's girlfriend Jane Walsh. "We're going to have dinner at this long table, just he and Chet and Stan and me ... I look over, and Chet's face is on the dining room table; he's nodded out. I immediately called Wigt and said, 'You'd better meet us in Paris tomorrow. Either he goes home or we go home'."[25]

The other members of the band, meanwhile, were discovering first hand what life was like in Saudi Arabia. "I remember thinking this is about as far away as possible from where I grew up," said Victor Lewis. "One day I was reading the guide to the hotel and I see that they have a swimming pool. So I get my trunks, get my towel, and head down to the pool. I go to walk in, and this guy steps in front of me and blocks me from going in. I said, 'Oh, is this the pool here?' He said, 'Yes'. I said, 'Well, I'm going swimming'. He stopped me again. 'Is it open?' 'Yes', he replied. I said, 'Fine!' and started heading in. He stops me again. I said, 'Is something wrong?' 'Yes', he said, 'Today's Tuesday. Tuesday is women's day'. They served us non-alcoholic beer at the hotel. That was pretty strange, not getting my beer after the gig!"[26]

When the band eventually returned to Paris, Getz again confronted Wim Wigt. "Stan told us, 'I don't want to play with him any more. He's taking too many drugs, and I don't want to deal with him'," explained his wife, Ria Wigt. "That may have been true, but he was doing the same thing! He was just trying to use his position to lean on us. At that point we had to make a decision. After discussing the situation with several promoters we decided that we would take Chet off the tour, and let Stan continue. We paid Chet in full for the tour—even the part he didn't play. He said, 'Nobody has ever done this to me before. This is very generous of you, Wim. I can hardly believe it'. He was so pleased. 'You know what', he said. 'Put it in the bank for me. Open a bank account for me'. It was a very cute thing to hear from Chet. When I told people about this story they said, 'Really! Chet said that!'"[27]

Around the time the tour ended, there were tentative plans for a reunion tour with Russ Freeman, Chet's original pianist in the Chet Baker Quartet in the early 1950s; sadly, the plans never materialised. With no tour dates organised, Wim Wigt suggested Chet take part in a recording session with the pianist Kirk Lightsey, who had played with Chet on the notorious Richard Carpenter recording sessions in the summer of 1965.

By this time, Lightsey had settled in Europe, where he had just finished a tour with the legendary tenor saxophonist Dexter Gordon. Wim Wigt had agreed to record the Kirk Lightsey Trio for his record label Timeless, and invited Dexter Gordon and Chet Baker to join the session as special guests. In the event, Dexter Gordon never showed up for the recording session, opting to spend his time enjoying the nightlife in Amsterdam.

Lightsey and Baker were staying at the same hotel, and ran into one another the day before the proposed recording session. "We spoke, and talked about the recording next day," the pianist recalled. "I said, 'What do you want to play? Why don't you bring in some music, and I'll bring in some music, and we'll see what happens'. I kind of expected that we'd be sitting around waiting for him, but he showed up about two hours before we were due to start. He was sitting there waiting for us. He had warmed up all this time, and he was feeling primed. So when we got there, I said, 'Chet, what music did you bring? He went to his bag and pulled out these sheets, put them on the piano. It turned out to be the lyrics to 'Everything Happens to Me'. No music, just the lyrics. We fell on the floor laughing! That started off the date very happily. It was a nice date."[28]

The resulting album, *Everything Happens To Me*, was the first of many recording sessions that Chet made in Studio 44, a recording studio located in Monster, near The Hague in Holland. The studio belonged to Max Bolleman, a Dutch musician and recording engineer. It was a small, intimate studio, and Bolleman succeeded in creating a unique atmosphere than Chet genuinely appreciated. "When I started my studio, he was one of my first clients, so I had almost no experience on those first records," said Bolleman. "*Everything Happens to Me* and *Mr. B* were amongst the first I did, and they were all done in a very, very small studio with a small grand piano. There was no singing booth, and no booth for soft instruments. It was really more of a live situation in a small and cosy studio; maybe that's what Chet liked."

Bolleman recalled one awkward moment during the first recording session, when he was still getting used to the way in which Chet liked to work. "Chet had played one strange note in his first melody. I was a musician for a long time, and picked up on this. I said, 'Excuse me, Chet, I heard something on the second bar of the bridge ... maybe you should listen to it'. He said nothing for three or four minutes. I wondered what was happening, because I couldn't see him; I was sitting round the corner. So I said again, 'Chet … ' He said, 'Max, please. I know what I played. Don't say anything about what I played—please'. I was very taken aback. Later he made a kind of apology, and said, 'I know you meant well, but please leave me alone when I'm sitting and thinking about what I just played'. From that time on, I could do anything for him, and he was crazy about recording with me. We sometimes waited as long as ten minutes after we'd finished the song. Then he'd ask me, 'Well, Max, what do you think? Was it good enough?'"[29]

After the collapse of the tour with Stan Getz, an Italian promoter arranged a tour of Italy. The tour was supposed to feature pianist Michel Graillier, his wife Micheline on drums, and bass player Riccardo Del Fra. Shortly before the tour was due to begin, however, the French pianist got into a drunken rage with his wife and beat her. "Chet said, 'That's it; you're not staying with this guy. You're coming with me'," said Micheline. "I stayed on tour with him for the next three weeks."

Diane Vavra had not yet arrived from California, and Chet's 'elopement' with Micheline Graillier—the daughter of his best friend—caused the only real argument in their long friendship, which extended over twenty years. Micheline was coy about the full extent of their relationship, but seems to have fallen for him at this time. "It was not really a love affair, but we were such close friends, and sometimes we found each other alone," she revealed. "We got closer in Italy, and I think we both felt lonely. I'm very sentimental, and told Chet that I thought I loved him. 'Oh, no, Micheline, I don't want you to love me. I don't want you to be unhappy'."

After playing in Italy, Chet travelled to Denmark in May, where he reunited with the guitarist Doug Raney. He sat in with Raney's quintet, which included pianist Horace Parlan and bass player Jesper Lundgaard. "It didn't turn out to be such a good idea," said Raney. "He preferred that quiet trio setting and we ended up splitting the group up into smaller components—most of the time Chet played with myself and Horace; the saxophone player and the drummer only joined us for a couple of songs."[30]

Chet seems to have played a few gigs with Raney at this time. The final gig took place in Amsterdam in mid-May, with the band taking the train from Paris. They settled in a first-class carriage, Chet dressed entirely in black, sporting a black hat with a red band. A pair of elderly American tourists were clearly unsettled by the arrival of the motley crew of musicians, all travelling with their bulky instruments. The gentleman made the mistake of challenging Chet, asking him if he had a first-class ticket. Chet mumbled a reply, and after a few minutes of uncomfortable silence, the tourist turned to his wife and whispered, "I can't stand that smell." Chet's hearing was always superb, and he got up, and flung open the train window as wide as it would go, the cool breeze blowing straight on to the couple. Recovering his composure, the man eventually asked Chet, "Could you please close the window?" "The window stays open until the smell is completely gone," Chet replied. The tourist tried to reason with him. "We would all like to have a pleasant trip." Chet leaned over, and said, "Listen, asshole, if you fuck with me you'll have the most unpleasant trip you had in your life."

One of Chet's friends in Amsterdam was the American musician Irv Rochlin, a pianist who had a drug habit of his own. Rochlin showed Chet the delights of Zeedijk, the notorious red-light district that was also an easy place to score heroin at that time. He later introduced him to 'Robert', a local physician who was also liked jazz. He was a fan of Chet's music, and eventually became his local supplier.

By this time, Diane Vavra had arrived in Europe. Chet explained to Rochlin that he was thinking of making Amsterdam his home, and was looking to buy a new car. As luck would have it, Rochlin knew a local trumpet player by the name of Evert Hekkema who was looking to sell his Peugeot. "One day my telephone rang, and to my great surprise it was Chet Baker," said Hekkema. "He was looking for a car and had heard that I wanted to unload mine cheap. A little while later I drove with the car to the Crest Hotel in Buitenveldert, where he lived. He took it for spin around the hotel to see how he liked it, and then we agreed on a price. The car was not insured, but that didn't bother him."[31]

The two musicians hit it off, and arranged to meet for a beer later that evening. "Later, while we were drinking a beer at the hotel bar, I told him that when we were young, we used to admire his album covers, and would style our hair just like his," said Hekkema. "Once he had his hair combed back with brilliantine, another time a real short bebop haircut, and we copied it exactly. He was a true teen idol. Chet was moved to hear that. 'It never occurred to me that on the other side of the ocean people tried to act like me'."[32]

Chet later explained to Hekkema that he liked Amsterdam, and was looking for a place to stay when he passed through. Hekkema offered him a room in his four-bedroom apartment, situated on the second floor of a house at the Da Costakade, a delightful location near two intersecting canals. He charged him just one hundred guilders a week (approximately sixty dollars). Over the next few years, Chet stayed in the apartment for a few weeks each year until 1986.

Given Chet's condition at this time, it is hardly surprising to learn that Hekkema remembers Chet's behaviour in the apartment as being somewhat erratic. On one occasion, he recalled, Chet walked to the toilet, stopping in front of a mirror in the hallway. "Mirror, mirror, on the wall," he muttered, "Who's the fairest of them all?" He remained silent for a few seconds, examining his lined features. "Not you, motherfucker," he said to himself, continuing his way to the bathroom.

On another occasion, Chet left his house keys in the car, and then forgot where he had parked the car. He rang the doorbell of the downstairs neighbour, introduced himself, and explained what had happened. He asked if he could access the alleyway at the back of the house, then clambered up two floors, just as easily as he had broken into the Riverside Records warehouse back in 1958.

In late May, Wim Wigt invited Chet to make a solo recording for Timeless Records. Chet invited pianist Michel Graillier and bass player Riccardo Del Fra to accompany him, his argument over Michel's treatment of his wife evidently forgotten. Riccardo Del Fra believes that the trio recording marked something of a departure for Chet after the SteepleChase recordings from 1979. "I think that Michel, because of his more European style, or French approach, added to the individuality of the trio that we had," he explained. "We didn't invent anything special, but if you put Niels Henning, Doug Raney and Chet together, you inevitably get a more 'bop' approach. But playing with Michel and myself, he ended up with more of a hybrid style, perhaps—something different."[33]

The three musicians had not played as a trio that frequently at that point, but chose a selection of tunes they had played with Chet on a regular basis. "The tunes that we recorded were the ones we played during our concerts, even if we played shorter versions for the record," said Del Fra. "I remember we specifically discussed the length of the tunes, maybe so we could put more tunes on the record. We used to play 'Beatrice', 'Dolphin Dance', and Chet was happy for us to record these tunes."[34]

Chet was in great shape that day, and the recording session went very smoothly. "You can sense that Chet was very creative and efficient," the bass player continued. "There's a fantastic solo by Chet on 'Beatrice', the

Sam Rivers tune. I think it was the first take, and the solo was just perfect. If you want to examine it technically, there is just one G that is not correct; a G flat chord at the end of the form. That's the only little thing. Of course, it could be taken as a chromatic approach to something else. But the form of the solo is just perfect, even when you see it on paper; you notice all the rhythmic devices and variations that he chooses, the silences, and where they arrive, the use of triplets, is just fantastic. When you see this, you think that someone must have been thinking for months before playing such a solo. But no, this was just a natural thing. You can imagine it was hard; I had to take a solo after him. In a sense, you don't realise how perfect is until later; but you know that there is something strong going on, and then it's up to you. That's when you learn to play with silence, rather than overplay, and fill the space with less useful stuff."[35]

The recording session again took place in Studio 44 in Monster, and the recording engineer, Max Bolleman, did everything he could to make Chet feel relaxed in the studio. "Chet was very particular," he remembered. "He was always sitting on a chair, never standing up. He was blowing almost on the floor. He was bending over with his trumpet, and I had to put a microphone on a very low stand on the floor to record him. That made him comfortable. I was a musician for thirty-five years, and I know it's important to make the musicians feel easy-going and relaxed." Despite this, there were still some technical difficulties to overcome. "On the early record, in between his singing and playing, he was coughing like hell, so loud," he laughed. "I had to erase all these parts on the tape; there were only four tracks at that time, only a small machine. So it was a very hard job for me to do these records right."[36]

The resulting album, *Mr. B*, was one of Chet's finest later recordings. There are numerous highlights; the trio's mid-tempo read of 'Dolphin Dance' is always a delight to hear, as is the slow reading of 'Ellen and David', where you almost hear Graillier and Del Fra slow to meet Chet's measured pace. Last, but not least, it's worth paying attention to Chet's exquisite solo on 'Beatrice'. "The only thing that dates the record is the sound," said Del Fra. "I was just happy to be there at the time—now I am much more demanding in the studio. For me, sometimes the bass is not loud enough, not round enough, or there's too much of the pick-up, and not enough of an acoustic sound. You can hear the pick-up on *Mr. B*. Despite that, the record does have a timeless quality."

One week later, on June 4th, Chet flew to Sweden to take part in a local jazz festival, where he was due to perform with a twenty-three-year-old local pianist, Melker Isaksson, and his trio. "Some of the local musicians did their part to scare me by telling me how unfriendly and wicked Chet could be sometimes," said Isaksson. "I hadn't heard too many of his records, so I started to study his repertoire, buying his records and even rehearsing some of the arrangements so I would be able to cope with this 'tough guy'."[37]

On the night of the concert, rumours circulated that Chet was in a foul mood, berating the festival staff about the arrangements. But by the time he went on stage, his mood had apparently brightened. "He must have felt my nerves because he just sat down with me and said, 'Hello, I'm Chet. What would you like to play?' What a relief! We went on stage and then it was just ... I can't find the words; it was so fabulously easy to play with him. It felt as if there was some kind of musical warmth all over the stage that lifted me and the whole trio, and made us play as never since. It was simply one of the most important nights in my career as a musician. We played five sets with Chet that night, finishing at after four o'clock in the morning. It was incredible!"[38]

As the summer approached, Diane Vavra showed signs of concern over Chet's growing drug use. 'Robert', Chet's new contact in Amsterdam, had started to supply him with barbiturates as well as heroin. Ruth Young had known it was best to keep him away from barbiturates, but Diane learned the hard way. "They made Chet completely crazy," she said. "Boy, it was scary." As the only non-heroin user amongst Chet's close friends in Europe, she was starting to feel left out. One day she asked Riccardo Del Fra, who was still snorting at this time, how much she could inhale without getting hooked.

Things were made worse by the arrival in Europe of Chet's friend and drug buddy, Leo Mitchell, who joined Chet and Diane in Rome over the next few weeks. While they were staying in Rome, Chet used to stop by at a small club, the Manoia, where he would listen to a Brazilian pianist by the name of Jim Porto. "My music is bossa nova, and I didn't know much about jazz musicians," said Porto. "Somebody said, 'Do you know who's in the club tonight? Chet Baker!' I said, 'Who is Chet Baker?' They told me that he was one of the most famous jazz trumpeters in the world. He came to talk with me after my performance. He told me that he liked my music, and would come back the following night to listen to me. He came back the next night, and the next night, coming with his trumpet."[39]

Jim Porto was in the process of recording his first album, ironically working with fellow Brazilian Rique Pantoja, who had recorded and toured with Chet in the summer of 1980. Chet offered to play trumpet on the album. "I need to talk to the producer about the money," said Porto, "because I thought he'd be very expensive. He said, 'It's not about the money. There are two things that are important. I don't want to record on a precise day—I want to be available to record with you at some time. Secondly, I hate hotels. I've finished my tour, and I'm in a hotel, but I want to stay in this neighbourhood'. I lived in an area called Trastevere, which is like the Village in New York. I said, 'Listen, my house is not too big, but if you want to, you can come and stay in my house'. He said, 'Perfect. Can Diane stay as well?' I only have one bedroom, so I slept in the living room, and let them sleep in my bedroom."

The unusual living arrangements lasted for the next five or six weeks. "I was told he had a problem with drugs, but he never, ever talked about drugs with me," the pianist explained. "He was a very gentle man. But Diane used to talk about drugs; every day she complained, how they need to change their lifestyle. But she was using drugs too. They never disturbed me. The only problem was that the spoons in my house were always black!"[40]

Chet eventually told Jim Porto he was ready to record his solos, but on the day of the recording, his trumpet had mysteriously vanished. "He said, 'Jim, there's something I have to tell you—I don't have my trumpet'. I said, 'What? Your trumpet was in the living room'. He said, 'It's not there. I gave my trumpet to somebody. I was with Diane in the Campo di Fiori, and we needed money. I gave my trumpet as a deposit'. That's when I understood he'd given his trumpet to some dealer. I talked to Sandro (Melaranci), my producer. He was a nice person, and came to talk to Chet. Chet told him the story, and Sandro asked, 'Do you remember the person?' Chet said, 'Sure, he's always there, in front of the monument'. At that time I had a small Volkswagen, and the four of us got in the car and drove to the Campo di Fiori. Chet pointed, and said, 'That's the man, over there!' Sandro said, 'OK guys, I'll go over, you stay here'. Sandro went up to him and said, 'Listen, my uncle came here a few days ago and left his trumpet'. The dealer said, 'That old son of a bitch! He came here looking for drugs, but he had no money, so I asked him for his trumpet'. Sandro said, 'Listen, give him back the trumpet. He can't sleep at night because he can't play. He's breaking my balls. He's in mourning!' The dealer said, 'OK, if you give me a hundred dollars, I'll give it back to you'. The day after we went to the studio to record the first song. He played on four songs on my album."[41]

Jim Porto and Chet Baker, Rome, June 1983.

Chet was not in particularly good shape on the day of the recording. "When he recorded the song 'Arbour Way', he left to go to the bathroom two or three times. So we cut the song a few times—some were good, some were not good. Then one time he played beautifully, a wonderful improvisation, and I shouted out, 'Yeah, Chet, yeah, yeah!' They recorded my voice, too, and then you can hear me laugh. I was very happy!" But for Rique Pantoja, it was sad to see him in that state. "He'd play a bit, then hang his head. From a musical standpoint, it was disappointing to see him this way."

Away from the influence of his Italian dealer, Chet was in much better shape. He reunited with guitarist Philip Catherine and bass player Jean-Louis Rassinfosse for a series of concerts in Spain, starting with a show in Barcelona. "The Barcelona concert that we did together was fantastic, and it was because of this that we decided to record our first album [*Chet Baker—Philip Catherine—Jean-Louis Rassinfosse*] later that year," the bass player explained. The same promoter arranged a short tour of Spain with Art Blakey's Jazz Messengers and Tete Montoliu, the blind Catalan piano player. "That was interesting because Chet and Art were very friendly—they sat at the back of the bus together, talking about things. Chet was much more open with some musicians; with producers and concert organisers he could be quite quiet, quite shy. When he got to know you better, he was like an oyster. When you first touch the oyster, it stays closed for a long time. It gradually opens, and if there's no danger, it opens more."[42]

Later that month, Chet appeared at the jazz festival in Juan-les-Pins in the south of France. Paul Bley, who had played piano with Chet in early 1955, was also appearing at the festival and decided to look him up. "I found the hotel, called upstairs, and said, 'Chet, Paul Bley here, remember we played together in the 50s'. He said, 'Yeah, come on up'. When I went upstairs he was in bed with a lady alto player, very beautiful. So when I came up, he asked if I had brought anything with me for him, and I said, 'No', not knowing what he meant—but everybody else knew what he meant! And I said, 'First, Chet, I'd like to take this opportunity to thank you very much for the wonderful phone call you made from Los Angeles to New York to ask me to join the band at Jazz City. It was snowing in New York, the call came from out of the blue'. Chet turned to me and said, 'You called me!' Of course I called him ... I was freezing in New York, and he was in California. He didn't need to call New York for a piano player. I must have been a very ambitious young man!"[43]

In early August, Chet was booked to play one week at The Canteen, a small club at Covent Garden in London. His appearance attracted the interest of the English pop singer Elvis Costello, who was in the process of recording his eighth album, *Punch The Clock*. He had written a song called 'Shipbuilding' for the singer and musician Robert Wyatt, and had decided to record a version of his own.

"I had been speaking with the record company about who might play the solo on this thing," Costello explained in an interview with *Jazz Times*. "I had got it in my head that we wanted trumpet, and I didn't know any trumpet player in England that I thought would necessarily be right to do it—except maybe my father. There was definitely a sense that the sound I wanted was a particular plaintiveness that I was completely obsessed with—the "Round About Midnight' record by Miles; more than *Kind of Blue* or some more famous record. I actually had a conversation with Wynton (Marsalis) about doing it—this was kind of like when he had just made one record. We had one conversation on the phone, and I think he was totally bewildered some guy from England calls him to come play on a record, and he couldn't do it. It wasn't until later that I realised that, 'Hey, that's that guy I spoke to on the phone, that Wynton; that famous Wynton guy's this guy I talked to about doing the record'. So, Wynton's not going to do it; guess Miles isn't going to do it—who knew how to ask him? And there wasn't anybody in England I trust, and I open the *Melody Maker* and Chet Baker is playing the next day. And he's only my favorite trumpet player—as far as I can tell, alive—that I can actually get to speak to, or so I thought. Maybe if I go down there and ask if he'll play, all he can say is, 'No.'"[44]

The next night, Costello went down to the club with a view to asking him. "Everybody's talking right through everything," he recalled. "He's playing so beautifully. He isn't playing standards. He actually has a band that knows his material, which is very rare for him. And at the interval he just walked off the stand, and he went up to the bar and bought a drink and nobody bothered him—[the audience] just kept on eating and talking and yakking. I went up to him and introduced myself—he had no idea; he had never heard of me. I said, 'I'm a musician. Is there any way in the world you would consider coming and playing on a session'. He said, 'Well, yeah, I'll do it for scale'. I said, 'How about we give you double scale?'"[45]

Chet agreed to come to the recording studio next day. The song had an unusual chord structure, and the band—The Attractions—went through the tune a couple of times. Looking back, Costello's only regret was that he chose to add reverb to the trumpet solo. "I almost wanted to remix it," he admitted, "but then we'd have to remix all the other elements, and the record is very beautiful. And there is so much embellished playing on the record that's glorious."

At the end of the recording session, Costello handed Chet a copy of a single he had recorded by the name of 'Almost Blue'. "I wrote it in 1981 after spending a lot of time with a couple of Chet Baker's vocal albums. I fell in love with the Brown/Henderson composition 'The Thrill Is Gone' and resolved to write a song modelled on Chet's rendition of it. My version of 'Almost Blue' was recorded for the album *Imperial Bedroom*." Costello assumed that Chet would never have the chance to listen to the song, and was pleasantly surprised to be given a tape recording of Chet singing it at a club in Cannes, in the south of France—recorded just one year before his death. "It turned out to be from a scene in Bruce Weber's Baker documentary *Let's Get Lost*, where, not for the first time in his life, Chet was attempting to perform for an audience of drunken, self-satisfied idiots," he later wrote. "It was pretty much as I had first encountered him and all the more heartbreaking being that I was not able to thank him for even attempting to play my tune."

Costello found the vocal recording somewhat harrowing, and was disappointed that it did not include one of Chet's trumpet solos, as he had originally envisioned. He later heard a second version of the song from the excellent *Chet Baker in Tokyo* album, recorded one month later on his tour of Japan. "It finds Chet much more at ease with the tune," he noted. "It is to my great delight that this arrangement also includes a trumpet solo and that the song finally sounds pretty much as I dreamed it would."

Diane Vavra argued with Chet about his drug intake at this time. The incident that provoked the argument remains unclear, but it probably occurred when Chet again hocked his trumpet for drug money. Diane was also concerned about her own drug use, which had escalated in the three months she had been in Europe. She had messed around with heroin for several weeks, but disliked the side effects, complaining to Micheline Graillier that she was suffering from stomach and leg cramps. She made a conscious decision to quit heroin, but felt the need to return to California to clear her head.

As a consequence, Chet travelled to Norway alone to play at a jazz festival in Vadsø, which was close to the Russian border. He was scheduled to play with the Norwegian pianist Per Husby, and his trio, which consisted of Terje Venaas on bass and Ole Jacob Hansen on drums. "Chet was wearing beach sandals, a newly acquired Stetson-type hat, corduroy jeans and a thin sweater," the pianist later recalled. "All very well for most places, but not for a place situated at the same latitude as Point Barrow, Alaska, and having Murmansk, Russia, as the nearest major city. Chet was visibly hurt when [a] stupid lady approached him and claimed he was wearing the hat "to look special." "I don't think I need a hat to be special," he remarked."[46]

Chet had turned up to the festival without his trumpet, prompting a panic as the organisers tried to find a replacement amongst the town's four thousand inhabitants. "The horn arrived about twenty-five minutes before the concert, which gave us exactly fifteen minutes for a combined sound check and rehearsal for a one-and-a-half hour concert," said Husby.[47]

Opening the concert, Chet wandered on to the stage, turned to the trio, and said, "Let's play 'Dig'." He proceeded to count out the tempo, and then started playing 'Mr. B', to the confusion of the band. The music quickly ground to a halt. "What's the matter—did I start in the wrong key?" he asks. "No, wrong tune." "Oh!" He turned back and addressed the audience, way off mike. "As you'll gather, we've got this concert timed to the nearest split second!"

After the initial confusion, Chet played well, and the band's performance was well received. Chet expressed dissatisfaction with his own playing, however, promising Husby, "I can play better than that."

Two days later, he kept his promise, returning to Oslo to play at the 'Hot House' club. On this occasion Husby borrowed a trumpet from his next door neighbour, who played for a local big band in his spare time. The man spent most of the afternoon washing and polishing his trumpet to leave it in the best possible condition for Chet. "People still come up to me to this day and say that the evening was electrifying, and their best jazz club experience ever," said Husby. "He had such stamina. He was playing long solos, and with such control. Quite a few people were very surprised by hearing his technical control. They had thought he would be lyrical, but not technically that good. There were quite a few trumpeters in the audience who commented on his command of the instrument. My sense was that he was very dependent on the people he was playing with, and of course the state he was in. But when he was comfortable, and there was no pressure on him one way or the other, he was a brilliant instrumentalist."

Chet had evidently promised Diane he would try to stay away from heroin while she was away. Per Husby remembers joining Chet for breakfast one morning at the hotel, and noticing he had a glass of methadone at the table. "I said to him, 'What happens to you when you take that?' He said, 'If I take it, I stay normal'. I said, 'What would happen if I took one?' He said, 'It would send you through the roof; I would never give you one'." This helps to explain why Chet was in relatively good shape on this tour, and played with such intensity.[48]

Wim Wigt had tried to line up some other gigs for Chet late summer, but when they fell through, Chet ended up returning to Norway—this time touring the west of the country with pianist Erling Aksdal and bass player Bjorn Alterhaug. "I toured with Chet Baker twice," Aksdal recalled. "A short tour in 1983, and a longer tour in 1984. It was like touring with two different people. The first tour he was in tremendous shape, and very, very nice. He was energetic, looked well, and a great guy in all respects, and he played beautifully. On the second tour, he was strung out. He brought Diane Vavra with him, but they kept fighting. So they were two different experiences, both musically and personally."[49]

One week later, Chet returned to Oslo where he reunited with Per Husby's trio, and played one night at Club 7. "The concert was advertised as starting at 9 p.m.," said Husby."Earlier, I had told the booking manager at the club that I could not be there before about 9.15 due to another engagement. He said to me that this was quite OK with them, they would just postpone the start of the programme till I arrived. When I came in, however, Chet was already on stage sitting at the piano singing, accompanying himself together with bass and drums. It turned out that due to some administrative cock-up, the people in charge that night had not been informed about the delay from the booking manager, and they had been very cross with me for not turning up on time. At the interval, Chet told me 'They seemed a bit annoyed so I just went up to cover for you till you arrived. I don't understand why they made such a fuss about it—I thought I was doing OK up there!' I always thought this was yet another sweet little gesture—he did it to save my ass, so to speak, but did not want to start the real gig without me. Also he seemed concerned the people in the club didn't think what he was doing was good enough."[50]

Back at Chet's hotel, Husby and the band's drummer, Ole Jacob Hansen, were watching the 1980s soap opera *Dynasty* on TV. "Chet was giving away these hilarious, alternative lines for people to say. I said to Chet, 'When you turn sixty, you should start writing scripts for comedy'. He just looked at me and said, 'I'll never reach sixty!' Unfortunately, he was right."[51]

In September, Chet returned to Paris. He initially reunited with pianist Michel Graillier and bass player Riccardo Del Fra—the trio that had recorded the excellent *Mr. B* earlier that year. A bootleg-style recording, *A Trumpet For The Sky*, was made of their gig at Club 21 in Paris on September 2nd. Chet's playing that night was superb—crisp, clean solos, full of ideas, supported by fine, responsive musicians. Unfortunately, the poor sound quality means that these recordings are virtually unlistenable, much of the fine music buried beneath the sound of Del Fra's bass.

Later that month Chet teamed up with two Belgian musicians, guitarist Philip Catherine and bass player Jean-Louis Rassinfosse. They had been playing together on an occasional basis for two-and-a-half years, and had reached the stage where there was a growing empathy between the musicians.

Catherine readily admits that he initially had little interest in playing with Chet Baker. His background was in fusion and rock. "I played with Chet for the first time in 1981," he said. "At the time I thought he was only a mediocre musician—a spent veteran, living off his former fame. The guy had a bad reputation at the time. But his playing still had something magical, and it was a fantastic concert. The second concert took place in Switzerland. After twenty minutes, it started to go so well that I got into a kind of trance. It was as if everything was going by itself."[52]

Given Catherine's background, it took time for the musicians to find a common repertoire. "He played the jazz standards, and at the beginning of the 1980s that was not my strong suit," he admitted. "Chet was notorious for rarely arranging things for his sidemen beforehand. He just sat down and started to blow. Fortunately, he never did that with me. I said right off at the first concert, 'Chet, if you want to play something that I don't know, you have to rehearse it with me briefly'. And so he always chose things that we all knew."[53]

After a magical concert in Barcelona in early July, the three musicians agreed that they should reconvene in September to record an album together. The recording session was scheduled to take place in Brussels, for a small Belgian record label. Chet turned up to the studio strung out, however, in no fit state to play. "The first time he was really fucked up, he couldn't play well, you know," said Philip Catherine. "And we decided we were not going to release an album like that."[54]

To his credit, Chet felt guilty about what had happened, and offered to make amends. "A few days later he called me," said Jean-Louis Rassinfosse. "He said, 'We should do it again. I don't think I was in very good shape for the recording. I won't charge you this time'. I booked a good studio in Brussels, owned by a friend of mine, but then we discovered a big problem. At 3 p.m. someone called me to let me know that Philip and Chet were traveling from Paris, but couldn't make it to Brussels because of a train strike. I ended up driving the 300km to Paris to pick them up, returned to Brussels, and started the recording session at 10 p.m."[55]

Despite the late start, the recording session went fairly smoothly second time around. "It was very relaxed, we just played on the spot," recalled Rassinfosse. "For instance, Philip had never played 'Cherokee' before. We were playing in the same room. Philip was playing with no amp, I was playing a strange electric contrabass that I had been using at that time, and Chet was playing without headphones, and could hear almost nothing. We had a small timing problem in the middle of 'Cherokee', but it came back very naturally, as we followed his timing. It was unbelievable—his timing was just impeccable. This was the first tune we played; we played quite fast, and it was clear his chops were in good shape."[56]

The only problem occurred a couple of hours into the recording session, when Chet announced that he needed to take heroin. "I had to arrange a connection for him," Rassinfosse said. "He was getting a bit nervous for a while. This led to a long break in the session, but aside from that, it went well, and nearly all of the recordings were first takes."[57]

The album was later released as *Chet Baker—Philip Catherine—Jean-Louis Rassinfosse*, and is the first—and probably the best—of the numerous albums the trio recorded together. Highlights include a gentle amble through Horace Silver's 'Strollin', with Catherine taking a pleasing solo, Rassinfosse offering fine support before taking a solo of his own. Richie Beirach's 'Leaving' is another gem; listen to the way Catherine responds to Chet's introduction for an example of how the chemistry worked within the band. 'Estaté', from João Gilberto's 1977 album *Amoroso*, brings the album to a close, the gentle samba fitting in with the relaxed feel of the session.

In late September, Chet returned to Sweden to play with pianist Åke Johansson's trio, which comprised of bass player Kjell Jansson and drummer Göran Levin. The tour had been arranged by Göran Levin, who had evidently contacted Wim Wigt about his availability. Chet met with the band at the Nefertiti jazz club in Gothenburg, where the band rehearsed for one day before embarking on a ten-day tour. As with his previous Scandinavian tours earlier that year, Chet was in good shape—sticking to methadone, rather than heroin, and his chops in good shape as a result of playing on a regular basis.

"Chet was very reliable, no problems at all," recalled Kjell Jansson. "He was very good with us, and we had a great time on the road. The band played with many American musicians in the 1980s and 1990s, and he was one of the best—both as a musician and as a person. The audience reaction was very good—they loved him. There were many people everywhere, and they came with their records they wanted him to sign."[58]

The tour was captured on a live recording at the Nefertiti Jazz Club in Gothenburg on the last night of the tour. "I was quite nervous because there were so many people," recalled Jansson. "Even in the back room we didn't have any space, no time for ourselves, because it was packed!" The album—released on Sweden's Dragon Records—is not one of Chet's better-known recordings from the 1980s, and deserves wider recognition. The recording quality is superb, capturing every nuance of the music played that night, and the material is excellent, with fine versions of Sam Rivers' 'Beatrice' and Charlie Haden's 'Ellen David'.

The following month, Chet reunited with pianist Michel Graillier and bass player Riccardo Del Fra for a three-week tour of Italy. They were accompanied by flute player Nicola Stilo, who was becoming a regular member of Chet's band, and American drummer Leo Mitchell. Chet also invited his Dutch landlord Evert Hekkema, a fellow trumpet player, to join the tour. "That's true, but he wasn't really in the band," said Stilo. "He just played a few songs, from time to time. I'm not sure the exact reason he joined us, but Chet used to spend a lot of time in Amsterdam."[59]

The atmosphere on this tour—unlike his tours of Scandinavia—was somewhat heavy. Chet, Graillier, Stilo and Mitchell were full-blown heroin addicts, and Del Fra was an occasional user, too. "Sometimes I was the only one who was awake," said Del Fra. "I'd have to take care of the tickets, because everyone else was loaded." The tour also involved extensive travelling, with the band driving as much as three hundred miles between gigs. Michel Graillier and Evert Hekkema shared most of the driving, with Chet resting in the back of the van with his girlfriend Diane Vavra.[60]

Despite the difficult logistics, Del Fra and Stilo remember the tour fondly from a musical perspective. "We played in nice little theatres," said Del Fra. "We didn't have arrangements organised, as you would do it today, but we got organised little by little by playing, almost by tacit convention. In this way it was authentic jazz, emerging from a jazz session. We'd develop an idea here, an idea there, then we'd use those ideas in the next concert, and after a while, they'd stay. It was a nice period from that point of view." Stilo also welcomed the consistency, playing with a steady line-up for the first time since he had started playing with Chet.[61]

"We arrived late only once, and that was the grandest gig of the whole tour. In the Conservatory of Turin, an enormous domed hall," Evert Hekkema said. "We reached the city on time, but Chet still had to buy something, and finally we were an hour late. A whole crowd of men were sitting in tuxedos, and ladies in evening gowns. The Italian manager who had organised the concert was there too, completely stressed out. He was furious at us. He wouldn't talk to Chet. Chet said laconically, 'Don't worry. We'll tell him that a headlight broke'. 'I think that's rather a lame excuse', I said. 'It's good enough', Chet answered casually."[62]

Chet finally made it on stage more than one hour after the scheduled start of the concert. He looked terrible, wearing a red sweater, dotted with dark bloodstains where he had injected himself in the neck before the show, and hotel bathroom slippers. "He sat down and started with 'Beatrice', a piece by Sam Rivers," Hekkema recalled. "After the first note an ovation broke out.

Everyone was so glad he was finally playing. And the trumpet sounded so fantastic in that gigantic space."[63]

The only record of the tour was a low-key studio recording in Milan, which was later released as *At Capolinea.* The band had played several nights at the Capolinea Club in Milan, one of the older jazz clubs in the city. The club's owner had a small recording studio at the back of the club, and invited the band to record and album. The session was noteworthy for two main reasons. First of all, Chet invited Diane Vavra to join the recording session, the first and only occasion she recorded with Chet. She was comfortable playing with the band in hotels and backstage, but still suffered from a lack of self-confidence. The album also marks the growing maturity of Nicola Stilo, who sounds more confident than on his earlier recordings, and contributes two compositions of his own.

"We recorded for two days, but worked well into the night, with Michel and I working on arrangements," recalled Stilo. "Diane was a very good musician, but she was a little nervous about recording with the band. She had a good relationship with the band, especially with me, over the first couple of years. After that, things changed, and she had some problems with Chet's lifestyle. We did two or three takes of some tunes, and Diane played differently on each version. When we came to mix the record, Chet and I made a choice between the different recordings. Diana was not pleased with some of the choices we'd made, and thought she'd played better on some of the other versions. But we made the choice based on the performance of the whole band, not just Diane's playing."[64]

Whilst *At Capolinea* is a fine recording, bass player Riccardo Del Fra still feels it failed to capture the band playing as well as they had done on stage. "I have nice memories of the recording," he recalled, "but the concerts we were playing were even better! We played together every night in a different city, and really felt like we were progressing. It's a shame they were not recorded."[65]

After the tour of Italy, Wim Wigt had arranged a twenty-date tour of Europe, this time accompanied by a 'Danish' band—bass player Jesper Lundgaard and American pianist Duke Jordan, a long-term resident of Copenhagen. The tour was something of a disaster, however. Chet was exhausted by the tour of Italy, and only showed up for five of the scheduled concerts. The situation was probably exacerbated by the continued presence of Leo Mitchell, a fellow addict. Three of the concerts were recorded for the Japanese record label Marshmallow, and they make for something of a mixed bag. "When he showed up, Chet sounded beautiful," said Lundgaard. "The recording of 'September Song' in Paris was a nice and concentrated experience."[66]

Chet's poor condition on this final tour should not detract from what had been a successful year, both in terms of his recorded output, and the overall quality of his playing. After the 'annus horribilis' of 1982, when Chet allowed his renewed addiction to take over his life, culminating in the breakdown of his relationship with Ruth Young, he had been able to get his life back on track, at least within the confines of his condition. To some extent he had Wim Wigt to thank for this; the abortive tour with Stan Getz once again raised Chet's profile in Europe. Wigt had, of course, arranged for two excellent studio recordings, *Everything Happens To Me*, with Kirk Lightsey, and *Mr. B*, with Michel Graillier and Riccardo Del Fra. Subsequent tours arranged by Wigt had met with mixed success, but showed that when Chet stayed relatively clean—as he did in Scandinavia—he could still play to the highest standard.

For Wigt himself, it had been a steep learning curve. "In the first year, he was completely unreliable," he told Dutch author Jeroen de Valk. "He didn't show up for half the gigs, a cancellation rate of 50%. Little by little, things got better. Because I got used to him. I took his habits into account. I learned that you always had to give him ample time to get somewhere. I learned to factor in the ups and downs of his frame of mind."

"You have to picture it like a curve—a curve with valleys during the times when he used too much and spun out of control," he continued. "Then he would fly to America to relax, and after a few months would return."

As the year came to and end, Diane flew back to the United States to spend some time with her son, and escape the pressures of life on the road. Chet stayed in Europe, blissfully unaware of the valley that was approaching.

Chapter Eighteen

DIANE
1984–1985

"Prince—I've never heard of him."
"He's a little like Michael Jackson."
"OK, I've heard of him ... "—Chet Baker, in conversation with Micheline Graillier[1]

In early 1984, Chet began his descent into one of the 'valleys' Wim Wigt referred to, and would not emerge until his return from the United States in early 1985. The period was marked by a reduced reliance on methadone, which tended to moderate Chet's behaviour, and increased use of heroin, which made him more unpredictable, capable of wild mood swings and even memory loss.

Nicola Stilo also noted that Chet was starting to mix different cocktails of drugs. "He had different doctors everywhere," said Stilo. "It was not just a problem of heroin or cocaine; he was taking pills, everything." One of Chet's preferred cocktails was a 'speedball', which refers to the combined use of heroin and cocaine in the same syringe. The theory is that the cocaine acts as a stimulant, negating the sedatory effects of the heroin, and allowing the user to stay awake, and enjoy the euphoria associated with the heroin without nodding out. But Stilo noted that the cocaine had an intense impact on Chet, resulting in extreme paranoia. It was also a dangerous game to play—speedballs have been associated with many celebrity deaths in recent years, including John Belushi, Lowell George, River Phoenix and Hillel Slovak, to name but a few.[2]

Chet was also taking more amphetamines, courtesy of his new supplier in Amsterdam. The side effects included hallucinations, as witnessed by Chet's landlord at this time, Evert Hekkema. Diane Vavra stayed in California in the winter of 1983/84, but Chet was convinced that Hekkema had hidden her in the house. He ran into the attic, calling her name, and when that failed he ran barefoot and wild-eyed into the icy streets. "Diane! I know you're there!"

The problem was probably exacerbated by the fact that Diane was less adept at handling Chet's problems than his previous girlfriend Ruth Young. Whilst Ruth was also prone to wild, hysterical behaviour of her own, she was more in tune with Chet's day-to-day requirements. She had known to keep Chet away from barbiturates, for example, and the problems they could cause.

In addition, Ruth was a more constant presence in Chet's life, and rarely left his side in the nine years they were together. Diane, by contrast, would return to the United States when times got tough, leaving Chet to fend for himself for months at a time—something he was ill-equipped to do. Left to his own devices, Chet would inevitably seek solace in drugs, his behaviour becoming more extreme, more anti-social, as the years went by.

Micheline Graillier had an alternative explanation for Chet's growing drug use at this time. She was convinced that Wim Wigt's extensive tour schedules were taking their toll on Chet's health.

This last explanation seems a little harsh. Wigt himself realised that he needed to take Chet's lifestyle into account, and adapted his tour schedules accordingly. In later years, he even appointed an individual tour manager, Peter Huijts, to look after Chet's day-to-day requirements. "There may have been times when Chet had to take long, tiring trips, but he wanted to work," explained Wigt's wife, Ria Wigt. "But my husband is one of the best bookers in the world, and made sure Chet had a lot of bookings. For some people, it may have been tiring, but Chet was happy about it."

It might be more reasonable to suggest that Chet's lifestyle was finally beginning to catch up with him. Chet was now fifty-four years old. In addition to his high drug intake, he had a poor diet. Norwegian pianist Per Husby remembers Chet as eating very little on his first tour of Norway in 1983. "I've got to stop losing weight like this," he once remarked, "but I have no appetite at all." Indeed, photographs from this era suggest that Chet was looking increasingly frail, his hollowed cheeks, furrowed face and unkempt appearance suggesting he was closer to seventy years old.[3]

Chet is thought to have spent Christmas 1983 in California. According to an interview in *Musica Jazz*, he was scheduled to appear at a show at Carnegie Hall on 21st January 1984, but there are no records of this show having taken place, and he seems to have returned to Europe at this time. Diane opted to stay in California for a few more weeks, and did not return to Europe until April.[4]

Chet was not particularly active over this period. He spent a few weeks in Amsterdam, after which he went to Paris, where he played a gig at the Petit Opportun club with pianist Michel Graillier and bass player Riccardo Del Fra. In February, he spent a few weeks living with Giampiero Giusti in Florence, but Chet's drug use prompted one of the few arguments between the two old friends. "I let Chet use my car from time to time, and after a while, I found out he was driving hundreds and hundreds of miles, driving to Rome, to see Nicola Stilo, to score, or to Switzerland, where he knew a doctor," said Giusti.[5]

His Italian tour manager put together a tour of Italy in March. Chet's regular bass player at this time, Riccardo Del Fra, seems to have been unavailable for much of the tour, presumably due to a prior engagement. For most of the concerts, the band consisted of a quartet of Chet Baker, Nicola Stilo on flute, Michel Graillier on piano, and Enzo Pietropaoli on bass. The tour seems to have taken in a number of regional Italian cities, including Rimini, Bergamo, Cusercoli, Torino, San Severino and Pescara, before concluding with four nights in Florence and one night in Rome, at the Music Inn. The tour was witnessed by the Italian photographer, Francesco 'Cecco' Maino, who noted that Chet was in very poor shape. "He kept nodding all the time as if he wanted to go to sleep," he said, "then finally one night he fell down from his stool to the ground."[6]

Diane returned to Europe in April, and joined Chet for a one-month tour of Sweden. Following the success of their tour in 1983, Göran Levin, drummer with the Åke Johansson Trio, contacted Wim Wigt about Chet's availability for an extensive tour, taking in twenty-four towns and cities. Diane's return seems to have stabilised Chet's drug intake, and he was in better shape on this tour. "Chet didn't talk very much, he was quite a silent person," recalled the band's bass player Kjell Jansson. "We had some fun, going out to restaurants and enjoying a drink." Chet's relationship with Diane also seemed to be on an even keel as a result. "They seemed to be very close," Jansson recalled. "They had their problems, too, but it must be tough for two people to live that kind of life, sharing a hotel room, travelling in a bus."[7]

The biggest problem on the tour seems to have been the loss of Göran Levin, who suffered from a stroke after the first few gigs. "I had to drive him to hospital in Västerås," said Jansson. "He was the road manager for the whole tour. We had a lot of trouble getting a replacement—I think we had three other drummers for the rest of the tour. I had to take over as road manager, and did most of the driving. The piano player, Åke Johansson, was blind, so we had to take care of him, too."[8]

From a musical perspective, the tour was a success, however. "He was the first musician I've played with who played behind me when I was playing bass solos," said Jansson. "He played small phrases behind me. I'd never seen this before; normally when a soloist stops playing he leaves the stage, or waits for his things, but Chet was in the band all the time. Sometimes he'd shout, 'Yeah!' when he heard a good phrase on the piano. It was good to hear things like that."

This brief period of stability was all that Chet could handle, it seems, and he returned to Amsterdam between tours to get high. Diane Vavra confronted him about his behaviour, but found it difficult to persuade him to change his ways. She gave some insight into Chet's thought process—and indeed her own—in an interview with Bruce Weber for the documentary *Let's Get Lost* in 1987. "He's so obsessed with getting high that he can't have a, quote, 'normal kind of life'," she explained. "He just can't. That really is his first priority, getting high. And you can't have a family, you can't have a home and still get high every day. It's too expensive, for one thing. He knows that, and he's told me time and time again … he's going to stop. He will stop. 'Can't you see, I'm not using as much as I was before? You know, give me some slack. I'll stop'. But we both know he's not going to stop. We're playing a game with pretend. He's pretending that's he's going to stop and I'm pretending that he's going to stop."[9]

Chet's tour of Norway with the pianist Erling Aksdal in 1983 had been a success, and as a result, Wim Wigt arranged a longer, three-week tour in May 1984. "Chet behaved differently from the very beginning," said Aksdal. "He seemed tired and unfocused. The first gig was actually cancelled. I came straight from New York where I'd met the trumpeter John McNeil. I told him that I was going to play with Chet, and that Diane was coming. John said to say 'hello' to Diane, because they had gone to school together. I met Chet at the soundcheck, and Diane was there. We exchanged the regular greetings, and I said hello from John McNeil to Diane, and Chet immediately changed. 'Where do you know John McNeil from?' She explained that they had gone to school together, but he just grabbed her and went straight to the hotel, and didn't come back. So we just played as a duo, and made a jam session out of it. They were fighting terribly, and never came out of the hotel room. When we were supposed to leave the hotel next day, Diane had a black eye."[10]

Aksdal wasn't sure whether Chet was strung out, suffering from withdrawal symptoms because he was back on methadone, or if it was the result of chemical imbalances in his system. Either way, it seemed to be affecting his sleeping patterns, too, and he regularly asked Aksdal for sleeping pills to help him rest. Chet continued to suffer from violent mood swings. A few days into the tour, Chet had problems when he was checking out of a hotel in Bergen. "He'd run up a small bill for a couple of beers, or something, from the night before, and he was asked to pay," said Aksdal. "Chet pushed his hands into his pockets and said, 'There's no money here. How am I supposed to pay?' He pushed his hand deep into his pockets until the pocket ripped, at which point he got so mad, he started tearing his pants apart. Eventually, with his pants torn to shreds, he took his trousers off and threw them in the face of the receptionist. At this moment, five Japanese businessmen entered the room, and they were shocked! Then he took his bag, walked into the restaurant, and changed his pants in front of all the people in the restaurant. I had to go around the corner, I was laughing so much!"

But Chet's violent mood swings were not always so amusing. Next day, the band had to take a ferry between gigs. Chet and Diane had been arguing again, and sat far apart on the boat. When they eventually docked, Chet approached Diane and asked for the money, which she had been looking after. "They were carrying a lot of money; the equivalent of $30,000, I think," said Aksdal. "Diane was trembling as she took the money out, and it was really windy that day. Chet grabbed her hands, and a handful of the money just flew up in the air. It was crazy, there was a cloud of notes! We collected most of it, but some of it flew into the water. Chet said to Diane, 'Why don't you go home?' She said, 'How am I going to get home if you take all the money?' 'You can fucking swim!' he yelled."[11]

The gig that night was terrible, with Chet in poor shape, physically and mentally. "That night I was sitting with Chet for hours," Aksdal recalled. "He was really having a tough time. He got a separate room for Diane. He didn't want to go to sleep, because he couldn't sleep. Next morning, we were supposed to go to Oslo, but he had disappeared. Through some contact we had at SAS airlines we found out that he had left very early in the morning for Amsterdam."

Chet had indeed returned to Amsterdam. He stopped by his apartment, and woke his landlord Evert Hekkema, leaving a bag by the side of his bed. "Just look after this for a while," he instructed him. The bag contained notes from all over Europe, but contained approximately $15,000, by Hekkema's estimation. Given Aksdal's estimate that he had been carrying closer to $30,000 just two days earlier, the remainder was presumably spent on drugs.

This conclusion is born out by pianist Erling Aksdal, who reconvened with Chet in Oslo the following night. "He made the gig in Oslo a little late, but by then he was a completely different person," he said. "It was like he was drunk—which he wasn't—but the gig was not good, and he was crazy the whole night."[12]

It was hard to get hotel rooms in Oslo at this time, and the owners of the jazz club—the Hot House—asked the Norwegian jazz critic and unofficial ambassador for Norwegian jazz, Randi Hultin, if Chet Baker and Diane Vavra could spend the night with her. She regularly invited American jazz musicians to stay with her, and had known Chet since the mid-1960s, so she readily agreed. "What he had bought in Holland must have been potent stuff, but obviously he hadn't begun using any of that until next day," she later wrote. "At *my* house. He became very unbalanced, and got angry and jealous of Diane for no reason. She asked me to go along with her to the Hot House that evening as well. 'When he's like this, I don't know what he's going to do', she said. 'He does everything he can to make me upset'."[13]

Chet was scheduled to play a second gig at the Hot House on May 22nd. Randi Hultin did her best to revive Chet in time for the show, but he was still in bad shape. "We arrived a little late and had to sober Chet up on plenty of black coffee," she explained. "His playing was not, unfortunately, what it could have been, although he did complete the last set."[14]

The next day, Chet was booked to play a studio session with pianist Erling Aksdal and bass player Bjorn Alterhaug for the local radio station. "I made him promise to take it easy," said Hultin. "Diane borrowed the washing machine, and I took two suitcases of clothes downtown to be dry-cleaned. They hadn't washed anything in two months."[15]

Despite Hultin's best efforts, Chet was still two hours late for the recording sessions, which was scheduled to last for three hours. As a consequence, the band only had time to record two tunes. "But he was a totally different person, like twenty years younger," said Aksdal. "He was so sweet, so nice, and he played beautifully. From then on, everything was fine, but I don't think he had the energy that he had the year before. Even at his worst, Chet never had a bad word to say to me, to Bjorn (Alterhaug), or the other musicians. He was usually on time, except for that one gig that he missed, and he was really easy to deal with in all respects."

Another musician that met him on that tour, pianist Per Husby, made a similar observation; that if you could get past Chet's addiction, and relate to him as a person, he was still a sweet man. "I came down to see him at the Hot House," he recalled. "I just wanted to give him a couple of pictures I'd taken of him and Getz. I said, 'I can't really stay because I've got another gig, but I wanted to drop by and give you these photos'. He gave me a hug, and said, 'I just want to tell you that you're one of my favourite people'. He didn't know me very well, but was impressed by everyday things. Because everything else with Chet was so non-everyday. A simple gesture—giving him a picture, or sending him a Christmas card—meant a lot to him. He was so bombarded with people who had no interest in Chet the person, the human being. They just wanted to be around Chet, say that they'd talked to him. If you met him on a personal level he was just a sweet, friendly guy."[16]

A couple of days later, Chet played a gig with the Erling Aksdal Trio at Trondheim, which the pianist remembers as being the best gig they ever played together. "He was so agile, and he really took chances," said Aksdal. "Sometimes he would play really fast and strong lines, not just the regular kind of Chet that you hear, but more intricate, less cool in a way. He did that on some tunes, and it was really amazing. The power, the creative power, and the control of his horn and the music." Excerpts from the concert were eventually released on CD by EMI Norway in 2006, and are well worth the search.[17]

Chet had been touring for almost two months solid, living most of that time out of a suitcase. He seems to have decided to take some time off, dividing his time between Amsterdam, Liege, Paris, Florence and Rome. "Sometimes Chet would disappear for a little while," said Ria Wigt, "and we wouldn't hear from him, then he'd call out of the blue, and request some bookings." He played the occasional gig in Italy over the summer, and also made the occasional festival appearance—joining the Steve Houben Quartet at the Middleheim Jazz Festival in Antwerp. But for the most part, he was happy to hang out with his drug buddies, including Jacques Pelzer, Nicola Stilo, and Michel and Micheline Pelzer.

These were difficult times for Diane Vavra, who started to resent some of the members of Chet's 'inner circle', including Micheline Pelzer, particularly when they left to score together. Nicola Stilo's growing presence also caused tension, both with Diane Vavra and Micheline Pelzer, who thought that he occasionally outstayed his welcome.

Chet accepted the offer of some lucrative film soundtrack work in mid-September, recording the theme to *Le Jumeau*, a French face starring Pierre Richard. The soundtrack, by Vladimir Cosma, was written with Chet Baker in mind, and also features the fine bass playing of Niels-Henning Ørsted Pedersen—a regular on Denmark's SteepleChase Records.

Later that month, Chet was called by Gerrie Teekens, the owner of Criss Cross Records, who suggested a recording with the 'cool school' tenor saxophonist, Warne Marsh. "Marsh was in Holland for a tour, and it struck me as being an intriguing combination," said Teekens. "So I called Chet, who also thought it was a good idea. He said he had always admired the guys from the Tristano movement because they were such honest musicians—Marsh especially. They didn't genuflect before the almighty dollar. It seemed quite natural for Marsh to work with Chet—who was straight, clean and sober. The negotiations went smoothly. I arranged with him by telephone: 'Next Sunday at six o'clock in the evening in Max Bolleman's studio in Monster, near The Hague'. Chet said, 'Alright, I'll be there'."[18]

As the scheduled date approached, Teekens began to have his doubts. Chet had a 'difficult' reputation, and the negotiations had gone a little too smoothly for his liking. "I finally managed to reach him in Paris," said Teekens. "I got a woman on the line, probably his friend Diane. Chet was sleeping. I introduced myself, and explained why I was calling. Then she asked me, 'What time is it?' 'Four o'clock', I said. 'Daytime or nighttime?' she asked. You see, that's how these people lived. They no longer knew whether it was day or night. Later, Chet came to the telephone. 'Don't worry', he said. 'If I say I'll come, then I'll be there'."[19]

Quite by chance, the American pianist Hod O'Brien—who had known Chet since the late 1950s—happened to be in Holland at this time, and was invited to join the recording session. "That was my first time to go to Europe," said O'Brien. "My wife was working with Jon Hendricks at that time—he was composing the *Vocalese* album that he did with Manhattan Transfer, and had his group stay in Aix-en-Provence. I needed to see my wife, and I had friends in Holland, and knew Al Levitt in France. So I played some gigs with Al Levitt in the south of France, and then met up with a good friend of mine, who was an arranger, in Holland. He introduced me to Gerrie Teekens, who re-introduced to me Chet."[20]

On September 30th, the day of the recording session, Chet travelled by car from Rome without a break, arriving at the studio just before 6 p.m.. "That shows how well he knew the European highways," said Teekens. "He retired for a brief time to fight his tiredness with a few medications, and then we got going."[21]

The band that day consisted of Chet, Warne Marsh, Hod O'Brien, bass player Cecil McBee and drummer Eddie Gladden. Teekens tried to give the session some direction, suggesting they try a blues number, or an up-tempo tune, but for the most part, Chet was happy for Warne Marsh to lead. "Chet didn't have any strong ideas about what we were going to do, and Warne was much more the leader type," said O'Brien. "Warne just picked some tunes, like 'What Is This Thing Called Love' and 'The Way You Look Tonight', and just did his thing. Warne's approach was to keep improvising on the chord changes of the tune, take a solo, and then end the tune. Sometimes he'd give the tune an original title and it becomes an original that he can publish under his own name, as the composer."[22]

Whilst the pairing of Chet Baker and Warne Marsh might not seem obvious on paper, there was always more to Warne Marsh's playing than the 'cool school', much as Chet was far more than a 'West Coast' musician. The opening track, 'Well Spoken', is a Marsh original that sees both men gravitate to a more bop-oriented sound, Chet playing muted trumpet, with both men delivering strong solos. Marsh drops out for a gorgeous version of 'If You Could See Me Now', which features delicate brush-work by Madden, and a fine solo by pianist Hod O'Brien. 'We Know It's Love' and 'Looking Good Tonight' are both recorded as Chet originals, but were simply improvisations based around the chord changes of 'What Is This Thing Called Love' and 'The Way You Look Tonight', respectively. The session was later released as *Blues For A Reason*, and represents another high point amongst Chet's later recordings.

In October 1984, Chet is thought to have returned to North America. Wim Wigt suggested that he used to fly to the United States to 'relax', but this does not appear to have been the case on this occasion. He played a few gigs in Canada at this time, including one week at the Bourbon Street jazz club in Toronto, and a one-off gig at the Renaissance II club in Buffalo, New York. He also played for one week at the Lush Life in New York just before Christmas. This suggests it was a pre-arranged tour, presumably booked by his US agent Linda Goldstein. Chet did not have a regular US band at this time, and relied on a combination of old friends—such as saxophonist

Sal Nistico, bass player Dennis Irwin, drummer Artt Frank—and pick-up musicians, such as guitarist Lorne Lofsky, who played at Bourbon Street and the Renaissance II.

Chet must have been aware that the tour would impinge on his ability to spend time with his children in Oklahoma, and invited his eldest son, Dean, to join him on part of the tour.

Chet no longer had an apartment in New York, and stayed with the pianist Hod O'Brien, who also accompanied him at Lush Life on that tour. "I used to worry about whether he'd make it to the gig at night," the pianist recalled. "He'd get up and say, 'I'm going out to get a toothbrush'. I never saw him until the gig that night, but there he was, he always made it. He wasn't always on his game, but some nights he was fantastic, very focused."[23]

He returned to Oklahoma over the holiday season to visit his mother, and Carol and the children. Chet never used to spend long visiting his family; Vera used to harass him about his drug use, and he continued to clash with Carol, particularly over money. In addition, he felt cut off from his regular 'connections', which weighed on his mind. After a week or so, Chet would tend to make his excuses and leave, a fact that did not escape his children. In the documentary *Let's Get Lost*, director Bruce Weber asked Chet's daughter Missy, "If you were to take a vacation with him, what would it be like and where would you go?" She said, "Mmm, probably a cruise, because he couldn't get off the ship. He couldn't disappear. For a few days we'd be able to track him down somewhere. To an island, you know, a small island. That would probably be the best vacation."[24]

In mid-January, Chet left Oklahoma for Texas where he is thought to have stayed with Joe Ellis, the doctor who looked after him while Luis Gasca was managing him in late 1982. While he was staying there, he agreed to sit in with an old acquaintance, vibraphonist Fred Raulston, who was playing a gig at Ratcliffe's Jazba Club in Dallas. Raulston was responsible for the club's music programme, and on Sunday 13th January he was scheduled to feature with his own quartet, along with a singer by the name of Martha Burks.

The owner of a local record company, Bill Craig, found out that Chet was due to appear. He asked Chet if it was possible to make a live recording at the club, then a studio recording next day. He reached an agreement with Chet and Raulston to issue one record, combining the best of the live and studio recordings. Craig later recalled that Chet was high and "having a lot of problems with his chops"; certainly he doesn't sound in the best of shape, mumbling his way through 'When I Fall in Love', his playing inconsistent from song to song. The studio recording, initially released as 'Would You Believe', is even worse; Chet is tired, and angry with Bill Craig for suggesting repeated takes. Unfortunately Craig reneged on his original agreement with both Chet Baker and Fred Raulston, selling the tapes in their entirety to the Italian record label I.R.D., which later released four albums.[25]

Chet was reminded of the recording session by the Dutch author Jeroen de Valk in the autumn of 1987, and it is quite clear the session meant nothing to him other than a cash payment. "I can barely remember the whole thing," he said. "I never knew it was released. At least the other companies still release good records. 'Mr. B' on Timeless, with Michel and Riccardo, and the records with Philip Catherine … " (*Chet Baker—Philip Catherine—Jean-Louis Rassinfosse*).[26]

Chet and Diane spent the remainder of the month in California, genuinely relaxing, before returning to Europe, where the Dutch promoter Wim Wigt had laid on an extensive touring schedule. 1985 was a highly successful year for Chet; he emerged from the 'valley' of the previous year, which was marked by increased use of heroin and erratic performances, and for the most part played with renewed vigour and consistency. As with his 'decline', it's hard to pinpoint what brought about this change in fortune, but it is worth noting that he relied on promoter Wim Wigt more heavily, meaning that he played on a regular basis, which kept his chops in better shape. He also spent much of the year playing with a fairly consistent line-up—Catherine and Rassinfosse for the most part, Graillier and Del Fra later in the year—musicians who were very familiar with Chet's requirements, and tended to bring out the best in him.

The first stop was Reykjavik in Iceland, a city he had not played since his ill-fated European tour of 1955. The concert had been organised by Jazzvakning, an association of jazz enthusiasts, who had arranged for Chet to play with a local band, including bass player Tómas Einarsson.

"Chet and Diane were supposed to fly from Los Angeles to Iceland, via New York," explained Einarsson. "Their luggage went with the right plane but they themselves did not catch the plane in LA. That meant that if they went to New York, they would be too late for the Icelandair flight and would not come to Iceland early enough for the concert. They were then sent on a plane to London where they had 45 minutes to get to the Icelandair plane. One of the members of Jazzvakning, Jónatan Garðarsson, was in touch with the head of the Icelandair office in London, and he managed to get the head of the Heathrow Icelandair office to postpone the flight to Iceland until Chet and Diane were safely on board. But their luggage never appeared in Iceland, and that explains why Chet was lightly dressed and Diane in shorts and T-shirt when they finally arrived in Iceland!"[27]

Jónatan Garðarsson called Wim Wigt to explain what had happened, and asked him if he would be willing to buy new clothes for Chet and Diane, which he refused to do. With the show fast approaching, and most of the stores closed for the night, Garðarsson called a friend who was a jazz fan, and owned a clothing store. The shop owner had seen Chet play in 1955—an event which Chet did not recall—and opened his store especially. The owner told Chet that his favourite song was 'My Funny Valentine'. Chet explained that he did not always like to play standards, but "I will do anything for you". "In that case," the owner said, "'My Funny Valentine' will be the payment for the clothes."

Chet was scheduled to play with a local trio—Kristján Magnússon on piano, Tómas R. Einarsson on bass, and Sveinn Óli Jónsson on drums. "The three of us had played together on and off for some years," said Einarsson. "I suggested Sveinn Óli Jónsson because he was the most unobtrusive drummer in Reykjavík, playing very softly. I knew that Chet was not fond of drummers in general and hated 'busy' drummers."[28]

Whilst the band only rehearsed for twenty minutes, Einarsson had done his homework and listened to many of Chet's recent recordings. "He told us that we might play this tune and this tune, so we at least knew about the half of the programme," he said. The concert, which was partially broadcast on radio and television, was well received. "The audience was delighted," he continued. "People had not expected him to be in such good shape, he was of course always strong on the ballads and in lyrical tunes, but he also played impressive eight-note runs, often with an unexpected aggressiveness. The composer Jón Múli Árnason, who ran weekly jazz programs on the Icelandic State Radio for various decades, said that his trumpet playing was so good that he could forgive him all the singing!"[29]

After the show, pianist Kristján Magnússon and his wife, Pálína Oddsdóttir, cooked dinner for Chet and Diane, the band, and two members of Jazzvakning, Jónatan Garðarsson and Vernharður Linnet. "Chet had his share of food and drink and was very relaxed and in a good humour. He told us about his stay in the Italian prisons, which he described as 'a torture', and that his old colleague Gerry Mulligan was not a very nice person," said Einarsson. Interestingly, Chet was upset that Mulligan had refused to join him on a lucrative tour of Japan, an event that has not been previously documented. When Vernharður Linnet asked him about male singers in jazz, Chet replied, 'It's only me and Louis Armstrong!' Chet was not a big drinker, and that night the free-flowing wine and gin may have got the better of him.

Chet in Reykjavík, Iceland, 3rd February 1985, in the home of Kristján Magnússon and Pálína Oddsdóttir. From left to right, Chet Baker, Tómas R. Einarsson, Kristján Magnússon, Sveinn Óli Jónsson. Photograph by Pálína Oddsdóttir.

The record that Chet had made with Philip Catherine and Jean-Louis Rassinfosse was released on CD in early 1985. "This was the first Belgian-produced CD in jazz history," explained Rassinfosse. "It cost a lot of money, of course, as I discovered whilst producing. The cost of making the CD was ten or fifteen times more than it is now."[30]

The band reconvened to play some shows in Belgium and Luxembourg to promote the CD. "Chet was in quite good shape, and liked the band," said Rassinfosse. "He felt that Philip was bringing something different to the music, something other than the restrictions of bebop. His way of playing is somewhat influenced by the rock scene—he has a voice of his own, that's for sure, so you immediately recognise who's playing. Chet liked this thing that we had."

On February 18th, Chet played briefly with the former Weather Report bassist, Jaco Pastorius. Pastorius had parted ways with Weather Report in early 1981, and had subsequently made a second solo album, *Word Of Mouth*. In early 1985, he was touring Holland with drummer Brian Melvin. He and Chet shared the same promoter, Wim Wigt, and happened to be staying in the same hotel in Amsterdam.

"They met in the lobby and greeted one another," said Rassinfosse, "and Jaco asked what he was doing. Chet explained that we were playing at the De Kroeg club, and said, 'Why don't you drop by and sit in?' That evening he walked in while we were playing, and was quite rude—he walked right through the audience, who asked him to be quiet. He walked straight on to the stage, trod on the cord of the bass, and pulled the plug out of the bass, so there was no sound any more. The music just stopped. Chet announced gently, 'The gentleman who just walked on to the stage is Jaco Pastorius'. Some people started booing, because he had killed the atmosphere of the club. Jaco wanted to throw some chairs into the audience, because of their reaction, which was quite funny. Finally he sat in, but Jaco played very loud, turning his amp up to number ten. Chet would not have enjoyed this, but didn't say anything. Jaco was obviously taking something strong, and Chet recognised the impact this could have. Jaco stopped playing after one or two tunes, and sat on the stage, listening to the band for the rest of the set."[31]

In late February, Chet returned to Sweden, where Wim Wigt had booked ten dates with the Åke Johansson trio. "Chet was in good shape for playing," recalled bass player Kjell Jansson. "He had a hard life, he looked like he'd been living, but he still had a good physique. In the town, when he was out walking, he did not seem like an old man."[32]

The highlight of the tour was a one-off concert with the Belgian harmonica player, Jean 'Toots' Thielemans, who had witnessed Chet playing in Los Angeles in 1953, at the time of the Gerry Mulligan Quartet, but never played with him. "The manager of the Stockholm Jazz Festival fixed this," explained Jansson. "I don't know how he came on this idea, but it was kind of strange. The first concert we played, they recorded. I didn't know it was going to be recorded, so of course we were very nervous. We hadn't really rehearsed, and there we were on the stage with two giants. It was a full house, and we didn't know what we were going to play!"[33]

In the event, Jansson need not have worried. Whilst it seemed an unlikely pairing, Chet and 'Toots' shared a love of harmony. They played together to good effect on a number of the songs from Chet's repertoire, including 'Beatrice' and 'Lament'; Thielemans plays a lovely version of 'When I Fall In Love', leaving Chet to play an excellent version of 'Broken Wing' with the trio. "What I remember most is his total concentration, which was not unlike that of Bill Evans or Jaco Pastorius," said Thielemans. "Every note counted, with nothing to add or to take out. He had a guru-like way to put you face to face with yourself."[34]

The next day, Chet and Diane flew to Copenhagen, where Chet was due to make another recording with SteepleChase Records. The label's owner, Nils Winther, had heard that Chet was playing in Sweden, and after a few phone calls, managed to track him down in Gothenburg. He explained that pianist Paul Bley was also in town, and that he would like to record them as a duo. "He said, 'Why?' 'I think that would be nice', I told him," said Winther. "'Are you sure?' Apparently he had played as a duo with Paul at the Juan-les-Pins festival, and he said it was the strangest musical experience he had ever had. He really thought it was terrible. I told him I still thought it was a good idea, and Chet said, 'Well, it's your money'."[35]

Paul Bley had no such reservations, and even changed his schedule to make time for the recording. Nils Winther booked a recording studio, and arranged to meet Chet at the airport on February 27th, only to find he hadn't made the flight. "I didn't know what to do, so I went back to my office in the city," said Winther. "He didn't arrive on the next flight, either, so I called Scandinavian Airlines out at the airport and told them I was looking for someone who was supposed to be on a particular flight. 'We can't give that kind of information', I was told. 'Well, it's kind of important, I'm waiting to meet a jazz musician'. 'Oh, is it Dexter?' the girl said. And then I worked out that I must be speaking to one of Dexter's old girlfriends. 'Who is it?' she asked. 'It's Chet Baker'. 'Well, he's just landed'. I gave her the address of the studio, because we were running late, and told her to tell him to take a taxi straight to the studio."[36]

Chet eventually showed up at the studio with a bottle of vodka and a bottle of juice, along with his girlfriend Diane. "He was in a good mood, and we had a long chat," Winther recalled. "The first tune they recorded was 'Everytime We Say Goodbye', and Paul was playing all over the place. He was playing so much, there was no room for Chet whatsoever. It was terrible. Chet turned to me, and said, 'I told you'. I took Paul aside and had a long talk with him. 'If you'd be kind enough to listen to Chet, leave him some space to play, just play some nice chords when Chet is playing'. 'Oh, do you think I played too much?' he said. I said, 'Yeah!' Then they went in to play a second take, the version that was on the record, and it was such a beautiful take."[37]

The only vocal recording on the session was 'You Go To My Head' by J. Fred Coots and Haven Gillespie. Chet couldn't remember all of the lyrics, so Diane wrote the lyrics out, and held them in the studio while Chet was singing, which may help to explain the slightly uncertain vocal.

After the initial problems, the session went very smoothly. 'If I Should Lose You' is taken at an extremely slow pace, the two musicians using the silence to create a quiet melancholy. Later in the session, Chet suggested a couple of more playful tunes to break things up, and they settled on 'Pent-up House' by Sonny Rollins. "I think the whole session was no more than three hours, no more than that," said Winther.

The musicians were delighted with the recording. "After the session, Paul came up to me and embraced me, saying, 'Thank you for saving the record date by telling me what to do'," said Winther. "It was really nice, and made me feel good."[38]

The album was released as *Diane*, and is rightly regarded as one of Chet's landmark recordings from the 1980s. Interestingly, Nils Winther—who had been working with Paul Bley since 1974—also regards the record as a major turning point for the pianist. "Before that time he was playing his own music, free music, or just improvising on chord changes," he explained. "I got him back playing standards which he appreciated. We recorded a lot of standards over the next few years. He also played a tune around 'Diane', which is on that record—he improvised on that tune, without playing the melody, and named it 'The Lady Of Chet'."[39]

Chet stayed in Copenhagen the next day, and reunited with a number of local musicians for a concert at the Jazzhus Montmartre. Although he had played with all of the musicians before—guitarist Doug Raney, bassist Jesper Lundgaard and drummer Aage Tanggaard, Chet was feeling tired that night, and the music never really gelled. The atmosphere was not helped by the fact that Chet called a number of tunes the band didn't know, and even took a ragged piano solo on one tune. The concert was taped by an amateur, and later sold to Enja Records, who wanted to release it on two or three CDs after Chet had died. Guitarist Doug Raney persuaded them against this, and hand-picked the best tunes from the evening for a single CD, entitled *I Remember You.*

Chet and Diane returned to the United States in March. Whilst the reason for the trip has not been documented, it may have been to finalise arrangements for a proposed tour of Japan. He certainly discussed this with pianist Hod O'Brien, who recalls collecting Chet from the airport in mid-March. "Leo Mitchell came up," the pianist explained. "We couldn't get Dennis Irwin to come, he was busy, so we asked David Finck to stand in on bass. So we had this rehearsal, but after a few songs, Leo went into the bathroom, shot up, and overdosed. After that, he couldn't play! I never heard any more about the tour of Japan. I heard that when he came back from the first tour, somebody asked him how he found Japan. Chet said, 'Hell, man, they all speak Japanese!'"[40]

They returned to Europe late March, and spent a couple of weeks living with the Belgian bass player Jean-Louis Rassinfosse, who had just become a father. "Most of the time we had fun when Chet stayed with us," he said. "We used to go to the movies, I cooked for him, and sometimes he cooked for me. He used to help around the house—he was a nice person to get along with. One time his denture broke and I fixed it with superglue, so that he didn't have to go to the dentist to get a new one. I remember we went to see the movie *Amadeus* together, and it was interesting to see a genius of melody watch a genius of composing. He liked the movie, and laughed at Mozart's rebellious streak in the middle of an organised society. In many ways, Chet was a bit like this, too."[41]

In April, the trio—with Philip Catherine on guitar—went on tour in Italy. "We went on tour with my wife and child, with Chet in the car," said Rassinfosse. "It was the first time we had got away from home with the baby, and people were always amazed to see Chet Baker on tour with a baby! They were not expecting this, with the reputation he had."[42]

After touring Italy, they enjoyed a few days off in Milan and Venice with their families, before resuming their tour in Germany, Austria and Holland. Guitarist Philip Catherine remembers he started to experiment with electronics more on this tour. "Chet never complained about it," he said. "He came on stage one night and saw me with all my pedals and so forth. 'Wow', he said under his breath. That was all. He gave me complete freedom."[43]

In early June, Gerrie Teekens, the owner of Criss Cross Records, approached Chet about doing a studio recording with Philip Catherine. Whilst Chet had been touring with Jean-Louis Rassinfosse for two months, Teekens suggested using a different bass player, Hein van de Geijn. "I had heard so many good things about him," Teekens later explained. "And Hein plays acoustic bass. Jean-Louis Rassinfosse, who formed a regular trio with Chet and Catherine, always played on a Van Zalinge bass, this electronic contrabass without body. I didn't like that."[44]

In the event, the studio recording did not work out as well as hoped. Chet was having problems with his dentures that day, and even when they were re-glued, it took some time to get his chops back, and he ended up playing muted trumpet to hide the problems he was having. "What we ultimately got on tape wasn't bad, but I was a little disappointed," admitted Teekens.

According to the recording engineer, Max Bolleman, Chet also had some problems adapting to the style of Hein van de Geijn's playing—although he stopped short of blaming him in any way. "He was very used to Jean-Louis Rassinfosse, who was used to playing without drums, and was a very steady timekeeper on the bass," Bolleman explained. "Hein was very lyrical, but not such a supportive player. As a result, Chet's playing was not as fluid as usual, his lines were more broken than normal."[45]

Gerrie Teekens was confident he had enough good material to release an album, but was confronted by Philip Catherine, who was not happy with the session. "I said to Gerry Teekens, 'Man, I am working with Chet Baker every day, and now we have a record which is not representative of what he is doing during the whole year'. And so he agreed to have the record done again, and we did it the second time with Jean-Louis Rassinfosse on bass."[46]

Later that month, Teekens later approached Chet about re-recording the session. "I asked him how he thought the session went. 'Oh, pretty well', he muttered without much conviction. 'I know it could have been better'." Teekens suggested re-recording the album. "Well, fine, let's do it over," Baker replied. "What's it going to cost me?" asked Teekens. "I don't have an unlimited budget. 'It'll cost you nothing at all', he said. I thought that was a fantastic gesture on the part of someone who went through money so quickly."[47]

The second recording session took place on June 25th, and went smoothly right from the start. "Chet came by car from Paris directly, but he was on top form," recalled the engineer Max Bolleman. "The second session went from about nine o'clock at night until about one, and for each piece we did one, at most two takes. To make sure that he would show up rested and well fed in the studio I went with him and Diane to a Chinese restaurant. We gossiped a little about old and mutual friends in the States. That was a good idea. Chet has a tendency to neglect himself."[48]

The album was eventually released as *Chet's Choice*. When it was eventually released on CD, Teekens added two tracks from the earlier recording session, which featured Hein van de Geijn. "I like the record very much, it captures the group feeling very well," said Rassinfosse. "The title is interesting, too, because it was finally Chet's choice that the album was recorded with me."

In between the two recording sessions, the trio played at a jazz festival in Münster in Germany, but Chet was in poor shape that day. The concert was recorded, and released posthumously by Enja Records as *Strollin'*. "Chet had better days, and we never thought this would be used as an album," said Rassinfosse. "We were never paid. The producer claimed he gave our money to Chet, which was easy to say, as Chet was dead at that time. Philip eventually took the producer to court over this—we were planning to do something together, but eventually Philip did it on his own and got paid. In the end, I couldn't be bothered to go any further." Records like this helped to dilute the reputation of Chet's later recordings, and it's better to stick with the official releases by the trio, such as the first recording from 1983, or *Chet's Choice*.

Wim Wigt had booked the trio to tour Sweden, but guitarist Philip Catherine was unavailable at the last moment, so pianist Michel Graillier took his place. This line up was recorded in Stockholm for a television show and album called *Candy*. "It was nice, because bass player Red Mitchell was there," said Rassinfosse. "Red was *the* major influence on my playing, so it was nice that I could meet him again. I was also lucky to be able to play in front of him, because he was in the front row of the audience, looking at me all the time!"[49]

Red Mitchell interviewed Chet as part of the television broadcast. "It was a nice interview, because it showed his sense of humour," said Rassinfosse. "He didn't laugh out loud, but you could see the laughter in his eyes." At one point, Mitchell demonstrates some new chords he had devised for Roger and Hart's 'My Romance'. Chet played a chorus, and then lowered his horn. "I think I'm a little too tired," he said. "I've got to play at midnight. And I've got a plane to catch at seven-thirty in the morning."

Chet's reply is interesting, and suggests that his lifestyle was starting to catch up with him. The constant touring and travelling would be tough enough for younger musicians, but age—coupled with his addiction and malnutrition, of course—was starting to take its toll. Equally insightful was Diane's response. "Everybody was going, 'Oh, the poor little thing'," she said. "But it was true. He was tired. He was in misery. I don't think he was just saying it to … Oh, who knows. Maybe he was." It sounds as though Diane's patience with Chet was gradually being eroded. She had heard him promise on so many occasions that he would reduce his drug intake, that he wanted to live a more settled life—but those promises had been diluted by time, and she no longer knew what to believe.[50]

Chet flew to Italy next morning, where he had agreed to perform with Mike Melillo a New Jersey-born pianist who had been living in Italy since 1983. Melillo had long dreamt of working with a full orchestra, and was persuaded by Paolo Piangiarelli—a local jazz lover and promoter—to arrange a series of concerts featuring Chet. Chet never made it to the rehearsals, which upset the musicians in the orchestra. He eventually turned up thirty minutes before the first show, and told Melillo not to worry. "I can't read music too well," he explained. "I only play by ear."[51]

In the days that followed, Chet played a series of concerts with the orchestra, one of which was taped and later released as *Symphonically* on Soul Note records. Unfortunately, Melillo's arrangements are somewhat heavy-handed and slushy, and the production leaves Chet sounding somewhat cavernous. In short, it's one of the less significant recordings made by Chet that year.

Later that month, Chet was invited to record one song on the movie soundtrack to *'Round Midnight*, which was put together by pianist Herbie Hancock in conjunction with the film maker Bertrand Tavernier. "On my first meeting with Herbie, we immediately agreed on certain principles. We wouldn't try to immediately duplicate the music of the fifties. 'Otherwise', declared Herbie, 'we might just as well use the Blue Note records'. We wanted to avoid a rigid of scholarly approach to the musical style. Herbie and Dexter Gordon chose most of the musicians, while I suggested Pierre Michelot, the rigorous bassist who had played with Bud Powell and Miles Davis."[52]

Herbie Hancock had never worked with Chet previously, and was profoundly impacted by the recording session. "He was asked to sing and play on one song ('Fair Weather')," Hancock later revealed. "The vocal performance was exactly what we needed and his trumpet solo was brilliant. I had forgotten that Chet didn't read music. I remember how fresh his first take was. He followed the chords as if he had known them all his life. The notes became pivots connecting the chords. His intuition was flawless, his musical choices were perfect. It was then that I personally discovered the greatness of Chet Baker. I'll always remember his heart pouring through those well chosen notes, and the warmth I felt inside as I listened to him play, for what was to be the last time."[53]

The reasons for Diane Vavra's growing turmoil became more apparent later that month. Chet was due to appear at a concert with the trio on the French island of Corsica. The show itself was uneventful, but with a one-week gap between this and the next concert, which was supposed to take place in Münster in Germany, Chet and Diane decided to take a short holiday. "Chet invited us to join them," said Rassinfosse. "He said, 'Why don't you ask your wife to come too?' So our child stayed with my wife's mother, the first time we had been away on our own. After the gig, Philip went back, but the four of us stayed on in Corsica."

Chet managed to stay off heroin on this trip, sticking to methadone, but over-compensated for this by taking too many barbiturates. "We had a nice dinner, went to our rooms, and a few minutes later there was chaos," said Rassinfosse. "Diane came and knocked at our door. She was crying, and it was clear they had had some kind of physical disagreement, and he had hit her. She was bleeding a little, and had a black eye. She was saying, 'He's going crazy, you have to help me'. We let her in, and she told us, 'I want to call the police; look what he did to me'. I tried to calm her down, and told her that calling the police straight away was not the best thing to do, that she should calm down a little first, and then decide what to do. The first thing to do was find a doctor."[54]

Thirty minutes later, Chet knocked on the door of Rassinfosse's hotel room, demanding to see Diane. "'Now's not the moment' I told him," said the bass player. "'Let her calm down a little, then talk things over in the morning'. He got aggressive with me at that point, saying, 'Open the door or I'll kill you'. I took him out into the garden, and tried to calm him down. He shouted, 'If you weren't so big and strong, I would kill you!' I said,

'You can do what you want, but I won't let you into my room to see her right now'. He disappeared at that point, and next morning he was gone."

The holiday had been ruined, and next day, Rassinfosse purchased tickets for the three of them to return to Belgium. Vavra decided she would return to California at this stage, but before she had the chance to book a ticket, Chet telephoned. "I thought it would be alright for them to speak on the telephone," said Rassinfosse. "They talked, and two hours later he was there. They hugged, and were the best of friends again. This incident was a complete surprise to me. I had never seen him behave like this before, but under the circumstances, thought it was best if he moved out of our house. He understood, they moved out next day, and I think they went back to Jacques's place."[55]

The following month, Chet was invited to play the inaugural Free Jazz festival in Rio de Janeiro in Brazil. 'Free' was a local cigarette brand, rather than the style of jazz, and the festival featured a number of big-name players, including Sonny Rollins, McCoy Tyner, Pat Metheny and Phil Woods. Chet had been chosen to headline the closing night, however, due to his popularity in Brazil, and the influence he had on many of the local bossa nova musicians. "Caetano Veloso, the famous Brazilian singer and writer wrote about the festival in the Fohla de Sao Paulo newspaper that Chet was a 'genius' and that he was 'amazed to be in the same room as the man who influenced bossa nova'," said the pianist and composer Rique Pantoja, who accompanied Chet at the festival. "He also wrote that João Gilberto was influenced in his singing style by Chet Baker; the close-miked, intimate singing, with no vibrato."[56]

Chet's festival appearance was not particularly memorable. "The concert in Rio was not great; from what I remember, we had to arrange a repertoire especially for the show, because Rique Pantoja was not a jazz musician," said flute player Nicola Stilo, who had accompanied Chet from Europe. "That night we mostly played Rique Pantoja tunes, but also two old songs by Jobim, 'Corcovado' and 'Solitude'. Aside from that, we played just two or three very easy jazz tunes."[57]

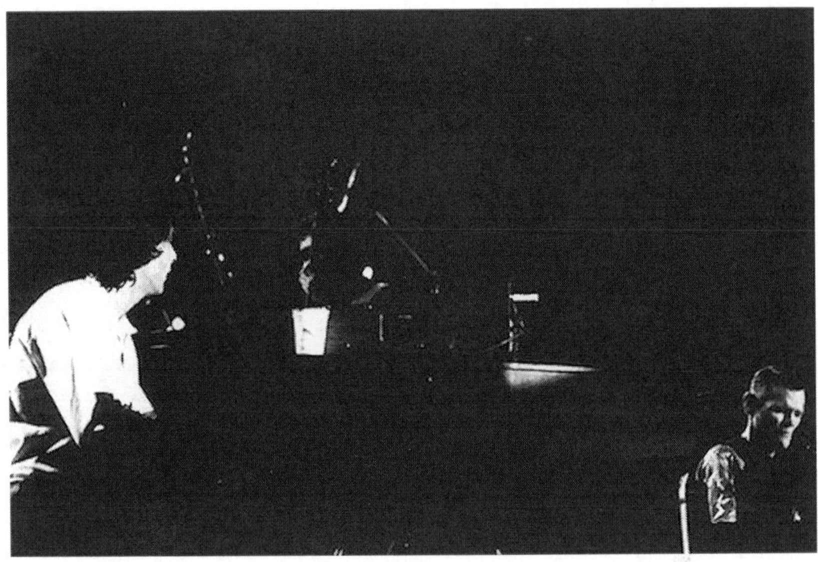

Chet Baker at the Free Jazz Festival, Rio de Janeiro, August 1985. Photograph courtesy of Rique Pantoja.

But Pantoja blamed his lacklustre performance on Chet's chemical intake, rather than the music they had selected. "The concert itself went relatively well," he said. "There were some great moments, but Chet's playing was patchy. It really depends on your standpoint; if you were a jazz lover, and admired and respected Chet Baker, you would capture the beauty of his playing. But if you only knew Chet from *Chet Baker Sings*, and you love his playing and his voice, and then you pay $45 to see him play at a festival, and he just sits in his chair—it was disappointing. When he played, he played beautifully, but he didn't treat it like a big event. It was like he didn't care."[58]

After the show at the festival, Chet joined Rique Pantoja on stage at a local club. "After the concert we played at Jazzmania, and a lot of people came along to see the show," said Pantoja. "But other people gave him other stuff, and his behaviour became strange."

Chet Baker on stage with Rique Pantoja at Jazzmania, Rio de Janeiro, August 1985. Photograph courtesy of Rique Pantoja.

Later that night, the real problems started. "At around 3 a.m., Diane called me and said, 'You've got to come over. Chet's threatening to kill me. He said I stole his money. I'm locked in the hotel room'," said Pantoja. "I drove to the hotel in my car, and he again threatened to kill her. I said, 'Man, you can't do this'. 'I don't give a fuck!' 'Maybe there's been some mistake'. 'No, she went through my wallet, and took my money'."

At some point during the dispute, Diane changed her story. "To make Chet mad, she told Chet she was having an affair with me," said the Italian flute player Nicola Stilo. "Believe me, it never happened. I was a deep friend of Chet's, and I took hold of him and said, 'Listen, man, it's not true!' Why did Diane play me against Chet? She thought I gave the coke to Chet. But it's not true—I knew Chet's problem with that stuff, and knew it would create a problem, knew that it could be dangerous for him."[59]

Rique Pantoja began to despair. He knew that Chet could react negatively to certain drugs, like cocaine and amphetamine, and his mood could change violently. But he also saw Diane taking drugs, and noticed that she occasionally set out to provoke him. "Eventually I took Diane back to my apartment, and she stayed there, while Chet stayed at the hotel," he explained. "Next morning Chet came over, and I had to babysit Diane, staying in the same room while Chet came over. It was a neurotic relationship."[60]

While Chet was in Rio, he made a small contribution to Rique Pantoja's new album, *Rique Pantoja and Chet Baker.* They sung a duet on a song he had composed by the name of 'So Hard To Know'. Chet's vocal is poor, but he contributes some fine playing that helps to liven up the album. One of the highlights is 'Arbor Way', a recording that dated back to Jim Porto's album from the summer of 1983; the vocal has been edited out, and Chet's trumpet overdubbed in its place. Chet liked the tune, and it became a part of his repertoire in the final years of his life.

Around the same time, Chet was also invited to play on *One For The Soul*, the fifth album by the pioneering art-school 'No Wave' singer, Lizzy Mercier Descloux. Combining elements of funk, soul and Brazilian music, together with her own wayward, off-key singing, it's something of an acquired taste. Chet plays on five tracks, including an unusual read of 'My Funny Valentine'.

Chet's popularity in Brazil was such that the organisers booked a second concert in the city of San Paulo. By that stage, Chet had exhausted his supply of methadone, a drug that was unavailable in Brazil. Rique Pantoja had played with Chet on a number of occasions over the years, and discussed Chet's likely requirements with Monique Gardenberg, the festival's manager. "In the end I had a doctor friend of mine help him out, to make sure he got morphine, as methadone was not available," Pantoja explained. "My friend, Walter Almeida, said he gave him enough morphine for three days, but that Chet had taken it in just one day. 'Rique, this amount in one day would put a horse to sleep'. Even after taking so much morphine, he seemed normal. We went out for dinner, told stories, had a pleasant conversation. It was normal. He didn't get high from the drug."[61]

The two concerts in San Paulo were the highlights of the Brazilian tour. "The concert in San Paulo was much better," said Pantoja. Despite his erratic behaviour, the pianist admitted that Chet's playing was far better than when they had met in the summer of 1983.

Chet did experience some problems in San Paulo, however. "Before the final show, some other musicians got hold of Chet, and took him somewhere," said Pantoja. "I was concerned, because I had arranged for another doctor to give morphine, and was putting his reputation as a doctor on the line. If something went wrong, if he were to die, my name and the doctor's name would be stained. It was a very delicate situation. I loved the music, but I did not want this event to mess up my life."

Later that night, one of the festival organisers, Paulo Albuquerque, was woken from his sleep, and summoned to Chet's hotel room. There he found the doctor, Walter Almeida, desperately trying to revive Chet, who had apparently overdosed on a combination of morphine, coke, and potentially amphetamines too.

Chet returned to Europe in September 1985. He had committed to a concert with an Italian jazz band, the Jazz Studio Orchestra. Unusually, Chet made it in time for a rehearsal, one day before the event. The concert was recorded by Paolo Piangiarelli of Philology Records, and later released as *Ten Years Of Jazz Studio Orchestra* and *Goodbye, Chet*, whilst selections from a later concert were issued as *Naima—Unusual Chet, Vol. 1*. As with many of the Philology recordings, these records are inessential, and hardly worthy of release.

Chet stayed in Italy for a few more gigs before returning to Belgium, where he stayed with Jacques Pelzer in Liege. He had been approached by Evert Hekkema, his landlord in Amsterdam, to be the guest soloist on a studio recording by the Dutch band, the Amstel Octet. "The date was set for September 22nd, and for a couple of days I found myself asking, 'Will he come?'" said one of the band's trumpet players, Edu Ninck Blok. "That Sunday morning Evert told me that Chet had phoned him from Liege where he stayed with the Pelzer family and that he would come to the studio. At 2 p.m. he arrived in an Alfa Romeo."[62]

Chet was a little late, and there was no time for a rehearsal. A number of the compositions were technically complex, and the band only had time to play them through two or three times. "On the tune 'Hazy Hugs' he played three solos, and we made a compilation, and glued parts of the three solos together," explained Hekkema. "If you listen very carefully, or know it, you can hear it. It's a difficult tune. But he had great ears, and picked it up fast."[63]

On another tune, 'Tergiversation', Chet had problems navigating the chord changes, but managed to negotiate his way through by ear. "It's a tune with an AABA structure," explained the band's bass player, Hein van de Geijn. "The B section is quite complicated harmonically. The arranger was smart, and wrote for Chet over the A sections. The band leader was quite nervous, and said to Chet in his best English, 'Chet, maybe you can play over the two A sections'. Chet said, 'Oh, that's cool'. And then the band leader added, 'Of course, if you want to take a whole chorus … ', meaning he could also play over the B section and the final A section, ' … that's fine too'. He just wanted to please Chet. My toes curled, because I knew Chet would not be able to follow all those changes; they were difficult chord progressions. But Chet was relaxed, almost fearless. When you listen to the recording, it's quite amazing. Chet plays melodically over the chord changes; technically what he is playing is wrong, yet what he plays is so strong that it sounds like the rest of the band is wrong. It was beautiful. He had such a strong sense of inner logic—his soloing was totally instinctive."[64]

The band was pleased with the outcome, and the album was issued as *Hazy Hugs* on Limetree Records. "The guy who organised it promised to give Chet one thousand guilders," said Hekkema. "He was so nervous. He took the money from his pocket, and counted it in front of Chet, and found there was an extra one hundred guilders. He said, 'What shall I do with this?' Chet grabbed it, and said, 'Give it to me!' He was a street-boy!"[65]

In late September, Chet had a chance encounter with the American R&B star Prince, who had become a major star after his 1984 album and movie *Purple Rain*. In September 1985, he moved to France to begin shooting a second movie, *Under The Cherry Moon*, which was filmed on location in and around Nice, in the south of France. During a break from the filming, the singer and his extensive entourage made their way to Paris. When he heard that Chet was playing at the 'New Morning' club, Prince sent his bodyguard into the club, while he remained in the limousine outside.

"A huge bodyguard came into the club and requested that everyone leave the club," said Micheline Pelzer. "The concert had been arranged by Wim Wigt, who would pay according to attendance. I had been counting the number of people in the club, which was full—there must have been around five hundred people. There was no way we were going to ask everyone to leave. The manager found a quiet place for him to sit behind the bar, on top of the refrigerator, but after a while, word got around. 'Isn't that Prince behind the bar, sitting on the fridge?' At the end of the evening, I had to explain to Chet that he had a special guest. 'I've never heard of him', he told me. I explained that he was a bit like Michael Jackson. 'OK, I've heard of him', he said."[66]

In early October, Wim Wigt arranged for Chet to return to the recording studio with his trio of Michel Graillier and Riccardo Del Fra, this time adding Dutch drummer John Engels to the line-up. The session had been arranged by a Japanese record producer, Makoto Kimata, who liked to record American and European artists for the Japanese market, where jazz was still very popular. "It was like a commission—they even had the title of the record," said Del Fra. "They gave us a list of tunes when we recorded that album—they sent us forty or fifty standards. Chet chose the songs, and I helped a little with the arrangements. His choice was not just musical, but also related to the lyrics. He would not sing lyrics that did not speak to him."[67]

This last point is interesting. Chet's old girlfriend, Ruth Young, always felt that the melody was important to Chet, but that the lyrics meant very little. Riccardo Del Fra is adamant that this was not the case. "I spoke with Chet about this, and remember him saying, 'Those lyrics are nuts!' when he didn't like a particular song," he explained. "Likewise when he chose 'I'm a Fool to Want You' for Bertrand Fèvre's movie, it was because he was at that point in his life where he wanted to speak about love."[68]

It has been suggested that the album placed an emphasis on Chet's vocals because his chops were in bad shape, but that is not the case. He was playing regularly at this time, and his trumpet playing on the album is good, even if the solos are brief. Riccardo Del Fra admits that he prefers the earlier records he made with Chet, which were more bop-oriented. "On records like *Chet Baker Sings Again* or *Chet's Romance*—I'm sorry to say it—he sounded more romantic, melancholic."[69]

Whilst *Sings Again* is undoubtedly less bop-oriented, it is one of the best of Chet's later vocal recordings. Makoto Kimata wanted to capture the feel of Chet's early 1950s Pacific Jazz vocal recordings, and whilst one or two songs sound somewhat under-rehearsed, most of the tunes are excellent. It's also worth noting that engineer Max Bolleman does a super job of capturing the intimate style of Chet's singing, and Chet himself is on good form, his intonation clear and singing in key. Finally, it's worth noting that Chet had not left his bop influences behind altogether. His condition and his energy levels may have fluctuated in his final years, and he sometimes fell back into a slower, more poetic style, but he was still capable of playing at the highest level until the very end, as albums like *Chet Baker In Tokyo*—recorded less than one year before his death—clearly illustrate.

After the *Sings Again* sessions, Chet was supposed to reunite with Jean-Louis Rassinfosse and Philip Catherine for around twenty-five concerts. The atmosphere within the band had become somewhat strained after the incident in Corsica, however, and they struggled to capture the earlier magic. The band effectively fell apart during a one-week stint at the New Morning club in Paris. Philip Catherine missed one night, because he had another gig booked, and failed to inform Chet. Chet fired the guitarist over the incident, and one of his most successful bands effectively disintegrated.

Wim Wigt tried to intervene at this point, as a further twenty gigs had been booked. He persuaded Philip Catherine to stay on, and effectively replaced Jean-Louis Rassinfosse with Riccardo Del Fra. Rassinfosse was upset by the incident, but felt that Wigt simply chose to keep Philip in the band because he was the bigger name. "Naturally, I also have a lot of memories on a personal level—after all, we worked together more than ten years," he said. "For me he was, quite literally, an outstanding person; he avoided the beaten track, he didn't care about outmoded rules. And he had a generosity, a humanity about him which existed independently from the person that life had treated so badly. He had, in spite of all that, retained a kind of naivety. Sometimes he appeared to me like a medieval knight, with his incredible sense of justice and honour, his amazement at the fact that there were people who were ripping him off."[70]

Wigt brought the new-look trio back to the studio on October 20th, but Chet was in poor shape that day, and the record had to be aborted. "We were supposed to record at six o'clock in the evening, and right on time he rang my bell, and said, 'Here I am!'" explained the recording engineer, Max Bolleman. "He had no shirt on, just a leather jacket on top, a hat on his head, and a pair of sandals. He also turned up with no trumpet; he had sold his trumpet on the road for drugs. I asked him, 'Where did you come from?' He said, 'I came from Naples'. 'Naples? When did you leave?' 'I left yesterday night', he replied. 'That's impossible!' 'I'm a hard guy; I drive and drive, and only stop for fuel and a cup of coffee'. He'd had nothing to eat, so I made something for him. He only wanted ice cream, some sugar because of his heroin problem. I made him some coffee, and some strong tea. The boys were already there."[71]

Two tracks from this recording session—'White Blues' and 'Father X-mas', eventually surfaced on a CD issue of *Mr. B*, which had been recorded back in May 1983. Soon after, the recording session had to be abandoned as Chet was in no state to continue. "Chet had started to cry later that evening, and didn't want to play on," Bolleman recalled. "He was saying, 'I'm a shit motherfucker, I cannot play. I don't want to play. Give me some drums to play on the record'. I called Wim Wigt and said, 'He doesn't want to play any more. I had my drums in the car in front of the studio. Wim said, 'Take the drums out, make him comfortable. Maybe later he'll want to play again'.

I said to Chet, 'I don't think you should record this—people want to hear you play the trumpet'. 'I don't give a shit', he replied. 'I want to play the drums!' I never knew what the problem was, as Chet never really shared his feelings. It may have been related to his drug problem, but I think he was just so tired from driving."[72]

The tour continued through early November. The Dutch bass player Hein van de Geijn remembers standing in for Riccardo Del Fra in Grenada, Spain, one evening, when the harmonica player Jean 'Toots' Thielemans joined the trio onstage. "To be in Grenada, the old Moorish town, was special, but in the evening we were on this immense stage, with one or two thousand people there," the bass player explained. "The four of us were so close together on the stage that they could touch each other. Chet and 'Toots' played such amazing melodic music, with Philip playing so tastefully on the side, and me supporting with the bass—that sound and image will be in my mind forever."[73]

Around this time, Chet informed Philip Catherine that he wanted to end their collaboration after the tour was over. "I think it stopped for few different reasons," Catherine explained. "One reason was I guess that I did not know enough tunes. The second was I was too expensive for him. Anyway he told me at Brussels airport at the end of October. He was extremely uptight that morning. I remember he arrived like a missile with Jacques Pelzer at the airport. I can still see him speaking aggressively to the check-in girl. He told me that he wanted to stop playing together, but at the same time reassured me that it was not for musical reasons. He was in great shape that following concert, as if he felt liberated."[74]

Philip Catherine played the occasional concert with Chet in 1996 and 1997, mostly at the request of promoters. "But it was not the same magic any more," he revealed. "He was not in such a good physical and mental state."

But in late 1985, at least, Chet was still at the top of his game—most of the time at least. In November, Chet toured with pianist Michel Graillier and bass player Massimo Moriconi, with Riccardo Del Fra otherwise engaged. This line up is captured on the superb *Live From The Moonlight*, recorded in Macerata, Italy. Chet was on majestic form that night, playing lengthy solos that are bristling with ideas. Highlights include a mournful rendition of 'Polka Dots and Moonbeams', a superb version of 'Estaté', with a flawless solo from Chet, and Richie Beirach's 'Broken Wing'. The quality of the recording is below average, and bass player Massimo Moriconi is not always clearly audible. This is a minor complaint, however, since this is one of Chet's finest live recordings of the 1980s.

Micheline Graillier regards the albums her husband recorded with Chet in 1985—*Sings Again* and *Live From The Moonlight*—as being the finest of their long partnership. "Michel and Chet were close, like family," she revealed. "It was almost like a father-son relationship. Chet could hear that he was a great musician, and helped him a lot. He kept saying to him, 'What are you trying to prove? You have nothing to prove; don't play so many notes'. Chet helped him musically, and his best solo work was because of Chet. When I met him, he had a much busier style, like Keith Jarrett or McCoy Tyner. Later his style was closer to that of Bill Evans."[75]

Later that same month, Chet appeared at Ronnie Scott's in London, accompanied by John Horler on piano, Lennie Bush on bass and Tony Crombie on drums. Chet was being supported by the British jazz trumpet player Guy Barker, who was playing with pianist Stan Tracey. "I remember Chet looked pretty frazzled," Barker later recalled, "but he played great, and what really knocked me out was his stamina. I remember sitting with Gil Evans, listening to Chet playing 'There'll Never Be Another You', and he played this solo that just went on and on. Every chorus, Gil would sigh, and at the end of the solo he turned to me and said, 'My God, did you hear that? Everything, the way it built, the strength of it all'. And it was, it was amazing."[76]

Chapter Nineteen

AS TIME GOES BY
1986

"I'm never going to play with that Paul Bley again!"—Chet Baker[1]

In late 1985, Chet and Diane returned to the United States for a well-earned break from the relentless touring schedule in Europe. They initially travelled to Oklahoma, which marked the first time he had introduced Diane Vavra to his mother. She was met with a surprisingly warm reception, and Diane even confided in her about some of Chet's more negative behavioural traits, including his drug abuse and occasional bouts of violence. Vera may have sensed a kindred spirit, and admitted that she had been disappointed by Chet's behaviour herself. "Chet could have been a celebrity," she said.

After a couple of weeks in Oklahoma, they travelled to Houston, Texas, where they were again the guests of Dr Joe Ellis, a trumpet player himself and lifelong Chet Baker fan.

On Chet's previous visit, one year earlier, Ellis had introduced him to a number of local musicians, including a keyboard player by the name of Joe LoCascio. "One day Joe calls me up and says, 'I'm bringing Chet out tonight, where are you playing?' At the time I was doing a lounge-type gig, just something to put the bread on the table. I said, 'Well, we're playing at Pete's Pub, which was a lounge in a hotel. And Chet came and sat in with us. I remember being struck by how gaunt he looked, very thin, cadaverous I guess. You couldn't help but notice the man walk into the room."[2]

A few days later, LoCascio got another call from Ellis, who was arranging a recording session in his home studio. "He said, 'Do you want to bring your own trio down?' I said, 'Absolutely!' We went down there, and we started playing, and after we had put down two or three tunes, Chet walked over to me and said, 'You can play!' I was a little stunned, and said, 'What do you mean?' 'I was confused', he said. 'When I saw you on that gig, I didn't realise you could play'. But then again, we were doing like Top 40, variety-type stuff, it wasn't a jazz gig. In a short time we put down like fourteen tunes, had a lovely dinner together, and kind of hung out."[3]

Two weeks later, in late January 1985, Chet requested LoCascio join for a second recording session. "This time I brought who I thought was the best drummer and the best bass player in the city," he explained. "I knew it would be risky, because they didn't get along, but thought, 'If this hits, it'll be a fun group'. We got through one tune, and started 'Milestones', and the bass player and drummer stopped the take, and started debating with each other about who was rushing, who was dragging, which was a totally uncool thing to do in the studio. I kept watching Chet, who was getting darker and darker, his head sinking lower, until finally he put his trumpet down. Finally they finished their little banter, and said, 'OK, we're ready, where's Chet?' I said, 'He's gone, and he's not coming back'. I don't pretend to know Chet intimately, but I've been around him enough to know that he was totally disgusted."[4]

Later that year, LoCascio's manager approached Chet about appearing on his own album *Sleepless*. Whilst LoCascio was aware that Chet generally played standards, he proposed a more fusion-oriented album. "At that time, straight-ahead jazz was almost nowhere, everyone was doing fusion," he explained. "I was a complete unknown. I played in the area, I was playing a lot of jazz, but I had no credibility. We were discussing realistically what kind of product we could sell. Even though Chet and I had a lot of fun playing standards, by the time the album came around, it seemed to me that we'd stand our best shot in the fusion market."

LoCascio sent Chet some music, but he never received the tapes. As a result, his mood was somewhat dark on the first day of the recording session. "He thought we were going to do standards. I remember him saying, 'Geez, I didn't think we were going to record stuff like this', when he heard the tracks. But when we started recording, everything was fine. He really did come in and play his ass off on this stuff, and most of the stuff were his original takes."[5]

LoCascio picked Chet up next day, and found he was in a good mood, exuberant and animated. He played tapes of some of his recent recordings, and left LoCascio with a pile of cassettes to listen to in his own time. "It was kind of a gruelling day in the studio, and at the end, Candee Christoforides, the executive producer, came in and handed him an envelope, because he asked for cash. He took one peak in the envelope and said, 'OK, who's up for dinner, I'm buying?'"

Sleepless met with generally favourable reviews on its release, and whilst it sounds somewhat dated now, LoCascio looks back on the session fondly. "It did do well on the airplay charts, it got a fair amount of press," he explained. "It secured me a contract with a good West Coast label, and I've been releasing an average of one album every year or two, and as a result, I am able to make a living as a jazz musician."

In early January, Chet made his way to Louisiana for a recording session with alto saxophonist Christopher Mason. Mason had first met Chet in a police cell in the late 1960s, and had stayed in touch over the years. Mason had eventually married a French lady, and caught up with Chet while visiting her family in Paris in late 1985, even sitting in with him at the New Morning. Later that year he called Chet to wish him a happy Christmas, and mentioned that he was thinking of recording a Christmas album. "It was something I wanted to do for some time, a little jazzy, not Jingle Bell Rock and all that crap, but something gentle, or as Chet put it, 'Something a little reverently'."[6]

Mason couldn't pay much for the date, but offered to give Chet his MG Midget sports car. "I'd spent a couple of grand on it over the year, so it was in pretty good order. He loved the idea. He'd had Alfa Romeos and Maseratis, that's one of the reasons he never had any money. He'd spend it on sports cars, he'd buy a car and if it broke down he'd leave it. That's what he eventually did with the MG; he drove it to Pennsylvania, the transmission went, and he just left it."[7]

The recording date was set for January 7th in Mason's hometown of New Orleans. The musicians were told that Chet Baker may show up at the session, and whilst some had doubts that he would appear, he turned up on time and in good shape. "He didn't touch the needle or anything else all the time we were in the studios. He was on methadone and had taken some to get him through, but after the session, while we were running the tape back and checking things, he was so tired he laid down on the floor and went to sleep. I'd say he was 99.9% straight while doing the album and he had never done any of the songs before. It went real well, we didn't have to chase the engineer or re-balance or anything like that, it just went so smooth."[8]

Like *Sleepless*, it's hardly an essential item in Chet's discography, but it does contain some delicate readings of some old favourites. Mason was understandably pleased with the results. "It's such a sensitive performance by Chet, isn't it? When he played that first note on 'Silent Night' he just knocked everybody out and put the musicians on form, they all played so well."[9]

Chet and Diane drove from New Orleans to New York, where Chet had two engagements. The first was a photo shoot with the renowned photographer Richard Avedon, who was the lead photographer at *Vogue* magazine, and had photographed most of the covers since 1973. In addition to his fashion photography, Avedon was known for his revealing portraits, and was interested in how portraiture captures the personality of its subject. His portraits are easily distinguished by their minimalist style, where the person is looking squarely in the camera, posed in front of a sheer white background.

Avedon would often look to evoke reactions from his subjects by asking them probing, uncomfortable questions, but when Chet walked in with his drug buddy Leo Mitchell, he knew he had all the material he needed. In the photographs, Chet looks ten to fifteen years older than his fifty-six years of age, his cheeks caved in through heroin use and dental problems, the deep furrows on his brow mirroring those of his father, twenty-five years earlier. The eyebrows are raised, Chet looking puzzled as to why he might still be of interest to a photographer after all these years. The eyes have a wistful, faraway look, but there's still a slight twinkle apparent. It's not the effect of the flash—there was just the faintest hint of the teenage rebel, the young man that had irked Gerry Mulligan by blasting on his horn.

The photographs were published posthumously in the French magazine *L'Egoiste*, accompanied by text from the French writer, Phillipe Adler. "The European public is stricken with a profound, sensitive and respectful love for this eternal wanderer, this voyager without any baggage except his trumpet case," he wrote. He went on to describe how he was once "as beautiful as an angel, with fragile, childlike features, a vulnerable air, sweet, romantic," but was hit by tragedy, "teeth broken, jaw fractured, trumpet vanished … " But Adler felt that there was a quiet triumph in Chet's final years. "From the damaged lips of this broken, defeated, skinny, pathetic man emerges, night after night, a music sublime, luminous, and lyrical. From his voyage to the ends of hell, Chet Baker has resurrected, in the day, the blue diamonds of jazz, the blue vapours of the trumpet."[10]

Night after night was an exaggeration, sadly, as demonstrated by Chet's appearance at Fat Tuesday's in New York, a few days after the photo shoot.

Chet was accompanied by Hod O'Brien on piano, Dennis Irwin on bass and Leo Mitchell on drums. "For some reason he didn't like my comping that night," said O'Brien. "I don't think he always felt that way, but there were times he would say, 'Why don't you swing more?' At one point, Sheila Jordan came in to the club, and Chet said, 'Why don't you come and play the piano? This guy can't comp for shit!' There were times I didn't know what he was asking for. But I think I'm a good comper. Everyone else digs my comping! Other times I heard that he'd told people that I was one of his favourite piano players! But that night he was fishing around a lot, trying a lot of stuff, but nothing particularly interesting was coming out."[11]

The club's manager, Steve Getz—son of the tenor saxophonist—confirmed he was in poor shape that night. "He was struggling to play the trumpet," he said. "He was staggering, nodding off on the bandstand. He had a drink by the stool, and he kept knocking it on the floor with his foot."

Chet hardly played in the weeks that followed, and would regularly try to call old friends in New York to ask for cash. "Gerry Teekens was staying with me, because he did record dates in New York," said Hod O'Brien. "Chet called us on the phone, asking us both for money. We tried to get out of it, saying, 'I can't meet you now, I have to do this', making excuses. Finally he called round when we were at home one day. We told him to come up, and he started yelling at us. So we gave him the money! That was a scene! A good friend of mine, a piano player I love to play with, has a tape of what went down."[12]

Chet finally returned to Europe in late February, playing in Sweden, before flying to Copenhagen for what would be his final recording session with SteepleChase Records. "I had to send him money to get here, he couldn't pay his own way," said Nils Winther, the owner of the record company. "I arranged a TV show for him with Danish television, which was taped at a club in the Tivoli Gardens, playing with the same band we used on the record date. He was in such bad shape that they ended up using basically nothing from what they had taped. He was sitting on a stool, falling asleep. He barely played, and his chops were completely gone. He was suffering from all kinds of chemical imbalances; he was really bad. It was the only time I'd seen him in bad shape."[13]

Over the next three days, Winther arranged three to four hours of rehearsal a day, in a desperate bid to get Chet into shape for the recording session, which was booked for February 23rd. "His chops were still not that great on the recording session," he explained, "but compared with a few days earlier, the difference was amazing."

The band, which comprised Butch Lacy on piano, Jesper Lundgaard on bass and Jukkis Uotila on drums, worked hard at rehearsals, getting to grips with Lacy's compositions. "Despite that, it was difficult in the studio—there were a lot of takes, and there were a lot of splicings," recalled Winther. "We did five takes of the first tune, 'You'd Be So Nice To Come Home To', four takes of 'Isn't It Romantic'. There were a lot of takes for what was not a long record. There were no unissued tunes, and we had to work on the various takes to make them musical. Chet's chops were not that good, but I think it works because there's a certain fragile beauty to the music. It was like what they used to say about Miles—we were walking on eggshells. I think there's a special feeling on that record. This record may not show the best side of Chet, as a musician, but maybe as an artist, you know ... "[14]

Over the next few weeks Chet played on a more regular basis, getting his chops back into shape for a forthcoming trip to Japan. The arrangements had been made through Wim Wigt's agency. "We had a number of good relationships in Japan, and had been looking to take Chet there since 1976," confirmed his wife Ria Wigt. "We spoke to them several times, and finally someone was willing to put up the money."

In fact, planning for the tour had started as far back as mid-1984. Naoki Tachikawa, a Japanese record producer, and writer for the local culture magazine *Brutus*, was commissioned to write an article about the European jazz scene. "The editor suggested I go to Paris for about three weeks. I admired and loved jazz very much, and thought it would be interesting to focus on Chet Baker for a couple of reasons. In the early 1980s, Miles Davis came to Japan, and a number of other famous jazz musicians, but Chet had never come over. In addition, nobody in Japan knew where Chet was, or what kind of life he was leading. I thought that it would be interesting for the readers, and for myself, too. I also wanted to make a record with Chet Baker, and started to contact concert promoters and record industry people to arrange an appointment with him. No one seemed to know how to reach him. At one stage I was told he had a gig in the Netherlands, but next day, no one seemed to know where he'd gone!"[15]

Tachikawa eventually tracked him down to Los Gatos, near San Jose, and made arrangements to meet Chet at Bimbo's club in San Francisco, where Chet planned to sit in with another jazz musician. "We went to the club. It was a very cold day, and we waited two or three hours in the car for Chet to arrive, but he never showed up," he explained.

With the help of William Hames, a local photographer who spoke Japanese, they spoke to Chet next day, who suggested they drive out to Los Gatos. "The house looked old and seedy, with abandoned cars outside," said Tachikawa. "Chet looked like he had just got out of bed, with his hair a mess, and said, 'Did I have an appointment with you yesterday? I'm sorry, I totally forgot about it'. Although he looked a wreck, he still had an incredible presence, a 'coolness' about him. We talked over coffee, and got along very well. Chet suggested that we meet up next day at Bimbo's, and could join him at a local radio station, where he was making a guest appearance."[16]

The radio show was scheduled to take place in Pacifica, just south of San Francisco. The Japanese producer explained that William Hames wanted to take some pictures for *Brutus* magazine. Chet suggested they take some photographs of him driving his car. "He drove out to the highway, took the car up the full speed, with the needle showing over 120mph," explained Tachikawa. "'I love speed!' said Chet. 'Why do they regulate the speed over here? There are a lot of freeways with no regulations in Europe. I want to buy a Ferrari when I can afford it!'"

Tachikawa thought that Chet was on good form that day. "The dark side of Chet felt like a myth," he said, "and we got on very well". He also felt that Chet still had a mischievous sense of humour. When they arrived at the radio station, Chet agreed to play 'Now's The Time', accompanied by a pianist, who was an old friend. "They played the theme," the producer explained, "but when it was time for Chet to take a solo, he simply tapped his feet. The pianist looked embarrassed, and kept playing. They tried another tune, but the same thing happened; Chet played the theme, but nothing more. Afterward, I asked him why he didn't solo. 'If they pay me only $200, that's the equivalent of playing the theme! I'm going to buy some marijuana on the way back with this money'."[17]

On the way back to San Francisco, Tachikawa asked Chet if he would consider playing a concert in Japan. "I'd like to play there," he said. "Why don't you invite me?" The Japanese record producer was a little concerned about Chet's criminal record, because Japan had quite strict regulations. "After I got back, I asked somebody to bring me details of all of his police records, to find out whether he would be allowed into Japan," he said. "Although he had been arrested eight times, he had never been accused of a serious offence, so the immigration department would let him in." In fact, Chet had been arrested for numerous drug-related offences, but presumably enough time had elapsed since his last arrest that he was no longer considered a serious risk.

Promotional document for Chet Baker's Tokyo concerts in March 1986, courtesy of John Engels.

Wim Wigt Productions were involved in the final negotiations, and arranged for their tour manager, Peter Huijts, to accompany Chet. Huijts was a soft-spoken family man, whose calm manner and efficiency enabled him to cope with the most demanding of musicians. Huijts had worked with Chet on previous tours, and was surprised he was so excited and animated about his first trip to Japan.

Chet had already carried out an ill-fated rehearsal with Hod O'Brien and Leo Mitchell in New York, and had invited countless others, but eventually settled on pianist Michel Graillier, bass player Riccardo Del Fra and drummer John Engels. The inclusion of John Engels was an interesting choice, and goes a long way towards explaining why many musicians respected Chet's underlying kindness and humanity, despite his own personal problems.

"One night (in July 1984) I got a call, asking me if I'd like to play with Chet Baker, which had always been one of my dreams," Engels explained. "One of the first recordings I ever bought was Charlie Parker and Chet Baker, and I always hoped I would eventually be good enough to play with him. My wife was very sick at this time, and passed away in September 1984. I played Chet's music at the funeral—I played 'She Was Too Good To Me'. I later heard from some good friends that when Chet heard about this, he started crying himself. He really saved my life at this time, because I was in a bad way. He heard about it, told me he liked my playing, and offered to take me to Japan."[18]

Naoki Tachikawa arranged to meet Chet at Narita Airport, and was nervously awaiting his arrival. "I remember seeing his passport at Los Gatos, and it looked as though it had been immersed in water, and wrung out," he laughed. "I'd never seen a passport like it in my life! When he arrived in Japan, he had virtually no luggage at all—just some hand luggage and his trumpet case."[19]

Peter Huijts had been informed of Japan's strict drug laws, and had arranged for a three-week supply of methadone. Chet genuinely appreciated the warm welcome he received in Tokyo. "People had been waiting for him to play for many years," explained Riccardo Del Fra. "*Mr. B.* had sold really well in Japan, although it was issued under the name *Twilight Ennui* there. We had also recorded *Chet Sings Again* for the Japanese market."[20]

The first concert took place at the Parco Theatre, in Shibuya, Tokyo. "There was a strange hush as the audience was eagerly anticipating the first concert in Japan of such a legendary figure," Tachikawa later recalled. "His appearance was very unassuming, but the instant Chet issued a sound, a shiver was felt."

"The music on that tour was amazing," confirmed the drummer, John Engels. "He brought me to another dimension. You know, we didn't talk so much, but we talked when we were playing and that's one of the secrets."[21]

Next day, Chet played a smaller gig at a club in Harajuku, Tokyo. "We decided it would be a good idea to arrange a special event, and laid on a Y10,000 (approximately $100) per head dinner, including champagne," said Tachikawa. "It was a special concert, and the two hundred seats sold out in less than one hour. I remember the audience being very hip and fashionable that night, a very unique atmosphere. Chet was on time, and seemed to really appreciate that the audience respected and cherished the music. After the show, Chet seemed to enjoy flirting with some of the girls, but later he asked me, 'Next time I come to Japan, can I bring my girlfriend?' Something in his manner reminded me of a mischievous boy."[22]

Chet Baker in Liège, March 1986. Photograph by Jacky Lepage.

Pianist Michel Graillier later told his wife Micheline that Chet had arrived in Tokyo with very few clothes, and was surprised how cold it was. "He bought a lot of clothes in Tokyo, including an Italian jacket," she said. "He was always in Italy, and never bought a jacket, but he bought an Italian jacket in Tokyo!" By the end of the trip, Chet was looking forward to returning to Europe. "Michel told me that the last night he played in Japan, he was in such a hurry to get back that he went to play in pyjamas," said Micheline. "He had a one-piece nightsuit, made of green velvet. It was very comfortable to wear, and they didn't really look like pyjamas, but he had worn them to sleep in for three weeks, and they had started to get a little dirty. And he wasn't wearing any underwear! For most of the tour he had been in good shape, but for the last night of the tour he let himself go."

Chet returned to Europe in late March, spending a few days with his friend Jacques Pelzer, before embarking on a brief European tour with Michel Graillier and Riccardo Del Fra. By this stage, Chet was commanding a minimum fee of $1,000 per night, prompting Wim Wigt to estimate that he was earning over $200,000 per annum—none of which was taxed. "I don't believe there is anyone who has spent so much money on drugs in one lifetime," he told the Dutch author, Jeroen de Valk. "The Six Million Dollar Man! He sometimes seemed to be quite proud of it. Most addicts spend less money and die earlier."

Chet returned to the United States in May 1986, for what was to be one of his final tours. On May 9th, he played at the Jazz Showcase in Chicago, where he was reunited with a young pianist by the name of Bradley Young. They had first met five years earlier, when he was in the audience to watch Chet play at the same club. "I was a great fan and I brought along all of my Chet Baker records," he later recalled. "I went up to Chet before the set, introduced myself, and asked if he could sign my albums. Not only was he gracious enough to sit at my table and sign the records but, as he went through each of the old albums, he would reminisce and tell us stories about each one. I was on cloud nine. After a while, he left to get ready to play. About three or four minutes later, he returned to the table to tell me that pianist Barry Harris was late and asked if I wanted to open the set with his group."[23]

The pianist found himself on stage with Chet Baker, fellow trumpet player Art Farmer, saxophonist Charles McPherson, bassist Milton Suggs and drummer Wilbur Campbell, trying to keep up on 'Star Eyes'. "I believe

I was in over my head, no question, but I made it through the tune which at the time I barely knew."

Next morning, Young received an unexpected phone call from Chet. They ended up dining together, after which Chet jammed for several hours with the pianist's trio. Chet was scheduled to travel to Milwaukee next day for a gig at the Jazz Gallery, and the pianist offered to drive him. "I brought along a boom box for the trip and a bunch of cassettes of Chet's music. It was truly magical, driving up to Milwaukee with Chet, as he shared memories of the different musicians he had played with over the years. I was such a fan of his that I knew all of his solos and scatted along. I'll never forget the funny grin on his face!"[24]

Bradley stayed in touch, and five years later, Chet again invited him to sit in with the band. "I felt a lot better about my playing (by this time)," the pianist explained. "At the end of the night I spontaneously suggested that we go into the studio and make a record. When he agreed, I had just two days to find a studio and get a band together. We had no preparation, and recorded everything in one afternoon." Despite the short notice, the pianist put together a first-class band. Drummer Rusty Jones had played with George Shearing between 1972 and 1978, whilst bassist Larry Gray has played with numerous artists over the years, most recently working with the Ramsey Lewis Trio. Tenor saxophonist Ed Petersen was also persuaded to sit in on four tracks.[25]

Twenty-two years later the session was finally released as *Chet Baker in Chicago* as part of Enja's 'Legacy' series. Whilst it's hardly a classic, Chet sounds as lyrical as ever on ballads such as 'We'll Be Together Again' and 'My Funny Valentine'. The real joy of this relaxed session, however, is to hear his spirited playing on bebop classics such as Charlie Parker's 'Ornithology' and Miles Davis' 'Sippin' At Bells'.

Back in Europe, Chet again picked up with his regular trio of Michel Graillier and Riccardo Del Fra. One night of the subsequent tour was captured by two filmmakers, Steven Cleary and Robert Lemkin, who arranged to film a concert at the London jazz club, Ronnie Scott's. The filmmakers invited the English pop singer Elvis Costello to join them, with a view to performing a couple of tunes with the band, including 'The Very Thought of You' and 'You Don't Know What Love Is'. "He had that drummerless trio, which was him and a bass player and a pianist, a French and an Italian guy," Costello later recalled. "I went to rehearsals and they didn't even know I was coming. Chet wasn't there, so I had to teach them the numbers; we didn't have any language in common. They were very good musicians."[26]

On his way to the rehearsal, Costello ran into the Irish R&B singer Van Morrison. "Van was right outside my front gate," said Costello. "(He) lived around the corner at the time. He said, 'Where are you going?' I said, 'I'm going to play a television [sic] at Ronnie's with Chet Baker, believe it or not'. He said, 'Can I come with you?' which was about the most unlikely thing—Van would never say that normally. So he walked in with me, and the two young guys that taped this thing had been trying to contact Van for about six months to do something with him and, I dunno, Nina Simone or something. So they got Van to sing with the band (during soundcheck) as well. So Van did, like, 'Send in the Clowns', which was just the most bizarre thing; Van doing 'Send in the Clowns' without a drummer and Chet playing 'Send in the Clowns'. They taped the soundcheck, which is just as well because (Van) never showed up for the gig."[27]

Van Morrison knew the song, but had presumably never sung it before. Whilst he had been influenced by many jazz singers, including Mose Allison, his performance came across as stilted and under-rehearsed—which was hardly surprising, under the circumstances. "Van Morrison is a good artist, but I don't think Chet had heard of him," explained the bass player Riccardo Del Fra. "I don't think Chet appreciated his singing. I remember him saying, 'He's shouting!' There was no conflict, but stylistically they were so different."[28]

There was no such stylistic conflict with Elvis Costello, who had been influenced by Chet's early vocal recordings, and worked with him during the recording of *Punch The Clock* three years earlier. "Elvis Costello was very nice, and of course, he's a very good singer," said Del Fra. "'The Very Thought of You' was very well done, and in keeping with the rest of the music we recorded. I was also touched by Elvis Costello's attitude when interviewing Chet—he was very careful, very sensitive."[29]

Riccardo Del Fra has fond memories of the show. "I wasn't very happy with the sound," he admits. "The sound of the bass was too electric, and I prefer a more acoustic sound, but aside from that, I think it's a nice document. Apart from the tunes we shared with the singers, we chose the tunes we wanted to play." The performance was let down by Chet, whose playing is listless, and who looks on the verge of falling asleep. "Chet didn't play his best, it's true, but the general ambience and mood was a fair reflection of the way we were playing in that period; the rhythmic figure without drums, still playing with silence."

In early July, Chet was scheduled to play at the Montreal Jazz Festival with Paul Bley, presumably in recognition of the superb album they had recorded together for SteepleChase Records the previous year. The organisers were well aware of Chet's reputation. Chet was staying with Jacques Pelzer in Liege, who had agreed to put him on a train to Paris. They had also arranged for Wim Wigt's wife, Ria Wigt, to meet him in Paris and make sure he got on the plane to Montreal.

When Chet arrived in Montreal, he was greeted by Paul Bley, who had known Chet since 1955. "Chet said, 'Can we go find something?' I said, 'Well, sure'. So we got in the car and found something. That was the afternoon of the gig. The problem was that about six o'clock at night he wants to go find something again. So we went to find something again."[30]

The problem was exacerbated by the fact that the show was not due to start until late. "It was a very big-time gig, in a sense, because Montreal pays the bar bill for the reporters," Bley explained. "So every reporter was there, and not only the reporters, but the editors—they wanted to be in on that themselves because of the bar bill. Everyone was looking for a good time!"[31]

Around midnight, the two musicians went on stage together. "He sits down on a high stool, just near the orchestra pit," said Bley. "So that was a little unnerving to start with. I went over and said, 'Chet, this is going to be a real easy gig. What we're going to do is you pick any tune you want, I'll play a little bit of an intro, and you come in, you just play the melody. If you don't feel like keeping playing, I'll take up as many choruses as you need. And then just look at me, we'll play some chords, and we can finish the tune'. He said, 'Fine, fine'. So I play the introduction, but I don't hear any trumpet playing, and I figured, well, I'll start playing a bit of a solo. But there was still no trumpet playing, so I stop the tune, and get up from the piano, walk over to where he was on the stool and said, 'Chet, did you not like that tune? Would you rather play another tune?' He said, 'OK'. So we picked another tune. I played the introduction, same thing—looked over, no music."[32]

By this stage the audience was starting to get restless. Some members of the audience started to jeer, and a few bottles were thrown towards the stage. "I'm sitting in the line of fire, so I get up from the piano and say, 'Chet, we're going to take a break now'. So we both leave the stage, and he's thinking it's an intermission. We got to the wings and I cornered the promoter and said, "Listen, there's only one way you're going to save this concert, because all the world's press is here. If we don't do the concert tonight, they're all going to report that you hired this guy, and there'll be a scandal. What you're going to do is take Chet to his dressing room, walk him in the room, lock him in his dressing room, and if he finds his way back to the stage, I'm leaving the building. Forget about my fee, I'm going home, and the gig is over. If he's locked up in his dressing room, I will go back on the stage and finish the concert without him. So that's exactly what happened; they locked him in his dressing room, and I finished the concert. A hundred people left, and a hundred new people came in. They had to refund a hundred tickets. The gig went on, and the festival was saved. At three in the morning I heard that Chet had left. They'd unlocked the door, let him out of his room, and he came downstairs and said, 'I'm never going to play with that Paul Bley again!'"[33]

Word of Chet's disastrous appearance in Montreal soon got back to his Dutch promoter, Wim Wigt. "Two days later we managed to talk to him," explained Ria Wigt. "But now he's in New York without any money. He calls to ask whether we could send money for a new ticket. Which was pretty difficult since he didn't have an account and the weekend had just begun."[34]

Back in Europe, Chet returned to Amsterdam where he finally fell out with his landlord, Evert Hekkema. In the three years he'd been renting a room, Chet had never paid on a regular basis. "Sometimes he gave me five hundred francs, or he'd give me some Norwegian money! Never guilders! Sometimes I didn't see him for a month or so, sometimes he came unexpectedly, always giving the doorbell a long ring. He had a key, but lost it."[35]

One night in July, he was disturbed by Chet and Diane, who were constantly fighting. "He was yelling at his girlfriend in the middle of the night," Hekkema recalled. "I didn't know what the problem was, so I knocked on the door a couple of times, until he yelled, 'Stay out!' I finally phoned my girlfriend and slept there, and next morning I came back and said, 'I had to cancel two students, and I had to cancel a tennis match'. Chet replied, 'So your tennis match is more important than our friendship?' I said, 'You call this friendship? You shit all over the place!'"[36]

Hekkema insisted that they leave the apartment. Chet packed, shaking with anger. As he handed him the front door keys he shouted, "Fuck you, and don't ever talk to me again."

One week later, Chet ran into Hekkema at the Bim Huis, a jazz club in Amsterdam. "I can understand why you did it," said Chet, hugging him. He continued to drop by the apartment in the months that followed, because it was a convenient place for him to shoot up, close to the Zeedijk district where he would score. By this stage, Hekkema was wise to his tricks. "I recognised the distinctive way he rang the doorbell," he explained, "so then I knew not to open the door."

In mid-July, Chet and Diane made their way down to Italy, where they were the guests of Lillo Quarantino, an Italian bass player who was an old friend of Chet's former band member, flute player Nicola Stilo. On the flight to Rome, Chet had an altercation with an obese passenger sitting in front of him, who moved his seat abruptly and caused Chet's drink to spill. "On that occasion my father called upon his friend, a judge, to help out, and the next morning we went to pick him up," said Quarantino. "He was upset, and feeling low, but grateful and smiling." Thereafter, Chet became friends with his father, and would occasionally join them for lunch.[37]

Chet seemed to enjoy the break from his hectic touring schedule. One afternoon he sat down on window ledge and took out his horn to practice. Trees surrounded the house, and Chet assumed that no one else could hear him play. "The elderly man who lived next door came to his window and started to protest, saying he was trying to sleep," said Quarantino. "Chet was upset, and swore under his breath, but out of respect for the old man, he took the mouthpiece off the horn, and in perfect tune, blew a beautiful ballad. I was astounded that even without his instrument, he was perfectly in tune."[38]

The atmosphere at the house took a turn for the worse when Nicola Stilo returned from Brazil, almost exactly one year after he had gone there with Chet. For Stilo, it had been an intense musical experience. "After the Brazilian experience I felt more sure about my playing," he explained. "The last years with Chet were wonderful; I played a lot of guitar, a lot of piano, and I felt my playing got better and better."[39]

But there was another, darker aspect to his return that worried Diane Vavra. He had always messed around with heroin, but he returned from Brazil a full-blown addict. In the early years, Chet had always tried to discourage him from using. "He tried," explained the guitarist, "but I wanted to do it. Then, of course, we became closer."

Quarantino noticed that Diane Vavra seemed suspicious of Stilo, as though she were worried that Chet would spend more time with him than with her. But the suspicion ran both ways, and Chet could become intensely jealous over the smallest things. "He had terrible fears that Diane was involved with someone else," explained Evert Hekkema. "He knew Diane a long time, since 1970 or so. For about nine years after that they did not see each other, and that disturbed him terribly. Because, who knows, maybe she was up to something with other men in the meantime."[40]

Peter Huijts was convinced that Chet's drug use exacerbated his behaviour in this respect. "I never completely understood Diane," he admitted. "How can anyone stay together with a man for so long who causes so many problems? Who is practically asocial? And Chet was so jealous. Probably we all have such feelings, but if you're a junkie those fears are reinforced."[41]

So why did Diane tolerate Chet's moods? A large part of their connection was musical. Chet respected both her knowledge of music and her abilities, and tried to encourage her to play on a more regular basis. "He offered me $3,000 to play with him on the first Japanese tour," Vavra later admitted. "I simply was not prepared. Just as an athlete must train every day for months in preparation for a performance, a musician must commit himself to a rigorous practice schedule to be prepared for public performance. Since our lifestyle was one of almost constant travel, it made rehearsal virtually impossible. This was, to say the least, a constant source of frustration. It was during these moments that Chet talked about renting our own home … where we could practice together, write tunes together, and just rest for six months. The other six months, of course, would be our time for touring."[42]

Peter Huijts also thought there were other factors that bound them together, beyond the music. "I think they needed each other," he said. "Diane found it hard to make decisions independently. Life with him certainly had its agreeable side. All the touring, you see many countries and get to know people. She was not such a strong personality."[43]

On this occasion, Diane seems to have been jealous of Chet's 'inner circle' of drug buddies, which included Nicola Stilo and Michel Graillier, and made a decision to return to the United States for a few weeks.

Chet was scheduled to play one gig at the opening of a theatre in the town of Latina. Chet's regular bass player, Riccardo Del Fra, was unable to make it, and Chet suggested that Lillo take his place. "The others were worried at first, but they ended up accepting when they saw how enthusiastic I was," said Quarantino. "Michel Graillier was very generous, and played for almost fifteen hours non-stop with me, running through all the tunes the group usually played in concert. I learned them all by heart because, as Michel told me, Chet never announced the songs ahead of time. I was very nervous, but the following evening I did a decent job, and everyone was pleased."[44]

Chet Baker with Paul Witte (bass) and Leo Mitchell (drums) at the Thelonious, Rotterdam, August 30th, 1986. Photograph by Hajo Piebenga, used with permission.

Over the next couple of months, Chet toured Europe with a core quartet of Michel Graillier on piano, Nicola Stilo on flute, and occasionally guitar, Joachim 'Rocky' Knauer on bass and Leo Mitchell on drums—although the line-up did vary from night-to-night.

In an interview with the Dutch author Jeroen de Valk, Chet explained why he generally preferred to play with Riccardo Del Fra or Jean-Louis Rassinfosse on bass in his later years. "Rocky is very laid back. Sometimes a little too much," he revealed. "He has a tendency to slow the tempo down. We often play without drummers, and that is very hard for a bass player. Because you don't have anyone else to support you. You have to set the time. And a feeling for tempo—either you have it or you don't. Bass players who don't have the time fixed in their head need a drummer to lean on. They need the hi-hat—tschick, tschick, tschick, tschick. The hi-hat on the two and the four."

By contrast, he praised the time keeping of Riccardo Del Fra. "Riccardo is an outstanding bass player without a drummer. Because his time is very well fixed. So he doesn't need the support of a drummer. Jean-Louis is also a good bass player, but his timing is not as strong as that of Riccardo. I always look for bass players who play precisely on the beat, with a good attack and a sound that resounds up to the next attack. Good bassists cost a lot of money and are hard to find."[45]

In October 1986, Chet returned to Santa Cruz, just south of San Francisco, for the funeral of Diane Vavra's mother. He played a moving, unaccompanied version of 'For All We Know', which had been a hit for bandleader Hal Kemp in the 1930s, and was also covered by Dinah Washington and Nat 'King' Cole.

Vavra's friends were worried by her 'dependence' on Chet. Her old friend Gary Howe, who owned the jazz club called La Bohème in Saratoga, had heard countless stories of Chet's verbal and physical abuse, and had long encouraged her to pluck up the courage to leave him.

When Chet flew down to Los Angeles for a day, Howe again pleaded with Diane to leave him. Chet phoned later that day, and asked for Diane to collect him from the airport. She had rehearsed the conversation again and again in her head, swallowed hard, and told him she had reached a difficult decision. "Chet, these last few years have been too much," she said. "I can't go on with you any more" Chet begged her to stay, explaining that he couldn't go on living without her, but she stood her ground and finally put down the phone, tears streaming down her face.

Howe gave her a big hug, and suggested they go out for dinner that night to celebrate. As they drove home later that night, Vavra had a strange feeling. She said goodnight, and as she walked into her room, she saw Chet's silhouette in the dim light. "I'm sorry I've been such an asshole," he said, reaching out to hold her.

"We both knew he was lying," Vavra later claimed. "I thought to myself, 'Oh my God, it's starting all over again!' And all I could do was hold him." Despite her best efforts, their suffocating codependency lived to fight another day.[46]

Chapter Twenty

LET'S GET LOST
1987

"Oh, honey, it's a fiction! They made me play on the roof of a building ... "
Chet Baker on the Bruce Weber movie Let's Get Lost[1]

In November 1986, Chet made what was to be his final appearance at a club in New York. The Whippoorwill had just opened, and was located in a basement on West 18th Street, near 5th Avenue. The owners had spent a great deal on the décor, but to Chet's old friend Jim Coleman, it looked tasteless, like a high-end bordello.

Chet had promised Diane he would stop getting high, a promise he broke as soon as he reached New York. He moved into the infamous Hotel Chelsea on West 23rd Street, whose long-term residents had included Jack Kerouac, Bob Dylan, Charles Bukowski, Janis Joplin and Tom Waits—to name but a few. Chet hocked his trumpet for drugs, and borrowed a cheap Yamaha trumpet from Jim Coleman. "I'd lent him trumpets in the past, but this time it was four or five months," he said. "It was my second or third trumpet, and I was happy that Chet was using it—it didn't mean that much to me."[2]

Chet's initial band at the club was a fairly unfamiliar line-up—Walter Davis Jr. on piano, Alex Blake on bass and Ben Riley—best-known for his work with Thelonious Monk—on drums.

Despite his disastrous appearance at Fat Tuesday's earlier in the year, Chet's appearance in New York attracted considerable attention. One visitor to the club was Joyce Tucker, Chet's old girlfriend from 1953—when he was still married to Charlaine Souder. She was delighted to catch up with him, and even proposed that she manage his US career. Chet politely declined her offer, and explained that he spent most of his time living in Europe.

After a few days, Walter Davis Jr. was replaced as the pianist by Kenny Kirkland, who had played with Wynton Marsalis, but also with the pop musician Sting—playing on *The Dream of the Blue Turtles* and *Bring on the Night*. His association with Chet did not last long. "Kenny Kirkland was late coming in one night, and he didn't speed his pace up as he walked in the room and hit the bandstand," explained Joanne Klein, the manager of pianist Kenny Barron. "Chet just glanced over at him, and ignored the whole thing. Then Kenny made a couple of fumbles in the music and Chet stood up, turned around with his back to the audience, and said, 'If you're going to show up late, at least you can play the music like you know it'. He fired him on the spot. Someone in the audience said, 'It's OK, leave the kid alone!' Chet gave the audience a glare, before turning around and asking, 'Is there a piano player in the house?' Harold Danko was in the audience, and walked up and played."[3]

Harold Danko had not seen Chet for a number of years, but remembered most of the songs in Chet's repertoire, and fitted in very naturally. "It was an honest thing on my part," Danko explained. "I wasn't aware that there was a problem going on with the piano player. When I showed up, Chet greeted me real warmly, and said 'Get in here and play!' I know that there were some piano players who would have been vying to get into that position."[4]

Danko saw that Chet looked much older, more weathered, than when they had last met, but noted that he still held an appeal to some women—despite his appearance. "That was the gig where I remember some beautiful young girls in the front row, probably in their early twenties, just looking at him with their mouths open, gawping," he recalled. "I remember thinking they must be seeing some image he's able to create for them, if they're looking at the same physical presence that I'm seeing. He would sit there, hunched over with his legs crossed, all gnarled up, and these women were just dazed."[5]

Another visitor to the club that week was the bass player Jon Burr, who had last played with Chet in 1978. "I had been with Tony Bennett for about five years, and had gotten a Broadway show," he revealed. "After the pit, I stopped down to the Whippoorwill and Chet was in town, working. Harold Danko was working with him. I sat in, and he asked me to join him."[6]

Jon Burr had struggled with heroin addiction for a number of years, and visited Chet at the Hotel Chelsea at this time. They shot up, but Burr noticed a large abscess on Chet's hip. The abscess was raw and oozing pus, and left the bass player feeling nauseous as he left the apartment. He passed out in the elevator, and the doorman found him out cold as the doors opened in the lobby. Later that night at the club, Chet told him he had been evicted from the hotel as a result of the incident—which was no mean feat at that particular hotel. As a result of this incident, the bass player invited Chet to stay at his apartment on 96th Street.

Chet's initial stint at the Whippoorwill was a success, and the club's owners invited him back for a second stint in early December. "Chet always filled the room, and the nights I was there, it was always crowded," confirmed Chet's pianist Harold Danko.

Chet enjoyed working with the new-look band, and invited them to Europe to take part in a recording session that had been commissioned by Naoki Tachikawa, the Japanese promoter who had helped to arrange his first visit to Japan earlier that year. "Organising a tour was not enough for me, and I wanted to arrange a recording, so again, I arranged to meet Chet in America," said Tachikawa. "When it came to arranging a deal, Chet wasn't interested in royalties, he just wanted cash. 'If we're going to record for two days or so, $5,000 is my fee'. We discussed a possible list of songs. I suggested 'Blue Moon', as arranged by Billie Holiday. He liked Billie Holiday, and agreed to this idea."[7]

Tachikawa soon discovered that negotiating with Chet wasn't always that simple; there was still a part of him that was a "street boy", as his former landlord, Evert Hekkema, once described him. "In all of the negotiations with Chet Baker, I felt that he paid considerable attention to detail, although with a 'jazz' touch," said Tachikawa, smiling at the memory. "Chet was supposed to sing five songs. After the second song, he said, 'If I'm going to sing as well, my fee is going to double'."[8]

The recording took place at Max Bolleman's studio in Monster, in Holland. "He was flown in specially from the US to my studio," said Bolleman. "I'm very proud of that session. The Japanese producers who got the idea thought, 'Just let Bolleman take care of it—he knows how to handle Chet'. Someone like Rudy van Gelder doesn't have the patience. No time to fool around, just play. I'm the opposite. I don't look at the clock, even if it becomes night work. You have to make sure the musicians feel good, that they have as much time as they need to make something decent out of it."[9]

The band recorded enough material for two CDs, which were later released as *Singin' in the Midnight* and *Love Song in Japan*, and as *Cool Cat* and *As Time Goes By* on Timeless Records in Europe. Harold Danko has mixed feelings about the recordings. "We did two albums in two days, and again, I wished we had had more time," he revealed. "I think what they were doing was that the Japanese producers wanted Chet to sing these songs, these standards, that Chet had never really sung before. The studio guys were transcribing the words off of the records, so Chet was basically reading the words on some of these songs. It was a treat for me to be able to record with Ben Riley. I'd played with him a couple of occasions in New York, but just to record with him was fun. He was a great drummer."[10]

Unfortunately, Ben Riley only stayed in the band for a few weeks. "When we went to Europe we were scheduled to tour with the infamous Wim Wigt, a producer from Holland who sends you all over the place as cheaply as he can," he said. "When we arrived in Amsterdam, we got a cab, and Chet took us straight to a drug house so he could cop. You talk about angry—I blew my top. I said, 'Boy, if we get arrested I'm gonna get done for murder, because I'm gonna kill you! You could have dropped us off at the hotel, and then go and take care of your business. Don't get us involved in it'. Later he wanted me to go to Japan, and I said, 'No', because I didn't like the situation he had put us in. I left the band in Amsterdam, cancelled, and went back to New York. I was in Sphere at that time with Charlie Rouse—we had some gigs coming up, and I decided to stay at home, and wait for the gigs. It's a pity, because Chet was a nice person—he was just bad on himself. He did himself an injustice."[11]

Chet returned to New York after the recording session to start work on a new project—a documentary movie to be directed by the fashion photographer, Bruce Weber.

Bruce Weber was a former model turned fashion photographer, whose work first appeared in *GQ* in the late 1970s. He became famous as a result of the images he captured for Calvin Klein's advertising campaigns in the early 1980s; black-and-white shots of scantily-clad young men and women that helped to usher in a new age of sexual permissiveness in advertising. There was also a distinct homoerotic edge to his photography, which prominently featured toned, athletic young men, including iconic images of Olympic athlete Tom Hintnaus.

In fact, Weber had been influenced by William Claxton's photographs of the young Chet Baker in the mid-1950s. He later explained that he had come across a copy of *Chet Baker Sings and Plays with Bud Shank, Russ Freeman and Strings* "That's sort of the way I always wished I'd looked," he admitted. "I grew up in a farm town in Pennsylvania, and I heard a sound on that record that was beckoning me to go west. It was that sound you felt when you listened to the ocean, when you were at the beach late in the afternoon. It was almost like you feel when you look at a surfing magazine, you know?"[12]

Weber gave up modelling in the late 1960s, and started taking photographs of his own. His career started to take off in 1973, when he teamed up with Nan Bush, a former representative of the photographer Francesco Scavullo. Although Weber was openly gay, Bush became his live-in companion, with Weber referring to her as his 'wife'. He hosted his first solo exhibition, Body Builders, in 1974, and later secured a contract with Federated Department Stores to shoot the 1978 Bloomingdales catalogue. This elevated his status in the fashion world, resulting in Calvin Klein and Ralph Lauren signing him for their advertising campaigns. By the mid-1980s, Weber was a star in his own right, charging up to twenty thousand dollars per day.

In late 1986, Weber was in the process of completing a movie called *Broken Noses*, a documentary about teenage boxers featuring Andy Minsker—a former Golden Gloves champion, who was teaching young boxers in a small town near Portland. Weber was convinced that Minsker was the spitting image of the young Chet Baker.

One of Weber's assistants at this time was a lady by the name of Cherry Vanilla. Born Kathleen Anne Dorritie, she had first encountered the young Weber in the mid-1960s, when she had just finished high school. She was working as the casting director at an advertising agency, and he was working as a model. "He had a kind of out-of-date style—collegiate, 1950s—but it had a certain small-town-boy charm," she recalled. "I don't think I ever used him for TV, but I put him in touch with the print department at the agency and I think he got some work there. We became friends."[13]

Cherry Vanilla later wrote a gossip column in the music magazine *Creem* ('Cherry Vanilla with Scoops for You'), and went on to work as a publicist for a young David Bowie. She became known for her outrageous marketing strategies, which included an open offer to perform oral sex on any DJ who would play Bowie's records. In 1976, she became a punk singer, and secured a contract with RCA Records in the UK. At one point her band even included the future members of The Police, Gordon 'Sting' Sumner on bass and Stewart Copeland on drums.

She started to work with Weber around the time of the *Broken Noses* movie, but admitted she could never fully understand the attraction of Andy

Minsker. "Bruce is a photographer, and supposed to have an eye. He thought that Andy looked like a young Chet. No way! But hey it was his movie, so he could do what he wanted with it."

Looking back, she wondered if Weber was interested in the theme of 'damaged beauty'. Whilst the models that he normally photographed were not 'damaged', he did express an interest in what he described as "that destroyed quality". "Maybe Bruce liked the loser aspect, the 'couldda been a contender' thing, the heartbreak and how life can change so fast and one's whole life gets based on that one moment, something like that ... who knows. Attraction is a chemical thing and Bruce found Andy attractive."[14]

With the movie close to completion, Bruce Weber wanted to include a photograph of Chet Baker in it, as well as including his music on the soundtrack. Cherry Vanilla managed to get hold of some Chet Baker recordings from Bobby Krivitz, the owner of a gay bar in Greenwich Village called the 'Ninth Circle'. "He had a great Chet Baker record collection, even managed Chet for a little while years earlier," she recalled."I had gotten some rare Chet tracks from Bobby, and Bruce loved them. Then Bobby told me Chet was coming to play at the Whippoorwill."

Cherry Vanilla introduced herself to Chet on the first night of his second stint at the club. With her cherry-red hair she cut a distinctive figure as she walked up to the stage.

She relayed Bruce's offer to pay one thousand dollars for a photo session. Chet readily agreed, and later that evening, Weber turned up at the club with his camera. Weber took a number of pictures that evening. One memorable image showed Chet and Diane in a warm embrace, Diane holding Chet to her neck; nearly fifty-seven, Chet looks fifteen years older. But he also looks vulnerable, as though he needs her attention. The photograph captures his dependence on Diane at that time of his life. Whether deliberate or not, it also closely resembles William Claxton's earlier portrait of Chet in the arms of Liliane Cukier, taken more than thirty years earlier.

Another notable feature of the session is that Weber arranged for Chet to wear designer clothes that he had been given from a recent fashion shoot, which give the images a highly stylised feel. He adopted a similar approach in the subsequent movie *Let's Get Lost*, with Chet often seen wearing the latest Agnès B outfits, a far cry from his normal look.

Weber was hooked, and returned to the Whippoorwill next night with his entourage. "Bruce also wanted to get a cassette recording of Chet doing 'My Foolish Heart' at the club that night," recalled Cherry Vanilla. "Chet agreed to everything easily. We said we would pay him for the recording. That night we went there with a bunch of friends and co-workers, caught the show and got the tape. Then we made arrangements to go to Jon Burr's apartment a few days later to photograph and film Chet."[15]

The following Sunday, Weber, his cinematographer Jeff Preiss and Cherry Vanilla were driven to Jon Burr's apartment on 96th Street. "I believe Jon was also using at the time, so here we were, collegiate-teenage Bruce, wanting to dig on the debauched musicians," Cherry Vanilla recalled. "Jon's apartment was up on the West side, far up for Bruce. It was very sparsely furnished, typical musician, typical junkie atmosphere—at least to Bruce. I had probably had a bit more experience with places like that, so I was not scared or shocked. The lighting was terrible, with a bare light bulb in the kitchen. I remember we laughed that on the table was a box of LU cookies. Bruce thought that was so odd and so funny—expensive French imported cookies in those surroundings."[16]

Bruce Weber presented Jon Burr with a cheque for the use of his apartment. Burr immediately cashed the cheque at a place on the street corner, and then returned to the apartment. Chet informed Weber that he needed to get something, and asked if he could borrow the car and the chauffeur. "So they left with the chauffeur and we sat there and waited for them to come back," said Vanilla. "It was awkward and strange, and we worried about where they had taken the chauffeur. Finally, they came back, shot up in the bathroom and then Chet was ready for his close-up."

Weber arranged for Chet to wear a crisp, white shirt and shot photographs of him against a bare wall. "Chet was dreamy and cooperative," Vanilla recalled. "He sort of didn't care what Bruce wanted to do, just sat there, closed his eyes and let him shoot."

A few days later, Weber made the decision to film a documentary. He was lying on the bed of his apartment with Nan Bush, Jeff Preiss and Cherry Vanilla, viewing the black-and-white footage that Preiss had shot. The deep lines embedded in Chet's face suggested a life of turmoil, and Bruce wanted to show what lay behind his shattered beauty. Cherry Vanilla pushed him to pursue the project. "This guy is fifty-seven years old," she said. "The way he lives, who knows how much longer he's going to be around."

When Chet returned from Europe, Weber proposed the project to him, promising a substantial sum of money in return. Chet threw his arms around the photographer and embraced him. "I think his beauty was so much about his openness to people he liked," Weber later revealed to *Interview*. "That's what I think engaged you about him first—that easiness, pretty much like all great lovers have." Weber's comments reveal the extent to which he was living in a fantasy world, and help to explain the 'fantasy' he built around the musician in the weeks that followed.[17]

Cherry Vanilla finalised the arrangements for the documentary, handing Chet a cheque for $4,400. In return, he signed away perpetual rights to his "name, likeness, voice, story" for use in a film, album, book, merchandising and advertising campaign—just as he would accept the cash payment for a recording. He asked Vanilla if the contract was OK, and signed it without reading a word.

Weber approached bass player Jon Burr as to whether he would like to appear in the movie. "We were hanging out, and things were really getting nuts," said Burr. "I had a girlfriend and we were engaged. I was afraid of the plenitude—when there's more around, dependence increases. That was frightening. How do you come back from that? In the meantime, Chet had found a world-class enabler in the form of Bruce Weber. He would give Chet whatever he asked for—he enabled the hell out of him. It was the worst period of my life; it's always darkest before the dawn. It was that period that led to what came after for me." Soon after, Burr entered rehab, and kicked his habit once and for all.[18]

Weber's next call was to William Claxton, the Los Angeles-based photographer who had come to prominence as a result of his work for Pacific Records in the 1950s. Weber had long admired his photographs of Chet Baker, but also his subsequent work with Steve McQueen. Weber explained that he had just met Chet, and was planning a documentary movie. "What did you think of him?" Claxton asked. "Oh, he sounds wonderful and looks wonderful," Weber enthused. "He *looks* wonderful?" asked a bemused Claxton, before agreeing to meet Weber at his studio the following week.[19]

Weber and his entourage flew to LA the following week. He arranged for Chet and Diane to stay at the Shangri-La, an art deco hotel in Santa Monica. In the meantime his line assistant, Emie Amemiya, booked a recording studio, Sage And Sound, with a view to filming a recording session with Chet.

Weber's first stop was to visit William Claxton. He lovingly eyed Claxton's black-and-white prints, and requested copies of many of the photographs for use in the movie. Admiring the way he looked in his younger years, Weber asked Claxton what he thought about clothes. "Chet thought nothing of clothes," the photographer replied. Undeterred, Claxton ordered a whole wardrobe of clothes for Chet from Agnès B, the French fashion designer.

As if dressing Chet in designer clothes were not enough of a fantasy, Bruce Weber set about recruiting a number of 'lookalikes' to appear in the movie alongside Chet. They included retro-pop star Chris Isaak, for whom Weber had photographed an album cover; the boxer Andy Minsker, star on *Broken Noses*; and the bass player from an up-and-coming funk-rock band, the Red Hot Chili Peppers, Michael 'Flea' Balzary. "It was all so stupid," said Cherry Vanilla. "I mean the whole movie is just a creation of Bruce's dream life of a junkie jazz musician. And don't get me wrong—I love it. It holds good memories for me, and it is dreamy and romantic. But these guys had absolutely nothing to do with Chet's life. It's Bruce's fantasy. Personally, I always thought it was embarrassing and so misguided for him to compare these guys to Chet or put them in his league. In a way, he liked the attention of these younger guys, but he didn't like that Bruce kept comparing them to him."[20]

The decision to include Melbourne-born Flea is not quite as left-field as it sounds. He was originally a jazz trumpet prodigy, idolising musicians such as Miles Davis, Louis Armstrong and Dizzy Gillespie. He only switched to playing bass in his later high school years at the suggestion of guitarist Hillel Slovak, one of the founder members of the Red Hot Chili Peppers. His meeting with Chet led to several uncomfortable moments, however. "One time when I was playing trumpet, someone told me 'Well, Chet Baker plays a lot like Miles Davis'. What do you think about that?" asks Flea. "Well, they can say that," replied Chet, slowly. "People that don't have enough ears to be able to tell the difference between Miles and me, and Miles and Clifford Brown, and Miles and Dizzy Gillespie, or Lee Morgan." In the same way, Chet was less than amused by the childish laughter about his story that the trumpet player Lee Morgan was in fact shot by his own (common-law) wife. The two musicians only seemed to bond over Clifford Brown, when it becomes apparent that Flea is familiar with Brown's solo on 'Joy Spring', which appears to take Chet by surprise.

Other 'stars' in the movie included Lisa Marie, a teenage model who had featured in one of Weber's Calvin Klein ads for Obsession perfume, Cherry Vanilla herself, and a glamorous-looking lady that Weber had met in the lobby of the Shangri-La Hotel. "I always liked the way Italian directors from the thirties, forties and fifties just threw people in their films for no reason," he later revealed.

Chet was scheduled to go to the Sage And Sound recording studio one afternoon, and Weber arranged to film him in a Cadillac convertible, driven by George Dorritie—Cherry's nephew, and chauffeur for the production. Cherry Vanilla and the lady from the Shangri-La Hotel took turns making out with Chet in the back seat of the car. "Again, it was just Bruce's idea of romantic," revealed Cherry Vanilla. "He had us putting our hands through Chet's hair and so forth. It was completely silly, a Calvin Klein ad, ridiculous ... but to Bruce it was 'jazz', 'cool' and very 'Chet'. I was high on pot and enjoying being close to Chet. And Chet, as long as we kept him stoned on heroin and pot, and Bruce kept giving him cash, Chet went along with almost anything. He once told me how silly he thought it all was, but he just didn't care. He needed the drugs and they cost a lot. And Chet, being a star and a man, also kind of liked the attention at times."[21]

The recording session was led by pianist Frank Strazzeri, who had first encountered Chet in Las Vegas in the late 1950s. "He came to my door, looking for dope," he recalled. "We didn't even know each other. He obviously came into town and was looking for someone who played jazz, hoping he could find a connection, and came over to my house. I recognised him, I knew who he was, but I didn't know what to say to him."[22]

Chet later hired Strazerri to work with him in Los Angeles in the late 1960s. The call to work with him again came out of the blue, apparently at Chet's suggestion. "He hired me for the Bruce Weber movie, and said, 'It's about time people heard you play'. Strazzeri assumed this was Chet's way of making things right with him, having burned him on the money almost twenty years earlier. "It was the nicest job I ever had in jazz, at least financially. I picked all the songs on the CD, *Let's Get Lost*, songs like 'Portrait In Black And White'. Bruce Weber didn't give me any credit for that, but I hired the rhythm section, chose the tunes and arranged the music. That left a bad taste in my mouth. If Chet had been alive, I don't think he'd have let that slip by."[23]

Bruce Weber wanted to focus on Chet's singing, rather than his playing, and Strazerri proposed a range of standards including 'Imagination', 'Everytime We Say Goodbye' and 'Moon and Sand'. When Chet was not familiar with the lyrics, Diane Vavra would sing the song to him. "He'd never heard 'Moon and Sand' before in his life, and asked me how it went," explained Strazzeri. "I played it for him once, then he asked me to play it again. The second time he read through the words as I played. After I'd finished he said, 'Let's do it', just like that. We did it on the first take. See if you could do that! He blew me away in that respect."[24]

Nevertheless, Chet was not in the best of moods in the recording studio. Weber had invited along a number of guests, including photographer William Claxton and singer Chris Isaak, and this, coupled with the presence of cameras, resulted in a fairly unnatural recording environment, the opposite of what he had experienced in Holland in mid-December. He also felt that some of the takes felt under-rehearsed.

In between the LA recording sessions, Weber arranged for various interviews to take place. The first interview with Chet took place at the Shangri-La hotel, Chet dressed for the occasion in a white designer sweater. Most of the questions were written and asked by his assistant, Cherry Vanilla. "Although Bruce often overdubbed his voice in the movie, asking the questions, or just left mine out—which was fine by me," she said. She found it helped to get Chet stoned, to loosen him up so that he would start to talk about himself. This had an unfortunate side-effect, however. "I remember I was so stoned, it was hard for me to say 'Twardzik'," she laughed.

The interview was not particularly revealing. Chet had nothing positive to say about his first wife, Charlaine Souder, referring to her as "a whore" on camera. Weber found out that she was married to a lawyer, and still living in Los Angeles. He also heard that she was an alcoholic, and when he tried to contact her, she was barely coherent. In the end, all mention of her name was edited out of the movie.

Chet spoke fondly of his second wife, Halema Alli, referring to her as a "beautiful lady". She refused to participate in the movie, however, preferring to keep her distance after all that Chet had put her through. Carol Baker was barely mentioned, and although Chet had the grace to mention that they were still married, the tone of his voice betrayed the fact that any feelings between them had long since died.

Somewhat surprisingly, he has little to say about Ruth Young, despite the close emotional bond they enjoyed for the best part of ten years. "I don't think Chet mentioned me in the movie," she admits. "He was still pissed off with me for leaving him." But when Cherry Vanilla was trying to track down some of Chet's old friends, he recommended she call Ruth, describing her as a "great girl". When they eventually tracked her down, she became one of the stars of the movie, her wit and charisma lighting up the screen.

Chet's children also get very little mention, which is perhaps less surprising, given the limited amount of time he had spent with them. "They're not really into music," he tells Weber, suggesting that the only way to get to know him was through music—or drugs. Only his first child, Chesney Aftab, arouses him from his drug-induced haze. "He has a very nice singing voice," Chet reveals.

Bruce Weber tried to inject an element of West Coast glamour into the interview, by asking Cherry Vanilla to show Chet some pictures taken by the Romanian photographer André de Dienes, who had moved to California in 1944, and became known for his pictures of nude women in an outdoor setting. Vanilla was embarrassed to be involved in the shooting of this particular scene, asking Chet if he'd known women like this in the 1950s. "He could have said, 'What the fuck are you showing me this for?'" she laughed.

The fantasy world that Weber had dreamed up came to an abrupt end in February 1987, when Chet returned to Europe to go on tour with Jon Burr and two of his friends, pianist Rob Schneiderman and drummer Mike Clark. Even in Chet's absence, Weber continued to act as an 'enabler'; the accounting log for the movie shows that Chet received an additional $10,000 on March 5th for "additional recording and filming", on April 13th, a further $1,000, and on April 25th, $1,500.

The tour with Jon Burr lasted for around six weeks, and he remembers it as being an unpleasant experience. "Chet had some serious substance problems in Europe," he revealed. "He got into barbiturates, which rendered him incapable of performing more than once." Chet also clashed badly with the pianist, Rob Schneiderman.

There were some good nights on the tour, but they were few and far between. "The good times have to be seen in the context of Chet's addiction," said Burr. "I can remember one night where there weren't any barbiturates in the picture, but there was some heroin, and Chet just played his ass off, just chorus after chorus. The heroin just lit him up, and the music had this incredible intensity. So the good times were when the shit was good."[25]

Looking back on the times he spent playing with Chet, Jon Burr feels that Chet did not make the most of the amazing gift that he had. "It's so sad, he had such a great musical mind," he explained. "He played so in tune that notes became transparent, a transcendental quality that he was capable of, but only under certain conditions. He could have had the world."[26]

Burr was finally able to kick his own addiction. "Today we manifest two of the possible three outcomes of addiction. Chet is dead. I am sober. The third outcome is institutionalisation, as in jails, hospitals, etc. I thank God for my sobriety." His only regret is that he was unable to show Chet that there was a way to cure addiction—but in all likelihood, Chet was too far gone.[27]

In Chet's absence, Cherry Vanilla was asked to "research" the movie, tracking down old friends, archive photos and video footage. Several close friends, including Jacques Pelzer, his daughter Micheline, and Chet's old girlfriend Liliane Rovère, refused to take part in the movie.

Chet's old schoolfriend, trumpet player Jack Sheldon, was happy to oblige. Pianist Frank Strazzeri remembers Sheldon walking into a room in Los Angeles to meet his old friend for the first time in many years. "What happened to Chettie's face?" he asked. "Those are laugh lines, Jack," explained Strazzeri. "Shit! Nothing's that *funny*!" said Sheldon. The trumpet player later spoke of his envy at Chet's natural talent, and his outrageous memories of Chet's young, carefree days, before addiction took hold.

Joyce Tucker also agreed to be interviewed for the movie, but was disappointed that Bruce Weber only seemed interested in the details of her affair with Chet. "Bruce wanted dirty talk, and I wouldn't give it to him," she said. "He got mad at me. He really came on to me, romanced me with all kinds of nice things. But it wasn't my idea of a documentary about Chet."

Bruce Weber got all the dirty talk he needed from Ruth Young, who Cherry Vanilla finally tracked down in St. Thomas, where she was living on a boat with her boyfriend. Weber arranged to fly her to New York, and arranged to interview her in a studio in Manhattan.

Weber loosened her up for the interview, just as he had with Chet a few months earlier. "The first thing he asked me was 'What do you like to do?'" Ruth revealed. "'Vodka, scotch, coke?' I said. 'I'll take some Absolut and the coke, that sounds great'." Weber arranged for Ruth to wear an elegant black cocktail dress for the occasion. The studio lighting capturing her long, blonde hair, dangling earrings and wafting cigarette smoke, the perfect 'torch singer' look that Weber was looking for.

Young revealed that she had first met Chet at the Half Note in 1973, how he "completely reveal(ed) himself—to look so horrible, to sound so terrible, but to be standing there and trying." In so doing, Ruth completely revealed herself, too; she was still in love with Chet, five years later, and tears welled up at the memories it brought back.

She recalled how Chet became manipulative over time, and sang an excerpt from the standard, 'My Foolish Heart', that explained how she felt. "Love and fascination … you said it, baby. That's the mystique. But that isn't necessarily real. And that's what takes a long, long time to figure out."[28]

Looking back on her time with Chet, one felt that Ruth had few regrets. "I'm just lucky that those years that I did spend weren't fruitless, finally," she revealed. "Because my ears were open, my heart was open, and my head was open. Well, my legs were open too once in a while!"[29]

Bruce Weber was convinced that Ruth Young had star quality. "At one point, all I could think about was doing a feature and having Ruth as an actress," he admitted. He booked some time in a recording studio, with a view to recording a double CD of Chet Baker and Ruth Young singing, and even made enquiries about getting her a record deal. According to Cherry Vanilla, Bruce Weber started to have his doubts after arranging for her to sing at a birthday celebration. "He had her play live at a show in the Adirondacks, where he has a house ... and she completely blew it. She said she needed coke to go on and there was just none up there. Well, somebody found some eventually—but she just sat backstage and cried and said she couldn't go on. Everyone left quite disappointed. It was a complete bust."

Ruth may still have suffered from a lack of self-confidence on stage, but at least that did not come across in the movie. "When I take a look at *Let's Get Lost*, I think I handled it quite well," she said. "I really think I came across a lot better than most people."[30]

Ruth certainly came across much better than Carol Baker, who was living in Stillwater, Oklahoma with her three children—now twenty-five, twenty-two and twenty-one. Weber had not told Chet of his intention to approach Carol, and his mother, Vera, and Chet was evidently angry when he found out.

Carol's initial response was one of suspicion, but Weber assured her it would be a fond tribute to Chet. He promised a payment of $600, a higher fee than he would have paid under normal circumstances, and promised to bring items of clothing for the children—which included a cowboy hat for Melissa, and a leather jacket for Paul.

When the film crew arrived in Oklahoma, they were taken aback by the family's poor living conditions—sharing a cramped apartment in a house. "I pictured them living on this little farm, the kids working on the farm, Carol cooking, the sons are repairing the fence," Weber later admitted. "We got there and it was totally different. They didn't have ice water in the icebox. We were kind of shocked and stunned." Cherry Vanilla was also surprised to note that there was not a single Chet Baker record in the house, suggesting that she did not hold Chet's music in particularly high regard.

Cherry Vanilla had the impression that Weber quickly dismissed Carol as "trailer trash". "I really think it was more about money than anything," she said. "He wanted to make her seem extra trashy—that he could buy her off for some groceries, beer and a few hundred bucks. He didn't want her claiming any rights to the movie. I think he wanted everyone to have the same opinion of her as he was portraying, so if anything did come up, sentiment would be on his side."[31]

Weber arranged to interview Carol seated on a garden chair in the middle of a huge field of weeds, a far cry from the more glamorous setting he had provided for Ruth Young. He began by asking if there was a special moment she could share from her early days with Chet. Carol responded with a blank stare, and eventually shook her head. "I can't think of anything," she replied. The contrast with Ruth, who called Chet her "Picasso", and Diane Vavra, who referred to him as a "Greek god" when they met, could not be more pronounced.

She became more animated when Weber mentioned Ruth Young's name. "You mean you interviewed that bitch?" she said. "That was his downfall, let me tell you. *That* was when he started taking drugs. She was a very, *very* destructive force in his life." She saw the movie as her chance to finally get revenge on her rival. Ruth later discovered that her own mother had been in touch with Bruce Weber, upset with the way in which her daughter had been portrayed. "Bruce had his office send her something saying, 'May, you have to realise that Ruth could not possibly have been responsible for the accusations Carol made, but I had to show things this way to make my point'. I hope to this day that everyone can see through Carol's behaviour in the movie."[32]

Worse was yet to come. Weber interviewed Carol and the children together, seated on the sofa in their apartment. Melissa told the story of how she had broken into Ruth's New York apartment, stolen clothes and jewellery, and pawned them for just ninety dollars. "That scene in the film is one of the most relevant on the human condition that I've ever seen—a mother giggling and looking proud while her daughter is telling a story about selling the jewellery of someone her father was involved with for $90," said Ruth. "He pans over the sofa, and you can tell they live in their own little world; the vicious evil, the emptiness. It's incredible!"[33]

Cherry Vanilla also interviewed Chet's seventy-seven-year-old mother, Vera, while they were in Oklahoma. She proudly recalled Chet's brilliance when he was young, but the film suddenly becomes more exploitative when Weber handed Vanilla a question—a question he was later overdubbed as asking. He wanted to know if Chet had ever let her down as a son. The camera hovers over her face as she hesitated. The pause seems to last an age, before she finally admitted that he had. "Yes. Mm, hmm, yes. But … let's don't go into that." Away from the camera, it was clear that Vera was still embarrassed by her son's involvement with drugs. "You're not going to show this film here, are you?" she asked Weber.

Looking at the footage they brought back from Oklahoma, Nan Bush was horrified by Carol's behaviour.

Cherry Vanilla was a little more sympathetic towards Carol Baker. She felt that she had done the best she could for the children, and even helped to look after Chet's mother, who was becoming frail. At one point, she even suggested that Bruce and Nan give the royalties from the movie soundtrack to Chet's children, but they refused, pointing out that they still needed to pay an allowance to Chet.

Chet eventually reunited with the film crew in Paris in May 1987, where he recorded part of the movie soundtrack. The recording session took place at Studios Davout in Paris, a venue chosen by Baker himself. "His main reason was it was near a place where he could get drugs," said Weber in an interview with the *S.F. Weekly*. "And the studio had a real bad feel to it. Some of the musicians were fighting amongst each other, provoked by Chet." Some of this footage was eventually used in the opening to the movie.[34]

Cherry Vanilla effectively supervised the recording session. Weber had no real experience in the recording studio, and reluctantly let her take charge.

In addition, he had revealed his lack of knowledge about jazz by constantly pestering Chet to record a Tom Waits song, 'Jersey Girls', which he had heard performed by Bruce Springsteen. "I tried to explain to Bruce why it was not a jazz progression, not for Chet—and actually a kind of insult to ask Chet to sing it," Vanilla explained. "Chet was polite to Bruce and only smiled whenever he was asked—and Bruce asked him over and over. One day Chet asked me why Bruce kept asking him to do 'Jersey Girls'. I told him because it was Bruce's favourite song. Chet was such a gentleman. Even then, he didn't make any nasty comments; he just gave me that look he would give over the top of his glasses, and he didn't have to say a word. That look spoke of all of the disappointment in what was wrong with the world, what people didn't understand, what sensitivity was missing. Bruce knows nothing about music."[35]

Cherry Vanilla proposed a collaboration with both Van Morrison and Elvis Costello. "I suggested some Van Morrison songs and put forth the idea that we should ask Elvis and Van to each produce a track for the album," she explained. "At first Bruce said OK. I contacted managment for both of them. Van's people said 'Yes', and I was so excited—I am a huge Van Morrison fan. But Elvis' people said his schedule wouldn't allow it at the time. So, then Bruce decided we shouldn't go with Van either. My heart broke. I had to call Van's people and tell them we wouldn't be pursuing the recording."[36]

It was Vanilla that suggested Chet record the Elvis Costello song 'Almost Blue'—the song that Costello had given him a copy of four years earlier. "I knew it was perfect for Chet. Chet had played on another Elvis tune, and I figured Elvis would like it if Chet recorded 'Almost Blue'," she said. "It's a shame we didn't get Elvis and Van to have more involvement. It would have been historical, them getting together with Chet for the movie soundtrack. But Chet did an amazing job on 'Almost Blue', and at least there is that." [37]

She was also angry to discover that Weber had tinkered with the soundtrack recording after the recording session. "Chet decided to do 'You're My Thrill' with just bass and guitar, with Nicola Stilo," she revealed. "They did it in one take—it was beautiful. After Chet died, Bruce had Frank Strazzeri overdub piano on the track. I hated Bruce doing that. It was not what Chet wanted. It was beautiful, sparse and did not need piano. Chet knew that. I have a cassette tape of the recording with guitar and bass only, and I just love it. But the public never got to hear it the way Chet wanted it heard. Again, I think Bruce's big ego had a lot to do with it."[38]

Chet met up with his old friend Micheline Graillier in Paris, and told her about the movie project. "'Oh, honey, it's a fiction!' he told me. 'They made me play on the roof of a building … ' If Chet had seen that movie, I'm sure he would killed Bruce Weber—not literally, of course, but I can imagine him saying, 'I'm gonna kill that motherfucker'. I think Bruce was in love with Chet. I never met Bruce, but I read some letters from the production company, and they left a very odd feeling. You feel it when you see the movie, as well—there's some weird things going on."[39]

Micheline laughed when she saw some of the clothes that Chet had brought with him. "As he was working in the fashion industry, Bruce would always give him sweaters from Agnès B, ties from Paul Smith," she explained. "I would say, 'Wow, that's Agnès B! That's pure cashmere, Chet'. Or he'd have Armani pyjamas. 'Chet, do you know what they cost? Your pyjamas cost $1,000'. He'd say, 'What? I wish he'd just give me the money!'"[40]

A few days later, Weber invited Chet Baker and Diane Vavra to the Cannes Film Festival, where his movie, *Broken Noses*, was scheduled to premiere. They were accompanied by Nicola Stilo, who seemed to be his constant companion in his final year. "Maybe I made the choice just to live the same life he was doing, you know?" he said. "We were like brothers, maybe sometimes fighting, but really taking care of each other."[41]

It was Nicola Stilo, not Diane Vavra, that took care of Chet in Cannes. The band—with Frank Strazzeri on piano and John Leftwich on bass—was booked to perform at the Majestic Hotel to celebrate the screening of Weber's new movie. When Cherry Vanilla checked up on them mid-afternoon, she found Chet pacing up and down in his hotel room, with Stilo lying on the bed sweating. They had run out of heroin, and couldn't find a supplier in the town. "The story about Bruce Weber giving money to Chet Baker to buy drugs is plainly true," said Stilo. "I was there when it happened in Cannes. I remember Chet was a little sick, and had run out of dope, and we took a car from Cannes to Turin and I bought some drugs to give him when I got back. I don't know what arrangement they'd reached about money. But after that, Chet felt better and everything was cool."[42]

The audience that night consisted of movie stars, movie industry players, models and paparazzi, most of whom had no interest in jazz. "There were a lot of young people there, who didn't know anything about jazz or Chet

Baker, eating and talking during the music," Stilo explained. "Chet stopped the music during the first song and said, 'Listen, we are playing, and we'd love to have some silence'. He was not happy." Later that evening Chet introduced the song 'Almost Blue'—the first time he'd played it on stage. "Well, we've come to the time of the evening when's there's not much time left", he said, the shouting and whooping from the crowd clearly audible. "And we'd appreciate it if you could try to be quiet, because it's that kind of tune, you know'".[43]

Chet also ran into the Danish actor Lars Bloch at Cannes. They had not met in over twenty-five years, since Chet's time in Italy in the late 1950s. "At that time I met Bruce and Nan Bush, and told them that Chet and I had done this movie together in 1959," he said. "They were excited about this, and sent Cherry Vanilla to see me in Italy. I found that old movie for her, and a tape of Chet playing in San Marino in 1956, which nobody knew he had done. Some of that footage we had to steal! I also sent Cherry to see people who had Chet Baker material, including a Danish painter called Hans Henrik Lerfeldt. Chet used to stay with him in Copenhagen. He was huge, and could barely get out of the door, and only used to leave his house when Chet was playing in Copenhagen. So I helped them a lot with the movie."[44]

Cherry Vanilla thought that Chet and Diane seemed close at this time describing their relationship as "sweet and sad". Bruce Weber captured that contradiction in the movie. Diane Vavra was interviewed while they were staying in Cannes, and recalled the time when she first met her 'Greek god'. "He was very gentle, very sweet, very charming," she revealed. "I guess that's what it was. The mystique about him."[45]

Over time, she realised that Chet's addiction made it difficult to trust him. She told Weber an interesting anecdote about one of their return trips to Santa Cruz. "Shortly before my mother died, Chet was doing his number about having to get high, and finally got some money out of my brother. I had left the home by that time, I couldn't take any more. So I went to a women's shelter to get away from it. And I spoke to my brother on the phone and he said, 'Well I told Chet to leave. He's full of shit, I never want to see him again'. Because Chet cons people, he has this ability to elicit sympathy from people, and it's all a big act. Like he came to my brother, and put his arms around him. 'Oh, I can't make it. I wait every morning for the sun to come up, and it's agonising, and I'm hurting so bad'. And my brother fell for it and gave him $50, so he could go cop. And after that he realised he was being conned, because Chet said, 'How was I, was I pretty good? I should have been an actor'. So you never know when Chet is being sincere."[46]

Her final remark in the movie revealed the underlying sadness of her life with Chet Baker. "You can't really rely on Chet. And if you know that, then you can pull through."

After the Cannes Film Festival, Chet played a few dates in Italy, before embarking on a second trip to Japan, which had been arranged by Wim Wigt. Chet was aware that he could only bring methadone into Japan, and made an effort to kick heroin—albeit temporarily—before the tour.

The side effects of Chet's cold turkey kicked in during a concert at Green Leaves, a nightclub in Porto Recanati on Italy's Adriatic Coast. Chet's mood that night was not helped by the noisy crowd, many of who were there to dance—not listen to jazz. He managed to play just one tune, 'For Minors Only', before returning to his hotel room, his body burning up with a fever of forty-two degrees.

Against all odds, Chet was able to play the following night at the Shalimar Club in Senigallia. It was not one of his better nights, however, and he was clearly in no fit state to play. The concert was recorded by Paolo Piangiarelli of Philology Records, and issued after Chet's death as *A Night At The Shalimar*. "The record was not supposed to come out, as Chet had made no agreement with Paolo Piangiarelli," explained Nicola Stilo. "Later I went to him and said, 'It's not right'. I went to the police, and finally, after several years, we reached an agreement, and he had to pay me and the rest of the band."

The band accompanying Chet on his Japanese tour was only finalised at the last minute. The original plan was to invite the band he had last played with in New York—pianist Harold Danko, bass player Jon Burr and drummer Ben Riley. The Japanese tour organisers had apparently requested this line-up because of the success of the two records they had made in late 1986, *Singing in the Midnight* and *Love Song*. But Ben Riley had left the band after the incident in Amsterdam, and it was not clear he wanted to go on tour, and Chet had evidently fallen out with Jon Burr after their European tour earlier that year.

Chet invited the Italian bass player Riccardo Del Fra to replace Jon Burr, but he turned down the invitation because Wim Wigt still owed him money from an earlier tour. In the end, Chet invited the Dutch bass player

Hein van de Geijn at the very last moment. "Around that time I was asked to do a television show with Chet in Holland; it was just to record one tune for a late-night show," the bass player explained. "It was just Chet, Nicola Stilo and me. Chet and Nicola had disappeared for some time, I felt sure it was something to do with drugs, and I picked up my bass to leave. Then Chet came up to me and said, 'Hein, would you like to come to Japan with me'. I was flabbergasted, but said, 'Of course!" At that stage I didn't know the dates, or anything. I called Wim Wigt, quickly got my visa together, and went. I thought that I would meet Chet, Harold and Ben Riley there. I arrived one day early, jet-lagged, and next day there was a knock on the door, and who was there but my good friend, the drummer John Engels. I couldn't believe it! I said, 'John, what are you doing here?' 'Ben Riley couldn't make it', he told me."[47]

As with the previous trip to Japan, Chet was accompanied by Wim Wigt's road manager, Peter Huijts. He noticed that the switch to methadone had a significant impact on Chet's personality and his playing. "He became quite a friendly guy, who played much better, much more powerfully," said Huijts. "But if you talked to him, he didn't seem too happy about it. 'Do you see that you can do it—go three weeks without taking anything?' He said, 'Yeah, sure, but I don't get a kick from methadone'. Methadone gives a mild high and prevents withdrawal symptoms. It kept him from being sick. But he didn't feel good with it. His tone really developed in Japan. In Europe, you never knew how he was going to play."[48]

Chet's appearance also improved on the tour. Day by day, the colour started to return to his cheeks. He even wore a dark suit, a shirt and tie to the concerts, his hair slicked back as it had been in the 1950s. John Engels attributed the changes to the presence of Peter Huijts. "I believe he would still play in a good suit and look like a young god if Peter had stayed with him," he told the Dutch author Jeroen de Valk.[49]

The atmosphere within the band was excellent. "Before the tour Chet told me, 'You're really going to enjoy these guys'," said the band's pianist, Harold Danko. "And I really did. It became a real band, as opposed to good musicians who hadn't quite gelled as a band. I think he was really enjoying that. There are similarities with Bill Evans, and his last band with Marc Johnson and Joe LaBarbera; Bill just seemed to be part of the band, and enjoy the whole environment."[50]

As with Bill Evans, the new band seemed to bring out the best of Chet.

"Musically he was from another planet," confirmed the drummer John Engels. "He got better and better every night, and his playing improved every night on the tour." The Japanese audiences tended to be knowledgeable about jazz, and would treat Chet and the band to a lengthy standing ovation at the end of each show.[51]

Away from heroin, Chet even became more sociable offstage too. The Japanese tour organisers took the band to the best restaurants in town. Chet was not particularly keen on sushi, but enjoyed the teriyaki and other meat dishes. He also enjoyed the occasional cognac after the show. "It was funny to see him have a couple of drinks, as he became a little more extroverted," recalled Danko. "I remember we'd go to clubs, after the gig, and sit in. At one club I remember he sat in and played drums!"[52]

According to Hein van de Geijn, one of the gigs outside Tokyo was recorded. "We played in one small club, and they asked us if they could record the concert," he said. "A small fee was negotiated, which was accepted. Only then could I see that all the microphones were wrong, we were much too close together. I thought it would be a disaster, and hoped the recording would never come out."[53]

A few nights later, on June 14th, the band was taped for a television show at Tokyo's Hitomi Kinen Kodo Hall. "I think Tokyo captured the band at its peak," claimed van de Geijn. "That night we played some tunes we'd never played before. You can hear that somehow, but there was so much mutual trust by that stage that we just went for it. 'Seven Steps to Heaven', for example, we'd never played before. It was great!"[54]

The tour organisers later contacted Wim Wigt and explained that the club recording did not work out, and sought the band's permission to use the sound from the television recording for a record. "I talked with John and Harold and we agreed that this was a good idea, not knowing that those records would be so legendary," said van de Geijn.

Chet's playing was really quite extraordinary on that tour, as the recording clearly illustrates. Chet was no stranger to hard bop, as albums like *In New York* and *Boppin'* clearly illustrate, but Chet had never sounded so convincing, so assured, as he does on Jimmy Heath's 'For Minors Only' and Miles Davis' 'Seven Steps To Heaven'. His solos on ballads such as 'My Funny Valentine' and 'Arborway' are quite superb, effortlessly combining the dazzling natural ability of his early years with the improvisational skill and emotional depth that marked the best of his later recordings.

Staying off heroin was good for Chet's health and his playing, but ironically the pressure of staying clean seemed to have a negative effect on his relationship with his girlfriend Diane Vavra. "Boy, those Japanese tours, you'd better stay out of his way, because that's when his temper would really flare," she said. "Oh man, it was terrible." But his mood swings never seemed to affect his relationship with the rest of the band. "I remember once, Chet was screaming at Diane at the airport," said Danko. "I thought, 'Gosh, Chet's in a bad mood'. But then he came up to us, was joking around, perhaps because Hein, myself and John Engels had bonded so much over there. He was really hanging, he was one of the guys."[55]

The tour had been an enormous success from both a musical and a commercial perspective, and tour manager Peter Huijts hoped that Chet would stay clean on his return to Europe. Chet was having none of it. "I can't wait to get back to Holland and get fucked up!" he muttered. Danko could barely hide his disappointment. "I just thought, 'He doesn't get it … '"

In July, Chet and Diane returned to San Jose for a few days, staying in the Number 9 motel. The two of them had another violent argument, which culminated in Chet throwing the television out of the window. The owner had Chet arrested, and rather than call a lawyer, he placed a call to Nan Bush, Bruce Weber's partner. Weber not only posted bail, but also agreed to give Chet an additional $1,000.

While Chet was behind bars, Diane Vavra again took refuge in a women's shelter. Chet eventually managed to track her down, and persuaded her to come back. Later that day she knocked on the door of Chet's hotel room, only to be greeted by his drug dealer. She waited for him to shoot up in the bathroom, and came across a handwritten note inside his trumpet case. In the note he claimed that Diane's rejection had caused him to lose his will to live, and he was taking ever larger speedballs, with a view to eventually killing himself. She was convinced that Chet had intended her to find the note, and this was just another attempt at emotional blackmail. For now, at least, their codependence would continue.

While he was in California, Chet heard from Carol that his daughter Melissa had been raped. He bought himself a motorcycle, and rode all the way to Oklahoma, badly burning his arms in the sun along the way. "He worried that the children were suffering," claimed his old friend Micheline Graillier. "He was hurt when he heard about Melissa, but had no money to spend at the time." This was the classic junkie excuse, of course; Chet had just completed a lucrative tour of Japan, but as usual, had spent all of the money on drugs with no thought for the future. Chet stayed in Oklahoma for ten days, and left the motorcycle as a gift to his eldest son Dean.

Chet returned to Europe with Diane Vavra in late July, and played a few concerts in Italy. After a gig in Florence he met up with his friend Giampiero Giusti, and explained that Diane was suffering badly with hay fever. Giusti explained that his son suffered from the same problem, and that he had the perfect medicine to treat her. "Chet took the medicine back to his hotel, and left Diane to sleep," said Giusti. "He came back to my house, and we stayed up all night talking. He had just got back from Japan, and was now back in Europe. After that he told me he wanted to settle down in Santa Monica, and buy or rent a house by the sea. 'I have stayed with you so many times here in Florence', he told me. 'Once I have a house in Santa Monica, you should come and stay with me for two weeks, one month. It will only be twenty or thirty meters from the sea!' This was the last time I saw him."[56]

Chet discussed the idea of buying or renting a house with several people in the final year of his life. The relentless touring was placing a strain on his relationship with Diane, and she wanted to settle down, find a place where they could relax between tours and play music together. In an interview with the Dutch author Jeroen de Valk in September 1987, Chet claimed he was seriously considering renting a property in Amsterdam. "We're in the process of looking for a place now. We're thinking about Amsterdam. We might rent the top floor above [music club] De Stip from [the owner] Tom [Mandersloot]," he said. "We're still discussing that at the moment. It has to be polished up a little. It is a nice big room. I'm thinking of maybe giving workshops there. We've already talked it over with someone from Muziekpakhuis (a music school in Amsterdam)." But Chet's closest friends, Nicola Stilo and Micheline Graillier, always felt that this was just a pipe dream; Chet would say things like this to appease Diane, but was quite incapable of planning more than a few weeks ahead.

In August 1987, Chet resumed his 'never-ending' tour of Europe, forming a new band centred around Nicola Stilo, who now tended to play both flute and guitar on stage, and bass player 'Rocky' Knauer. They would occasionally be joined by a pianist—Larry Porter played a few dates that month, but was later replaced by Michel Graillier. Most of the time, Chet kept to the 'drummerless' format that he enjoyed in later years. Around this time, Chet explained to Jeroen de Valk that playing without a drummer affects the whole mood. "The music becomes a lot quieter," he explained. "I don't have to play so loudly in order to be heard. You know, cymbals ringing all the time. I like to play as softly as possible. The drums bring the volume up. Drummers are often too emphatic."[57]

Later that month, the German vibraphonist Wolfgang Lackerschmid approached him about recording an album of his compositions—many of which had been written with Chet in mind. The recording took place in an intimate studio in Germany, complete with an open fire. Three tunes were recorded as a trio, with Günter Lenz on bass, including a new version of 'Why Shouldn't You Cry'. Nicola Stilo joined on flute on two tracks, including a somewhat cluttered version of Lackerschmid's 'Christmas Waltz', which sounds under-rehearsed. There were also two Latin-tinged tunes, 'Gloria's Answer' and 'Volta Trais', where the band was joined by two Brazilian musicians, Peri and Edir dos Santos.

"Chet was in a very good mood at this recording, also enjoying the company of Diane Vavra," Lackerschmid later recalled. "I really loved his interpretations of my tunes. Chet also started to write some lyrics for some of them. It's really sad that he had no chance to sing them any more."[58]

Friends of Chet noticed that his appearance started to deteriorate after his return from Japan; the colour quickly drained from his face, his cheeks started to cave in, giving his face a ghostly, cadaverous look. "Maybe he had other physical conditions that we don't know about, that weren't being treated," suggested pianist Harold Danko, who was shocked by his physical deterioration. "I remember the AIDS thing had just broken, and he said, 'I probably have all that shit, but I keep all those motherfuckers so stoned. They don't even know what they're going to do in my body!'"[59]

Diane Vavra also expressed her concern, and urged Chet to take an AIDS test, given that he had been known to share needles. He refused; he made a point of shooting up first, he told her. "If you really loved me, you wouldn't care if I had AIDS," he once told her. "You'd get it from me, and we'd die together." Diane didn't want to take any such chances, and was tested regularly on her return visits to the United States. She stayed clean, and it is likely that Chet's physical deterioration was due solely to his lifestyle.

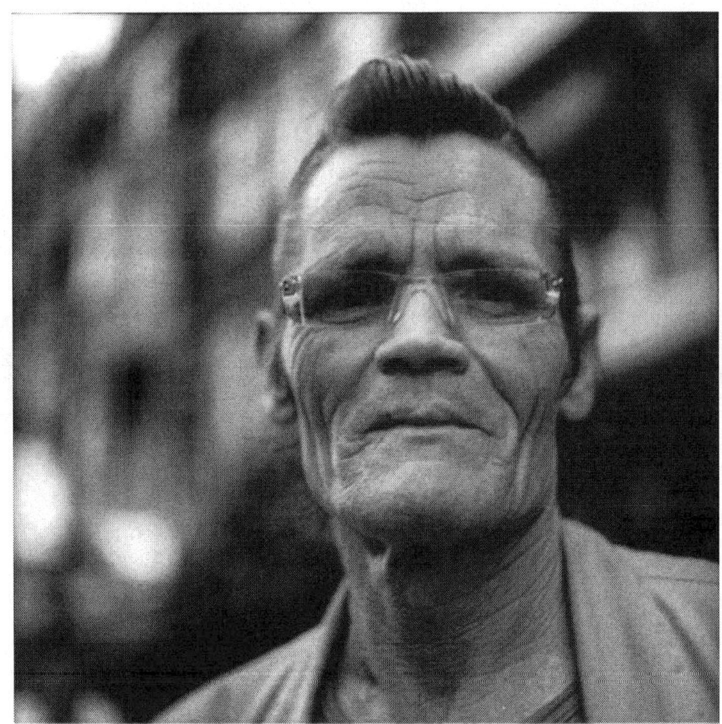

Chet Baker in Amsterdam, September 22nd 1987.
Photograph by Gert de Ruyter.

Chet's favourite way to get high in his later years was a 'speedball'. "The kind of high that scares other people to death," he explained to Bruce Weber, a faint smile on his face. "That first rush of coke is, um, a devastating feeling. I mean, scary."[60]

But Chet's increased use of cocaine increased his paranoia, and exacerbated his tendency to feel jealous over the slightest issue. It could also result in hallucinations, which was a common side-effect of the drug. In October 1987, Chet and Diane stayed in the apartment of a cocaine dealer in Paris by the name of François. After a few days, Chet was convinced that Diane was sleeping with him, and when the accusations became too much to bear, she fled the apartment, and spent the night with Micheline Graillier. Next day, she flew back to California in another desperate attempt to break the spell Chet held over her.

It was Diane's second attempt to leave Chet in just three months, which may have added to his sense of desperation. When he was unable to find his passport, he was convinced that Diane must have stolen it. He even wondered if François was somehow involved, and was planning to elope with Diane to the United States.

In the absence of someone to take care of his daily needs, he grew desperate. At one point, he even telephoned Ruth Young, begging her to come back to him. She refused. In the end, Micheline Graillier took him to the American embassy in Paris, and helped him to apply for a new passport.

Chet Baker and Diane Vavra, Rennes, France, November 19th 1987. Photograph by Richard Dumas.

Diane had returned to Europe in November 1987, and reunited with Chet in Italy. While Chet was in Rome, he was contacted by Giovanni Bonandrini, the founder of Soul Note Records. Charlie Haden was touring Italy with the Ornette Coleman/Don Cherry Quartet, and had a day off. Haden was a big fan of Chet's playing, heard that he was in town, and wanted to suggest a recording session. Bonandrini suggested that pianist Enrico Pieranunzi join them; he knew that Pieranunzi had played with Chet on a number of occasions, and was a big fan of his playing.

Despite the strong line-up, the recording session was plagued with difficulties. Chet had been arguing again with his girlfriend, Diane, which made for a tense atmosphere. He also insisted on shooting up in the recording studio, which did not sit well with the studio's owner, and may help to explain the plodding pace and ponderous solos on tunes such as Charlie Haden's 'Silence' and Monk's ''Round About Midnight'. Pieranunzi's playing shines, and shows the degree to which his playing had developed since he first met Chet, but it is not one of Chet's finest moments.

Two days later, and Chet was in fine form. He had been booked to play a concert with the NDR Big Band, the resident orchestra of Norddeutscher Rundfunk (North German Radio), which was established in 1945. Over the years, the orchestra had played with an array of visiting jazz stars, and even counted two veterans of the West Coast scene—Herb Geller and Walter Norris—among its ranks. The band's former producer, Wolfgang Kunert, had worked with Chet previously, and invited him to play with the band at a concert at the Audimax Hall at Hamburg University.

Kunert was aware of Chet's reputation, and sent him a non-refundable ticket. Chet missed the flight that had been booked, presumably because of the recording session with Charlie Haden, and tried to take the flight next day. When he found out the ticket was non-refundable, he paid for the flight out of his own pocket. Despite this, Chet made it to the rehearsals on time, much to the relief of all concerned.

Horst Mühlbradt had written a new arrangement for 'Look for the Silver Lining'. "We started playing the arrangement, and in the second eight bars, he used some alternative harmonies," explained alto saxophonist Herb Geller. "I saw Chet suddenly stop playing, listen, and then start again, a little bit unsure. He called an intermission, came over to me, and said, 'What happened in the second eight with those changes? That's not the way I know the song'. So I introduced him to Horst, and said, 'Maybe you could make a couple of changes'. He said to Chet, 'Well, what changes do you want?' And Chet sat down at the piano and played a chord, didn't know what it was, and said, 'This is the chord I want'. I looked at Horst and said, 'It's a C9!' And then he went through a diminished chord and said, 'I don't know what that is, either'. I said, 'F sharp'. He knew the chords, but he just couldn't tell you what they were. If you wrote a chord scheme for him, he'd just have to hear it."[61]

Pianist Walter Norris made a similar observation about Chet's technical limitations. "I don't want this to sound the wrong way; in fact I am paying Chet a tremendous compliment to say this," he said. "He did not read music, and did not read chord symbols. He would look at the music in front of him, and he would play intuitively by ear, and do everything magical like no-one else could do. So we did a Herbie Hancock title, 'Dolphin Dance'; well it sounds similar in a few places to another title. Well, that's what happened with Chet. He was playing it, and he played some notes where I could tell he was reminded of this other title. He was getting lost in it, just for a moment, just for a phrase. And he catches himself; he doesn't stop, and think, 'I've made a mistake'. He just holds the note, it's kind of wrong, and just bends it a little bit, adds a few more notes, and virtually no musician would know that there was a moment where he was kind of sidetracked. It turned out beautifully, and they kept it on the tape."[62]

The concert that took place the following evening was the sole jazz event of the first Hamburg Music Fair. The arrangements, most of which had been written for the occasion, were superb. There were a number of interesting touches that livened up even the best-known standards, but there was still plenty of space for Chet to stretch out. Chet responded to the challenge of playing with a big band, his tone sounding bright, and his solos more fluid than in Rome two days earlier. The highlights included a delightful version of 'All Of You', which brings the audience to its feet, and a fine arrangement of Miles Davis' 'All Blues', which Chet endeavoured to make his own. The concert was later released on CD after Chet's death as the *The Legacy, Volume 1* on Enja Records, and lives up to its billing.

There wasn't much time to catch up with his old friends on this occasion, but Geller remembered that Chet seemed quite upbeat, telling him about his girlfriend Diane Vavra. "He was telling me she played soprano sax, and that if he could bring her over, maybe I could give her a couple of lessons," said Geller. "I said, 'Sure, any time!'" After the show, the saxophonist and his wife drove Chet back to his hotel. "We all embraced, then Chet turned to my wife and said, 'Please look after Herb'. She started crying."[63]

Pianist Walter Norris spoke with Chet the following night at a local jazz club, Birdland, and got a rather more worrying glimpse of Chet's lifestyle at that time. "We all went over there, and later Chet was talking to the owner, a very nice gentleman who ran a construction firm, who loved jazz, and had built this club," recalled Norris. "He said, 'Chet, I'd love to have you come in and play with the local rhythm section'. He looked in his calendar, and said, 'Maybe in about four months'. Chet said, 'Listen, I'm just trying to get through the next month. What part of the next month can you put me in? I don't want to talk about four months from now. I'm trying to get through this month'. It was tragic; he was just desperate to get enough work for the next month, and that's the way his life was. He was just one step away from being a street person." The problem was not a shortage of work; Chet is thought to have earned well over $200,000, tax-free, in 1987. But he spent the money on drugs as fast as he could earn it, with no thought beyond the weeks ahead.[64]

Chet had captured the imagination of a young French photographer and filmmaker, Bertrand Fèvre, a graduate of the Conservatory of French Cinema. In late 1986, he heard a recording of Chet singing 'The Touch Of Your Lips' on the radio, and immediately went out to buy the record, and find other Chet Baker recordings.

One year later, Fèvre had the chance to see Chet play at the New Morning club in Paris, where he was appearing with pianist Alain Jean-Marie, flautist and guitarist Nicola Stilo and bass player Riccardo Del Fra. Fèvre found Chet as mesmerizing to watch as he was to listen to. "It was Friday, February the 13th 1987—a full moon night," he later recalled. "That night, I discovered the perfect incarnation of the music I was already fascinated by. Chet was physically as exceptional as his music was. A particular beauty where strength and fragility were one, where elegance and despair could join to express an unlimited sensitivity."[65]

At the end of the evening, Fèvre approached Chet with the idea of making a short movie. He had already worked as the assistant director on several films, and figured he could film Chet and his band on a relatively modest budget. "I told him I would like to make a film with him, without any precise script in mind," he said. "He just said yes to the idea, trusting me right away. I guess he felt instinctively that I could offer him an honest and respectful treatment as a filmmaker. Chet always trusted me and treated me with care and affection all the way until the end of the story."

On November 25th, Fèvre filmed Chet singing 'I'm A Fool To Want You', accompanied by Alain Jean-Marie, Riccardo Del Fra and American bebop drummer George Brown, who was living in Paris. To Fèvre the song captured the sound of a man who was addicted "to a person, love, music, or drugs, and the suffering behind it."

The footage was shot in black and white in a Paris studio, which resembled an empty, ageing theatre. Chet was dressed elegantly for the movie in a black, turtleneck sweater, his hair neatly slicked back for the occasion. Curling cigarette smoke floats across the screen, adding to the late-night club feeling that Fèvre wanted to capture. The beauty of the film is its simplicity; it looks stylish, not stylised, and allows the well-lit close-ups of Chet to tell their own story.

Looking back, Fèvre felt that drugs helped Chet to escape the pain and despair he was feeling, but that his soul was laid bare when he was performing. "On stage or during recording sessions, he was concentrated on his emotions that he expressed with feeling, improvising through his voice and trumpet, with as much beauty and depth he could give to the audience," he said.[66]

He entitled the movie *Chet's Romance*, and made sure that Chet approved the film before it was released. "I didn't realise I had so many lines," said Chet, before nodding his approval. "He later told me how proud he was of that film," said Fèvre. The film went on to win the prize for the best documentary at the French César Awards in 1989. The DVD is currently available as part of an EMI compilation entitled *Prince of Cool: The Pacific Jazz Years*.

Fèvre recalled that Chet seemed happy with Diane at this time, and even drove them around the ninth arrondissement of Paris, where Chet dreamed of finding an apartment. "I'm definitely a romantic," Chet told him in an interview before the movie was filmed. "I don't think life is really worth all the pain and effort and struggling if you don't have somebody that you love very much."

Diane Vavra desperately wanted to believe him, but too often she felt relegated to second place behind Chet's inner circle of drug buddies. Chet's band at the tail end of 1987 included pianist Michel Graillier, bass player 'Rocky' Knauer, Nicola Stilo and drummer George Brown. As the only clean member of the band, Knauer was also starting to feel the strain and considered leaving the band.

On New Year's Eve, Chet was scheduled to play at De Kroeg in Amsterdam, a tiny, dingy club belonging to Tom Mandersloot. With a capacity of just sixty people, the fee was only small, but Mandersloot let the musicians stay in the room above the club. Knauer took one look at the room—which consisted of a small kitchen area, a table and chairs, and some mattresses on the floor—and decided to quit the band. He was replaced by one of Chet's other regular bass players, Riccardo Del Fra.

In the days leading up to the gig, Vavra watched in horror as Chet got high with the other band members.

Both Nicola Stilo and Michel Graillier's wife, Micheline, distinctly remember Chet suffering from hallucinations as a result of the cocaine in the speedballs he was taking. Micheline remembers Chet opening the window, and shouting at an imaginary enemy in the tree outside. Stilo remembers his paranoia, and on one occasion having to physically stop Chet from climbing out of the window to 'escape'. At times like this, Vavra must have realised that Chet would never be ready to settle down in an apartment and live a normal life, teaching students for six months a year.

The New Year's Eve gig was filmed by a Dutch TV crew, VPRO-TV. They later combined the footage with an interview to make a fifteen-minute documentary about Chet. He explained to the film crew that he enjoyed life in Holland, compared with countries like Germany, Switzerland and Belgium, which were less relaxed. "Holland is another thing … coming to a country where there's a permanent, twenty-four-hour party going on all year," he revealed. Chet had been partying for several days before the gig, and he was not at his best that night, sweat pouring off his forehead under the TV lights. He recognised as much when he spoke to the audience between songs. "We played five nights at a very big club and you could hear a pin drop," he said. "I'm not playing well enough for that tonight. But I don't know—you guys have more enthusiasm."

The band celebrated the arrival of the New Year by getting high on cocaine, but after a few hours the mood turned ugly, with Chet getting into a bitter dispute with drummer George Brown over money. Chet took a handful of notes from his pocket, and threw them at the drummer, who stormed out of the room.

A few minutes later, Chet realised that the keys to his Alfa Romeo were still in Brown's jacket pocket. He ran down the stairs, closely followed by Micheline, and searched the surrounding streets for the drummer. They eventually found him in the red-light district of Zeedijk, where he was surrounded by drug dealers. They retrieved the keys before returning to the room above De Kroeg.

Earlier that day, the film crew had asked Chet how he felt about his prospects for the year ahead. "1987 continued to bring me a wonderful gift, and that is … that I got through it," he laughed. "I managed to survive. And of course, I've had Diane with me all this year, and that was another gift that a man can really appreciate. And I've had a lot of success all over Europe this year, every club, every auditorium … has been full. It doesn't have to get any better; if it just stays as good as '87, it will be fine."[67]

Chapter Twenty-One

THE LAST GREAT CONCERT
1988

"It doesn't have to get any better; if it just stays as good as '87, it will be fine." —Chet Baker[1]

In the final chapter of his own illustrious career, Miles Davis sought to reinvent himself—not once, but twice. In the mid-1980s, he moved towards a less jazz-oriented, more stripped-back eighties funk sound. This can be heard to good effect on his covers of pop songs like Cyndi Lauper's 'Time After Time' and Michael Jackson's 'Human Nature' from the album *You're Under Arrest*, and from the albums he recorded with bass player and arranger Marcus Miller—most notably *Tutu* and *Amandla*. Miller even recalls being called by Miles, who wanted to do 'Spitti Monitti'. "Oh, you're talking about Scritti Politti … that's a pretty extreme choice," said Miller. "Just do it, motherfucker," said Miles, before hanging up the phone.[2]

Even as he was dying in the early 1990s, Miles tried to reinvent himself one last time, keen to work with the new 'hip-hop' sounds he occasionally picked up from the bedroom of his apartment. Whilst 'Doo-Bop' proved to be something of a disappointment, it was interesting to note that Miles wanted to stay 'current' until the very end.

Chet Baker had no desire to follow Miles along this route. "The average person isn't interested in trying to think about the music too much," Chet told French journalist Gerard Rouy. "That's probably why sooner or later jazz will become a lost art. Everything will go electronic and people will make records by themselves with a synthesiser."[3]

Chet was also fairly scathing about the new generation of trumpet players that had emerged in the last ten years. "I can't tell the young trumpeters apart," he told Dutch author Jeroen de Valk in late 1987. "They all play like Freddie Hubbard or Woody Shaw. They all sound alike, as if they all come from Berklee." When asked about Wynton Marsalis, who had joined Art Blakey's Jazz Messengers in 1980, and won Grammy awards in 1983 and 1984, he was equally dismissive, claiming that Marsalis had "a lot of technique but no soul."[4]

Whilst Chet remained a musical conservative, he was not afraid to explore new directions, and his first two studio recordings in 1988 were albums of poetry. The first of these albums, *Chet On Poetry*, was recorded in Rome, and primarily consisted of Chet reciting and singing the verses of two Italian poets, Maurizio Guercini and Gianluca Manzi, accompanied by Nicola Stilo. In a slightly bizarre footnote, Enzo Pietropaoli is credited with playing bass on the album, but overdubbed his contribution at a later date. "The record was recorded with another bass player," he later explained. "I'm not sure whether it was Chet or the producer, but they decided they wanted to re-record the bass. I went to the studios and listened on the headphone to the music, without the bass track, and played along, all alone. So I played with Chet that day, but I didn't play with him physically!"[5]

The second project was even more obscure. Chet recorded an album with the Norwegian 'jazz poet', Jan Erik Vold, accompanied by guitarist Philip Catherine, Egil Kapstad on piano and Terje Venaas on bass. It was not the first time Vold had recorded with jazz musicians. One of his first records was with Norwegian saxophonist Jan Garbarek, and he had also made a record with the bass player Red Mitchell. Despite this, he was nervous about approaching Chet, and asked the jazz critic Randi Hultin whether she would be prepared to approach him. She got her chance when Chet played at the Musikkflekken club in Sandvika, Norway, in late January. Randi handed Chet a letter, and he agreed immediately, explaining that he would be in Paris between 17th and 20th of February. He also told Randi, "It would be nice if you could come along; it would make it extra nice."[6]

Hultin called Vold to relay the good news, and he arranged the musicians. The recording session was booked for 17th and 18th of February at a small, cosy studio, Studio Sysmo, on the outskirts of Paris. As was often the case, the musicians waited nervously to see if Chet would remember to show up. A phone call to Chet's hotel revealed that he was booked to stay there, but had not yet arrived. "He usually lives here," the receptionist explained helpfully, "but we never know." The man put them in touch with the guitarist Philip Catherine, who was due to play with Chet at the New Morning club later that week. Hultin had known the guitarist for many years, and asked if he'd be willing to join the recording session. "We don't have a lot of money to offer you," she explained, "just great musicians." Catherine agreed to come along, and joined the other musicians at the hotel next morning. To everyone's relief, he brought good news. "Chet is on his way! He got in by train from Rome."

Jan Erik and Egil selected a number of jazz compositions that would accompany the poetry. They also brought along the word to a children's lullaby, 'Blåmann, Blåmann, Bukken Min', written by Anne Haavie. Before the recording session, Chet insisted on hearing a translation of the poems so that he could grasp the mood of words and play in an appropriate manner. Hultin remembers the recording process as proceeding smoothly. "In a room by himself, Jan Erik stood swaying to and fro, shifting his weight from his toes to the balls of his feet, as he read his poetry. He was immersed in the event, and it was like going to church each time we went into the technician's room to hear a playback."[7]

At the end of the recording session, Chet invited everyone in the studio to the New Morning club that evening, even asking Terje Venaas and Egil Kapstad if they would like to join him on stage. He was as good as his word, finding them in the audience after the first set, and announcing them both to the crowd, before they joined him on 'Solar' and 'Just Friends'.

In between these two recording sessions, in late January, Chet appeared on a Danish TV show, *Jazz Masters*, in which he was interviewed by the show's American host, Leonard Malone. The interview took place in the gardens of the Ny Carlsberg Glypotek, an art museum in Copenhagen. At one point, Malone asked if Chet really believed the sentiment of the song he had recorded, 'You Can't Go Home Again'. "I still have some hope that may be true," he replied, after a long pause. "But on the other hand, I seem to be getting further and further from what I call home. And my desire is really not too strong to go back, you know. Oklahoma is really a cultural wasteland, and most of the states around it … I'd rather be in Europe any time."

Malone also raised the subject of drug addiction, asking Chet why he thought jazz and drugs were so closely tied. "I think maybe it's an attempt to put your head in a different place, in order to block out a lot of things," Chet explained, without elaborating on the issues he had tried to block out over the years—his father's abuse, the suffocating love of his mother, who wanted so much for her son to succeed, the pressure associated with his early success and the guilt he felt over the loss of Dick Twardzik.

"I'm not sorry," he stated firmly. "And I don't apologise for anything. I've never done anything to hurt anyone. And, uh, I don't think I've hurt myself too much. I'm fifty-eight years old, I'm still here, and I'm still playing." It was one thing to underestimate the pain he had caused his children; his relationship with Carol had effectively ended almost fifteen years earlier, and he kept communication to the bare minimum. But he severely underestimated the hurt felt by his girlfriend Diane Vavra; the strain of living her life out of a suitcase, of trying to control Chet's reckless drug use, the physical and verbal abuse she suffered, and the hurt she felt when she played second string to his drug buddies like Nicola Stilo and Micheline Graillier. On February 14th 1988, she flew back to California, claiming she had to make an insurance payment on her car, and wanted to catch up with her family. And this time she had no plans to return.

Chet did not know that this was her intention, and pressed ahead with his tour schedule. In late February, Chet travelled to the Marche region of Italy, where Paolo Piangiarelli, owner of the Philology record label, had arranged a five-day tour with the Italian pianist Enrico Pieranunzi and his band, Space Jazz Trio.

Pieranunzi's playing had developed significantly in the preceding years. "He forced me, silently, to use less notes, to choose the notes with care, to build melodies," he later admitted. "Before playing with him I was mostly an 'harmonic' and rhythmical player, but after meeting him I turned to the melody. Chet was an unbelievable storyteller, able to play and sing the essential. I tried to learn his secret and transfer it to my piano playing. It was a very long process, of course. He opened me to a new musical world where any improvisation becomes an opportunity to tell your own story, not just to show your chops. I learned from him to let the piano sing, to give the instrument a 'vocal' tone that's not easy at all at the piano."[8]

Baker and Pieranunzi played one performance as a duo on February 28th in Ascoli, before recording an album next day at a small studio in Recanati. *The Heart Of The Ballad* is slightly disappointing after Chet's duo album with Paul Bley, *Diane*, from 1985. Perhaps Pieranunzi was too respectful, and did not push Chet in the same way, or perhaps Chet was simply feeling unwell. He sounds weary on many of the tunes, and resorts to singing, rather than playing. The album still has its moments—Chet's playing on the final take of 'But Beautiful' is excellent; 'Here's That Rainy Day' has a fragile beauty; and 'The Thrill Is Gone' captures his singing to good effect.

Against all odds, Chet delivered a much stronger studio recording the very next day. Chet was sick after the duo recording, and Enrico Pieranunzi almost cancelled the concert that evening. In the end Chet decided to play, and put on a fine performance. They were scheduled to record an album next day with Pieranunzi's band Space Jazz Trio, and Chet was on fine form. There's a rare chance to hear Chet perform Miles Davis' 'Blue In Green', from *Kind Of Blue*, and Chet takes the opportunity to slow the pace, lingering over the melody. 'Old Devil Moon' is taken at a faster pace than usual, and Wayne Shorter's 'House Of Jade', a regular in Chet's repertoire, is given a swinging reading. Another highlight is the title track, a tune that Chet had rarely played since it was recorded for 'Embraceable You' back in 1957, with Chet delivering a dreamy vocal. The album was later released as *Little Girl Blue*.

Chet Baker in Ancona, Italy, March 2nd 1988.
Photograph by Carlo Pieroni.

Over the next few days, Chet toured the surrounding area with Pieranunzi and his band. The pianist was well aware of Paolo Piangiarelli's reputation for making illegal recordings, and used to check carefully for hidden microphones before they played. "I remember during those days my partners Pietropaoli and Sferra and I used to have fun looking for mikes everywhere," he laughed. "We were almost sure to find some, even in the toilet!"[9]

By this stage, Diane had been back in Santa Cruz for two weeks. Chet telephoned her from Italy, begging her to come back. When she sounded hesitant, Chet told her that he had just recorded 'The Thrill Is Gone' on his new album with Enrico Pieranunzi. "Chet was very devious," Diane later revealed. "I said, 'Are you trying to tell me something, Chet?' He said, 'Oh, it's the way the melody went, it reminds me of us'."[10]

When he failed to persuade her to return, he wired nine hundred dollars to her account in early March. Chet became convinced that Diane had left him for another man, and placed a call to Bruce Weber in New York, asking for his help. "I sent a guy out to Carmel to see her," Weber later revealed, "and there she was, living totally alone, broke, with nothing to her name. Chet always had these weird things going on his head."[11]

Chet left Italy for Belgium, spending a few days with his close friend Jacques Pelzer. Pelzer had been experiencing problems of his own in recent months with his pharmacy business. In the mid-1980s, an investigation was launched into his pharmacy records, revealing that he had regularly provided codeine to friends without prescription. He escaped with a fine, but the pharmacy eventually closed in November 1987 after Pelzer's assistant was caught stealing from the business.

It was Pelzer's daughter, Micheline, that Chet turned to in his darkest hours. "On two occasions, he made me listen in on the conversation he was having with Diane," she revealed. "He said, 'Micheline, you're a woman. Tell me, when she talks like that, do you think she's telling me the truth?' It was hard for me, I had a big responsibility. I told him the truth, because I was first and foremost his friend. I didn't want to bullshit him, and told him I thought she wasn't going to come back unless he changed. 'I've tried to change, but she wants me to go to the United States. I want to stay here and play'. You could feel he was so sad that she had left him, and I think he made a conscious decision to let himself go."[12]

In the weeks that followed, Chet's drug use spiralled out of control, often with alarming consequences. "I didn't want to leave him alone at that time," she said. "Even two months before he died, I knew he was not in a good state."

In mid-March, Chet played two concerts with tenor saxophonist Archie Shepp, who was best known for his passionate, Afro-centric recordings for Impulse! Records in the 1960s. It looked an unlikely combination on paper, and so it proved. "Chet had no real relationship with Archie Shepp," recalled

Ria Wigt, the wife of promoter Wim Wigt. "They met each other from time to time when they were in the same place. A festival organiser in Frankfurt thought it would be a nice idea to bring those people together. We thought it would make sense to have each musician play with his own quartet, but festival organisers always look for something special, to help them sell the festival."[13]

A rehearsal had been scheduled on the day of the concert at noon, but at the last minute, Chet decided to fly to Italy to buy a new cream-coloured Alfa Romeo sports car. Peter Huijts, Wim Wigt's road manager, tried to persuade Chet that this was crazy, but he promised he would be back in time for the concert that evening. Amazingly, he made it, but tired and under-rehearsed, he and Shepp struggled to make sense of one another's playing. "At the start, it was very stressful," recalled Huijts. "Chet needs space. He would play a phrase, wait a few bars and then resume. While Archie blew non-stop. If Chet just paused for a moment, Archie immediately came in with a big surge of sound. And then Chet sat there with an expression as if to say, 'Fine, go ahead, if it's so important to you'."[14]

A second concert had been booked the following night at the New Morning in Paris. In order to ensure that Chet arrived in good shape, Peter Huijts arranged to swap his airline ticket for Chet's car keys. As a consequence, Chet had more time to rest between the two shows. Huijts also spoke to Archie Shepp before the concert in Paris. "'This is how Chet is,' I said. 'If you go on like this, we won't get much music out of him'. That evening things went a little better."[15]

The second night was indeed considered a success by all concerned, and Wim Wigt arranged for the two stars to play a third concert in Laren, Holland, on May 13th. When Chet failed to show up for that final show, Huijts knew that something must be wrong.

Chet returned to Italy on March 17th for a studio recording with a number of Italian musicians, including pianist Enrico Pieranunzi, his close friend Nicola Stilo, and members of Space Jazz Trio, bass player Enzo Pietropaoli and drummer Fabrizio Sferra. Pietropaoli remembers the atmosphere being very intense. "I loved Chet, but when you were not involved with drugs you felt very different," he explained. "I felt very sad and very uncomfortable. One day Chet called me and asked me if I was free, and I told him, 'Chet, I'm sorry, I cannot play, I have another concert'. And it was not true. It was very sad for me, because playing with Chet is one of the most wonderful things that ever happened to me. In the end it was too hard for me to find the balance—the drugs had become more important than the music."[16]

For Nicola Stilo, the music and drugs were hopelessly entwined, but he still felt a deep connection to Chet when they played together. "Musically, that period was very important to me," he claimed. "Each night was a spiritual thing." But he could see the changes his friend was going through. "I never saw Chet as sad as those last few weeks," he said. "He didn't react in a positive way."[17]

On April 1st, Chet played at a jazz festival at the Theaterhaus in Stuttgart, a concert that was being broadcast for German TV. Chet seemed to be in poor shape that night, forgetting some of the words to 'I'm A Fool To Want You', and getting into an angry dispute with the sound engineer. Gudrun Endress, publisher of the German jazz magazine *Jazz Podium*, witnessed the concert. "The music is the only thing that kept him alive," she later claimed. "I didn't even dare to approach him. He seemed so broken and sad."

A few days later, Chet returned to Italy to play a short stint at the Music Inn in Rome. He stayed on for a few days, accompanied by his close friends—Michel and Micheline Graillier, and Nicola Stilo. Before long, they had burned through all the money they had earned from the engagement, and found themselves penniless. Chet suggested that Micheline call pianist Amadeo Tommasi, and ask him to lend her money—he had long since stopped lending money to Chet, knowing the money would never be paid back.

Micheline called Tommasi, who she had known all her life, and explained that she was stranded in Rome, with no money for food. Tommasi arranged to meet her for dinner, and when he arrived, found Chet Baker, Michel Graillier and Nicola Stilo there too. As the evening progressed, the mood turned progressively dark. "I asked Chet how he was doing," recalled the pianist, who had played with Chet when he was released from prison in Italy. "At my age, it's time to die," he said. "I want to drive into a wall in my car at high speed. It's no longer necessary to live."[18]

After dinner, Tommasi invited them all to his studio. He sat at the piano and played 'Ballad for Micheline', a tune he had written when she was just a small child. Micheline was reduced to tears. "Chet said to me, 'Amadeo, you've made her cry'. That was the last time I saw him."

Next day, Michel Graillier suggested they make some money busking on the streets of Rome—a sad state of affairs for musicians of their calibre. He set up a small battery-operated keyboard, and was joined by Chet on trumpet, Nicola Stilo on guitar and his friend Lillo Quaratino on bass. They soon attracted a sizeable crowd, and after thirty minutes, Chet passed his hat around the crowd, raising about one hundred dollars in Italian lire.

A few days later, on April 15th, Chet drove to Milan. That night, he stopped by the Capolinea club to hear his old friend, tenor saxophonist Gianni Basso, play with his band. "I asked him to join me, but he'd forgotten his trumpet," said Basso. "'I might come along tomorrow night', he said. Next day he joined my quartet for one set. After the set he took me outside to show me his new Alfa Romeo. He seemed happy, and proud of his new car. 'You're earning too much money', I told him! Chet was leaving for Germany next day, but said to me, 'Gianni, I'm thinking about getting a place, but I'm not sure where to live—Paris or Rome—what do you think?' 'Oh, Paris', I said. 'Well, next time I come back to Italy, I'll play with you'."

On April 17th, Chet drove to Rosenheim for a concert with a new-look quartet; he was appearing with the Italian pianist Luca Flores, Nicola Stilo, who played both flute and guitar, and a bass player by the name of Marc Abrams. Chet played well that evening, and seemed to form a strong bond with Flores. "Luca Flores, who committed suicide in 1993, was a great piano player who Chet loved very much," said Stilo. "They were close friends. I think he was one of Chet's favourite pianists."[19]

A recording of the concert was later released as *Live in Rosenheim—Last Recordings As Quartet*. Unfortunately, the sound quality is poor. The microphone captures Marc Abrams and Nicola Stilo quite clearly, but Chet is low in the mix. On 'Portrait in Black and White', for example, Chet sounds as though he is playing offstage; we can barely hear his trumpet, and only get to hear him more clearly when he sits down at the piano. There's a lengthy version of Rique Pantoja's 'Arborway', but the tape is badly edited in the middle of the tune. Finally, some of Nicola Stilo's flute solos are overlong, which is made worse by his prominence in the mix. Recordings like this should have stayed in the vault, but understandably attracted a certain morbid curiosity after Chet's death a few weeks later.

Chet's swansong took place on April 29th 1988—a concert with the Norddeutscher Rundfunk Big Band and the Hannover Radio Orchestra at the elegant Grosser Sendesaal Hall in Hannover. The event had been carefully planned for several months. Kurt Giese, a Hamburg-based radio producer and director, had long dreamed of creating a showcase for his musical hero, and wanted to reinvent *Chet Baker with Strings*—his 1954 album—with the Hannover Radio Orchestra.

Chet had agreed terms some months earlier, and was apparently looking forward to the event. "(Recording with an orchestra) happens from time to time; not often because of the money involved, and because someone has to write the arrangements," he told an interviewer in Denmark earlier that year. "But when it does happen, it's a lot of fun. I think I'm supposed to do something with a string section in Hannover. Also I'm supposed to make a record for Japan in Amsterdam with the string section from the Concertgebouw theatre. All this music is being written, I have no idea who's writing the arrangements on these things. I just go there and play when they tell me, and stop when they tell me!"[20]

Giese had primarily selected songs from the early part of Chet's career, during his heyday recording with Pacific Jazz, including 'I Fall In Love Too Easily,' 'I Get Along Without You Very Well', and of course his signature tune, 'My Funny Valentine'.

There were supposed to five days of rehearsals, Monday to Friday, with the concert—which was a black-tie affair—taking place on Friday evening. For the first two days, the NDR Big Band—which still featured Chet's old West Coast friends, saxophonist Herb Geller and pianist Walter Norris—rehearsed their parts in Hamburg to save money.

Chet was supposed to meet with the Hannover Radio Orchestra on the Monday, but failed to show up. Wim Wigt received a number of angry phone calls that day, and spent several hours trying to track down the trumpet player. When he did finally reach him, it was clear he had no intention of attending the rehearsal. "I'm going on a little vacation with Micheline," he informed the promoter. "But if there's no rehearsal, there's no gig," Wigt told him, a warning that fell on deaf ears. The orchestra evidently began the rehearsal without him, and recorded the arrangements as playbacks.

By Tuesday morning, there was still no sign of Chet, and the radio producers started to panic. "It wasn't easy for them to get a nice comfortable setup with budgets for two orchestras," explained the executive producer, Matthias Winckelmann, "and if the concert didn't take place, a lot of heads would roll."[21]

Around 5 p.m. on Wednesday, Chet called Kurt Giese from his hotel room. He claimed to have come two hours earlier, but the security guard did not recognise him, and would not let him in. The Radio Orchestra and Big Band had left at this stage, but Giese arranged for Chet to come to the studio, and play along to the tapes the orchestra had recorded earlier that day. He was apparently having trouble with his dentures that evening, and could hardly play. “The next morning I went into the studio to hear the playbacks,” said Walter Norris, pianist with the NDR Big Band. “The man who sets up the microphones was saying, ‘Who is this man? He’s just ruined his health, he has no teeth!’ He could not believe how tragic it was.”[22]

Late morning on the Thursday, Chet pulled into the parking lot in his Alfa Romeo, and to the relief of all concerned, he seemed to be in good shape. That afternoon, Chet’s dentures stayed in place, and he played beautifully.

“I remember that time I sat in for Gerry Mulligan,” recalled saxophonist Herb Geller. “I’d been playing at The Lighthouse, and Max Roach brought in an arrangement for ‘Conception’ that was actually based on Gil Evans’s harmony from ‘Birth of the Cool’. I really liked that tune. We called a little rehearsal, and I said, ‘Chet, let me show you this tune called “Conception”’. I wrote it out for him, wrote out the changes. He wasn’t a very fast reader—he could read, but slowly. He had to hear it. It was a very difficult song, especially in the 1950s! The keys were all over the place. Chet took it a little bit slow, and the chords didn’t mean much to him. He stumbled round a little bit. We did a second time, and the third time he nailed it, he played fantastic. At the concert in Hanover, the producer went up to Chet and myself and said, ‘How about doing one of the tunes you used to play together?’ I looked at Chet and said, ‘Hey, remember “Conception”?’ He said, ‘Yeah, let’s do that’. So I wrote it out real quick for the rhythm section and we did it on that date.”[23]

The only hitch came later that day, when a camera crew wanted to film some footage to promote the forthcoming concert. Chet initially refused to participate, but was eventually persuaded it would only take a few minutes. “So they played for three minutes, and the TV crew said, ‘Listen, we had a little trouble with the camera, can you do that again?’” explained Walter Norris. “Chet said ‘That’ll be five thousand’. He wanted additional money. They started bargaining, and he wasn’t going to play. It was embarrassing. Well, eventually they persuaded him, but that’s how stubborn he could be about money. I guess one becomes that way because of the drugs, and the need for money for drugs.”[24]

Around five o’clock that afternoon, the producer invited a few of the musicians, including Walter Norris, to join him for coffee. Chet was quiet, but started to open up when Norris asked him a few questions. He was evidently worried his French driving would not be renewed because of his numerous arrests. He also complained how long it could take him to cross the border, given his history, when driving to countries like Italy and Germany. "He was exhausted from all of the hassle that went along with his daily life, but he still had energy, which is the locomotive that keeps us going," said Norris. "I think he suffered from depression, but not necessarily like anyone else. He was depressed, but he was annoyed that he couldn't do what he wanted to do; which is better than being depressed in a very passive way. Depressed, but he could fight back, and had the energy to keep going. I was very surprised to hear about his death just two weeks later. I don't think it was suicide."[25]

On Friday, the day of the concert, the musicians had one final rehearsal. "Everything was peaches and cream," recalled Matthias Winckelmann. "He just went over the heads of the tunes since he wanted to save his lip for that night. Of course, he knew these songs perfectly, and the way it worked out his solos were very spontaneous."[26]

After the final rehearsal, Chet had a long chat with Herb Geller, who had a more negative impression of his state of mind. "He was more depressed than when I'd seen him in Hamburg in late 1987," the saxophonist recalled. "He was having a lot of trouble with his teeth. At the rehearsal he had to stop playing because his upper teeth were sliding around; he had to get his denture glue and call an intermission. He told me his lower teeth were starting to go. 'When that happens, I've got to stop playing'. Also I heard that his girlfriend was supposed to join him, but had just broken up with him. That's why I think he had a sort of death wish."[27]

For the concert that evening, the whole sixty-two-piece band was wearing tails, and the auditorium was full. "Chet came in wearing tennis shoes that were broken, and old Levis that were torn," recalled Geller. Chet sat down in his chair on the stage, the NDR Big Band on one side, and the Hannover Radio Orchestra on the other. "We were all holding our breath," the saxophonist claimed.

Chet's playing was somewhat below par on the first few tunes, including 'All Blues' and 'My Funny Valentine'. He had been having problems with his teeth, and may have worried whether they would stay in place, or he may simply have been tired. Either way, his playing and singing improved steadily as the concert progressed. His playing is a delight on Brubeck's 'In Your Own Sweet Way', and he delivers memorable versions of two of his early vocal recordings, 'I Fall In Love Too Easily' and 'I Get Along Without You Very Well'. "He played just beautifully that night," said Geller.

The arrangements and recording quality are also superb, providing a fitting farewell to one of the jazz greats—the last great concert.

After the concert, Chet jumped in his Alfa Romeo, and is thought to have driven to Amsterdam, where he reunited with Nicola Stilo. On April 30th, he performed a concert in Calais, France. "In Calais, Chet gave his last good concert," claimed promoter Wim Wigt. "Afterwards he was so oppressed by drugs that things really didn't go any more." That night, Wigt paid him for the last time—$2,500 for the concert in Calais, and a further $4,000 as part of the payment for the recordings with Archie Shepp in mid-March.[28]

After the concert, Chet drove to Liège, staying with his old friend Jacques Pelzer. He was accompanied by Nicola Stilo, Michel Graillier and his wife Micheline. The next three days were incredibly harrowing, according to Nicola Stilo, who could barely bring himself to discuss the events, even twenty years later. "He was a man completely lost, you understand?" he said. "He was crying for help, asking somebody to show him a minimum reason to live."

Chet briefly discussed getting clean, bringing Diane Vavra back to Europe and finding a place to settle down—but deep down, he knew it was just a dream. "Did Chet want to give up drugs?" mused Micheline, looking back on his final days. "'The feeling of a speedball, coke and heroin, that's what I love'. He told me that many times. Maybe love could have saved him, but he was too far gone, I think. For his body, it was too late. Sharing a house with Diane would never have worked—it was impossible. Chet needed to live the way he always lived. Moving, driving, playing, sharing his life with a woman—that was his life. Eating sometimes!"[29]

As the realisation sunk in that Diane was never going to return, Chet buried the pain the only way he knew, taking ever larger speedballs. Again, the cocaine caused him to hallucinate. At one point he telephoned Bruce Weber in New York. "I just want you to know that if something happens to me, you know, that there are these guys who have been after me."[30]

When he settled down to sleep that night, Nicola Stilo stayed in the same room, knowing that Chet could not bear to be alone. Chet nodded off with a cigarette in his hand, and set fire to the pillow. Nicola Stilo awoke with a start, and tried to rouse his friend, who was deep in a dream. Micheline Graillier was also woken up by the commotion, and helped to put out the fire, throwing the pillow out of the window into the garden below.

Next day, Chet was in an emotional turmoil and could barely think straight. At one point, he couldn't find his heroin, which was stuck in the pocket of his jeans. He started to accuse Michel Graillier of stealing his drugs. "If Michel doesn't give me my bag back, I'm gonna drive my car in the garden, and burn it with myself inside!" I told him, "Michel has never stolen anything from you. Why don't you take off your pants? Stop this bullshit," said Micheline. "Of course, the heroin was there. He calmed down eventually, but he was not in a good way."[31]

Micheline also remembers that Chet was looking back on his failures, discussing his relationship with Diane Vavra, and his relationship with his children. "I'm going to die one day, and my kids won't even know who I am," he said.

Chet was scheduled to play two nights at the New Morning club in Paris, starting on May 4th, accompanied by pianist Alain Jean-Marie rather than Michel Graillier, Nicola Stilo and Jacques Pelzer. Chet had mistakenly invited two bass players to play with him in Paris, which was a fairly common occurrence. "I lived in England at the time, in Dover, and when the time came I took the ferry from Dover to Calais, drove three hours to Paris with my bass," recalled Hein van de Geijn. "I checked into the hotel Anna de France, the usual hotel for musicians playing at the New Morning. I checked the guest list to see if Chet had arrived, and saw the name of Marc Abrams, an American bass player that lived in Milan at the time. I thought, 'That's nice, Marc is in town'. I called his room, and said, 'Hey Marc, how are you doing, are you playing in Paris?' He said, 'I'm playing with Chet tonight'. I said, 'That's strange, I thought I was playing with Chet tonight!' It was the first and last time I was mad with Chet. I stormed up to his room and said, 'Chet, man, what the fuck is happening?' Chet looked at me, and said, 'Hein, we're all good musicians, we should be able to make some beautiful music together'. With that, what could I say?"[32]

But Chet was in no fit state to play. He wanted to take something to relax, and ended up taking fifteen valium. "I had to wake him up for the gig, which was very hard," explained Micheline. "He had taken the pills earlier that day, and it was almost impossible to wake him up."[33]

Chet was still struggling to stay awake when he took to the stage before the first set. "He was writing the set list, and was writing the song titles painstakingly slowly," said van de Geijn. "When he was halfway through one title, he nodded off, his pen still on the paper, and sat there for five or ten minutes. Then he opened his eyes, and continued where he had left off. It was quite scary to see."[34]

Chet finally roused himself to play, but was not on the best of form, his energy levels clearly low. "We started one tune, Chet turned to me after the theme, and gave me the first solo," recalled van de Geijn. "I played the solo, then went back to comping, and Marc and I tried to stay out of each other's way. But there was just too much going on, it wasn't really working. After the first tune I thought, 'Forget it!' I gracefully got off the stage, and said to Marc, 'I'll take the second set'. We did the same thing on the second night."[35]

Chet's old girlfriend, Liliane Rovère, was in the audience that night, and had the chance to talk to him between sets. "He was so high, I couldn't believe it," she recalled. "He told me he was sad, because Diane wouldn't join him because of the drugs. I said to him, 'Well I can understand it—she did ask you to stop taking drugs'. He told me he was also anxious because his hands were swollen. 'You should see a cardiologist', I told him. 'Your fingers are badly swollen, but it's not surprising given what you do'."[36]

After the concert, Chet approached Liliane and asked her if she would consider spending the night with him, holding him in her arms. She initially rejected his offer, thinking that Chet was trying to rekindle their old love affair, but soon realised that Chet was simply lonely and needed company. "He just wanted me to hold him in my arms, like a baby," she said. "He was living in a small hotel at the time. I said I would go with him, but asked Jacques Pelzer to join us. I didn't want to be alone with Chet, because I was afraid of him. I wasn't afraid that he would jump on me, and make love to me—that was a joke! I was afraid of him because with Chet, you never knew what would happen. In the hotel, after a while, Chet said, 'I'm going to take a shot'. I said to him, 'Please, Chet, be careful'. After that he was so high, and I was glad that I was with Jacques, and not alone with him. He was lying on the bed like a dead man, with his mouth open. I remember thinking, this is what he will look like when he dies. It's a very sad memory for me, because that was the last time I saw him. I got very scared, and I left. I still don't know what ate Chet, why he lived like that."[37]

Jacques Pelzer returned to Liège next day. At 7 p.m., Bertrand Fèvre's movie *Chet's Romance* premiered at a cinema in Montmartre. The director left a note at Chet's hotel that morning, and was disappointed when Chet failed to show up. "I kept an empty seat at my side in case he would appear during the three screenings," said Fèvre, "but the seat stayed empty."

Fèvre went along to the concert that night, the same venue where he had met Chet for the first time six months earlier. The difference was striking. "He appeared extremely weak that night, whispering with his lips stuck to the microphone," he said. "He seemed broken inside as I had never seen him before, almost hopeless."[38]

Fèvre stayed for the second set, and was struck by the overwhelming sadness and despair that seemed to be hanging over him. The rest of the audience could feel it too, and there was an uncomfortable atmosphere, as though they were intruding on a personal tragedy unfolding before their eyes. As the audience shuffled out in to the night, Chet remained slumped in his chair on the stage, looking as though he lacked the energy to leave the club. Fèvre took one of the white roses from a bouquet he had been given at the earlier premier, called Chet's name, and gave him the rose. Chet embraced him, and whispered, "Thanks". For Fèvre, it felt like an emotional farewell. "No-one could have rescued him at that point," he felt. "No drugs either."[39]

At the end of the evening, Chet drove back to Liège, accompanied by Nicola Stilo. "He came back to see my father and I," explained Micheline. "He was very down. I was his nurse, and wouldn't leave him alone for a second. The one time I went to sleep, just for one hour, he skipped the house, taking his car but leaving his trumpet and trumpet case." Despite his low energy levels, Chet is thought to have driven all the way back to Zeedijk to score.

Chet spent the night in Amsterdam. On the morning of Saturday, May 7th, he called Nicola Stilo in Liège, and requested that he bring his trumpet case to the port city of Rotterdam, where Wim Wigt had arranged a concert at short notice. "Chet hadn't called us for some time," explained Ria Wigt. "Then he called us out of the blue and said, 'I must have more concerts. I must play now, because I need the money'. We had some concerts arranged, but Chet wanted more—and earlier. Wim had a relationship with the owner of a club in Rotterdam who offered to help out at very short notice. We only got paid on the door, because he didn't want to take any risk."[40]

Hein van de Geijn and Chet Baker at Jazzclub Thelonious, May 7th 1988. Photograph by Hajo Piebenga.

The concert took place at the Jazzclub Thelonious, a dingy basement club located in a graffiti-covered shopping mall, the shops all shuttered for the night. Bass player Marc Abrams had returned to Italy after the New Morning gig, claiming he had to look after his girlfriend, who was sick. Hein van de

Geijn stayed on for the gig, but was depressed by the sleazy venue in which they were playing. "The club was run by a shady guy, and there were lots of other strange characters hanging round Chet," he said. "I'm sure there were lots of drugs going on. It was just a sad scene."[41]

The concert had been expected to sell out, but in the event, only a handful of paying customers showed up. "It was just the quartet with Chet, Nicola, Alain and me," the bass player explained. "But the music was not really there that night. The heart and soul of his sound and his melodies was still there, but he was less eloquent."[42]

At the end of the evening, the club's owner only paid Chet a fraction of the fee he had been expecting. "Chet got paid nothing, or almost nothing," said Wim Wigt. "Willem van Empel thought that Chet played so bad that he didn't have to pay him anything. Besides, attendance had been so poor that there was hardly any gate."[43]

The musicians left the club around 2 a.m. Chet was planning to leave with Nicola Stilo, while Alain Jean-Marie and Hein van de Geijn went their separate ways. "I walked over to say goodbye to Chet, and he looked so sad at that moment," the bass player recalled. "I put my arms around him. 'Thank you so much', I said. 'Be careful of yourself, because we need you'. I don't know why I said that. Perhaps intuitively I saw something in his eyes, but I felt a strong emotion I hadn't felt before."[44]

Chet and Nicola climbed the stairs to the street, but must have come in by a different entrance, because the street looked unfamiliar. They searched in vain for Chet's Alfa Romeo, but could not find it anywhere. Assuming it must have been stolen, they boarded a night train to Amsterdam. They scored from Chet's regular dealer, before checking in to the Capitol Hotel on the Nieuwe Zijds Voorburgwal in Amsterdam.

Over the course of the next thirty-six hours, Nicola Stilo watched in horror as Chet went crazy, injecting himself with pure cocaine. The high would only last for a short period, and then he would have to inject himself again, leaving the hotel room a bloody mess. The cocaine again resulted in paranoid delusions. At one point, Chet was again convinced that someone was out to kill him, and made a rush for what he thought was the door. The door was in fact a window, and Stilo had to use all his strength to pull the trumpet player back. The noise alerted a member of the hotel staff, who knocked on the door to check everything was under control.

By the morning of Monday, May 9th, Nicola Stilo couldn't take any more. He had already informed Chet that he needed to return to Rome because his wife was expecting a baby, but was worried about leaving his friend in such a fragile condition. "Chet, look at me," he said, one hand on each of his shoulders. "I'll be gone for the next few days. Please, man, try to stay strong."[45]

Stilo took the train to Liège, where he had left his guitar. He explained to Micheline what had happened in Amsterdam. "That was the beginning of the end," she said. "I knew I couldn't do anything any more. He was taking so much coke. He spent five thousand bucks in two or three days, so it was not surprising that he was hallucinating. Chet needed a woman next to him all of the time, and couldn't live by himself. Music and love—he didn't care too much for anything else. Money was what you needed to survive. By the time he realised Diane wasn't coming back, he didn't want to struggle any more. He just let himself go—that's the feeling I have."

Chet stayed alone in Amsterdam that night. On the morning of Tuesday, May 10th, he telephoned a bass player, Harry Emmery, about playing a concert the following week. According to Emmery, there was nothing out of the ordinary about the phone call.

After lunch, Chet took the train to Rotterdam, hoping to find his car. Sometime late afternoon, Wim Wigt received a phone call from a police station in Rotterdam. "They said, 'There's a gentleman called Chesney H. Baker. He is looking for his car, and says if we don't understand him properly, we should call you, because you are organising everything for him. Is that true?'" explained Ria Wigt. "Wim said, 'Yes, that's right'. It was a perfectly relaxed phone call, but even so, Wim started to worry. He knew that Chet regularly hid his drugs in the car, and that if the police found the car, they might discover his drugs. Also, the way Chet looked, it is easy to see how someone might not hold him in the highest esteem."[46]

Wim Wigt tried to call Willem van Empel, the owner of Jazzclub Thelonious, but was unable to reach him. When that failed, he called Robert van de Feyst, a former employee who lived near the station in Rotterdam. Van de Feyst was well-known in the Rotterdam jazz world; he had worked as a bartender in Jazzclub Thelonious, dealt in drugs, and also helped to house American jazz musicians who were passing through Europe. He had previously housed Chet's former drummer, 'Philly' Joe Jones, and in May 1988, he was looking after tenor saxophonist Frank Wright and trumpet player Woody Shaw. Van de Feyst had adopted the Americanised name of Bob Holland, which was easier for visiting musicians to remember. "Without asking me, Wim decided to call Bob Holland," said Ria Wigt. "I was not happy about it, because he had worked with us before, and had been extremely unreliable. Bob agreed to help, and went along to meet Chet at the police station."[47]

Holland agreed to help Chet look for his car. A policeman drove the two men around the streets near the club, and when they again failed to find it, dropped them off at Holland's apartment. There was a piano in the living room of the apartment, and photographs of jazz stars that Holland had met lining the walls. Chet surprised his host by pulling a small bag of heroin and cocaine from his socks, and asking if he could take a hit in the bedroom. "The man was a walking corpse," Holland later recalled. "He was only living for the stuff. Music was the last resort to get it." Holland was astounded by the amount he was taking, but Chet brushed off his concerns. "Bob, I'm fifty-eight years old. I've used this stuff for thirty years. You can't help me. I'm too far out."[48]

Later that evening, Chet decided he needed another fix. He was not familiar with the drug scene in Rotterdam, and asked Holland to score for him. He reached into the pockets of his trousers and pulled out a fistful of mixed banknotes, including Dutch guilders, French and Swiss francs. Holland estimated he was carrying around six thousand guilders, or four thousand US dollars—indicating he had already spent one third of the money he was given ten days earlier. Holland scored for him, waited for Chet to take another hit, and then took Chet and Frank Wright to a nearby Chinese restaurant. Woody Shaw had evidently just left the country to go on tour.

Around midnight, Chet informed Holland that he would like to play. They made their way to a bar called Jazzcafé Dizzy, where a jazz-rock band, Bad Circuits, was playing. Chet joined them for two songs in their final set—'R.C.', an abbreviation for 'Rhythm Changes', which was a tune based on 'I Got Rhythm', and 'On Green Dolphin Street'.

Holland later reported that Chet played "with a strength and intensity that I had never heard from him before."[49]

But the band's saxophonist was rather less charitable. "Chet Baker didn't have his best day, obviously; he looked bad, and his ideas only came out haltingly. It testified to some vigour that he took the initiative to play along, but apart from that, he made a sorry impression." He went on to elaborate about Chet's problems that night. "We had to gallantly make allowances, but we managed. Of course, we played rather 'heavy'. We immediately brought the volume down, otherwise we never could have heard him. A couple of times he whispered in my ear that he could play a lot better, and that he was having trouble with his chops. His playing still had a certain charm. He could express his ideas concisely. But I think that only for someone who had heard a lot of jazz was it clear what he wanted to express."[50]

The set finished around 1 a.m. and at Chet's request, Holland took the musicians to a dealer, but they were only able to score three grams of heroin. Chet needed more, so Wright took Chet back to the apartment while Holland went in search of more. He later reported that he returned home empty-handed at around three or four in the morning.

Chet slept in most of the morning of April 12th. He was scheduled to play a concert with Archie Shepp that evening, a live broadcast from the Singer-Konzertsaal in Laren, Holland for the anniversary of popular Sesjun radio show. The police called Bob Holland mid-morning to inform him they had found Chet's car. Holland offered to collect the car, and score some more dope while he was out, so Chet handed him the car keys.

Around midday, Peter Huijts, who worked with Wim Wigt, made a couple of telephone calls to Chet, and found him in a foul mood. "Without a regular drug intake, his behaviour would become unpredictable," Ria Wigt explained. "He told Peter that Bob Holland had left, had taken the car keys with him, and hadn't come back. Peter offered to come and meet Chet, and take him to the hotel in Amsterdam where they would meet before the concert. Chet eventually told Peter, 'I'm not waiting a second longer. I've had it with everybody. I'm coming to Amsterdam now!' He hung up the phone, and when Peter tried to call him back, there was no answer."[51]

Peter Huijts then called Ria Wigt to explain that Chet was on his way to Amsterdam. "When Peter told me what had happened, I felt right away that something bad was going to happen," she said. "Peter wanted to go after Chet, but lived too far away to meet Chet at the station—he couldn't do anything about it."

Chet gathered the pile of banknotes left on the living room table, left the apartment, and took the 1.32 p.m. train to Amsterdam. Sometime later that afternoon he checked in at the Hotel Prins Hendrik, just across from Amsterdam's Central Station, a few minutes walk from Zeedijk where he knew he could score.

It is not clear why Chet chose this particular hotel. Wim Wigt had booked both Chet Baker and Archie Shepp into the nearby Memphis Hotel, with a view to collecting the musicians by van at 6.30 p.m. The hotel had been chosen because it was close to Zeedijk, allowing Chet the opportunity to score before the show. Most likely, Chet had simply forgotten this arrangement, having left Rotterdam in a bad mood. He often used other hotels in the city—the Barbizon Palace, the Victoria—but those hotels may have been full, as it was a national holiday—Ascension Day. James Gavin has suggested that Chet may have chosen that hotel because he wanted to be alone; it seems more likely that he chose it because it was convenient and available. We do know that he had stayed in the hotel before, and used it to shoot up with Micheline Graillier. "He had a nice hotel booked further away, but he didn't want to wait any longer," concluded Ria Wigt. "This is the sort of thing that could happen to Chet if you didn't take good care of him."

Chet's room was C-20, located on the third floor of the hotel. It was a functional room, with bright yellow walls, a double bed, a night table and a small television. There were two sash windows overlooking the bustling streets below.

Chet telephoned Diane Vavra that afternoon, and informed her that he couldn't go on living without her, and would not be calling for some time. It sounded like a thinly veiled hint that he was considering suicide, but Vavra had heard similar threats on numerous occasions, and there was nothing in Chet's tone to suggest anything was different on this occasion.

At some point after his arrival in Amsterdam, Chet walked to Zeedijk, where he used most of his remaining cash to score both heroin and cocaine.

At around 6 p.m., Archie Shepp and his band started to assemble in the lobby of the Memphis Hotel. Ria Wigt called the hotel at this time to make sure that Chet had checked in. The van was supposed to depart at 6.30 p.m., but there was still no sign of Chet. "Everybody was waiting for Chet, and people were very upset that he hadn't shown up," said Ria Wigt. Peter (Huijts) had gone to Laren to see the concert, and when there was no sign of Chet, kept calling me every few minutes. I knew that if he hadn't made it to the concert, but was still in Amsterdam, that something very bad must have happened—my intuition told me right away."[52]

The other musicians left for Laren at 7 p.m., and when there was still no sign of Chet, went ahead with a soundcheck at 8 p.m. Chet's Alfa Romeo pulled up outside the venue a little later, but the driver was Bob Holland, not Chet. Wim Wigt was still expecting Chet to make a last-minute appearance, and asked him to drive the car to Laren.

As the evening wore on, Peter Huijts started to worry. "At the start of the concert, I was not especially concerned," he said. "He had failed to appear before. For the duration of the concert I was merely annoyed. But later in the evening I began to worry. Because in general, you would hear from him. Usually he would call in the course of an evening with some story or other about something that hadn't happened and why he hadn't come. He always had an excuse, a flat tire or something. But now there was nothing."[53]

Archie Shepp had agreed to perform a thirty-minute set with a vocalist, Annette Lowman. With no sign of Chet Baker, the organisers started to panic, and asked Shepp to play for longer, and fill the empty timeslot. He refused to do so without being paid an additional fee. As a consequence, he played a short, thirty-minute set, then returned to Lowman's dressing room, where they sat in an eerie silence. "We just sort of sat there looking at each other," the singer later recalled. "Peter Huijts is a miracle man—for Peter not to be able to round Chet up and get him there, we knew something was wrong."[54]

A little later, a furious argument erupted between the radio producers, Archie Shepp, and the promoter Wim Wigt. The producers blamed the saxophonist, and threatened to withhold part of his fee. Shepp argued forcefully that he had fulfilled his contract, and demanded to be paid in full. The producers then turned on Wigt, blaming him for Chet's absence.

In the meantime, his wife Ria Wigt had started to make a series of frantic phone calls. "I called everyone in Amsterdam that I could think of calling—hospitals, police officers," she said. "I don't know why, I just felt something was wrong. Normally, if Chet was in trouble, or needed help, he would call me. Sometimes he'd be nice, sometimes not nice, but he would call me when he wanted something."[55]

There was no sign of Chet until around 3 a.m. on Friday, 13th May. At that time, a man leaving a nearby Surinamese bar discovered a blood-stained body curled up on the sidewalk outside of the Hotel Prins Hendrik. He knocked on the front door of the hotel, which was locked for the night. The desk clerk was evidently in a different part of the hotel, and did not hear the commotion. But the noise was loud enough to wake another American guest staying at the hotel. He came down to the lobby, assumed it was just a drunk from one of the nearby bars, and returned to his room. A few minutes later, the police at nearby Warmoesstraat received a phone call, a man reporting that a body had been discovered.

Police officers arrived at the hotel a few minutes later. The police found the dead body of a man who had evidently jumped or fallen from the window of the hotel, hitting his head on one of the stone posts outside the hotel, which crushed the back of his skull. The man was wearing a long-sleeved shirt, with his sleeves rolled up, a pair of striped trousers, and was barefoot. Beside the body was a pair of tortoiseshell spectacles and a steel pin, which appeared to have come from one of the sash windows. A passport was also found in the man's trouser pocket. The police dragged the body onto a stretcher, and drove it to the morgue at the police station. The face was caked in blood, and the initial police report listed that the body of a thirty-year old man had been discovered.

Early next morning, Inspector Rob Bloos arrived for work at the Warmoesstraat police station. He was informed of the events of the previous night, and initially assumed he was dealing with a young addict. "From the needle tracks and what my colleagues found in the room, it soon became clear we were dealing with a drug addict," he told Dutch author Jeroen de Valk. "I come into the office, see the report, and think—a thirty year-old addict with the passport of an American almost sixty years old—this must be a junkie who robbed a tourist. And it happens often enough that a junkie registers in a hotel under an assumed name. In the hotel registry he had written the address of a Mr. Baker of Yale, Oklahoma. I immediately sent a telex to Yale asking if anyone knew of a theft that had taken place there."[56]

Around noon that day, Peter Huijts returned home from a shopping trip, and continued to puzzle over Chet's disappearance. Together with Wim and Ria Wigt, he had stayed up to midnight the previous night, telephoning hospitals and police stations. He worried that something still wasn't right. After a few phone calls, he was eventually put through to Inspector Bloos himself. "After some back and forth, the officer suddenly thought of something, and told me a very strange story. They had found a man about thirty years old—they didn't yet tell me he was dead—with a trumpet in his possession. I said, 'Damn, that can't be him, because he was much older. But if you found a trumpet, that could be his, and since there are problems, I am coming to Amsterdam anyway'." At that point, the Inspector informed Huijts that the man was dead, and that a pair of tortoiseshell glasses had been found at the scene. At this point, Huijts knew instinctively that Chet was dead.[57]

Huijts drove to Amsterdam with his wife, worried that he was too upset to go alone. They waited for two hours in the busy Warmoesstraat police station, sensing that the police were in no hurry to investigate yet another junkie death in the Zeedijk district. "They had hardly taken the time to investigate," he later revealed. "In the open trumpet case lay a piece of paper with my telephone number and that of the Memphis Hotel, and another telex from Wim Wigt. These they had completely overlooked."[58]

The police eventually took Huijts to the morgue, where he made a formal identification. "I thought 'It's going to be horrible to see him. The poor guy has fallen out of the window'. But in fact he looked quite uninjured because he had landed on the back of his head."

Later that day, he called Diane Vavra in California to inform her of the news. "I just went numb," she said. But she also felt a sense of relief, as though someone had lifted the monkey from her back. "I was addicted to him," she admitted. "Now that he was gone, I was free."[59]

Carol Baker exhibited rather less emotion when Huijts told her what had happened. "She was rather quiet—not very excited," he later recalled.

Whilst Peter Huijts expressed concerns over the speed of the initial police response, the final report into Chet Baker's death was incredibly thorough, running to more than thirty pages, and leaves little room for interpretation.

The door to Chet's room had evidently been locked from the inside, indicating that no one else had been in the room. It is possible that someone could have opened the door from the outside with a master key, but there was no sign of a disturbance in the room. Chet may have aged rapidly in the last year of his life, but he remained strong and wiry, as Nicola Stilo could verify after trying to hold him back in the Capitol Hotel a few days earlier.

Photographs of the room show that Chet had not slept in the room; the bedspread was undisturbed, and some clothing was laid out on the bed. Chet's trumpet case was on the ground, his borrowed Bach Stradivarius trumpet—loaned to him by the French Selmer company for the making of *Let's Get Lost* —was still inside. As Huijts indicated, there were also some papers in the trumpet case, including the telex from Wim Wigt. Also in the case was a Citizen Quartz watch, fifty-nine guilders, a cigarette lighter and a bracelet.

On the table, police found a large amount of heroin and cocaine, and two glasses. One contained traces of heroin and coke, indicating they had been mixed, presumably to make a speedball; the other contained a needle.

The window sash was old, and had been painted numerous times. It did not open easily, and only raised about two feet. It could be secured open by a metal pin, which was chained to the wall. At some point, Chet appears to have opened the window, and grabbed the chain in an attempt to stop himself from falling. The metal pin and part of the chain were found on the pavement below, the heavy sash window slamming shut behind him.

The autopsy revealed that Chet's skull and cheekbone had been smashed on the concrete post below the hotel window, which resulted in blood filling his cranial cavity. His ribs were also broken, creating haemorrhaging in his chest. A police spokesman, Klaas Wilting, later issued a statement. "He was alone and shoved the window open himself and either fell or jumped out … all we know is that there was no criminal activity involved."

Chet's closest friends are in no doubt that his death was an accident, rather than suicide. Micheline remembered that Chet had kept $5,500 in cash for three months, February through April, thinking he could rent an apartment if Diane eventually returned. "I'd never seen Chet do that," she said. "What happened was not suicide, but he left himself in a state and a mood where anything could happen. Nicola told me that for three days he was taking no heroin, just coke, perhaps thinking this might induce a heart attack. After that he started on heroin again until he died." In addition, she pointed to the fact that there were still drugs in the room when he died. "If a junkie wants to commit suicide, he'll take everything before he dies," she said. "He won't leave three grams in his room."[60]

In his biography *Deep In A Dream*, James Gavin suggests that Chet might have committed some sort of passive-aggressive suicide, sitting on the window ledge and waiting for death to take him. This theory "perfectly fit the profile of a man who, by his own admission, had never had the courage to confront tough decisions."[61]

But this theory also sounds a little fanciful. If Chet was simply sitting on the window sill, waiting to 'let death come to him', or even nodded off whilst sitting on the window ledge, why would he make an effort to grab the window pin, if not to prevent himself from falling?

The truth was rather more mundane. He appears to have taken a sizeable speedball, and after a while, the cocaine started to cause paranoid delusions—just as it had in Liège in early May, and again in Amsterdam on May 8th. Nicola Stilo agreed that this had most likely caused Chet's death. "The cocaine is absolutely the thing that caused the worst problems," he said.

Four nights earlier, Chet had been in a drug-crazed emotional turmoil, trying desperately to clamber out of the window, convinced it was a door.

On that occasion Nicola Stilo had been there to restrain him. But in the early hours of May 13th, he was on his own. Diane had made it clear she was not going to return, and this time, there was no one to hold him back. He fell to his death, frightened and alone.

Epilogue

CHET
1988

"I don't have any property or a bank account. I'm sure I'll die flat broke, and that's OK, because that's how I came into this world."—Chet Baker[1]

When news of Chet's death hit the news wires, Bruce Weber and his partner, Nan Bush, were in the process of editing their documentary *Let's Get Lost*. Weber called Carol Baker in Oklahoma to offer his assistance with the cost of the funeral. Whilst the movie had not yet been released, Carol Baker must have sensed Weber's dislike of her and her family, and made a conscious decision to use all the financial assistance she could, even if it meant turning Chet's funeral into something of a circus.

Chet had told Weber that when he died, he would like to be cremated. Weber offered to pay for a cremation, but Carol—at Chet's mother's request—insisted on a burial. Vera insisted on burying her son in Inglewood Park Cemetery, close to Los Angeles International airport, next to his father, Chesney Baker Senior, who had died in California back in 1967. She had also purchased a third lot, so that she might later be buried next to her son.

Peter Huijts, who worked with Wim Wigt, and had done so much to support Chet on many of his later tours, also telephoned Carol Baker to offer his support. "Chet was very negative about Carol, but never had the money to get a divorce," explained Ria Wigt. "We thought that Carol was still his official wife, and that we should do what we could to help them. Chet may not have been able to do much to help his children when he was alive, but perhaps something good could come out of this." Wim Wigt offered to help pay the cost of flying Chet's body back to Europe, a cost that was eventually shared with Bruce Weber and the US Embassy. He also offered to help Chet's family by paying royalties on Chet's final recording, with the NDR Big Band

and Hannover Radio Orchestra.[2]

Huijts also proposed that a memorial service be held for Chet in Europe, ahead of his burial in Los Angeles. The body was only released after five days, the delay caused by the autopsy and the paperwork associated with flying the body overseas, and the service was held on May 18th. Huijts and Wigt had wanted to dress Chet in jeans and a casual shirt, the way in which he normally dressed, but Carol insisted that he be dressed in a three-piece suit. The casket was open for the service, revealing a waxen face, heavy with makeup to hide the bruising to his cheek, his hair cut short and slicked back. Photos later revealed a distraught Jacques Pelzer among the mourners, kneeling down in prayer in front of his closest friend.

Next day, Huijts flew to Los Angeles with the body. The day after that, Carol, Vera and children also arrived, their flights and hotel paid for by Bruce Weber. Weber's producer, Emie Amemiya, made most of the arrangements for the ceremony, and met the family on their arrival, so they could view the body.

Later that evening, Peter Huijts met with the family at their hotel. He was initially met with a warm reception. He brought a number of Chet's albums, recorded in Europe, and shared some of his memories of working with Chet on some of his final tours, including the trips to Japan. Things turned sour when he mentioned Chet's recording in Germany. Wim Wigt felt that the royalties should be shared between Carol Baker, Chet's wife, and Diane Vavra, Chet's girlfriend in his final years. Huijts presented her with a draft contract, but Carol was livid, and refused to sign.

"It took us a lot of time to plan the recording, and to set up the rehearsal with the orchestra, but we had managed to get the recording done," Ria Wigt explained. "We were planning to release the record, which was also scheduled for release in Japan. Peter informed Carol that Chet was supposed to receive a good fee for the recording, and that part of it probably belonged to her now. In my mind I knew that Chet would not have been happy with such an arrangement, but I thought that we were trying to make the best of the situation. Carol turned down the offer of a cheque, and didn't know how to deal with the situation. She told Peter that she had to consult with her lawyer as to who was the rightful heir, and get the paperwork sorted out."[3]

One can see both sides. On the one hand, Wim Wigt was trying to do the right thing from a moral standpoint. On the other hand, the timing was insensitive. Emotions were no doubt running high, and the discussion should probably have taken place a few weeks after the funeral, not the day before.

On the morning of the funeral, Carol Baker was upset to learn that Bruce Weber had invited Diane Vavra to attend. At around 2 p.m., guests started to arrive, but Vavra kept her distance, standing at the back of the crowd. That didn't stop Chet's daughter Melissa from taunting her. Her behaviour was embarrassing to everyone but Carol, and eventually one of Chet's childhood friends put his hands on her shoulders and whispered, "Not now."

Also in attendance was Chet's second wife, Haleema Alli. She had refused to take part in the movie *Let's Get Lost*, but accepted Emie Amemiya's invitation to the funeral. She did not bring their son, Chesney Aftab, and left soon after the ceremony, keeping her dignity just as she had always done.

Other attendees included Russ Freeman, the original pianist in the Chet Baker Quartet, bass player Hersh Hamel, a childhood friend who had been interviewed for *Let's Get Lost*, another old friend, Bernie Fleischer, pianist Frank Strazzeri, saxophonist Christopher Mason and Peter Huijts. Conspicuous by their absence were Ruth Young, who thought it best to avoid the ceremony, given the long-standing animosity between her and Carol, and Bruce Weber, who worried the funeral would be an awkward occasion. Jack Sheldon was also unable to make it to the ceremony because of a prior engagement, but made it to a small gathering after the funeral.

In total, less than forty people turned up to the funeral, a far cry from the European ceremony, where hundreds had attended. But then, Chet lived most of his later years in Europe, which felt more like home to him. "It was a wretched funeral," said Peter Huijts, who was dismayed by the behaviour of Chet's family.[4]

There were brief eulogies from a number of his friends, including Bernie Fleischer. Later in the ceremony, Chris Tedesco, a young West Coast trumpeter who loved Chet's playing style, played an unaccompanied version of 'My Funny Valentine', reducing many of the guests to tears.

As the service ended, Melissa took a single white rose from a bouquet of flowers that Emie Amemiya had arranged, and placed it on her father's coffin. After the burial, the guests made their way out to the car park. Whilst Diane Vavra tried to keep her distance from Carol and the children, Melissa could not resist turning round to abuse her one last time. Looking back, Vavra tried not to judge her too harshly. "Well, she was just a little kid," she said, although Melissa was almost twenty-two years old. "Her father didn't treat her very well. Never was around."[5]

The mood brightened, as the guests made their way to the Ports O' Call restaurant in San Pedro, close to the Palos Verdes cliffs that Chet had climbed in his carefree teenage years. The venue had been booked by Emie Amemiya, who had carefully arranged the seating so as to separate Diane Vavra from Chet's family.

The musicians reminisced about Chet's life. He had "one helluva career", noted pianist Frank Strazerri, who told everyone he'd been playing with Chet on and off for thirty years. "And when I heard him play for the last time last year," Strazzeri said, "he was the same guy as when I first knew him. He never deviated from what he was."[6]

Jack Sheldon, Chet's childhood friend, made it for the reception and played a tender version of 'My Funny Valentine', prompting Carol Baker to present him with a white rose of his own. "We'd go down and climb the cliffs at Palos Verdes," Sheldon told the assembled guests, an impromptu memoir of the summer days the two young musicians spent together. "He'd do it and I'd follow. Chetty taught me how to play the trumpet, he taught me how to sing—he taught me everything I know about playing and singing." Jack shook his head as though there were quite a few other things he learned from Chet. "I could never catch up with him."[7]

In the weeks that followed, the apparently mysterious nature of Chet's death—falling from an Amsterdam hotel window in the middle of the night—prompted widespread speculation as to what had happened that night, most of it uninformed, and not in keeping with the facts.

Robert van de Feyst, more commonly known as Bob Holland, heard a couple of theories. One was that Carol Baker had arranged to have her husband murdered for the insurance money; but this was patently ridiculous, as Chet had never opened a bank account, let alone taken out life insurance. The second was at least plausible— that Chet had overdosed in his room, and had been dumped out of the window on the street by hotel staff. Even so, this seems unlikely; police would have to thoroughly investigate the hotel room whether he had died inside or fallen from the window, so the hotel staff had nothing to gain by doing this.

George Brown, the American bebop drummer living in Paris, claimed that Chet fell to his death after finding himself locked out of his room. "George Brown is a crazy motherfucker, but a great drummer, plays like Elvin," said trombone player Ed Byrne. "He might have been the last person to see Chet alive. But George was saying there was a slug in the lock of his room, so he couldn't get in. The manager wasn't there, so he was out of luck. Knowing Chet he climbed up to the window to get his trumpet and his clothes, and fell." It is entirely possible Chet locked himself out of the room, but there was no slug in the lock.[8]

The police also dismissed the theory that Chet could have died trying to climb into the room. "Any child can see that it would be impossible to climb the front of that hotel, even a meter," said Inspector Rob Bloos, talking to Dutch author Jeroen de Valk. "And even if he had managed to do that, he would not have landed on his head but on the lower part of his body."[9]

Carol Baker felt strongly that Chet was murdered, either by drug dealers or one of the European record companies. In a Village Voice article entitled 'Jump, Fall or Push?' she claimed "it wasn't suicide, it was foul play … Chet deserves a proper investigation."[10]

Her second son, Paul Baker, went on to elaborate about how the family felt about his death. "The family has certain theories, certain ideas," he said. "I think he was killed. The man didn't *fall* out of the damn window. I think they shoved him. He had a metal peg in his hand from the window. You don't reach out and grab something if you're trying to commit suicide. My father wasn't a big guy. He often sat on the window ledge and played."[11]

He felt strongly that European record labels played a role in Chet's death. "I think SteepleChase had something to do with my father's death," he claimed. "The record companies, these were the people in his life. Companies like Timeless and Enja. I spoke to my father a few weeks before he died and he said he had ten reel-to-reel recordings—enough to put out two records a year for the next twenty years. I think they would have killed him for those tapes. Also, my father was the sort of guy who carried $10,000 in cash. The tapes were probably recorded in a studio. If my father didn't get paid, maybe he took them. Where did these tapes go? Also, the last time I spoke to my father, he told me that someone had taken his car. SteepleChase had introduced my father to this guy who supplied him, and he had taken his car. After his death, all of a sudden the car was returned."[12]

Paul Baker may have been confused by what his father had told him. Chet had indeed made a number of recordings before his death that had not yet been issued at that time—the recording with Charlie Haden from late 1987, with the NDR Big Band in Hamburg, two poetry albums, recorded in early 1988, the records made with Paulo Piangiarelli in Italy, the concert recording with Archie Shepp, and the final recording with the NDR Big Band and Radio Orchestra—enough material for eight to ten albums. But Chet was paid in cash for most of those recordings, and there is no evidence to suggest the tapes were ever stolen.

The suggestion that SteepleChase were somehow involved is even more ludicrous. A number of European labels did release unauthorised recordings of Chet after his death, but SteepleChase was not one of them. The only 'new' material they released after Chet's death were additional tunes and takes recorded at earlier recording sessions, made available when the original albums were released on CD.

The idea that labels like Enja and Timeless might somehow have been involved is equally ill-informed. Matthias Winckelmann of Enja actually worked closely with Carol Baker to release a series of 'Legacy' recordings after Chet's death. As Carol herself noted in the liner notes, "I would like to thank Matthias Winckelmann of ENJA records for being there for us since Chet's untimely and mysterious death."[13]

Carol continued to negotiate with Wim Wigt, owner of Timeless Records, after Chet's funeral. "Carol eventually called us, and said she needed some things from us," explained Wim Wigt's wife, Ria Wigt. "I need to go to hospital, and to pay some bills. Can you lend me the money ahead of the cheque you were going to give me?" So we lent her some money. Wim called her from time to time, to see how she was doing. A few weeks went by, and all of a sudden we heard that she would not deal with us over the orchestra recording—she was going to deal with someone else. Wim called her, and said, 'That's not what we agreed. We organised the whole event, the whole project, the recording. How can you do this to us?' Carol said that we didn't have the money. 'But we showed you a guaranteed cheque for $15,000, and said that we would try to negotiate more with the orchestra. This is not the way to deal with things.' 'I couldn't care less', said Carol. 'Then you should pay us back the money we lent you. You can't just treat us like trash after we have done for Chet'."[14]

Carol Baker refused to negotiate with Wim Wigt, and the NDR Big Band and Hannover Radio Orchestra recording was eventually released on Enja Records as *My Favorite Songs—The Last Great Concert* and *Straight From The Heart—The Last Great Concert*. "After a while, Carol tried to claim that all of the signatures on Chet's contracts had been forged," Ria Wigt continued. "At that moment, I asked her to return the money she owed us, in good faith, and only then would we consider talking to her. She never did. In some ways, her behaviour is totally understandable—Chet had not taken care of her and the children. She was probably thinking that now it was her time. Unfortunately, she was not a very smart lady. She could have had a better time, but you have to treat people decently. If you don't, it comes back to you. Every few years, a different lawyer would contact us. We had to explain that Chet signed a contract, he was well paid, he was very happy, we provided a lot of work for him. What more could we have done? We gave him five years of our time, day and night. Who did that? Not Carol Baker."[15]

Finally, Paul Baker's comments about Chet's car are yet another red herring. Robert van de Feyst had indeed dealt drugs, but he was introduced to Chet by Wim Wigt of Timeless Records, not SteepleChase Records. And whilst there are still some unanswered questions about Chet's movements in Rotterdam in the hours before his death, the delay in van de Feyst's return to his apartment—which ultimately prompted Chet's return to Amsterdam—was most likely caused by a futile hunt for heroin to appease his house guest, and nothing more sinister.

Carol Baker's negotiations with Wim and Ria Wigt set the tone for the next ten years, with the family establishing a website which was less a tribute to Chet than a warning to anybody looking to make money out of his name or image. In 2002, the site included a list of record labels they regarded as "bootleggers", who had "illegally" issued Chet Baker recordings over the years, including SteepleChase, Timeless Records and others. As the family discovered, however, Chet normally signed a contract for an upfront cash payment, with no future royalties.

They also approached a number of Chet's older record companies, from the 1950s, with a view to seeking the release of some of his earlier recordings. This approach was also unsuccessful. "His son, Paul, is the opposite of his father," claimed British promoter Jeffrey Kruger, owner of the Flamingo Club, and co-promoter of Chet's first European tour. "He's an arrogant, big-headed guy, who thinks he's going to sue the world for what they haven't done for his father. But he's a dreamer. I know that he was totally unrealistic. He came after us for the release of some of Chet's earlier works. I said to him, 'Listen. I've been in the business longer than you've been alive. I have the paperwork, and you'll end up just making a fool of yourself. You'd be better taking advantage of the situation and accepting royalties'. And we've not heard from him in five or six years, maybe more."[16]

They later established their own record label, CCB Records (Chet and Carol Baker), to release bootleg-style recordings of their own, including *Live at Pueblo, Colorado, 1966*. They even tried to auction the film rights to Chet Baker's life story on eBay for a minimum of five million dollars, plus royalties.

At the time of writing, the endless legal wrangling continued to drag on—almost twenty-five years after Chet's death. In 2011, the Chet Baker Estate was involved in a class action lawsuit against four record labels—Sony Music Entertainment Canada, EMI Music Canada, Universal Music Canada and Warner Music Canada—claiming copyright infringement and overdue royalties. The record companies eventually reached a settlement, agreeing to pay $45m in royalties—although only a small portion of that sum is thought to be owed to Chet Baker's estate. Even then, Paul Baker sent a letter to the judge, raising an issue about the right of his mother to enter into an agreement on his behalf.

In some respects, one can hardly blame Chet's family, who were left with nothing. But the manner in which they have gone about making their claims upset many people in the music industry, including those who had gone out of the way to help Chet when he was alive. "The family seems to think the world owes them a living," concluded Jeffrey Kruger.

Bruce Weber's movie, *Let's Get Lost*, debuted at the Toronto International Film Festival on September 15th, 1988—just four months after Chet's death.

The movie was edited down from around ninety hours of footage captured by cinematographer Jeff Preiss. Before the film was launched, Weber sent a release to his producer, Cherry Vanilla, who found her significant contribution had only been listed as 'cast member' and 'researcher'. She complained bitterly, claiming that Weber had promised she would be credited as 'writer-producer', but with no written contract the two parties ended up communicating through lawyers.

To this day, Vanilla still feels that Bruce Weber and Nan Bush tried to steal all the credit for the movie. "I got screwed on this film, so did Carol and the kids—so did Chet, in a way," she said. "Bruce would never give me a writer credit on the film, even though I wrote the interview questions and kept Chet stoned on grass and talking, even when he really didn't want to talk. Bruce is a producer of kiddy-porn fashion commercialism. He was lucky to have had this opportunity with Chet. He was lucky to have me. I don't think he will ever have the same combination of chemistry and events again ... obviously, the films he did before and after are pure crap. This one is the best and it is because of Chet and, dare I say, me. Bruce had never even listened to Elvis Costello before I played him 'Almost Blue'. Bruce knew nothing about musicians or about being high. Bruce is a lucky jerk and a manipulative control freak. I'm happy the movie exists, but at the same time ... I am really glad you and others are trying to delve more deeply into Chet's life and personality as it really was."[17]

Notwithstanding Vanilla's concerns over the credits for the movie, the film met with critical success, for the most part. "Surfaces are everything in *Let's Get Lost*, but they are gorgeously stylish surfaces, redolent of both contemporary notions of glamour and of the late 1950's jazz mystique of which Baker was a part," wrote Janet Maslin in the *New York Times*. "Mr. Weber, well known as a fashion photographer and as the director of one previous documentary, displays an unerring eye for the strikingly evocative image, using black-and-white cinematography to produce as varied a palette as other directors might achieve in color."[18]

Rex Reed also praised the movie in the *New York Observer*. "A tragic and dissolute life is vividly recalled in Weber's marvelous documentary ... Mark the date and make an effort to see this extraordinary homage not only to one of the most unusual musicians of all time, but also to the Doomed Youth of the cool jazz age that made him an icon. There has never been a film about a wayward hero in the smoke neon of jazz music quite like *Let's Get Lost* ... A film of small insights, large dimensions and plenty of soul, like the man himself."

One of the few negative reviews at the time came from Sheila Benson in the *Los Angeles Times*, who complained the documentary ignored Baker's music. "In a world centered around image, music takes a back seat to cutting-edge cheekbones," she wrote. "Weber has such little respect for Baker's music that he muscles in on the end of a phrase to have one of Baker's ex-old-ladies rag on another one, a wife or another ex-girl friend. Or Weber overrides the music so we can hear his precious questioner prod: 'Maybe you can tell me about your unfortunate encounter and how you got your teeth knocked out … '"[19]

The cinematography is undoubtedly gorgeous, and there are moments when Weber employs some interesting juxtaposition of images—flitting from Chet as a young man to Weber's epitome of 'damaged beauty', from a discussion of a drug overdose to the entry of Chet's charismatic ex-girlfriend, Ruth Young—as though going from death back to life. But one can't help thinking of the movie as a wasted opportunity. Far too much time is devoted to his sparring ex-lovers, and whilst they provide some insight into the damage caused by Chet's addiction, the issue of what made Chet important—his music, not his cheekbones—is what gets lost. Ultimately, the movie is stylish but highly stylised, a documentary about one man's obsession with Chet Baker, rather than Chet Baker himself.

'Stylish but highly stylised', one of the original movie posters from Let's Get Lost, *directed by Bruce Weber.*

One of the most fascinating aspects of the film is that it acts as a reminder in this 'pop idol' and 'reality TV' era that not everyone is cut out to be famous. Chet Baker was a reluctant star in his mid-twenties, ill-equipped to cope with fame; even then he was talking about buying a boat, escaping from everything, and when he started his comeback in the early 1970s, he was clearly more comfortable playing in a small bar than a large auditorium. "If there's a driving force to Weber's film, it seems to be delving into the nature and purpose of star quality and personal magnetism, which Baker had in droves but which didn't save him," wrote Carina Chocano in the *Los Angeles Times*. The parallels with the life of celebrities like Britney Spears or Amy Winehouse are all too clear.[20]

The movie was later nominated for an Academy Award for Best Documentary Feature in 1988. It was out of print for many years, but a newly restored print was screened at the Cannes Film Festival in 2008, which marked the twentieth anniversary of Chet's death. It was subsequently released on DVD for the first time.

Chet's closest friends were disappointed by the movie. Micheline Graillier agreed with Chet himself, and regarded the movie as a fiction, whilst her father, Jacques Pelzer, allegedly described it as "a piece of shit".

Nicola Stilo worked extensively on the movie with Chet, and gave a unique insight into what was filmed, and what was excluded from the movie. "Chet never saw the movie, but I am absolutely sure he would not have been happy with it," he revealed. "Chet was really generous showing the darker side of his life, giving an honest impression of himself. At the beginning, he was really happy to be working with Bruce, but at the end of the shooting, when we were in Cannes, he understood that Bruce was always giving him the same bullshit. He was not really interested in what Chet was trying to do with music, but his own image of the 'James Dean of jazz'. The movie also showed one hour of women fighting with each other; Diane with Ruth, Ruth with Carol, Carol with Diane. There was something very low about this, and Chet would not have been interested."[21]

Ultimately, Stilo felt the movie was too one-dimensional. "In just a few minutes, Bertrand Fèvre gave much more truth than Bruce Weber."[22]

Legacy

"Even if I could play like Wynton Marsalis, I wouldn't play like Wynton Marsalis"—Chet Baker

The issue of Chet's importance, both as a musician and a singer, remains a deeply divisive subject, almost twenty-five years after his death. Any debate is made more complex by the fact that Chet survived for as long as he did; had he have died of a drug overdose on his first European tour, in his mid-twenties, he would probably have been seen in the same terms as his contemporaries, the actor James Dean, or the jazz trumpet player Clifford Brown, both of whom left us with a small but enduring legacy. As a result, our image and memory of them remains trapped in time, and we are left wondering what might have been. By contrast, Chet's early good looks soon started to fade, and his musical legacy was tarnished by numerous poor quality recordings, often made for drug money or recorded illegally, and his erratic live performances in later years.

As a starting point for this discussion, I talked to the late Mike Zwerin, a musician who played with Miles Davis on the legendary *Birth Of The Cool* album, and who worked as a music critic for the *International Herald Tribune* for many years. "I really liked Chet a lot," he said. "I'm not talking about his personality, but his playing which is often ignored for the very obvious and rather brutal fact that he was white."[1]

Some years earlier, Zwerin had shared his views with Wynton Marsalis, the most famous jazz trumpeter of recent years, who currently serves as the Artistic Director for Jazz at Lincoln Center. "On a good night—and there weren't enough of them—towards the end of his life, in his 50s, Chet was playing jazz as well as anybody has ever played it. It's not a popular thing to say to Wynton Marsalis. I told him once, and he looked at me as if I was crazy."[2]

This was not the only time Marsalis played down the significance of white jazz musicians. In fact, he has frequently espoused a narrow, conservative view of jazz history. In the documentary *Jazz: A Film by Ken Burns*, for example, he discussed the history of jazz trumpet, and neglected to mention a single white musician.

More recently, perhaps reflecting criticism of his stance, he has amended his view. On his website, he discusses the greatest trumpeters of all time. Leaving aside the non-jazz musicians, Marsalis suggested the following: "Then you got the jazz musicians: Buddy Bolden, King Oliver, Freddy Keppard, Buddy Petit. Then you get to 'Red' Allen, and then you've got Louis Armstrong. From there, you get all the trumpet players influenced by him. Various trumpet players like Buddy Barry, Cootie Williams, Rex Stewart, Ray Nance, 'Sweets' Edison, Buck Clayton, Roy Eldridge, Doug Mascoll. There are a lot of people. Then you come up in the more modern era with Dizzy and Miles, Freddy Hubbard, Don Ellis, Don Cherry, Booker Little, Lee Morgan."[3]

Note that the 'modern era' stops around 1970. There's no mention on the list of Lester Bowie, Woody Shaw, Kenny Wheeler, Terence Blanchard, Roy Hargrove, Tomasz Stanko—to name just a handful of the most influential jazz trumpet players of recent years. To be fair, Hargrove and Blanchard are mentioned on the website as players that Marsalis recognises as 'interesting or promising', but one can't escape the feeling that he feels that nothing significant has happened in jazz in the last forty years.

Leaving aside Wynton Marsalis's somewhat blinkered view of jazz history, there are other reasons why he might have been dismissive of Chet Baker.

Firstly, Chet was not one of the innovators in the history of jazz trumpet. In the words of Jim Coleman, one of Chet's old friends, and a trumpet player himself, Chet did not break any new ground. "When you look at the lineage of jazz trumpet, from Louis Armstrong, Roy Eldridge, Dizzy Gillespie, and the guy who wrote the book after Dizzy, Fats Navarro. If you ever listen to anything Clifford Brown did, he copied note for note every solo that Fats Navarro ever played. Clifford Brown was a brilliant, healthy young guy, and if he'd have lived, who knows where he'd have gone. From Clifford Brown, the guy who replaced him in the Max Roach band was Booker Little, who died of a rare blood disease at a very young age. Booker Little took the trumpet to the next level, harmonically and rhythmically. And then Woody Shaw took it from there. Notice that Miles Davis did not fit in there. Miles was a great musician; he synthesised a lot of stuff that was around, but never had the chops that Dizzy had. Likewise, Chet did not break any new ground—what he did was take everything that Miles and Kenny Dorham did, and kept playing in that style."[4]

Coleman is not suggesting that Chet's playing stood still. On the contrary, he felt his playing continued to evolve, even if many people—Marsalis and Davis included—failed to appreciate it.

Secondly, whilst Miles Davis did not break new ground from a harmonic and rhythmic perspective, he was clearly a musical visionary, helping to change the direction of jazz on a number of occasions in his long career. Whilst it is now generally accepted that Gerry Mulligan was the main architect behind the 'Birth of the Cool' sound, it was Miles Davis who took it to the next level, working with arranger Gil Evans to produce 'orchestral jazz' albums such as *Miles Ahead* (1957), *Porgy and Bess* (1958) and *Sketches of Spain* (1960). Davis was also one of the key drivers of 'modal jazz', influenced by the composer George Russell. Modal jazz used musical modes rather than chord progressions as a harmonic framework; Miles Davis albums like *Milestones* (1958) and *Kind of Blue* (1959) paved the way for later modal compositions by the likes of John Coltrane, Herbie Hancock and Wayne Shorter, for example.

Miles Davis continued to search for new directions later in his career. He started to incorporate electric instruments into his recordings in the late 1960s, with Herbie Hancock playing electric piano and Ron Carter playing bass guitar on *Miles In The Sky* (1968). He was greatly influenced in this respect by the sound and commercial success of the funk band Sly and the Family Stone, and his melding of jazz with rock and funk rhythms eventually resulted in so-called 'jazz fusion' albums, such as *In A Silent Way* (1968) and *Bitches Brew* (1969), which paved the way for important artists such as Weather Report, Headhunters, The Mahavishnu Orchestra and Return to Forever in the 1970s.

An important contributing factor in these developments was Miles Davis's skill as a bandleader. His close relationship with Gil Evans was vital to the success of albums such as *Miles Ahead*, even if the concept came from Davis himself, whilst the development of fusion came about through his work with sympathetic musicians such as Wayne Shorter, Herbie Hancock, Chick Corea, Joe Zawinul and John McLaughlin. Even outside the key musical developments discussed above, he understood the importance of keeping a good band together for a prolonged period, allowing the music to develop over time.

By contrast, Chet was neither a musical visionary nor a strong bandleader. If there was a vision, it might be described as a "poetic vision", a term coined by his old friend, the vibraphonist Warren Chiasson. That vision did evolve over time, but could hardly be described as groundbreaking. Likewise, Chet was singularly ill-equipped to be a bandleader. Pianist Russ Freeman had to take charge of the finances on his first solo tour, or else Chet would not have set aside enough money to pay the band. In his later years, he formed a number of successful bands—whether it was the quartet with Markowitz/Brillinger/Lee in late 1978, or the trios with Catherine/Rassinfosse and Graillier/Del Fra in the mid-1980s, but these line-ups were often relatively short-lived. Too often, Chet was content to surround himself with drug buddies, or work with cheaper musicians to keep the costs down.

Thirdly, Wynton Marsalis would have found fault with Chet's technique. Marsalis was classically trained, and is one of the few jazz musicians to have successfully straddled the jazz and classical music worlds in a professional capacity. Hearing the then twenty-one-year-old Marsalis in London, the French classical player Maurice André pronounced him "potentially the greatest trumpeter of all time". Even Miles Davis, who had several run-ins with the young Marsalis, conceded that the younger man was "a hell of a trumpet player".

By contrast, Chet Baker was largely self-taught. He had a limited ability to read music, and was unable follow written chord changes, and as a consequence, played almost entirely by ear—as documented in this book by many of the musicians who worked with him.

In addition, Chet had a tendency to focus primarily on the lower register of the trumpet, even in his early years. "I like to play in the deep register," he later admitted. "I was never a high-note specialist. My range goes from the bottom of the horn up to around C or D. High D is about it for me. About two-and-a-half octaves, I think."[5]

In later years, of course, Chet Baker's technique was compromised by dental problems, the consequence of years of heroin abuse, which had rotted his teeth, and a severe beating in San Francisco in 1966. He had dentures fitted later that year, and had to adapt his embouchure and effectively relearn how to play the trumpet. "I worked hard at it," he told the Dutch author Jeroen de Valk. "I managed to get a sound from my trumpet again, and I practiced some more to get the sound that I envisioned. I worked three years on it. I played a lot, and I had a clear idea about the way I wanted to sound."

But technique isn't everything. The British jazz trumpeter Ian Carr, author of Miles Davis: The Definitive Biography, expressed the view that Marsalis was brilliant from a technical perspective. "But the most important thing about music is feeling; Miles could move people to tears." One could make the same argument about Chet's playing.[6]

Pianist Keith Jarrett has expressed a similar view of Wynton's playing. "I've never heard anything Wynton played sound like it meant anything at all," he claimed. "Wynton has no voice and no presence. His music sounds like a talented high-school trumpet player to me."[7]

Chet evidently felt the same way. "Even if I could play like Wynton Marsalis," he once said, "I wouldn't play like Wynton Marsalis."

Wynton Marsalis would surely have regarded Chet Baker as an ill-disciplined musician, too. Whilst Chet was blessed with an incredible natural talent, he did not like to practice, and took the view that playing on the bandstand at night gave him all the practice he needed. Even in his early years, Gerry Mulligan used to complain that he did not keep his chops in shape. As the years went by, this would periodically cause problems with his embouchure, particularly if he had not played a gig in a few weeks. Nils Winther of SteepleChase Records remembers the problems this caused during the recording of 'When Sunny Gets Blue' in 1986. "I was worried about the recording session, because he had no chops whatsoever; he probably hadn't played for a month," he recalled. "I arranged a whole bunch of rehearsals with Chet and the band, so they played together for three or four hours a day. His chops were still not that great on the recording session, but compared with a few days earlier, the difference was amazing."[8]

The vibraphonist Gary Burton, who played with Chet occasionally in the 1960s, feels that Chet's ill-discipline made it difficult to compare his playing to that of other major players of the time, such as Miles Davis, Freddie Hubbard, Lee Morgan and Art Farmer. "My overall take on Chet is that he was the living embodiment of a certain stereotype of the jazz musician as drug addict/cool guy," he said. "He was a kind of genial version of James Dean, good-looking and boyish, always getting into trouble, getting through life by using his charisma, more than talent or hard work. But that's just my opinion."[9]

The last two reasons why Marsalis might have dismissed Chet Baker relate to jazz history. Firstly, there was a feeling amongst African-American musicians, particularly in the 1950s, that Chet Baker did not deserve the recognition that he received, either from the jazz critics or the general public. When Chet's debut solo recording received a five-star review in *DownBeat* magazine, Miles complained bitterly that Chet was being treated as "The second coming of Jesus Christ." Other members of Miles' band seemed to share this perspective, with pianist Horace Silver making a thinly veiled reference to the Chet Baker Quartet in an interview with *DownBeat.* "I can't stand the faggot-type jazz—the jazz with no … no guts," he told Nat Hentoff. "And the discouraging part is that the faggot-type jazz is getting more popularity than the jazz with real soul. The groups that play with a lot of guts are not making as much loot." As a keen student of jazz history, Wynton Marsalis would undoubtedly have been familiar with such views, and they may have coloured his own view.[10]

Secondly, he may have felt that Chet's career had been on a steady decline since the peak of his fame in the early–mid 1950s. This was certainly the view of Bud Shank, Chet's contemporary from the West Coast jazz scene. "Since the '50s it's all gone downhill for him … That's all there is to it, as everyone knows."[11]

Others share this opinion. When the movie *Let's Get Lost* was re-released in 2007, Terrence Rafferty was quick to dismiss the significance of Chet Baker's musical legacy. "Jazz history hasn't been kind to him; his talent, though real, was thin," he wrote in the *New York Times*. "Unlike his rival Miles Davis, he persisted, with a stubbornness that suggests a fairly serious failure of imagination, in playing the cool style long past the point at which it had begun to sound mannered and even a little silly. When you hear Mr. Baker's stuff, you can't help picturing his ideal listener as one of those lupine swingers of the Playboy era, decked out in a velvet smoking jacket and loading smooth platters onto the hi-fi to get a hot chick in the mood for love."[12]

I would certainly take issue with these views. For his own part, Chet was convinced that he continued to develop as a musician in his later years. If one listens some of his recordings from the late 1970s and early 1980s, there were significant changes to both the style of music he was playing, and to his soloing, which continued to evolve. "He never forgot to develop his own style," noted the bass player Riccardo Del Fra. "The way he played the trumpet in his last six or seven years is special and original, and completely different to the way he played when he was young."[13]

He started to experiment with a 'drummerless' trio, which is heard to good effect on the recordings he made for SteepleChase in 1979, and again in his classic trios with Riccardo Del Fra and Michel Graillier, and Philip Catherine and Jean-Louis Rassinfosse in the early–mid 1980s. This approach required a bass player with good timing, but allowed Chet to develop long, uncluttered lines in his solos. The music was frequently astonishing, a far cry from the 'cool style' of the mid-1950s that Rafferty refers to in his article.

The development in Chet's playing can be heard to good effect on *Chet Baker in Tokyo*, recorded less than one year before his death. It certainly supports Mike Zwerin's view that—on a good day at least—Chet was still capable of playing to the highest standard. The DVD was recently reviewed in the *New York Times*. "The performances are remarkable because they take in, at the highest level, everything that people said Chet could do—play ballads with almost painful, poetic eloquence—and what many said he could not: blow hard and tough enough so as to make the trumpet sound its essence," wrote John Vinocur. "The Tokyo Concert has fascinated and moved me the same way that Miles Davis, on the way down, was able to on *Time After Time*, or Stan Getz, not long before his death, did on his *Serenity* and *Anniversary* albums with Kenny Barron."[14]

If Chet Baker was not an innovator or a trendsetter, why was he more important than Wynton Marsalis would have us believe? I asked that question of Mike Zwerin, who loved Chet's playing. "It's that total honesty," he suggested. "He might be compared to Stan Getz. Neither one was musically literate, they didn't know chords, they just played. They played unlike anyone else, just like themselves, and they played fluently—when they were at their best. Again, it should be said—emphasised even—that at the end, Chet was not good most of the time. But when he played well, he played really well. It was the investment he made in music. Improvising was the way he expressed himself, and he put everything into it. He put his whole life into it—and when he played, you could tell."[15]

Zwerin expanded on this issue in an article he wrote back in 1983. "You do not feel like jumping up and shouting, 'Yeah!' after a Chet Baker solo. All that tenderness, turmoil and pain has driven you too far inside. He reaches that same part of us as a late Beethoven string quartet, a spiritual hole where music becomes religion ... To his fans, Baker becomes the measure by which to judge the honesty quotient in others. He goes for feeling first, with just as much technique as he needs. Other improvisers try and overwhelm the trumpet; blast it fast, screech down the walls of Jericho. Baker builds new walls. He needs them for protection. He always plays seated, folded in a question mark. Between solos he sits, trumpet rested on his crossed legs, without moving. You almost say to yourself, 'My God, he's passed away up there'. Then, ever so slowly, he raises the instrument to his lips and when those sweetly burned innocent notes bloom again it's a relief, almost as though you've made it through one more winter."[16]

Many of the musicians interviewed for this book expressed a similar view. The producer Don Sebesky felt that Chet stood for lyrical communication. "When he played, all the best stuff in him came out through his horn. It was seductive, and engaged you. You have to be grateful for that—anybody who plays like that can't be all bad! You want to remember Chet for what he gave you as a gift."[17]

Likewise the Brazilian keyboard player and composer Rique Pantoja felt that his playing encapsulated many of the problems he experienced in his personal life. "He and the trumpet were as one, and what came out was in his heart—the music is transparent, and carries his anguish, his pain, his suffering, his ability to love," he said. "That was his contribution to the world."[18]

Drummer John Engels, who played with Chet on his two Japanese tours, summarised his view very succinctly. "Chet is important because of the music. How can I explain? He made you cry inside. It has to do with the heart, the soul."[19]

The fact that Chet could bare his soul to the world through his playing was ironic in a number of respects. First of all, his drug addiction suggested he was trying to hide his pain, yet through his playing he revealed so much of himself. This was a point raised by the Australian jazz singer, Melissa Forbes. "Where Chet gets interesting for me is that, in my opinion, his drug addiction was a sign that he was in many ways desperate to escape himself and his own feelings, yet he sounds so true when he plays," she said. "In my song 'Broken Wings (For Chet)' I explored Chet's paradoxical nature—his life was full of so much ugliness, yet he was capable of creating incredible beauty, and above all, truth."

Chet was capable of being brutally honesty in his real life. Think back to the way he told his pregnant girlfriend, Ruth Young, that he had no interest in raising another child. "But that's what I loved about him, too," she said.

"He didn't pull any punches."[20]

There was also an honesty about the way Chet treated other musicians, even if it was occasionally harsh. "I've seen him take on someone whose playing he doesn't like and say, 'Stop doing that while I'm playing! Don't do all of that stuff'," said trumpet player Bobby Shew. "He'd generally do it in a kind way, but it would often get people rattled. But it was usually aimed at people trying to impress him with their skills, and it meant that there was too much stuff going on."[21]

But much of the time that honesty was suppressed by his day-to-day requirements as a drug addict. He would do or say anything required to get what he wanted, as Diane Vavra discovered to her own cost. "You can't rely on Chet," as she told Bruce Weber during the making of *Let's Get Lost*. "And if you know that, then you can pull through." Ultimately we got more truth from Chet as a musician than as a person, but as Don Sebesky points out, for that we should be grateful.

The comments above also address the issues raised by Ian Carr and Keith Jarrett. Jarrett felt that Wynton's playing did not sound like it meant anything, and had no presence. Yet these are qualities that many musicians do associate with Chet's playing. "There was a magic about Chet's playing," said pianist Paul Bley, who played with Chet in the mid-1950s and again in the mid-1980s. "Antibes was a festival, for instance, with maybe five or ten thousand people outdoors, by the ocean. We went up there and we played one ballad after another, very soft, and the audience wouldn't make a sound. He had them completely hypnotised, like a snake charmer in India. They were powerless to leave, to speak, even to applaud. How does a guy who plays this soft, without any change in dynamics, how does he manage to captivate what is by nature a rowdy audience? And cast his spell over them. And that was his magic. No-one else could do that, including Miles. Miles had so many talents—but Chet had this one talent, that he was the most romantic of players. And a great, great ballad player. From my point of view it was educational that he could do these things that no one else could do, and no one thought could be done. He did it everywhere he went, he did it in Los Angeles when I was with him. He was a magician. The great artists are magicians, finally, and they rise above explanation."

Another quality that many musicians highlighted was Chet's innate sense of melody. "If you boil down Chet's strength as a musician to its essential parameters, I think you will find a deep sense of melody," noted the Dutch bass player Hein van de Geijn. "And I feel it myself, very strongly. After playing with Chet, and allowing his influence to sink in, I believed more and more in the strength of a melody—a melody that speaks for itself, played with integrity and a beautiful sound; that's enough. You don't have to play your ass off; you just have to play with intensity, and melodic power, and the music will take care of the rest."[22]

The pianist and composer Clare Fischer, who crossed paths with Chet in the mid-1960s, agreed that this was one of Chet's great strengths. "He was definitely one of the major talents of that era—especially considering the fact that most jazz players only wanted to play a lot of notes for display," he said. "Chet was a melodist. He had a great natural ability for melodic invention. The one thing that Chet was very good at was picking fine notes out of the harmonic progressions; you might say the 'choice notes'."[23]

Singer Melissa Forbes believes that Chet's sense of melody is extremely important to singers, as well as musicians. "The most obvious point of attraction to Chet for me as a singer is his innate sense of melody, both when he plays through a head and when he solos," she revealed. "Naturally, singers love to be able to sing along and Chet's solos are mostly eminently singable. I believe his melodic ideas are so strong because they come from the gut rather than the head."[24]

Another important element of Chet's playing was that he developed his own, unique sound. In the mid-1950s, he was clearly influenced by Miles Davis, who he openly admitted was his favourite trumpet player. But his playing continued to evolve, and he was able to develop a style that was his own. "What's important to me about jazz, and what I always tell my students, is that it is about finding your own signature," said bass player Larry Ridley, who played with Chet briefly in the mid-1970s. "When you hear someone like Chet, you know his sound, you know it's him—just like with Miles Davis, or Dizzy Gillespie, or Louis Armstrong. When I listen to the musicians coming out of some of these so-called 'jazz programmes', they spend so much time studying things from an intellectual perspective, as opposed to how to develop themselves. It's like the dictionary; there are words in the dictionary. Shakespeare wrote differently to Hemingway. Students have to learn the language of jazz before they can craft something that becomes very personally their own."[25]

Ridley went on to explain how it takes time to develop one's own sound, and why it's important to recognise this fact in a world obsessed with instant gratification. "A lot of young players try to play exercises instead of learning how to play through chord sequences and really compose music; because that's one of the most important attractions of jazz, that you're called upon to be an instantaneous composer when you're performing," he explained. "What you played yesterday is not necessarily repeated today or tomorrow. The challenge is creating something that has some sort of compositional merit. Certainly it's a terrific challenge; not everybody is able to do it, but conceptually it has a lot to do with approaching from a spiritual level, rather than thinking they can take two bars from a Chet Baker solo, and follow it with two bars from a Miles Davis solo. I hear a lot of grafting going on with a lot of people. When we were growing up it was so scientifically analysed and choreographed. We learnt a lot by transcribing what some of our favourites did in their solos, and used that as a pivot point to developing your own sound. We'd take the various kinds of melodic, rhythmic and harmonic motifs, and learn how to utilise them to develop the language of jazz. Now there are all kind of books telling you to play this scale and that scale, telling you what to do over this type of chord. There have always been study books, so that when you study bop, you can understand the art of the fugue, but the trick is to learn how you can utilise that as the basis for developing something uniquely your own. That's what takes time."[26]

"We're in a world where people want instant success," he continued. "The *American Idol* concept that has brainwashed a lot of the young kids into thinking that copying one of their favourite recording artists will give them an opportunity to get a recording concept, or get them a suite, riding round in a stretch limousine. It's still about developing a craft."

The degree to which Chet had learned his craft, rather than studied it per se, is clear when one tries to analyse his solos. Whilst musicians like Stan Getz and Freddie Hubbard had a unique sound, they occasionally fell back on certain familiar phrases during their solos. Chet tried to play it differently each time, thinking of new ways to tell his story. "Chet could play some licks, but if you transcribe Chet's solos you'll find he played some common things here and there, but it's very occasional," said keyboard player Rique Pantoja. "By contrast when I transcribe Freddie Hubbard's solos, you see a lot of motifs that are repeated; he would play the same line and accents."[27]

Bass player Jean-Louis Rassinfosse noted that Chet's improvisational skills continued to develop as he got older, in contrast to musicians like Miles Davis, whose own playing stopped developing after he started playing 'fusion'. "With Miles Davis, the way he played on the *Birth of the Cool* is not so different to *Tutu*; he had the muted sound, right from the beginning, the same nice, long notes. The way he played the trumpet didn't change so much. This is what all musicians face—how to develop your art, how to develop your career by changing yourself, the people you work with, by composing. All artists have these questions in front of them. Some, like Miles, changed the personnel all the time but focused less on their improvising. Some compose a lot of material, hoping to change and develop their style over time. Some keep playing the same material over time, but develop different ways of treating the standards that everyone knows. People want something new all the time, so there is a technical aspect to art. But as an artist, the art now is not necessarily better than it was previously. In this way Chet was very much an influence on me; he showed that you can use the same material but tell different stories every time. Chet was an instant composer in his improvisation, an instant composer of melodies—he was very much a composer, even if he didn't put anything on paper."[28]

Part of Chet's unique sound, I think, was his use of space when playing. He had always been critical of musicians who tried to overplay, and encouraged them to keep things simple. He once explained to saxophonist Bob Mover that the stage was not a research laboratory, urging him to keep it simple. "It was a good lesson," Mover admitted, "because I was getting indulgent." In the same vein he felt Italian pianist Enrico Pieranunzi overplayed when he first started out, and preferred to tour with Dennis Luxion. Chet had a particular dislike for overemphatic drummers, and in the late 1970s started to experiment with a 'drummerless' trio, which worked to particularly good effect when the bass player could keep good time.

Bass player Hein van de Geijn felt that Chet's approach added a sense of drama to the music. "Drama in that he was capable of exploring into the magic of silence and quietness," he explained. "That understatement can result in a strength. I think European musicians, and perhaps European people in general, can embrace that more readily than an American. I lived long enough in America, and traveled there regularly; it's a generalisation, of course, but over there it felt like the survival of the fittest—you have to play your ass off. In Europe you don't necessarily think that way; you try to touch people's emotions. When you are touched by Chet in some way, by listening to Chet, or better still, playing with him, it leaves an incredible mark. I can really hear that in the German trumpet player, Till Bronner or the marvelous Italian trumpeter, Paolo Fresu. And I feel it myself, very strongly; after playing with Chet, and allowing his influence to sink in, I realised I also wanted to play less, and I wanted to play softer, more acoustic."[29]

It was a lesson that was absorbed by many of the musicians that played with Chet, including Enrico Pieranunzi. "He forced me, silently, to use less notes, to choose the notes with care, to build melodies," he later admitted. "Before playing with him I was mostly an 'harmonic' and rhythmical player, but after meeting him I turned to the melody. Chet was an unbelievable storyteller, able to play and sing the essential. I tried to learn his secret and transfer it to my piano playing. It was a very long process, of course." The results can be heard to great effect on Pieranunzi's recent solo recordings, not least his composition 'When All Was Chet' from the 2006 CD *Ballads*.[30]

That same use of space is apparent in Chet's singing, as noted by the jazz singer Kurt Elling. "I also listened to a lot of Chet Baker coming up," he wrote on his website. "He is a great teacher of how few 'extras' a great song needs to communicate with real depth. Chet was a master minimalist, and yet not one iota of emotive power is ever missing from his work. Though the work he did in his youth is the first most people think of when they think of Chet, I recommend 'Let's Get Lost', which he made in the year before his death."[31]

The fact that Chet employed the same minimalist approach to his singing is no great surprise, as he regarded his singing as being an extension of his trumpet playing. "If I hadn't been a trumpet player, I don't know if I would have arrived at singing that way," he said. "I probably wouldn't have. I don't know whether I'm a trumpet player who sings or a singer who plays the trumpet. I love to do both."

It was that same minimalist, natural approach to singing that attracted jazz singer and saxophonist Curtis Stigers. "I heard about Ella Fitzgerald, Sarah Vaughan and Frank Sinatra before I heard about Chet Baker," he admitted. "Chet had that resurgence in the 1980s, I guess. Someone turned me on to him around that time, and I heard *The Best of Chet Baker Sings*, with 'My Funny Valentine' and all that, and it just hit me. As a jazz singer, I suppose, I had been influenced by singers who were more 'show-offy'. I still love Sarah Vaughan and Mark Murphy, who are technically great singers, but what spoke to me with Chet was the way he told a story, the way he let the song do the work. The storytelling was what turned me on, the same way Sinatra did it, but without the big voice. There was something about his approach as a singer that seemed completely natural—it seemed to come out of him without much guile, without much artifice. It knocked me out."[32]

Chet's early vocal recordings for Pacific Jazz had their technical limitations, as discussed at length earlier in this book, and divided both fellow musicians and critics alike. But regardless of critical opinion, they have an enduring appeal, and have remained in print for many years. It's interesting to note that his singing, not just his playing, has influenced a wide range of jazz and pop musicians, from Antonio Carlos Jobim to Astrud Gilberto, Bebel Gilberto to Stacey Kent, Kurt Elling to Georgie Fame, Rickie Lee Jones to Elvis Costello.

Note that this list includes a number of Brazilian musicians. Chet Baker's influence on Brazilian music has not been discussed that widely, in part because he failed to capitalise on the bossa nova boom that took place in the 1960s, like Stan Getz, Bud Shank and even Frank Sinatra. "The bossa nova stars were greatly influenced by Chet Baker, Bud Shank and the whole West Coast movement," claimed Brazilian jazz trumpeter Claudio Roditi. "There was a record label in Brazil called Music Disc; that label issued the whole of the Pacific Jazz catalogue in Brazil, so those albums were available on Brazilian prints; they were much cheaper to buy than imported records, which cost an arm and a leg. As a consequence, everyone listened to those sounds, rather than the Blue Note artists, which were only available on import. The main influence on João Gilberto was a singer from Martinique called Henri Salvador, who was the first one to sing with that voice; he played some Latin-American style music and also played the guitar. To some degree Chet Baker may also have influenced him."[33]

Pianist João Donato confirmed that he and João Gilberto listened extensively to Chet in their formative years. "We listened to Chet Baker play with Russ Freeman," he said. "In those days we didn't have many records, and we didn't know how to copy. So João Gilberto and I used to fight over the Chet Baker records. He'd say, 'Let me borrow the record for one day, then I'll give it back to you!' Jobim, Gilberto and myself, we were close together. We used to get together every night. We grew up listening to Chet Baker, Stan Kenton, Shorty Hodges and Gerry Mulligan, and started to enjoy that kind of music. The sound of Chet Baker belonged only to him, it doesn't sound like anybody. He had a personality that made him different to any other kind of trumpet player. We all loved him in Brazil!"[34]

The fact that Chet sang like he played made him a very natural scat singer; in fact, several of the musicians interviewed in this book suggested that Chet was one of the few scat singers they could enjoy listening to. Curtis Stigers elaborated on this view. "When Chet sang a ballad, he would have played it the same way," he explained. "The way he attacked a note was so similar to the way he used his voice. Likewise his scat solos—although there weren't so many examples on record—were just amazing. They sound just like his trumpet solos. He even used that hard 'th' sound, the way he played his trumpet. That really intrigued me, because I was studying what it is that makes a person a jazz singer, rather than a pop singer."

One of the best examples of Chet's scat singing can be seen and heard on 'You'd Be So Nice To Come Home To' from *Chet Baker in Tokyo*, which is available on both CD and DVD. "The first time I heard him do a scat chorus I thought, wow, if everyone who said they were going to sing scat did it like that, it wouldn't cause the problems (with jazz musicians) that it does," noted British jazz trumpet player and composer Guy Barker. "I could never really get my head around the idea of scat singing, but when Chet does it, it's just beautiful."[35]

Chet's legacy is still seen as far greater in Europe than in the United States. "It's because he was here," explained Barker, "he was in Italy, in France, and he was part of the whole scene. The footprints he left on these countries just stayed there, and his influence remains strong. Everyone's got thousands of Chet Baker stories, wherever you go—but especially in Italy, France, and Scandinavia. All of the jazz musicians have first hand knowledge of Chet."[36]

It's probably fair to say that recognition of Chet's legacy has also grown over time. He left behind approximately two hundred recordings—including albums that were released posthumously. Richard Cook and Brian Morton, authors of the splendid Penguin Guide to Jazz Recordings, once admitted they were surprised by the scale of Chet's recorded output, and felt the need to re-evaluate his later recordings—which may have varied in quality, but included some hidden gems.

Chet's visual appeal, discussed at length in the opening chapter of the book, has certainly helped to keep him in the spotlight, giving him an iconic status. The photographer, William Claxton, published a book of his pictures of Chet, simply entitled *Young Chet*, and his image has been used in countless magazine articles over the years. The movie *Let's Get Lost,* directed by fashion photographer Bruce Weber, further added to the mystique, a black-and white study of Chet Baker as a 'damaged beauty', 'faded jazz star' or 'junkie cool', depending of your perspective.

But for all that, Chet's greatest legacy, and the reason I wrote this book, is the music he left behind. I'll leave the last words to the jazz guitarist John Scofield. "Chet had an absolute commitment to playing good and improvising and swinging—he was doing it night after night. There's this whole big thing about his romantic history with drugs, the beatnik James Dean-type thing—but that wouldn't have meant anything if it weren't for Chet's music. It was the way he played that made him who he was."[37]

Chet Baker: An Illustrated Discography

The discography included in this book is not intended to be complete; there are a number of records that are long out of print, and near impossible to find, and others that are little more than bootleg recordings. In addition, Chet's back catalogue has been reissued and compiled on a regular basis, a problem that has effectively snowballed as his older recordings have come out of copyright in Europe. I have excluded most compilations from the main body of the discography, except where the record or CD concerned includes a variety of recordings not available elsewhere, such as compilations of recordings made for television.

Given that Chet's recorded output is vast, I have also included a short section on 'where to begin'—'Ten Chet Baker Records Everyone Should Own', which will hopefully be of use to readers who only have one or two of Chet's recordings.

In my view, these CDs are the best place to start, rather than the many compilations that are now available. Many of the recent collections are of dubious quality—not necessarily taken from the original master tapes, badly compiled and poorly annotated. If you prefer to buy a compilation, I would stick with the original Pacific Jazz collections of Chet's earlier recordings.

For those looking to delve further, the best information source is still Thorbjorn Sjogren's excellent publication, *Chet: The Music of Chesney Henry Baker*. Whilst the book was last updated almost twenty years ago, it remains an invaluable source of information about his recorded output, his enormous repertoire, the musicians he worked with and the lengthy tours he undertook.

ABBREVIATIONS:

acc:	accordion
arr:	arranger
as:	alto saxophone
b:	bass
bs:	baritone saxophone
bcl:	bass clarinet
c:	cello
cond:	conductor
dr:	drums
elb:	electric bass
elp:	electric piano
fl:	flute
flh:	flugelhorn
frh:	french horn
g:	guitar
harm:	harmonica
key:	keyboard
p:	piano
perc:	percussion
ss:	soprano saxophone
syn:	synthesiser
tb:	trombone
tp:	trumpet
vib:	vibraphone
vo:	vocal

CHET BAKER: LIVE AT THE TRADE WINDS 1952

Personnel: Chet Baker (tp), Sonny Criss (as), Wardell Gray (ts), Dave Pell (ts), Jerry Mandell (p), Harry Babasin (c), Bob Whitlock (b), Lawrence Marable (dr).
Date: March 1952
Place: Trade Winds Club, Inglewood, California
Rating: 2.0

After his discharge from the army in the spring of 1952, Chet returned to Los Angeles. Although his reputation as a musician was growing, he was still struggling to find regular work. This CD, issued on the Fresh Sounds label, captures Chet playing at a jam session with the saxophonists Sonny Criss and Wardell Gray. Chet is only heard on one tune, 'Out of Nowhere'. *Live at the Trade Winds* is the earliest recording of Chet that has been released to date, and is therefore important from a historical perspective. The sound quality is poor, however, and whilst Chet's playing is fine, there's little to suggest the wonderful recordings that would follow later that year.

CHET BAKER AND CHARLIE PARKER: COMPLETE JAM SESSIONS

Personnel: Charlie Parker (as), Baker (tp), Sonny Criss (as), Harry Babasin (b), Al Haig (p), Russ Freeman (p), Lawrence Marable (dr).
Date: June 16 1952
Place: Trade Winds Club, Inglewood, California
Rating: 2.5

Recorded just a couple of weeks after Charlie Parker had opened with Chet at the Tiffany Club, this jam session found the quintet joined by Parker disciple Sonny Criss. Claxton later recalled that Bird seemed happy and healthy on this West Coast tour, and from the opening track, 'Indiana', it is clear that he is on good form, producing a flood of ideas throughout his lengthy solos. As you might expect, Chet sounds a little hesitant, but determined not to be overwhelmed by the occasion, concentrating hard to pull off brief, eloquent solos. The recording is interesting, rather than essential, marred by its bootleg-style sound quality and the occasional missed cue, inevitable in such informal jam sessions.

GERRY MULLIGAN QUARTET

Personnel: Gerry Mulligan (bs), Chet Baker (tp), Carson Smith (b), Chico Hamilton (dr).
Date: September 1952 and January 1953
Place:
Rating: 4.0

Before signing a contract with Pacific Jazz, Mulligan signed up for two sessions with San Francisco's Fantasy Records. These recordings are not always easy to find, but are well worth looking for; there is no overlap with the Pacific Jazz sessions, and it includes the original versions of songs that were important part of the band's repertoire at that time, such as 'Line for Lyons'. Most importantly, it includes the original studio recording of 'My Funny Valentine'; it provided the Quartet with its first big hit, and still sounds haunting to this day.

GERRY MULLIGAN QUARTET: THE ORIGINAL QUARTET WITH CHET BAKER

Personnel: Gerry Mulligan (bs, p), Chet Baker (tp), Bobby Whitlock (b), Carson Smith (b), Red Mitchell (b), Joe Mondragon (b), Chico Hamilton (dr), Larry Bunker (dr), Jimmy Rowles (p).
Date: Various, June 1952–May 1953
Place: Los Angeles, California
Rating: 4.5

More than fifty years on, it is worth remembering that Mulligan's 'pianoless' quartet was seen as ground-breaking at the time. The quartet's music provided a stark contrast to bop, with ordered, sometimes chamber-like arrangements in addition to its unusual instrumentation. The enduring appeal of the music can be partly explained by the relatively simply, uncluttered arrangements, and the extraordinary, if short-lived, chemistry between Mulligan and Baker. The absence of a piano, which grabbed the headlines at the time, allows the two horns to play off one another in a variety of different settings. Mulligan's original compositions, particularly in the early months of the quartet, included a number of gems such as 'Nights at the Turntable', 'Soft Shoe' and 'Walkin' Shoes'. An essential part of any Chet Baker collection.

GERRY MULLIGAN TENTET AND QUARTET: FEATURING CHET BAKER

Personnel: Gerry Mulligan (bs, p), Chet Baker (tp), Pete Candoli (tp), Bob Envoldsen (v tb), John Graas (fr h), Ray Siegel (tu), Don Davidson (bs), Bud Shank (as), Joe Mondragon (b), Carson Smith (b), Chico Hamilton (dr), Larry Bunker (dr).
Date: January 1953, May 1953
Place: Los Angeles, California
Rating: 4.0
"The tentet," Mulligan later explained, "is essentially my original quartet with Chet Baker on trumpet with the ensemble instrumentation of the Miles Davis nonet." Although there are considerable developments, tunes like 'A Ballad' and 'Rocker' bear some resemblance to the earlier 'Birth of the Cool' sessions. Others, like 'Walkin' Shoes,' are clearly influenced by the arrangements he was writing for the quartet. The CD pairs the eight tracks recorded by the tentet with five later tunes recorded by the quartet in May.

GERRY MULLIGAN QUARTET WITH LEE KONITZ: KONITZ MEETS MULLIGAN

Personnel: Gerry Mulligan (bs), Chet Baker (tp), Lee Konitz (as), Carson Smith (b), Larry Bunker (dr).
Date: January 1953
Place: Los Angeles, California
Rating: 3.5
Lee Konitz, who was playing with Stan Kenton's orchestra at the time, guests with Mulligan's quartet at The Haig. One would be forgiven for thinking this was a Lee Konitz date; the saxophonist was clearly enjoying his freedom from the confines of the orchestra, stretching out over lengthy solos, with Mulligan and Baker limited to supporting roles for the most part. The rhythm section occasionally slips from 'cool' to 'soporific', but with Konitz on such good form, this is a minor quibble. Also available on CD as *The Complete 1953 Haig Performances*.

CHET BAKER AND STAN GETZ: WEST COAST LIVE

Personnel: Chet Baker (tp), Stan Getz (ts), Carson Smith (b), Larry Bunker (dr), Russ Freeman (p), Shelly Manne (dr).
Date: June 1953, August 1954
Place: Los Angeles, California
Rating: 3.0
With Mulligan undergoing cold turkey, trying to quit heroin ahead of his trial, Haig owner John Bennett made the commercial decision to pair Baker with Getz. After the wonderful chemistry of the original quartet, the results are something of a disappointment. One can sense the clash of egos, with Baker eager to prove himself as more than just a sideman, and Getz keen to assert his leadership of the band. The recording does allow us to hear Baker stretch out as soloist, and one can also hear his growing confidence on the more up-tempo tunes. This double CD also includes three tunes recorded at the Tiffany Club the following summer.

CHET BAKER QUARTET: FEATURING RUSS FREEMAN

Personnel: Chet Baker (tp), Russ Freeman (p), Bob Whitlock (b), Carson Smith (b) Joe Mondragon (b), Bobby White (dr), Larry Bunker (dr), Shelly Manne (dr).
Date: December 1952, July 1953, October 1953
Place: Los Angeles, California
Rating: 4.5
Walter Norris claimed that the studio recordings of the Mulligan quartet failed to capture the 'sparkle and fire' that was heard on stage at The Haig. The studio recordings with Russ Freeman bear that out, and illustrate clearly how rapidly Chet had developed as a soloist in just one year. Listen to his performance on the Latin-tinged 'Maid in Mexico', or the dazzling solo on 'Bea's Flat'. In Freeman, Baker had found the perfect partner. A talented composer and arranger, he gave Baker the space to blossom as a musician, and the stability Baker needed to keep a band together. This CD includes the first four sessions recorded by the Quartet, and includes Chet's first vocal performances on 'The Thrill is Gone' and 'I Fall in Love Too Easily'.

CHET BAKER AND THE LIGHTHOUSE ALL-STARS: WITCH DOCTOR

Personnel: Chet Baker (tr), Rolf Ericson (tr), Bud Shank (as, bs), Jimmy Giuffre (ts), Bob Cooper (ts), Russ Freeman (p), Claude Williamson (p), Howard Rumsey (b), Max Roach (dr), Shelly Manne (dr).
Date: September, 1953
Place: The Lighthouse, Hermosa Beach, California
Rating: 3.0
The Lighthouse All-Stars, who at this stage consisted of Rumsey, Cooper, Ericson, Williamson and Roach, are joined for a jam session by a number of special guests, including Chet Baker, Jimmy Giuffre and Shelly Manne. The recording has been remastered well, but it is hard to escape the fact that this is little more than a good-natured jam session. One of the highlights is a lively reading of 'Winter Wonderland', which was recorded by the Chet Baker Quartet the following month, and became a staple of their live repertoire. A sister record, 'At Last', features Miles Davis with the All-Stars, with Chet featured on one track.

CHET BAKER: ENSEMBLE

Personnel: Chet Baker (tr), Russ Freeman (p), Herb Geller (as, ts), Jack Montrose (ts), Bob Gordon (bs), Shelly Manne (dr), Joe Mondragon (b).
Date: December, 1953
Place: Los Angeles, California
Rating: 3.0
Producer Dick Bock was looking for a showcase for his rising star, and paired Chet with arranger Jack Montrose, who had been rehearsing with his own band at the Haig. Whilst Mulligan played to Chet's strengths, the arrangements here sound fussy, and don't allow much space for the assembled line-up to shine. The standout track is probably the ballad 'Goodbye', one of the three tunes not composed by Montrose himself. The session is also available on Fresh Sound Records as 'Ensemble and Sextet'.

CHET BAKER: CHET BAKER & STRINGS

Personnel: Chet Baker (tr), Russ Freeman (p), Shelly Manne (dr), Bud Shank (as), Jack Montrose (ts), Zoot Sims (ts), Joe Mondragon (b), Strings.
Date: December 1953, February 1954
Place: Los Angeles, California
Rating: 3.0
Dick Bock was keen to show the world that Chet Baker was now a major recording artist, and when Columbia Records proposed a one-record deal, he suggested recording the trumpet player with a string section, trying to emulate Charlie Parker's recordings on Verve. Whilst some of the arrangements are a little cloying, there's enough going on to keep things interesting; Baker plays with maturity, the soloing by Bud Shank and Zoot Sims is excellent, and there are strong original compositions by Montrose ('A Little Duet for Zoot and Chet') and Freeman ('The Wind'). Although 'Chet Baker & Strings' was widely dismissed by the jazz critics, it went on to become one of his most successful albums.

CHET BAKER: CHET BAKER SINGS

Personnel: Chet Baker (tr, vo), Russ Freeman (p, celeste), Carson Smith (b), Jimmy Bond (b), Peter Littman (dr), Lawrence Marable (dr), Bob Neel (dr).
Date: February 1954, July 1956
Place: Los Angeles, California
Rating: 4.0
Chet's first vocal single proved to be a success, and Bock brought the quartet back to the studio to record a 10" LP in February 1954. Chet's singing divided the critics, then as now, but this remains one of the most popular items in his immense backlog. It's easy to see why; the choice of material is impeccable, Baker sings with a charm and boyish innocence that would be tarnished in later years, and Freeman frames his soft voice with delicate arrangements. Chet's playing on these sessions is good, lyrical, yet concise. The *Chet Baker Sings* CD bizarrely reverses the original recording sessions; more importantly, some issues did not use the original mono recordings, but remixed the songs with excessive echo, and added Joe Pass on rhythm guitar, overdubbed at a later date. It's far better to look for *The Best of Chet Baker Sings* on Pacific Jazz, which uses the original masters, and better illustrates how his voice control improved over time.

CHET BAKER QUARTET: THIS TIME.../ OUT OF NOWHERE / MY OLD FLAME

Personnel: Chet Baker (tr, perc.), Russ Freeman (p), Carson Smith (b), Bob Neel (dr), Larry Bunker (dr).
Date: August 1953, May 1954, July 1954, August 1954
Place: Los Angeles, California; Ann Arbor, Michigan; Santa Cruz, California
Rating: 4.0

The original live LP, *Jazz at Ann Arbor* is still available periodically, but has effectively been superseded by this three-volume set, which captures the Quartet playing live in Los Angeles, and on its first nationwide tour. Chet's improvisational and interpretative skills continued to evolve over the years, but listening to his solo on up-tempo numbers like 'Zing Went the Strings of my Heart' (Volume 3), it's easy to argue that his technique never got much better. The set includes a number of tunes associated with the Mulligan Quartet, such as 'Line for Lyons' and 'Lullaby of the Leaves', most of which got dropped by the time Baker left for Europe in 1955. The sound quality is mixed, in part reflecting degradation in the quality of the master tapes, but these CDs are highly recommended.

CHET BAKER QUARTET: BOSTON, 1954

Personnel: Chet Baker (tr, vo), Russ Freeman (p), Carson Smith (b), Bob Neel (dr).
Date: March 1954, October 1954
Place: Boston, Massachusetts
Rating: 3.5

A series of three FM radio broadcasts from the Storyville Club in Boston, this release gives us the chance to hear live recordings of 'Time After Time', 'Long Ago and Far Away' and Russ Freeman's 'Bea's Flat', none of which feature on the Pacific Jazz releases above. The band plays shorter versions of some tunes, presumably to fit in with the radio programme.

CHET BAKER: SEXTET

Personnel: Sextet: Chet Baker (tr), Russ Freeman (p), Bob Brookmeyer (v tr), Bud Shank (bs), Carson Smith (b), Shelly Manne (dr).
1957 session: Chet Baker (tr), James Buffington (frh), Gene Allen (bass clarinet), Bob Tricarico (bassoon), Seymour Barab (ce), Russ Savakus (b), David 'Buck' Wheat (g).
Date: September 1954, December 1957
Place: Los Angeles, California; NYC
Rating: 3.5

The original 10" *Sextet* LP featured arrangements by Johnny Mandel, Jack Montrose and Bill Holman, and as a result, lacked cohesiveness. Highlights are a swinging version of 'Tommyhawk', which Baker later played on his first European tour, and 'Stella by Starlight', which he had learned from Stan Getz some months earlier. To the best of my knowledge, Chet never again played the other four tunes from this date. The CD adds four rare Bob Zieff tunes taken from an aborted recording session from December 1957. Style-wise it's not a good fit, but these tracks are well worth hearing, and were only previously available on a long-deleted 4-CD box set, *The Pacific Jazz Years*. The sextet session is also available on the Pacific Jazz CD, *Big Band*, which includes ten tunes recorded in October 1956.

CLIFFORD BROWN/CHET BAKER: THE TWO TRUMPET GENIUSES OF THE FIFTIES

Personnel: Various.
Date: Various, 1954–1956
Place: NYC; Baden-Baden, Germany; Los Angeles, California.
Rating: 1.0

Paolo Piangiarelli's Philology label seems intent on releasing every Chet Baker recording they can lay their hands on. Whilst there are a handful of exceptions, most notably 'Live at the Moonlight', most of the albums are of dubious quality. *Trumpet Geniuses* includes a selection of tunes recorded for *The Tonight Show*, two songs taped for the *Stars of Jazz* KABC show in LA, two songs from a radio broadcast from the Blue Note in Chicago, and an informal recording taped in Germany. Whilst it is interesting to hear Chet's playing evolve in 1955, and the influence of Miles Davis start to make itself heard, most of the recordings are of very poor quality. The radio broadcast is virtually unlistenable, and the *Stars of Jazz* tape is running too fast, with no obvious attempt made to correct the speed. Hard to find, and not worth the effort.

CHET BAKER: SINGS AND PLAYS

Personnel: Chet Baker (tr, vo), Bud Shank (fl), Russ Freeman (p), Red Mitchell (b), Carson Smith (b), Bob Neel (dr), Corky Hale (harp), Ed Lustgarten (c), Ray Kramer (c), Eleanor Slatkin (c), Kurt Reher (cello).
Date: February 1955, March 1955
Place: Los Angeles, California
Rating: 4.0
In early 1955, Chet topped the *DownBeat* and *Metronome* readers' poll, beating Dizzy Gillespie, and leaving Miles Davis and rising star Clifford Brown trailing in his wake. Dick Bock noticed that *Chet Baker Sings* was outselling Chet's instrumental releases, and proposed a new 12" LP, *Chet Baker Sings and Plays*, to cash in his growing popularity. The album was recorded at two different sessions; the first, in February 1955, included Bud Shank on flute and Red Mitchell on bass, and featured a string section, whilst the second session featured the regular Quartet. One year after his first full vocal album, Chet's singing sounds more confident; his enunciation is still a little nasal, but far clearer. Highlights include a gorgeous reading of Gershwin's 'Someone to Watch Over Me', with Chet sounding every inch the 'little lamb that's lost in the woods', and a dreamy vocal on 'This is Always'. The album also features Chet's only known recording of 'Let's Get Lost', the title track of the Bruce Weber movie.

CHET BAKER QUARTET PLUS: THE NEWPORT YEARS, VOL. 1

Personnel: Various.
Date: Various, 1953–1956
Place: Los Angeles, California; Newport, Rhode Island; NYC; Baden-Baden, Germany
Rating: 1.5
This Philology compilation features Chet's appearance at the second Newport Jazz Festival in July 1955, where he reunited briefly with Gerry Mulligan, and a selection of rare material from TV appearances and recordings from his first European tour. The Newport recordings are disappointing, marred by murky sound and patchy playing by Baker himself, who sounds out of place in front of a boisterous festival audience. More interesting are two songs recorded with Caterina Valente in Germany, and an energetic version of 'Night in Tunisia' on *The Tonight Show*, where Chet sounds like he's out to prove a point to his critics.

CHET BAKER QUARTET: INDIAN SUMMER

Personnel: Chet Baker (tr, vo), Dick Twardzik (p), Jimmy Bond (b), Peter Littman (d).
Date: September 1955
Place: Amsterdam and Scheveningen, Holland.
Rating: 4.0

With Freeman reluctant to commit to a European tour, Boston-born Dick Twardzik was brought in as a replacement. 'Indian Summer' captures recordings made of the first two concerts of the European tour, in Amsterdam and Scheveningen. The Scheveningen concert had previously been released as *The Lost Holland Concert* (see below). This version, released by the Dutch Jazz Archive in 2007, has been well mastered from better quality source tapes, and sounds vastly superior. On both nights, the band opens with a brisk version of Mandel's 'Tommyhawk', before slowing things down with the ballad 'Indian Summer', which allows us to enjoy a lengthy, elegant solo from Twardzik. On the second night, Twardzik lends delicate support to Baker's fragile, slightly wobbly vocal on 'Someone to Watch Over Me'. European audiences were less familiar with Chet's singing, and it was a brave move to attempt this ballad at such a glacial pace; nevertheless, he is rewarded by rapturous applause from the crowd. It's apparent from Chet's playing, the selection of tunes, and the more dynamic rhythm section, that Miles Davis had become a more important influence since his first nationwide tour of the US in 1954.

CHET BAKER QUARTET: THE LOST HOLLAND CONCERT

Personnel: Chet Baker (tr, vo), Dick Twardzik (p), Jimmy Bond (b), Peter Littman (d), Rolfe Schnoebiegel (t—one track).
Date: September 1955
Place: Scheveningen, Holland; Mainz, Germany; Zurich, Switzerland
Rating: 3.5

In addition to the Scheveningen concert, discussed above, this CD also includes three songs recorded a few days later at Mainz, in Germany. The tape runs too fast, but on the opener, 'Walkin'', one can still hear the power of Baker's playing at this time, and the swing that Littman brought to the band. Twardzik's classically influenced introduction to 'All The Things You Are' is astonishing, just one example of the inventive touches that he brought to this wonderful, if short-lived band. Two songs recorded in Zurich, with a local rhythm section, are also included.

CHET BAKER QUARTET: KÖLN CONCERT

Personnel: Chet Baker (tr, vo), Dick Twardzik (p), Jimmy Bond (b), Peter Littman (d), Hans Koller (ts), Willi Sanner (bs).
Date: October 1955
Place: Cologne, Germany
Rating: 4.0
The Köln Concert, released on the budget European label, RLR Records, allows us to hear the Quartet's full set, rather than just the tunes recorded for a radio broadcast. The quartet has clearly evolved in the three weeks since the Dutch concerts; 'Tommyhawk' sounds more polished, Chet's singing sounds more confident, and recognising his contribution to the band, Twardzik is given a solo feature, 'Yellow Tango'. The local promoter was clearly expecting a Mulligan-influenced set, and struggled to come to terms with the swinging, hard-bop drumming of Littman or the idiosyncratic style of Twardzik. Despite occasionally muffled sound, this is a valuable document; just twelve days later, Twardzik was dead.

CHET BAKER: CHET IN PARIS, VOLUME 1

Personnel: Chet Baker (tr, vo), Dick Twardzik (p), Jimmy Bond (b), Peter Littman (d).
Date: October 1955
Place: Paris, France
Rating: 4.5
While he was in Paris, Chet signed a contract to record seven records for Barclay, a French record label. Dick Twardzik suggested they record a number of tunes by Bob Zieff, a Boston-based composer with whom he had worked extensively. The success of the subsequent recording sessions is partly explained by their differing approach to Zieff's intricate arrangements; Chet plays by ear, approaching the harmonies from an intuitive perspective, whilst the pianist adopts a more considered, intellectual approach, constantly surprising Chet with his invention. In Dick Twardzik, Chet appears to have found the ideal musical partner—someone who was prepared to push him beyond his comfort zone. Composer Bob Zieff agreed. "It was a landmark … he seems to have turned a corner with Dick Twardzik and my music. There were not many who could meet that challenge—and with such great artistic results." It would have been fascinating to see how this partnership developed, but when the quartet reconvened to record a follow-up, Twardzik was dead from an overdose, aged just twenty-four. These recordings are no longer in copyright, and are therefore available in a number of different formats; the Barclay box set (below), whilst expensive, is highly recommended for its remastered sound and elegant packaging.

CHET BAKER QUARTET: LARS GULLIN 1955–56, VOL. 1

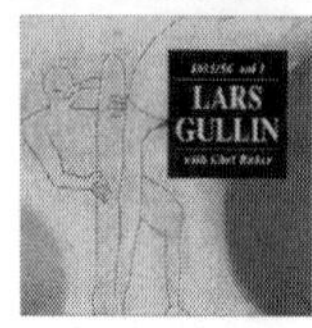

Personnel: Chet Baker (tr), Dick Twardzik (p), Jimmy Bond (b), Peter Littman (d), Lars Gullin (bs), Caterina Valente (vo).
Date: October 1955
Place: Stuttgart, Germany
Rating: 3.0
The last word from Twardzik, and a rare opportunity to hear a Bob Zieff tune played on stage. Swedish baritone saxophonist Lars Gullin and Italian singer Caterina Valente joined the Quartet for a few dates. Gullin joins the band for a brisk romp through Charlie Parker's 'Cool Blues'. The second tune is the Bob Zieff composition 'Brash', recorded just four days earlier. It is played by the Quartet alone, and offers a tantalising glimpse at how the band might have evolved had Twardzik lived. If Chet's solo sounds slightly hesitant, the pianist sounds at ease with the arrangement, producing a brief but imaginative solo; interesting to note the audience reaction, which is extremely favourable. Gullin returns for a slightly plodding version of 'Lover Man', before Valente scats her way through a forgettable 'I'll Remember April'.

CHET BAKER: CHET IN PARIS, VOLUME 2

Personnel: Chet Baker (tr, vo), Gerard Gustin (p), Raymond Fol (p), Jimmy Bond (b), Benoit Quersin (b), Nils-Bertil Dahlander (dr), Jean-Louis Viale (dr).
Date: October 1955, November 1955
Place: Paris, France
Rating: 4.0
Volume 2 comprises two sessions. The first of these was recorded on October 24th, just three days after Twardzik's death. With Rene Utreger unavailable at such short notice, Gerard Gustin plays piano, whilst Swedish drummer Bert Dahlander fills in for Littman on drums. The band sticks to standards, familiar to all of the musicians. Whilst the record opens with an uptempo version of 'Summertime', there is an unmistakable air of melancholy hanging over the session. There's an aching sadness to Baker's playing on 'You Go To My Head' and 'Tenderly'; he may have struggled to express his feelings in words, but one can hear the emotion he was going through in his playing. One month later, Baker returned to the studio with Raymond Fol on piano for a somewhat underrated session; only three of the six tracks recorded that day were originally released, and one, 'What Is There To Say', has since been lost. The highlight is probably 'Everything Happens To Me', the only vocal recording Chet made in Paris.

CHET BAKER: CHET IN PARIS, VOLUME 3

Personnel: Chet Baker (tr), René Urtreger (p), Francy Boland (p), Benoit Quersin (b), Eddie de Haas (b), Bobby Jaspar (ts), Jean-Louis Chautemps (ts), Armand Migiani (ts), Teddy Ameline (as), William Boucaya (bs), Benny Vasseur (trb), Jean-Louis Viale (dr), Charles Saudrais (dr), Pierre Lemarchand (dr).
Date: December 1955, February 1956, March 1956
Place: Paris, France
Rating: 3.5
The third volume of the Barclay/Emarcy recordings is probably the least essential, and illustrates the degree to which Chet benefited from a guiding hand in the studio. It comprises three separate recording sessions. The first is excellent, and features Bobby Jaspar on tenor and René Urtreger on piano. Sadly, the band only recorded four tunes; this may be down to time pressure, since Chet had just returned from Iceland. The second session was recorded in February with Chet's working band, which included Jean-Louis Chautemps on tenor. Again, only four tracks were recorded, and the existence of multiple takes suggests some frustration with the heavy-handed drumming of Saudrais. The final session features three songs composed for Chet by Pierre Michelot and Christian Chevalier, and later re-recorded for the Big Band LP.

CHET BAKER: CHET IN PARIS, VOLUME 4 —ALTERNATE TAKES

Personnel: Various, as above.
Date: October 1955, November 1955, December 1955, February 1956
Place: Paris, France
Rating: 2.0
The fourth and final volume of the original Barclay/Emarcy recordings features alternate takes from many of the original sessions, although it should be noted that none exists from the first session with Dick Twardzik. As one would expect, the inclusion of multiple takes does not make for great listening, and this volume is really for collectors only. The main point of interest is probably to hear the first four takes of 'Tasty Pudding', where Chet grows increasingly frustrated with the intrusive drumming of Charles Saudrais. Note how he plays far softer on take three than take two, before the band attempts the same tunes at a slower, almost funereal pace on take four. Saudrais is eventually excluded from the master take, which is featured on Volume 3.

CHET BAKER: IN PARIS—BARCLAY SESSIONS 1955–1956

Personnel: Various, as above.
Date: October 1955, November 1955, December 1955, February 1956
Place: Paris, France
Rating: 4.5

The first of these—*In Paris—Barclay Sessions, 1955–1956*, is a good, single-disc introduction to Chet's studio recordings in Paris. The sound has been remastered well, and offers greater clarity, and the accompanying booklet includes some elegant sepia photographs of Chet. *The Complete Barclay Sessions*, as the name suggests, contains every studio recording from Paris. The eight recording sessions have been separated out—quite unnecessarily—over eight CDs. As a result, the two recording sessions with Dick Twardzik are spread over two discs, each less than twenty minutes in length. Aside from this, the packaging is quite exquisite, with a large-sized, eighty-four page booklet complete with rare photographs, reproduced on glossy paper, essays by Francis Marmande and Alain Tercinet, and an interview with composer Bob Zieff. The high price will deter most buyers, especially now that these recordings are out of copyright, but the box set comes highly recommended.

CHET BAKER: MY FUNNY VALENTINE

Personnel: Chet Baker (tr), Ralph Schecroun (p), Eddie de Haas (b), Jean-Louis Chautemps (ts), Charles Saudrais (dr).
Date: December 1955
Place: Copenhagen, Denmark
Rating: 2.0

By far the weakest of Chet's recordings from the first European tour, this makes for fairly grim listening. Ralph Schecroun was no replacement for Twardzik; influenced by Errol Garner, he could only play in one or two keys, and had little experience playing with a band, where he was expected to lend support to the other musicians. Charles Saudrais replaced Littman, and lacked the subtlety that Chet typically looked for in a drummer; listening to his clumsy work on 'CTA', it's a wonder he stayed in the band as long as he did. Chet sounds uncomfortable, playing with a rare anger for much of the concert. The packaging is cheap, and contains no information about the band, or photographs from the tour.

CHET BAKER QUINTET: CONSERVATORIO CHERUBINI—COMPLETE CONCERT

Personnel: Chet Baker (tr, vo), Francy Boland (p), Eddie de Haas (b), Jean-Louis Chautemps (ts), Charles Saudrais (dr). Various on bonus disc.
Date: January 1956. Various on bonus disc.
Place: Florence, Italy. Various on bonus disc
Rating: 3.0
Originally released as *Exitus*, a two-volume set on an Italian label, Replica Records, the Conservatorio Cherubini concert is now available on CD. The CD does not feature the 'complete' concert, as billed, and excludes instrumental versions of both 'My Funny Valentine' and 'I Cover the Waterfront', both of which were excluded from the original LPs; a pity, because this is the only known recording of Chet playing the latter. Ralph Schecroun was replaced by the more sympathetic Francy Boland on piano. Chet sounds more relaxed with this line-up, delivering lengthy solos on a fairly bop-oriented set. His singing on 'You Don't Know What Love Is' and 'This is Always' also sounds good, suggesting he was growing in confidence by this stage. Saudrais remains the weak link, his wild thrashing occasionally marring a strong set. The sound quality is poor, captured by just two microphones according to de Haas, and his bass is barely audible for much of the concert. The bonus CD includes other recordings from Europe, and Baker's set at the 1955 Newport Jazz Festival, all of which are also available on the Philology label (Newport Years, Vol. 1).

CHET BAKER: CHET BAKER AND CREW / AT THE FORUM THEATER

Personnel: Chet Baker (tr, vo), Bobby Timmons (p), Phil Urso (ts), Jimmy Bond (b), Peter Littman (dr), Bill Loughbrough (chromatic tympani).
Date: July 1956
Place: Los Angeles, California
Rating: 4.0
Chet's first recording on his return to the U.S. saw him reunited with Peter Littman and Jimmy Bond, the original rhythm section from his European tour, and his old friend Phil Urso. Producer Dick Bock had not recorded Chet for almost eighteen months, and was keen to record Chet's 'hard' new sound. For the most part this is a fine, bop-oriented set; notable exceptions are two Zieff compositions, 'Slightly Above Moderate' and 'Medium Rock', the ballad 'Halema', written by Urso to appease Chet's new wife, and a rare vocal reading of 'Line for Lyons', with lyrics by percussionist Bill Loughborough. Additional material from these sessions is available on 'At the Forum Theater' and 'Cools Out', albeit with some overlap. The former includes more songs, including 'Night on Bop Mountain', and is probably the better bet.

CHET BAKER AND ART PEPPER: THE ROUTE

Personnel: Chet Baker (tr), Art Pepper (as), Richie Kamuca (ts), Pete Jolly (p), Leroy Vinnegar (b), Stan Levey (dr).
Date: July 1956
Place: Los Angeles, California
Rating: 3.0
Art Pepper had just completed a twenty-month jail sentence when he was invited to make a record with Chet Baker by Dick Bock. There was some disagreement over the material, with Pepper reluctant to play the Zieff compositions that Baker proposed. The result was a compromise, with Bock opting to record the two stars with a different band. The session included five strong sextet recordings, with Lester Young-influenced tenor saxophonist Richie Kamuca holding his own. Thereafter, the group splits, with Pepper supported by the trio on his own composition 'Ol' Croix', before playing stripped-back versions of 'I Can't Give You Anything But Love' and 'The Great Lie' with just bass and drums. Baker, Kamuca and Jolly each play a 'solo' piece to round off the record, with Chet recording 'Sweet Lorraine'. The fragmented nature of the session meant that the album was not released at the time, with Bock releasing several tracks on compilations over the years. With the aid of producer, Michael Cuscuna, the whole session was eventually unearthed and released as *The Route*.

CHET BAKER: BIG BAND

Personnel: Chet Baker (tr), Norman Faye (tr), Conte Candoli (tr), Frank Rosolino (tb), Bob Burgess (tb), Art Pepper (as), Bud Shank (as), Phil Urso (as, ts), Fred Waters (as), Bill Perkins (ts), Bob Graf (ts), Bill Hood (bs), Bobby Timmons (p), Jimmy Bond (b), Lawrence Marable (dr), Peter Littman (dr), James McKean (dr).
Date: October 1956
Place: Los Angeles, California
Rating: 4.0
Inspired by the eight-piece band recordings Chet made for Barclay in Paris (*Chet in Paris, Vol. 3*), Dick Bock wanted to capture Chet's lustier tone accompanied by a 'big band' sound. Seven tracks were recorded with a nonet, including 'Mythe', 'Not Too Slow' and 'V-line' which were composed and arranged for the March 1956 Paris session; a further three tunes were recorded by an eleven-piece band which included Art Pepper, Bud Shank and Phil Urso on saxophone. The arrangements are better suited to Chet's style than the earlier *Ensemble* and *Sextet* records, and swing easily. The CD adds six tunes that comprised the *Sextet* 10" LP from 1954.

CHET BAKER AND ART PEPPER: PLAYBOYS / PICTURE OF HEATH

Personnel: Chet Baker (tr), Art Pepper (as), Phil Urso (ts), Carl Perkins (p), Curtis Counce (b), Lawrence Marable (dr).
Date: October 1956
Place: Los Angeles, California
Rating: 3.5
Recording Chet for the fourth time in as many months, Dick Bock was either looking to make up for time 'lost' while Chet was in Europe, or was aware that his biggest star was developing a heroin habit that was spiralling out of control. One suspects the latter. Loughborough had quit the band in August, concerned that one of the band members might overdose. Saxophonist Jimmy Heath, responsible for some of the arrangements on 'Playboys', memorably described the session as 'an authentic junkie record'. He was in jail for possession at the time, Art Pepper had slipped back into his old ways, Urso and Baker were also using, and pianist Carl Perkins would be dead within two years. Despite their collective problems, Urso remembers the date as going "very, very well." Baker and Pepper were not close, but there is far greater chemistry in their playing than the earlier recording with Stan Getz. Urso arguably deserves greater recognition, and contributes some bright, inventive solos. The original, politically incorrect cover art has been replaced but is worth tracking down for fans of glove puppets.

CHET BAKER AND RUSS FREEMAN: QUARTET

Personnel: Chet Baker (tr), Russ Freeman (p), Leroy Vinnegar (b), Shelly Manne (dr).
Date: November 1956
Place: Los Angeles, California
Rating: 4.5
The final collaboration between Baker and Freeman, this was nominally a Russ Freeman session. The record opens with the stunning 'Love Nest', which was the theme to the popular Burns and Allen TV Show. After a number of aborted takes, Chet delivers a wonderful solo on muted trumpet. Another highlight is Russ Freeman's 'Summer Sketch', a ballad on a par with 'The Wind', and one of the pianist's favourite compositions. 'Say When', another Freeman original, features bright, vibrant solos from both Baker and Freeman, whilst Strayhorn's 'Lush Life' is given a fairly straight reading. 'Quartet' is probably the strongest of the numerous dates recorded with Freeman, in part reflecting the growing maturity of the musicians, but also because of the driving drumming of Shelly Manne on the more uptempo numbers. Highly recommended.

CHET BAKER AND BUD SHANK: THEME MUSIC FROM THE JAMES DEAN STORY

Personnel: Chet Baker (tr), Bud Shank (as), Don Fagerquist (fl), Ray Linn (tr), Milt Bernhart (trb), Charlie Mariano (as), Herbie Steward (as), Bill Holman (ts), Richie Kamuca (ts), Pepper Adams (bs), Claude Williamson (p), Monte Budwig (b), Mel Lewis (dr), Mike Pacheco (bongos).
Date: November 1956
Place: Los Angeles, California
Rating: 2.5
A 'musical tribute to the genius of the young man who had brought the promise of beauty to so many', according to the sleeve notes. Not Chet Baker, of course, but James Dean, who had died one year earlier at the age of just twenty-four. The documentary was co-directed by a young Robert Altman. The music was composed by Leith Stevens, a former child prodigy and prolific soundtrack composer, and was arranged by Johnny Mandel and Bill Holman. The playing features some pleasant solos from Baker and Shank, and the CD reissue includes a rare vocal performance of 'Let Me Be Loved'. Nevertheless, this remains an inconsequential item within Chet's crowded discography.

CHET BAKER QUARTET AND QUINTET: PRETTY/GROOVY

Personnel: Various
Date: Various
Place: Los Angeles, California
Rating: 2.0
Dick Bock, the owner and producer of Pacific Jazz Records, had a number of peculiar habits. He sometimes used alternative takes when issuing a 12" version of a 10" LP. When he reissued *Chet Baker Sings*, he drenched the original mono mix in echo, and overdubbed guitar. Another example of his strange approach to editing came with the 1957 release of *Pretty/Groovy*, which claims to feature 'previously unreleased dates with Bill Perkins, Jimmy Giuffre, and new guitarist David 'Buck' Wheat'. For the most part, Bock simply overdubs Bill Perkins' tenor sax in place of Chet's vocals on songs such as 'Time After Time' and 'My Funny Valentine', whilst Jimmy Giuffre's clarinet replaces Chet's vocal on 'There Will Never Be Another You.' The record presumably filled at a gap at a time when Chet was rarely in a fit state to record. Pretty/Pointless.

JACK SHELDON: JACK'S GROOVE

Personnel: Jack Sheldon (tr), Chet Baker (tr), Stu Williamson (trb), Herb Geller (as), Art Pepper (as), Harold Land (ts), Paul Moer (p), Buddy Clark (b), Mel Lewis (dr)..
Date: August 1957
Place: Los Angeles, California
Rating: 2.5
This good-natured swing session, recorded in August 1957, is available as *Jack Sheldon and His All Stars* or *Jack's Groove*. The line-up, which includes both Chet Baker and Art Pepper, suggests that Jack was calling in some favours. Chet can only be heard sparingly on this unremarkable record.

GERRY MULLIGAN QUARTET: REUNION WITH CHET BAKER

Personnel: Gerry Mulligan (bs), Chet Baker (tp), Henry Grimes (b), Dave Bailey (dr).
Date: December 1957
Place: NYC, New York
Rating: 3.5
Dick Bock travelled to New York in early December to supervise a number of recordings with Gerry Mulligan. When he learned of Chet's problems, he offered to lend a helping hand, including a potentially lucrative reunion with his old partner. Gerry Mulligan had his reservations, and when the trumpet player turned up late for the first recording session, his eyes hidden behind dark glasses, his worst fears were confirmed. This may help to explain why Chet's playing lacks focus on certain tracks, and Mulligan's somewhat detached, stilted tone. There are moments when the old chemistry comes through, however. 'Ornithology' sounds as fresh as the original quartet recordings, whilst 'All The Things You Are', which was not even included on the original LP, is superb. The alternate take of 'Gee, Baby, Ain't I Good To You' is another highlight, demonstrating the intuitive way in which Baker and Mulligan could play off one another.

CHET BAKER: EMBRACEABLE YOU

Personnel: Chet Baker (tp, vo), David 'Buck' Wheat (g), Ross Savakus (b).
Date: December 1957
Place: NYC, New York
Rating: 2.5

After consulting Mulligan, Dick Bock decided to abandon Chet's recording session with Bob Zieff after just four tunes had been completed. Perhaps inspired by the success of Julie London's 'Julie is Her Name,' Bock suggested the guitarist and bass player from that session stay on, and record a vocal session with Chet. In the event, the producer thought that the results were too depressing, and the session stayed in the vaults, unreleased bar one track, for over forty years. Chet is in relatively good voice, but there's a weary edge to his singing; Gershwin's 'They All Laughed' has rarely sounded so joyless. Whether his tone is down to the late hour—he was late for the original session—or Chet's lifestyle at that time is not clear. It may be that he was not particularly enamoured of the material suggested by Bock; he never again recorded 'The Night We Called it A Day', 'They All Laughed' or 'There's a Lull in My Life'. The session has its moments, most notably Chet's playing and that of the guitarist, David Wheat, but is too one-paced to be recommended that highly.

ANNIE ROSS: SINGS A SONG WITH MULLIGAN!

Personnel: Annie Ross (vo), Gerry Mulligan (bs), Chet Baker (tp), Art Farmer (tp), Henry Grimes (b), Bill Crow (b), Dave Bailey (dr).
Date: December 1957
Place: NYC, New York
Rating: 4.0

But only a handful with Chet Baker! Chet played on the first ten songs recorded for this session, of which only five made it to the original LP. "Chet just went to the bathroom and never came back," recalled Ross. "That's why we had to get Art Farmer." Chet's antics aside, she remembers the session fondly. "I loved the people who I worked with, and the whole atmosphere was relaxed and loving." Annie Ross selected the songs, which include a wonderful selection of standards, including 'Let There Be Love', 'It Don't Mean a Thing' and 'I've Grown Accustomed to Your Face'. Mulligan's arrangements are a delight. Chet's contribution may be limited, but fans of Mulligan or jazz singing will find plenty to enjoy.

STAN GETZ AND CHET BAKER: STAN MEETS CHET

Personnel: Stan Getz (ts), Chet Baker (tp), Jodie Christian (p), Victor Sproles (b), Marshall Thompson (dr).
Date: February 1958
Place: Chicago, Illinois
Rating: 2.0
One of the low points in Chet's long discography. In return for allowing Mulligan to record with Pacific Jazz records in December 1957, Dick Bock agreed that Chet be allowed to record one session with Norman Granz's Verve Records. Bock got the better deal. Norman Granz chose to pair Chet with fellow West Coast musician Stan Getz for what was to be their only studio session. Getz was on his way back from San Francisco, and met Chet in Chicago, where he was touring. Granz paired them with a local rhythm section, and with no time to rehearse, they agreed on a handful of songs. Getz plays well, but Baker was in no fit state to record. On the opening track, 'I'll Remember April', one of only two tunes they play together, Baker had to woken from the sofa to take his solo. On a solo feature, 'Autumn in New York', the trumpeter drops a huge clam in the opening bar; bizarrely, there was no second take. After the session, Baker was busted driving to Milwaukee, and then again in Harlem. A spell in the Lexington Federal Hospital beckoned.

CHET BAKER: IT COULD HAPPEN TO YOU

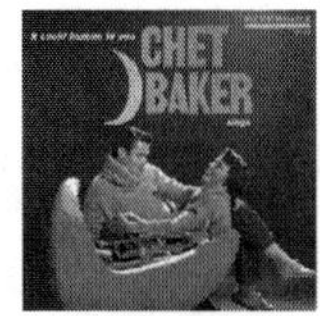

Personnel: Chet Baker (tp, vo), Kenny Drew (p), Sam Jones (b), George Morrow (b), Danny Richmond (dr), Philly Joe Jones (dr).
Date: August 1958
Place: NYC, New York
Rating: 2.5
The year Chet spent with Riverside in New York was a troubled period for the trumpeter; struggling to cope with his addiction, he was eventually sentenced to six months at Rikers Island in March 1959. Bill Grauer, who had been responsible for signing Baker to the label, hoped to win back Chet's fanbase with an album of romantic ballads, and paired Chet with pianist Kenny Drew. The resulting LP, *It Could Happen To You*, was slammed by the critics. "Can you carry a tune?" asked Martin Williams of *DownBeat*. On this evidence, it was a fair question. Chet turned up stoned for the first session, which was abandoned after two songs, including a slurred version of 'Old Devil Moon'. Two later sessions were more fruitful, but Chet's pitch is often wayward; whether this reflects a lack of rehearsal, or a choice of songs that was overambitious for his limited range, it is hard to say. The CD includes two additional tracks, one of which was apparently the tenth take. It seems Grauer tried his best, but the results lack the charm and innocence of his earlier recordings.

CHET BAKER: IN NEW YORK

Personnel: Chet Baker (tp, vo), Johnny Griffin (ts), Al Haig (p), Paul Chambers (b), Philly Joe Jones (dr).
Date: August 1958
Place: NYC, New York
Rating: 3.0
Bill Grauer's partner, Orrin Keepnews, was never a fan of 'cool' West Coast jazz, and after Baker's poor performance on the vocal LP, decided to 'bury him' in a hard-bop, 'East Coast' line up which included rising tenor star Johnny Griffin, and the young bass player Paul Chambers, who was playing with Miles Davis. Far from being buried, Chet holds his own, and makes a mockery of the East/West divide. 'In New York' is usually held to be the pinnacle of Chet's brief stay with Riverside, but in truth, it's fairly standard bop, with little to distinguish it from many other records released at the time. Whilst Chet sounded comfortable playing with Miles' sidemen, Miles himself had moved on, recording the ground-breaking 'Milestones' and 'Porgy and Bess' earlier that year. Nor did Chet's playing burn as brightly as that of Lee Morgan, the twenty-year-old Philadelphia trumpeter who had just recorded *Candy* for Blue Note records.

JOHNNY PACE: CHET BAKER INTRODUCES JOHNNY PACE

Personnel: Johnny Pace (vo), Chet Baker (tp), Herbie Mann (fl, bcl), Joe Berle (p), Vinnie Burke (b), Philly Joe Jones (dr), Ed Thigpen (dr).
Date: December 1958
Place: NYC, New York
Rating: 2.0
Given Chet's difficult relationship with Orrin Keepnews, it's a wonder this project ever got off the ground. Johnny Pace was an Italian-Irish singer, raised in New Jersey, and working the club circuit, where he occasionally got the chance to work with touring jazz musicians. Chet Baker met him in a small Pittsburgh night club, and persuaded Riverside to give him his big break. Pace's tone is pleasant on the ear, but his phrasing sounds like that of a nightclub, rather than a jazz singer. Chet's playing is good throughout, offering delicate support on 'This Is Always', one of the few standout tracks on this unremarkable record. Keepnews wondered what his partner was doing, recording this "cockamamie singer", and was not surprised when the record sank without trace.

CHET BAKER: CHET

Personnel: Chet Baker (tp), Pepper Adams (bs), Herbie Mann (fl), Kenny Burrell (g), Bill Evans (p), Paul Chambers (b), Connie Kay (dr).
Date: December 1958
Place: NYC, New York
Rating: 4.0
Keepnews was keen to salvage some worthwhile material from the last of the sessions with Johnny Pace, and persuaded Chet and Herbie Mann to stay on to make an album of ballads with the label's rising star, pianist Bill Evans. Evans and Chambers were working with Miles Davis at the time, and there are hints of the 'modal' playing heard on *Milestones*, and more prominently on *Kind of Blue* which was recorded just three months later. The smoky baritone of Pepper Adams is heard to good effect on several tracks, whilst Kenny Burrell makes telling contributions throughout. Critics have pointed to the slow, 'junkie' beat that pervades the sessions, but Mann remembered Chet as being on good form. The result was a late-night classic to rival Burrell's own *Midnight Blue*. The album received favourable reviews, and having hit upon a potentially winning formula at last, Riverside looked set to make a modest return on the investment they had made. Sadly it was not to be; weeks after the completion of the album, Chet was busted twice in quick succession, and sentenced to six months at Rikers Island prison.

CHET BAKER: PLAYS THE BEST OF LERNER AND LOEWE

Personnel: Chet Baker (tp), Pepper Adams (bs), Zoot Sims (as, ts), Herbie Mann (fl, ts), Bill Evans (p), Bill Evans (p), Bob Corwin (p), Earl May (b), Clifford Jarvis (dr).
Date: July 1959
Place: NYC, New York
Rating: 2.5
Before leaving for Europe, Chet had to fulfill his contract with Riverside, and recorded a tribute to Lerner and Loewe, the composers of 'My Fair Lady'. It sounds an unlikely project for Chet, who had only previously recorded two of their tunes; he recorded 'Almost Like Being In Love' with Mulligan, and 'I've Grown Accustomed to Her Face' with the singer Annie Ross. Despite a strong line-up, the session fails to gel. A couple of the tunes, 'I Could Have Danced All Night' and 'Show Me', don't work well as jazz standards, their cause not helped by cloying arrangements from Herbie Mann. Highlights include a duet with Pepper Adams on 'On the Street Where You Live', and the delicate ballad 'I Talk To The Trees', which would not have sounded out of place on the 'Chet' album.

CHET BAKER: IN MILAN

Personnel: Chet Baker (tp), Gianni Basso (ts), Clauco Masetti (as), Franco Cerri (b), Renato Sellani (p), Gene Victory (dr).
Date: September, October 1959
Place: Milan, Italy
Rating: 2.5
By the autumn of 1959, Chet was living in Italy, and desperate for cash to fund his growing Palfium habit. His manager arranged for him to record two LPs with local musicians. The first of these, *In Milan*, featured tenor saxophonist Gianni Basso. The band mostly sticks to bop standards such as Charlie Parker's 'Cheryl Blues' and Tadd Dameron's 'Lady Bird', and also revisits Mulligan's 'Line For Lyons'. For the most part, the results are fairly pedestrian, and lack any real spark. Baker's tone is not as clean as on his previous European recordings, most likely the result of his drug intake. 'My Old Flame', one of two tracks recorded as a quartet, is probably the highlight, but it falls far short of his previous peaks.

CHET BAKER: WITH FIFTY ITALIAN STRINGS

Personnel: Chet Baker (tp, vo), Mario Pezzotta (tb), Fausto Papetti (bars), Gianni Basso (ts), Glauco Masetti (as), Franco Cerri (b), Giulio Libani (p, cel), Gene Victory (dr), Orchestra, Len Mercer (arranger, conductor).
Date: September, October 1959
Place: Milan, Italy
Rating: 2.5
Around the same time as the *In Milan* sessions, Chet recorded an album with Len Mercer (real name Ezio Leoni) and his orchestra. It appears to have been a deliberate attempt to reproduce the Capitol-era Sinatra recordings, even including 'Angel Eyes' and Goodbye' from Sinatra's 1958 LP *Sings for Only the Lonely*. The album has its admirers, and has been reissued with different sleeves on numerous occasions. Chet's playing is strong, never overwhelmed by the orchestra, and he is in good voice on the five vocal tracks. The arrangements are extremely heavy-handed, however, and generally inferior to the earlier *With Strings* album recorded for Pacific Jazz.

CHET BAKER: ITALIAN MOVIES—MUSIC OF PIERO UMILIANI

Personnel: Chet Baker (tp), Nino Rosso (tp), Bill Gilmore (tb), Marcello Boschi (as), Livio Cervellieri (ts), Gino Marinacci (bars), Piero Umiliani (p), Berto Pisano (b), Jimmy Pratt (d), Various (Piero Umiliani's Big Band, Strings).
Date: Various, 1960, 1962
Place: Rome, Italy
Rating: 3.0
Something of an oddity in Chet's discography, the original LP included scores written and arranged by Piero Umiliani for two Italian movies, *Big Deal on Madonna Street* (1961) and *Smog* (1962). The arrangements vary, with some written for octet, others for a big band, whilst strings were added to two tracks. The results may be less compelling than Miles Davis's *L'Ascenseur pour L'Échafaud* (1957), but the arrangements are atmospheric, and it makes for a more interesting collection than either of the Milan records. There was clearly a great deal of mutual respect between Umiliani and Baker, and when they met in later years, Baker referred to him affectionately as 'Maestro'. The record was later reissued with three tracks recorded for the movie *Urlatori alla Sbarra*. Sadly, Chet's vocal recording of 'Arrivederci' was not included.

CHET BAKER: CHET IS BACK! / THE ITALIAN SESSIONS

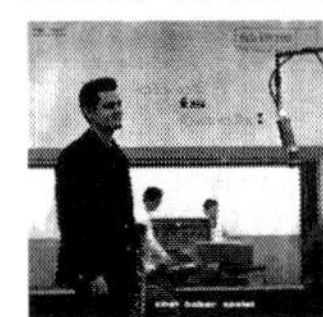

Personnel: Chet Baker (tp, vo), Bobby Jaspar (ts, fl), René Thomas (g), Amadeo Tommasi (p), Benoît Quersin (b), Daniel Humair (dr), Ennio Morricone (conductor), Orchestra, The Swingers (vo).
Date: January 1962
Place: Rome, Italy
Rating: 3.5
RCA Italiana offered him $10,000 for a one-year contract, and in early January, Chet entered RCA's new studio with a first-class band, including René Thomas on guitar, Bobby Jaspar on tenor and flute, and the emerging Italian pianist, Amadeo Tommasi. "Chet played very strongly, like Dizzy Gillespie," Tommasi later recalled, and indeed, his blowing on opening track 'Well, You Needn't' is barely recognisable. The set included uptempo bop, including Bird's 'Barbados', gentle ballads, such as 'These Foolish Things' and 'Over the Rainbow', and a strong original composition by the young pianist. A second session saw Chet record four tunes he had composed in prison, arranged by Tommasi, and recorded with a young Ennio Morricone. These romantic ballads included 'Chetty's Lullaby', written for his young son who had returned to live in the U.S. with his second wife, Halema. Aimed at the Italian pop market, and designed to cash in on Chet's image, the recordings are inconsequential and marred by syrupy arrangements.

CHET BAKER: STELLA BY STARLIGHT

Personnel: Chet Baker (tp), Jacques Pelzer (ss, as, f), René Thomas (g), Franco Cerri (b), Joe Harris (dr).
Date: 1962
Place: Brussels, Belgium
Rating: 2.5
Sleeve notes from this rare radio broadcast suggest it was recorded in Rome in 1964, but the actual recording took place for Belgian radio station BRT3 in 1962. The notes also mistakenly credit Glauco Masetti and Gianni Cazzola as playing saxophone and drums, respectively. Whilst Chet's playing is strong, the sound quality is somewhat muffled, and this recording is only really notable for the chance to hear a rare Chet composition, 'Theme for Freddy'. For collectors only.

CHET BAKER QUINTET: BRUSSELS 1964

Personnel: Chet Baker (tp, vo), Jacques Pelzer (as, f), René Urtreger (p), Luigi Trussardi (b), Franco Manzecci (dr).
Date: 1963
Place: Brussels, Belgium
Rating: 3.0
This CD has now been withdrawn, following legal action by Luigi Trussardi and René Urtreger; according to Trussardi, it captures the rehearsal for a Belgian TV show in 1963, and was withdrawn because the recording was issued illegally, and most of the musicians were not paid. Fortunately, the TV appearance is now available on DVD as part of the *Jazz Icons* series, pairing this with a 1979 concert in Norway. The highlight is a long, wistful version of 'Time After Time', Baker's singing far stronger than on his original 1954 studio recording. By contrast, the band's version of Miles Davis's 'So What' sounds under-rehearsed. The sound has also been well remastered compared with the original CD. A fascinating document from a year that otherwise produced no studio recordings.

TERRY RILEY: MUSIC FOR THE GIFT

Personnel: Terry Riley (composer, tape manipulation), Chet Baker (tp), Luis Fuentes (tb), Luigi Trussardi (b), George Solano (dr), John Graham (voice).
Date: June, 1963
Place: Paris, France
Rating: 2.5
One of the more peculiar items in Chet's discography; playwright Ken Dewey persuaded Chet to work with the experimental musician Terry Riley to create a soundtrack for an avant-garde theatre production. Riley asked the musicians to play a number of pieces, including Miles Davis's 'So What'. They were recorded as a group, and solo, and the music was then cut into loops and re-orchestrated. Other effects were also added, including a line from the play and a sound effect taken from one of Riley's previous works, 'Mescalin Mix'. The results are vaguely unsettling, and barely recognisable as the work of Chet. The use of repetition sounds crude here, but paved the way for Riley's groundbreaking composition 'In C', which helped to pave the way for the 'minimalist' movement. One can also hear occasional echoes of what Miles Davis would later achieve with Teo Macero on 'Bitches Brew', although the credit lies with Riley, rather than Chet Baker.

CHET BAKER: THE MOST IMPORTANT JAZZ ALBUM OF 1964/65

Personnel: Chet Baker (flh, vo), Phil Urso (ts, cl), Hal Galper (p), Jymie Merritt (b), Charlie Rice (dr)..
Date: May, 1964
Place: NYC, New York
Rating: 3.5
An important album for Chet Baker, at any rate, this album marked his return to the US, and his first studio recording in over two years. The album consists primarily of Tadd Dameron tunes, including 'Soultrane'. Was this an attempt to ally Baker with the music of John Coltrane, whose star had risen so dramatically in Chet's absence, or was Baker repaying Dameron for housing him on his return to New York? The explanation is probably more sinister; Baker was now being managed by Richard Carpenter, who 'owned' the right to Dameron's tunes; he is also dubiously credited with co-writing two other tunes on the record, including 'Walkin''. Released shortly after Lee Morgan's soul-jazz classic, 'The Sidewinder', and as Freddie Hubbard was flirting with the avant-garde on 'Breaking Point', the critics were quick to dismiss the record. Chet's switch to flugelhorn leaves him sounding slightly less assured than on his previous studio recording, 'Chet is Back!' but this is a fine album in its own right.

CHET BAKER: BABY BREEZE

Personnel: Chet Baker (flh, vo), Phil Urso (ts,) Frank Strozier (as, f), Hal Galper (p), Bob James (p), Bobby Scott (p), Kenny Burrell (g), Michael Fleming (b), Charlie Rice (dr).
Date: November 1964
Place: NYC, New York
Rating: 4.0
The follow-up, *Baby Breeze*, saw Chet move to Limelight, the new jazz division of Mercury Records. There's a greater emphasis on Chet's singing this time around, presumably at Carpenter's suggestion. He is accompanied by Bobby Scott or Bob James on piano on these songs; Chet apparently complained about Hal Galper's comping, a dispute which contributed to his leaving the band. Chet's singing is far more convincing than on his Pacific Jazz recordings, as 'Born to be Blue' and 'You're Mine, You' clearly illustrate. His playing on the flugelhorn also sounds more confident this time around; the sparkling on solo on Hal Galper's 'This is the Thing' contains echoes of the great Fats Navarro.

CHET BAKER: BAKER'S HOLIDAY

Personnel: Chet Baker (flh, vo), Alan Ross, Henry Freeman, Seldon Powell, Leon Cohen, Wilford Holcombe (reeds), Everett Barksdale (g), Hank Jones (p), Richard Davis (b), Connie Kay (dr).
Date: May 1965
Place: NYC, New York
Rating: 3.0
Whilst Chet reveals his admiration for Lady Day's unique and intimate vocal style in the sleeve notes, this project has all the hallmarks of another Richard Carpenter production; the 'big band' is relatively small in scale, and the arrangements are by one of his regular collaborators, Jimmy Mundy, who had previously worked with both Benny Goodman and Count Basie. Whilst Chet plays and sings with delicacy, one cannot help but feel that this was not a project that was close to his heart. Highlights are 'Travelin' Light' and 'That Ole Devil Called Love'.

CHET BAKER QUINTET: SMOKIN'/GROOVIN'/COMIN' ON

Personnel: Chet Baker (flh), George Coleman (ts,) Kirk Lightsey (p), Herman Wright (b), Roy Brooks (dr).
Date: August 1965
Place: Englewood Cliffs, New Jersey
Rating: 3.5
After the commercial failure of *Baker's Holiday*, manager Richard Carpenter effectively gave up on achieving 'pop' success with Chet Baker. He arranged one final, mammoth recording session for Prestige Records, taping thirty-two songs over just three days, enough to fill five LPs. Carpenter arranged for Chet to play opposite George Coleman, who had just recorded *Maiden Voyage* with Herbie Hancock. On paper, they make an unlikely pairing, but Chet's playing had acquired a lustier tone since his European travels, and they adapt well to each other's styles. The rhythm section all came from Detroit; Wright and Brooks lived in the same apartment building as Chet, the latter recruiting pianist Kirk Lightsey for the session. The resulting albums were named to echo the famous Miles Davis sessions for Prestige in 1956; *Smokin'* and *Groovin'* were eventually released in 1966—by which time Chet had left for California—and *Comin' On* in 1967. More judicious editing would have resulted in two or three excellent records, rather than the five good, but patchy, LPs that were released.

CHET BAKER QUINTET: COOL BURNIN'/BOPPIN'

Personnel: Chet Baker (flh), George Coleman (ts,) Kirk Lightsey (p), Herman Wright (b), Roy Brooks (dr).
Date: August 1965
Place: Englewood Cliffs, New Jersey
Rating: 3.5
More of the same. Highlights of *Cool Burnin'* include Tadd Dameron's 'The 490' and a beautiful version of 'Sleeping Susan', by Jimmy Mundy. Dameron's 'Lament for the Living' is probably the strongest tune on *Boppin'*, and includes elegant solos by Baker, Coleman and Lightsey. There's also a fine reading of 'On a Misty Night'. Sadly these were to be Chet's last worthwhile studio recordings until his 1970s comeback. It's worth noting that the five original releases from this session are available separately, but have also been re-released as three Prestige Session CD's; *Lonely Star*, *Stairway to the Stars* and *On a Misty Night*. The latest CDs are somewhat marred by poor mastering, which lends a slightly muffled tone to the horns, and a metallic edge to the piano.

THE MARIACHI BRASS FEATURING CHET BAKER: A TASTE OF TEQUILA

Personnel: Chet Baker (flh), The Mariachi Brass (personnel unknown), Jack Nitzsche (arr).
Date: Unknown, probably late 1965
Place: Los Angeles, California
Rating: 1.5

Effectively dropped by Richard Carpenter, and evicted from his New York apartment, Chet relocated to Los Angeles, where he teamed up with his old producer, Dick Bock. Bock had sold his faltering World Pacific label to Liberty Records in 1964, but stayed on as a salaried employee to head up the label. The Mariachi Brass was Bock's attempt to emulate the success of Herb Alpert's Tijuana Brass, whose 1965 recording *Whipped Cream and Other Delights*, went on to sell over six million copies. Their debut album, *A Taste of Tequila*, was derided by the jazz press, with *DownBeat* accusing Baker of "sounding as if he's on the point of collapse." It's no jazz album, certainly, but as easy listening records go, it has its moments. The arrangements, by Jack Nitzsche no less, give the recording a less anaemic feel than many of the Tijuana Brass albums, and it's interesting to note that it received quite warm reviews when it was finally released on CD in 2006.

BUD SHANK: MICHELLE

Personnel: Bud Shank (as, fl), Chet Baker (flh), others (personnel unknown), Bob Florence (arr, cond).
Date: December 1965
Place: Los Angeles, California
Rating: 1.0

Bud Shank's December 1965 recording, *Michelle*, consisted primarily of recent pop hits by the likes of the The Beatles, The Byrds and The Mamas and The Papas, arranged for the easy listening market by Bob Florence. Drenched in saccharine strings and given a choral backing, it proved to be a surprise hit, reaching #54 on the U.S. album charts. "Chet showed up late, and wanted to borrow twenty dollars," Shank later recalled. "Past that, everything was all right. He did exactly what he had to do and did it well."

JOE PASS: A SIGN OF THE TIMES

Personnel: Joe Pass (g), Chet Baker (flh), Frank Capp (d), others (personnel unknown), Bob Florence (arr, cond).
Date: December 1965
Place: Los Angeles, California
Rating: 1.0
Bob Florence weaves his magic again, this time for guitarist Joe Pass. Pass and Baker play well enough, but it doesn't make for easy listening for anyone interested in jazz.

BUD SHANK: CALIFORNIA DREAMIN'

Personnel: Bud Shank (as, fl), Chet Baker (flh), others (personnel unknown), Bob Florence (arr, cond).
Date: March 1966
Place: Los Angeles, California
Rating: 1.0
After the success of Michelle, Bud Shank and Bob Florence deliver more of the same; a selection of recent hits by The Mamas and The Papas (the title track, and 'Monday, Monday'), The Beatles ('Norwegian Wood') and by songwriters Bacharach and David ('What the World Needs Now', 'In Times Like These'). Bud Shank later defended his move away from jazz by arguing "that by this time jazz records were not selling. Jazz musicians weren't working in jazz clubs. It was a matter of survival."

THE MARIACHI BRASS FEATURING CHET BAKER: HATS OFF

Personnel: Chet Baker (flh), Herb Ellis (g), Frank Capp (d), The Mariachi Brass (personnel unknown), George Tipton / Jack Nitzsche (arr).
Date: Spring 1966
Place: Los Angeles, California
Rating: 1.0
After the modest success of the first Mariachi Brass LP, the Pacific Jazz A&R team assembled another strong line-up of session musicians, including Herb Ellis and Victor Feldman to record a follow-up, *Hats Off.* The format is less successful second time around; this partly reflects the formulaic nature of the sound, but also the fact that George Tipton, rather than Jack Nitzsche, handled the bulk of the arrangements. Don Nelson in *DownBeat* gave the LP a no-star rating, calling it 'a loser' and 'a wipeout'. *Hats Off* was only released on CD in 2006, paired with the first Mariachi Brass recording, *A Taste of Tequila*. The CD includes one previously unreleased tune—the 'Colonel Bogey March'—which was hardly suitable material for the mariachi sound.

CHET BAKER AND THE CARMEL STRINGS: QUIETLY THERE/INTO MY LIFE

Personnel: Chet Baker (flh), Various.
Date: June, October 1966
Place: Los Angeles, California
Rating: 0.5
On the sleeve notes to *Quietly There*, the first of Chet Baker's recordings with the Carmel Strings, *DownBeat* magazine's John Tynan suggests that Chet's romantic style is well suited to recording with strings, suggesting echoes of his 1953/1954 recording with Pacific Jazz. His colleague, Pete Welding, was rather closer to the mark. "Rarely … has Baker sounded as flaccid as he does against the keening strings and choral ooh-ings and aah-ings of these performances. He's a shade out of tune, too, for added drama." *Into My Life* is the weaker of the two recordings, with Chet's chops in bad shape after his July 1966 beating.

CHET BAKER: 'ROUND MIDNIGHT / LIVE AT GAETANO'S

Personnel: Chet Baker (flh, vo), Phil Urso (ts) Dave McKay (p) Chuck Domanico (b) Harry Kevis Jr. (d).
Date: Summer 1966
Place: Pueblo, Colorado
Rating: 2.5
This bootleg-quality recording captures Chet playing at Gaetano's Club in Pueblo, Colorado; the precise date of the recording is unknown. When the recordings were first released it was suggested that they were taped in December 1966, but as Carol Baker pointed out, Chet's chops were in poor shape at that time, suggesting it must have been earlier. Saxophonist Pete Christlieb, who was later replaced by Phil Urso, remembers the concert as being in 1965—most likely it was in the spring or early summer of 1966. The recording is interesting insofar as it proves that Chet was not completely lost to jazz at this time; the chemistry between Chet and Phil Urso remains as strong as ever, Chet is in good voice ('Forgetful'), and the tape captures the onstage banter between the band members, who sound as though they're having fun. Unfortunately the sound quality is poor, taken from a private recording made by drummer Harry Kevis Jr, so the saxophone and piano are barely audible. The music has been released under a variety of names and formats.

BUD SHANK: BRAZIL! BRAZIL! BRAZIL!

Personnel: Bud Shank (as), Chet Baker (flh), Laurindo Almeida (g), Joe Pass (g), João Donato (p), Clare Fischer (p), Others (unknown).
Date: Various, September 1966
Place: LA, California
Rating: 1.0
Brazil! Brazil! Brazil! was not a new Bud Shank recording, but effectively a reissue of several older sessions with Laurindo Almeida, Clare Fischer and João Donato, overdubbed with strings. The string arrangements were by Julian Lee, a blind Australian pianist, and were added by producer Dick Bock to cash in on the success of 'Michelle'. Baker only appears on one track, 'Summer Samba'. "It's my guess—I wasn't present at the string overdub—that Chet once again came by the World Pacific Studio to hit Dick Bock for more money," Shank later recalled. "Dick probably said, 'Here's $20, go play something on this track that they are overdubbing!' I can think of no other reason why this came about. His name is so prominently displayed on the album cover, however!" Fans of Bud Shank's Latin recordings are better off seeking the originals; otherwise this is for collectors only.

THE MARIACHI BRASS FEATURING CHET BAKER: DOUBLE SHOT / IN THE MOOD

Personnel: Chet Baker (flh), The Mariachi Brass (personnel unknown), George Tipton (arr).
Date: June, late 1966
Place: Los Angeles, California
Rating: 0.5

On the first of these recordings, Chet plays 'Dancing in the Street', 'Ring of Fire' and 'Danke Schoen'—hardly promising material for the 'mariachi' sound, and firm evidence that the concept was starting to wear very thin. 'In The Mood' was even worse, his chops yet to recover from the beating in San Francisco. "He was so out of shape, playing-wise, it was ridiculous," Bob Zieff later recalled. "He just couldn't get through anything." A few months later, Chet had dentures fitted, and had to rebuild his embouchure; he would not make another recording for one year.

BUD SHANK: MAGICAL MYSTERY

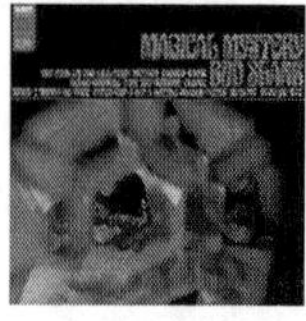

Personnel: Bud Shank (as, fl), Chet Baker (flh),Gary Barone (flh), Dennis Budimir (g), Herb Ellis (g), Robert West (b), John Guerin (b), Victor Feldman (perc).
Date: November 1967
Place: Los Angeles, California
Rating: 1.5

By late 1966, Chet's playing was in such poor shape he asked Dick Bock to pay for him to have dentures fitted. He struggled to play for several months, and eventually emerged one year later, appearing on a handful of songs on Bud Shank's *Magical Mystery* album. Chet's playing still sounds extremely tentative at times—the first few bars of his playing on 'Hello Goodbye' find him struggling to hold a note—and it is probably for this reason that a second recording session was arranged with a new band, this time featuring Gary Barone on flugelhorn. The arrangements, still by Bob Florence, are slightly more interesting than on Bud Shank's previous 'pop' albums, suggesting a move away from the 'easy listening' market to a more current, 'psychedelic' sound.

CHET BAKER: ALBERT'S HOUSE

Personnel: Chet Baker (tp), Barney Kessel (g), Paul Smith (p, org), Jim Hughart (b), Frank Capp (d).
Date: Mid-1968
Place: Los Angeles, California
Rating: 0.5
Albert's House is widely regarded as Chet's worst record, a dubious honour it probably shares with the Carmel Strings albums recorded two years earlier. TV Show host Steve Allen continued to promote Chet's records and inviting him to perform on his show, even when most club owners were reluctant to take the risk. When Chet asked to borrow $500, Allen offered to pay him in return for recording an album of his own compositions. He later recalled that Chet turned up to the recording session stoned, unfamiliar with the tunes, despite having been sent the music some weeks earlier. Chet sleepwalks his way through the session, his playing more confident than on *Magical Mystery*, but still weak. Whilst it's hard to excuse Chet's behaviour, it can't have been easy to summon much enthusiasm for Allen's bland, soulless compositions; the cheap-sounding organ on several tracks, and the poor quality overdubbing does not help matters. Despite this, the record has been re-released on several occasions. Buyer beware.

CHET BAKER: BLOOD, CHET AND TEARS

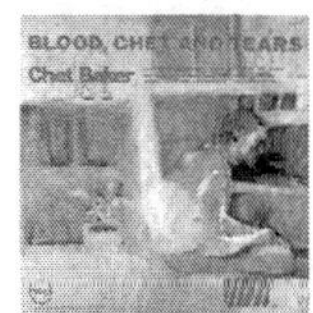

Personnel: Chet Baker (tr, vo), Tony Terran (tr), Ray Triscari (tr), Ollie Mitchell (tr), Plas Johnson (ts), Buddy Collette (reeds), Dick 'Slide' Hyde (tb), Miles Anderson (tb), George Roberts (tb), Joe Pass (g), Mike Deasy (g), Tommy Tedesco (g), Al Casey (g), Larry Knechtel (keyboards), Ray Pohlman (b), Hal Blaine (dr), Gary Coleman (perc), Sid Sharp (strings), Others (personnel unknown).
Date: July 1970
Place: Los Angeles, California
Rating: 1.0
This is Chet's MOR pop album; ten songs arranged in the style of a poor man's Blood, Sweat and Tears. Whilst it is true that Miles Davis released the groundbreaking fusion album *Bitches Brew* in 1970, it is worth remembering that most jazz musicians were struggling to make a living from jazz at this time; just one year earlier, Dizzy Gillespie had released a 'crossover' album entitled *It's My Way*, which featured the great bebop trumpeter playing covers of Jimmy Webb's 'Galveston' and a medley of songs from the musical *Hair*.

CHET BAKER AND LEE KONITZ: IN CONCERT

Personnel: Chet Baker (tr, vo), Lee Konitz (as), Michael Moore (b), Beaver Harris (dr).
Date: April 1974
Place: New York
Rating: 3.0

This record is something of an oddity amongst Chet's 1970s' recordings; it was taped before his 'comeback' recordings with CTI, but only released later on India Navigation. Lee Konitz had sat in one night with Chet at the Half Note, where he played for a couple of weekends with Warren Chiasson, and later suggested that he and Chet form a band. They played together on a couple of occasions, once with Keith Jarrett on piano (available on a rare LP), and once for this concert at Ornette Coleman's loft in New York. Konitz later claimed that Chet was feeling unwell that day, and that this recording does not capture him at his best, but he manages to pull off elegant solos on 'Body and Soul' and 'Willow Weep for Me'. The sound quality is patchy, with Chet wandering away from the microphone on occasion.

CHET BAKER: SHE WAS TOO GOOD TO ME

Personnel: Chet Baker (tr, vo), Paul Desmond (as), George Marge (afl, ob), Hubert Laws (fl, afl) Romeo Penque (cl, fl), Lewis Eley, Max Ellen, Barry Finclair, Paul Gershman, Harry Glickman, Emanuel Green, Harold Kohon, David Nadien, Herbert Sorkin (violin), Warren Lash, Jesse Levy, George Ricci (cello), David Friedman (vib) Bob James (el-p), Ron Carter (b) Steve Gadd (d), Jack DeJohnette (d), Don Sebesky (arr).
Date: July, October, November 1974
Place: Englewood Cliffs, New Jersey
Rating: 3.5

Creed Taylor was worried about the state of Chet's chops on his major label comeback, and surrounded him with the cream of the label's impressive roster of musicians, and to cushion his fragile tone with strings on two songs. With the exception of 'Funk in a Deep Freeze', producer Don Sebesky chose the material, opting for standards, rather than push Chet towards a more fusion-oriented sound. As a result, the album sounds like an exercise in nostalgia. From the opening track, 'Autumn Leaves', Chet sounds in good shape, his soft tone and melodicism intact, Paul Desmond's alto saxophone the perfect complement. The title track reveals Chet to be in fine voice, too, his singing a fraction deeper now. Hubert Laws replaces Desmond for a delightful version of 'Funk in a Deep Freeze'. The highlight of the album, however, is an exquisite reading of Johnny Mercer's 'Tangerine', Baker and Desmond playing off one another effortlessly.

GERRY MULLIGAN AND CHET BAKER: CARNEGIE HALL CONCERT

Personnel: Gerry Mulligan (bs), Chet Baker (tr, vo), Ed Byrne (tb), Bob James (p, el-p), Dave Samuels (vib, perc), John Scofield (g), Ron Carter (b), Harvey Mason (dr).
Date: November 1974
Place: NYC, New York
Rating: 3.5
Mulligan was always more business-minded than Chet, and effectively hijacked the second reunion, refusing to reunite the pianoless quartet, and dominating both the track-listing and the royalties. Chet still managed to draw the biggest applause of his night for his solo on 'My Funny Valentine', but the highlight is 'Line For Lyons', which showed they were still capable of creating fireworks onstage as well as off.

JIM HALL: CONCIERTO

Personnel: Jim Hall (g), Chet Baker (tr), Paul Desmond (as), Roland Hanna (p), Ron Carter (b), Steve Gadd (dr), Don Sebesky (arr).
Date: April 1975
Place: Englewood Cliffs, New Jersey
Rating: 4.0
Jim Hall's 'Concierto' is one of his finest recordings, and as a consequence, this is one of Chet's finest records of the 1970s. After their successful pairing on *She Was Too Good To Me*, Creed Taylor suggested Chet Baker and Paul Desmond for the session; Jim Hall was reluctant at first, having never previously played with Chet, but saw things fall into place quickly. The album opens with a swinging version of 'You'd Be So Nice To Come Home To', before Desmond drops out for two tracks, leaving Baker to shine. Sebesky's arrangement of 'Concierto de Aranjuez' is the album's highlight; he never tries to replicate Gil Evans' quasi-classical version, and resists the urge to add strings, keeping things simple. The musicians state the main theme simply, before breaking into a gentle, effortless swing. A triumph.

VARIOUS ARTISTS, FEAT. CHET BAKER: IT HAPPENED IN PESCARA...1969-1989

Personnel: Chet Baker (tr, vo), Kenny Drew (p), Larry Ridley (b), David Lee (dr).
Date: July 1975
Place: Pescara, Italy
Rating: 2.0
There are various bootleg-quality recordings available of Chet's European festival appearances in 1975; at the time of writing, this Philology compilation is the most readily available. Chet's playing is quite strong, especially on Bud Powell's 'Tempus Fugit', and the set was warmly received by the Italian audience. Unfortunately, the sound quality is appalling; the recording was made by somebody in the crowd, and the drums are barely audible. Avid collectors might also want to track down *The Fabulous Pescara Jam Sessions* on the same label, or *Live in Paris 1960-63*, *Live in Nice 1975*, but these are recordings that should have been left in the vault.

CHET BAKER QUARTET: I CAN'T GET STARTED—LIVE IN PALERMO 1976

Personnel: Chet Baker (tp, vo), Enzo Randisi (p), Giovanni Tommaso (b), Gianni Cavallaro (dr)
Date: January 1976
Place: Brass Club, Palermo, Italy
Rating: 2.5
This bootleg-style recording was only issued in 2011, and captures Chet on a short tour of Italy in 1976. The band had been assembled at short-notice by bass player Giovanni Tommaso, and included Enzo Randisi – primarily known as a vibraphone player – on piano. The sound quality is adequate, but somewhat muffled in places. The recording is primarily of interest to hear tunes like Charlie Parker's 'Buzzy' and 'I Can't Get Started', which rarely featured in Chet's vast repertoire. Tommaso remembers the atmosphere on stage as being tense, and when Chet asked him to play additional dates over the spring, he politely declined. For collectors only.

CHET BAKER: YOU CAN'T GO HOME AGAIN / THE BEST THING FOR YOU

Personnel: Chet Baker (tp, vo), Michael Brecker (ts), Paul Desmond (as), Hubert Laws (fl, bfl, piccolo), John Campo (basn), Kenny Barron (el-p), Richie Beirach (el-p, clav), John Scofield (g), Ron Carter (b), Alphonso Johnson (el-b), Tony Williams (d), Ralph MacDonald (per), David Nadien, Rochelle Abramson, Max Ellen, Paul Gersham, Diana Halprin, Harold Kohon, Charles Libove, Marvin Morgenstern, Matthew Raimondi (violin), Jesse Levy, Charles McCracken, Alan Shulman (cello), Don Sebesky (el-p, arr).
Date: February, May 1977
Place: NYC, New York
Rating: 3.0/3.5
A&M's Jerry Moss was worried that Chet Baker would be too 'jazzy' for the fusion-dominated market, so Don Sebesky was drafted in to make a more commercial album. If Sebesky showed uncharacteristic restraint on *Concierto*, he went the other way for *You Can't Go Home Again*, drenching the album with overdubbed strings and percussion after the initial recording session. The title track, again with Paul Desmond, is the highlight of the album; for the most part, the prominent electric piano makes the record sound fusion-lite, and lends it a very dated feel. The sessions produced enough material for two albums; *The Best Thing For You* consisted of outtakes from the original album, but without strings it has more of a swinging feel to it. These dates marked one of Paul Desmond's final recording sessions before his death from lung cancer.

CHET BAKER: ONCE UPON A SUMMERTIME

Personnel: Chet Baker (tp, vo), Gregory Herbert (ts), Harold Danko (p), Ron Carter (b), Mel Lewis (d).
Date: February 1977
Place: NYC, New York
Rating: 3.5
Aware that Chet was not entirely comfortable with the fusion-tinged sound that Sebesky had arranged, John Snyder took advantage of the downtime in the studio to squeeze in a straight-ahead jazz session. He retained Ron Carter on bass, and brought in Mel Lewis and Harold Danko. Highlights of the session are a version of Miles Davis/Wayne Shorter's 'ESP', with Chet playing mute, and the lengthy title track, which Chet played regularly in later years.

CHET BAKER: THE INCREDIBLE CHET BAKER PLAYS AND SINGS

Personnel: Chet Baker (tp, vo), Ruth Young (vo), Gianni Basso (ts), Jacques Pelzer (fl, ss), Bruce Thomas (p), Lucio Terzano (b), Giancarlo Pillot (d).
Date: March 1977
Place: Milan, Italy
Rating: 2.5
An interesting but uneven recording. The record marks Ruth Young's only appearance on record with Chet, and they sing duet on two songs, 'Autumn Leaves' and 'Whatever Possessed Me'; Ruth sings in Chet's key, however, leaving her uncomfortable, and it shows. Chet was suffering from kidney stones during the recording, which helps to explain the frail, airy tone to his playing, something that became more prominent in his later years. Whilst it is interesting to hear Chet reunited with the fine tenor saxophonist Gianni Basso, the rhythm section is less convincing; Bruce Thomas was a relatively inexperienced pianist, and drummer Giancarlo Pillot's touch is a little heavy for Chet's liking.

ASTRUD GILBERTO: THAT GIRL FROM IPANEMA

Personnel: Astrud Gilberto (vo), Chet Baker (tp, vo) James Buffington, John Trevor Clark, Earl Daniels (frh), Jay Beckenstein, Eddie Daniels, George Marge, David Tofani (reeds), Frank Owens (p) Jay Berliner, Gene Bertoncini (g), Ron Carter (b), Ronnie Zito (d), Rubens Bassini (per), Joey Dee, Mary Eiland, Maureen McElheron (back vo), Don Sebesky, Others (arr).
Date: Late 1977
Place: NYC, New York
Rating: 1.5
The precise recording date for this session is unknown, but it probably took place in late 1977, after Chet returned to New York. Astrud Gilberto had been a fan of Chet Baker since the mid-1960s, and had wanted to record with him for some time. Don Sebesky was one of four arrangers used for this album, and persuaded Chet to play on one of the songs she had composed, 'Far Away'. This is the only memorable moment on an otherwise grim record; the low point is undoubtedly the opening song, a disco version of 'The Girl from Ipanema'.

CHET BAKER: SINGS, PLAYS—LIVE AT THE KEYSTONE KORNER

Personnel: Chet Baker (fl, vo), Roger Rosenberg (bs, ss), Phil Markowitz (p), Jon Burr (b), Jeff Brillinger (d), Unknown (ts, two tracks).
Date: February 1978
Place: San Francisco, California
Rating: 2.5
1978 was a good year for Chet in many respects; *You Can't Go Home Again*, recorded with rising stars like Michael Brecker and John Scofield, had helped to put Chet back on the map with U.S. jazz fans. His chops were in good shape, and he was relatively clean. Just as important, he was able to put a band together with a relatively consistent line-up, which happened too infrequently in subsequent years. The recordings from the North American dates were made illegally, and do not capture the band at its best. Baker's playing is patchy on this set, recorded in San Francisco. He fluffs his entrance on 'Secret Love', and seems to disappear part of the way through 'Blues 'n' Boogie', presumably to fix his teeth. The notes to the *Keystone Korner* recording suggest that Chet had broken his dentures prior to the concert, but this is incorrect; that incident occurred at Sweet Basil in New York.

CHET BAKER: LOVE FOR SALE / THE RISING SUN COLLECTION

Personnel: Chet Baker (fl, vo), Roger Rosenberg (bs, ss), Phil Markowitz (p), Jon Burr (b), Jeff Brillinger (d).
Date: March 1978
Place: Montreal, Canada
Rating: 3.0
Three weeks later, the band was starting to gel more effectively; listen to Roger Rosenberg gently playing underneath Chet's vocal on 'Oh, You Crazy Moon', or playing off one another on 'Love For Sale'. Chet's chops are still not in the best of shape, and he opts for a lengthy but fine scat solo on ''There Will Never Be Another You'. Rosenberg is perhaps guilty of over-playing on some solos, something he now readily admits. "I listen to it now and think, 'Why didn't I take advantage of the fact that I was playing with one of the most lyrical trumpet players in the world?' Of course, I was twenty-five or twenty-six, and that's what saxophone players were doing back then." The sound quality is better than the *Keystone Korner* recording, although the balance is occasionally poor. It does offers a rare opportunity to hear Chet play 'Snowbound', best known as the title track of Sarah Vaughn's 1962 album for Roulette (check this).

CHET BAKER: LIVE IN CHATEAUVALLON, 1978 / LIVE IN FRANCE, 1978

Personnel: Chet Baker (tp, vo), Phil Markowitz (p), Scott Lee (b), Jeff Brillinger (d)..
Date: November 1978
Place: Chateauvallon, France
Rating: 2.5

In late 1978 Chet embarked on a European tour with a number of the U.S. musicians he had toured with earlier in the year. Saxophonist Roger Rosenberg opted to stay behind, given Chet's occasional erratic behaviour, whilst bass player Jon Burr chose to tour with Stan Getz, who was a bigger name in North America, and was replaced by Scott Lee. The tour was well documented; the first recording was made in the Centre Culturel in Chateauvallon in France. Chet's chops are not in the best of shape; he scats for much of opener 'Oh, You Crazy Moon', and his solos are unusually hesitant. It's interesting to note the band's influence on his repertoire, however; 'Love for Sale' is given an upbeat, funky reading, driven by Brillinger and Markowitz, whilst Wayne Shorter's wonderful 'Beautiful Black Eyes' becomes a regular part of the set list. The band is better documented on albums like *Live at Nick's* and *Broken Wing*, however, when Chet was on better form.

CHET BAKER: LIVE AT NICK'S

Personnel: Chet Baker (tp, vo), Phil Markowitz (p), Scott Lee (b), Jeff Brillinger (d).
Date: November 1978
Place: Laren, Holland
Rating: 4.0

Recorded at Nick Vollebregt's Jazz Café in Laren, Chet is in much better shape here, and this ranks as one of his finest recordings of the decade. It marks the first appearance on record of 'Broken Wing', written for Chet by pianist Richie Beirach, a tune that would become a staple part of his repertoire in his final years. There's also a fine reading of 'Beautiful Black Eyes', running to over 17 minutes, with Markowitz offering strong support. The music is well recorded, the tapes later purchased and produced by the excellent Gerry Teekens of Criss Cross records. The CD contains two extra tracks, 'I Remember You' and 'Love for Sale', and is highly recommended.

CHET BAKER: OH YOU CRAZY MOON

Personnel: Chet Baker (tp, vo), Phil Markowitz (p), Scott Lee (b), Jeff Brillinger (d).
Date: December 1978
Place: Ludwigsburg, Germany
Rating: 3.5
More of the same. This concert was recorded for German radio, and later released on Enja as part of the Legacy series, following Chet's death. The song selection is very similar to the live recording from Chateauvallon, although Chet's playing is far stronger. The highlight is an excellent version of 'Beautiful Black Eyes', but overall this performance is not on a par with those that bookmark it—the superior *Live at Nick's* and the fine studio recording *Broken Wing*. After this recording, bass player Scott Lee returned to the U.S. due to other commitments, and was replaced for the live dates by Jean-Louis Rassinfosse.

CHET BAKER: BROKEN WING

Personnel: Chet Baker (tp, vo), Phil Markowitz (p), Jean-François Jenny-Clark (b), Jeff Brillinger (d).
Date: December 1978
Place: Paris, France
Rating: 4.0
The quartet was playing in Paris when French record producer Gilles Gautherin suggested an afternoon recording session, replacing Jean-Louis Rassinfosse with the more experienced French bass player Jean-François Jenny-Clark. The result was Chet's best studio album of the decade, and a suitable monument to a memorable tour. The repertoire is similar to the preceding live shows, opening with a delicate version of 'Broken Wing', with Chet on muted trumpet. 'Black Eyes' follows, and although the studio recording is somewhat inferior to the live version on *Live at Nick's*, where Chet has more time to stretch out, there is compensation in the form of a wonderful solo from Jenny-Clark, which leaves you wondering why he did not work with Chet more frequently. 'Oh You Crazy Moon' is let down by an imperfect vocal from Chet, but there's a gentle swing to 'How Deep is the Ocean', which is far superior to the studio recording on *The Best Thing for You*. The album closes with a rare composition from Baker, 'Blue Gilles', a tribute to the French producer; it's little more than a slow studio jam, but it's enjoyable enough. The CD comes with alternate takes of both 'Black Eyes' and 'How Deep is the Ocean'. Unfortunately no one recorded the concert that evening at Chappelle des Lombards. "Chet was totally burning that night," Markowitz later recalled.

CHET BAKER: TWO A DAY

Personnel: Chet Baker (tp, vo), Phil Markowitz (p), Jean-Louis Rassinfosse (b), Jeff Brillinger (d).
Date: December 1978
Place: Paris, France
Rating: 3.0

Unbeknown to Gilles Gautherin, the band had agreed to record a second studio album that day, after the show at Chappelle des Lombards in Paris; hence the title of the album, which has nothing to do with Chet's drug intake, as is commonly believed. "*Two A Day* sounds a little tired," Markowitz admits, "which we were, starting the recording at two in the morning." The album kicks off with a rare Chet Baker original composition, named after the record itself, and there's a sprightly version of 'If I Should Lose You'. The tempo begins to sag on 'Blue Room', however, and by the time we get to Chet's vocal on 'This Is Always' it sounds as though he's finally ready to call it a day.

CHET BAKER AND WOLFGANG LACKERSCHMID: BALLADS FOR TWO

Personnel: Chet Baker (tp), Wolfgang Lackerschmid (vib).
Date: January 1979
Place: Stuttgart, Germany
Rating: 3.5

Chet continued his run of fine recordings with *Ballads for Two*, an album made with the young German vibraphonist Wolfgang Lackerschmid. Chet's tone sounds more aerated here, not dissimilar to the effect heard on *The Incredible Chet Baker Plays and Sings*, recorded two years earlier. He may simply have been tired after his long European tour; it may have been the effect of his 'long weekend' in the aftermath of that tour. Either way, it was a sound that Chet enjoyed and felt comfortable with, and increasingly returned to in his later years. This is probably an underrated item in Chet's long discography, predating the 'drummerless' recordings made for SteepleChase, and later with Philip Catherine and Jean-Louis Rassinfosse; records that form a vitally important part of Chet's legacy. *Ballads for Two* was an early digital recording, and whilst the sound is occasionally a little harsh, for the most part it captures the soft tone of the horn and the ringing quality of the vibes to good effect. Highlights include Lackerschmid's composition 'Why Shouldn't You Cry', and a delicate reading of 'Softly As In A Morning Sunrise'.

CHET BAKER WITH ORCHESTRA: SOUNDTRACK FOR FLIC OU VOYOU

Personnel: Chet Baker (tp), Hubert Laws (fl), Hubert Rostaing (cl) Rene Benedetti, Herve Berrien, Jean-Charles Capon, Hubert Varron (vln) Will Lockwood, Francois Rabbath (vlc), Maurice Vander (harp), Larry Coryell (g), Ron Carter (b), Billy Cobham (d).
Date: March 1979
Place: Paris, France
Rating: 3.5
Flic ou Voyou ('Cop or Hood'), was a French crime movie from 1979, starring the popular actor Jean-Paul Belmondo. The movie was a box office success, drawing four million viewers, which made it the second most successful release of the year. The soundtrack is not a Chet Baker album, but consists of a series of miniatures written for the movie by Philippe Sarde. Chet was invited to play on the record, and was joined by a number of the other CTI regulars, including Ron Carter. Chet's playing is not particularly prominent, but really shines on 'Tender Variations', one of the main themes.

CHET BAKER: THE TOUCH OF YOUR LIPS

Personnel: Chet Baker (tp, vo), Doug Raney (g), Niels-Henning Ørsted Pedersen (b).
Date: June 1979
Place: Copenhagen, Denmark
Rating: 4.0
Chet's first record with the Danish SteepleChase label was a studio recording with Doug Raney and NHØP. It was landmark recording for Chet in a number of respects. Firstly, it was one of the first 'drummerless' recordings he made, a format that he enjoyed; it allowed him to develop long, uncluttered lines, a style that was particularly effective on the ballads that he tended to favour. It required a bass player who was a good timekeeper, like NHØP, and it is unfortunate that they did not record together more frequently. Second, the album was released on a bigger label, which enjoyed wider distribution; in the sleeve notes, Ira Gitler mentions that Chet's records had not been widely distributed in the U.S. since his CTI days. The SteepleChase records helped to raise Chet's profile once more, at least temporarily. Highlights include a slow, drawn-out vocal from Chet on 'The Touch of Your Lips', a song requested by Nils Winther, and some lovely interplay between Chet and Doug Raney on 'Blue Room'. It's not a flawless record; Chet's chops were not in the best of shape for the sessions, but there is considerable chemistry between the musicians, lending the record a special feel.

CHET BAKER: RENDEZ-VOUS/ALL BLUES / 'ROUND MIDNIGHT

Personnel: Chet Baker (tp), Henry Florens (p), Jean-Paul Florens (g), Jim Richardson (b), Tony Mann (d) Rachel Gould (vo).
Date: September 1979
Place: London, England
Rating: 3.0
A patchy studio session, recorded in London, with enough good material to fill one LP, but spread a little thin over two. Chet's playing is excellent, demonstrated to good effect on a lovely reinterpretation of 'My Funny Valentine'. There is some strong interplay between Chet and guitarist Jean-Paul Florens on ''Round Midnight' and the guitarist's own composition, 'Phil's Bossa'. Singer Rachel Gould pops up on three tracks, including 'All Blues', but Tony Mann's drumming sounds a little too heavy-handed for Chet on certain tracks, such as 'Secret Love'. The sessions were originally released on two LPs on Bingow Records, but are now available as a single CD, *'Round Midnight*. Be warned that there are several releases with this title under Chet's name; the correct cover for this release is shown above.

CHET BAKER QUARTET: NO PROBLEM

Personnel: Chet Baker (tp, vo), Duke Jordan (p), Niels-Henning Ørsted Pedersen (b), Norman Fearrington (d).
Date: October 1979
Place: Copenhagen, Denmark
Rating: 4.5
Another outstanding studio session on SteepleChase that occasionally recalls some of the excellent recordings Chet made with Russ Freeman in the 1950s. Nils Winther had already booked Chet to record him live in a trio format the following day, and asked him if would be interested in recording an album of Duke Jordan's own compositions. It was an inspired move; Duke Jordan's lyrical but melancholic style was well suited to Chet's own playing. Chet's chops were in better shape than on the previous studio session with SteepleChase, and it's interesting to hear him play with a muted trumpet on some tracks. 'Sultry Eve' is taken at a slow pace, suggesting a hushed intimacy, whilst there's a playful bounce to the waltz-time 'Glad I Met Pat' that brings to mind the style of Bill Evans. Another highlight is the dark, brooding 'Kiss of Spain', which opens with the drums and the bowed bass of NHØP, before Chet enters on muted trumpet, echoing the sound of earlier Miles Davis. Highly recommended.

CHET BAKER TRIO: DAYBREAK / THIS IS ALWAYS / SOMEDAY MY PRINCE WILL COME

Personnel: Chet Baker (tp, vo), Doug Raney (g), Niels-Henning Ørsted Pedersen (b).
Date: October 1979
Place: Copenhagen, Denmark
Rating: 4.0
After the success of their studio recording *The Touch of Your Lips*, Nils Winther reunited the trio for a live recording at Copenhagen's Jazzhus Montmartre. Chet's playing was superb, for the most part, his chops in good shape after playing regularly for several weeks. Most of that period had been spent touring with Doug Raney and Jean-Louis Rassinfosse, so there was probably a better understanding with the guitarist second time around. Over the course of one evening, there was enough material for three LPs, with one or two additional songs surfacing when the music came out on CD. Highlights include 'Broken Wing' and Miles Davis's 'One' (*Daybreak*), whilst *This is Always* includes a lengthy version of 'How Deep Is The Ocean', where Chet seems to produce an endless stream of ideas, and a breezy version of Wayne Shorter's 'House of Jade'. Bob Zieff's 'Sad Walk' is one of the high points of the third LP, as is the title track, 'Someday My Prince Will Come', which features some incredible phrases from Chet.

CHET BAKER / WOLFGANG LACKERSCHMID

Personnel: Chet Baker (tp, vo), Wolfgang Lackerschmid (vib), Larry Coryell (g), Buster Williams (b), Tony Williams (d).
Date: November 1979
Place: Stuttgart, Germany
Rating: 3.0
Guitarist Larry Coryell had proposed a trip recording with Baker and Lackerschmid, but Gaby Kleinschmidt insisted on recruiting a rhythm section; unfortunately they add little to the proceedings. The arrangements sound cluttered and under-rehearsed, for the most part, and one can't help but feel that a more stripped-back sound would have produced a better record. Better to stick with the original duo recording, or look for *Why Shouldn't You Cry*, part of the Enja Legacy series, which includes highlights from Chet's three sessions with Lackerschmid, plus a song recorded as a tribute to Chet, 'Chet's Ballad'.

CHET BAKER AND ENRICO PIERANUNZI: SOFT JOURNEY

Personnel: Chet Baker (tp, vo), Enrico Pieranunzi (p), Maurizio Giammarco (ts), Riccardo Del Fra (b), Roberto Gatto (d).
Date: December 1979, January 1980
Place: Rome, Italy
Rating: 3.5
Chet first met the Italian pianist Enrico Pieranunzi in late 1979, and through him met bass player Riccardo Del Fra, who went on to accompany Chet for a number of years. The album, *Soft Journey*, primarily consists of original compositions by the pianist. The title track and 'Fairy Flowers' are both lovely tunes, although Chet was particularly taken with 'Night Bird', which became a regular part of his repertoire in the years that followed. Saxophonist Maurizio Giammarco contributed one song, entitled 'Animali Diurni' ('Daytime Animals'); although it has a pretty melody, the lyrics sound somewhat superfluous. Chet also performs a duet with Pieranunzi, which is particularly notable for Chet's beautiful muted trumpet solo—a device he rarely employed. Chet thought that Pieranunzi was occasionally guilty of overplaying in early years; the only real evidence on this album is on 'My Funny Valentine', where his fills are somewhat floral, but for the most part this a relaxed, enjoyable session.

CHET BAKER AND STEVE HOUBEN

Personnel: Chet Baker (tp, vo), Steve Houben (as), Bill Frisell (g), Dennis Luxion (p, elp), Kermit Driscoll (b), Bruno Castellucci (d).
Date: February 1980
Place: Brussels, Belgium
Rating: 3.0
A pleasant session with Belgian alto saxophonist, Steve Houben, who was the nephew of Chet's old friend Jacques Pelzer. Houben had attended the Berklee College of Music in Boston, and on his return to Belgium formed a band with some of his college friends, which included a young Bill Frisell and Kermit Driscoll. That band was on the verge of splitting, with Frisell about to return to the U.S., when Houben was offered the chance to make a record with Chet. There's a good version of 'Beatrice' by Sam Rivers, and a lovely vocal by Chet on 'Deep in a Dream', where the saxophonist plays gently beneath Chet's singing. The session was eventually released on CD as *Almost Blue* (West Wind 2126), which pairs this session with some of the live recordings made in Tokyo in 1987; the CD claims the Houben session was recorded live in Paris in October 1984, which is incorrect.

CHET BAKER: BURNIN' AT BACKSTREET

Personnel: Chet Baker (tp), Drew Salperto (p), Mike Formanek (b), Artt Frank (d).
Date: February 1980
Place: New Haven, Connecticut
Rating: 3.5
Recorded at a low-key gig at the Backstreet Club in New Haven, Connecticut, this CD captures Chet in explosive form, both on and off the trumpet. The gig turns into an inadvertent tribute to Miles Davis, kicking off with 'Tune Up' and 'Milestones', and playing 'Stella by Starlight' as an audience request later in the show. Supported by a good band, including old friend Artt Frank and the excellent bass player Mike Formanek, Chet's playing is fiery and aggressive, right from the open, playing with an intensity rarely captured on his 1980s' recordings. Unfortunately, the CD also illustrates some of Chet's less admirable characteristics; lacking a regular band for much of the time, and reluctant to rehearse, he relied on pick-up musicians who were not always so familiar with his repertoire. This results in an explosive argument with the pianist during 'Milestones', and a tense atmosphere for the remainder of the show. The poor sound quality means that this record may not be the best place to start, but it is warmly recommended nonetheless.

CHET BAKER QUARTET: IN YOUR OWN SWEET WAY / JUST FRIENDS

Personnel: Chet Baker (tp, vo), Nicola Stilo (fl), Dennis Luxion (p), Riccardo Del Fra (b).
Date: March 1980
Place: Cologne, Germany
Rating: 2.0
Riccardo Del Fra remembers many good nights at this time, with Chet in relatively good shape, relishing the drummerless format and delivering lengthy, bop-style solos. This concert, recorded at the Subway Club in Cologne, was not one of Chet's better nights. The first record opens with a twenty-six-minute version of Russ Freeman's 'No Ties', with Baker's opening solo lasting for fourteen minutes; Chet seems to lose his thread part of the way through the solo, and can be heard cursing. The second LP, *Just Friends*, contains just two tracks—the title track and 'Doodlin'', both running at over twenty minutes. Releases like this helped to spoil the reputation of Chet's later recordings, with *DownBeat* describing them as "shambling efforts in which Baker, alternately, beguiles one with snatches of excellence, then stultifies with long stretches of aimlessness." Released on Colgne's Circle Records, they are hard to find. Let's hope it stays that way.

CHET BAKER: LEAVING

Personnel: Chet Baker (tp, vo), Nicola Stilo (fl), Dennis Luxion (p), Riccardo Del Fra (b).
Date: April 1980
Place: Munich, Germany
Rating: 3.0
A little-known studio recording by Chet's young quartet, recorded in Munich for Intercord records, *Leaving* features four original compositions by the band's pianist, Dennis Luxion. The most memorable of these is the haunting 'Blues for C.R.'; others, like 'You've Flipped Out', sound somewhat under-rehearsed. The record also features Chet's first studio recording of the title track, written by Richie Beirach, which would be a staple of his repertoire going forward. Chet's vocal on the closing song, 'When I Fall In Love', is not one of his better efforts, the phrasing poor. The record is beautifully recorded. Unfortunately, 'Leaving' has not yet been released on CD, and the vinyl is hard to track down.

RON CARTER: PATRÃO

Personnel: Ron Carter (b), Chet Baker (tp), Kenny Barron (p), Aloisio Agoiar (p), Amaury Tristao (g), Nana Vasconcelos (per), Edison Machado (d), Jack DeJohnette (d).
Date: May 1980
Place: Englewood Cliffs, New Jersey
Rating: 3.0
A slightly lukewarm Latin set from Ron Carter. Aloisio Agoiar's piano sounds somewhat insipid on the opening track 'Ah Rio', whilst the percussion is also strangely lifeless. Kenny Barron plays piano on three of the five cuts, and helps to lift the proceedings. Ron Carter was always a fan of Chet's playing, and he does not disappoint, playing well throughout, including a beautiful muted solo on 'Nearly'.

CHET BAKER: NIGHT BIRD / TUNE UP / CONCEPTION/IT NEVER ENTERED MY MIND

Personnel: Chet Baker (tp, vo), Karl Ratzer (g), Nicola Stilo (fl), Riccardo Del Fra (b), Al Levitt (dr).
Date: June 1980
Place: Paris, France
Rating: 2.5

Another set of vaguely dispiriting releases from Circle Records. Chet played at Le Dreher in Paris for fifteen nights; Dennis Luxion had left the band, and was effectively replaced by Karl Ratzer on guitar, whilst Al Levitt joined on drums. Two nights of music were recorded and eventually released on four LPs. There are some fine moments; Chet's solo on Russ Freeman's 'No Ties' (*Tune Up*) is one of his longest on record, and never seems to run out of ideas, and 'Leaving' (also *Tune Up*) is also worth hearing. "If you listen to these records," said Del Fra, "he plays like a bopper. It's very different to what we did later." The records are let down by the atrocious recording quality; Chet's vocal on 'There Will Never Be Another You' is barely audible, and at times, the audience is more closely recorded than the musicians. A selection of the material recorded over the two nights was later released on CD as *At Le Dreher*.

CHET BAKER MEETS NOVOS TEMPOS: SALSAMBA

Personnel: Chet Baker (tp, vo), Rique Pantoja Leite (key), Richard Galliano (acc), Michel Peratout (elb), José Boto (d).
Date: July 1980
Place: Paris, France
Rating: 2.5

Chet probably missed his best opportunity to record more bossa nova when he returned to the US in 1964; the prospect of Chet recording with the likes of João Gilberto or Antonio Carlos Jobim would have been a mouth-watering prospect. Chet's 1980 recording with Novos Tempos, a young Brazilian quartet featuring keyboard player Rique Pantoja, is something of a mixed bag. The Fender piano and electric bass lend the record a dated feel, and one or two of the tunes are a little too close to 'smooth jazz' for my liking. The album has its moments, however; 'Inaïa' and 'Seila', both of which were composed by Pantoja, are the highlights. Chet's vocal on 'Forgetful' is just that, a somewhat lazy rendition, but the solo that follows is wonderful.

CHET BAKER QUARTET: LIVE AT FAT TUESDAY'S

Personnel: Chet Baker (tp, vo), Bud Shank (as), Phil Markowitz (p), Hal Galper (p), Ron Carter (b), Ben Riley (d).
Date: April 1981
Place: NYC, New York
Rating: 3.0
Chet had flown back from Europe shortly before this gig. A radio broadcast had been scheduled, so pianist Phil Markowitz arranged a brief rehearsal at his apartment. By the evening, jet lag was beginning to kick in, and when Chet ran into saxophonist Bud Shank at the club, he asked him if he could sit in with the quartet. The set opens with just the quartet, and a weary-sounding Chet sounds uninspired on 'You Can't Go Home Again', with Markowitz's playing the highlight. During a break for the radio broadcast, Chet ran into his old pianist Hal Galper, and asked him to sit in for a couple of songs, leaving a disgruntled Markowitz on the sidelines. Bud Shank does his best to reinvigorate the proceedings, and is on fine form, particularly on a lengthy reading of 'In Your Own Sweet Way'. Chet's vocal on 'There Will Never Be Another You' brings a ripple of applause, but when he returns for his solo, he sounds flat and tired, missing several notes.

CHET BAKER: MY FUNNY VALENTINE / 'ROUND MIDNIGHT / I REMEMBER YOU

Personnel: Chet Baker (tp, vo), Jon Eardley (flh), Bob Mover (as, ss), Dennis Luxion (p), Rocky Knauer (b), Burkhart Ruckert (d).
Date: May 1981
Place: Cologne, Germany
Rating: 3.0
Another set of three vinyl releases from Germany's Circle Records, this time recorded at the Salt Peanuts Club in Cologne. By this stage, pianist Dennis Luxion had returned, and is joined by Bob Mover on saxophone and Chet's old friend, Jon Eardley, on flugelhorn. This is by far the best of the numerous Circle releases; the recording quality is of a much higher standard, and there's some nice counterpoint between the horns. Bob Mover recalls that some of the better tracks from those evenings were not released; hopefully that will be fixed if these sessions ever make it to CD.

CHET BAKER: LIVE IN PARIS

Personnel: Chet Baker (tp, vo), René Utreger (p), Pierre Michelot (b), Aldo Romano (d).
Date: November 1981
Place: Paris, France
Rating: 3.5

Having made a series of wonderful recordings in late 1978 and 1979, a period accompanied by relative stability in his personal life, Chet failed to capitalise on this, at least from a recording standpoint. There were a variety of reasons for this; firstly, after his European tour of 1978, he started to hire more local musicians—in some cases, they were considerably less experienced than Chet, and this impacted the quality of his output. Secondly, Chet became a more important commodity to European record companies, who were keen to cash in on his resurgence; Chet was not always good at 'taking care of business', as he would say, which is probably why we ended up with more recordings on Circle Records than on SteepleChase. Finally, in part because of his higher income, Chet gradually moved away from methadone, increasing his heroin intake as the period progressed. This live recording, with the fine René Utreger on piano, was probably the best album released in this period; Chet's chops are in relatively good shape, although he does scat at some length on 'But Not For Me' and 'Just Friends', and the recording quality is of a high standard. The CD was released on Norma records, and can be hard to find, but it's worth the look.

MICHEL GRAILLIER: DREAM DROPS

Personnel: Michel Graillier (p), Chet Baker (tp).
Date: November 1981
Place: Paris, France
Rating: 3.0

Chet only appears on the title track of Michel Graillier's solo LP, an album that also features Michel Petrucciani and Jean-Francois Jenny-Clark. The melody was written by Michel's wife, Micheline, for Chet, and was recorded on the second take.

CHET BAKER: PEACE

Personnel: Chet Baker (tp), David Friedman (vib, marimba), Buster Williams (b), Joe Chambers (d).
Date: February 1982
Place: NYC, New York
Rating: 4.0
Matthias Winckelmann of Enja Records approached David Friedman about making a record with Chet. The resulting album, *Peace*, is Chet's most significant studio album since the SteepleChase recordings in late 1979. It opens with the complex, angular 'Syzygies', a tune which was later renamed '3+1=5'. It was the first time Chet had recorded a tune without a harmonic basis, and proved to be quite a challenge. Chet sounds more comfortable with the Horace Silver composition 'Peace', where he lingers over the melody to good effect. The lengthy 'Lament for Thelonious' opens with a sad refrain from Chet, building gradually as the bass enters, then Friedman, to develop the elaborate melody. Buster Williams is a key part of the equation, carrying the chord changes and providing muscular support. 'Shadows', another Friedman original, is another highlight, a simple duo with Chet that works well.

CHET BAKER: BUT NOT FOR ME

Personnel: Chet Baker (tp, vo), Howard Johnson (tuba), James Newton (fl), Kenny Barron (p), Charlie Haden (b), Ben Riley (d).
Date: April 1982
Place: NYC, New York
Rating: 3.5
Despite a fine line-up, this studio session remained in the vaults until 1994, six years after Chet's death. It's hard to see why; Chet's playing sounds a little tired, but the material is excellent, the arrangements interesting, and with support from Charlie Haden and Kenny Barron, it's hard to go wrong. The album opens with 'Lament', based on the spiritual, 'Sometimes I Feel Like A Motherless Child'. Kenny Barron plays the introduction, before solos from both Chet and James Newton on flute. There's an unusual arrangement of 'Four' to follow, with Chet singing over the bass, before a solo by Howard Johnson on tuba. Chet rounds things off, with Johnson playing softly beneath him, much as Mulligan used to. There are conscious reminders of the Mulligan Quartet on 'Line for Lyons', too, with Johnson taking Gerry's role in proceedings. Haden's 'Ellen David', from *Closeness* (1976) follows, with Chet playing well. Recommended.

CHET BAKER—JIM HALL—HUBERT LAWS: STUDIO TRIESTE

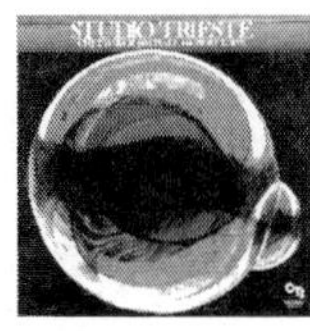

Personnel: Chet Baker (tp, flh), Hubert Laws (fl), Jim Hall (g), Jack Wilkins (g), Kenny Barron (key), Jorge Dalto (key), George Mraz (b), Gary King (elb), Steve Gadd (d), Sammy Figueroa (perc), Don Sebesky (arr).
Date: March/April 1982
Place: NYC, New York
Rating: 3.0
Creed Taylor suggested the line-up for this record; "Hall, Baker and Laws have the innate and unmistakable ability to know what to leave out," he comments in the liner notes. As the title suggests, there's a Latin tinge to the album, a likely deliberate attempt to recreate the feel of Jim Hall's *Concierto*. 'Malaguena' opens the proceedings, a vehicle for Jim Hall, keyboard player Jorge Dalto and percussionist Sammy Figueroa; the keyboard sound has dated badly, unfortunately. 'Django' is an improvement, with solos from Hall, Law, Chet, then Kenny Barron on electric piano. Hard to know what Tchaikovsky would have made of Sebesky's arrangement of 'Swan Lake', but I'm not sure he would have approved of the electric piano. The overall effect is less delicate and understated than the earlier *Concierto*. Finally there's a Spanish-tinged reading of Miles Davis's 'All Blues', which is probably the highlight of the album, featuring enjoyable solos from the three leads. An enjoyable session, but on which has not held up as well as Chet's earlier sessions on CTI.

ROLAND HANNA: GERSHWIN CARMICHAEL CATS

Personnel: Roland Hanna (p), Chet Baker (tp), Larry Coryell (g), Rufus Reid (b), Jimmy Madison (d), Don Sebesky (arr).
Date: June/July 1982
Place: NYC, New York
Rating: 2.0
A forgettable studio session for CTI from pianist Roland Hanna. There's little in the way of sleeve notes, but presumably we have Creed Taylor to thank for including Lloyd-Webber's 'Theme from Cats (Memory)'. Chet plays on only one track, Hoagy Carmichael's 'Skylark', but it's not particularly memorable.

CHET BAKER: OUT OF NOWHERE

Personnel: Chet Baker (tp, vo), Frank Adams (fl, as), Frank Brown (g), Ted Adams (b), Ron Adams (elb), Wade Robertson (d).
Date: December 1982
Place: Tulsa, Oklahoma
Rating: 2.0
After a brief tour, managed by Luiz Gasco, Chet returned to Oklahoma to visit his family. He ended up staying for several weeks—one of his longer visits—and played briefly on Oklahoma City itself. There he received a call from Tulsa-based saxophonist Frank Adams, who invited Chet to sit in with his own band as the 'special guest' when playing a club date booked for Christmas Eve at the now defunct Nine of Cups Club in Tulsa. There was no rehearsal, Chet simply playing tunes called by Frank Adams from his lengthy repertoire. Chet's playing is fine, Frank Adams acquits himself well, and the rest of the band try their best to keep up, reading the changes where necessary. The sound quality is poor, and it's sad that a label such as Milestone felt the need to ever release such a recording. For collectors only.

STAN GETZ & CHET BAKER: THE STOCKHOLM CONCERTS

Personnel: Stan Getz (ts), Chet Baker (tp, vo), Jim McNeely (p), George Mraz (b), Victor Lewis (d).
Date: February 1983
Place: Stockholm, Sweden
Rating: 3.0
The tour with Stan Getz was arranged by Wim Wigt, and was originally scheduled to last for thirty-five dates. Excerpts from the Stockholm Concert, which took place about one week into the tour, were originally released as 'Line for Lyons'. The two shows are now available in their entirety on Verve Records as a three- CD set. By all accounts, Chet's chops were not in good shape before the tour, and he seems to take time to warm up here. His vocal on 'Just Friends' and 'My Funny Valentine' is weak, and the video footage shows that Getz was not impressed. The second show was an improvement; Getz plays quietly beneath Chet's vocal on 'Valentine', and there is a spirited 'Line for Lyons', one of a handful of songs that the two leaders play together, where they unite without the aid of the rhythm section. The sets by Stan Getz, played with his regular quartet, are good. Pianist Jim McNeely remembers playing on autopilot that evening, suffering from severe jet lag, but Getz is on masterful form, most notably on 'How Long Has This Been Going On'. Chet's playing may have been patchy, his relationship with Getz a little frosty, but there's still plenty to enjoy here.

STAN GETZ & CHET BAKER: QUINTESSENCE, VOLUME 1 & 2

Personnel: Stan Getz (ts), Chet Baker (tp, vo), Jim McNeely (p), George Mraz (b), Victor Lewis (d).
Date: February 1983
Place: Baerum, Norway
Rating: 3.5

The following night of the tour, captured for Norwegian radio, is significantly better. 'Just Friends' and 'But Not For Me', both on Volume 1, find Chet's voice in much better shape. McNeely contributes more this time, delivering sparkling solos on the likes of 'We'll Be Together Again' (Volume 2). Even Getz seems to have thawed somewhat, perhaps sensing the improvement in Chet's contribution. The sound quality on these CDs, released on Concord, is also superior, making this the better bet for most buyers.

KIRK LIGHTSEY TRIO WITH CHET BAKER: EVERYTHING HAPPENS TO ME

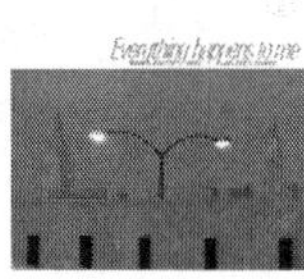

Personnel: Kirk Lightsey (p), Chet Baker (tp, vo), David Eubanks (b), Eddie Gladden (d).
Date: March 1983
Place: Monster, Holland
Rating: 3.5

After the abortive tour with Stan Getz, Wim Wigt paid Chet for the remainder of the concerts, and set about organising a number of other bookings. He also arranged a studio date with Chet's old pianist, Kirk Lightsey, for Timeless Records. Dexter Gordon was also supposed to show, but apparently preferred to enjoy the darker side of Amsterdam. Chet plays on just two songs—a brisk read of 'Ray's Idea', and a gorgeous, slow version of the title track. Chet lingers over the vocal, before an elegant solo from Lightsey, and then a solo by Chet on trumpet. The recording engineer for Timeless, Max Bolleman, always seemed to have the knack of recording Chet intimately, and this was the first of several excellent recordings they made together.

CHET BAKER TRIO: MR. B

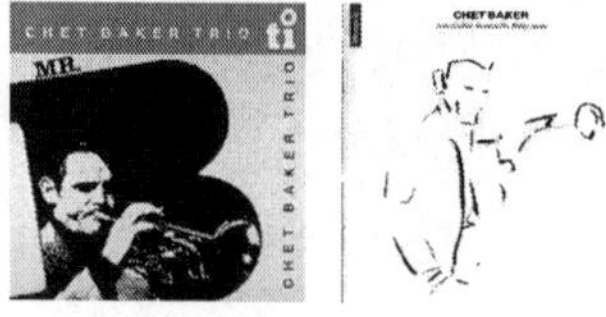

Personnel: Chet Baker (tp), Michel Graillier (p), Riccardo Del Fra (b).
Date: May 1983
Place: Monster, Holland
Rating: 4.5

Chet returned to Max Bolleman's studio with his trio in May to record one of his finest albums of the 1980s, *Mr. B*. Chet had gradually moved away from the 'bop' sound that can be heard on the early SteepleChase records, and indeed the albums he recorded with Riccardo Del Fra for Circle Records. He had developed a softer, more melancholy tone, first glimpsed in 1977 when he was suffering from kidney stones. The transition partly reflects Chet's own desire to experiment with this style, which he felt comfortable with, but Del Fra believes it also reflected the more 'French' approach of Graillier, who was less bop-oriented than the likes of NHØP and Doug Raney. The recording was also successful because the trio recorded songs that they had been playing in concert, such as 'Dolphin Dance' and 'Beatrice'; they deliberately chose to record shorter versions than they would play in a concert setting, so they could fit more songs on the record. Again, the sensitive recording style of the producer played a part, carefully editing out Chet's occasional coughing. There are numerous highlights; the trio's mid-tempo read of 'Dolphin Dance' is always a delight to hear, as is the slow reading of 'Ellen and David', where you almost hear Graillier and Del Fra slow to meet Chet's measured pace. Finally, it's worth flagging Chet's exquisite solo on 'Beatrice'. The CD comes with extra tracks; usually two songs rescued from an aborted session from October 1983, one of which—'Father X-Mas'—also features Philip Catherine on guitar. Essential.

JIM PORTO: RIO

Personnel: Jim Porto (vo), Chet Baker (tp), Alberto Corvini (tp), Oscar Valdambrini (tp), Claudio Corvini (tp), Tommaso Vittorini (tb), Virgilio Fraternali (tb), Dino Piani (tb), Ferrucio Corsi (as), Nicola Stilo (fl), Michele Ascolese (g), Rique Pantoja (elp), Mauro Dolci (b), Marco Fratini (b), José Boto (d), Roberto Gatto (d), Stefano Rossini (perc).
Date: May/June 1983
Place: Rome, Italy
Rating: 2.0

A disappointing album with Brazilian singer Jim Porto on which a sub-standard Chet contributes solos to just two tracks; 'Somos Todos Colossal' and a Rique Pantoja composition, 'Arbor Way', which became part of Chet's repertoire.

ELVIS COSTELLO: PUNCH THE CLOCK

Personnel: Elvis Costello (vo, g), Chet Baker (tp), Steve Nieve (p), Bruce Thomas (elb), Pete Thomas (d).
Date: July 1983
Place: London, England
Rating: 3.0
Elvis Costello was looking to add a trumpet solo to 'Shipbuilding', a song that he had written for the English musician Robert Wyatt. He had already asked Wynton Marsalis, who was unavailable, when he saw an advert that Chet was playing at the Canteen Club in London. Chet agreed to do the session, and recorded a couple of takes with the band. "The one thing I regret is in the mix that we added echo,“ Costello later recalled, "and I almost wanted to remix it." At the end of the session, Costello handed Chet a copy of the song 'Almost Blue', a song that he had written after listening to Chet's version of "The Thrill Is Gone'. Chet later recorded 'Almost Blue' on *Chet Baker in Tokyo* in 1987, and a stark, more harrowing version for the movie soundtrack to *Let's Get Lost*.

CHET BAKER: THE IMPROVISER

Personnel: Chet Baker (tp), Per Husby (p), Terje Venaas (b), Bjorn Kjellemyr (b), Ole Jacob Hansen (d), Espen Rud (d).
Date: August 1983
Place: Oslo, Norway
Rating: 3.0
Chet toured Norway quite extensively in August 1983, playing first with Per Husby's trio, then touring the west of the country with Erling Aksdal, before reuniting with Husby in Oslo. He was reportedly in good shape for the tour, taking only methadone, although he plays on a trumpet borrowed from a local musician. This bootleg-style recording captures three songs recorded at Oslo's Hot House. The sound quality is adequate, but it is clear that Chet is in fine form, delivering a delicate version of 'Beatrice', and playing astonishing long, clear lines on Tadd Dameron's 'Gnid' and Hal Galper's 'Night Bird', with Husby's band offering strong support. The CD also has two songs recorded two weeks later at Club 7, this time with a different rhythm section. The sound is not as good for the second date, the bass too loud, and the piano buried deep in the mix, but Chet is again playing well, 'Polka Dots and Moonbeams' the standout. Great music, but the poor recording means that this is not the best place to begin.

CHET BAKER TRIO: A TRUMPET FOR THE SKY, VOLUMES 1 & 2

Personnel: Chet Baker (tp, vo), Michel Graillier (p), Riccardo Del Fra (b).
Date: September 1983
Place: Paris, France
Rating: 2.0
Chet reunited with Michel Graillier and Riccardo Del Fra for a gig at Club 21 in Paris. Once again, his playing is superb—crisp, clean solos, full of ideas, supported by fine, responsive musicians. Under normal circumstances this would be an ideal opportunity to hear the band that recorded *Mr. B* in a concert setting, playing extended versions of some of the key tunes in Chet's repertoire. Unfortunately, the poor bootleg-style sound quality means that these recordings are virtually unlistenable, much of the fine music buried beneath the sound of Del Fra's bass. Avoid.

CHET BAKER TRIO: CHET BAKER—PHILIP CATHERINE—JEAN-LOUIS RASSINFOSSE

Personnel: Chet Baker (tp), Philip Catherine (g), Jean-Louis Rassinfosse (b).
Date: September 1983
Place: Brussels, Belgium
Rating: 4.5
Chet's rich vein of form continued on this, the first of the celebrated recordings with Philip Catherine and Jean-Louis Rassinfosse. Inspired by an excellent concert in Barcelona earlier that summer, they decided to record their first album together. Chet was in poor shape for the first session, but is in fine fettle second time around. His tone has again softened, revealing how his playing would be impacted by the shape he was in, but also by his sidemen; Catherine's background was in jazz-rock, so there was a less bop-oriented feel to the trio, very different to the SteepleChase recordings with NHØP and Doug Raney. There's a relaxed feel to the recording, which open's with Charlie Mariano's 'Crystal Bells'; as the tempo picks up, Chet responds with some long, clean runs. Next up is a gentle amble through Horace Silver's 'Strollin', Catherine taking a pleasing solo, Rassinfosse offering fine support, before taking a solo of his own. Richie Beirach's 'Leaving' is another highlight; listen to the way Catherine responds to Chet's introduction for an example of how the chemistry worked within the band. 'Estaté', from João Gilberto's 1977 album *Amoroso*, brings the album to a close, the gentle samba fitting in with the relaxed feel of the session. The electric contrabass used by Rassinfosse gives the album a slightly dated feel, but this is a minor quibble. Highly recommended.

CHET BAKER: LIVE IN SWEDEN WITH ÅKE JOHANSSON TRIO

Personnel: Chet Baker (tp, vo), Åke Johansson (p), Kjell Jansson (b), Göran Levin (d).
Date: September 1983
Place: Gothenburg, Sweden
Rating: 3.5
Recorded at the end of a tour of Sweden with pianist Åke Johansson's excellent trio, this is a superb live recording, capturing every nuance of the music played that night at Gothenburg's Nefertiti Club. The band opens with J.J. Johnson's 'Lament', Chet's blowing sweetly over some fine brush work by Levin. Johansson plays the next solo, before Jansson takes over with a mournful bowed bass, finally handing back to Chet. Chet's vocal on 'My Ideal' is not one of his best, but is sung with feeling, but 'Beatrice' is excellent, his blowing a joy to listen to. Charlie Haden's 'Ellen David' is gorgeous, again featuring Kjell Jansson's bowed bass to good effect. The CD version comes with three extra songs, including 'Milestones', but the best tracks were probably selected for the original LP. An underrated recording that deserves greater recognition.

CHET BAKER: AT CAPOLINEA

Personnel: Chet Baker (tp), Nicola Stilo (fl), Diane Vavra (ss), Michel Graillier (p), Riccardo Del Fra (b), Leo Mitchell (d).
Date: October 1983
Place: Milan, Italy
Rating: 3.5
Recorded in the middle of a somewhat chaotic tour of Italy, *At Capolinea* is not a live recording, as has been suggested, but a studio recording from Milan. The album is notable for the growing maturity of Nicola Stilo, who sounds more confident than on earlier recordings, and contributes two compositions of his own, but also because of the appearance of Chet's girlfriend Diane Vavra, who plays soprano saxophone on two tracks. The album opens with a long version of Bruno Martino's 'Estaté', the larger band giving the tune a very different flavour to the version recorded with Philip Catherine one month earlier. Vavra's solo on 'Dream Drop' sounds nervous; she apparently preferred one of the alternative takes, but the band sounded better overall here, according to Stilo. 'Lament' is again one of the highlights, with a lovely opening from Del Fra, before Chet states the theme, eventually giving way to a lengthy flute solo from Nicola Stilo. Graillier follows, before handing back to Chet to wrap things up.

CHET BAKER: SEPTEMBER SONG/LIVE AT NEW MORNING/STAR EYES

Personnel: Chet Baker (tp, vo), Duke Jordan (p), Jesper Lundgaard (b), Leo Mitchell (d).
Date: November 1983
Place: Paris, France / Lauwe, Belgium / Arnhem, Holland
Rating: 3.0

The tour of Italy left Chet in poor shape, and he only turned up for five of the scheduled fifteen concerts with Duke Jordan and Jesper Lundgaard the following month; the continued presence of Leo Mitchell, his old friend from New York, was no doubt a contributing factor. Odd, then, that these five shows should be represented by three live recordings, all made by the Japanese record company Marshmallow. The albums are something of a mixed bag. On 'September Song', Chet demonstrates why he rarely attempted to sing the Kurt Weill tune, but then delivers a splendid solo. 'My Funny Valentine' is much better, Chet understandably sounding more at ease. The *New Morning* album features more songs from the same show, apparently a later set, with Mitchell sitting in on drums. *Star Eyes* is more of a bop-oriented set; Chet fluffs the introduction to 'Walkin'', but concentrates hard to pull off a strong solo, before a good version of Miles Davis' 'Solar'. The sound quality is excellent on these recordings, many of which are only available on import from Japan.

CHET BAKER: MY FUNNY VALENTINE

Personnel: Chet Baker (tp, vo), Erling Aksdal (p), Bjorn Alterhaug (b), Kjell Johansen (d).
Date: May 1984
Place: Oslo / Trondheim, Norway
Rating: 4.0

A fascinating document from Chet's Norwegian tour of May 1984, this double-CD was only released by EMI in Norway in 2006, and deserves a wider audience. Chet had not been in the best of shape on that tour, suffering from chemical imbalances, and arguing constantly with his girlfriend, Diane. He was in better shape for a radio recording which took place on May 23rd, despite being two hours late, and recorded three songs, all presented here for the first time. Chet plays well on 'Nightbird', but sounds a little tired, before delivering a gorgeous vocal on 'My Foolish Heart'. Two days later he performed in Trondheim, a show which pianist Erling Aksdal remembers as the best gig of the tour. There are three songs from the concert, of which 'Broken Wing' and 'Nightbird' are the standouts, Chet delivering long, intricate lines on his solos. The CD also includes one track recorded with Norwegian jazz poet Jan Erik Vold, recorded in February 1988. The second CD is a *Best Of Chet Baker*, taken from his Pacific Jazz recordings, 1952 through 1957.

CHET BAKER: SOUNDTRACK TO LE JUMEAU/PLAYS VLADIMIR COSMA

Personnel: Chet Baker (tp, vo), Maurice Vander (p), Herve Sellin (p), Niels-Henning Ørsted Pedersen (b), John Guerin (d), Vladimir Cosma (comp, cond), Various horns/reeds/strings.
Date: September 1984
Place: Paris, France
Rating: 2.0 / 3.0
Le Jumeau was a French farce starring Pierre Richard as a humble greeting-card vendor who pretends to have a twin brother when he meets twin American heiresses, and decides to seduce them both. The soundtrack, by Vladimir Cosma, was written with Chet Baker in mind, and also features the fine bass-playing of NHØP. Themes such as 'Le Jumeau', 'Matthias-Mathieu' and 'Two Much' are interesting but inessential. Elsewhere, the keyboard and synthesiser of 'Les Bigames' and 'La Folle Journee' have dated badly. It's better to look for *Chet Baker Plays Vladimir Cosma/Sentimental Walk in Paris*, which are more jazz-oriented; they exclude a number of songs included on the soundtrack which did not feature Chet, and include other songs recorded at the same sessions that were later included in other movies, such as 'Diva' and 'Nous Irons Tous Au Paradis'. Note that some of the songs included on this record are identical to those included on *Le Jumeau*, but the song titles have been changed; 'Hoobylog', for example, is 'Matthias-Mathieu'.

CHET BAKER QUINTET FEATURING WARNE MARSH: BLUES FOR A REASON

Personnel: Chet Baker (tp), Warne Marsh (ts), Hod O'Brien (p), Cecil McBee (b), Eddie Gladden (d).
Date: September 1984
Place: Monster, Holland
Rating: 4.0
An inspired meeting with Warne Marsh. It might not seem like an obvious pairing on paper, but there was always more to Warne Marsh's playing than the 'cool school', much as Chet was far more than a 'West Coast' musician. Opening track, 'Well Spoken', is a Marsh original that sees both men gravitate to a more bop-oriented sound, Chet playing muted trumpet, with both men delivering strong solos. Marsh drops out for a gorgeous version of 'If You Could See Me Now', which features delicate brush-work by Madden, and a fine solo by pianist Hod O'Brien. 'We Know It's Love' and 'Looking Good Tonight' are both recorded as Chet originals, but were simply improvisations based around the chord changes of 'What Is This Thing Called Love' and 'The Way You Look Tonight', respectively. Chet drops out for 'Imagination', before returning for the title track. Highly recommended.

CHET BAKER: LIVE AT THE RENAISSANCE II/I REMEMBER YOU

Personnel: Chet Baker (tp, vo), Sal Nistico (ts), Lorne Lofsky (g), Chris Conners (b), Artt Frank (d).
Date: November 1984
Place: Buffalo, New York
Rating: 3.0
Originally released on CCB Records, *Live at the Renaissance II* is one of the better 'bootleg' recordings issued by Chet's family after his death in 1988. Recorded at a small club in Buffalo, New York, belonging to jazz trumpeter Sam Noto, it features Chet's old friends Sal Nistico on tenor saxophone and Artt Frank on drums. Lorne Lofske, who recalls playing with Chet in Toronto around this time, joins on guitar. The set opens with 'Stella by Starlight', which features overlong solos by the sidemen. Chet's vocal on 'I Remember You' is poorly recorded, but he sounds in good voice, and there are strong solos from the whole band, Sal Nistico in particular. The highlight is 'Night Bird', a composition by Enrico Pieranunzi, that originally featured on the 1980 album *Soft Journey*. There's some nice interplay between the horns, and a strong solo by Chet, who delivers strong, clean bop-like lines before handing over to the saxophonist, who sticks to a rather more mellow delivery. The sound quality is adequate, but a notch above many of the other unofficial recordings released in recent years.

CHET BAKER: THE SESJUN RADIO SHOWS

Personnel: Chet Baker (tp, vo), Jacques Pelzer (fl), Cameron Brown (b), Scott Lee (b), Frank Tusa (b), Jan Voogd (b), Jean-Louis Rassinfosse (b), Philip Catherine (g), Harold Danko (p), Phil Markowitz (p), Michel Graillier (p), Wolfgang Lackerschmid (vib), Jeff Brillinger (dr), Alphonse Mouzon (dr), John Engels (dr).
Date: Various, 1976–1985
Place: Various, Netherlands
Rating: 4.0
This 2010 2-CD release is a fine addition to any Chet Baker CD collection. It contains selections from a series of five performances recorded for live broadcast for Tros Sesjun, a weekly Dutch radio programme that featured live jazz that ran between 1973 and 2004. Chet was typically in good shape, performing a warm up set before the live broadcast began, and the sound quality is superb. Of the five line-ups featured, it's particularly interesting to hear Chet's early 'drummerless' quartet with pianist Harold Danko, recorded in February 1976, and a 50-minute set by his trio with Philip Catherine and Jean-Louis Rassinfosse, from February 1985. The CD includes informative line notes from Chet Baker biographer Jeroen de Valk.

CHET BAKER: MISTY/MY FOOLISH HEART/TIME AFTER TIME/ WOULD YOU BELIEVE

Personnel: Chet Baker (tp, vo), Martha Burks (vo), Fred Raulston (vib), Floyd Darling (p), Kirby Stewart (b), Paul Guerrero (d).
Date: January 1985
Place: Dallas, Texas
Rating: 2.0
A series of ragged recordings with vibraphonist Fred Raulston's band, recorded on stage at The Jazba in Dallas, Texas, and then later a nearby studio. Local record company owner Bill Craig reached an agreement with Chet to make one record, combining the best of the live and studio recordings. Craig later recalled that Chet was high and "having a lot of problems with his chops"; certainly he doesn't sound in the best of shape, mumbling his way through 'When I Fall in Love', his playing inconsistent from song to song. The studio recording, initially released as *Would You Believe*, is even worse; Chet is tired, and angry with Bill Craig for suggesting repeated takes. Unfortunately Craig reneged on his original agreement with both Chet Baker and Fred Raulston, selling the tapes in their entirety to the Italian record label I.R.D., which released four albums, later appearing as three CDs. Avoid.

ÅKE JOHANSSON TRIO WITH CHET BAKER & TOOTS THIELMANS: CHET & TOOTS

Personnel: Chet Baker (tp, vo), Toots Thielemans (harm), Åke Johansson (p), Kjell Jansson (b), Rune Carlsson (d).
Date: February 1985
Place: Stockholm, Sweden
Rating: 3.5
In February 1985, Chet reunited with Swedish pianist Åke Johansson; the manager of the Stockholm Jazz Festival suggested they perform a few concerts with the legendary Belgian harmonica player Toots Thielemans, who had originally made his name as a jazz guitarist, sharing the bandstand with Charlie Parker, and touring with Benny Goodman and George Shearing. It seemed an unlikely pairing, and they had never played together before, but they shared a love of harmony. The final concert was recorded for Swedish radio and later released on CD as *Chet & Toots*. They play together to good effect on a number of the songs from Chet's repertoire, including 'Beatrice' and 'Lament'; Thielemans plays a lovely version of 'When I Fall In Love', leaving Chet to play an excellent version of 'Broken Wing' with the

trio. The last two tunes are rather less effective; 'For Minors Only' does not seem to gel, and Chet's vocal on 'My Foolish Heart' is badly distorted. For the most part, however, this is an enjoyable concert which captures him in good shape, playing with a responsive band.

CHET BAKER: DIANE

Personnel: Chet Baker (tp, vo), Paul Bley (p).
Date: February 1985
Place: Copenhagen, Denmark
Rating: 4.5

One of Chet's landmark recordings from the 1980s, *Diane* sees him reunited with SteepleChase Records, and with the Canadian pianist Paul Bley, who was living in Copenhagen at the time. Bley was not playing many standards at this time, and is careful to allow Chet plenty of space. The first track they recorded was 'Every Time We Say Goodbye'; listen to how Bley plays a flurry of notes to introduce the song, before slowing the tempo, and playing with the lightest of touches as Chet comes in. That set the tone for a warm, relaxed session. 'If I Should Lose You' is taken at an extremely slow pace, the two musicians using the silence to create a quiet melancholy. Chet's vocal on 'You Go To My Head' sounds uncertain—he was apparently reading from Diane's hand-scrawled lyrics in the studio—and he lingers over the lyrics, just as he did in the breathy solo to the first song. Chet suggested a couple of more playful tunes to break things up, and they settle on 'Pent-up House' by Sonny Rollins. Essential.

CHET BAKER: I REMEMBER YOU

Personnel: Chet Baker (tp, p, vo), Doug Raney (g), Jesper Lundgaard (b), Aage Tanggaard (d).
Date: February 1985
Place: Copenhagen, Denmark
Rating: 2.5

Recorded the night after the *Diane* session at the Café Montmartre, this is a sub-par concert that should probably have remained in the vaults. Chet called a couple of tunes the band were not familiar with; for the most part the rhythm section try their best to follow, but during 'Deep In A Dream' Chet tries to teach them the tune, sitting at the piano. That performance was never released, but Chet's frustration is plain to hear; he takes a piano solo during a ragged version of 'But Not For Me'. The recording was made by an amateur, the tapes later sold to Enja Records after Chet's death. The company originally hoped to release two or three CDs of material, but Doug Raney persuaded them to keep it to one, picking out the highlights of an evening that most would rather forget. For Enja to release this as part of their *Legacy* series and for Carol Baker to refer to Enja picking out "only the best" of Chet's unreleased recordings simply reveals that neither party cares much about Chet's legacy, just the money.

CHET BAKER: CHET'S CHOICE

Personnel: Chet Baker (tp, vo), Philip Catherine (g), Jean-Louis Rassinfosse (b), Hein van de Geijn (b).
Date: June 1985
Place: Monster, Holland
Rating: 4.5

Chet had been touring for several weeks as a trio with guitarist Philip Catherine and bass player Jean-Louis Rassinfosse. Producer Gerrie Teekens suggested recording an album for Criss Cross with Hein van de Geijn on acoustic bass, rather than Rassinfosse, who played an electronic contrabass. However, Chet was not in the best shape at the initial recording session, and his playing was less fluid than usual. Chet agreed to re-record the album a few weeks later for no additional fee, but suggested they use Rassinfosse on bass; he was more accustomed to playing without a drummer, and was a steady timekeeper. Chet's playing on the second session was crisp and focused, his tone expertly captured by engineer Max Bolleman. Catherine is more playful than Doug Raney was on the earlier SteepleChase recordings, livening up the proceedings with elements of funk and electronic effects. When the album was released on

CD, producer Gerrie Teekens added two of the stronger songs from the earlier session. The title of the album refers to the fact that Chet eventually chose his own bass player for the album; the result was one of his finest later recordings.

CHET BAKER: STROLLIN'

Personnel: Chet Baker (tp, vo), Philip Catherine (g), Jean-Louis Rassinfosse (b).
Date: June 1985
Place: Monster, Holland
Rating: 3.5
A live recording of the trio from the 7th Jazz Festival at Munster in Germany. The concert was originally broadcast on the radio, but later released on vinyl—without the knowledge of Catherine and Rassinfosse—by Enja Records. Chet is not in such good shape as the studio session, and the sound is not as good. Still, the album has its moments, including fine versions of the Horace Silver's title track, 'Sad Walk' by Bob Zieff, and 'Leaving' by Richie Beirach.

CHET BAKER: CANDY

Personnel: Chet Baker (tp, vo), Michel Graillier (p), Jean-Louis Rassinfosse (b), Red Mitchell (p).
Date: June 1985
Place: Stockholm, Sweden
Rating: 4.0
An intimate, relaxed session recorded at the Sonet Library in Stockholm, with pianist Michel Graillier filling in for Philip Catherine, who was unavailable on that day. Highlights include a melancholic version of 'Bye Bye Blackbird', Chet playing slightly behind the beat, and a more upbeat read of Bob Zieff's 'Sad Walk', the tune becoming brighter as the pace picks up. Veteran bass player Red Mitchell was on hand to interview Chet for a TV broadcast of the show. As a result, the trio plays a version of Mitchell's own composition, 'Red's Blues', whilst the video/DVD also includes a version of 'My Romance', with Mitchell accompanying Chet on piano.

MIKE MELILLO AND CHET BAKER: SYMPHONICALLY

Personnel: Chet Baker (tp, vo), Mike Melillo (p, arr, cond), Massimo Moriconi (b), Giampaulo Ascolese (dr), Orchestra Filarmonica Marchigiana.
Date: July 1985
Place: Porto Recanati, Italy
Rating: 2.0
Mike Melillo, a new Jersey-born pianist, had been living in Italy since 1983. He had long dreamt of working with a full orchestra, and was persuaded by Paolo Piangiarelli—a local jazz lover and promoter—to arrange a series of concerts featuring Chet Baker, who was scheduled to tour Italy. One of the final concerts was recorded, and later released as *Symphonically* on Soul Note records. Unfortunately Melillo's arrangements are somewhat heavy-handed and slushy, and the production leaves Chet sounding somewhat cavernous. The only real highlight is a pleasant vocal on 'My Foolish Heart'.

VARIOUS ARTISTS: 'ROUND MIDNIGHT

Personnel: Chet Baker (tp, vo), Herbie Hancock (p), Pierre Michelot (b), Billy Higgins (dr).
Date: July 1985
Place: Epinay Sur Seine, France
Rating: 3.5
Herbie Hancock arranged and produced the soundtrack to Bertrand Tavernier's acclaimed 1986 movie *Round Midnight*. They agreed that it was important to capture the 'feel' of jazz, rather than to recreate the authentic sound of jazz in the 1950s. Despite the presence of Freddie Hubbard, Dexter Gordon, Wayne Shorter, John McLaughlin—to name but a few—Chet's rendition of Kenny Dorham's 'Fair Weather' is one of the highlights. "The vocal performance was exactly what we needed and his trumpet solo was brilliant," Hancock later recalled. "I had forgotten that Chet didn't read music. I remember how fresh his first take was. He followed the chords as if he had known them all his life. The notes became pivots connecting the chords. His intuition was flawless, his musical choices were perfect. It was then that I personally discovered the greatness of Chet Baker."

RIQUE PANTOJA AND CHET BAKER

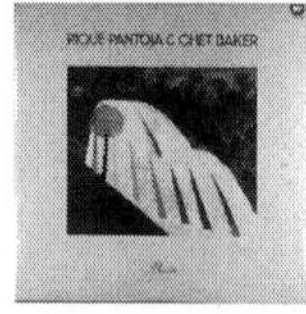

Personnel: Chet Baker (tp, vo), Rique Pantoja (p, key, vo), Sizao Machado (b), Bob Wyatt (dr), Silvano Michelino (perc). (Except 'Arborway'): Chet Baker (tp), Rique Pantoja (key), Michele Ascolese (g), Marco Fratini (b), Roberto Gatto (d), Stefano Rossini (perc).
Date: August 1985
Place: Rio de Janeiro, Brazil
Rating: 2.5

Rique Pantoja, who had known Chet since Novos Tempos days in 1980, arranged for Chet to play at the Free Jazz festival in Rio de Janeiro. While Chet was in Brazil, they discussed singing a duet on Pantoja's new album, a song he had composed by the name of 'So Hard To Know'. Chet's vocal is poor, but he contributes some fine playing to liven up some otherwise dull Latin-jazz arrangements. The highlight is 'Arborway', a Pantoja composition that had originally appeared on Jim Porto's 1983 album *Rio*; it is reproduced here, with Porto's vocal edited out. Chet liked the tune, and it became a part of his repertoire in the final years of his life.

LIZZY MERCIER DESCLOUX: ONE FOR THE SOUL

Personnel: Lizzy Mercier Descloux (vo), Chet Baker (tp, vo), Moacyr Marques Da Silva (bcl), Leonardo Gandelman (as, ts), Michel Cron (vln), Sivuca (accor), Vincent Bouvot (key), Doudeth 'Neco' DeAzvedo (g), Vitor Biglione (g), Harry Bruce (b), Jorge Degas (b), Jamil Jones, Dos Santos Zeppa (b, g), Paulo Braga (dr), Billy Perry (dr), Djalma Correa (per), Alceu Maia (per), Paulo 'Chacal' Perira (per), Marcelo Salazar (per).
Date: August 1985
Place: Rio de Janeiro, Brazil
Rating: 3.0

Something of an oddity in Chet's discography. While he was in Rio, Chet was invited to play on *One For The Soul*, the fifth album by the pioneering art-school 'No Wave' singer, Lizzy Mercier Descloux. Combining elements of funk, soul and Brazilian music, together with her own wayward, off-key singing, it's something of an acquired taste. Chet plays on five tracks, including an unusual read of 'My Funny Valentine'. Sadly, Mercier Descloux passed away in 2004, and this album has become something of a collector's item. It's no jazz album, but it's a grower.

AMSTEL OCTET AND CHET BAKER: HAZY HUGS

Personnel: Chet Baker (tp), Edu Ninck Blok (tp), Evert Hekkema (bar horn), Kees van Lier (as), Dick de Graaf (ts), Jan Vennik (bs), Bert van den Brink (p), Hein van de Geijin (b), John Engels (d).
Date: September 1985
Place: Loenen an de Vecht, Holland
Rating: 3.0
Back in Europe, Chet was invited to perform as the guest soloist on a recording by the Amstel Octet, a Dutch band that primarily played in Holland and Belgium. Chet had been renting a room in Amsterdam from the band's baritone horn player, Evert Hekkema, and had even invited him on a tour in Italy in October 1983. Chet had also met the other band members when they were rehearsing their first album the previous summer. Chet plays on four of the six tunes, having missed the beginning of the recording session. His solo on 'Someday You'll Leave Me', an original by Hein van de Geijn, is pieced together from three different solos, whilst on 'Tergiversation' he bluffs his way through the complex chord changes. Despite the lack of rehearsal, Chet picked up on the tunes quickly, and played well. The resulting album, *Hazy Hugs*, has a relaxed, easy feel to it; it's far from essential, but highly enjoyable nonetheless.

CHET BAKER: SINGS AGAIN

Personnel: Chet Baker (tp, vo), Michel Graillier (p), Riccardo Del Fra (b), John Engels (d).
Date: October 1985
Place: Monster, Holland
Rating: 3.5
It has been suggested that *Sings Again* placed an emphasis on Chet's vocals because his chops were in bad shape, but that is not the case. He was playing regularly at this time, and his trumpet playing on the album is good, even if the solos are brief. The album was commissioned for the Japanese market; jazz vocal albums have always been popular in Japan, and there was a desire to capture the feel of Chet's early vocal albums for Pacific Jazz. Chet chose the songs from a list of standards that had been suggested, and whilst one or two tunes sound under-rehearsed, the result is one of Chet's finer vocal recordings from later years. Engineer Max Bolleman does a super job of capturing the intimate style of Chet's singing, and Chet himself is on good form, his intonation clear and singing in key. The band—which included old friends Michel Graillier and Riccardo Del Fra—lend strong support. Whilst the album has tended to divide the critics, I love the record, which includes an exquisite version of 'My Funny Valentine'.

CHET BAKER AND PHILIP CATHERINE: THERE'LL NEVER BE ANOTHER YOU

Personnel: Chet Baker (tp, vo, p, dr), Philip Catherine (g), Allan Praskin (as).
Date: October 1985
Place: Zagreb, Yugoslavia
Rating: 2.5

Chet's superb trio with Philip Catherine and Jean-Louis Rassinfosse fell apart in late 1985. Rassinfosse left the band after a misunderstanding at a gig at the New Morning in Paris in late September. Philip Catherine stayed on for the remaining gigs of the tour; Riccardo Del Fra occasionally filled in on bass, but at this gig in Zagreb, Baker and Catherine mostly play as a duo. After the fine studio albums, this set is something of a disappointment—one that should have stayed in the vaults. Chet does not sound in the best of shape—he plays piano on some tracks—and most of the tunes are meandering, featuring overlong solos by Catherine. Chet's vocal on 'My Foolish Heart' is pretty, but when he starts to play drums behind saxophonist Allan Praskin, you know it's not going to be one of his finer nights.

CHET BAKER: LIVE FROM THE MOONLIGHT

Personnel: Chet Baker (tp, vo), Michel Graillier (p), Massimo Moriconi (b).
Date: November 1985
Place: Macerata, Italy
Rating: 4.5

"Towards the end, on a good night, he could play jazz just as well as it has ever been played," claimed musician and jazz critic Mike Zwerin. "There were not enough good nights." This was one of the good nights, a recording from the Moonlight Club in Macerata. The CD includes a recording of the band's rehearsal, and three full sets—a total of two-and-a-half hours of music. Chet is on majestic form, playing lengthy solos that are bristling with ideas. Highlights include a mournful version of 'Polka Dots and Moonbeams', a superb version of 'Estaté', with a flawless solo from Chet, and Richie Beirach's 'Broken Wing'. The quality of the recording, courtesy of Paulo Piangiarelli (Philology records), is below average, and bass player Massimo Moriconi is not always clearly audible. This is a minor complaint, however, since this is one of Chet's finest live recordings of the 1980s. The CD is out of print at the time of writing, but is well worth tracking down from the one of the numerous online stores.

JOE LOCASCIO FEATURING CHET BAKER: SLEEPLESS

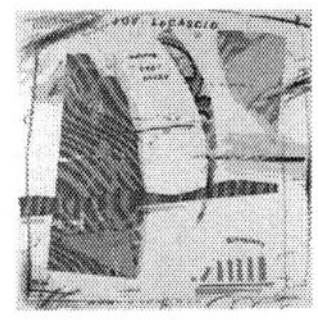

Personnel: Joe LoCascio (p, syn), Chet Baker (tp), Tom McClaren (b), George Weimmer (dr, perc), Alonzo Alonzo (perc), Terri Meason (vo).
Date: December 1985
Place: Houston, Texas, USA
Rating: 2.5
Chet was staying in Texas with a friend over the Christmas period when he was invited to record an album with a local keyboard player, Joe LoCascio. The album primarily consists of fusion-oriented, 'crossover' material, which was selling well in the U.S. in the mid-1980s. The title track has dated badly, and sounds more 'new age' than fusion, but on the more acoustic tunes Chet's playing shines. The opening track, 'Old and Lost Rivers', has a beautiful melody, and 'For Amanda', a duet with LoCascio on piano, is another highlight. The album did not sell particularly well, and is hard to find, but did help to make LoCascio's name as a musician, and secure him a contract with a bigger label.

CHET BAKER & CHRISTOPHER MASON: SILENT NIGHTS

Personnel: Chet Baker (tp), Christopher Mason (as), Mike Pellera (p), Jim Singleton (b), Johnny Vidacovich (dr).
Date: January 1986
Place: New Orleans, Louisiana, USA
Rating: 3.0
Alto saxophonist Christopher Mason has first met Chet in a police cell in the late 1960s, but stayed in touch with him over the years. Mason eventually moved to New Orleans, and married a French lady. He was visiting his wife's family in Paris in late 1985, and caught up with his old friend at the New Morning jazz club. A few weeks later, back home in the U.S., he called Chet and told him that he was thinking of recording a Christmas album. Chet agreed to join the session, provided the tunes were played "a little reverently". The session comprises delicate arrangements of seasonal favourites, including two delightful versions of 'Silent Night', and spirituals such as 'Nobody Knows The Trouble I've Seen' and 'Swing Low, Sweet Chariot'. The resulting album, *Silent Nights*, is hardly an essential album in Chet's long discography, but is highly enjoyable nonetheless.

CHET BAKER: WHEN SUNNY GETS BLUE

Personnel: Chet Baker (tp, vo), Butch Lacy (p), Jesper Lundgaard (b), Jukkis Uotila (dr).
Date: February 1986
Place: Copenhagen, Denmark
Rating: 3.0
Chet's final recording on SteepleChase, and the weakest of them all. Chet arrived in Copenhagen in a sorry state; he had barely played in the preceding weeks, and his chops had completely gone. A planned recording for a TV show was scrapped, with Chet barely playing a note, nodding off on the bandstand. His condition had improves somewhat by the time the album was recorded, but Chet's playing was not up to his normal standard, and numerous takes were required; in the end, Chet's solos had to be spliced together from the various takes. Despite its numerous shortcomings, the record has its moments; pianist Butch Lacy's arrangements are interesting, and there's still a fragile beauty to Chet's playing, even on a bad day. "The record may not show the best side of Chet as a musician," claimed producer Nils Winther, "but maybe as an artist, you know."

CHET BAKER WITH THE BRADLEY YOUNG TRIO: CHET IN CHICAGO

Personnel: Chet Baker (tp, vo), Bradley Young (p), Larry Gray (b), Rusty Jones (dr), Ed Petersen (guest—ts).
Date: May 1986
Place: Chicago, Illinois, USA
Rating: 3.5
Chet was playing at the Jazz Showcase in Chicago, in what was to be his final performance in that city, when he was invited to record an album with local pianist Bradley Young. When Chet agreed to make the record, Young had just two days to assemble a band a book a recording studio. He was able to secure a fine rhythm section—drummer Rusty Jones had played with George Shearing between 1972 and 1978, whilst bassist Larry Gray has played with numerous artists over the years, most recently working with the Ramsey Lewis Trio. Tenor saxophonist Ed Petersen was also persuaded to sit in on four tracks. Chet's chops are in far better shape this time around, and he sounds as lyrical as ever on ballads such as 'We'll Be Together Again' and 'My Funny Valentine'. The real joy of this relaxed session, however, is to hear his spirited playing on bebop classics such as Charlie Parker's 'Ornithology' and Miles Davis' 'Sippin' At Bells'. The session went unreleased for more than twenty years, and was finally issued as part of Enja's Legacy series in the autumn of 2008.

CHET BAKER: NIGHTBIRD/LIVE AT RONNIE SCOTT'S

Personnel: Chet Baker (tp, vo), Michel Graillier (p), Riccardo Del Fra (b), Van Morrison (vo), Elvis Costello (vo—DVD only).
Date: June 1986
Place: London, UK
Rating: 2.5
This is one of Chet's best-known sessions from his later years, in part because it has long been available on DVD, but also because of the appearance of two special guests, Elvis Costello and Van Morrison. Although Chet was playing in the drummerless format that he enjoyed, with two fine, supportive musicians—Michel Graillier and Riccardo Del Fra—Chet's playing and singing sounds tired and uninspired. Van Morrison was only recorded at the soundcheck, and his version of 'Send in the Clowns' sounds sloppy and under-rehearsed as he struggles to remember the lyrics. Elvis Costello was more familiar with Chet's repertoire, and contributes moving versions of 'The Very Thought Of You' and 'You Don't Know What Love Is'. The DVD includes a lengthy interview with Chet, conducted by Costello himself.

CHET BAKER: COOL CAT/AS TIME GOES BY/HEARTBREAK

Personnel: Chet Baker (tp, vo), Harold Danko (p), Jon Burr (b), Ben Riley (dr).
Date: December 1986
Place: Monster, Holland
Rating: 3.5 (Heartbreak 2.0)
Chet played in Japan for the first time in March 1986. One of the organisers of that tour, Naoki Tachikawa, also wanted to record two albums for the Japanese market, again featuring Chet's singing. He arranged to fly Chet's band to Max Bolleman's studio in Monster, in the Netherlands. Chet was not familiar with all of the songs suggested by the Japanese production team, and they hurriedly transcribed the lyrics to some of the songs. Despite the lack of preparation, this is an enjoyable session. Chet's phrasing on some of the vocals occasionally sounds tired, but for the most part, he is in good shape, and his playing is strong. The albums were released in Japan as *Singing in the Midnight* and *Love Song*. The sessions were also licensed to Timeless records in Europe, where they were released as *Cool Cat—Chet Baker Plays*, *Chet Baker Sings* and *As Time Goes By*. After Chet's death, Timeless added strings to certain songs from this session, and the earlier *Sings Again* record, and released an album entitled *Heartbreak*. The editing on this album is poor, however; far better to look for the original albums.

CHET BAKER: SINGS AND PLAYS FROM THE FILM LET'S GET LOST

Personnel: Chet Baker (tp, vo), Frank Strazzeri (p), Nicola Stilo (g, fl), John Leftwich (b), Ralph Penland (dr).
Date: January 1987, May 1987
Place: Los Angeles, California, USA; Paris, France
Rating: 3.5

The soundtrack to Bruce Weber's movie, like the movie itself, tends to divide both fans and critics alike. Chet had never previously played with either John Leftwich or Ralph Penland, but he apparently insisted on using his old friend Frank Strazzeri on piano. Some of the material is also unfamiliar; Chet had never heard 'Moon and Sand' before the recording session, but was still able to record it first take. There is also considerable emphasis on Chet's singing, which is closely recorded, presumably to capture the ageing tone of his voice. Despite these issues, the soundtrack does effectively capture the world-weariness that increasingly weighed on Chet in the final years; the effect of hearing him whisper songs like 'Imagination', 'Blame It On My Youth' and 'Almost Blue' is almost heartbreaking, comparable in some respects to hearing Billie Holiday's final recordings.

CHET BAKER: A NIGHT AT THE SHALIMAR CLUB

Personnel: Chet Baker (tp, vo), Mike Melillo (p), Luca Flores (p), Nicola Stilo (fl), Furio Di Castri (b).
Date: May 1987
Place: Senigallia, Italy
Rating: 2.0

One of the bad nights. Chet was struggling to kick heroin, and pulled out of the previous night's concert at Porto Recanati midway through the first set, his body burning with fever. He made it to Senigallia next day, but was in no fit state to play. Despite this, Paulo Piangiarelli, the founder of Philology records, recorded the concert without the band's knowledge and released the album after Chet's death. "Later I went to him and said, 'It's not right'," recalled Nicola Stilo. "I went to the police, and everything, and finally after several years we reached an agreement, and he had to pay me and the rest of the band." One to avoid.

CHET BAKER: CHET BAKER IN TOKYO

Personnel: Chet Baker (tp, vo), Harold Danko (p), Hein van de Geijn (b), John Engels (d).
Date: June 1987
Place: Tokyo, Japan
Rating: 5.0
From the ridiculous to the sublime. Chet stayed off heroin in Japan, taking only methadone, and as a consequence his playing became more powerful, his tone less fragile, and his execution cleaner, even at faster tempos. Chet was no stranger to hard bop, as albums like *In New York* and *Boppin'* clearly illustrate. But Chet had never sounded so convincing, so assured, as he does here on Jimmy Heath's 'For Minors Only' and Miles Davis' 'Seven Steps To Heaven'. His solos on ballads such as 'My Funny Valentine' and 'Arborway' are quite superb, effortlessly combining the dazzling, natural ability of his early years with the improvisational skill and emotional depth that marked the best of his later recordings. The Tokyo concert was recorded at the end of the tour, by which time Chet had forged a strong relationship with his band, which included his old friend Harold Danko. The material was originally released on two albums, *Memories* and *Four*, but is now available on a double CD, *Chet Baker in Tokyo*. The concert is also available on DVD. "Towards the end, on a good night, he could play jazz just as well as it has ever been played," wrote Mike Zwerin in *The Parisian Jazz Chronicles*. Here's the proof.

CHET BAKER AND WOLFGANG LACKERSCHMID: WELCOME BACK

Personnel: Chet Baker (tp), Wolfgang Lackerschmid (vib), Nicola Stilo (fl, g), Günter Lenz (b), Rocky Knauer (b), Peri dos Santos (g), Edir dos Santos (dr).
Date: August 1987
Place: Bischofsmais, Germany
Rating: 3.0
Chet reunited with Wolfgang Lackerschmid in August 1987 for a relaxed, low-key session recorded at an intimate studio, complete with an open fire. Three tunes are recorded as a trio, with Günter Lenz on bass, including a new version of 'Why Shouldn't You Cry'. Nicola Stilo joins on flute on two tracks, including a somewhat cluttered version of Lackerschmid's 'Christmas Waltz', which sounds under-rehearsed. There are two Latin-tinged tunes, 'Gloria's Answer' and 'Volta Trais', where the band are joined by two Brazilian musicians, Peri and Edir dos Santos. Chet apparently started to write lyrics to some of the tunes, but sadly, none of these pieces were recorded. The album was originally released as *Originals* on a label called

'Art and Sound', but has subsequently been re-released as *Welcome Back* on Westwind, and ASOJ (Another Side of Jazz) in Japan. The Japanese version is recommended for its superior mastering.

CHARLIE HADEN: SILENCE

Personnel: Charlie Haden (b), Chet Baker (tp, vo), Enrico Pieranunzi (p), Billy Higgins (b).
Date: November 1987
Place: Rome, Italy
Rating: 2.5
A great line-up, but a disappointing album. Charlie Haden was touring Italy with the Ornette Coleman/Don Cherry quartet, and arranged a recording session with Chet on a day off while he was in Rome. The session, which started late on November 11th, was plagued with difficulties. Chet had been arguing with his girlfriend Diane, which made for a tense atmosphere. He also insisted on shooting up in the recording studio, which may help to explain the plodding pace and ponderous solos on tunes such as Charlie Haden's 'Silence' and Monk's ''Round About Midnight'. Pianist Enrico Pieranunzi shines, however, contributing an elegant tune, 'Echi', as well as some delightful solos. Worth looking out for Pieranunzi's more recent meeting with Charlie Haden, *Special Encounter*, recorded for Cam Jazz in 2003.

CHET BAKER WITH THE NDR BIG BAND: THE LEGACY

Personnel: Chet Baker (tp), Lennart Axelsson (tp), Heinz Habermann (tp), Manfred Moch (tp), Paul Kubatsch (tp), Wolfgang Ahlers (tb), Hermann Plato (tb), Manfred Grobmann (tb), Egon Christmann (bass tb), Herb Geller (as), Jochen Ment (as), Stan Sulzman (ts), Harald Ende (ts), Werner Rönfeldt (bs), Walter Norris (p), John Schröder (g), Lucas Lindholm (b), Alex Riel (dr), Dieter Glawischnig (cond).
Date: November 1987
Place: Hamburg, Germany
Rating: 4.0
What a difference a day makes. Well, two days to be precise. The NDR Big Band, the resident orchestra of Norddeutscher Rundfunk (North German Radio) was established in 1945. Over the years, the orchestra had played with an array of visiting jazz stars, and even counted two veterans of the West Coast scene—Herb Geller and Walter Norris—among its ranks. The band's former producer, Wolfgang Kunert, had worked with Chet previously, and invited him to play with the band at a concert at the Audimax Hall at Hamburg University. Chet arrived

two days later than scheduled, probably because of the recording session in Italy, but still made it in time for a day of rehearsals. The arrangements are excellent; a number of interesting touches that liven up even the best-known standards, yet leaving plenty of space for Chet to stretch out. Chet responds to the challenge of playing with a big band, his tone sounding bright, and his solos more fluid than in Rome two days earlier. Highlights include a delightful version of 'All Of You', which brings the audience to its feet, and a fine arrangement of Miles Davis' 'All Blues', which Chet endeavours to make his own. The album was eventually released as the first volume of Enja's Legacy series. Highly recommended.

CHET BAKER: IN ITALY—UNISSUED 1975–1988

Personnel: Chet Baker (tp, vo), Larry Ridley (b), Kenny Drew (p), David Lee (dr), Various others.
Date: Various, 1975–1988
Place: Italy
Rating: 2.5
A collection of unissued bootleg-style recordings from various Italian tours, courtesy of Palo Piangiarelli, owner of Philology Records. Highlights include 'For Minors Only', recorded at Pescara in 1975, 'Blue Room'—an early recording with Michel Graillier and Jean-Louis Rassinfosse from January 1979, and Chet trading ideas with Italian trumpet player Enrico Rava from April 1988. This compilation has its moments, but the sound quality and performances are of varying quality. Again, for collectors only.

CHET BAKER: CHET ON POETRY

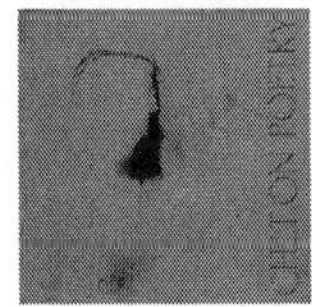

Personnel: Chet Baker (tp, vo), Nicola Stilo (fl, g, p, synth), Paul Cantos (fl), Enzo Pietropaoli (b), Roberto Gatto (dr), Diane Vavra (vo), Carla Marcotulli (vo).
Date: January 1988
Place: Rome, Italy
Rating: 2.0
Rare, and destined to stay that way. Most tracks consist of Chet reading poems by two Italian poets, Gianluca Mauri and Maurizio Guercini. Chet also sings 'Almost Blue', accompanied by Nicola Stilo on guitar.

CHET BAKER AND JAN ERIK VOLD: BLÅMANN! BLÅMANN!

Personnel: Jan Erik Vold (vo), Chet Baker (tp, vo), Philip Catherine (g), Egil Kapstad (p), Terje Venaas (b).
Date: February 1988
Place: Paris, France
Rating: 2.0
Another album of poetry, this time with Norwegian 'jazz poet' Jan Erik Vold. Vold had previously recorded with both Jan Garbarek and Red Mitchell, and was delighted when Chet agreed to work with him. Guitarist Philip Catherine was scheduled to play with Chet at the New Morning in Paris, and was invited to the recording session at the last minute. Chet was extremely professional, and asked to hear a translation of the poems before the recording session, so that he could capture the appropriate mood. For all that, it's not an easy listen unless you are familiar with the Norwegian language.

CHET BAKER AND ENRICO PIERANUNZI: THE HEART OF THE BALLAD

Personnel: Chet Baker (tp, vo), Enrico Pieranunzi (p).
Date: February 1988
Place: Recanati, Italy
Rating: 2.5
The Heart of the Ballad is incorrectly billed is Chet's last studio album. Paulo Piangiarelli had arranged a brief tour for Enrico Pieranunzi and his band, Space Jazz Trio, and invited Chet to play with the band. Chet and Enrico played one performance as a duo on February 28th in Ascoli, before recording next day at a small studio in Recanati. It's a disappointing album after Chet's album with Paul Bley from 1985; perhaps Pieranunzi was too respectful, and did not push Chet in the same way, or maybe it was wrong to expect too much from Chet so late in the day. Perhaps it was the multiple takes of 'But Beautiful', but Chet sounds weary on many of the tunes, and resorts to singing, rather than playing. The album has its moments—Chet's playing on the final take of 'But Beautiful' is excellent, 'Here's That Rainy Day' has a fragile beauty, and 'The Thrill Is Gone' captures his singing to good effect.

CHET BAKER MEETS SPACE JAZZ TRIO: LITTLE GIRL BLUE

Personnel: Chet Baker (tp, vo), Enrico Pieranunzi (p), Enzo Pietropaoli (b), Fabrizio Sferra (dr).
Date: March 1988
Place: Recanati, Italy
Rating: 3.5
Against all odds, Chet delivered a much stronger studio recording the very next day. Chet was sick after the duo recording, and Enrico Pieranunzi almost cancelled the concert that evening. In the end, Chet decided to play, and put on a fine performance. They were scheduled to record an album next day with Pieranunzi's band Space Jazz Trio, and Chet was on fine form. There's a rare chance to hear Chet perform Miles Davis' 'Blue In Green', from *Kind Of Blue*, and Chet takes the opportunity to slow the pace, lingering over the melody. 'Old Devil Moon' is taken at as faster pace than usual, and Wayne Shorter's 'House Of Jade', a regular in Chet's repertoire, is given a swinging reading. Another highlight is the title track, a tune that Chet had rarely played since it was recorded for *Embraceable You* back in 1957, with Chet delivering a dreamy vocal. The CD version includes on extra track, 'I Thought About You', which sounds like a warm-up, but is bizarrely placed first in the running order.

CHET BAKER AND ARCHIE SHEPP: IN MEMORY OF

Personnel: Chet Baker (tp, vo), Archie Shepp (ts, vo), Horace Parlan (p), Herman Wright (b), Clifford Jarvis (dr).
Date: March 1988
Place: Frankfurt, Germany and Paris, France
Rating: 2.5
It looked an unlikely combination on paper, and so it proved. The idea was originally proposed by a festival organiser in Frankfurt, after which Wim Wigt arranged a second concert the following night in Paris. Unfortunately, Chet missed the rehearsal for the festival, having impulsively decided to fly to Rome to buy a new car. As a consequence, he looked exhausted and the band was under-rehearsed. Material like 'Bessie Smith's Blues' was ill-suited to Chet's playing, and Shepp's bluesy shouting must have left him wishing he were elsewhere. In addition, Archie Shepp struggled to come to terms with Chet's playing style, filling every pause with a surge of notes. The second night was much better. Peter Huijts, Wim Wigt's right-hand man, insisted that Chet fly to Paris, instead of driving, so he was in better shape; he also took the trouble to talk with Shepp, and explain the way Chet normally played. The

second night was successful enough that they were booked to play at a concert in Laren on May 13th. When Chet failed to show, Huijts knew something was wrong.

CHET BAKER: LIVE IN ROSENHEIM

Personnel: Chet Baker (tp, vo, p), Nicola Stilo (fl, g), Luca Flores (p), Marc Abrams (b).
Date: April 1988
Place: Rosenheim, Germany
Rating: 2.5
Live in Rosenheim was issued posthumously, and is billed as 'Chet Baker's last recording as a quartet'. It has been suggested that Chet's performance is tired and lacklustre, but he sounds on fairly good form. The biggest problem is the bootleg quality of the recording; the microphone captures Marc Abrams and Nicola Stilo quite clearly, but Chet is low in the mix. On 'Portrait in Black and White', for example, Chet sounds as though he is playing offstage; we can barely hear his trumpet, and only get to hear him more clearly when he sits down at the piano. There's a lengthy version of Rique Pantoja's 'Arborway', but the tape is badly edited in the middle of the tune. Finally, some of Nicola Stilo's flute solos are overlong, which is made worse by his prominence in the mix. One that should have stayed in the vaults.

CHET BAKER: THE LAST GREAT CONCERT

Personnel: Chet Baker (tp, vo), Lennart Axelsson (tp), Heinz Habermann (tp), Bob Lanese (tp), Manfred Moch (tp), Wolfgang Ahlers (tb), Hermann Plato (tb), Manfred Grossmann (tb), Egon Christmann (tb), Herb Geller (as), Emil Wurster (as), Andreas Boether (ts), Harald Ende (ts), Klaus Nagurski (ts), Walter Norris (p), Wolfgang Schlüter (vib), John Schröder (g), Lucas Lindholm (b), Aage Tanggaard (dr), Hanover Radio Orchestra, Dieter Glawischnig (cond).
Date: April 1988
Place: Hanover, Germany
Rating: 4.0
The Last Great Concert saw Chet reunited with the NDR Big Band, this time accompanied by the Hanover Radio Orchestra. Kurt Giese, a former drummer, worked as a radio producer for NDR, and had long dreamed producing an updated version of *Chet Baker With Strings*. Although Chet missed the first two days of rehearsals, he arrived in time to listen to the recordings the orchestra had made, and memorise the arrangements. Chet's playing sounds somewhat below par on the first few tunes, including 'All Blues' and 'My Funny Valentine'.

He had been having problems with his teeth, and may have worried whether they would stay in place, or he may simply have been tired. Either way, his playing and singing improves steadily as the concert progresses. His playing is a delight on Brubeck's 'In Your Own Sweet Way', and he delivers memorable versions of two of his early vocal recordings, 'I Fall In Love Too Easily' and 'I Get Along Without You Very Well'. The arrangements and recording quality are also superb, providing a fitting farewell.

TEN CHET BAKER RECORDS EVERYONE SHOULD OWN.

Gerry Mulligan Quartet: The Original Quartet with Chet Baker (1952–1953)

Where it all began…

Chet Baker Quartet: Featuring Russ Freeman (1952–1953)

A good introduction to the Chet Baker Quartet.

Chet Baker: The Best of Chet Baker Sings

The best of Chet's vocal-oriented albums. His later vocal recordings tend to be more of an acquired taste.

Chet Baker: In Paris - Barclay Sessions (1955–1956)

Chet's legendary quartet with Dick Twardzik, and lots more…

Jim Hall: Concierto (1975)

One of guitarist Jim Hall's finest albums, featuring a fine arrangement of 'Concierto de Aranjuez' by Don Sebesky. Chet's playing shines, and it is probably the best of his 1970s recordings.

Chet Baker Trio: Mr. B (1983)

A great example of Chet's 'drummerless' trio recordings, featuring pianist Michel Graillier and bass player Riccard Del Fra. Chet has moved away from the 'bop' oriented sound of the late 1970s and early 1980s to a softer, more melancholic tone that tended to be a feature of his later recordings.

Chet Baker: Diane (1985)

A tough call, but Chet's duo album with Paul Bley is probably the pick of his fine recordings for SteepleChase.

Chet Baker: Chet's Choice (1985)

The best recording by Chet's trip with guitarist Philip Catherine and bass player Jean-Louis Rassinfosse, the sound well captured by engineer Max Bolleman.

Chet Baker: Live From The Moonlight (1985)

The sound quality on this live trio recording is below par, but Chet was on majestic form, delivering lengthy solos that are bristling with ideas.

Chet Baker: Chet Baker in Tokyo (1987)

"Towards the end, on a good night, he could play jazz just as well as it has ever been played," wrote Mike Zwerin in 'The Parisian Jazz Chronicles'. Here's the proof.

Acknowledgements

First of all, I would like to acknowledge the support of Ruth Young, without whom this book would never have been written. Her encouragement, warmth, humour and unflinching honesty provided an invaluable insight into Chet's character, and helped to bring the story to life. Likewise Micheline Pelzer, who generously gave her time, told me some wonderful anecdotes, and was kind enough to invite me to her family home.

A special mention must also be made of certain people who went out of their way to help me. Bob Whitlock, who provided an invaluable insight into Chet's formative years, and was kind enough to send me details of an old interview he had given. Liliane Rovère, who had fond memories of the time she spent on tour with Chet in the 1950s. The late Phil Urso, who took me back to his younger days, and had some amazing tales to tell. Hod O'Brien, who sent me a cassette tape of stories – some of them funny, some of them sad, but all delivered with warmth and good humour. Jean-Louis Rassinfosse, who patiently put up with my endless questions, and Riccardo del Fra, who helped to explain what made some of Chet's later recordings so special. Nicola Stilo, who was a kind host, and introduced me to so many of Chet's friends in Rome. Francesco 'Cecco' Maino, who remembered so much about Chet's time in Italy, and gave me a copy of the court transcripts from Chet's trial in Lucca. Pia Richardson and Serenella Martufi, who kindly translated the manuscripts. Peter Mansell, who's phenomenal work updating Chet's long discography hopefully prevented me from making too many errors in this book. And Guy Barker, who shared with me his fond recollection of Chet, and was kind enough to help with the launch of the book.

Thanks to the many friends and musicians who agreed to be interviewed for *Funny Valentine* – your help was greatly appreciated, and I hope you enjoy the book. Erling Aksdal, Giampaolo Ascolese, Robert Badgley, Colin

Bailey, Paul Baker, Alexander Bally, Gary Barone, Paul Bley, Lars Bloch, Max Bolleman, Jeff Brillinger, Till Brönner, Jon Burr, Gary Burton, Ed Byrne, Graham Carter, Philip Catherine, Jack Chambers, Warren Chiasson, William Claxton, Jim Coleman, Brian Cooke, Larry Coryell, Elvis Costello, Ron Crotty, Michael Cuscuna, Harold Danko, Margaret Davis, Hein Van De Geijn, Riccardo Del Fra, João Donato, Tómas Einarsson, John Engels, Georgie Fame, Bertrand Fèvre, Clare Fischer, Donna Fischer, Robb Fisher, Melissa Forbes, Artt Frank, Bob Freedman, David Friedman, Paolo Fresu, Hal Galper, Luiz Gasca, Herb Geller, Gianpiero Giusti, Johnny Griffin, Henry Grimes, Eddie de Haas, Chico Hamilton, Evert Hekkema, Bill Holman, Steve Houben, Jim Hughart, Daniel Humair, Sandi Hummer, Per Husby, Dennis Irwin, Melker Isaksson, Bob James, Kjell Jansson, Hans Kennel, Stacey Kent, Joanne Klein, Ken Koenig, Jeffrey Kruger, Rolf Kuehn, Wolfgang Lackerschmid, Victor Lewis, Kirk Lightsey, Joe LoCascio, Lorne Lofsky, Bill Loughborough, Jesper Lundgaard, Dennis Luxion, Jimmy Madison, Phil Markowitz, Rod McKuen, Ron McLure, Jim McNeely, Martin Montenegro, Jack Montrose, Bob Mover, Stephanie Nakasian, Walter Norris, Rique Pantoja, 'Sebby' Papa, Enrico Pieranunzi, Enzo Pietropaoli, Jim Porto, Lillo Quarantino, Doug Raney, Danilo Rea, Rufus Reid, Larry Ridley, Ben Riley, Claudio Roditi, Gabriel Rosati, Roger Rosenberg, Annie Ross, Cicci Santucci, John Scofield, Don Sebesky, Bud Shank, Jack Sheldon, Bobby Shew, John Snyder, Curtis Stigers, Olafur Stephenson, Frank Strazzeri, Naoki Tachikawa, Aage Tanggaard, Lilian Terry, 'Toots' Thielemans, Amadeo Tommasi, Giovanni Tommaso, Luigi Trussardi, Joyce Tucker, Cherry Vanilla, Paul Warburton, Ria Wigt, Pinky Winters, Nils Winther, Ingo Wulff, Bob Zieff and Mike Zwerin.

I would also like to thank the numerous photographers who gave me permission to use their images, and individuals who allowed me to use their personal snapshots, including Graziano Arici, Ray Avery, William Claxton, 'Cecco' Maino, 'Sebby' Papa, Eddy Posthuma de Boer, Pieter Boersma, Cecil Charles, Hans Kumpf, Jacky Lepage, John Engels, Denis Alex, Bertrand Fèvre, Jak Kilby, Paolo Gant, Hajo Piebenga, Tómas Einarsson and Ruth Young.

It's also important to mention the help and inspiration I took from other authors who have written about Chet Baker over the years. Michael Cuscuna introduced me to 'Chet – A Discography' by Thorbjorn Sjogren, which was not only an invaluable resource, but got me started on this whole project.

Jeroen de Valk's biography, 'Chet Baker – His Life and Music', was a useful source of information and rare interviews, and even more importantly, has done much to boost the popularity of Chet's later recordings. James Gavin's biography, 'Deep in a Dream', set the benchmark for detailed research, and inspired me to dig deeper in search for original content for this book. Last but not least, William Claxton's book of photos and anecdotes, 'Young Chet', was pleasing on the eye, and several of the photographs from that book have been included in *Funny Valentine.*

Mosaic Records has provided jazz fans around the world with countless treasures over the years. I was lucky enough to pick up second hand copies of their Original Gerry Mulligan Quartet box set, and their two Chet Baker/ Russ Freeman collections in Tokyo back in 1994, and the long-term love affair started there. Michael Cuscuna and the late Charlie Lourie were kind enough to chat with me when I was passing through Stamford, and later provided me with my first leads when starting this book.

Thank you to everyone at Melrose Books – for your faith in the book, and helping to make my dream a reality. Especially Jill de Laat, who managed the project as a whole, production co-ordinator Gwyn Law, editor Nick Smith and marketing co-ordinator Rachel Hutchinson.

At times it felt like this book would never be completed, especially since I had to combine my writing with a time-consuming day job. Thanks to the many friends around the world who encouraged me to persevere, including Todd Martin, Phil Barnes, Sean Hughes, Peter Guy, Mike Kukreja, Markus Thielen, Maria Abbonizio, Tom and Jane Welch, Amanda Bradford, Jane Foran, Brian Brown, Dean and Sally Cashman, Clarence Chang, Natalie Tong and Rudi Leung, John Fildes, Alistair and Catherine Gough, Rupa Graham, Bethan Hutton, Chris Newton and Masyuki Koito.

Thanks to my Mum and my late father, who taught me right from wrong, and always believed in me. My sister, Louise, for being the best sister and a great friend. And last, but not least, my family, for the love, support and encouragement over the years. This book is dedicated to you.

Notes

Prologue

1 Frank Wilkinson, letter to Charles Neighbors, September 14th 1981.
2 Ruth Young, interview with author, June 2007.
3 Bob Whitlock, excerpt from an interview with Gordon Jack.
4 Orrin Keepnews, sleevenotes to *Chet*, Keepnews collection edition.
5 Colin Bailey, interview with author, October 2009.
6 Micheline Graillier, interview with author, April 2006.
7 Bud Shank, excerpt from *Chet Baker: His Life and Music* by Jeroen de Valk.
8 Mike Zwerin, excerpt from an interview by Farah Nayeri, *Bloomberg News*.
9 Riccardo Del Fra, interview with author, April 2006.
10 Chet Baker, excerpt from *Young Chet* by William Claxton.
11 Ruth Young, ibid.

Chapter One

1 Carol Baker, excerpt from the Introduction to *As Though I Had Wings*.
2 Lee Tanner, excerpt from a magazine article *Chet Baker in Black & White*.
3 Ron McClure, interview with author, January 2006.
4 William Claxton, excerpt from *Young Chet*.
5 Carol Baker, excerpt from an interview with Jerry Jazz Musician.
6 Rod McKuen, e-mail to author May 2008.
7 William Claxton, ibid.
8 William Claxton, ibid.
9 'Story of Chet Baker', excerpt from *DownBeat* magazine, 12th August 1953.
10 Excerpt from 'Soul on Ice, And a Twist', *Newsweek*, 12th March 2007.
11 Gary Burton, e-mail to author February 2006.
12 Terrence Rafferty, *New York Times*, 3rd June 2007.
13 Chet Baker, excerpt from *As Though I Had Wings*.
14 Headline in *The Daily Oklahoman*, 27th September 1931.
15 Chet Baker, excerpt from a conversation with Lisa Galt Bond, 1980.
16 The (Oklahoma City) Journal record, Part IV – Oklahoma City during the 1930s.
17 Chet Baker, 'The Trumpet and the Spike—A Confession by Chet', date unknown.
18 Chet Baker, excerpt from *As Though I Had Wings*.
19 Chet Baker, ibid.
20 Chet Baker, excerpt from an interview in *Jazz Hot* magazine, November 1983.
21 Chet Baker, 'The Trumpet and the Spike—A Confession by Chet', date unknown.
22 Dr Alan R. Lang, 'The Addictive Personality', *New York Times*, 18th January 1983.
23 Diane Vavra, excerpt from *Deep in a Dream* by James Gavin.
24 Ruth Young, interview with author, April 2007.
25 Dr Leon Wurmser, 'The Addictive Personality', *New York Times*, 8th January 1983.
26 Diane Vavra, from *Deep in a Dream* by James Gavin.
27 Carol Baker, excerpt from *Chet Baker—His Life and Times* by Jeroen de Valk.

28 Ruth Young, ibid.
29 Ruth Young, ibid.
30 Chet Baker, excerpt from a conversation with Lisa Galt Bond, 1980.
31 Chet Baker, from an interview with Gudrun Endress, *Jazz Podium* magazine, 1980.
32 Diane Vavra, excerpt from *Deep in a Dream* by James Gavin.
33 Chet Baker, excerpt from *As Though I Had Wings*.
34 Chet Baker, interview with Gerard Rouy, *The Wire*, November 1985.

Chapter Two

1 Chet Baker, interview with Les Tomkins, Roundhouse, London, March 1979.
2 Chet Baker, excerpt from *As Though I Had Wings*.
3 Chet Baker, ibid.
4 Chet Baker, ibid.
5 Sebastian 'Sebby' Papa, excerpt from Berlin-Brigade website.
6 Sebastian 'Sebby' Papa, interview with author, June 2008.
7 Jim Coleman, interview with author, January 2006.
8 Chet Baker, ibid.
9 Bob Badgley, e-mail to author, July 2008.
10 Chet Baker, ibid.
11 Ted Gioia, *The History of Jazz*, excerpt from Chapter Six: Modern Jazz'
12 Chet Baker, interview with Les Tomkins, Roundhouse, London, March 1979.
13 Chet Baker, excerpt from *As Though I Had Wings*.
14 Chet Baker, ibid.
15 Bernie Fleischer, excerpt from *Deep in a Dream*, by James Gavin.
16 Chet Baker, excerpt from *As Though I Had Wings*.
17 Chet Baker, excerpt from '30,000 Hell-Holes in My Arm', *Today*, February 2nd 1963
18 Chet Baker, interview with *L'Europeo*, 1961.
19 Art Pepper, excerpt from *Straight Life*, by Art and Laurie Pepper.
20 Jack Sheldon, interview with author, May 2007.
21 Bill Holman, interview with author, May 2007.
22 Bill Holman, ibid.
23 Jack Sheldon, from *Let's Get Lost*, directed by Bruce Weber.
24 Chet Baker, excerpt from *As Though I Had Wings*.
25 Jack Sheldon, ibid.
26 Bill Holman, ibid.
27 Jack Sheldon, ibid.
28 Hersh Hamel, excerpt from *Straight Life*, by Art and Laurie Pepper.
29 'Everything Happens To Me'; Music by Matt Dennis, lyrics by Thomas Adair.
30 Chet Baker, excerpt from *As Though I Had Wings*.
31 Chet Baker, interview with Les Tomkins, Roundhouse, London, March 1979.
32 Bob Whitlock, interview with author, June 2007.
33 Bob Whitlock, ibid.
34 Bob Whitlock, excerpt from *Deep in a Dream*, by James Gavin.
35 Bob Whitlock, interview with author, June 2007.
36 Bob Whitlock, excerpt from an interview with Gordon Jack.
37 Bob Whitlock, interview with author, June 2007.
38 Bob Whitlock, ibid.
39 Bob Whitlock, ibid.
40 Chet Baker, excerpt from *As Though I Had Wings*.
41 Bob Whitlock, ibid.

42 Chet Baker, excerpt from *As Though I Had Wings*.
43 Bob Whitlock, ibid.

Chapter Three

1 Chet Baker, interview with Brian Case, *Melody Maker*, 14th April 1979.
2 Ted Gioia, excerpt from *West Coast Jazz*.
3 Harry 'Sweets' Edison, from *Blues for Central Avenue*, directed by Lois Shelton, 1986.
4 Howard Rumsey, *Jazz on the West Coast: The Lighthouse*' directed by Ken Koenig.
5 Howard Rumsey, interview with Dick Williams, *LA Mirror*, October 16th 1954.
6 Ken Koenig, interview by Whitney Youngs, *The Beach Reporter*, 24th August 2005.
7 Chet Baker, excerpt from *As Though I Had Wings*.
8 Chet Baker, ibid.
9 Bob Whitlock, interview with author, June 2007.
10 Jack Sheldon, interview with author, June 2007.
11 Jack Sheldon, excerpt from *Let's Get Lost*, directed by Bruce Weber.
12 Chet Baker, excerpt from *As Though I Had Wings*.
13 Chet Baker, from *All That Jazz, All Those Girls, All That Dope!* date unknown.
14 Bob Whitlock, ibid.
15 Herb Geller, interview with author, October 2005.
16 Jack Sheldon, excerpt from *Deep In A Dream* by James Gavin.
17 Jack Sheldon, interview with author, June 2007.
18 Chet Baker, excerpt from *As Though I Had Wings*.
19 Bob Whitlock, ibid.
20 Chet Baker, ibid.
21 Bob Whitlock, ibid.
22 Chet Baker, interview with Les Tomkins, Roundhouse, London, March 1979.
23 Chet Baker, excerpt from *As Though I Had Wings*.
24 Chet Baker, excerpt from *Let's Get Lost*, directed by Bruce Weber.
25 Bob Freedman, interview with author, June 2008.
26 Bob Freedman, ibid.
27 Bob Freedman, ibid.
28 Bob Freedman, ibid.
29 Bob Freedman, ibid.
30 Bob Freedman, excerpt from *Deep In A Dream* by James Gavin.
31 Chet Baker, excerpt from *As Though I Had Wings*.
32 Russ Freeman, excerpt from liner notes to Mosaic Box Set MR4-122.
33 Bob Whitlock, interview with author, August 2008.
34 Chet Baker, excerpt from *As Though I Had Wings*.
35 Chet Baker, ibid.
36 Ted Gioia, excerpt from *West Coast Jazz*.
37 Teddy Edwards, excerpt from interview in Cadence, April 1994.
38 Teddy Edwards, ibid.
39 Chet Baker, excerpt from *As Though I Had Wings*.
40 Bob Whitlock, ibid.
41 Jack Sheldon, interview with author, May 2007.
42 Charlie Parker, excerpt from *The History of Jazz*, by Ted Gioia.
43 Chet Baker, excerpt from *As Though I Had Wings*.
44 William Claxton, excerpt from his book *Young Chet*.
45 William Claxton, ibid.
46 William Claxton, ibid.

47 Bob Whitlock, interview with author, September 2008.
48 Bob Whitlock, ibid.
49 Chet Baker, excerpt from *As Though I Had Wings*.
50 Chet Baker, ibid.
51 Bob Whitlock, interview with author, June 2007.

Chapter Four

1 Chet Baker, interview with Gudrun Endress, *Jazz Podium magazine*, 1978.
2 Gerry Mulligan from an interview with M. Abramson, *Telegraph*, November 20th 1959.
3 Gerry Mulligan from *Jeru: In the Words of Gerry Mulligan*, Library of Congress.
4 Gerry Mulligan from *Jeru: In the Words of Gerry Mulligan*, Library of Congress.
5 Gerry Mulligan from *Jeru: In the Words of Gerry Mulligan*, Library of Congress.
6 Miles Davis from *Miles, The Autobiography*.
7 Miles Davis from *Miles, The Autobiography*.
8 Gerry Mulligan from *Jeru: In the Words of Gerry Mulligan*, Library of Congress.
9 John Carisi from *West Coast Jazz*, by Ted Gioia.
10 Miles Davis from *Miles, The Autobiography*.
11 Gerry Mulligan from *Jeru: In the Words of Gerry Mulligan*, Library of Congress.
12 Miles Davis from *Miles, The Autobiography*.
13 Gerry Mulligan from *Jeru: In the Words of Gerry Mulligan*, Library of Congress.
14 Gerry Mulligan from *Jeru: In the Words of Gerry Mulligan*, Library of Congress.
15 Gerry Mulligan from *Jeru: In the Words of Gerry Mulligan*, Library of Congress.
16 Winthrop Sargeant from *Jazz Hot and Hybrid.*
17 Bob Whitlock, interview with author, July 2007.
18 Gerry Mulligan from an interview with Gordon Jack, *Jazz Journal International.*
19 Gerry Mulligan from *Jeru: In the Words of Gerry Mulligan*, Library of Congress.
20 Bob Whitlock, interview with author, July 2007.
21 Bob Whitlock, interview with author, June 2007.
22 Bob Whitlock, interview with author, June 2007.
23 Jack Montrose, interview with author October 2005.
24 Dick Bock, liner notes to Mosaic Records MR5-102.
25 Bob Whitlock, excerpt from an interview by Gordon Jack.
26 Gerry Mulligan from *Jeru: In the Words of Gerry Mulligan*, Library of Congress.
27 Bob Whitlock, interview with author, June 2007.
28 Chet Baker from *As Though I Had Wings*.
29 Buddy Collette from J*azz Generations: A Life in American Music and Society*.
30 Bob Whitlock, interview with author, June 2007.
31 Gerry Mulligan from *Jeru: In the Words of Gerry Mulligan*, Library of Congress.
32 Gerry Mulligan from *Jeru: In the Words of Gerry Mulligan*, Library of Congress.
33 Bob Whitlock, interview with author, June 2007.
34 Bob Whitlock, interview with author, June 2007.
35 Dick Bock, liner notes to Mosaic Records MR5-102.
36 Bob Whitlock, interview with author, June 2007.
37 Gerry Mulligan from *Jeru: In the Words of Gerry Mulligan*, Library of Congress.
38 Gerry Mulligan, excerpt of an interview with Gordon Jack.
39 Bob Whitlock, excerpt of an interview with Gordon Jack.
40 Ralph Gleason from *DownBeat*, October 22nd 1952.
41 Bob Whitlock, excerpt of an interview with Gordon Jack.
42 Bill Holman, interview with author, June 2007.
43 Bob Whitlock, excerpt of an interview with Gordon Jack.

44 Bob Whitlock, ibid.
45 Chet Baker, interview with Brian Case, *Melody Maker*, April 14th 1979
46 *DownBeat* magazine, January 14th 1953
47 Bob Whitlock, interview with author, June 2007.
48 Walter Norris, interview with author, October 2005.
49 Bob Whitlock, interview with author, July 2007.
50 Bob Whitlock, interview with author, July 2007.
51 Excerpt from 'The Hollywood Beat', *DownBeat* magazine, May 20th 1953.
52 Jack Montrose, interview with author October 2005.
53 Walter Norris, interview with author, October 2005
54 Chico Hamilton, excerpt from *Fifties Jazz Talk*, by Gordon Jack.
55 Chet Baker from *As Though I Had Wings*.
56 Bob Whitlock, interview with author, June 2007.
57 Bob Whitlock, interview with author, June 2007.
58 Excerpt from *DownBeat*, April 8th 1953.
59 Joyce Tucker, interview with author, July 2006.
60 Joyce Tucker, interview with author, July 2006.
61 Joyce Tucker, interview with author, July 2006.
62 Gerry Mulligan, liner notes to Mosaic Records MR5-102.
63 Chico Hamilton, excerpt from *Fifties Jazz Talk*, by Gordon Jack.
64 Excerpt from *DownBeat*, October 7th 1953.
65 Walter Norris, interview with author, October 2005.
66 Excerpt from *Time* magazine, February 2nd 1953
67 Walter Norris, interview with author, October 2005.
68 Excerpt from *DownBeat*, April 8th 1953.
69 Excerpt from *DownBeat*, April 8th 1953.
70 Bob Brookmeyer, interview by Alyn Shipton, *Jazzwise* magazine, May 2007.
71 Excerpt from *DownBeat*, January 1989.
72 Bill Crow, from *Jazz Heroes* by John Fordham.
73 Walter Norris, interview with author, October 2005.
74 Chet Baker from *As Though I Had Wings*.
75 Herb Geller, interview with author, October 2005.
76 John O'Grady from O'Grady: *The Life & Times of Hollywood's No. 1 Private Eye*.
77 Chet Baker from *As Though I Had Wings*.
78 Excerpt from *Los Angeles Mirror*, April 14th 1953.
79 Chet Baker from *As Though I Had Wings*.
80 Joyce Tucker, interview with author, July 2006.
81 Joyce Tucker, ibid.
82 Bill Loughborough, interview with author, April 2006.
83 Walter Norris, interview with author, October 2005.
84 Bob Whitlock, interview with author, June 2007.
85 Bob Brookmeyer, interview with Alyn Shipton, *Jazzwise* magazine, May 2007.
86 Bob Whitlock, interview with author, June 2007.
87 Nat Hentoff, excerpt from *DownBeat* magazine, September 1953.
88 Chet Baker, excerpt from *As Though I Had Wings*.
89 Chet Baker, interview with Jeroen Reece, *Jazz Hot*, November 1983.
90 Bob Whitlock, excerpt from an interview by Gordon Jack.

Chapter Five

1 Herb Geller, interview with author, October 2005.
2 Excerpt from *DownBeat* article, August 12th 1953.
3 Saundra Hummer, *The Birthplace of Cool: A Look at the Lighthouse California*, 2005.
4 Saundra Hummer, ibid.
5 Dick Bock, liner notes to Mosaic Records MR4-122.
6 Russ Freeman, liner notes to Mosaic Records MR4-122.
7 Ibid.
8 Ibid.
9 Doug Ramsey, liner notes to Mosaic Records MR4-122.
10 Bill Loughborough, interview with author, April 2006.
11 William Claxton, excerpt from *Young Chet*, originally published 1993.
12 Ruth Young, interview with author, March 2007.
13 Excerpt from *DownBeat* magazine, 10th August 1955.
14 Robert Gordon, excerpt from *Jazz West Coast*, p83.
15 Ron Crotty, interview with author.
16 Herb Geller, interview with author, October 2005.
17 Dick Bock, liner notes to Mosaic Records MR4-122.
18 Herb Geller, Ibid.
19 Jack Montrose, interview with author, October 2005.
20 Jack Montrose, from *Jazz Generations* by Buddy Collette.
21 Jack Montrose, interview with author, October 2005.
22 Chet Baker, interview with Mike Nevard, *Melody Maker*, November 21st 1953.
23 Excerpt from *DownBeat* magazine, July 14th 1954.
24 Russ Freeman, from *Chet Baker: His Life and Music*, by J. de Valk.
25 Liliane Rovere, interview with author, April 2006.
26 Ibid.
27 Miles Davis, excerpt from *Miles: The Autobiography*.
28 Excerpt from *DownBeat* magazine, October 31st 1956.
29 Ben Riley, interview with author, June 2007.
30 Excerpt from *DownBeat* magazine, June 2nd 1954.
31 Liliane Rovere, interview with author, April 2006.
32 Ibid.
33 Ibid.
34 Bill Holman, interview with author, June 2007.
35 Excerpt from *DownBeat* magazine, December 29th 1954.
36 Russ Freeman, from *Chet Baker: His Life and Music*, by J. de Valk.
37 Ibid.
38 Excerpt from *Bird Lives!* (R. Russell).
39 Phil Urso, interview with author, May 2005.
40 Ibid.
41 Phil Urso, from a taped interview, taken from *Chet: A Discography* by T. Sjogren.
42 Phil Urso, interview with author, May 2005.
43 Phil Urso, ibid.
44 Phil Urso, ibid.
45 Paul Bley, interview with author, March 2005.
46 Phil Urso, from a taped interview, taken from *Chet: A Discography* by T. Sjogren.
47 Phil Urso, interview with author, May 2005.
48 Bob Whitlock, interview with author, June 2007.
49 Ibid.

50 Ibid.
51 Russ Freeman, liner notes to Mosaic Records MR4-113.
52 Bob Whitlock, e-mail to author, August 2008.
53 Paul Bley, interview with author, March 2005.
54 Paul Bley, ibid.
55 Bob Whitlock, interview with author, June 2007.
56 Bob Whitlock, e-mail to author, August 2008.
57 Paul Bley, ibid.
58 Excerpt from *DownBeat* magazine, August 10th 1955.
59 Excerpt from *Metronome* magazine, August 1955.
60 Excerpt from *DownBeat* magazine, April 6th 1955.
61 Excerpt from *'Cool and Hot' in Jazz Journal*, May 1955.
62 Bill Coss, excerpt from *Metronome* magazine, July 1955.
63 Liliane Rovere, ibid.
64 Russ Freeman, excerpt from *Deep In A Dream*, by James Gavin.
65 Bob Freedman, excerpt from *Deep In A Dream*, by James Gavin.

Chapter Six

1 Chet Baker, from *Let's Get Lost*, directed by Bruce Weber.
2 Russ Freeman, liner notes to *Trio*, PJ-1212.
3 Anecdotes from *Bouncin' with Bartok—The Incomplete Works of Richard Twardzik*, by Jack Chambers.
4 Jack Chambers, excerpt from *Bouncin' with Bartok.*
5 Excerpt from *Bouncin' with Bartok* by Jack Chambers.
6 Crystal Joy, from *Deep in a Dream* by James Gavin.
7 Crystal Joy, from *Bouncin' with Bartok* by Jack Chambers.
8 Chet Baker, from *As Though I Had Wings*.
9 Dr Jeffrey Kruger, interview with author, April 2006.
10 Excerpt from *Melody Maker*, September 24th 1955.
11 Excerpt from *Bouncin' with Bartok* by Jack Chambers.
12 Chet Baker Quartet: The Lost Holland Concert (RLR Records).
13 Liliane Rovère, interview with author, April 2006.
14 Ibid.
15 Dr Jeffrey Kruger, interview with author, April 2006.
16 Louis Scali, from *Actualité Musicale*.
17 Excerpt from autobiography of Dr Jeffrey Kruger (unpublished).
18 Dr Jeffrey Kruger, interview with author, April 2006.
19 Richard Twardzik, from *Bouncin' with Bartok* by Jack Chambers.
20 Excerpt from *Bouncin' with Bartok* by Jack Chambers.
21 Chet Baker, from *As Though I Had Wings*.
22 Bob Zieff, interview with author, March 2006.
23 Bob Zieff, excerpt from *Bouncin' with Bartok* by Jack Chambers.
24 Excerpt from *Bouncin' with Bartok* by Jack Chambers.
25 Bob Zieff, interview with author, March 2006.
26 Excerpt from *Revenge of the Underground Composer* by Jack Chambers.
27 Excerpt from autobiography of Dr Jeffrey Kruger (unpublished).
28 Ibid.
29 Dr Jeffrey Kruger, interview with author, April 2006.
30 Eric van Aro, excerpt from *Bouncin' with Bartok* by Jack Chambers.
31 Also available on CD on *Chet Baker Quintet: Conservatorio Cherubini.*

32 Lars Resberg, *Estrad*, December 1955.
33 Excerpt from 'The Trumpet and the Spike', *Today* magazine, date unknown.
34 Daniel Humair, interview with author, April 2006.
35 Ibid.
36 Excerpt from *Bouncin' with Bartok* by Jack Chambers (unpublished).
37 Chet Baker, interview by Chet (jpgchet.jpg) © Pär Rittsel 1985–2000.
38 Roger Guérin, from *Une Vie dans le Jazz*, by Roger Guérin and Laurent Rieu.
39 Excerpt from *Bouncin' with Bartok* by Jack Chambers (unpublished).
40 Eddie de Haas, interview with author, December 2005.
41 Ibid.
42 Excerpt from autobiography of Dr Jeffrey Kruger (unpublished).
43 Ibid.
44 Dr Jeffrey Kruger, interview with author, April 2006.
45 Excerpt from *Deep In A Dream* by James Gavin, 2002.
46 Liliane Rovère, interview with author, April 2006.
47 Excerpt from 'Young Man Without a Horn', *Melody Maker,* October 29th 1955.
48 Dr Jeffrey Kruger, interview with author, April 2006.
49 Eddie de Haas, interview with author, December 2005.
50 Chet Baker, from '30,000 Hell-Holes in My Arm', *Today*, February 2nd 1963.
51 Ibid.
52 Laurie Pepper, excerpt from *Straight Life* by Art and Laurie Pepper.
53 Gérard Gustin, from Alain Gerber's sleevenotes to the *LP House of Jazz Vol. 11*.
54 Eddie de Haas, interview with author, December 2005.
55 Excerpt from *Melody Maker*, November 12th 1955.
56 Oli Stephenson, interview with author, December 2005.
57 Dr Jeffrey Kruger, interview with author, April 2006.
58 Jimmy Bond, interview in *Chet's Choice Vol. V, No. 4*.
59 Oli Stephenson, interview with author, December 2005.
60 Eddie de Haas, ibid.
61 Oli Stephenson, ibid.
62 Giancarlo Testoni, from *Chet Baker a Milano*, Musica Jazz.
63 Excerpt from *DownBeat* magazine, May 2nd 1956.
64 Jean-Louis Chautemps, liner notes to *The Complete 1955–1956 Barclay Sessions*.
65 Cicci Santucci, interview with author, April 2006.
66 Jean-Louis Chautemps, ibid.
67 Ibid.
68 Eddie de Haas, ibid.
69 Jean-Louis Chautemps, ibid.
70 Liliane Rovère, interview with author, April 2006.
71 Adriano Mazzoletti, liner notes to *The Complete 1955–1956 Barclay Sessions*.
72 Ibid.

Chapter Seven

1 Miles Davis, excerpt from *DownBeat* magazine, November 2nd 1955.
2 Nat Hentoff, excerpt from *DownBeat* magazine, November 28th 1956.
3 Charlie Mingus, excerpt from *DownBeat* magazine, November 30th 1955.
4 Miles Davis, excerpt from *Miles: The Autobiography* by Davis/Troupe.
5 George Avakian, liner notes to 1997 reissue of *Miles Ahead*.
6 Halema Alli, from *Deep in a Dream* by James Gavin.
7 Ibid.

8 Bob Zieff, interview with author, March 2006.
9 Phil Urso, interview with author, May 2005.
10 Ibid.
11 Graham Carter, e-mail to author, May 2005.
12 Bill Loughborough, interview with author, April 2006.
13 Ibid.
14 Nat Hentoff, excerpt from *DownBeat* magazine, April 4th 1957.
15 Bill Loughborough, interview with author, April 2006.
16 Chet Baker, excerpt from 'The Trumpet and the Spike', *Today*, 1963.
17 Phil Urso, excerpt from *The Philosophy of Urso* by T.R. Witcher.
18 Chet Baker, excerpt from '30,000 Hell-Holes in my Arm', *Today*, February 1963.
19 Chet Baker, from 'Les Confidences de Chet Baker', *Jazz Hot*, November 1983.
20 William Claxton, from *Young Chet* by William Claxton.
21 Jimmy Heath, from *Chet Baker, His Life & Music* by Jeroen de Valk.
22 William Claxton, from *Young Chet* by William Claxton.
23 Jeroen de Valk, from *Chet Baker: His Life And Music.*
24 Excerpt from *Jade Visions: The Life And Music of Scott LaFaro* by Helene LaFaro-Fernández.
25 Shelly Manne, from *Jazz West Coast* by Robert Gordon.
26 Excerpt from *Jade Visions: The Life And Music of Scott LaFaro* by Helene LaFaro-Fernández.
27 Ibid.
28 Paul Warburton, interview with author, October 2009.
29 Ibid.
30 Available on CD. *Two Trumpet Geniuses of the Fifties: Brownie and Chet* (Philology Records).
31 Phil Urso, interview with author, May 2005.
32 Excerpt from *Jade Visions: The Life And Music of Scott LaFaro*, by Helene LaFaro-Fernández
33 Rolf Kühn, interview with author, April 2008.
34 Albert Heath, excerpt from *Deep In A Dream* by James Gavin.
35 L.A. Times, May 1st 1957, *Dallas Morning News*, May 10th 1957.
36 Phil Urso, interview with author, May 2005.
37 John Tynan, excerpt from *DownBeat* magazine, August 22nd 1957.
38 Donald Friedman, from *Deep in a Dream*, by James Gavin.
39 Chet Baker, excerpt from *As Though I Had Wings*.
40 Chet Baker, Ibid.
41 Jack Sheldon, interview with author, May 2007.

Chapter Eight

1 Chet Baker, from 'All That Jazz, All Those Girls, All That Dope', *Today*, March 1963.
2 Bob Belden, excerpt from liner notes to Mosaic Records MQ11-164.
3 Ira Gitler, excerpt from liner notes to Thelonious Monk with John Coltrane (JLP-46).
4 Eddie de Haas, interview with author, December 2005.
5 Ibid.
6 Ibid.
7 Bob Zieff, excerpt from *Deep in a Dream*, by James Gavin.
8 Hod O'Brien, interview with author, November 2005.
9 Ibid.
10 Bob Zieff, interview with author, April 2006.

11 Ibid.
12 Ibid.
13 Ibid.
14 Ibid.
15 Gil Evans, excerpt from *Revenge of the Underground Composer* by Jack Chambers.
16 Bob Zieff, interview with author, April 2006.
17 Released as *Chet Baker—Embraceable You* (Pacific Jazz CDP 7243 8 31676 2 3).
18 Henry Grimes, courtesy of Margaret Davis, interview with author.
19 Annie Ross, interview with author, January 2006.
20 Martin Williams, excerpt from *DownBeat* magazine, 1958.
21 Chet Baker, excerpt from *As Though I Had Wings*.
22 *A test of the maturation hypothesis with respect to opiate addiction*, John C. Ball, Richard W Snarr, January 1969.
23 Chet Baker, excerpt from 'All That Jazz, All Those Girls, All That Dope!'
24 Jim Coleman, interview with author, January 2006.
25 Orrin Keepnews, excerpt from liner notes to *Chet* (Keepnews Collection).
26 Ibid.
27 Ibid.
28 Martin Williams, excerpt from *DownBeat*, January 1959.
29 Dinah Washington, excerpt from *DownBeat*, April 1959.
30 Orrin Keepnews, Ibid.
31 Giampiero Giusti, interview with author, April 2007.
32 Ibid.
33 Excerpt from *DownBeat*, July 1959.
34 Jack Sheldon, interview with author, May 2007.

Chapter Nine

Much of the source material for this chapter came from the court transcriptions that were published after Chet was sentenced in Lucca, Italy, in April 1961. Special thanks must go to Francesco 'Cecco' Maino, who went to considerable trouble to obtain these records, and was kind enough to let me take a copy and help me with my research. Thanks also to Pia Richardson and Serenella Martufi for translating the court records.

1 Chet Baker, excerpt from *As Though I Had Wings*.
2 Epoca magazine, 21st February 1960.
3 Gianni Basso, interview with author, April 2006.
4 Amadeo Tommasi, interview with author, April 2006.
5 Cecco Maino, e-mail to Chet Baker Yahoo chat group.
6 Cecco Maino, interview with author, April 2007.
7 Amadeo Tommasi, ibid.
8 Giovanni Tommaso, interview with author, April 2006.
9 Giampiero Giusti, interview with author, April 2006.
10 Cecco Maino, e-mail to Chet Baker Yahoo chat group.
11 Chet Baker, *Jazz Di Ieri e Di Oggi*, translated by Cecco Maino.
12 Excerpt from *Deep In A Dream* by James Gavin, 2002.
13 Roberto Capasso, *Jazz Di Ieri e Di Oggi*, translated by Cecco Maino.
14 Giovanni Tommaso, ibid.
15 Cicci Santucci, interview with author, April 2006.
16 Cicci Santucci, ibid.
17 Lars Bloch, interview with author, August 2006.
18 Lucio Fulci, excerpt from *Chet Baker in Italy*, by Paola Boncompagni/Aldo Lastella.

19 Cecco Maino, e-mail to Chet Baker Yahoo chat group.
20 Cicci Santucci, ibid.
21 Giovanni Tommaso, ibid.
22 Cecco Maino, e-mail to Chet Baker Yahoo chat group.
23 Gianni Basso, ibid.
24 Chet Baker, excerpt from *As Though I Had Wings*.
25 Gianni Basso, ibid.
26 Ibid.
27 *Il Vedovo—Music by Armando Trovajoli:* CD by Cam Original Soundtracks.
28 Cecco Maino, e-mail to Chet Baker Yahoo chat group.
29 Chet Baker, excerpt from *As Though I Had Wings*.
30 Chet Baker, letter to *Playboy* magazine, August 1961.
31 Chet Baker, ibid.
32 Carol Baker, interview by Jerry Jazz Musician.
33 Ibid.
34 Ibid.
35 Lilian Terry, e-mail to author, November 2008.
36 Lilian Terry, ibid.
37 Chet Baker, letter to *Playboy* magazine, August 1961.
38 Carol Baker, from *Let's Get Lost*, directed by Bruce Weber.
39 Amadeo Tommasi, interview with author, April 2006.
40 Chet Baker, excerpt from *As Though I Had Wings*.
41 Amadeo Tommasi, ibid.
42 Ibid.
43 Cecco Maino, interview with author, April 2007.
44 Chet Baker, letter to *Playboy* magazine, August 1961.
45 Ibid.
46 Amadeo Tommasi, ibid.
47 Ibid.
48 Excerpt from *Il Telegrafo*, August 22nd 1960.
49 Chet Baker, excerpt from *As Though I Had Wings*.
50 Lars Bloch, ibid.
51 Dino Grilli, excerpt from *Il Telegrafo*, April 11th 1961.
52 Giovanni Tommaso, ibid.
53 Cecco Maino, e-mail to Chet Baker Yahoo chat group.
54 Excerpt from court transcriptions, translated by Pia Richardson.
55 Renzo Battiglia, excerpt from *Giornale del Mattino*, April 12th 1961.
56 Sergio Frosali, excerpt from *La Nazione*, April 12th 1961.
57 Excerpt from court transcriptions, translated by Pia Richardson.
58 Ibid.
59 Chet Baker, excerpt from *As Though I Had Wings*.
60 Amadeo Tommasi, ibid.
61 Chet Baker, letter to *Playboy* magazine, August 1961.
62 Excerpt from *Il Telegrafo*, September 9th 1961.

Chapter Ten

1 Chet Baker, excerpt from *As Though I Had Wings*.
2 Don DeMichael, excerpt from *DownBeat*, 1960.
3 Jack McKinney, excerpt from *Metronome* magazine, October 1960.
4 Ornette Coleman, liner notes to *Change of the Century*, Atlantic Records.

5 Miles Davis, excerpt from *Jazz Masters of the 50s*, Joe Goldberg.
6 Giovanni Tommaso, liner notes to *Chet is Back!* CD reissue.
7 Giovanni Tommaso, interview with author, April 2006.
8 Daniel Humair, interview with author, April 2006.
9 Amadeo Tommasi, interview with author, April 2006.
10 Daniel Humair, ibid.
11 Daniel Humair, ibid.
12 Amadeo Tommasi, ibid.
13 Francesco 'Cecco' Maino, liner notes to *Chet is Back!* CD reissue.
14 Giampiero Giusti, interview with author, April 2007.
15 Giovanni Tommaso, interview with author, April 2006.
16 Giovanni Tommaso, ibid.
17 Chet Baker, excerpt from *As Though I Had Wings*.
18 Amadeo Tommasi, ibid.
19 Giovanni Tommaso, ibid.
20 Amadeo Tommasi, ibid.
21 Giovanni Tommaso, ibid.
22 Chet Baker, excerpt from *As Though I Had Wings*.
23 Chet Baker, ibid.
24 Giovanni Tommaso, ibid.
25 Chet Baker, excerpt from The Trumpet and the Spike, *Today*, date unknown.
26 Chet Baker, excerpt from *As Though I Had Wings*.
27 Carol Jackson, excerpt from *Giornale del Mattino*, April 16th, 1961.
28 Chet Baker, excerpt from 'The Trumpet and the Spike', *Today*, date unknown.
29 Halema Alli, excerpt from 'Deep in a Dream', James Gavin.
30 Chet Baker, excerpt from 'The Trumpet and the Spike', *Today*, date unknown.
31 Excerpt from *Heroin Addiction Care and Control*, H.B. Spear, 2002.
32 Chet Baker, excerpt from *As Though I Had Wings*.
33 Chet Baker, ibid.
34 Chet Baker, excerpt from *Melody Maker* article, September 1st 1962.
35 Chet Baker, ibid.
36 Chet Baker, excerpt from 'The Trumpet and the Spike', *Today*, date unknown.
37 Chet Baker, excerpt from *As Though I Had Wings*.
38 Chet Baker, excerpt from '30,000 Hell-Holes in My Arm', *Today,* February 2nd 1963.
39 Chet Baker, ibid.
40 Giovanni Tommaso, ibid.
41 Chet Baker, excerpt from *As Though I Had Wings*.
42 Chet Baker, ibid.
43 Johnny Griffin, interviewed on Mel Martin's Jazz and Saxophone website.
44 Johnny Griffin, interview with author, March 2006.
45 Chet Baker, excerpt from 'The Trumpet and the Spike', *Today*, date unknown.
46 Chet Baker, excerpt from 'The Trumpet and the Spike', *Today*, date unknown.
47 Johnny Griffin, interview with author, March 2006.
48 Chet Baker, excerpt from interview in The Wire, November 1985.
49 Luigi Trussardi, interview with author, December 2006.
50 Hans Keller, interview with author, April 2006.
51 Alex Bally, interview with author, November 2006.
52 Hans Keller, ibid.
53 Alex Bally, ibid.
54 Chet Baker, excerpt from 'The Trumpet and the Spike', *Today*, date unknown.

55 Hans Keller, ibid.
56 Terry Riley, interviewed by Robert Dean, CD version of The Gift,
57 Terry Riley, ibid.
58 Terry Riley, ibid.
59 Terry Riley, ibid.
60 Luigi Trussardi, ibid.
61 Hans Keller, ibid.
62 Chet Baker, from *Born Under The Sign Of Jazz*, by Randi Hultin.
63 Hans Keller, ibid.
64 Chet Baker, excerpt from 'Chet Baker's Tale of Woe', *DownBeat*, July 30th 1964.
65 Amadeo Tommasi, interview with author, April 2006.
66 Luigi Trussardi, ibid.
67 Alex Bally, ibid.
68 Alex Bally, ibid.
69 Luigi Trussardi, ibid.
70 Alex Bally, ibid.
71 Alex Bally, ibid.
72 Luigi Trussardi, ibid.
73 Chet Baker, excerpt from 'Chet Baker's Tale of Woe', *DownBeat*, July 30th 1964.
74 Chet Baker, excerpt from *As Though I Had Wings*.
75 Lothar Lewien, excerpt from *Chet Baker Blue Notes*.
76 Chet Baker, excerpt from 'Chet Baker's Tale of Woe', *DownBeat*, July 30th 1964.

Chapter Eleven

1 Chet Baker, liner notes to Baby Breeze, Limelight Records, LM 82003.
2 Chet Baker, excerpt from *New York Daily News*, March 5th 1964.
3 Chet Baker, excerpt from 'Chet Baker's Tale of Woe', DownBeat, July 30th 1964.
4 Excerpt from *Time* magazine, April 17th 1964.
5 Chet Baker, excerpt from 'Chet Baker's Tale of Woe', DownBeat, July 30th 1964.
6 Chet Baker, ibid.
7 Jim Coleman, interview with author, January 2006.
8 Ron McClure, interview with author, January 2006.
9 Ira Gitler, excerpt from *DownBeat*, May 21st 1964.
10 Excerpt from *Time* magazine, April 17th 1964.
11 Phil Urso, excerpt from *Chet: A Discography* by Thorbjorn Sjogren.
12 Chet Baker, excerpt from 'Chet Baker's Tale of Woe', *DownBeat*, July 30th 1964.
13 Chet Baker, liner notes to Baby Breeze.
14 Phil Urso, interview with author, May 2005.
15 Phil Urso, ibid.
16 Phil Urso, ibid.
17 Hal Galper, interview with author, May 2005.
18 Hal Galper, ibid.
19 Hal Galper, ibid.
20 Excerpt from *DownBeat*, October 4th 1964.
21 Hal Galper, ibid.
22 Hal Galper, interview by David Udolph, July/August 1991 edition, 'Letter From Evans'.
23 Gary Burton, e-mail to author, February 2006.
24 Excerpt from Jazz Journal, UK, September 1964.
25 Hal Galper, ibid.
26 Phil Urso, ibid.

27 Carol Baker, from liner notes to Live at Pueblo.
28 Hersh Hamel, excerpt from *Deep in a Dream* by James Gavin.
29 Vera Baker, letter to Chet Baker dated July 2nd 1964.
30 Vera Baker, ibid.
31 Vera Baker, ibid.
32 Michael Fleming, excerpt from *Deep in a Dream* by James Gavin.
33 Hal Galper, ibid.
34 Excerpt from *Time* magazine, 31st July 1964.
35 Astrud Gilberto, from her website.
36 Gary Burton, e-mail to author, February 2006.
37 Hal Galper, ibid.
38 Hal Galper, ibid.
39 Harvey Siders, excerpt from *DownBeat* magazine, March, 25th 1965.
40 Phil Urso, excerpt from *The Philosophy of Urso* by T.R Witcher, Denver Westword.
41 Kirk Lightsey, interview with author, September 2005.
42 Kirk Lightsey, ibid.
43 Chet Baker, interview with Richard Williams, *Melody Maker*, 21st July 1973.

Chapter Twelve

1 Chet Baker, excerpt from *As Though I Had Wings*.
2 Vera Baker, letter to Chet Baker, 2nd July 1964.
3 Excerpt from *DownBeat* magazine, date unknown.
4 Bud Shank, excerpt from 'Bud Shank: A New Image', Jazz Forum, March 1987.
5 Bob Whitlock, interview with author, July 2007.
6 Bob Whitlock, ibid.
7 Sandy Jones, excerpt from *Deep In A Dream* by James Gavin.
8 Bob Whitlock, ibid.
9 Don Nelson, excerpt from *DownBeat* magazine, 25th August 1966.
10 Pete Welding, excerpt from *DownBeat* magazine, 1st December 1966.
11 Colin Bailey, interview with author, October 2009.
12 Colin Bailey, ibid.
13 João Donato, interview with author, January 2006.
14 João Donato, ibid.
15 João Donato, ibid.
16 Ralph J. Gleason, excerpt from *San Francisco Chronicle*, 1st July 1966.
17 João Donato, ibid.
18 Chet Baker, excerpt from *New York Times*, 9th August 1966.
19 Chet Baker, excerpt from *Melody Maker*, 20th August 1966.
20 Chet Baker, excerpt from *DownBeat* magazine, 22nd September 1966.
21 João Donato, ibid.
22 João Donato, ibid.
23 João Donato, ibid.
24 Bud Shank, from *Chet: A Discography* by Thorbjorn Sjogren.
25 Pete Christlieb, excerpt from *Jazz Journal International*, March 2000.
26 Pete Christlieb, ibid.
27 Phil Urso, interview with author, May 2005.
28 Larry Bunker, excerpt from *Chet's Choice* newsletter, Vol. 5, No. 2.
29 Colin Bailey, interview with author, October 2009.
30 Carol Baker, excerpt from *Chet's Choice* newsletter, Vol. 1, No. 1.
31 Carol Baker, ibid.

32 Chet Baker, excerpt from *Jazz Hot* magazine, November 1983.
33 Carol Baker, excerpt from de Valk
34 Carol Baker, excerpt from *Chet's Choice* newsletter, Vol. 1, No. 1.
35 Artt Frank, interview with author, April 2005.
36 Artt Frank, ibid.
37 Bob Whitlock, ibid.
38 Bob Whitlock, ibid.
39 Bob Whitlock, ibid.
40 Carol Baker, excerpt from *Chet's Choice* newsletter, Vol. 1, No. 1.
41 Artt Frank, ibid.
42 Artt Frank, ibid.
43 Carol Baker, ibid.
44 Chet Baker, letter to Harry Kevis, March 1968.
45 Chet Baker, ibid.
46 Jim Hughart, interview with author, September 2005.
47 Jim Hughart, ibid.
48 Jim Hughart, ibid.
49 Jack Sheldon, interview with author, May 2007.
50 Bob Whitlock, ibid.
51 Artt Frank, ibid.
52 Christopher Mason, interviewed on *Time for Jazz*, BBC Radio Kent, October 1988.
53 Bob Whitlock, ibid.
54 Bob Whitlock, ibid.
55 Bob Whitlock, ibid.
56 Artt Frank, ibid.
57 Leonard Feather, *Los Angeles Times*, 11th February 1969.
58 Giovanni Tommaso, interview with author, April 2006.
59 Artt Frank, interview with author, May 2007.
60 Art Pepper, excerpt from *Straight Life: The Story of Art Pepper*.
61 Artt Frank, interview with author, April 2005.
62 Bill Loughborough, interview with author, April 2006.
63 Bill Loughborough, ibid.
64 Diane Vavra, from *Let's Get Lost*, directed by Bruce Weber.
65 Ron Crotty, interview with author, November 2008.
66 Brian Cooke, interview with author, November 2008.
67 Robb Fisher, interview with author, November 2008.
68 Ralph J. Gleason, excerpt from *San Francisco Chronicle*, 27th May 1970.
69 Artt Frank, interview with author, April 2005.
70 Artt Frank, ibid.
71 Brian Cooke, ibid.
72 John Wasserman, excerpt from *San Francisco Chronicle*, 17th July 1970.
73 Brian Cooke, ibid.
74 Brian Cooke, ibid.
75 Brian Cooke, ibid.
76 ONDCP Drug Policy Information Fact Sheet on Methadone, April 2000.
77 Paul Baker, interview with author, February 2002.

Chapter Thirteen

1 Carol Baker, excerpt from *Chet Baker: His Life and Music* by Jeroen de Valk.
2 Ed Byrne, interview with author, December 2005.

3 Ibid.
4 Steve Houben, interview with author, October 2005.
5 Phil Urso, interview with author, May 2005.
6 Phil Urso, ibid.
7 Harold Danko, interview with author, October 2005.
8 Phil Urso, ibid.
9 Harold Danko, ibid.
10 Phil Urso's memory may have let him down on this issue. Turk Mauro's real name is Mauro Turso, and his brother Ron Turso played drums during the first week at the Half Note. Mel Lewis played in the final week of the engagement.
11 Harold Danko, excerpt from *Chet's Choice* newsletter, Vol. 3, No. 1.
12 Harold Danko, interview with author, October 2005.
13 Richard Williams, excerpt from *Melody Maker*, 21st July 1973.
14 Phil Urso, ibid.
15 Rex Reed, *New York Daily News*, 8th July 1973.
16 Bob Micklin, *New York Newsday*, 23rd July 1973.
17 Ruth Young, interview with author, March 2007.
18 Ruth Young, from *Let's Get Lost* directed by Bruce Weber.
19 Ruth Young, interview with author, March 2007.
20 Ruth Young, ibid.
21 Jimmy Madison, interview with author,
22 Ruth Young, ibid.
23 Harold Danko, interview with author, May 2005.
24 Bob Mover, interview with author, May 2005.
25 Jimmy Madison, interview with author, September 2006.
26 Jimmy Madison, ibid.
27 Jimmy Madison, ibid.
28 Ruth Young, ibid.
29 Ruth Young, ibid.
30 Ruth Young, ibid.
31 Patrick Tafoya, excerpt from artist's homepage.
32 Ed Byrne, interview with author, December 2005.
33 Ed Byrne, ibid.
34 Ruth Young, ibid.
35 Warren Chiasson, interview with author, May 2005.
36 Warren Chiasson, ibid.
37 Lee Konitz, excerpt from *Chet's Choice* newsletter.
38 Lee Konitz, ibid.
39 Bud Shank, excerpt from *Chet Baker: His Life and Music* by Jeroen de Valk.
40 Ed Byrne, ibid.
41 Ed Byrne, ibid.
42 Ruth Young, ibid.
43 Ed Byrne, ibid.
44 Ruth Young, interview with author, May 2007.
45 John Snyder, interview with author, May 2005.
46 John Snyder, ibid.
47 John Snyder, excerpt from *Chet's Choice* newsletter, Vol. 3, No. 2.
48 Don Sebesky, interview with author, May 2007.
49 Warren Chiasson, ibid.
50 Ed Byrne, ibid.

51 John Snyder, ibid.
52 John Scofield, interview with author, November 2005.
53 John Scofield, ibid.
54 John Scofield, ibid.
55 Ed Byrne, ibid.
56 Ed Byrne, ibid.
57 Chet Baker, interview with Les Tomkins, Roundhouse, 1979.
58 Ed Byrne, ibid.
59 Ed Byrne, ibid.
60 Ed Byrne, ibid.
61 Bob Mover, ibid.
62 Ed Byrne, ibid.
63 Hod O'Brien, interview with author, November 2005.
64 Hod O'Brien, ibid.
65 Ed Byrne, ibid.
66 Jimmy Madison, ibid.
67 Jimmy Madison, ibid.
68 Don Sebesky, ibid.
69 Don Sebesky, ibid.
70 Artt Frank, interview with author, April 2005.
71 Hod O'Brien, ibid.
72 Ruth Young, interview with author, March 2007.
73 Bob Mover, ibid.
74 Bob Mover, ibid.
75 Ed Byrne, ibid.
76 Ruth Young, ibid.
77 Ruth Young, ibid.
78 Ruth Young, ibid.
79 Ruth Young, ibid.
80 Ed Byrne, ibid.
81 Bob Mover, ibid.
82 Ruth Young, ibid.
83 Chet Baker, interview with Giulio Palumbo, *Paese Sera*, 16th July 1975.

Chapter Fourteen

1 Chet Baker, excerpt from *Chet Baker: His Life and Music* by Jeroen de Valk.
2 John S. Wilson, 'Mulligan, Baker in Jazz Reunion', *NY Times*, 26th November 1974.
3 Costanzo Costantini, unknown Italian newspaper, 17th July 1975.
4 Larry Ridley, interview with author, March 2006.
5 Ruth Young, interview with author, April 2007.
6 Ruth Young, ibid.
7 Ruth Young, ibid.
8 Ruth Young, ibid.
9 Chet Baker, interview with *Jazz Press*, 17th September 1975.
10 Ruth Young, ibid.
11 Micheline Pelzer, interview with author, April 2006.
12 Ruth Young, ibid.
13 Dan Morgenstern, excerpt from *DownBeat* magazine, 18th December 1975.
14 Maarten Derksen, excerpt from *Chet Baker: His Life and Music* by Jeroen de Valk.
15 Bob Mover, interview with author, May 2005.

16 Bob Mover, ibid.
17 Ruth Young, ibid.
18 Artt Frank, interview with author, February 2005.
19 Carol Baker, letter to Chet Baker, 7th October, 1977.
20 Harold Danko, interview with author, October 2005.
21 Bob Mover, ibid.
22 Ruth Young, interview with author, March 2007.
23 Harold Danko, ibid.
24 Ruth Young, ibid.
25 Giovanni Tommaso, interview with author, April 2006.
26 Giovanni Tommaso, ibid.
27 Chet Baker, excerpt from interview in *DownBeat* magazine, July 30th 1964.
28 Chet Baker, excerpt from *Chet Baker: His Life and Music* by Jeroen de Valk.
29 Riccardo Del Fra, interview with author, April 2006.
30 Mike Zwerin, excerpt from *The Parisian Jazz Chronicles*.
31 Branford Marsalis, excerpt from *The Parisian Jazz Chronicles* by Mike Zwerin.
32 Chet Baker, interview by Gudrun Endress, *Jazz Podium* magazine, 1978.
33 Ria Wigt, interview with author, May 2006.
34 *Musica Jazz*, June 1976 edition.
35 Hal Galper, interview with author, May 2005.
36 Ruth Young, interview with author, April 2007.
37 Lilian Terry, e-mail to author, November 2008.
38 Jean-Louis Rassinfosse, interview with author, March 2006.
39 Jean-Louis Rassinfosse, ibid.
40 Roger Rosenberg, interview with author, February 2006.
41 John Snyder, interview with author, May 2005.
42 Chet Baker, interview with Gudrun Endress, *Jazz Podium* Magazine, 1978.
43 Don Sebesky, interview with author, May 2007
44 Roger Rosenberg, ibid.
45 John Scofield, interview with author, November 2005.
46 Ruth Young, ibid.
47 Excerpt from *DownBeat* magazine, 4th May 1978.
48 Excerpt from *Playboy* magazine, May 1978.
49 John Snyder, 'Ethics, soul and a conscience…' from *Elsewhere* website
50 Hod O'Brien, interview with author, November 2005.
51 Ruth Young, ibid.
52 Ruth Young, ibid.
53 Micheline Pelzer, interview with author, April 2006.
54 Micheline Pelzer, ibid.
55 Ruth Young, ibid.
56 Ruth Young, ibid.
57 Micheline Pelzer, ibid.
58 Micheline Pelzer, ibid.
59 Ruth Young, ibid.
60 Steve Houben, interview with author, October 2005.
61 John Snyder, interview with author, October 2005.
62 John Snyder, excerpt from *Deep In A Dream,* by James Gavin.
63 John Snyder, interview with author, October 2005.
64 Micheline Pelzer, ibid.

Chapter Fifteen

1 Chet Baker, excerpt from an interview with Brian Case, *Melody Maker*, 14th April 1979.
2 Jeff Brillinger, interview with author January 2006.
3 Roger Rosenberg, interview with author, February 2006.
4 Phil Markowitz, interview with author, May 2005.
5 Phil Markowitz, ibid.
6 Roger Rosenberg, ibid.
7 Roger Rosenberg, ibid.
8 Jim McNeely, interview with author, June 2005.
9 Vera Baker, letter to Chet Baker, 16th April, 1978.
10 Ruth Young, interview with author, May 2007.
11 Jim McNeely, ibid.
12 Jeff Brillinger, ibid.
13 Roger Rosenberg, ibid.
14 Jeff Brillinger, ibid.
15 John Snyder, ibid.
16 Ruth Young, ibid.
17 Jeff Brillinger, ibid.
18 Jon Burr, interview with author, June 2005.
19 Roger Rosenberg, ibid.
20 Phil Markowitz, ibid.
21 Jean-Louis Rassinfosse, interview with author, March 2006.
22 Jean-Louis Rassinfosse, ibid.
23 Jean-Louis Rassinfosse, ibid.
24 Ruth Young, interview with author, April 2007.
25 Chet Baker, excerpt from *Deep In A Dream* by James Gavin.
26 Jean-Louis Rassinfosse, ibid.
27 Jean-Louis Rassinfosse, ibid.
28 Phil Markowitz, ibid.
29 Jean-Louis Rassinfosse, ibid.
30 Micheline Pelzer, interview with author, April 2006.
31 Jeff Brillinger, ibid.
32 Wolfgang Lackerschmid, interview with author, May 2005.
33 Wolfgang Lackerschmid, excerpt from *Chet Baker In Europe* by Ingo Wulff.
34 Wolfgang Lackerschmid, ibid.
35 Wolfgang Lackerschmid, interview with author, May 2005.
36 Francesco Maino, interview with author, April 2007.
37 Giampiero Giusti, interview with author, April 2007.
38 Giampiero Giusti, ibid.
39 Ruth Young, ibid.
40 Ruth Young, ibid.
41 Ruth Young, ibid.
42 Jean-Louis Rassinfosse, ibid.
43 Rene Magron, from *Stern*, taken from *Deep In A Dream* by James Gavin.
44 Phil Markowitz, ibid.
45 Jean-Louis Rassinfosse, ibid.
46 Wolfgang Lackerschmid, interview with author, May 2005.
47 Doug Raney, excerpt from *Chet Baker In Europe*.
48 Nils Winther, interview with author, May 2007.
49 Doug Raney, interview with author, May 2007.

50 Ruth Young, ibid.
51 Doug Raney, excerpt from *Chet Baker In Europe*.
52 Jean-Louis Rassinfosse, ibid.
53 Doug Raney, interview with author, May 2007.
54 Philippe Gaviglio, excerpt from sleevenotes to *All Blues*.
55 Doug Raney, excerpt from *Chet Baker In Europe*.
56 Doug Raney, ibid.
57 Doug Raney, excerpt from *Chet Baker In Europe*.
58 Nils Winther, ibid.
59 Jean-Louis Rassinfosse, ibid.
60 Nils Winther, ibid.
61 Dennis Luxion, interview with author, August 2006.
62 Doug Raney, interview with author, May 2007.
63 Wolfgang Lackerschmid, interview with author, May 2005.
64 Enrico Pieranunzi, interview with author, November 2005.
65 Riccardo Del Fra, interview with author, April 2006.
66 Enrico Pieranunzi, ibid.
67 Carol Baker, letter to Chet Baker, 26th November 1979.
68 Dennis Luxion, ibid.

Chapter Sixteen

1 Chet Baker in a conversation with Rique Pantoja, summer 1981.
2 Ruth Young, excerpt from *Deep In A Dream* by James Gavin.
3 Ruth Young, ibid.
4 Ruth Young, interview with author, May 2007.
5 Nicola Stilo, interview with author, September 2005.
6 Nicola Stilo, ibid.
7 Ruth Young, interview with author, May 2007.
8 Giampiero Giusti, interview with author, April 2007.
9 Chet Baker, letter to Dean Baker, January 14th, 1980.
10 Riccardo Del Fra, interview with author, April 2006.
11 Steve Houben, interview with author, October 2005.
12 Artt Frank, letter to Chet Baker, December 10th, 1978.
13 Artt Frank, liner notes to *Burnin' At Backstreet*.
14 Dennis Luxion, interview with author, August 2006.
15 Nicola Stilo, interview with author, September 2005.
16 Pete Welding, excerpt from *DownBeat* magazine, March 1985.
17 Nicola Stilo, ibid.
18 Francesco 'Cecco' Maino, interview with author, April 2007.
19 Francesco 'Cecco' Maino, ibid.
20 Dennis Luxion, ibid.
21 Riccardo Del Fra, ibid.
22 Riccardo Del Fra, ibid.
23 Jean-Louis Rassinfosse, interview with author, March 2006.
24 Rique Pantoja, interview with author, June 2007.
25 Rique Pantoja, ibid.
26 Rique Pantoja, ibid.
27 Richard Galliano, sleevenotes to *Chet Baker and the Boto Brazilian Quartet*.
28 Ruth Young, ibid.
29 Carol Baker, letter to Chet Baker, June 12th 1980.

30 Carol Baker, letter to Chet Baker, July 22nd 1980.
31 Melissa Baker, telephone conversation with Ruth Young, date unknown.
32 Rique Pantoja, ibid.
33 Rique Pantoja, ibid.
34 Enzo Pietropaoli, interview with author, April 2006
35 Ruth Young, ibid.
36 Enzo Pietropaoli, ibid.
37 Ruth Young, ibid.
38 Enzo Pietropaoli, ibid.
39 Ruth Young, ibid.
40 Ruth Young, ibid.
41 Advertisement in *Jazz Podium* magazine, October 1980.
42 Ruth Young, interview with author, August 2007.
43 Ruth Young, interview with author, April 2007.
44 Warren Chiasson, interview with author, May 2005.
45 Excerpt from *Deep In A Dream* by James Gavin.
46 Dennis Irvin, e-mail to author, August 2007.
47 Dennis Irwin, ibid.
48 Ruth Young, interview with author, May 2007.
49 Peter Pavia, 'Let's Get Lost', New York *Daily News*, December 21st, 1997.
50 Bob Mover, interview with author, May 2005.
51 Phil Markowitz, interview with author, May 2005.
52 Phil Markowitz, ibid.
53 Don Nelson, New York *Daily News*, May 1st 1981.
54 Dennis Luxion, ibid.
55 Bob Mover, ibid.
56 Bob Mover, ibid.
57 Dennis Luxion, ibid.
58 Claudio Roditi, interview with author, May 2007.
59 Chet Baker, interview with Maggie Hawthorne, *DownBeat* magazine, summer 1981.
60 Chet Baker, ibid.
61 Chet Baker, ibid.
62 Ruth Young, interview with author, May 2007.
63 Ruth Young, ibid.
64 Dennis Irwin, ibid.
65 Dennis Luxion, ibid.
66 John Snyder, interview with author, May 2005.
67 Ruth Young, ibid.
68 Kirk Lightsey, interview with author, September 2005.
69 David Friedman, interview with author, August 2006.
70 David Friedman, ibid.
71 David Friedman, ibid.
72 Ben Riley, interview with author, June 2007.
73 Hod O'Brien, interview with author, November 2005.
74 Ruth Young, ibid.
75 Ruth Young, ibid.
76 Melissa Baker, excerpt from *Let's Get Lost*, directed by Bruce Weber.
77 Ruth Young, ibid.
78 Ruth Young, ibid.
79 Ruth Young, ibid.

80 Ruth Young, ibid.
81 Ruth Young, ibid.
82 Ruth Young, excerpt from *Deep In A Dream* by James Gavin.
83 Ruth Young, interview with author, May 2007.
84 Ruth Young, ibid.
85 Ruth Young, ibid.
86 Ruth Young, ibid.
87 Ruth Young, ibid.
88 Ruth Young, ibid.

Chapter Seventeen

1 Chet Baker, in a conversation with Luis Gasca, late 1982.
2 David Friedman, interview with author, August 2006.
3 Ruth Young, interview with author, April 2007.
4 Diane Vavra, except from *Deep In A Dream* by James Gavin.
5 Luis Gasca, interview with author, April 2006.
6 Luis Gasca, ibid.
7 Luis Gasca, ibid.
8 Luis Gasca, ibid.
9 Luis Gasca, ibid.
10 Luis Gasca, ibid.
11 Jane Walsh, excerpt from *Stan Getz: A Life In Jazz* by Donald L. Maggin
12 Wim Wigt, excerpt from *Chet Baker: His Life And Music* by Jeroen de Valk.
13 Wim Wigt, sleevenotes to *Stockholm Concerts.*
14 Per Husby, interview with author, August 2005.
15 Victor Lewis, interview with author, July 2005.
16 Victor Lewis, ibid.
17 Jim McNeely, interview with author, June 2005.
18 Jim McNeely, ibid.
19 Jim McNeely, sleevenotes to *Stockholm Concerts.*
20 Wim Wigt, excerpt from *Chet Baker: His Life And Music* by Jeroen de Valk.
21 Victor Lewis, ibid.
22 Jim McNeely, ibid.
23 Victor Lewis, ibid.
24 Jim McNeely, ibid.
25 Jane Walsh, excerpt from *Stan Getz: A Life In Jazz* by Donald L. Maggin.
26 Victor Lewis, ibid.
27 Ria Wigt, interview with author, May 2006.
28 Kirk Lightsey, interview with author, September 2005.
29 Max Bolleman, interview with author, September 2005.
30 Doug Raney, interview with author, May 2007.
31 Evert Hekkema, interview with author, July 2005.
32 Evert Hekkema, ibid.
33 Riccardo Del Fra, interview with author, May 2006.
34 Riccardo Del Fra, ibid.
35 Riccardo Del Fra, ibid.
36 Max Bolleman, ibid.
37 Melker Isaksson, interview with author, October 2005.
38 Melker Isaksson, ibid.
39 Jim Porto, interview with author, November 2005.

40 Jim Porto, ibid.
41 Jim Porto, ibid.
42 Jean-Louis Rassinfosse, interview with author, March 2006.
43 Paul Bley, interview with author, March 2005.
44 Elvis Costello, excerpt from 'Elvis in Ireland: Costello's Jazz Tones', *Jazz Times.*
45 Elvis Costello, ibid.
46 Per Husby, liner notes to *The Improviser.*
47 Per Husby, ibid.
48 Per Husby, ibid.
49 Erling Aksdal, interview with author, September 2005.
50 Per Husby, interview with author, August 2005.
51 Per Husby, ibid.
52 Philip Catherine, interview with author, May 2006.
53 Philip Catherine, excerpt from *Chet Baker: His Life And Music* by Jeroen de Valk.
54 Philip Catherine, interview with author, May 2006.
55 Jean-Louis Rassinfosse, ibid.
56 Jean-Louis Rassinfosse, ibid.
57 Jean-Louis Rassinfosse, ibid.
58 Kjell Jansson, interview with author, July 2005.
59 Nicola Stilo, interview with author, October 2005.
60 Riccardo Del Fra, ibid.
61 Riccardo Del Fra, ibid.
62 Evert Hekkema, excerpt from *Chet Baker: His Life And Music* by Jeroen de Valk
63 Evert Hekkema,, ibid.
64 Nicola Stilo, ibid.
65 Riccardo Del Fra, ibid.
66 Jesper Lundgaard, interview with author, July 2005.

Chapter Eighteen

1 Chet Baker, in a conversation with Luis Gasca, late 1982.
2 Nicola Stilo, excerpt from *Deep In A Dream* by James Gavin.
3 Per Husby, sleevenotes to *The Improviser*, 1983.
4 Musica Jazz, November 1983.
5 Giampiero Giusti, interview with author, April 2007.
6 Francesco 'Cecco' Maino, interview with author, April 2007.
7 Kjell Jansson, interview with author, July 2005.
8 Kjell Jansson, ibid.
9 Diane Vavra, excerpt from *Let's Get Lost*, directed by Bruce Weber.
10 Erling Aksdal, interview with author, September 2005.
11 Erling Aksdal, ibid.
12 Erling Aksdal, ibid.
13 Randi Hultin, excerpt from *Born Under The Sign Of Jazz.*
14 Randi Hultin, ibid.
15 Randi Hultin, ibid.
16 Per Husby, interview with author, August 2005.
17 Erling Aksdal, ibid.
18 Gerrie Teekens, excerpt from *Chet Baker: His Life And Music* by Jeroen de Valk.
19 Gerrie Teekens, ibid.
20 Hod O'Brien, interview with author, November 2005.
21 Gerrie Teekens, ibid.

22 Hod O'Brien, ibid.
23 Hod O'Brien, ibid.
24 Melissa Baker, excerpt from *Let's Get Lost*, directed by Bruce Weber.
25 Bill Craig, excerpt from *Chet's Choice* newsletter, Volume 3.
26 Chet Baker, excerpt from *Chet Baker: His Life And Music* by Jeroen de Valk.
27 Tómas Einarsson, interview with author, October 2005.
28 Tómas Einarsson, ibid.
29 Tómas Einarsson, ibid.
30 Jean-Louis Rassinfosse, interview with author, March 2006.
31 Jean-Louis Rassinfosse, ibid.
32 Kjell Jansson, interview with author, July 2005.
33 Kjell Jansson, ibid.
34 Jean 'Toots' Thielemans, e-mail to author, August 2005.
35 Nils Winther, interview with author, May 2007.
36 Nils Winther, ibid.
37 Nils Winther, ibid.
38 Nils Winther, ibid.
39 Nils Winther, ibid.
40 Hod O'Brien, interview with author, November 2005.
41 Jean-Louis Rassinfosse, ibid.
42 Jean-Louis Rassinfosse, ibid.
43 Philip Catherine, interview with author, May 2006.
44 Gerrie Teekens, ibid.
45 Max Bolleman, interview with author, October 2005.
46 Philip Catherine, ibid.
47 Gerrie Teekens, ibid.
48 Max Bolleman, ibid.
49 Jean-Louis Rassinfosse, ibid.
50 Diane Vavra, excerpt from *Deep In A Dream* by James Gavin.
51 Chet Baker, excerpt from *Musica Jazz*, July 1988.
52 Bertrand Tavernier, sleevenotes to *'Round Midnight.*
53 Herbie Hancock, sleevenotes to *Let's Get Lost.*
54 Jean-Louis Rassinfosse, ibid.
55 Jean-Louis Rassinfosse, ibid.
56 Rique Pantoja, interview with author, June 2007.
57 Nicola Stilo, interview with author, April 2006.
58 Rique Pantoja, ibid.
59 Nicola Stilo, ibid.
60 Rique Pantoja, ibid.
61 Rique Pantoja, ibid.
62 Edu Ninck Blok, excerpt from *Chet Baker In Europe* by Ingo Wulff.
63 Evert Hekkema, interview with author, November 2005.
64 Hein van de Geijn, interview with author, May 2006.
65 Evert Hekkema, ibid.
66 Micheline Pelzer, interview with author, April 2006.
67 Riccardo Del Fra, interview with author, April 2006.
68 Riccardo Del Fra, ibid.
69 Riccardo Del Fra, ibid.
70 Jean-Louis Rassinfosse, excerpt from *Jazz in Time*, July/August 1989.
71 Max Bolleman, ibid.

72 Max Bolleman, ibid.
73 Hein van de Geijn, ibid.
74 Philip Catherine, excerpt from notes for a BBC radio interview.
75 Micheline Pelzer, interview with author, April 2006.
76 Guy Barker, interview with author, May 2008.

Chapter Nineteen

1 Chet Baker, speaking after the Montreal Jazz Festival, July 2006.
2 Joe LoCascio, interview with author, February 2005.
3 Joe LoCascio, ibid.
4 Joe LoCascio, ibid.
5 Joe LoCascio, ibid.
6 Christopher Mason, interview by Roger Dalleywater for Time for Jazz, BBC Radio Kent.
7 Christopher Mason, ibid.
8 Christopher Mason, ibid.
9 Christopher Mason, ibid.
10 Phillipe Adler, excerpt from *Le Jazz en chute libre,* L'Egoiste, 1988.
11 Hod O'Brien, interview with author, November 2005.
12 Hod O'Brien, ibid.
13 Nils Winther, interview with author, May 2007.
14 Nils Winther, ibid.
15 Naoki Tachikawa, interview with author, September 2005.
16 Naoki Tachikawa, ibid.
17 Naoki Tachikawa, ibid.
18 John Engels, interview with author, May 2007.
19 Naoki Tachikawa, ibid.
20 Riccardo Del Fra, interview with author, April 2006.
21 John Engels, ibid.
22 Naoki Tachikawa, ibid.
23 Bradley Young, excerpt from sleevenotes to *Chet in Chicago.*
24 Bradley Young, ibid.
25 Bradley Young, ibid.
26 Elvis Costello, excerpt from 'Elvis in Ireland: Costello's Jazz Tones', *Jazz Times.*
27 Elvis Costello, ibid.
28 Riccardo Del Fra, ibid.
29 Riccardo Del Fra, ibid.
30 Paul Bley, interview with author, March 2005.
31 Paul Bley, ibid.
32 Paul Bley, ibid.
33 Paul Bley, ibid.
34 Ria Wigt, interview with author,
35 Evert Hekkema, interview with author, November 2005.
36 Evert Hekkema, ibid.
37 Lillo Quarantino, interview with author, April 2006.
38 Lillo Quarantino, ibid.
39 Nicola Stilo, interview with author.
40 Evert Hekkema.
41 Peter Huijts, excerpt from *Chet Baker: His Life And Music* by Jeroen de Valk.
42 Diane Vavra, excerpt from *Chet Baker In Europe* by Ingo Wulff.

43 Peter Huijts, ibid.
44 Lillo Quarantino, ibid.
45 Chet Baker, excerpt from *Chet Baker: His Life And Music* by Jeroen de Valk.
46 Diane Vavra, excerpt from *Deep in a Dream* by James Gavin.

Chapter Twenty

1 Chet Baker, speaking after the Montreal Jazz Festival, July 2006.
2 Jim Coleman, interview with author, January 2006.
3 Joanne Klein, interview with author, October 2005.
4 Harold Danko, interview with author, October 2005.
5 Harold Danko, ibid.
6 Jon Burr, interview with author, June 2005.
7 Naoki Tachikawa, interview with author, September 2005.
8 Naoki Tachikawa, ibid.
9 Max Bolleman, interview with author, October 2005.
10 Harold Danko, ibid.
11 Ben Riley, interview with author, June 2007.
12 Bruce Weber, excerpt from *Deep In A Dream* by James Gavin.
13 Cherry Vanilla, interview with author, June 2006.
14 Cherry Vanilla, ibid.
15 Cherry Vanilla, ibid.
16 Cherry Vanilla, ibid.
17 Bruce Weber, interview with Cyn Zarrow, *Interview*, February 1989.
18 Jon Burr, ibid.
19 William Claxton, excerpt from *Deep In A Dream* by James Gavin.
20 Cherry Vanilla, ibid.
21 Cherry Vanilla, ibid.
22 Frank Strazerri, interview with author, August 2007.
23 Frank Strazerri, ibid.
24 Frank Strazerri, ibid.
25 Jon Burr, ibid.
26 Jon Burr, ibid.
27 Jon Burr, excerpt from *Chet Baker in Europe* by Ingo Wulff.
28 Ruth Young, excerpt from *Let's Get Lost*, directed by Bruce Weber.
29 Ruth Young, ibid.
30 Ruth Young, interview with author, April 2007.
31 Cherry Vanilla, interview with author, June 2006.
32 Ruth Young, ibid.
33 Ruth Young, ibid.
34 Bruce Weber, interview with Andrew O'Hehir, *S.F. Weekly*, May 31st 1989.
35 Cherry Vanilla, interview with author, June 2006.
36 Cherry Vanilla, ibid.
37 Cherry Vanilla, ibid.
38 Cherry Vanilla, ibid.
39 Micheline Pelzer, interview with author, April 2006.
40 Micheline Pelzer, ibid.
41 Nicola Stilo, excerpt from *Deep In A Dream* by James Gavin.
42 Nicola Stilo, interview with author, September 2005.
43 Chet Baker, excerpt from *Let's Get Lost*, directed by Bruce Weber.
44 Lars Bloch, interview with author, August 2006.

45 Diane Vavra, excerpt from *Let's Get Lost*, directed by Bruce Weber.
46 Diane Vavra, ibid.
47 Hein van de Geijn, interview with author, May 2006.
48 Peter Huijts, excerpt from *Chet Baker: His Life And Music* by Jeroen de Valk.
49 John Engels, excerpt from *Chet Baker: His Life And Music* by Jeroen de Valk.
50 Harold Danko, interview with author, October 2005.
51 John Engels, interview with author, May 2007.
52 Harold Danko, ibid.
53 Hein van de Geijn, ibid.
54 Hein van de Geijn, ibid.
55 Harold Danko, ibid.
56 Giampiero Giusti, interview with author, April 2007.
57 Chet Baker, excerpt from *Chet Baker: His Life And Music* by Jeroen de Valk.
58 Wolfgang Lackerschmid, interview with author, June 2005.
59 Harold Danko, ibid.
60 Chet Baker, excerpt from *Let's Get Lost*, directed by Bruce Weber.
61 Herb Geller, interview with author, October 2005.
62 Walter Norris, interview with author, October 2005.
63 Herb Geller, ibid.
64 Walter Norris, ibid.
65 Bertrand Fèvre, interview with author, May 2006.
66 Bertrand Fèvre, ibid.
67 Chet Baker, excerpt from *Hoop*, VPRO-TV (Netherlands), January 1988.

Chapter Twenty-One

1 Chet Baker, excerpt from *Hoop*, VPRO-TV (Netherlands), January 1988.
2 Marcus Miller, excerpt from *Uncut* magazine, September 2011.
3 Excerpt from *Chet Baker*, Paris: Editions du Limon, 1992.
4 Chet Baker, excerpt from *Chet Baker: His Life And Music* by Jeroen de Valk.
5 Enzo Pietropaoli, interview with author, April 2006.
6 Chet Baker, excerpt from *Born Under The Sign Of Jazz* by Randi Hultin.
7 Randi Hultin, excerpt from *Born Under The Sign Of Jazz* by Randi Hultin.
8 Enrico Pieranunzi, interview with author, November 2005.
9 Enrico Pieranunzi, ibid.
10 Diane Vavra, excerpt from *Deep In A Dream* by James Gavin.
11 Bruce Weber, excerpt from 'Horn Loser' by Dylan Jones, *The Face*, December 1988.
12 Micheline Pelzer, interview with author, April 2006.
13 Ria Wigt, interview with author, May 2006.
14 Peter Huijts, excerpt from *Chet Baker: His Life And Music* by Jeroen de Valk.
15 Peter Huijts, ibid.
16 Enzo Pietropaoli, ibid.
17 Nicola Stilo, interview with author, April 2006.
18 Amadeo Tommasi, interview with author, April 2006.
19 Nicola Stilo, ibid.
20 Chet Baker, interview with Ib Skovgaard, January 29th 1988.
21 Matthias Winckelmann, interview in liner notes to *The Last Great Concert* CD.
22 Walter Norris, interview with author, October 2005.
23 Herb Geller, interview with author, October 2005.
24 Walter Norris, ibid.
25 Walter Norris, ibid.

26 Matthias Winckelmann, ibid.
27 Herb Geller, ibid.
28 Wim Wigt, excerpt from *Chet Baker: His Life And Music* by Jeroen de Valk.
29 Micheline Graillier, interview with author, April 2006.
30 Chet Baker, excerpt from *Deep In A Dream* by James Gavin.
31 Micheline Graillier, ibid.
32 Hein van de Geijn, interview with author, May 2006.
33 Micheline Graillier, ibid.
34 Hein van de Geijn, ibid.
35 Hein van de Geijn, ibid.
36 Liliane Rovère, interview with author, April 2006.
37 Liliane Rovère, ibid.
38 Bertrand Fèvre, interview with author, May 2006
39 Bertrand Fèvre, ibid.
40 Ria Wigt, ibid.
41 Hein van de Geijn, ibid.
42 Hein van de Geijn, ibid.
43 Wim Wigt, excerpt from *Chet Baker: His Life And Music* by Jeroen de Valk.
44 Hein van de Geijn, ibid.
45 Nicola Stilo, ibid.
46 Ria Wigt, ibid.
47 Ria Wigt, ibid.
48 Chet Baker, excerpt from *Deep In A Dream* by James Gavin.
49 Robert van de Feyst, *Vrij Nederland*, May 21st 1988.
50 Jasper Blom, excerpt from *Chet Baker: His Life And Music* by Jeroen de Valk.
51 Ria Wigt, ibid.
52 Ria Wigt, ibid.
53 Peter Huijts, excerpt from *Chet Baker: His Life And Music* by Jeroen de Valk.
54 Annette Lowman, excerpt from *Deep In A Dream* by James Gavin.
55 Ria Wigt, ibid.
56 Rob Bloos, excerpt from *Chet Baker: His Life And Music* by Jeroen de Valk.
57 Peter Huijts, ibid.
58 Peter Huijts, ibid.
59 Diane Vavra, ibid.
60 Micheline Graillier, ibid.
61 James Gavin, excerpt from *Deep In A Dream* by James Gavin

Epilogue

1 Chet Baker, excerpt from an unknown interview.
2 Ria Wigt, interview with author, May 2006.
3 Ria Wigt, ibid.
4 Peter Huijts, excerpt from *Chet Baker: His Life and Music* by Jeroen de Valk.
5 Diane Vavra, excerpt from *Deep in a Dream* by James Gavin.
6 Frank Strazerri, from *Makes No Difference How I Carry On'* by Tony Gieske.
7 Jack Sheldon, from *Makes No Difference How I Carry On'* by Tony Gieske.
8 Ed Byrne, interview with author, December 2005.
9 Inspector Bloos, excerpt from *Chet Baker: His Life and Music'* by Jeroen de Valk.
10 Carol Baker, excerpt from 'Jump, Fall or Push?', *Village Voice*, by Richard Linnett, August 1988.
11 Paul Baker, interview with author, February 2002.

12 Paul Baker, ibid.
13 Carol Baker, excerpt from liner notes, *Chet Baker—The Legacy*, Enja Records.
14 Ria Wigt, ibid.
15 Ria Wigt, ibid.
16 Jeffrey Kruger, MBE, interview with author April 2006.
17 Cherry Vanilla, interview with author, June 2006.
18 Excerpt from 'The History of a Musician's Disintegration', Janet Maslin, *New York Times*, March 24th 1989.
19 Excerpt from 'Documentary Ignores Baker's Music—It's Not Photogenic', Sheila Benson, *Los Angeles Times*, May 25th 1989.
20 Excerpt from '*Lost* traces jazz legend's shocking descent', Carina Chocano, *Los Angeles Times*, January 11th 1988.
21 Nicola Stilo, interview with author, September 2005.
22 Nicola Stilo, excerpt from *Deep in a Dream* by James Gavin.

Legacy

1 Mike Zwerin, interview with author, April 2008.
2 Mike Zwerin, excerpt from an interview by Farah Nayeri, *Bloomberg News*
3 www.wyntonmarsalis.org/about/faq/
4 Jim Coleman, interview with author, January 2006.
5 Chet Baker, excerpt from *Chet Baker: His Life And Music* by Jeroen de Valk.
6 Excerpt from 'Blowing Up A Storm' by Maya Jaggi, *The Guardian*, 25th January, 2003.
7 Excerpt from an article by Andrew Solomon, *New York Times Magazine*, February 9th 1997.
8 Nils Winter, interview with author, May 2007.
9 Gary Burton, interview with author, February 2006.
10 Horace Silver, excerpt from interview with Nat Hentoff, *DownBeat*, October 31st 1956.
11 Bud Shank, excerpt from *Chet Baker: His Life and Music* by Jeroen de Valk.
12 Terrence Rafferty, excerpt from 'A Jazzman So Cool You Want Him Frozen at His Peak', *New York Times*, June 3rd 2007.
13 Riccardo Del Fra, interview with author, April 2006.
14 John Vinocur, excerpt from 'A glorious moment in Chet Baker's twilight', *New York Times*, February 22nd 2008.
15 Mike Zwerin, interview with author, April 2008.
16 Mike Zwerin, excerpt from *Close Enough For Jazz*, 1983.
17 Don Sebesky, interview with author, May 2007.
18 Rique Pantoja, interview with author, June 2007.
19 John Engels, interview with author, May 2007.
20 Ruth Young, interview with author, May 2007.
21 Bobby Shew, interview with author, May 2007.
22 Hein van de Geijn, interview with author, May 2006.
23 Clare Fischer, interview with author, September 2005.
24 Melissa Forbes, interview with author, May 2007.
25 Larry Ridley, interview with author, March 2006.
26 Larry Ridley, ibid.
27 Rique Pantoja, ibid.
28 Jean-Louis Rassinfosse, interview with author, March 2006.
29 Hein van de Geijn, ibid.
30 Enrico Pieranunzi, interview with author, November 2005.
31 Kurt Elling, taken from: http://kurtelling.com/news/faq.html

32 Curtis Stigers, interview with author, October 2006.
33 Claudio Roditi, interview with author, May 2007.
34 João Donato, interview with author, January 2006.
35 Guy Barker, interview with author, May 2008.
36 Guy Barker, ibid.
37 John Scofield, interview with author, November 2005.

Index

About the Author

MATTHEW RUDDICK is a Hong Kong based author. Over the last few years, he was a regular music critic for a variety of publications, including HK-listings magazine Beats, and the author of 'Music On The Move', a music column in Escape travel magazine. Born in England, Matthew has been living in Hong Kong for eight years, and works in the finance industry.

Matthew can be contacted via his website www.funnyvalentine.org